The Complete History of
Jack the Ripper

The Complete History of
Jack the Ripper

PHILIP SUGDEN

Carroll & Graf Publishers, Inc.
NEW YORK

Carroll & Graf Publishers, Inc.,
260 Fifth Avenue
New York, NY 100001

Copyright © Philip Sugden 1994

Philip Sugden asserts the moral right to be identified as the
author of this work.

First Carroll & Graf edition 1994

A copy of the Cataloguing in Publication Data for this title is
available from the Library of Congress.

ISBN 0–7867–0124–2

Printed and bound in the UK

10 9 8 7 6 5 4 3 2 1

Contents

Acknowledgements

During the research and writing of this book I have had the help of many people and it is a great pleasure to be able to thank them.

I owe a considerable debt of gratitude to the following persons for according me facilities to study, replying to my inquiries or granting me access to archives: the staff of the Public Record Office, Chancery Lane and Kew; Miss J. Coburn, Head Archivist, and her staff at the Greater London Record Office and Library; Mr James R. Sewell, City Archivist, and his staff at the Corporation of London Records Office; the staffs of the British Library, Bloomsbury, and the British Newspaper Library, Colindale; the staff of the Guildhall Library; Miss K. Shawcross, City of Westminster Archives and Local Studies, Victoria Library; Richard Knight, Local Studies Library, Holborn Library; Paul Burns, Public Record Office of Northern Ireland; Myrtle V. Cooper, Metropolitan Police Archives Department; Miss Rhoda Edwards, St Olave's and St Saviour's Grammar School Foundation; Mr P. R. Evans and Mrs J. V. Thorpe, Gloucestershire Record Office; Michael Farrar, County Archivist, Cambridgeshire Record Office; Robin Gillis, Metropolitan Police Musuem; Stephen Humphrey, Southwark Local Studies Library; David A. Leitch, Curatorial Officer, Royal Commission on Historical Manuscripts; C. J. Lloyd, Local History Librarian, Globe Town Neighbourhood, Bancroft Road Library; Keith A. Miller, Executive Administrator, World Association of Document Examiners, Chicago, USA; Michael Page, Surrey Record Office;

Mark Purcell, Senior Library Assistant, Bodleian Library; Miss G. Sheldrick, Hertfordshire County Record Office; Miss J. G. A. Sheppard, Wellcome Institute for the History of Medicine; Mr Jonathan Evans, Archivist, Royal London Hospital Archives and Museum; Mr Maurice D. Jeffery, formerly Administrator, Friern Hospital; Mr H. P. Dulley, Trust Project Manager, Horizon NHS Trust; Miss J. M. Smyth, General Services Manager, and Mr Bernard Cousens, Fire Prevention Officer, Springfield Hospital.

Even within a field as notorious for its cranks and charlatans as Ripper research there are knowledgeable and responsible students dedicated to the pursuit of truth. I am particularly indebted to four of the latter: Nick Warren, for guidance on the medical aspects of the case; Jon Ogan, for innumerable suggestions and especially for information on criminal psychological profiling; Stewart Evans, for dispelling my confusion as to the site of George Yard Buildings and for information on the Littlechild letter; and Keith Skinner, for generously agreeing to read my extracts from the Aberconway notes.

Extracts from Crown Copyright records in the Public Record Office and the Corporation of London Records Office appear by permission of the Controller of Her Majesty's Stationery Office. Material from Gloucestershire Quarter Sessions records in the Gloucestershire Record Office appears by permission of Mr David J. H. Smith, the County and Diocesan Archivist.

I am grateful for this opportunity to express my thanks to Nick Robinson, my publisher, and to Jan Chamier and Eryl Humphrey Jones at Robinson Publishing, for their patience and understanding and for their expertise in steering this project through its various stages of production. To my editor, Tim Haydock, I owe a special debt of gratitude. Tim's impressive knowledge of the Whitechapel murders and boundless enthusiasm for this book were most formidable factors in sustaining me over the last mile. I also wish to thank Richard Corfield, Sue Aldridge and Mick Wolf at Oxford Illustrators Ltd, for their preparation of the maps.

Thanks are long overdue to my friend Derek Barlow, formerly of the Public Record Office, for his generosity, encouragement and support over many years. My greatest debt, finally, is to my brother, Dr John Sugden of Coventry, who unstintingly spared time from his own research projects to discuss or assist this one and who, ten years ago, first insisted that I write this book.

Philip Sugden
Hull, England, 1994

Picture credits: 1, 4–5, 7–8, 13, 16–17, Public Record Office, MEPO 3/140 and MEPO 3/3155; 3, 6, 9, 22, 24, Greater London Photograph Library; 2, 19, British Library; 11, 14–15, 18, British Newspaper Library; 10, Royal London Hospital Museum and Archives; 12, Metropolitan Police Museum; 21, Hull City Museums and Art Galleries.

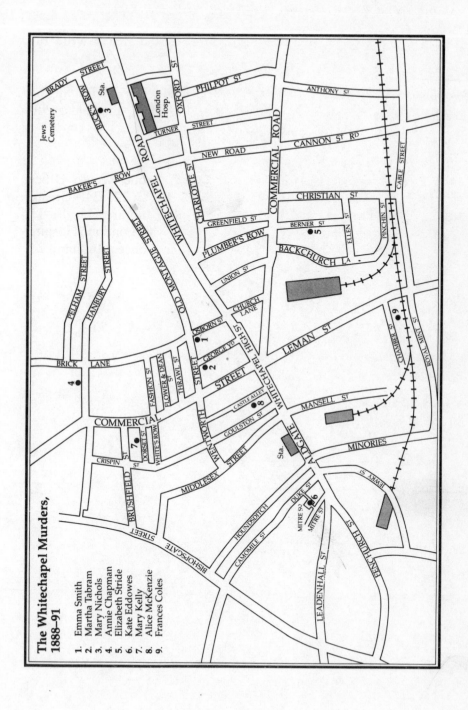

The Whitechapel Murders,
1888–91

1. Emma Smith
2. Martha Tabram
3. Mary Nichols
4. Annie Chapman
5. Elizabeth Stride
6. Kate Eddowes
7. Mary Kelly
8. Alice McKenzie
9. Frances Coles

1

A Century of Final Solutions

JACK THE RIPPER! Few names in history are as instantly recognizable. Fewer still evoke such vivid images: noisome courts and alleys, hansom cabs and gaslights, swirling fog, prostitutes decked out in the tawdriest of finery, the shrill cries of newsboys – 'Whitechapel! Another 'orrible murder! Mutilation!' – and silent, cruel death, personified in the cape-shrouded figure of a faceless prowler of the night, armed with a long knife and carrying a black Gladstone bag.

The Victorian murderer who slew a handful of women in London's East End has become a worldwide symbol of terror, his fame celebrated in story and song, on the stage and on film, in art and in opera, his tale told in languages as diverse as English and Russian, Spanish and Swedish, German and Japanese. Robert Bloch, the American author of *Psycho*, has said that Jack the Ripper belongs to the world as surely as Shakespeare. It is not an undue exaggeration.

Why our perennial fascination with the Ripper case? After all, tragic and gruesome as his crimes undoubtedly were, they are by no means unique or even spectacular in the lengthening roll of serial murder. The victims were comparatively few. They were drawn from only one small class of the population. And they were slain within an area less than a single square mile in extent.

True, they have their niche in history. In 1888 they embarrassed Lord Salisbury's second Conservative administration, contributed to the resignation of Sir Charles Warren, Commissioner of the Metropolitan Police, and, by spotlighting the living conditions of the poor, inaugurated a brief period of redevelopment in Spitalfields, at the heart of the murder district.

More important for our own day, perhaps, the Ripper heralded the rise of the modern sexual serial killer. He was not the earliest such offender. But he was the first of international repute and the one that first burned the problem of the random killer into police and popular consciousness.

The Ripper's contemporaries were baffled by the lack of conventional motive, whether gain, jealousy or revenge, in his crimes. Casting about for an explanation, some turned to the far past. 'It is so impossible to account . . . for these revolting acts of blood,' commented one, 'that the mind turns as it were instinctively to some theory of occult force, and the myths of the Dark Ages rise before the imagination. Ghouls, vampires, bloodsuckers, and all the ghastly array of fables which have been accumulated throughout the course of centuries take form, and seize hold of the excited fancy.' Others, sensing that the Ripper's origins lay in the social and economic upheavals of the new industrial age, glimpsed the future. 'Suppose we catch the Whitechapel murderer,' queried the *Southern Guardian*, 'can we not, before handing him over to the executioner or the authorities at Broadmoor, make a really decent effort to discover his antecedents, and his parentage, to trace back every step of his career, every hereditary instinct, every acquired taste, every moral slip, every mental idiosyncrasy? Surely the time has come for such an effort as this. We are face to face with some mysterious and awful product of modern civilization.'[1]

Those who hunted the Ripper, too, believed they were confronting a new and frightening phenomenon. 'I look upon this series of murders as unique in the history of our country,' Warren told Henry Matthews, the Home Secretary, at the height of the scare. George Lusk, President of the Mile End Vigilance Committee, formed to assist the police, agreed. 'The present series of murders,' he assured the Home Office, 'is absolutely unique in the annals of crime . . . and all ordinary means of detection have failed.'[2]

But none of this explains the Ripper's continual hold on popular imagination, his most potent legacy to the world. Some would have it that those who read or write about the murders are misogynists. I am not a misogynist. Nor, for that matter, is any serious student of the case personally known to me. It should be obvious from the most cursory glance at the literature, moreover, that what really fascinates people about the story is the question of the killer's identity. After a series of horrific murders Jack the Ripper disappeared, as if 'through a trapdoor in the earth' as a contemporary put it, and left behind a mystery as impenetrable as the fog that forms part of his legend. He left us, in short, with the classic 'whodunnit.'

It is this that lies at the root of our enduring fascination with the case. Good mysteries become obsessive. A century ago Percival Lowell spent a fortune in building the Lowell Observatory in Arizona specifically to find the canals of Mars. In the 1960s Tim Dinsdale, monster hunter extraordinaire, abandoned his career as an aeronautical engineer to search the waters of Loch Ness. And, driven by similar irresistible urges to know the truth, amateur sleuths in at least three continents still seek final proof of the identity of Jack the Ripper.

The Metropolitan Police file on the murders was officially closed in 1892. Since then we have had an ever-growing mountain of books and a welter of theories. Looking at the size of that mountain and the dramatic finality of many of the titles that form it – *The Final Solution*, *The Mystery Solved*, etc. – the general reader might well ask: is there anything new to be said about Jack the Ripper? The answer, surprisingly, is an emphatic 'Yes'! For the fact is that the conventional story of the murders, as passed down to us in these books, is shot through with errors and misconceptions and that, with very few exceptions, their authors have taken us, not towards, but away from the truth.

The whole subject is now a minefield to the unwary. Even true crime experts venture there at their peril. 'No new books will tell us anything more than we already know'. This was the confident claim of Brian Marriner, reviewing the Ripper case in his valuable book, *A Century of Sex Killers*. Unfortunately, Marriner's account of the murders, brief as it is, proceeds to repeat a number of old canards.[3] And where an author as knowledgeable as this stumbles, one is tempted to caution the general reader, approaching the groaning shelf of Ripper books for dependable information, with those famous words from Dante: 'Abandon hope, ye who enter here!'

There are several reasons for the lamentable state of Ripper studies.

One has been the tendency of writers to draw the bulk of their primary source material from newspaper reports and later reminiscences of police officers and others. This practice should not have survived the 1970s, when police and Home Office records on the Ripper case were first opened to the public, but it continues because of the relative accessibility of newspapers and memoirs. Every sizeable library has its microfilm backfile of *The Times*, and published memoirs are readily available through interlibrary loan services. Unfortunately, as sources of factual information on the crimes and police investigations, they are simply not reliable.

At the time of Jack the Ripper it was not the policy of the CID to disclose to the press details about unsolved crimes or their inquiries respecting them. Reporters were not even permitted to enter premises in which such a crime had been committed. Naturally, they resented it. 'The police authorities observe a reticence which has now apparently become systematic, and any information procured is obtained in spite of them,' carped one. 'However much or little they know, the police devote themselves energetically to the task of preventing other people from knowing anything,' fumed another.[4]

The purpose of the police precautions will be discussed later. Primarily it was to prevent villains being forewarned as to what the CID knew and might do. But at present the rationale behind the policy concerns us less than the effects of its application upon newsmen. It placed them in an impossible predicament. For they were confronted at the height of the Ripper scare by a massive public clamour for information and possessed few legitimate means of satisfying it.

Gathering news at that time was a particularly frustrating business. Sometimes, by following detectives or hanging about police stations, reporters were able to identify and interview important witnesses. We will have cause to thank them when we encounter Israel Schwartz and George Hutchinson. But more often press reports were cobbled together out of hearsay, rumour and gossip, picked up at street corners and in pubs or lodging houses.

There seems to have been no shortage of informants. A *Star* reporter, investigating the Miller's Court murder in November 1888, found the locals basking in their new-found importance, anxious to please and ready to regale him with 'a hundred highly circumstantial stories', most of which, upon inquiry, proved 'totally devoid of truth'. Even true anecdotes might be passed from mouth to mouth until they became unrecognizable. Sarah Lewis, who stayed in Miller's Court on the fatal night, had heard a cry of 'Murder!' By the time the *Star*'s man got to the scene of the crime her story had got round and 'half a dozen women were retailing it as their own personal experience', a circumstance which may explain why Sarah's story is sometimes credited, in aberrant forms, to a Mrs Kennedy in the press.[5]

Inevitably much of the press coverage was fiction. Inevitably, too, the press were happy to blame the police. 'We were compelled in our later editions of yesterday,' observed the *Star* after the Hanbury Street murder, 'to contradict many of the reports which found admittance to our columns and to those of all our contemporaries earlier in the day. For this the senseless, the endless prevarications of the police were to blame.'[6] But journalists themselves, determined to exploit the astonishing runs on the papers after each murder, were more than usually willing to invent copy of their own.

Perhaps the most important myth created by the press was Fairy Fay.

The first trace of her appeared in a verse broadsheet, *Lines on the Terrible Tragedy in Whitechapel*, printed at the beginning of September 1888. This referred vaguely to an early and unnamed victim of the murderer, killed 'twelve months ago', i.e. in 1887. However, it was the *Daily Telegraph* that really got the ball rolling. In its issues of 10 and 11 September 1888 it stated that the first victim of the Whitechapel murderer had been slain in the vicinity of Osborn and Wentworth Streets at Christmas 1887. A stick or iron instrument had been thrust into her body. She had never been identified. The story was repeated again and again – in newspapers and broadsheets, in a parliamentary question of November 1888, and in Dr L. Forbes Winslow's widely read memoir, *Recollections of Forty Years*, published in 1910. Terence Robertson, writing for *Reynold's News* in 1950, embroidered the tale still further. He gave the unknown woman a name – Fairy Fay – and said that she was killed on Boxing Night 1887, when she was taking a short cut home from a pub in Mitre Square.

No such event occurred. There is no reference to it in police records. No mention of it can be found in the local or national press for December 1887 or January 1888. And a search of registered deaths at St Catherine's House reveals no woman named Fay or anything like that murdered in Whitechapel during the relevant period. There is no doubt that the *Telegraph* story was a confused memory of the known murder of Emma Smith in the spring of 1888. Emma was attacked in Osborn Street and a blunt instrument, perhaps a stick, was savagely thrust into her. She died the next day in the London Hospital. Obviously the *Telegraph*'s writer recalled this incident very hazily. He remembered, for example, that it had occurred on a public holiday and opted for Christmas 1887. The correct date was the night of Easter Monday, 2–3 April 1888.[7]

Today writers still regularly list both Fairy Fay *and* Emma Smith as possible victims of Jack the Ripper. But Fairy Fay is a phantom, born of sloppy journalism back in 1888.

The deficiencies of newspaper files cannot be redressed from reminiscent evidence, whether memoirs of retired policemen or interviews with aged East End residents. These sources, although often readily accessible, have special problems of their own.

Over time our memories deteriorate more profoundly than many people inexperienced in the use of historical evidence realize, and reminiscences recorded long after the event are characteristically confused on chronology and detail. There is a very human tendency, too, for us to 'improve' upon our memories, to make a better story, to explain away past mistakes, or simply to claim for ourselves a more impressive role in past dramas than we have acted in life.

In 1959 a ninety-year-old Mr Wright could still show broadcaster Dan Farson the spot in Buck's Row where one of the murders took place. He had lived in Buck's Row as a boy, he explained, and it was he who had washed the blood from the pavement. Contemporary records reveal that there was, in fact, very little blood and that what there was was washed down by a son of Emma Green, who lived adjacent to the murder site.

At the time of the murders a greengrocer called Matthew Packer told police that on the night Liz Stride was killed in Berner Street he had sold grapes to her killer. More than seventy years later an aged Annie Tapper remembered the story and retold it for Tom Cullen. She insisted, however, that as a girl of nine *she* had sold the grapes to Jack the Ripper and, of course, she remembered him perfectly. 'I'll tell you what he looked like as sure as this is Friday,' she said. But her murderer was a fantasy, disguised in a black, pointed beard and togged out in a bobtail coat and striped trousers.

At a more exalted level Sir Robert Anderson, head of CID in 1888, made the preposterous suggestion in his memoirs that his policy of withdrawing police protection from prostitutes drove them from the streets and thereby put an end to street murders in the Ripper series. Not true. Contemporary evidence demonstrates that the policy was never implemented and could not have worked.

In producing reminiscences there is also a tendency for our memories to become contaminated by later stories and influences. A case in point is Mary Cox. Mrs Cox lived in Miller's Court in 1888. She knew Mary Jane Kelly, usually regarded as the Ripper's last victim, and saw her with a man only hours before she was murdered. Many years later Dan Farson interviewed Mrs Cox's niece at her home off the Hackney Road. According to the niece's story, Mrs Cox remembered the man as a gentleman, a real toff: 'He was a fine looking man, wore an overcoat with a cape, high hat . . . and Gladstone bag.' Now this is very like the classic villain in Victorian melodrama. And by then that is precisely how East Enders had come to think of Jack the Ripper. But it is poles apart from the man Mrs Cox *really* saw, the one she described before detectives and at the inquest back in 1888. Then she spoke of a short, stout man, a man with a carroty moustache and blotchy face, a man who dressed shabbily and carried only a quart can of beer.[8]

'I can remember it now as though it were yesterday.' Such protestations are common enough in reminiscent accounts. I urge my readers not to be fooled. Rather, take to heart the words of John Still: 'The memories of men are too frail a thread to hang history from.'

Sadly, the misinformation propagated in books today is not simply a product of reliance upon untrustworthy sources. For, as far as most Ripperologists are concerned, the truth runs a very poor second to selling a pet theory on the identity of the killer. This means that evidence in conflict with the theory is liable to be suppressed or perverted, that fiction is frequently dressed up as fact, and that evidence in support of the theory is sometimes completely invented. There is a long history of dishonesty and fraud in Ripper research.

We have had some notable cock-and-bull stories in recent years.

Many readers will remember Stephen Knight's bestseller, *Jack the Ripper: The Final Solution*, published in 1976. In Knight's complex tale, Mary Jane Kelly witnesses the secret marriage of Prince Albert Victor, Queen Victoria's grandson and Heir Presumptive to the throne, to a shop-assistant called Annie Elizabeth Crook, and then bands together with a group of fellow East End whores to blackmail the government. Salisbury, the Prime Minister, is alarmed. Annie Crook is a Catholic. And anti-Catholic sentiment is rife amongst the population at large. So if it comes out that the prince has taken a Catholic bride the very future of the monarchy itself might be endangered! Without further ado Salisbury hands the problem to Sir William Gull, Physician-in-Ordinary to the Queen, and Gull, assisted by Walter Sickert, the artist, and John Netley, a sinister coachman, promptly tracks down and slices up the black-mailers.

The falsehoods and absurdities in this yarn have been exposed in many books and there is no need to repeat them here. Even Joseph Sickert, who told Knight the story in the first place, denounced the Jack the Ripper part of it 'a hoax . . . a whopping fib' in 1978. What is disconcerting about the whole episode, however, is the attitude of Stephen Knight himself. His research is now known to have uncovered evidence which proved that the story was untrue. Yet he shamelessly chose to suppress it.

Later Joseph Sickert retracted his confession and supplied further material to Melvyn Fairclough, who used it in his book *The Ripper and the Royals*. It included three diaries supposedly written by Inspector Frederick George Abberline between 1892 and 1915 and given by him to Walter Sickert in 1928. Abberline is well known to students of the Ripper case. In 1888 he co-ordinated the hunt for the murderer in Whitechapel and he died in Bournemouth in 1929. I do not know whether the diaries have been subjected to competent forensic examination. I do know they are not true bill. The diaries, which incriminate a galaxy of public figures, including Lord Randolph Churchill, Sir William Gull and James K. Stephen, Prince Albert Victor's tutor at Cambridge, conflict with Abberline's known views on the identity of Jack the Ripper. On one page, reproduced by Fairclough, the detective's name is incorrectly signed 'G. F. Abberline.' Still more telling, biographical notes on four of the murder victims, set down in the diaries, supposedly by Abberline, appear to have been cribbed, sometimes almost word for word, from a research article published in *True Detective* in 1989![9]

It is in this context that we must view the recent 'discovery' of the alleged Jack the Ripper diary.

This document is a black-and-gilt calf-bound volume containing sixty-three handwritten pages. It is signed 'Jack the Ripper'.

The owner of the diary is Mike Barrett, a one-time scrap-metal dealer who lives in Liverpool. It was Barrett who brought the diary to the offices of Rupert Crew Ltd., a London literary agency, in April 1992. Its commercial potential was obvious. The publishing rights were snapped up by Smith Gryphon Ltd and on 7 October 1993 the diary hit the bookshelves amidst a blaze of hype. '7 October 1993,' ran the pre-launch publicity, 'the day the world's greatest murder mystery will be solved.'

Unfortunately, it isn't solved. And the diary is an impudent fake.

Forensic examination of the diary is as yet inconclusive. There seems no doubt that the volume itself is genuinely Victorian. This, of course, proves nothing. Family and business archives contain many used and partly used Victorian diaries, ledgers and notebooks. They frequently come on the market and can be bought at market stalls and from antiquarian book dealers. Significantly, the first forty-eight pages of the Ripper diary are missing, apparently cut out with a knife. Rectangular stains on the flysheet suggest that the volume was originally used for mounting photographs.

Tests on the ink have been made. It should be noted, however, that there is little difference between Victorian iron-gall blue-black ink and modern permanent blue-black ink and that comprehensive and diverse tests are necessary to distinguish the two. In any case it is not difficult to age ink artificially. Amalia and Rosa Panvini, the forgers of the Mussolini diaries in 1967, used modern ink. Nevertheless, they fooled the experts by baking the diaries at low heat in a kitchen oven for half an hour, a process which aged the ink so perfectly that no scientific test was able to fault it. The evaluation of the Ripper diary will doubtless continue. But at least two out of three experts who have already made tests on the ink have concluded that it is of later than Victorian age.

The diary has no pedigree before May 1991. Mike Barrett says that it was given to him at that time by a friend, a retired printer called Tony Devereux, and that Devereux refused to account for its history or explain how he came by it. Devereux died a few months later. His family insist that he never mentioned the diary to them.

All this raises a crucial question. If the diary is genuine where has it been for the last century? No one knows. It purports to be the diary of James Maybrick, a wealthy cotton broker, and identifies Maybrick as the Ripper. Maybrick will already be familiar to devotees of true crime. He died at Battlecrease House in Aigburth, a suburb of Liverpool, in May 1889, and his wife Florence was accused of poisoning him with arsenic extracted from flypapers. Florence was convicted and sentenced to death but her sentence was commuted to one of penal servitude for life. She was released in 1904 and died in the United States in 1941. Battlecrease House still stands. It has been speculated that the diary may have been found under the floorboards during rewiring work in 1990 or 1991. But neither the present owner of the property nor the electricians involved have any knowledge of such a discovery.

The diary itself contains nothing to persuade me that it was written by the Whitechapel murderer. Like most charlatans, its author gives little substantive information to check. What there is is scarcely impressive.

The diarist repeats, for example, the myth that the murderer left two farthings with the body of Annie Chapman. He makes several errors in recounting the murder of Mary Kelly in her lodging at 13 Miller's Court. We are told that the various parts of her body were strewn 'all over the room', that her severed breasts were placed on the bedside table and that the killer took the key of the room away with him. None of these statements are true. They are errors that were published in the Victorian press and have been repeated in books many times since. But the real murderer would have known better. The diarist's claim to have penned the famous 'Jack the Ripper' letter and postcard sent to the Central News in 1888 does nothing for his credibility. As I will demonstrate in this book, there is no reason whatever to suppose that these communications were written by the murderer. Besides, the handwriting of the letter and postcard does not match that of the Maybrick diary.

Presumably the hoaxer pitched upon Maybrick because his death in 1889 would neatly explain the mysterious cessation of the Ripper crimes. In other ways, though, he is an unlikely choice. Contemporary evidence suggests that the Whitechapel murderer was a man in his twenties or thirties, a man who lived in the East End of London and possessed some degree of anatomical knowledge. None of this fits Maybrick. He was a fifty-year-old cotton broker and lived at Battlecrease House at the period of the murders. Yes, he may have made regular visits to Whitechapel, but there is no evidence of it.

There are other difficulties. If Maybrick was the killer and, as the diary alleges, confessed everything to his wife, why didn't Florence mention it in her defence at her trial? Surely she could have argued that she poisoned Maybrick because she had learned that he was the Ripper and feared for her life? And if Maybrick wrote the diary why does the handwriting in this document not conform to that in Maybrick's known signatures, recorded on his marriage certificate and will?[10]

By now it should be obvious that we are dealing with a transparent hoax. The unacceptable provenance of the diary, the missing front pages, the factual inaccuracies and the implausibility of Maybrick as a Ripper suspect – even without forensic tests we have learned enough to set a whole belfry of warning bells ringing. A reading of the diary still leaves me baffled as to how any intelligent and reasonably informed student of the Ripper case could possibly have taken it seriously. There were those well versed in the subject, men like Nick Warren, Tom Cullen and Melvin Harris, who saw through the hoax from the beginning. Yet it is astonishing how many experts were fooled and allowed their names to be used in the promotional literature. They remain there, preserved like flies in amber, warnings to the complacent and the credulous.

Once errors creep into the literature they are repeated in book after book. This is because Ripperologists have always drawn heavily, sometimes exclusively, upon the work of their predecessors. Assertions of fact, however erroneous, thus travel down the years virtually unchallenged. A single example will suffice.

It is more than fifty years since William Stewart's *Jack the Ripper: A New Theory* was published. In this work we are told that Mary Kelly was three months pregnant at the time she was slain.[11] Now, there is no reason to believe any unsupported statement in Stewart. He was an uncaring fictioneer and his book is one of the worst ever written on the subject. Even inquest testimony is reported wrongly. Sometimes he invents testimony for real witnesses. Sometimes he invents witnesses as well as testimony! Especially is this assertion about Mary Kelly suspect. For it was Stewart's contention that the crimes were the work of a midwife and a pregnancy among the victims would have bestowed credibility upon his theory.

In 1959 Stewart was followed by Donald McCormick. His *Identity of Jack the Ripper* sets out to be a factual study, but does McCormick query the fable of Mary Kelly's pregnancy? Not a bit, he repeats it. Furthermore, he claims to quote the findings of Dr George Bagster Phillips, a Metropolitan Police surgeon, that Mary was 'in the early stages of pregnancy and that she was healthy and suffering from no other disease except alcoholism.'[12]

Such confident assertions sound convincing. Not surprisingly, they have found their way into numerous books and are still trotted out today as hard fact. But they are entirely made out of wholecloth. In 1987 original post-mortem notes came to light which proved that Mary was not pregnant when she died. Years before this, however, obvious questions should have been asked. Where did these writers come by their information? And were there credible sources for it?

Faulty primary sources, dishonest research and the sheepish repetition of printed folklore have taken us very far from the truth about Jack the Ripper. I do not wish to imply that there have not been worthwhile books on the subject and happily acknowledge my debt to them.[13] But this whole field of research has degenerated into a mass of conflicting claims and is now held in widespread and well-earned disrepute.

In the early seventies the rash accusations of Ripperologists against all and sundry prompted a Bill Tidy cartoon. It shows Sherlock Holmes, backed by two stalwart constables and kneeling before a dismayed and distinctly unamused Queen Victoria. 'I have reason to believe,' he says, 'that you are Jack the Ripper.' *The Truth* sent up the industry again in 1988. Reviewing the credentials of suspects as diverse as Lord Tennyson and George Formby, its contributors eventually plumped for Sooty, an 'evil little criminal mastermind' who understood that being an eight-inch-high glove puppet of a bear he might pass through the cesspits, pubs and gutters of Whitechapel unnoticed.[14]

It is time to attempt a rescue.

When I began this book I realized that a new study of the Whitechapel murders would have to do two things. First, it must have the courage to dispense with the books and research the subject from scratch. And second, it must proceed without any preconceived theory. In short, the conclusions must follow from the facts and not the other way around.

I have, of course, benefited from the work of other bona-fide students. But essentially my account rests upon a completely fresh overhaul of primary sources. A mass of documents in police, Home Office, inquest, court, hospital, prison, workhouse and genealogical records, some still closed to general public access, have been searched. And from them I have fashioned the most comprehensive and accurate reconstruction of the case ever placed before the public. Areas of research generally neglected in the literature have been explored. Victims, for example, are accorded as much priority as suspects in this book. I have also described and assessed the methods taken by the police to capture the criminal and explained their difficulties with both Home Office and press.

A century ago the identity of Jack the Ripper aroused as much passion and debate amongst senior detectives as it does today amongst the world's amateur sleuths. Sir Melville Macnaghten accused a barrister who threw himself into the Thames in December 1888. Sir Robert Anderson remained steadfast to his belief that the Ripper was a Polish Jew committed to a lunatic asylum in 1891, while in the opinion of Inspector Abberline, Jack the Ripper died on the scaffold in Wandsworth Prison in 1903, convicted under another pseudonym of the murder of his wife.

On the strength of my findings the most important police suspects are identified and assessed. Some, like Montague John Druitt, are already well-known. Others, like Oswald Puckridge and Nikaner Benelius, have never been fully dealt with in any book before. In rejecting the names dangled before us by Macnaghten in 1894 I have challenged the whole drift of serious Ripper studies since 1959. This has not been prompted by any desire for sensation. I have simply followed where the evidence has led me.

If you are looking for another shoddily-researched 'final solution', with a cast list of disgraced royals, Czarist secret agents, black magicians and deranged midwives, you had best put this book down now.

If you prefer facts to journalism, if you want to know the truth about Jack the Ripper and are tired of being humbugged, read on!

2

Mysterious Murder in George Yard

BANK HOLIDAY MONDAY, 6 August 1888. It was the last holiday of the summer. Some Londoners, rising early and determined to spend this last day in the country or by the sea, ventured out to Epping Forest, Rye House, Hampton Court, Kew or the Kent and Sussex coasts. But as the day wore on an increasingly dull and leaden sky presaged yet more rain. It seemed to have done little else that summer. Rainy, thundery weather had persisted until the end of July, and August had begun wet and changeable. Not surprisingly, then, most holiday folk elected to shelter in the capital. To its attractions they resorted in shoals.

Tussaud's, the zoological gardens in Regent's Park, the People's Palace in the East End, the South Kensington museums and the Tower all enjoyed brisk patronage. At Alexandra Palace holidaymakers gathered in their thousands in the drizzle to watch intrepid Professor Baldwin ascend in his balloon to 1000 feet and then parachute to the ground. More than 55,000 opted for Crystal Palace. There the entertainments ranged from organ recitals to military bands, from Keen the cyclist, matching his bicycle over 20 miles against horses, to Captain Dale, the 'well-known Aeronaut', from a monster fireworks display to a 'Grand Fairy Ballet'. And when the day's activities were done London's rich night life, its pubs, theatres and music-halls, ensured conviviality and spectacle for those still anxious to postpone the damp journey home.

Amidst the holiday crowds that day were Joseph and Elizabeth

Mahoney, a young married couple. Their lives, like those of most East Enders, were hard. Joseph was a carman. His wife worked from nine o'clock in the morning to seven at night in a match factory at Stratford. And their combined earnings supported a frugal existence at No. 47 George Yard Buildings, a block of model dwellings occupied, as the *East London Observer* tells us, by 'people of the poorest description', in George Yard (present Gunthorpe Street), off Whitechapel High Street.

The Bank Holiday thus came as a kind if brief respite, and in defiance of bad weather the Mahoneys made the most of it. It was not until about 1.40 on the Tuesday morning that the weary couple arrived home. They went straight up to their room but Elizabeth, after taking off her hat and cloak, slipped out again for some provisions for their supper. Every night the gas jets illuminating the wide, stone staircase in George Yard Buildings were turned out at eleven, so it was completely dark on the stairs as she descended to the street. She was away but a few minutes. It was perhaps about 1.50 when she returned, having purchased provisions from a chandler's shop in nearby Thrawl Street, and after supper had been disposed of the Mahoneys went to bed. Elizabeth had seen no one in descending or ascending the stairs, and that night the couple slept undisturbed.

Alfred George Crow was a licensed cab-driver. He, too, rented a lodging, No. 35, in George Yard Buildings. Crow got home that night at 3.30 a.m. Although he carried no light his eyes were good, and when he reached the first floor landing he saw someone lying there. It was not unusual to find vagrants sleeping on the landing so he took no notice of the silent figure and went straight up to his room, where he sought the comfort of his bed. Like the Mahoneys he heard no noise during the night.

It was another tenant, waterside labourer John Saunders Reeves from No. 37, who discovered the murder. Because he had to be up early for work, Reeves retired at about six on the Bank Holiday evening. The next morning he left his lodging at about 4.45. It was already getting light as he descended the stairs. And on the first floor landing he was horrified to come upon the body of a woman, lying on her back in a pool of blood. A few details – the absence of blood from the mouth, the clenched hands and the disarranged clothes, torn open at the front – registered in his brain before he stumbled down into the street to find a policeman.[1]

Reeves was soon back, leading PC Thomas Barrett 226H up the

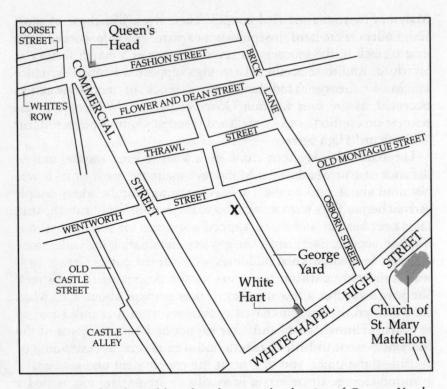

George Yard and neighbourhood. × *marks the site of George Yard Buildings, where Martha Tabram was found dead, 4.45 a.m. on 7 August 1888*

stairs to the landing. The body was that of a middle-aged woman, plump and about five feet three inches in height. Her hair and complexion were both dark. Her clothes, a black bonnet, long black jacket, dark-green skirt, brown petticoat and stockings, and pair of 'side-spring' boots, were old and worn. She lay on her back, her hands lying by her sides and tightly clenched, her legs open. 'The clothes,' Barrett told the inquest two days later, 'were turned up as far as the centre of the body, leaving the lower part of the body exposed; the legs were open, and altogether her position was such as to at once suggest in my mind that recent intimacy had taken place.'[2]

The woman was plainly dead. Nevertheless, Barrett sent immediately for a doctor and Dr Timothy Robert Killeen of 68 Brick Lane arrived in George Yard at about 5.30 a.m. His hurried examination of the body revealed for the first time the awful extent of the woman's injuries. She had been stabbed no less than thirty-nine times! The doctor concluded that she had been dead for about three hours and gave instructions for the body to be at once removed to the mortuary. Since there was no public mortuary in Whitechapel the police conveyed it to the deadhouse belonging to the workhouse infirmary in Old Montague Street.

At the mortuary Killeen conducted a post-mortem examination. His findings, presented to the inquest jury on 9 August, described the woman's fearful wounds in detail. Upon opening the head he had found an effusion of blood between the scalp and the bone. The brain was pale but healthy. There were at least twenty-two stab wounds to the trunk: 'the left lung was penetrated in five places, and the right lung in two places, but the lungs were otherwise perfectly healthy. The heart was rather fatty, and was penetrated in one place, but there was otherwise nothing in the heart to cause death, although there was some blood in the pericardium. The liver was healthy, but was penetrated in five places, the spleen was perfectly healthy, and was penetrated in two places; both the kidneys were perfectly healthy; the stomach was also perfectly healthy, but was penetrated in six places; the intestines were healthy, and so were all the other organs. The lower portion of the body was penetrated in one place, the wound being three inches in length and one in depth . . . there was a deal of blood between the legs, which were separated. Death was due to hemorrhage and loss of blood.'[3]

Killeen disagreed with Barrett on one point. He saw no reason to believe that sexual intercourse had recently taken place. But he did proffer some clues as to the modus operandi of the killer. There was no evidence of a struggle. One of the wounds, he contended, might have been made by a left-handed person, but the rest appeared to have been inflicted by a right-handed person. And two different weapons had been used. Now, much has been made of Killeen's testimony on this last point. It is worded differently by different reporters. The *East London Observer* quoted the doctor thus: 'I don't think that all the wounds were inflicted with the same instrument, because there was one wound on the breast bone which did not correspond with the other wounds on the body. The instrument with which the wounds were inflicted, would most probably be an ordinary knife, but a knife would not cause such a wound as that on the breast bone. That wound I should think would have been inflicted with some form of a dagger.' In the *Daily News* his evidence is a little more specific: 'In the witness's opinion the wounds were not inflicted with the same instrument, there being a deep wound in the breast from some long, strong instrument, while most of the others were done apparently with a penknife. The large wound could have been caused by a sword bayonet or dagger.'[4]

Inspector Edmund Reid, the 'Local Inspector' (Head of CID) in the Metropolitan Police's H or Whitechapel Division, took charge of the investigation. From the outset the case promised to be a difficult one. The dead woman was not known to any of the tenants of George Yard Buildings. There was no clue to the author of the crime and no obvious motive for it. And despite the ferocity of the murder no inhabitant of the buildings had heard the slightest disturbance during the night. The last point is one of some significance. Inspector Ernest Ellisdon, in a report written only three days after the murder, explicitly stated that no blood was found on the stairs leading to the landing. This means that the victim was killed where her body was discovered. Yet, in a crowded tenement block, no one seems to have heard a sound. Francis Hewitt, the superintendent of the dwellings, occupied an apartment with his wife close to the spot where Reeves found the body. Indeed, for the benefit of one journalist, he took a foot rule and measured the distance between the two. They were only twelve feet apart. 'And we never heard a cry,' he told the reporter. Mrs Hewitt said that she heard a single cry of 'Murder' but that was early in the evening, and although it echoed through the building it did not seem to emanate from there. In any case, as the Hewitts explained, 'the district round here is rather rough, and cries of "Murder" are of frequent, if not nightly, occurrence in the district.' The Hewitts' comment suggests a possible solution to the problem. But there is another – that the victim's cries were stifled by strangulation before or during the knife attack. That, according to the *Illustrated Police News*, is what happened: 'The difficulty of identification arose out of the brutal treatment to which the deceased was manifestly subjected, she being throttled while held down and the face and head so swollen and distorted in consequence that her real features are not discernible.' Unfortunately, with the bulk of the police files now lost, it has proved impossible to corroborate this particular detail.[5]

Hastily-compiled press reports soon apprised the general public of the tragedy. One of the earliest, printed in the *Star*, appeared on the day of the murder:

A Whitechapel Horror

A woman, now lying unidentified at the mortuary, Whitechapel, was ferociously stabbed to death this morning, between two and four o'clock, on the landing of a stone staircase in George's-buildings, Whitechapel.

George's-buildings are tenements occupied by the poor laboring class. A lodger going early to his work found the body. Another lodger says the murder was not committed when he returned home about two o'clock. The woman was stabbed in 20 places. No weapon was found near her, and her murderer has left no trace. She is of middle age and height, has black hair and a large, round face, and apparently belonged to the lowest class.[6]

The East End, accustomed as it was to everyday violence, was shocked by the ferocity displayed in this killing. Morbid sightseers visited George Yard Buildings to gaze at the crimson-stained flags where the body had been found. The victim, in the view of one local newspaper, had been 'literally butchered', the 'virulent savagery' of her killer 'beyond comprehension'. Another spoke of the 'feeling of insecurity' occasioned by the realization that 'in a great city like London, the streets of which are continually patrolled by police, a woman can be foully and horribly killed almost next to the citizens peacefully sleeping in their beds, without a trace or clue being left of the villain who did the deed.' Indeed such was the consternation in and about George Yard that a few days after the murder about seventy local men held a meeting and appointed a committee of twelve to watch certain streets, chiefly between eleven at night and one in the morning. The St Jude's Vigilance Committee, as it was called, was the first of several spawned by the Whitechapel murders. It comprised both working men and students from Toynbee Hall and met once a week to receive reports and concert recommendations for the better order and security of the district. The honorary secretary was Thomas Hancock Nunn.[7]

If the public hoped for clues to emerge at the inquest they were disappointed. Wynne E. Baxter, Coroner for the South Eastern District of Middlesex, was on holiday in Scandinavia, so it was George Collier, the deputy coroner, who opened the proceedings in the library of the Working Lads' Institute, Whitechapel Road, on the afternoon of Thursday, 9 August. He sat beneath a magnificent portrait of the Princess of Wales by Louis Fleischmann. Other paintings, royal portraits and landscapes, adorned the library walls in profusion. Collier was flanked on his right by Inspector Reid, smartly dressed in blue serge, and Dr Killeen, and on his left by the inquest jury. The general public had been excluded, but popular interest was reflected in the unprecedentedly large number of summoned jurymen who attended, twenty in all, and in the atmosphere that prevailed throughout the court. It was, commented the *East London Advertiser*'s reporter, 'painfully quiet'.[8]

But there were to be no major revelations that day. A succession of tenants from George Yard Buildings were called as witnessses – Elizabeth Mahoney, plainly clad in a 'rusty-black' dress and black woollen shawl and speaking so softly that she was ordered to stand next to the jury; Alfred George Crow, the young cab-driver with the 'beardless, but intelligent face' and close-cropped hair, dressed in a shabby green overcoat; and John Saunders Reeves, he who found the body, a short man wearing a black overcoat, corduroy trousers and ear-rings, his face 'pale and contracted' but sporting a slight, dark beard and moustache. Together with PC Barrett they did no more than detail the circumstances surrounding the discovery of the body. The only other important witness was Dr Killeen, who presented the medical evidence.

The inquest, then, established the fact and cause of death. But of whom? Even the identity of the victim still remained a mystery. A woman wearing a blue dress and black hat, and holding a baby in her arms, sat before the deputy coroner throughout the proceedings. She had been taken to view the body at the mortuary and had identified it as that of an acquaintance named Martha Turner. But she was only one of three women who had purported to identify the deceased and each had named her differently.

In view of the uncertainties still surrounding the case Collier adjourned the inquest for two weeks. 'It was one of the most dreadful murders anyone could imagine,' he heatedly told the court in terminating the afternoon's proceedings. 'The man must have been a perfect savage to inflict such a number of wounds on a defenceless woman in such a way.'[9]

The puzzle of the dead woman's identity was resolved by Henry Samuel Tabram of 6 River Terrace, East Greenwich, a foreman packer at a furniture warehouse. On Monday, 13 August, he saw the victim's name printed as 'Tabram' in a newspaper, and the next day identified the body as that of his wife Martha, from whom he had been separated for thirteen years. At the time of her death she was 39 years old and a prostitute.

Apparently Martha told Mary Bousfield, her landlady in 1888, that her real name was Staples or Stapleton. In fact, it was Martha White and she was born at 17 Marshall Street, London Road, Southwark, on 10 May 1849, the daughter of Charles Samuel and Elisabeth (née Dowsett) White. The family are recorded at the same address in the 1851 census. By then Charles Samuel, a warehouseman, had sired five children: Henry (aged 13), Esther (11), Stephen (9), Mary Ann (4) and Martha (1). Henry was an errand boy and Esther and Stephen were still at school.

Martha's life was dogged by tragedy from an early age. On 15 November 1865, when she was sixteen, her father died suddenly and unexpectedly. William Payne, Coroner for the City of London and Borough of Southwark, held an inquest three days later at the Gibraltar public house in St George's Road and his papers, now preserved at the Corporation of London Records Office, afford us a glimpse into the circumstances of Martha's family at this time.

Her parents had separated and since about May 1865 Charles White had been lodging alone at the house of Mrs Rebecca Grover of 31 Pitt Street, St George's Road. His health there was uncertain. In October he suffered a severe attack of diarrhoea. When Mr Henry O'Donnell, a surgeon, came to treat him, he found him troubled by his family problems and complaining of poor circulation and cold. Mary Ann, Martha's sister, told the inquest, too, that their father had recently complained of a weak back and had been unable to work.

Tragically, Charles White died at a time of reconciliation with his wife. Four days before his death Elisabeth White visited him for the first time since he had moved into Mrs Grover's house. During the next few days she came several times and, on the evening of 15 November, both Elisabeth and Mary Ann had supper with Charles at his lodging. The meal was frugal – bread, butter and beer – but Charles was pleased to see his daughter and the three were happy together. Indeed, according to Mrs Grover, who saw him that evening, he 'seemed more cheerful and better than I had ever seen him.' Then, at about ten, Charles got up to go to bed, began to take off his waistcoat and fell over backwards to the floor.

Unable to speak, he died there without another word, one arm out of his waistcoat. O'Donnell, summoned by Mary Ann, arrived about fifteen minutes later. He found the dead man's face pale and his body so cold that it 'was as if he had been dead two hours'. There were, nevertheless, no suspicious appearances and he concluded that death had been occasioned by syncope. The inquest recorded a verdict of death by natural causes.[10]

We know nothing of Martha's relationship with her father. But the break up of the family home and the death of its breadwinner at the early age of fifty-nine were presumably important destabilizing factors in the life of the growing girl. Her own marriage four years later should have provided her with the basis for a fresh start. Charles White had been a relatively sober person. His youngest daughter, sadly, was not. And it was drink more than anything else that turned the rest of her life into a chapter of accidents.

Martha married Henry Samuel Tabram at Trinity Church in the parish of St Mary, Newington, on Christmas Day 1869. At the time of the marriage the couple were already living together in Pleasant Place but by February 1871 they had moved to 20 Marshall Street, only a few doors from the house in which Martha had been born. Although blessed by two sons – Frederick John in February 1871 and Charles Henry in December 1872 – the union was short-lived. It foundered upon the rock of Martha's heavy drinking and Henry left her in 1875. For about three years after that he allowed her twelve shillings a week. Then, because she was given to pestering him for money in the street and had taken up with another man, he reduced her weekly allowance to only 2s. 6d.

The other man was a carpenter named Henry Turner. Martha lived with him, on and off, for about twelve years, her drinking habits the cause of occasional separations. 'Since she has been living with me,' Turner told the resumed inquest on 23 August, 'her character for sobriety was not good. If I gave her any money she generally spent it in drink. In fact, it was always drink.' While they were together Martha usually came home about eleven in the evening but there were occasions when she stayed out all night. Her excuse invariably was 'that she was subject to hysterical fits, had been overtaken with one and taken to a police-station or hospital.' Turner himself had witnessed her in such fits. They generally occurred, he said, when she was drunk.

By 1888 Turner was out of regular employment and he and

Martha were earning a living as hawkers, selling trinkets, needles and pins, menthol cones and other small articles. For about four months they lodged in the house of Mrs Mary Bousfield of 4 Star Place, Commercial Road. There Mrs Bousfield found Martha a rather reserved woman but one who, though not habitually drunk, would 'rather have a glass of ale than a cup of tea.' About a month or six weeks before the murder the Turners left without giving any notice and owing rent. Exhibiting a curious twinge of conscience, Martha returned one night, unbeknown to Mrs Bousfield, and left the key of her room. The George Yard tragedy, of course, etched Martha's name indelibly into the memory of the Bousfield household. In 1964, when Tom Cullen was researching his book on Jack the Ripper, he appealed through the East End press for people who could remember and perhaps shed light upon the crimes to come forward. One of those who responded was James W. Bousfield. Eighty-three years old, he was Mary's son, and he still owned one of the key chains Martha Tabram had hawked about the streets and which he had preserved as a souvenir after the murder.

Turner last broke with Martha about three weeks before her death. She seems to have tried to support herself by hawking and prostitution but many of her pitiful earnings were probably spent on drink. Her last known address, 19 George Street, Spitalfields, was a common lodging house. On Saturday, 4 August, Turner met Martha in Leadenhall Street. She was then in a destitute condition and he gave her 1s. 6d. to buy stock 'with which to earn a few ha'pence.' He never saw her alive again.

So the victim was identified. But what of the killer? Inspector Reid had turned up two important witnesses. The first was Thomas Barrett, the constable on duty near George Yard on the night of the murder. Early on the morning of 7 August, at about two o'clock, he saw a soldier loitering in George Yard. When Barrett challenged his presence there at so late an hour he replied that he was waiting for his chum who had gone with a girl. Notwithstanding the fleeting nature of this encounter in the dark the constable was able to furnish his superiors with a detailed description of the man. He was a private of the Grenadier Guards with one good conduct badge but no medals. His age was 22 to 26, his height five feet nine or ten inches. He had a fair complexion, dark hair and a small dark-brown moustache turned up at the ends.[11]

Reid lost no time in following up this lead. That very day, 7

August, he took Barrett to the Tower, where the sergeant-major of the garrison showed him several prisoners confined in the guardroom, presumably for indiscretions committed on the Bank Holiday. When the constable failed to identify any of them a parade of all the Grenadiers who had been absent or on leave at the time of the murder was arranged. It took place at the Tower on the morning of 8 August.

The ensuing fiasco was fully described by Reid in a report of 25 September to the Assistant Commissioner (CID) of the Metropolitan Police.[12] Before the parade he cautioned Barrett 'to be careful as to his actions because many eyes were watching him and a great deal depended on his picking out the right man and no other.' While the men were being mustered the constable was kept out of the way by the sergeant's mess. When all was ready Reid directed him to walk along the rank and touch the man he had seen in George Yard. Slowly Barrett worked his way along the line from left to right. About the centre of the line he stopped, stepped forward and touched a private wearing medals. As PC Barrett walked back to report to his chief Reid came out to meet him. Barrett said that he had picked out the man, but Reid wanted him to be certain and told him to return to the rank and have another look. Passing once more along the line Barrett picked out a second man. 'I asked him how he came to pick out two,' reported the inspector, 'when he replied "the man I saw in George Yard had no medals and the first man I picked out had."'

Both suspects were escorted to the orderly-room. There the constable insisted that he had made a mistake in picking out the soldier with medals. His name was not taken and he was dismissed. The second suspect, John Leary, denied that he was Barrett's man and gave a detailed account of his own movements on Bank Holiday night. He had, he said, gone on leave with Private Law that night. They visited Brixton and stayed there drinking until the pubs closed. Leary went to the rear of one of them to relieve himself. When he returned Law had disappeared so he set off alone to Battersea and Chelsea, and from thence past Charing Cross into the Strand. There he met Law at about 4.30 a.m. They walked together to Billingsgate, where they had a drink, and arrived back at barracks at 6.00 a.m.

When Law was brought into the orderly-room he was not permitted to speak to Leary. His statement, nevertheless, corroborated that of his companion 'in every particular' and the case against the accused man collapsed. 'I felt certain in my own mind,' wrote Reid, 'that [the] PC had made a great mistake and I allowed the men to leave the orderly room.'

The next day Corporal Benjamin, who had been absent from the Tower garrison without leave since 6 August, turned up for duty. His bayonet and clothing were inspected but no trace of bloodstains could be found on them. Benjamin protested that he had spent Bank Holiday night with his father, the landlord of the Canbury Arms, Kingston-upon-Thames, and when the police checked his alibi it was confirmed.[13]

On the face of it Reid's dismissal of John Leary, the man Barrett picked out, may seem complacent, for only Private Law could corroborate any part of his statement and it is probable that if the two men had been involved in the murder they would have concocted an alibi between themselves before returning to barracks. However, Barrett's selection of two men certainly suggests that he was not very confident in his identification and Reid was obviously highly sceptical of its worth. It is not possible for us to identify Barrett's final choice satisfactorily because there were two privates named John Leary then serving in the third battalion of Grenadier Guards stationed at the Tower. Their attestation and discharge papers, preserved at the Public Record Office, suggest that both were men of good character. One, a Glamorganshire man, served in the ranks between 1877 and 1898. At the time of the murder he was thirty-one. Like the man Barrett saw in George Yard, he was five feet ten inches tall and had dark-brown hair and a fair complexion. But he had been decorated for service in Egypt in 1885 (Barrett's man wore no medals) and his conduct is described as 'exemplary.' The only offences noted against him are nine cases of drunkenness between 1877 and 1885. The other private, from Macroom in Cork, served with the colours or in the reserve from 1886 to 1902. Although, at nearly six feet one inch, he was taller than Barrett's man, he was a good fit in other respects. Of dark brown hair and fresh complexion, he was twenty-five years old at the time of the identity parade.[14]

Reid's second important witness, a tall, masculine-looking prostitute, her face reddened and soddened by drink, walked into Commercial Street Police Station on 9 August and said that she had been in the company of the deceased on Bank Holiday night. Her name was Mary Ann Connelly but she was known on the streets as Pearly Poll. Poll had known Martha Tabram by the name of 'Emma' for several months. On 6 August, together with two soldiers, they had walked and drunk about Whitechapel from 10.00 to 11.45 in the evening. The soldiers were guardsmen, one a corporal, the other a private. When the foursome broke up at 11.45 Poll took her client, the corporal, up Angel Alley. Emma and the private went up George Yard together. About thirty or forty minutes later, at the corner of George Yard, Poll and her corporal separated. He set off 'Aldgate way' and Poll walked towards Whitechapel. Apparently there had been no animosity between the four. 'There was a quarrel about money, but not with the deceased,' Poll would tell the inquest on 23 August. 'We parted all right, however, and with no bad words; indeed, we were all good friends.'[15]

Poll stated that she would know both men again and promised the police that she would attend an identity parade at the Tower on Friday the 10th. But neither on that day nor the next could she be found. Without telling them she had, in fact, gone to spend a couple of days with her cousin, a Mrs Shean of 4 Fuller's Court, Drury Lane, and it was not until the following Sunday that they contacted her again. The soldiers of the Tower garrison were eventually paraded before her at 11 o'clock on the morning of Monday, 13 August, but Poll failed to pick anyone out. A colourful if apocryphal account of this bizarre episode was printed in the *East London Observer*:

> Inspector Reid, accompanied by 'Pearly Poll', proceeded to the Tower on Monday afternoon (sic), where she was confronted with every non-commissioned officer and private who had leave of absence at the time of the outrage. They were paraded at the back of the Tower, unseen by the public – of whom on Monday there was a large number frequenting the historic structure – and 'Pearly Poll' was asked, 'Can you see either of the men you saw with the woman now dead?' 'Pearly Poll', in no way embarrassed, placed her arms akimbo, glanced at the men with the air of an inspecting officer, and shook her head. This indication of a negative was not sufficient. 'Can you identify anyone?' she was asked. 'Pearly Poll' exclaimed, with a good deal of feminine emphasis, 'He ain't here.' The woman was very decided on this point, and the men were then dismissed.[16]

Poll now, however, disclosed the information that her soldier companions of Bank Holiday night had white bands around their caps. This suggested that they had been men of the Coldstream Guards and a parade of all the corporals and privates of that regiment who had been absent or on leave at the time of the murder was held at Wellington Barracks, in Birdcage Walk, on 15 August. The proceedings began auspiciously enough. Poll identified two men, one as the corporal who had been with her and the other as the private with whom 'Emma' had gone up George Yard. Unfortunately the man picked out as the 'corporal' turned out to be a private named George. Besides three good conduct badges he had an alibi. George insisted that he had been with his wife at 120 Hammersmith Road from eight o'clock on the evening of 6 August to six o'clock the following morning and subsequent police enquiries verified his statement. Poll's second man, another private named Skipper, protested that on the night of the murder he had been in barracks. When the regiment's books demonstrated that this had, indeed, been the case, that he had been in barracks from 10.05 p.m. on 6 August, he too was cleared.[17]

Police officers later spoke disparagingly of Pearly Poll's efforts. Walter Dew was a CID officer in 1888, attached to the H or Whitechapel Division of the Metropolitan Police. When he wrote his memoirs fifty years later he accused Poll of deliberately identifying the wrong men out of pique. Sir Melville Macnaghten, who joined the Metropolitan Police in 1889, heard a similar story. In a confidential note he prepared upon the Whitechapel murders in 1894 he asserted that she 'failed, or refused, to identify' the soldiers.[18] There are grounds for such suspicions for Poll's behaviour during the investigation did sometimes seem to exhibit the distrust of authority characteristic of her class. She thus went to stay with her cousin without troubling to inform the police, even though she was required for the identity parade at the Tower, and to one person who enquired where she was going she allegedly replied that she was going to drown herself. Later, when testifying before the inquest on 23 August, she displayed the same diffidence. On this occasion, complaining that her chest was 'queer', she gave her testimony through an officer. Yet all this does not necessarily mean that Poll deliberately sabotaged the investigation. She drank heavily on Bank Holiday night. Her recollections of that evening may well have been hazy. At the inquest she insisted that the two men whom she had picked out were, to the best of her belief, the ones who had been with her and Tabram, and if she was mistaken it is well to remember that PC Barrett enjoyed no better success. Why, moreover, did Poll volunteer her information in the first place if she did not wish to assist the police?

By 23 August, when George Collier reopened the inquest at the Working Lads' Institute, the police investigation had thus ground to an ignominious halt. Popular excitement had now begun to wane and at two o'clock p.m., when the proceedings commenced, only a small crowd had gathered outside the Institute. As on the previous occasion the general public were excluded from the court, but they carefully scrutinized the witnesses as, one by one, they passed into the building.

The evidence heard inside identified the victim as Martha Tabram and dwelt at some length upon her character and history. On the circumstances surrounding her death, however, the only important witness was Pearly Poll. Wrapped in an old green shawl and speaking in a low, husky voice, she told the inquest of her Bank Holiday night out in Whitechapel with Martha and the two soldiers. And that being all, the proceedings came to an end.

In his concluding remarks to the jury Collier left them in no doubt as to what their verdict must be. 'This was one of the most horrible crimes that had been committed for certainly some time past,' he reminded them. 'The details were very revolting, as they would remember from the doctor's evidence on the last occasion, and the person who had inflicted the injuries could have been nothing less than a fiend.' Martha Tabram had clearly been 'foully and brutally murdered'. They could bring in no other verdict than one of wilful murder.[19]

The jurors returned a unanimous verdict of wilful murder against some person or persons unknown, and when Martha's death was registered two days later, that was recorded as the cause of death. 'Wilful murder against some person or persons unknown' . . . words which would become frighteningly familiar to the people of the East End that autumn.

The facts of the Tabram slaying, like those relating to almost all of the Whitechapel murders, have been obscured by generations of supposition and invention. It is important to be clear about them. Tabram was stabbed thirty-nine times. A special report upon the case, prepared in September 1888 by Chief Inspector Donald S. Swanson, noted that she had been stabbed 'on body, neck and private parts with a knife or dagger', and press versions of Dr Killeen's inquest testimony indicate that there were no fewer than nine stab wounds to the throat.[20] But there is no evidence that carotid arteries had been severed, the throat cut or the abdomen extensively mutilated.

The notion now sometimes expressed that the George Yard murderer displayed anatomical knowledge is a myth. It sprang, apparently, from the remarkable statements which Donald McCormick, in his book *The Identity of Jack the Ripper* (1959), placed in the mouth of Dr Killeen. According to McCormick, the doctor tentatively identified the murder weapons as a long-bladed knife and a surgical instrument, and told the police that 'whoever it was, he knew how and where to cut.'[21] Anyone who cares to examine the contemporary evidence will soon discover that these were not Killeen's views. At the inquest he said that the murderer had employed two weapons. All but one of the wounds had evidently been inflicted with an ordinary penknife, but the wound on the breast bone had been inflicted with a strong long-bladed weapon, possibly a dagger or a bayonet. There is no reason to suppose that the doctor changed his mind upon this point. The records of the Metropolitan Police still contain a contemporary digest in tabular form of all the official reports made upon the case.[22] In one column, headed 'Nature and description of wounds as given in surgeon's report', is written the comment 'twenty wounds on breast, stomach and abdomen apparently inflicted with a penknife.' As for the killer's supposed anatomical knowledge, there is no record that Killeen ever expressed an opinion upon the subject. To judge by what we know of the case the question would scarcely have arisen. There had been no systematic mutilation. Instead, in an apparent frenzy, the murderer had repeatedly stabbed his victim through and through. We know of no police inquiries amongst doctors, or even butchers and slaughter men, at this time, which in itself suggests that Killeen had given the CID no reason to suspect that the murderer might be possessed of anatomical knowledge.

The 'fiend' responsible for the outrage was never identified. Yet a view that the crime was perpetrated by soldiers has taken root in conventional Ripperology and will now be very difficult to shift. Paul Harrison's optimistically titled *Jack the Ripper: The Mystery Solved* endorsed it as recently as 1991: 'To this day the crime remains unsolved, though the Grenadier Guard theory seems highly probable since the wounds inflicted upon the body of Martha Turner/Tabram were like those caused by a bayonet.'[23] My discerning readers will already know better. The truth is that there is no persuasive evidence against the soldiery.

Certainly Martha Tabram was last seen alive on Bank Holiday night, walking up George Yard with a soldier. But that was at

11.45 p.m. Dr Killeen estimated the time of her death as about 2.30 the following morning, an estimate that is consistent with the testimony of both Elizabeth Mahoney and Alfred Crow. Between 1.40 and 1.50 that morning Elizabeth climbed or descended the staircase in George Yard Buildings three times and saw nothing on the first floor landing. Crow noticed a body, almost certainly Martha's, there at 3.30. Almost three hours thus elapsed between the time Pearly Poll last saw Martha alive and that of the murder, ample time for her to have ventured out again into Whitechapel Road or Commercial Street, found herself another client and returned to the relative seclusion of George Yard. The police realized this very well and their identity parades at the Tower and Wellington Barracks are evidence less of their conviction that the murderer was a soldier than of their diligence in following up the only leads they had.

Certainly, too, sergeants and corporals were then permitted to carry side-arms when on leave and Dr Killeen told the inquest that *just one* of Martha's wounds might have been inflicted with a bayonet. But it is important to note that he did not positively assert that a bayonet had been used, only that the wound on the breast bone had been inflicted with a strong, long-bladed weapon which *could have been* a bayonet *or* a dagger. And even if, for the sake of argument, we assume that a bayonet was one of the guilty weapons, such a circumstance would not unequivocally have incriminated a soldier. The police, too streetwise to attach much importance to the alleged bayonet, explained this at the time to the *East London Advertiser*: 'The police state that they should not be at all surprised to find that the murder was not entirely the work of soldiers or that soldiers had a [i.e. no] hand in the crime at all . . . Old bayonets, they assert, can at any time be bought in Petticoat Lane, and at the old iron stalls there, for about a penny each, and they have frequently been seen as playthings in the hands of the children.'[24]

A view propagated by some modern writers that the murderer was ambidextrous has even less to recommend it. It was suggested, of course, by the killer's use of two weapons. However, Killeen's testimony made it clear that although one wound *might* have been inflicted by a left-handed person the others all appeared to have been inflicted by a right-handed person. And the only sensible conclusion we can draw from that is that the murderer was right-handed.

Back in August 1888 no one seems to have feared that the George Yard murder might herald a series of such atrocities. There had, however, already been three murderous attacks on women in the area that year.

The first, and in the context of the Tabram murder by far the most interesting, occurred on Saturday, 25 February 1888. At 5.00 p.m. that day Annie Millwood, widow of Richard Millwood, a soldier, was admitted to the Whitechapel Workhouse Infirmary from 8 White's Row, Spitalfields. In infirmary records the cause of her admission is simply given as 'stabs'. But an *Eastern Post* report is more revealing: 'It appears . . . the deceased was admitted to the Whitechapel Infirmary suffering from numerous stabs in the legs and lower part of the body. She stated that she had been attacked by a man who she did not know, and who stabbed her with a clasp knife which he took from his pocket. No one appears to have seen the attack, and as far as at present ascertained there is only the woman's statement to bear out the allegations of an attack, though that she had been stabbed cannot be denied.'

Annie recovered from her wounds. On 21 March she was discharged to the South Grove Workhouse, Mile End Road, but on 31 March, while engaged in some occupation at the rear of the building there, she suddenly collapsed and died. An inquest was held before Coroner Baxter five days later. It attributed Annie's death to 'sudden effusion into the pericardium from the rupture of the left pulmonary artery through ulceration'. In other words, she died from natural causes and not from the effects of the stab wounds.[25]

We are not told whether Annie was a prostitute or not but, although only thirty-eight, she was a widow and may have been maintaining herself in this way. White's Row, off Commercial Street, was only a few minutes away from George Yard. And Annie was attacked by a stranger who wounded her 'numerous' times in the legs and lower torso with a knife. Annie's case thus has much in common with Martha's. Both women could easily have encountered the same man.

The victim of the second attack was Ada Wilson, a 39-year-old machinist of 9 Maidman Street, Burdett Road, Mile End. At about 12.30 on the night of 27–28 March Ada was about to go to bed when she heard a knock at the door. Opening it, she was confronted by a man, a total stranger. He looked about thirty, his face was sunburnt and he had a fair moustache. He was about 5 feet 6 inches tall. His clothes included a dark coat, light trousers and a wideawake hat. The man demanded money and told Ada that if she did not at once produce the cash she had but a few moments to live. Then, when Ada refused to give him anything, he immediately drew a clasp knife from his pocket and stabbed her twice in the throat. Fortunately her screams attracted help and, after Dr Wheeler of Mile End Road had bound up her wounds, she was sent to the London Hospital. It had been a very dangerous attack indeed. Press reports of the incident commented: 'it is thought impossible that the injured woman can recover.' But Ada baffled their expectations and on 27 April, after thirty days in hospital, she was discharged as cured. Her assailant, who had probably been scared off by the screams, was never traced.[26]

Robbery seemed to have been the motive for the attack on Ada Wilson. The fatal assault upon Emma Smith, less than a week later, was less easy to explain. Emma Elizabeth Smith, a 45-year-old widow, lived in a common lodging house at 18 George Street, Spitalfields. At seven o'clock on the evening of Easter Monday, 2 April 1888, she went out. Nine or ten hours after that she staggered back into the lodging house and told the deputy keeper, Mrs Mary Russell, that she had been set upon and robbed of all her money. She certainly looked in a dreadful state. Her head and face were injured, her right ear had nearly been torn off and she complained of pains in the lower part of her body. Mrs Russell immediately took Emma to the London Hospital. But her injuries were severe and she did not long survive them. A blunt instrument had been inserted into her vagina with great force and had ruptured the perineum. At nine o'clock on Wednesday morning she died of peritonitis.

Two days later, on 6 April, the *News* gave its version of the murder: 'Yesterday the authorities of the London Hospital informed the coroner of the death in that institution of Emma Elizabeth Smith, aged 45, a widow, lately living at 18, George-street, Spitalfields. It appears that the deceased was out on Bank Holiday, and when returning home along Whitechapel-road early on Tuesday morning she was set upon by some men and severely maltreated. The men made off, leaving the woman on the ground in a semi-conscious condition, and have not yet been apprehended. She was taken home, and subsequently conveyed to the hospital, where she died.'[27] This account leaves many questions unanswered. So what really did happen to Emma Smith in the nine hours or so after seven on Easter Monday?

At about 12.15 a.m. Margaret Hayes, who lodged at the same address, saw her with a man at the corner of Farrance Street and

Burdett Road in Limehouse. The man was of medium height and wore a white silk handkerchief around his neck and a dark suit. More important, however, were the dying statements of Emma herself. Piecing together the fragments of information gleaned from her by Mary Russell and George Haslip, the house-surgeon at London Hospital, we can learn something of the fatal attack. Emma was walking home along Whitechapel Road about 1.30 on the Tuesday morning. By St Mary's Church she saw three men coming towards her. Although she crossed the road to avoid them they followed her into Osborn Street, attacked and raped her, and made off with what little money she had. She remembered nothing of her assailants except that one was a youth, apparently about nineteen years old.[28]

Emma Smith was entered in the hospital records as married and a charwoman. In reality she was a friendless widow who supported herself at least partly by prostitution. She told Haslip, indeed, that she had not seen any of her friends for ten years. According to Walter Dew, writing fifty years later, she was once asked why she had broken so completely with her old life and friends. 'They would not understand now any more than they understood then,' she replied wistfully. 'I must live somehow.' Like Martha Tabram her living was made on the streets. Yet, by Dew's account, the vestiges of a respectable past never entirely deserted her. 'There was something about Emma Smith,' he wrote, 'which suggested that there had been a time when the comforts of life had not been denied her. There was a touch of culture in her speech unusual in her class.' If Dew was not wearing the rose-coloured spectacles of age Emma must have fallen far by 1888 for contemporary records depict little refinement in her appearance or behaviour. Her clothing was in such a dirty and ragged condition that the police, who inspected it for clues, were unable to tell if any part of it had been freshly torn. And Mrs Russell often saw the consequences of her dissipated lifestyle. When she had been drinking she behaved like a madwoman. She frequently returned home with black eyes given her by men and one night came home and told Mrs Russell that she had been thrown out of a window.

There were certain similarities between the Smith and Tabram murders. Both seem to have been unprovoked attacks and both took place on Bank Holiday nights. They were committed within 100 yards of each other. And the victims had much in common. Both women were prostitutes and both were residents of common lodging houses in George Street. Emma Smith lived at No. 18. Martha Tabram's last known address was No. 19. It is interesting too that Martha Tabram sometimes masqueraded under the name 'Emma'.

Yet it is most unlikely that the same hand slew both women. As far as we know Tabram was murdered by a lone killer. Smith was the victim of a gang of bullies. Tabram's murderer used two weapons, a penknife and a long-bladed weapon like a dagger or bayonet. The injuries upon Emma Smith were inflicted, not with a knife, but with some blunt instrument, possibly a stick. Most telling of all was the apparent difference in purpose displayed by the attackers. Although the perpetrators of a particularly nasty street robbery and sex attack, the assailants of Emma Smith probably did not intend murder. Had they done so they would scarcely have allowed her to totter away and tell what she knew. It is very likely that they were intoxicated and left her unaware of the real extent of the injuries they had inflicted. But there can be no such doubts about the man who accompanied Martha Tabram into George Yard Buildings. No common street robber or drunken lout would have evinced the relentless fury of that attack. Her slaying bore all the hallmarks of a maniacal killer.

There is no evidence that the police or the press linked the Smith and Tabram murders as early as August. Although the inexplicable savagery of the Tabram slaying shocked East London it seems to have been regarded as an isolated, freak tragedy; no one suggested that the George Yard murderer might strike again. Prostitutes, from among whose ranks both victims had been chosen, plied the streets as brazenly as though nothing had happened. Heavy rain ushered out one of the wettest and coolest summers on record. On Thursday, 30 August, the showers were sharp and frequent and accompanied by loud peals of thunder and vivid flashes of lightning. That night two fires broke out in the London docks, reddening the sky above the East End with a great glow. Art traditionally depicts monsters fresh from Hell in just such settings, but no sense of foreboding, no premonition of disaster touched Polly Nichols as she tramped the streets that night.

Polly was a prostitute. Her life oscillated between the common lodging house, the workhouse and the pavement. And like Smith and Tabram before her she was middle-aged, destitute and frequently drunk. Witnesses later recalled glimpses of her on Thursday night and Friday morning.[29] At about 11.00 p.m. she was seen in the Whitechapel Road and at 12.30 a.m. leaving the Frying Pan public house in Brick Lane. For about six weeks Polly had shared a room in a common lodging house at 18 Thrawl Street with an elderly married woman named Ellen Holland. About a week before she had moved to another common lodging house in Flower and Dean Street but at 1.20 on the morning of Friday, 31 August, she was back at 18 Thrawl Street. Polly was the worse for drink and wearing a new black straw bonnet trimmed with black velvet. When the lodging house deputy turned her away because she did not have 4d. for a bed she was far from dispirited and asked the deputy to keep her bed for her while she went out to get the money. Then she turned away, laughing. 'I'll soon get my "doss" money,' she cried, 'see what a jolly bonnet I've got now!'

About an hour later Ellen Holland met Polly at the corner of Whitechapel Road and Osborn Street. Ellen was on her way home after going to see the fire that had broken out that morning at Shadwell Dry Dock. Polly had come down Osborn Street and was alone. She was very drunk. The two friends talked at the corner for perhaps seven or eight minutes. As they did so the clock at St Mary's, across the road, struck 2.30. Mrs Holland tried hard to persuade Polly to come home with her but she was determined to earn her 'doss' money. 'I have had my lodging money three times today,' she boasted, 'and I have spent it . . . It won't be long before I'll be back.' They parted. And that was the last time Mrs Holland saw Polly alive, a small, lonely figure, staggering eastwards along the Whitechapel Road.

3

Without the Slightest Shadow of a Trace

AT ABOUT 3.40 on the morning of Friday, 31 August, a carman was walking to work along Buck's Row, Whitechapel. He was Charles Cross of 22 Doveton Street, Cambridge Heath Road, Bethnal Green, and he had worked at Pickford's for more than twenty years. Buck's Row seemed deserted. Cross was on the north side of the street and was walking towards Baker's Row. The morning was chilly and still very dark.

For much of its length Buck's Row was narrow, cobbled and mean. Beyond the board school it became wide and open. It was as he approached the end of the narrow section that Cross saw something on the opposite side of the street, a large object lying across the entrance to a stable yard. At first he thought it was a tarpaulin, but when he got halfway across the street he realized that he was mistaken. It was the body of a woman. Standing uncertainly in the middle of the street the carman then heard the approaching footsteps of another workman. The newcomer, walking in the same direction as Cross, was also a carman, Robert Paul by name, of 30 Foster Street, Bethnal Green. Cross went up to him and tapped him on the shoulder. 'Come and look over here,' he said, 'there's a woman lying on the pavement.'

Together they gingerly approached the silent form. She was lying on her back, her skirts raised almost to her stomach. Cross felt her hands. They seemed cold and limp. 'I believe she's dead,' he ventured. Paul was not so sure. He found her face and hands cold and when he

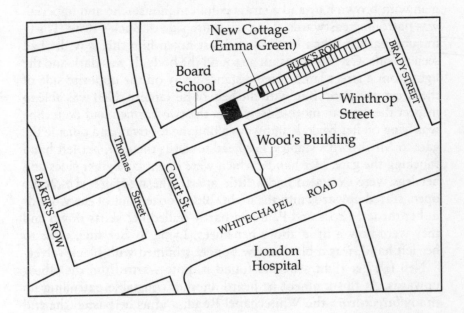

The vicinity of Buck's Row. × marks the spot where the body of Mary Ann Nichols was found, at 3.40 a.m. on 31 August 1888

crouched down and tried to hear her breathe he could detect nothing, but touching her breast fancied there was slight movement. 'I think she's breathing,' he said, 'but very little if she is.' He suggested that they prop her up but Cross would not touch her. In the gloom neither of them noticed the ferocious gashes in her throat that had nearly severed her head from her body. And, callously, neither were prepared to lose more time to the matter. Paul said that he would fetch a policeman except that he was behind time, and Cross was late himself. So, after attempting to pull down the woman's skirts, they nonchalantly proceeded on their way intending to tell the first constable they might see. In Baker's Row, at the junction of Hanbury and Old Montague Streets, they met PC Mizen 55H and told him of their discovery. 'She looks to me to be either dead or drunk,' enlarged Cross, 'but for my part I think she is dead.'[1]

In the meantime the body had also been found by a policeman on the beat. At about 3.45 PC John Neil 97J, a tall fresh-complexioned man with brown hair and a straw-coloured moustache and imperial, was patrolling eastwards along the south side of Buck's Row. Thirty minutes earlier, when his beat had last taken him this way, he had seen no one. On this occasion he found the body. It was dark and the light from a street lamp some distance away on the opposite side of the street was poor. But, with the help of his lantern, Neil was able to inspect the woman more closely than the two carmen had done. She was lying on her back, lengthways along the footway and outside the gate to Mr Brown's stables, her head towards the east, her left hand touching the gate. Her hands, which were open, lay by her sides and her legs were extended and a little apart. The woman's eyes, wide open, stared upwards into the night. Blood oozed out of the wounds in her throat. Cross and Paul had partly pulled her skirts down and they were now a little above her knees. Lying by her side, close to her left hand, was a black straw bonnet trimmed with black velvet.

Neil felt her right arm and found it quite warm from the elbow upwards. At this moment he heard another constable patrolling up Brady Street from the Whitechapel Road, and as he passed the end of Buck's Row Neil called him and flashed his lantern. It was PC John Thain 96J. 'Here's a woman has cut her throat,' said Neil, 'run at once for Dr Llewellyn.' When PC Mizen arrived soon after, hotfoot from Baker's Row, Neil sent him for an ambulance and further assistance from Bethnal Green Police Station.

While awaiting the doctor PC Neil scouted around. The gate, some nine or ten feet high, was closed. To the west of the stable yard was a board school, to the east a row of shabby two-storey houses inhabited, for the most part, by respectable working people. On the north side of the street, opposite the gateway, was Essex Wharf. When Neil rang the bell at the wharf the face of Walter Purkis, the manager, appeared at an upper window. The constable wanted to know whether anyone had heard a disturbance in the street but Purkis and his wife had heard nothing. Neil was soon reinforced by Sergeant Kirby. The sergeant knocked up Mrs Green, who lived at New Cottage, the house immediately to the east of the gateway, but she too had heard no disturbance. And when Neil examined the road with his lantern he discovered no trace of wheel marks or any other clue.

Dr Rees Ralph Llewellyn of 152 Whitechapel Road, called out by PC Thain at or shortly before four, quickly arrived on the scene. When he made a preliminary examination of the body he noted the severe injuries to the throat and pronounced life extinct. But although the woman's hands and wrists were cold, the doctor discovered that her body and legs were still warm and he did not think that she could have been dead for more than half an hour. By this time early morning sightseers were already beginning to collect, including three horse slaughterers from Barber's slaughterhouse in nearby Winthrop Street, and Llewellyn decided that the body should be moved. 'Move her to the mortuary,' he told the police officers. 'She is dead and I will make a further examination of her there.'

The relatively small amount of blood left at the place where the dead woman had been found was later to be the subject of some speculation. Dr Llewellyn, in a statement issued to the press later in the day, spoke of a small pool of blood on the footway, 'not more than would fill two wine glasses, or half a pint at the outside.' And constables Neil, Thain and Mizen subsequently told the inquest of a patch of congealed blood about six inches in diameter, some of which had run towards the gutter. This blood on the pavement had apparently trickled from the wounds in the throat. Some of it, however, had been absorbed by the woman's clothes. PC Thain was one of those who lifted the body onto the ambulance. Her back appeared to be covered with blood which, Thain believed, had flowed from her neck as far as her waist, and his hands became smeared in the stuff. Neil, Mizen and Kirby went with the body to the mortuary while Thain waited in Buck's Row for Inspector John Spratling. When Spratling arrived Thain showed him the spot where the woman had lain. By that time the blood was being washed away by one of Mrs Green's sons who worked at the stables but Spratling could still see traces of it between the paving stones.

It was a discovery by Inspector Spratling that brought Dr Llewellyn tumbling from his bed for the second time that night. From Buck's Row the inspector quickly repaired to the mortuary in Old Montague Street. He arrived to find the place locked up and the body still on the ambulance in the yard. But the keeper of the mortuary had been sent for and while waiting for him to come Spratling began taking a description of the dead woman. At some time between 5.00 and 5.20 Robert Mann, the keeper, turned up with the keys and the body was moved into the mortuary. There Spratling completed his description of the deceased and, upon lifting her clothes, discovered that her abdomen had been savagely ripped open from as high as the breast bone and that her intestines were exposed. Dr Llewellyn, hastily summoned by Spratling, made a fresh examination of the woman and was appalled at the extent of her injuries. 'I have seen many terrible cases,' he would tell the press, 'but never such a brutal affair as this.'[2]

The character of the wounds do not appear to have been identical to those which had been inflicted upon Martha Tabram. But, unfortunately, no report from Dr Llewellyn on the Buck's Row murder has survived. We must gather what we can from the brief references in police reports and from press notices of the doctor's inquest testimony.

The earliest report on the case in the records of the Metropolitan Police is signed by Inspector John Spratling and dated 31 August 1888. At this time Llewellyn had made two preliminary examinations of the body, one in Buck's Row and the other at the mortuary, but he had not yet conducted a full post-mortem. The inspector summarized Llewellyn's findings thus:

... her throat had been cut from left to right, two distinct cuts being on left side, the windpipe, gullet and spinal cord being cut through; a bruise apparently of a thumb being on right lower jaw, also one on left cheek; the abdomen had been cut open from centre of bottom of ribs along right side, under pelvis to left of the stomach, there the wound was jagged; the omentum, or coating of the stomach, was also cut in several places, and two small stabs on private parts; [all] apparently done with a strong bladed knife; supposed to have been done by some left handed person; death being almost instantaneous.

Subsequent police reports added only one significant detail to this information. Chief Inspector Donald S. Swanson, writing on 19 October, noted: 'At first the Doctor was of opinion that the wounds were caused by a left-handed person but he is now doubt-ful.'[3]

On the morning of Saturday, 1 September, Llewellyn carried out a post-mortem examination. His evidence, presented to the inquest the same day, can now only tentatively be recovered by a comparison of the various newspaper versions.

There was bruising about the face. A bruise running along the lower part of the jaw on the right side of the face might have been caused by a blow from a fist or by the pressure of a thumb. On the left side of the face was a circular bruise. Llewellyn thought that this might have been caused by the pressure of fingers.

There were two incisions in the throat. One, about four inches long, began on the left side of the neck at a point immediately below the ear and ran about an inch below the jaw. The second was about eight inches long and encircled the throat. It commenced on the left side of the neck about an inch in front of the first, ran about an inch below the first incision and terminated at a point about three inches below the right jaw. This cut had severed both carotid arteries and all the tissues down to the vertebrae. Both incisions had been made from left to right. They must have been inflicted, thought the doctor, with 'a strong-bladed knife, moderately sharp, and used with great violence.'

And there were further severe cuts in the lower part of the abdomen. Two or three inches from the left side was a long, very deep and jagged wound which had cut through the tissues. Several incisions ran across the abdomen. On the right side were three or four similar cuts running downwards. The abdominal injuries had been inflicted with a knife used violently and downwards.

On the murderer himself Llewellyn offered very few clues. He had inflicted all the wounds with the same weapon and might have been left-handed. Replying to questions, the doctor added that the murderer 'must have had some rough anatomical knowledge, for he seemed to have attacked all the vital parts. The murder could have been executed in just four or five minutes.[4]

At first the identification of the woman promised to be difficult. Apart from a small scar on the forehead and three missing teeth, one at the front of the upper jaw and two in the left side of the lower, there were no distinguishing marks on the body itself. She was small – not more than five feet two or three inches tall – end middle-aged. Her dark-brown hair had been in the process of turning grey, her eyes were brown and her complexion dark. Her face was bruised and very much discoloured. The woman's few belongings – a comb, a piece of looking glass and a white pocket handkerchief – afforded no clue to her identity. And most of her clothing was equally anonymous. The main items were a reddish-brown ulster, somewhat the worse for wear, with seven large brass buttons; a brown linsey frock, apparently new; a white chest flannel; two petticoats, one of grey wool, the other flannel; a pair of brown stays; a pair of black ribbed woollen stockings; a pair of men's side spring boots, cut on the uppers and with steel tips on the heels; and a black straw bonnet trimmed in black velvet.

Yet within twenty-four hours of the murder the victim had been named. As news of the crime spread throughout the East End various women came forward to identify the deceased and it soon transpired that a woman of her appearance had been living in a common lodging house at 18 Thrawl Street. Ellen Holland, fetched from there, identified the body as that of 'Polly', a woman who had once shared her room at Thrawl Street. But the real breakthrough occurred when the police examined the dead woman's petticoats and found the mark 'Lambeth Workhouse, P.R. [i.e. Prince's Road]' upon them. At 7.30 on the evening of 31 August Mary Ann Monk, an inmate of the Lambeth Workhouse, was taken to Old Montague Street and she gave the deceased a name. The victim was Mary Ann Nichols and she had been a resident of the workhouse as late as May 1888. With this information the police soon traced the relatives. Edward Walker, Mary's father, and William Nichols, her husband, both identified her body the next day.

Mary Nichols, or Polly as she was known to her friends, is conventionally regarded as the first victim of Jack the Ripper. Perhaps for this reason her sad career of drunkenness and decline has been documented more thoroughly than that of any other victim in the Whitechapel murder series.[5] The daughter of Edward Walker, a locksmith, and his wife Caroline, Polly was born in Dean Street, off Fetter Lane, on 26 August 1845. She married William Nichols, a printer's machinist, at St Bride's, Fleet Street, on 16 January 1864.

After lodging briefly in Bouverie Street the couple went to live with Polly's father at 131 Trafalgar Street, Walworth. They seem to have stayed there for about ten years. Then, in about 1874, they set up home for themselves at 6D Peabody Buildings, Stamford Street, just off Blackfriars Road. There were five children: Edward John (1866), Percy George (1868), Alice Esther (1870), Eliza Sarah (1877) and Henry Alfred (1879). Notwithstanding all of which the marriage ended acrimoniously in 1880.

The pain of that break-up seems to have permanently embittered relations between Nichols and his father-in-law. Walker told the inquest that the cause of the marriage's failure was Nichols' affair with Polly's nurse when Polly was last confined, that the couple separated (the eldest boy subsequently living with Walker and the four remaining children staying with their father) and that Nichols later sired another family by the nurse. This tale smeared Nichols in 1888 and, since it continues to be regularly trotted out in the books, still does today. Yet it was a considerable distortion of the truth and when Nichols himself appeared before the inquest he moved swiftly to refute it. 'No, sir, that is false,' he told the foreman of the jury, 'I have a certificate of my boy's birth two years after that.' Curiously, neither here nor anywhere else does Nichols seem to have denied that an affair had actually taken place, merely that it had been the direct cause of the failure of his marriage. And certainly, if – as Nichols implies – his affair occurred when Polly was pregnant with Eliza Sarah in 1877 then the marriage survived it by at least three years. Interviewed by the press, Nichols elaborated: 'I did not leave my wife during her confinement and go away with a nurse-girl. The dead woman deserted me four or five times, if not six. The last time she left me without any home, and with five children, the youngest one year and four months. I kept myself with the children where I was living for two and a half years before I took on with anybody, and not till after it was proved at Lambeth Police Court that she had misconducted herself.'

Walker's statement that Edward John, Polly's eldest child, was living with him in 1888 inspired a news report that Nichols had had so little to do with his son that when they met at Polly's funeral he did not recognize him. It has also led modern writers to infer that the boy decisively took his mother's part when the marriage of his parents disintegrated. This, too, may be inaccurate. In his press statement Nichols insisted that Edward John remained with him until as late as 1886: 'He left home of his own accord two years and a half ago, and I have always been on speaking terms with him. Only two or three months ago I saw him, and last week received two letters from him asking me if I knew of any work for him.'

From 6 September 1880 to 31 May 1881 Polly lived in the Lambeth Workhouse. There is then a gap of nearly a year in her record. During this time perhaps she took up with another man. In any event we know that Nichols paid Polly an allowance of 5s. a week which he stopped in 1881 or 1882 upon learning that she was living with another man. Apparently the Guardians of the Parish of Lambeth, to whom Polly then became chargeable, summonsed him to show cause why he should not be ordered to contribute to her support but his plea that she had been living with someone else prevailed and the summons was dismissed. Thereafter Polly lost touch with her husband. In a statement made at the Mitcham Workhouse on 13 February 1888 she declared that she didn't know where he had been living for the last six or seven years, and on 3 September Nichols informed the inquest that he had not seen Polly at all for three years.

Many of Polly's remaining years were spent in workhouses and doss-houses. Between 24 April 1882 and 24 March 1883 she sheltered continuously in the Lambeth Workhouse or its infirmary and she returned there for another twelve days on the following 21 May. Her name then disappears from workhouse records for another four years. The gap, again, reflects an attempt by Polly to better herself. For a short time she lived with her father. She was not 'fast' with men, he recalled, and was not in the habit of staying out late, but she drank heavily and they did not get on. Eventually they quarrelled and Polly left home. After that Walker heard that his daughter was living with a blacksmith named Thomas Stuart Drew in York Mews, 15 York Street, Walworth. He saw her for the last time in June 1886. His son had been burned to death in the explosion of a paraffin lamp and Polly attended the funeral. The quarrel still rankled too much for either of them to attempt a crossing of the gulf that had opened up between them and they did not speak to each other. It was nevertheless apparent from her respectable dress that her circumstances had improved.

Her movements during the last year of her life are rather better documented. For one day – 25 October 1887 – she stayed in St Giles Workhouse, Endell Street. Then, from 26 October to 2 December 1887, she found refuge at the Strand Workhouse, Edmonton. On 19 December she reappeared at the Lambeth Workhouse but was turned out ten days later. The Mitcham Workhouse, run by the Holborn Board of Guardians, admitted her on 4 January 1888. She was sheltered there for more than three months but on 16 April was transferred to Lambeth, her place of settlement. Polly remained at the Lambeth Workhouse until 12 May. She then made a last attempt to pull the threads of her life together.

Polly left the workhouse to take up a position as domestic servant with Samuel and Sarah Cowdry, Ingleside, Rose Hill Road, Wandsworth. And she tried to reforge the broken links with her kinsfolk by writing a letter to her father:

I just write to say you will be glad to know that I am settled in my new place, and going on all right up to now. My people went out yesterday, and have not returned, so I am left in charge. It is a grand place inside, with trees and gardens back and front. All has been newly done up. They are teetotallers and religious, so I ought to get on. They are very nice people, and I have not too much to do. I hope you are all right and the boy has work. So good-bye for the present. – From yours truly,

POLLY

Answer soon, please, and let me know how you are.[6]

Walker sent a kind reply but heard nothing more. He did not learn, for instance, that on 12 July Polly absconded from her employer stealing clothing worth £3 10s. A few days later she took lodgings at 18 Thrawl Street. Apart from a day in the Grays Inn Road temporary Workhouse at the beginning of August Polly shared a room with Ellen Holland at Thrawl Street for something like six weeks. Mrs Holland liked Polly. She told the inquest that she had seen her the worse for drink on two or three occasions but had otherwise found her clean, quiet and inoffensive.

Polly left Thrawl Street about a week before her death. Her last few days are extremely mysterious. When Mrs Holland saw her in the early hours of 31 August, however, she gathered that Polly had been staying at the 'White House', a common lodging house in Flower and Dean Street.[7] We do know that on the night of her murder she tried to return to 18 Thrawl Street and was turned out because she did not have her lodging money. Ellen Holland was the last person apart from the killer who is known to have seen her alive. That was at the corner of Osborn Street and Whitechapel Road at 2.30 on the morning of 31 August. Mrs Holland wanted Polly to come home with her but she was then still sanguine about raising the money and reeled drunkenly off along the Whitechapel Road. Just over an hour later and less than three-quarters of a mile away her dead and mutilated body was found in Buck's Row. It was just a few days after her forty-third birthday.

Inadequate, impoverished, a prostitute, probably an alcoholic – Polly Nichols was all of these but she inspired affection in those who came to know her best. Despite his differences with his daughter Edward Walker waived away her faults at the inquest on 1 September. 'I don't think she had any enemies,' he said, 'she was too good for that.' On the same day William Nichols, Polly's estranged husband, was taken to Old Montague Street to identify her body by Inspector Abberline. Nichols was a pale man with a full, light-brown beard and moustache. Wearing a long black coat, dark trousers, a black tie and a tall silk hat, and carrying an umbrella, he appeared at the mortuary looking very gentlemanly and dignified, but when the lid of the coffin was removed and he saw the dead face of his wife he was much affected. 'I forgive you, as you are,' he told her, 'for what you have been to me.' And Polly's friend Ellen Holland was greatly moved by her death. At the inquest proceedings of 3 September the following exchange took place between her and Mr Horey, the foreman of the jury:

> Mr HOREY: 'What name did you know her by?'
> Mrs HOLLAND: 'Only as "Polly".'
> Mr HOREY: 'You were the first one to identify her?'
> Mrs HOLLAND: 'Yes, sir.'
> Mr HOREY: 'Were you crying when you identified her?'
> Mrs HOLLAND: 'Yes, and it was enough to make anybody shed
> a tear, sir.'[8]

Inspector Reid, Head of CID in H Division, had conducted the investigation into the George Yard murder. The body of Polly Nichols, however, had been discovered within the jurisdiction of the newly created J or Bethnal Green Division and Inspector Joseph Helson, Reid's counterpart in Bethnal Green, took charge of the inquiry. This third murder of an East End prostitute, moreover, evoked a response from Scotland Yard in the portly form of Inspector Frederick George Abberline.

Police records describe Abberline as a fresh-complexioned man, five feet nine and a half inches in height, with dark-brown hair and hazel eyes. In 1888, it might equally truthfully have been said, he was forty-five and overweight, his thick moustache and bushy side-whiskers serving to accentuate the balding condition of his pate. Modest and soft-spoken, he reminded Walter Dew more of a bank manager or a solicitor than a detective-inspector first class. But Abberline's track record befitted his rank. He had served twenty-five years in the Metropolitan Police, fourteen of them in the slums of Whitechapel. And during his years as H Division's 'Local Inspector' (1878–1887) he had built up an unrivalled knowledge of the East End and its villains and his even-handed and meticulous methods of work had won him the admiration and affection of his colleagues. In December 1887, after Abberline had been transferred to Scotland Yard at the express wish of James Monro and Adolphus Williamson, Assistant Commissioner (CID) and Chief Constable (CID) respectively, a large company of Whitechapel citizens and ex-colleagues gathered to honour him with a presentation dinner at the Unicorn Tavern in Shoreditch. George Hay Young then spoke of him as 'the very ideal of a faithful, conscientious and upright officer' and Superintendent Arnold, Head of H Division, lamented Abberline's loss to Whitechapel 'for a better officer there could not be.' They presented him with a gold keyless hunting watch inscribed: 'Presented, together with a purse of gold, to Inspector F. G. Abberline by the inhabitants of Spitalfields, Whitechapel, etc., on his leaving the district after fourteen years' service, as a mark of their esteem and regard.'9 But Abberline was not out of the district for long. Ability and experience alike qualified him to investigate the Whitechapel murders. Hence it was, that in the autumn of 1888, he was sent to the East End to co-ordinate the work of the divisional detectives. In the ensuing months no officer would be more intimately involved in the investigation of the crimes. Few indeed would acquire such an encyclopaedic knowledge of the case.

The most strenuous efforts of Abberline and the detectives of J Division, however, yielded not the slightest clue to the identity of Polly Nichols' murderer.

The Buck's Row killer had left nothing except Polly's body to mark his passing. On the day of the murder several officers searched Buck's Row and its vicinity. Between five and six in the morning Spratling sent PC Thain to examine all the premises near the spot where the body had been found. The constable subsequently told the inquest that he 'searched Essex Wharf, the Great Eastern Railway, the East London Railway, and the District Railway as far as Thomas Street' but discovered neither weapon nor bloodstain. At eleven or twelve Spratling himself looked for clues in Buck's Row and Brady Street but he, too, returned empty-handed. Later, with Sergeant Godley, he made a futile search of the Great Eastern Railway yard and of the premises of the East London and Metropolitan District Railways. Inspector Helson also examined the area. He discovered only one stain which 'might have been blood' in Brady Street.10

Extensive enquiries in the locality proved equally fruitless. No one in Buck's Row seemed to have seen or heard the killer. Three residents who lived very close to the spot where the body had been found were Mrs Emma Green, a widow, and Mr and Mrs Purkis. Emma Green lived with her three children at New Cottage, Buck's Row, adjoining and east of the stable gateway where Polly had lain, but no one in the house had heard anything untoward during the night. Mrs Green shared a front room on the first floor with her daughter and the first intimation that they had of the tragedy was Sergeant Kirby's sharp knock on the street door about four in the morning. Walter Purkis, the manager of Essex Wharf, lived with his wife in a house that fronted on Buck's Row, almost opposite the stable gateway. They occupied the front room on the second floor. His wife was awake most of the night; Purkis himself only slept fitfully and was awake between one and two. Yet, again, it was a policeman – this time PC Neil – who apprised them of the atrocity. Until then the street had been very quiet. And neither the keeper of the board school, immediately to the west of the stable yard, nor the watchmen at Browne & Eagle's wool warehouse and Schneider's cap factory, across the road, had heard anything suspicious.

At the time of the murder there had been men at work in nearby Winthrop Street – three slaughtermen at Harrison, Barber & Co. Ltd and a watchman guarding a sewage works for the Whitechapel District Board of Works. None could shed the faintest light upon the mystery. Even those who had discovered Polly's body, apparently within minutes of her death, could not contribute a crumb of information on the perpetrator of the crime. Cross had neither seen nor heard a person or vehicle leave the body. Paul had seen no one running away. And until he found Polly's body PC Neil had seen and heard nothing suspicious. Yet his beat had never taken him far from Buck's Row. 'The farthest I had been that night was just through the Whitechapel Road and up Baker's Row,' he told the inquest.

Polly may have died without a cry of any kind. The proximity of the railway, however, might explain why no one heard a scream. Inevitably, too, one questions the efficacy of the local watchmen. Patrick Mulshaw, the Board of Works watchman, may not have been the only slacker. He went on duty at about 4.45 p.m. on 30 August, watching some sewage works in Winthrop Street, at the back of the Working Lads' Institute, and was relieved at about 5.55 the next morning. He saw no one between three and four and heard no cry for help but admitted at the inquest to having dozed at times during the night. 'I suppose,' asked the coroner, '[that] your watching is not up to much?' 'I don't know,' replied the old man truculently, '[but] it is thirteen long hours for 3s. and find your own coke.'[11]

In the absence of genuine clues suspicion momentarily fell upon the three horse slaughterers who had been working at the yard of Harrison, Barber & Co. Ltd. in Winthrop Street on the night of the murder. These men had turned up in Buck's Row at some time after four and had stood as onlookers while Dr Llewellyn examined the body. One of them, Henry Tomkins of 12 Coventry Street, Bethnal Green, spoke on 3 September at the inquest. He related how he and his mates, James Mumford and Charles Britton, had worked at the slaughterhouse from between 8.00 and 9.00 p.m. on 30 August until 4.20 the next morning. They had learned of the murder, he explained, from PC Thain, who had called at the yard for his cape on his way for Dr Llewellyn, and after finishing work they had gone to see the body. PC Thain, testifying before the inquest a fortnight later, denied having alerted the slaughtermen to the murder, but apart from their presence in the vicinity and the nature of their calling there was nothing to connect them with the crime. Interrogated separately by the police, they all maintained that they had been working in Winthrop Street at the time of the murder, and since PC Neil had seen them there at 3.20 they were dismissed.[12]

The police made enquiries at common lodging houses, at coffee stalls and amongst prostitutes, but the search for Polly's killer was completely barren of result. Surviving police reports leave us in no doubt of that. On 7 September Helson conceded that 'at present not an atom of evidence can be obtained to connect any person with the crime.' Twelve days later Abberline reported that 'not the slightest clue can at present be obtained.' And reviewing the case on 19 October Chief Inspector Swanson acknowledged that the 'absence of the motives which lead to violence and of any scrap of evidence either direct or circumstantial, left the police without the slightest shadow of a trace.'[13]

There was little public criticism of the police investigation at this stage but later commentators have judged it wanting. Certainly the body could have been screened off and subjected to a more thorough examination in Buck's Row, and it would have been possible to carry out a more systematic and comprehensive search of the area. But in a busy part of the East End, just off the Whitechapel Road, these operations would have been difficult, perhaps ineffective, and however deficient the police procedures might appear in the context of modern standards of criminal detection they do not seem to have departed from Victorian conventions. When a body was discovered in the street it was incumbent upon the police to move it and in none of the Whitechapel murders did they waste much time in doing so.

The other frequently repeated allegation – that untrained mortuary officials stripped and washed the body before it could be properly examined – requires some qualification. It is true that Whitechapel had no public mortuary and that the body had of necessity to be taken to the workhouse mortuary in Old Montague Street, where the attendants – Robert Mann and his assistant James Hatfield – were both pauper inmates of the workhouse. It is also true that the attendants stripped and cleaned the body before the post-mortem. However, Mann and Hatfield were probably mistaken when they told the inquest that they received no instruction to leave the body alone and stripped it without a policeman being present. The attendants did not give their evidence until 17 September, nearly three weeks after the event, and were in any case both unreliable informants. Hatfield, for example, told the inquest that Polly had not been wearing stays, an assertion that was immediately disproved:

> CORONER: 'Would you be surprised to find that there were stays?'
> HATFIELD: 'No.'
> A JURYMAN: 'Did not you try the stays on [the body] in the afternoon to show me how short they were?'
> HATFIELD: 'I forgot it.'
> CORONER: 'He admits that his memory is bad.'
> HATFIELD: 'Yes.'

Mann's testimony commanded equally scant respect from Coroner Baxter who informed his jury that the keeper was subject to fits and cautioned them that 'neither his memory nor statements are reliable.'[14] The assertions of the mortuary attendants were in direct conflict with those of senior police officers. Spratling told the inquest that he instructed the attendants not to touch the body without authorization and Helson added that he was actually present when the body was stripped. The testimonies of these officers were taken as early as 3 September and we have no reason to disbelieve them.

What, then, really happened to Polly Nichols in the early hours of 31 August 1888? The failure of the police investigation has left us very little evidence upon which to speculate and that little has been distorted or lost over the past century by generations of myth makers. Some 'Ripperologists' have hidden deficient research amidst a wealth of fiction. Others have distorted what they have read in order to buttress a favourite theory. Few have deemed it necessary to verify the facts. Looking up the Nichols murder in a book on Jack the Ripper we are thus likely to be misinformed about the place, time and manner of it, the nature of the weapon used and the degree of surgical skill employed, in short about almost every aspect of the case. After a century of misrepresentation and falsehood it is time to return to the original evidence. By treating it with respect and by carefully marshalling such clues as we have we can learn something of Polly's fate. We can recover a little of the elusive truth.

Stephen Knight, in his bestseller *Jack the Ripper: The Final Solution*, tried to persuade his readers that Polly had been the victim of three men. One was John Netley, a villainous coachman, in whose carriage she accepted a lift. Once inside she was fed poisoned grapes and slaughtered by the other two – the artist Walter Sickert and Sir William Gull, onetime Physician-in-Ordinary to Queen Victoria! Their grisly task accomplished, Netley deposited the body where it was found and the terrible trio jogged merrily away. Knight's tale was the wildest fiction but the view that Polly had not been killed in Buck's Row at all, that she had been slain elsewhere, dressed after death and carried to the spot where she had been found or dumped from some passing vehicle was seriously considered in 1888. Indeed, the relatively small amount of blood found at the spot and the manner in which Polly lay on her back with her legs extended – 'as though she had been laid down' – led Dr Llewellyn to form precisely this opinion when he first examined the body in Buck's Row.[15] Other circumstances lend colour to the view. There were no cuts or slashes in Polly's clothing and no one in the vicinity of Buck's Row heard a disturbance or scream.

But these arguments do not carry conviction. There was certainly little blood where Polly's body was found but much of that from the throat had been absorbed by her dress and ulster and Llewellyn's post-mortem examination satisfied him that the blood from the abdominal mutilations had flowed into the abdominal cavity. The absence of cuts in Polly's clothing proves nothing. Her skirts, as the carmen saw, had been thrown up by the murderer. Her stays, which might have been expected to protect her abdomen, were indeed found fastened and undamaged. But Spratling and Helson, both of whom saw Polly's body before it was undressed, agreed at the inquest that the abdominal wounds could have been inflicted without the removal of the stays. Spratling said that they did not fit tightly and that he was able to see the wounds without unfastening them. Helson asserted that although the stays were fastened fairly tightly they were too short; all the abdominal wounds were visible with the stays on and he discovered no wounds beneath the stays.[16]

It is almost certain that Polly died where she was found. Inspector Helson considered that her clothing had been too little disarranged for her to have been carried far. More telling though was the absence of a trail of bloodstains in the street for it is inconceivable that anyone could have carried Polly's body without clearly marking his progress in crimson splashes. It is just possible, although very unlikely, that she was deposited from a vehicle. A trap or cart may not have left wheelmarks on the cobbled street but it would surely have made a noise, especially in the peace of the early hours, and Charles Cross, the first to discover the body, heard no sounds of a vehicle. The time of death, however, provides the most compelling evidence for the murder having taken place in Buck's Row. At about 3.40 the carman Paul touched Polly's breast and thought he detected movement. Five minutes later PC Neil found her right arm warm above the elbow. And, despite the abdominal injuries, the loss of blood and the exposure of Polly's legs to the cold air, Dr Llewellyn discovered warmth in her body and legs soon after four and concluded that she had not been dead for more than half an hour. Polly seems to have died, then, only minutes before Cross came upon her and it is entirely on the cards that he unwittingly scared her attacker away.

Inspectors Helson and Abberline shared the belief that Polly had been killed outside the stable gateway in Buck's Row. As early as 2 September Helson told the press that 'both himself and Inspector Abberline had come to the conclusion that it [the murder] was committed on the spot.' He reaffirmed this view at the inquest the next day and again in his report of 7 September. And on 19 September Abberline reported that he had 'no doubt' that Polly Nichols and the later victim Annie Chapman had both been murdered where the bodies had been found.[17] Even Dr Llewellyn, whose initial impression was that the body had been deposited outside the stable, came to accept that he had been mistaken.

Polly thus met her end at the entrance to the stable yard in Buck's Row. At 3.15 PC Neil patrolled the street and saw no one about. Twenty-five minutes later Cross came upon Polly's body, so soon after her death that he might easily have disturbed the murderer. If, as Llewellyn averred at the inquest, the crime could have been executed in four or five minutes Polly died between 3.30 and 3.40 a.m. When Mrs Holland last saw her, only an hour earlier, Polly was tipsy, in search of her 'doss money' and reeling eastwards along the Whitechapel Road. Further along that road she met her assassin and they retired to Buck's Row. The eastern end of the street was dismally lighted, narrow and tenanted on the south side only. High warehouses dominated the north side. Dark and relatively secluded, it was the regular resort of prostitutes.

The injuries inflicted upon Polly Nichols were unlike Martha Tabram's but exhibited a similarly pointless ferocity. In two gashes the throat had been cut from ear to ear right back to the spinal column. Inspector Spratling was evidently incorrect when he reported that the spinal cord itself had been cut through but the vertebrae had been penetrated. More, cruel abdominal mutilations had laid the belly open from a point just below the breastbone to the lower abdomen. Either the injuries to the throat or those to the abdomen would have been sufficient to cause death. But, and the point would assume importance later, no part of the viscera was missing.

The manner in which these injuries were inflicted must be largely speculative. There were no signs of a struggle. The throat was cut from left to right. Dr Llewellyn at first held the view that the murderer had attacked Polly from in front. With his right hand he pushed her head back, his thumb bruising her right lower jaw and his fingers her left cheek, and with his left hand he held the knife that cut her throat.[18] More recently several writers, notably Donald Rumbelow (on the strength of an opinion of James Cameron, the pathologist) and Arthur Douglas, have promulgated the view that the killer attacked Polly from behind. If this was the case he could have gripped her head with his left hand and used the knife with his right, the bruise on her left cheek resulting from the pressure of his left thumb and that along her right lower jaw from the pressure of his fingers. Polly's attempts to pull away from him, moreover, would have facilitated his efforts to expose her throat to the knife.[19]

The evidence of the bloodstains can help to resolve this problem for us. If Polly's throat were cut while she was erect and alive a strong jet of blood would have spurted from the wound and probably deluged the front of her clothing. But in fact there was no blood at all on her breast or the corresponding part of her clothes. Some of the flow from the throat formed a small pool on the pavement beneath Polly's neck and the rest was absorbed by the backs of the dress bodice and ulster. The blood from the abdominal wounds largely collected in the loose tissues. Such a pattern proves that Polly's injuries were inflicted when she was lying on her back and suggests that she may already have been dead.

The probable explanation of this evidence is that Polly was throttled before she was mutilated. Although she went to Buck's Row anticipating sexual intercourse neither Polly nor her killer are likely to have been lying down in the street, especially after the previous day's showers. She would presumably have expected to complete that transaction standing against a wall. It is possible that she was felled by a blow and in her besotted condition she would have proved an easy victim. But the fact that Polly's throat was severed when she was lying down and with so little spillage of blood, together with the apparent absence of any scream, points to prior strangulation. There are indications of this, too, in the medical evidence. We know from police reports that Polly's face was discoloured and her tongue slightly lacerated. And Dr Llewellyn's inquest deposition mentions a small bruise on the left side of her neck and an abrasion on the right.[20]

We can safely dismiss the notion that Polly's murderer cut her throat from behind. Whether he was left or right-handed, however, is impossible to determine. If he was kneeling by Polly's head, facing her feet, he would have gripped her face with his left hand and severed her throat (from left to right) with a knife held in his right hand. This technique would have directed the flow of blood from the left carotid artery away from him and is certainly consistent with the evidence of the facial bruises. Llewellyn himself came to doubt his earlier view of a left-handed killer.

Both the nature of the murder weapon and the degree of surgical skill exhibited by the murderer are now commonly misconceived. The error relating to the weapon dates back to contemporary press notices of the inquest proceedings. Some of these, including that in the prestigious *Times*, wrongly reported Dr Llewellyn as identifying the weapon as 'a long-bladed knife, moderately sharp.' The belief that the Buck's Row killer displayed expert surgical skill seems to have originated in Donald McCormick's *Identity of Jack the Ripper*, published over thirty years ago. By McCormick's account Llewellyn testified that the abdominal injuries had been 'deftly and fairly skillfully performed.'[21] These errors have been perpetuated and even embroidered in the literature of the case. Thus, in the recent study by Colin Wilson and Robin Odell, the mutilations inflicted upon Polly were 'deftly and skilfully performed' (note the loss of the word 'fairly') and the weapon was an 'exceptionally long-bladed knife.'[22]

A comparison of contemporary police reports, press interviews and press notices of the inquest demonstrates that Llewellyn actually spoke of the weapon as a 'strong-bladed knife, moderately sharp.' It was not his contention that the knife had a particularly long blade. Indeed, in an interview reported by *The Times* on 1 September, he specifically refuted that view: 'The weapon used would scarcely have been a sailor's jack knife, but a pointed weapon with a stout back – such as a cork-cutter's or shoemaker's knife. In his opinion it was not an exceptionally long-bladed weapon.'[23] No contemporary substantiation has been discovered for McCormick's assertion that Llewellyn testified that the mutilations were 'deftly and fairly skilfully performed.' At the inquest the doctor credited the murderer with 'some rough anatomical knowledge', in other words he knew roughly what was where, but nothing whatsoever was said about his surgical skill.

Since Polly was undoubtedly lying down, and probably strangled, before the knife attack took place, the killer need not have been greatly bloodstained. The presence of so many slaughterhouses in the area, moreover, may have allayed suspicion when he made his escape. At that time Whitechapel Road was already busy. Even in Brady Street PC Thain saw one or two men walking to work in the direction of Whitechapel Road shortly before he was hailed by PC Neil. But no one suspected Polly's killer as he merged with the early morning's market traffic.

Polly Nichols had been a pauper. Few believed robbery a credible motive for the crime. This suggested a link between her death and the equally purposeless killings, in the same area, of Emma Smith and Martha Tabram. For the first time police, press and public alike began to speak of a new and chilling possibility – that the purlieus of London's East End harboured a deranged killer who would strike again. It was a thought that quickly found expression in street literature. One verse broadsheet, sung to the tune of 'My Village Home', regaled East Enders with *Lines on the Terrible Tragedy in Whitechapel*:

> Come listen to a dreadful tale I'm telling,
> In Whitechapel three murders have been done;
> With horror many hearts they now are swelling,
> Those fearful deeds that now to light have come.
>
> Twelve months ago a woman was found lying,
> In death's cold arms, how dreadful to relate,
> What agony they suffered here when dying
> They were nearly all found in the same state.
>
> The first poor creature's death they all are thinking
> The same hand took her life that fatal night,
> Poor people now with fear they are shrinking
> Oh! may this crime be quickly brought to light.
>
> Now scarcely had the news of that foul murder,
> Which filled all hearts with sorrow and dismay,
> When – sad to tell – the fate of Martha Turner,
> Poor soul, she met her fate near the same way.
>
> 'Twas thought that soldiers had killed that poor creature,
> And on them many people laid the blame,
> When found 'twas hard to recognise a feature.
> To leave her so, oh! what a cruel shame.
>
> And now poor Mary Nicholls' death relating,
> In Buck's Row, Whitechapel there did lie,
> While in the dark her body lay awaiting
> And no one there to see that poor soul die.
>
> By workhouse clothes the body recognising,
> That cruel deed all around will show
> Who could have done that deed they are surmising,
> And murdered Mary Nicholls in Buck's Row?[24]

4

Leather Apron

POLLY NICHOLS WAS the first victim of Jack the Ripper. Such is the conventional wisdom amongst students of the case. The earlier murders are dismissed as irrelevancies, products of the everyday violence of the East End.

This view would have found little favour in 1888 for although Emma Smith seemed to have been slain by drunken ruffians there had been nothing at all everyday about the murder of Martha Tabram. Her wounds had not been identical to those of Polly Nichols but both killings shared characteristics that set them apart from routine crime. Neither murder appeared to have had any connection with domestic quarrels, drunken affrays or street robberies. In both cases the murderer had left no clue to his identity. And both crimes, even amidst the violence of the Victorian East End, had been remarkable for their savagery.

The last point, perhaps, was more evident then than it is now and the Ripper buffs of today, who so casually disregard the George Yard tragedy as 'just another murder', would do well to consider the impact that it made upon Martha Tabram's contemporaries. In his summing up George Collier, the deputy coroner, spoke of it as 'one of the most brutal [crimes] that had occurred for some years . . . almost beyond belief,' and newsmen appeared genuinely appalled and bewildered by the rage of Martha's killer. 'The wound over the heart was alone sufficient to kill,' puzzled the *Illustrated Police News* of 18 August, 'and death must have occurred as soon as that was inflicted. Unless the perpetrator was a madman, or suffering to an unusual extent from drink delirium, no tangible explanation can be given of the reason for inflicting the other thirty-eight injuries, some of which almost seem as if they were due to thrusts and cuts from a penknife.' This journal, admittedly revelling in the sensational, devoted six drawings on its front page and more than a column of small print inside to the crime. But in the East End too the manner of Martha's death evoked unusual horror. Thus, on 11 August, the *East London Observer* devoted nearly two columns to a murder it considered 'so unique and mysterious.'[1]

At the beginning of September it was the general belief of the press that at least Martha Tabram and Polly Nichols had been slain by the same hand. And although we have no authoritative statement from the police on this point such clues as can be gleaned from the press indicate that they, too, were now seriously considering the possibility that all three Whitechapel murders were linked.

Three theories were current. One – that the murders had been perpetrated by a gang of thieves – originated in the report of a robbery in Whitechapel circulated by the Central News Agency.[2] According to this tale a woman, leaving the Foresters' Music Hall, Cambridge Heath Road, on the night of Saturday, 1 September, was accosted by a well-dressed man. Inveigling himself into her company, he walked a short distance with her but, not far from the spot where Polly Nichols had been killed, suddenly seized her by the throat and dragged her down a court. The villain was immediately joined by both male and female confederates. They brutally assaulted their victim and despoiled her of her necklace, ear-rings, brooch and purse. She opened her mouth to scream but was silenced by a bloodcurdling threat from one of the gang. Laying a large knife across her throat he warned: "We will serve you as we did the others." The whole story was, apparently, a newspaper fiction, but even before it was publicly discredited it should have been obvious that there was a world of difference between its affluent if luckless heroine and the penniless whores slaughtered in George Yard and Buck's Row. Robbery could not plausibly be advanced as the reason for their deaths. The police themselves evidently toyed with the theory that Smith, Tabram and Nichols had been the victims of a 'High Rip' gang which levied blackmail upon prostitutes and then took vengeance upon such as failed to pay them a proportion of their earnings.[3]

The most widely held view, however, was that the killer was a lunatic. As early as 31 August the *Star* fostered this theory in screaming headlines:

A REVOLTING MURDER.
ANOTHER WOMAN FOUND HORRIBLY
MUTILATED IN WHITECHAPEL.
GHASTLY CRIMES BY A MANIAC.

A day later it returned to the theme. The Osborn Street, George Yard and Buck's Row outrages, it insisted, had been committed by a single madman: 'In each case the victim has been a woman of abandoned character, each crime has been committed in the dark hours of the morning, and more important still as pointing to one man, and that man a maniac, being the culprit, each murder has been accompanied by hideous mutilation . . . All three crimes have been committed within a very small radius. Each of the ill-lighted thoroughfares to which the women were decoyed to be foully butchered are off turnings from Whitechapel Road, and all are within half a mile. The fact that these three tragedies have been committed within such a limited area, and are so strangely alike in their details, is forcing on all minds the conviction that they are the work of some cool, cunning man with a mania for murder.'[4]

There was undoubtedly news value in such a theory. But there was substance too, as the *East London Observer*, commenting on the Tabram and Nichols murders, ponderously elaborated: 'The two murders which have so startled London within the last month are singular for the reason that the victims have been of the poorest of the poor, and no adequate motive in the shape of plunder can be traced. The excess of effort that has been apparent in each murder suggests the idea that both crimes are the work of a demented being, as the extraordinary violence used is the peculiar feature in each instance.'[5] For whatever reason, the notion of a homicidal maniac stalking the streets quickly took hold of the press and by 8 September, when both the leading East End weeklies endorsed it, their voices did little more than add volume to a chorus.

Talk of this kind naturally stoked the fire of excitement already kindled in the East End by the Buck's Row murder. In the week after Polly's death morbid sightseers came in groups of two or three to gaze at the gaudy green gates of the workhouse mortuary. Small crowds, twenty or thirty strong, gathered in Buck's Row to inspect the murder site. And the latest details of the outrage were hungrily devoured and discussed at street corners throughout the East End.

In Buck's Row a *Daily News* reporter mingled with the crowds on 4 September. He found groups of women clustered together, bending over what they supposed to be the bloodstained paving stones, gossiping nervously but insatiably about the murder, and men, for the most part sullen and taciturn, puffing at their pipes, hands thrust deep in their pockets. The reporter's account, if coloured, preserves for us something of the flavour of the common talk in those early September days of 1888.⁶ Mixed emotions – compassion for the victim, anger against her killer and fear for themselves – repeatedly surfaced amidst the gossip.

Reflections upon the character of the deceased were met with such emphatic expressions of compassion that the critic was invariably abashed into silence. 'No matter what she was, poor thing,' one woman chided, "taint for the likes of us to judge her now.' 'No, that's right enough,' agreed another, 'whatever she was it was an awful cruel thing to do to her.'

The story that the murders had been committed by a gang of robbers had been published that morning in the papers and was widely credited by the gullible Buck's Row tattlers. But one bystander dismissed it. 'That's a got up yarn,' he scoffed. 'I rather wish it was true. If there was a gang like that, one or t'other of 'em 'd split before long, and it'd all come out. Bet your money this ain't been done that way.' No one was betting anything but this observation stimulated a lively discussion amongst the females as to what they would like to see done to the killer if it did come out. By general acclamation it was agreed that he deserved to be turned out in the midst of the Whitechapel women and then, 'seemingly forgetful of all the pain and pathos of the dreadful event, [the] women squeezed their elbows and clenched their fists, and went through a mimic performance on the person of the murderer.'

It was an anger fuelled by apprehension for the womenfolk were alert to the danger that the killer would strike again. 'Thank God I needn't be out after dark!' exclaimed one. 'No more needn't I,' chimed in another, 'but my two girls have got to come home latish and I'm all of a fidget till they comes.' A little woman with a rosy cherub face summed up the general view: 'Life ain't no great thing with many on us,' she said, 'but we don't all want to be murdered, and if things go on like this it won't be safe for nobody to put their 'eads out o' doors.'

Pity, anger, fear – but, above all, fascination. The murder held the collection of gossips and loafers in Buck's Row as if by a spell. Some dropped away but their places were taken by fresh sightseers and every time new arrivals joined the crowd the supposed bloodstains were pointed out to them and the whole affair was avidly discussed again. And if the talk temporarily faltered the crowd 'stood and silently stared at the pavement and the brickwork of the adjacent house and minutely examined the scratches and other marks in the wall, as if these things helped them to realise the horror of it all.'

Polly Nichols was buried in the City of London Cemetery, Ilford, on the afternoon of Thursday, 6 September.[7] The collection of the body proved complicated because although the time at which the cortege was to start had been kept a profound secret the date of the funeral had not and a large crowd had assembled about Old Montague Street. In order to get the body out of the mortuary, therefore, the undertaker resorted to stratagem. A two-horse, closed hearse was observed jogging eastwards along Hanbury Street. The crowd made way for it to turn into Old Montague Street but instead it passed on into Whitechapel Road and, doubling back, entered the mortuary by the back gate in Chapman's Court. The ruse worked. There was not a soul about when the undertaker's assistants placed the coffin into the hearse.

The coffin was of polished elm and bore a plate inscribed with the words: 'Mary Ann Nichols, aged 42; died August 31, 1888.' It was driven to Hanbury Street, probably to No. 87, the house of Mrs Henry Smith, the undertaker, and there awaited the mourners. They were late in arriving, however, and by the time the cortege was ready to start news that the body was in the hearse had been passed around the district and the vehicle was surrounded by curious onlookers. With a police guard to keep the crowd at a distance the little procession – the hearse and two mourning coaches – at length set off for Ilford. It turned into Baker's Row, passed the corner of Buck's Row and entered Whitechapel Road, where police, stationed at intervals of several yards, ensured its passage. The mourners included Edward Walker, Polly's father, William Nichols, her husband, and Edward John Nichols, her son, but the entire community appeared united in grief. Everywhere the greatest sympathy was expressed for the relatives and all the houses in the neighbourhood had their blinds drawn. 'The expenses of the funeral,' noted *The Times*, 'were borne by the relatives of the deceased, her father, husband, and son.'

When Polly was murdered Parliament had been in summer recess for eighteen days and would remain so until 6 November. Her death, nevertheless, sent the first ripples of alarm washing into the Home Office. For on 31 August, the day of the murder, L. & P. Walter & Son of Church Street, Spitalfields, manufacturers of clothing for export, sent a newspaper clipping and the following letter to Henry Matthews, the Home Secretary:

> We beg to enclose you [a] report of this fearful murder & to say that such is the state of affairs in this district that we are put to the necessity of [having] a nightwatchman to protect our premises. The only way in our humble opinion to tackle this matter is to offer at once a reward.

At this time neither Matthews nor his advisers can possibly have anticipated the furore the murders would ultimately visit upon them and they considered a brief reply, barren of explanation, sufficient to exculpate them from further concern in the matter. Signed by Edward Leigh-Pemberton, Legal Assistant Under-Secretary at the Home Office, and dated 4 September, it curtly informed Walter & Son that 'the practice of offering rewards for the discovery of criminals has for some time been discontinued; and that so far as the circumstances of the present case have at present been investigated, they do not in his [i.e. Matthews'] opinion disclose any special ground for departure from the usual custom.'[8]

The direct responsibility for laying the killer by the heels fell to the Metropolitan Police. They were ill-prepared to meet the challenge. Nevertheless, in the context of the murder investigation, the extent and nature of their difficulties have been almost universally misconstrued. Assuredly the regime of General Sir Charles Warren, Chief Commissioner of the Metropolitan Police from 1886 to 1888, was a troubled one. For while at loggerheads with his immediate superior, Henry Matthews, he made a determined effort to tighten up the structure and discipline of the force and was confronted by the need to police increasingly formidable demonstrations by socialists and the unemployed. The details of these much published differences do not concern us.[9] Their impact upon the detective problem in

Whitechapel does and that, contrary to popular belief, seems to have been negligible.

Take 'Bloody Sunday'. On Sunday, 13 November 1887, the police, assisted by detachments of Life and Grenadier Guards, successfully held Trafalgar Square against converging processions of socialists, radicals and Irish Home Rulers intent upon holding a rally there in defiance of a ban by the Commissioner. As regular as clockwork we are told that Warren's stern policing of meetings of socialists and the unemployed, culminating in this fierce battle, embittered relations between the police and working-class people, and are led to infer that this somehow impeded their investigation of the murders. In some districts, it is true, 'Bloody Sunday' lingered as a bitter memory for more than twenty years. And Warren himself received hate mail. 'Beware of your life you dog' began one such communication. 'Dont venture out too fur [sic]. Look out. This is yours – ' and a drawing of a coffin followed.[10] But not one jot does any of this seem to have affected police operations in the East End. There, as we shall see, large numbers of people had reasons of their own for avoiding the police but neither that nor Warren's attempts to preserve public order at the expense of free speech prevented them from co-operating with them to ensnare Jack the Ripper. The murderer's victims were drawn from the weakest and most vulnerable members of the community, 'the poorest of the poor', as the *Observer* reminds us, and impelled by a sense of common outrage as well as rapidly increasing reward money, East Enders not only organised themselves into a proliferation of local vigilance committees to assist the police but flocked to them in such numbers with information that Abberline, co-ordinating the inquiry at ground-level, almost broke down under the strain of processing it. Even in October 1888, when Warren sanctioned a massive house-to-house search north of Whitechapel High Street/Whitechapel Road, and when he feared that the socialists might orchestrate determined opposition to such an arbitrary measure, the community willingly accorded the police access to their homes. Both Warren, in a press notice of 17 October, and Robert Anderson, then head of CID, in a confidential minute six days later, happily acknowledged the fact, and for once the press agreed: 'the greatest good feeling prevails towards the police, and noticeably in the most squalid dwellings the police had no difficulty in getting information.'[11]

The skirmishing between Matthews and Warren was much more than a clash of uncongenial personalities because the two held widely divergent views on the extent of the Home Secretary's authority over the force and on matters of general policy. Again, however, although they ultimately produced Warren's resignation in November 1888, their squabbles did not exert a significant effect upon the conduct and prospects of the murder hunt. The records of the Whitechapel investigation do attest to the state of tension and distrust that existed between the two men. But Matthews supported a succession of initiatives proposed or endorsed by Warren – the experiment with bloodhounds, the house-to-house search and, belatedly, the offer of a pardon to any accomplice of the murderer who would betray him – and vetoed only one, the offer of a government reward. The reward question was a complicated one. However, there were good reasons for the rejection of such a proposal and the nature of the crimes, together with the failure of substantial City and private rewards, suggests that a government offer would not have been successful.

Exactly what the impact of Warren's reforms within the force itself was is more difficult to judge. At the time the central complaint of the radical and opposition press was that under Warren the police were being transformed from a civil into a military force primarily intended, not for the prevention and detection of crime, but for the policing of political rallies and demonstrations of the poor and unemployed. The results, according to the exponents of this view, had been far reaching and pernicious – increasingly centralized control of the police, an emphasis upon drill and discipline, the discouragement of individual initiative throughout the force, the diversion of manpower and resources from the pursuit of criminals to political work and the consequent neglect of the CID.[12] But the fact that such politically inspired vituperation was widely credited in 1888 does not oblige us to believe it now. Warren's regime at Scotland Yard is badly in need of reappraisal and until some diligent research student undertakes the task we have few firm facts to go on. The little we do know, however, suggests that the embattled Commissioner may have been grossly maligned.

Certainly Warren's appointment was followed by those of five other army officers, three as chief and two as assistant chief constables, and certainly, to improve discipline, he greatly increased the number of inspectors and sergeants. It is also true that Sir Charles quarrelled with some of his colleagues, including Sir Richard Pennefather, the Receiver for the Metropolitan Police District, and James Monro, the Assistant Commissioner in charge of CID. The

Warren – Monro feud is especially significant here in that it is held to have left the detective branch leaderless and demoralized at the very time that it was confronted by the Whitechapel murders.

There were several sources of conflict between the two men.[13] One lay in Monro's dual role as Assistant Commissioner (CID) and Secret Agent. In the latter capacity he was the head of a small cadre of four CID inspectors designated Section D. Engaged entirely in political intelligence work, they were funded not from Metropolitan Police but Imperial funds, and Monro, as their chief, reported not to Warren but direct to the Home Office. Now Warren held the view that the position of Chief Commissioner was analogous to that of the general in the field, subject to higher authority for general purposes but in complete control of the internal administration and discipline of his force. Naturally, then, he resented the independence of Section D and considered its existence subversive of good discipline. Monro, on the other hand, strove to retain his independence as Secret Agent and even to extend it to his functions as Assistant Commissioner in charge of CID, and became increasingly exasperated by Warren's attempts to restrict his freedom of action. There were other difficulties. Since the CID was undermanned and overworked, Monro proposed the creation of a new post of Assistant Chief Constable (CID) and nominated his friend Melville Macnaghten for the job. Warren suggested that Monro shed his secret service duties instead. In March 1888 the Home Office agreed to the appointment but when Warren objected that Macnaghten was unsuitable for the post quickly rescinded it. Eventually, in August, Monro resigned in protest against the 'change of policy and system' which the Chief Commissioner was seeking to impose.

Notwithstanding all this, the view that Warren was a military despot, alienating his men, is greatly overdone. It assumes that the alleged proofs of Warren's militarization of the police were all accurate which they were not. He did not, for example, greatly increase the number of army reserve men in the force since the Chief Commissioner had for several years been restricted to the employment of only 500 such at any one time. And it ignores Warren's not inconsiderable leadership qualities, demonstrated over many years of active service abroad. An early riser, he had an immense capacity for work; a strong disciplinarian, his strictness was tempered by humour and by a solicitous care for the welfare of his men; and a courageous soldier, he had displayed a disposition to lead by example, to share the dangers and privations of his command. Such qualities do not foment disaffection, at least among the rank and file.

Writing in 1910, Robert Anderson, Monro's successor, conceded that at first there was a 'dangerous want of sympathy' between Warren and his men. But when Sir Charles stoutly defended the force from Home Office imputations after 'Bloody Sunday' the constables forgot their grievances so that, by the time Anderson joined the service, the Chief Commissioner's 'popularity with the uniformed force was established'. The deputation of police super-intendents that called at Warren's home to pay him tribute after his resignation in November 1888 suggests that this was indeed the case. Superintendent Draper, their spokesman, admitted that Warren had been a stickler for discipline but 'repudiated the idea that such discipline was in any degree distasteful to the force so long as the regulations were administered with the fairness and equity which had characterized Sir Charles Warren's tenure of office.'[14]

In the CID, admittedly, things may have been a little different. Monro's resignation took effect on 31 August, the day that Polly Nichols died in Buck's Row. His successor, Dr (later Sir) Robert Anderson, possessed a keen analytical mind, twenty years' experience in intelligence work for the Home Office and supreme self-conceit. Within days he advised Warren that the murder could be successfully grappled with if systematically taken in hand and even went so far as to boast that 'I could myself in a few days unravel the mystery provided I could spare the time and give undivided attention to it.' But he came to the Yard suffering from fatigue and was in such poor health that Dr S. J. Harvey of Harley Street immediately prescribed him three months' leave for overwork. 'This, of course, was out of the question,' Anderson related in his memoirs. 'But I told Mr Matthews, greatly to his distress, that I could not take up my new duties until I had had a month's holiday in Switzerland. And so, after one week at Scotland Yard, I crossed the Channel.'[15]

Yet even these upheavals do not seem to have seriously prejudiced the murder inquiries. It should not be supposed, for example, that the departure of Anderson left the Ripper hunters leaderless. In the East End Inspector Abberline co-ordinated their activities, while at the Yard central continuity of supervision had been provided for in the appointment of Chief Inspector Donald Sutherland Swanson to oversee the investigation. This appointment had been one of the few administrative decisions Anderson had taken during his first week at

Scotland Yard. Swanson, a shrewd Scot with twenty years' service in the Metropolitan Police, was freed from all other duties. He was given an office to himself. And he was to see 'every paper, every document, every report [and] every telegram' relating to the inquiry. 'I look upon him,' said Anderson, 'as the eyes and ears of the Commissioner in this particular case.'[16]

When Anderson succeeded Monro he found some CID officers smarting over the treatment accorded their late chief. But the rift between Warren and the detective branch was but temporary. Anderson soon established a harmonious working relationship with the Chief Commissioner. 'My relations with Sir Charles were always easy and pleasant,' he wrote later. 'I always found him perfectly frank and open, and he treated me as a colleague, leaving me quite unfettered in the control of my department.' In the East End detectives showed no lack of commitment to the murder hunt. To judge from their reminiscences Abberline and Dew nearly exhausted themselves in the effort. And after the double murder of 30 September even the radical *Star*, ever eager to disparage Warren and his force, felt obliged to acknowledge their diligence: 'The failure of the police to discover the Whitechapel murderer is certainly not due to inactivity. No one who has had occasion to visit the police offices whence the investigations are being conducted can escape the impression that everybody is on the move, and it is probably a fact that very few of the chief officials and detectives have had their regular rest since last Sunday morning. One hears no complaint against the demand for extra duty, except in instances where the pressure is unevenly applied, for the police are individually more interested in the capture of the murderer than anyone else.'[17]

The general troubles of the Metropolitan Police, then, scarcely touched the Ripper investigation, and those writers who have sought in them some explanation of the killer's escape have largely misdirected their efforts. More, by dwelling upon them they have diverted attention away from the real causes of the police failure, which lay specifically in the nature of the detective problem in Whitechapel. The murders posed a most formidable challenge to the fledgling CID. Their difficulties stemmed from the character of Whitechapel and Spitalfields, the area of the atrocities, from the primitive state of Victorian methods of criminal detection and, most of all, from the nature of the crimes themselves. Together these factors operated to stack the odds in favour of the murderer from the first.

Throughout the century Whitechapel and Spitalfields had been reputedly criminous as well as poor. For the criminal a residence on the border between the City and Metropolitan Police jurisdictions was highly advantageous and the Whitechapel-Spitalfields district lay just outside the City's north-eastern boundary, on and beyond the arc from Bishopsgate round to Aldgate. The market in Petticoat Lane, moreover, afforded ample facilities for the disposal of stolen goods. 'If the King's crown were to come within half a mile of Petticoat Lane,' boasted one thief in 1835, 'money would be found in an hour for its purchase.'[18]

The main refuge of the poor, criminal and non-criminal alike, lay in a maze of dirty streets, courts and alleys between Petticoat Lane and Brick Lane. But by 1888 the area was being transformed by the demolition contractor and by Jewish immigration into the East End.

The cutting of Commercial Street in the 1840s and the redevelopments inaugurated by the Artisans' Dwelling Act of 1875 cleared much slum housing. At the same time blocks of tenement flats, like the first Peabody Buildings in Commercial Street in 1864, were being erected to provide decent homes for the working poor. The effects of such developments were not entirely beneficial. Slum clearances tended to drive the poor into surrounding streets which were themselves overcrowded, and model dwellings offered accommodation at rates only the most prosperous artisans could afford to pay.

Jewish immigration is generally held to have improved the character of some streets. A colony of Iberian Jews, rich and respected Jews of the Sephardim, settled in London during the Protectorate and in the reign of Charles II. The Ashkenazim settlement in the capital dates from the close of the 17th century and their first synagogue, in Duke's Place, Aldgate, was established in 1722. Thereafter every continental upheaval in which the Jews were sufferers brought influxes of refugees into England. The Russian pogroms of 1881–1882 and Bismarck's expulsion of alien Poles from Prussia in 1886 encouraged a new wave of immigration from Eastern Europe. Low rents, the proximity of the central business district and the presence of an existing Jewish community drew the newcomers in large numbers to Whitechapel, where the streets they overran became, by and large, quiet, law-abiding and clean. 'They have already taken one end of Great Pearl Street,' wrote Charles Booth, 'and it is probably the Jews alone who will turn out the prostitutes from the end that is still bad.'[19]

Notwithstanding these changes crime and prostitution lingered amidst the poverty and squalor, especially in parts of Spitalfields. On Booth's 'Descriptive Map of London Poverty 1889' Dorset Street, Flower and Dean Street, Thrawl Street, George Street and Great Pearl Street were all marked in black, denoting that they were occupied by the lowest class, that they were 'vicious, semi-criminal'. In these overcrowded, labyrinthine slums, where policemen were traditionally greeted with suspicion if not outright hostility, the Whitechapel killer had chosen a perfect hunting ground.

The methods by which the police were obliged to seek their quarry within this human warren were relatively crude. Although detectives had been appointed at Scotland Yard as early as 1842 the popular opposition to the use of plain clothes men as spies and agent provocateurs among their fellow citizens and the organization of the Metropolitan Police as a preventive force retarded the growth of the detective branch. The CID had been established in 1878 but there were still few aids to detection beyond photography and plaster of Paris for taking impressions of footprints. The second, in the Whitechapel context, was irrelevant and photography would be employed but sparingly during the investigation of the murders. It was not even the usual practice, for example, to photograph the bodies of victims before they were moved and in only one of the murders (that of Mary Jane Kelly) does it seem to have been done. It was possible in 1888 to identify blood as mammalian but not to prove that it was human or classify it by blood group. Galton would not publish his work on fingerprints until 1892, the year after the last of the Whitechapel murders, and there would be no scientific laboratory at Scotland Yard until 1934.

Where inquiry into the history and circumstances of the victim revealed possible motives for murder these, in turn, suggested suspects. Otherwise the success of the Victorian detective largely rested upon a thorough knowledge of the local villains, upon the evidence of informers, and upon much legwork tracing and interviewing witnesses.

The Whitechapel murderer, however, may not have been a professional villain and probably worked alone. With only one possible exception there were no eye-witnesses to his attacks because they were committed at dead of night and in secluded locations. Indeed his victims, prostitutes all, accustomed to accosting men and taking them to dark or unfrequented byways and yards for sex, greatly facilitated his crimes. Most baffling of all to the Victorian detectives, there was no obvious motive.

In the age of Albert DeSalvo (the Boston Strangler), Peter Sutcliffe (the Yorkshire Ripper) and Ted Bundy we are familiar with the phenomenon of the sexual serial murderer but to our ancestors in the 1880s it was relatively unknown. Precedents of the Whitechapel or Jack the Ripper murders are alleged from the United States and Continental Europe but they are ill-researched and seem to have acquired only local notoriety. Certainly there had been nothing like the Whitechapel crimes in recent English experience. There our most ancient citizens would have had to think back nearly eighty years, to the Ratcliff Highway murders of 1811, in order to recall murders at all comparable. Even then, horrific as the slaughter of the Marr and Williamson households had undoubtedly been, the motive for the atrocities had evidently been the obvious one of plunder. More, the Ratcliff Highway murderers had obligingly left their weapons behind them and it was the tracing of one of these, a bloodstained maul, to the Pear Tree public house in Wapping that eventually fixed suspicion upon John Williams, a seaman who lodged there.[20] The Whitechapel killer, on the other hand, evinced no obvious motive and left no clue. In such a case orthodox police methods were almost futile.

During the investigation of the murders the police displayed a marked reluctance to share their knowledge with the press or with coroners' inquiries. The late Stephen Knight thought that this secrecy was unique to the Whitechapel killings and read into it evidence that the police were party to a government sponsored 'cover-up' of the Jack the Ripper affair. Knight – and for that matter most other writers on the case – was altogether ignorant, however, of the Yard's policy on press publicity in the 1880s.

The fact is that where the publication of information might secure the arrest of a *known* culprit the police were only too willing to make disclosures to the press. 'The press is a power in the detection of crime which we must not omit to take into account,' wrote Howard Vincent, the first Director of the CID, '. . . and when publicity is desirable their help is invaluable. Indeed, if the identity of a culprit is clear, and the importance of a case is sufficient, the question of his capture is reduced to a mere question of time and money.'[21] Perhaps the first instance of this was the case of Percy LeFroy, the murderer of Isaac Gold in a train on the London–Brighton line in 1881. LeFroy was arrested after police had issued a portrait of him to the press.

But during the hunt for a killer whose identity had not yet been established it was not the general policy of the CID to make known its discoveries. Vincent himself had laid down that rule:

Police must not on any account give any information whatever to gentlemen connected with the press, relative to matters within police knowledge, or relative to duties to be performed or orders received, or communicate in any manner, either directly or indirectly, with editors, or reporters of newspapers, on any matter connected with the public service, without express and special authority . . . The slightest deviation from this rule may completely frustrate the ends of justice, and defeat the endeavour of superior officers to advance the welfare of the public service. Individual merit will be invariably recognized in due course, but officers who without authority give publicity to discoveries, tending to produce sensation and alarm, show themselves wholly unworthy of their posts.[22]

From the first the police adhered to this principle in their investigation of the Whitechapel murders. The *East London Advertiser*, hungry for details about the Tabram case, complained on 18 August that the police were 'very reticent upon the matter generally' and 'not disposed to assist in the publication of details.' Three weeks later, fishing for copy on the Nichols murder, the *Advertiser* encountered the same attitude: 'the authorities are extremely reticent and guarded in all the information they tender, and most of the particulars and information has to be obtained from other sources.'[23]

On Saturday, 1 September, Mr Wynne E. Baxter, Coroner for the South Eastern District of Middlesex, opened the Nichols inquest at the Working Lads' Institute. Baxter, fresh from his Scandinavian tour, attended resplendent in black and white checked trousers, dark coat, dazzling white waistcoat and crimson scarf. In ferreting out the facts of the case he was indefatigable. And his zeal was, of course, troublesome to the detectives who wished to suppress the details of their inquiries. Three witnesses, Edward Walker, PC Neil and Dr Llewellyn, were heard on the first day. At the end of the proceedings Inspector Abberline asked for a lengthy adjournment 'as certain things were coming to the knowledge of the police and they wished for time to make inquiries.' The coroner and his jury, however, wanted to hear more so Baxter did not accede to the request.

Instead he adjourned the inquest until the following Monday, the next working day. It was only after the second day's proceedings, during which another eight witnesses made depositions, that the coroner consented to adjourn the inquest for a fortnight in order to provide the police with 'an opportunity of obtaining further evidence.'[24]

Today pedlars of the 'cover-up' theory represent police secrecy in the Ripper case as an integral part of a sinister conspiracy of silence designed to conceal the involvement of persons close to the throne. Back in the 1880s it was naturally resented by journalists and they roundly condemned the force for being 'either sulkily silent or barrenly communicative on topics concerning which the public, through their journalistic delegates, justifiably demand ample information.'[25] There were, nevertheless, some perfectly sound reasons for the CID's policy.

In a practical context, for example, it was crucial for the detectives to pursue their inquiries before memories faded or clues were obliterated and their frustration at having to spend precious days dallying in attendance at the coroner's court is understandable. The publication of evidence, moreover, was not invariably in the public interest. In the case of sensational atrocities like those in Whitechapel there was a real danger that publicity would foster panic and that the publication of detailed medical evidence would inspire imitators. The Ripper murders were, as we shall see, to generate copy killings and the baleful influence of Whitechapel began to appear soon after the Buck's Row tragedy. The first such incident concerned Henry Hummerston, a Hoxton labourer, and his mistress Eliza Smith. Hummerston came home drunk, quarrelsome and sporting a black eye. He asked Eliza who had given him his black eye and she replied that she did not know. The befuddled labourer then insisted that she had done it and commenced to abuse and beat her. Eliza fled into the back yard but Hummerston caught her there, knocked her down and kicked her. He then drew a table knife across her throat and swore that he would make a second 'Buck's Row murder' out of it. This attack, fortunately, was not fatal. Eliza was rescued by her neighbours and suffered only a slight cut which passed halfway round her throat on the right side. Hummerston himself was sentenced on 5 September at Worship Street to six months' hard labour for assault. But at the very least it demonstrated the sinister effect that gruesome murders can exert upon weak or disturbed minds.[26] Finally, as Howard Vincent had pointed out, there was always the possibility that a police investigation might be hindered by the publicity accorded to the activities of detectives. A notable instance of this, at the beginning of the Whitechapel investigation, occurred in the case of 'Leather Apron'.

During the hunt for Polly Nichols' killer police inquiries amongst prostitutes revealed that the Whitechapel whores walked in fear of a man they knew as 'Leather Apron'. His real name was Jack Pizer and in various parts of the metropolis he had for some time been levying tribute from prostitutes and beating those who resisted his demands. Obviously the detectives were anxious to trace him, if only to eliminate him from their inquiries, and a careful search of common lodging houses began. But then, whether from street gossip or from the unguarded remarks of some policeman, the press learned of 'Leather Apron'.

The *Star* was the prime offender. On 5 and 6 September it devoted long and lurid articles to the subject. The first was headlined:

'LEATHER APRON.'

THE ONLY NAME LINKED WITH THE WHITECHAPEL MURDERS.

A NOISELESS MIDNIGHT TERROR.

The Strange Character who Prowls About
Whitechapel After Midnight – Universal
Fear Among the Women – Slippered Feet
and a Sharp Leather-knife.

It is difficult in a short space to do justice to the *Star's* articles on Leather Apron. They seem to have been pieced together from the title tattle of whores, lodging house proprietors and tradesmen and almost no reliable substantiation exists for any part of them.

Leather Apron, according to the *Star*, was a Jewish slipper maker who had abandoned his trade in favour of bullying prostitutes at night. The women did not know his real name. But they were able to furnish the newspaper with a description: 'From all accounts he is five feet four or five inches in height and wears a dark, close-fitting cap. He is thickset, and has an unusually thick neck. His hair is black, and closely clipped, his age being about 38 or 40. He has a small, black moustache. The distinguishing feature of his costume is a leather apron, which he always wears, and from which he gets his nickname. His expression is sinister, and seems to be full of terror for the women who describe it. His eyes are small and glittering. His lips are usually parted in a grin which is not only not reassuring, but excessively repellent.' A George Yard grocer, who had supposedly known Leather Apron for six years, added that he was 'unquestionably mad' and that 'anybody who met him face to face would know it . . . his eyes are never still, but are always shifting uneasily, and he never looks anybody in the eye.'

The reputation the *Star* bestowed upon Leather Apron was as villainous as his face. For several years he had subjected the prostitutes of Whitechapel to a reign of terror. His method was to go to public houses after midnight, peep in through the window to select his victim and then wait outside in the dark for them to come out. The hapless whores rarely knew of his presence until he was upon them for, although they could not tell what he wore on his feet, he had the uncanny ability to tread quite noiselessly about the streets. Victims were kicked, bruised, injured and terrified but not, as far as the newspaper could determine, cut. It was told, however, that Leather Apron always carried a sharp knife, the kind used to trim leather, and that he frequently menaced women with it. Thus when 'Widow Annie' encountered him, two weeks since as she was crossing the square near the London Hospital, he drew his knife upon her and threatened, with his ugly grin and malignant eyes, to 'rip her up.'

The *Star* was as ignorant as the police as to the whereabouts of Leather Apron. He was everywhere and he was nowhere. According to the newspaper he had even been temporarily in police custody on Sunday, 2 September, but there is no corroboration of it in police records. At the fourpenny lodging house off Brick Lane, where he frequently slept, the people denied he was there and appeared disposed to shield him. Rumour was rife. One of the *Star*'s informants claimed to have seen him lately in Leather Lane, Holborn. Another swore that she descried him crossing London Bridge into Southwark, 'as stealthily as usual, with head bent, his skimpy coat turned up about his ears, and looking as if he were in a desperate hurry.' Two women in Philpot Street told the *Star*'s reporter that Leather Apron would most likely be found in Commercial Street, opposite the Princess Alice Tavern. 'It will be necessary,' they added, 'to look into all the shadows, as if he is there he will surely be out of sight.'27

Having read these hair-raising articles few of the *Star*'s patrons can have doubted that Leather Apron and the Whitechapel killer were one. Yet the only direct evidence offered by the paper was a piece of false gossip to the effect that Leather Apron had been seen walking in Baker's Row with Polly Nichols on the morning of her murder. Contemporary police reports, indeed, contain no corroboration of the *Star*'s allegations other than the bare acknowledgement that Pizer bullied prostitutes for money, and they took pains to point out that there was no evidence implicating him in the killings. 'At present,' wrote Helson on 7 September, 'there is no evidence whatever against him.' Twelve days later Abberline concurred: 'there was no evidence to connect him with the murder.'[28]

The effect of the press campaign against Leather Apron was twofold. It alerted Pizer to the fact that he was being sought by the police and it stirred up popular feeling against him. The prospect of falling victim to mob vengeance scared him more than the police and he went into hiding amongst his relatives. In this way the best efforts of the detectives were frustrated.

The arm's length policy applied by the CID to the press rested, therefore, upon bitter experience and sound reasoning. But it had its disadvantages and some of the detectives of the time, notably Walter Dew and Sir Melville Macnaghten, later publicly disavowed it.[29] In particular the CID, by embracing such a policy, largely denied itself the undoubted benefits that publicity can bestow upon police investigations. Just how valuable the publication of clues can be, even in cases in which the identity of the culprit is unknown, has been dramatically demonstrated in our own day by the spectacular success since 1984 of the BBC's *Crimewatch UK*. The first 28 programmes, covering 288 cases, resulted in 81 arrests and 9 people were charged with murder.[30] The attitude of the police to the press, moreover, exacerbated the already strained relationship between the two. On the part of the police it implied mistrust which the responsible press found galling. And journalists, unable to satisfy their inquiries at the police stations, were reduced to all manner of dubious practices in order to fill their columns – trying to loosen the tongues of police constables with drink and bribes, shadowing detectives to discover and interview their witnesses, scavenging gossip and hearsay about the streets and, of course, romancing shamelessly.

Since the Clerkenwell explosion of 1867 the number of constables on the beat had been increased. By 1888, moreover, most police stations had been connected by the telegraph, and that autumn saw the appearance in the metropolis of ten experimental 'police alarms'. These were telephone boxes, affixed to houses or stout posts, to which constables were provided with keys. But such improvements had brought no sense of increased security to the citizens of East London. There, even before the murders, the inadequacy of police protection had been a frequent complaint, one that the lurking menace of a homicidal maniac immediately revived in the autumn of 1888. Henry Tibbatts, a local man with business premises within a stone's throw of Whitechapel church, was writing in the *Daily News* as early as 3 September about 'shamefully inadequate' policing. 'I myself have witnessed street fights amounting almost to murder,' he contended, 'in the neighbourhood of Osborn Street, Fashion Street, &c., and never at any of these critical periods are the police to be found.'[31] Not yet, however, had disquiet turned into panic. Those primarily responsible for the policing of the metropolis were content to leave the matter to their subordinates. Matthews was enjoying his respite from parlimentary duties. Warren was on vacation in the south of France. And on 7 September Dr Anderson left the capital on his way to Switzerland.

It was the lull before the storm. On the morning of Saturday, 8 September, the *East London Advertiser* ventured a prediction that was pregnant with foreboding. 'The murderer must creep out from somewhere,' it ran, 'he must patrol the streets in search of his victims. Doubtless he is out night by night. Three successful murders will have the effect of whetting his appetite still further, and unless a watch of the strictest be kept, the murder of Thursday will certainly be followed by a fourth.'[32]

So it proved. For in the early hours of that same morning, after those words had been written but before they appeared on the streets, the body of another woman was discovered in the back yard of a house in Hanbury Street, Spitalfields. She had been mutilated more horrendously than any of the others. Close by, saturated with water, lay what appeared to be a clue. It was a piece of a leather apron.

5

Dark Annie

TO HER FRIENDS the fourth victim was known simply as 'Dark Annie'.

She is identified in police records as Annie Chapman, alias Annie Siffey. A sad, broken-down little prostitute, she lived a precarious and semi-nomadic existence on the streets and in the common lodging houses of Spitalfields. She was forty-seven years old.[1]

At one time Annie's future must have seemed secure enough. On 1 May 1869 she married a coachman named John Chapman. The place of residence of both is recorded on the marriage certificate as 29 Montpelier Place, Brompton, where Annie's mother lived until her death in 1893, but the newly weds soon set up home at 1 Brook Mews, Bayswater, and then at 17 South Bruton Mews, Berkeley Square. By 1881 they had moved to Windsor, where John had taken a position as head domestic coachman to Josiah Weeks, a farm bailiff, at St Leonard's Mill Farm Cottage. There were children. Emily Ruth was born in 1870, Annie Georgina in 1873 and John in 1881.

But tragedy dogged Annie throughout the eighties and her life disintegrated under a catalogue of disasters. Her little boy was a cripple and Emily Ruth died of meningitis when she was only twelve. In 1888 John junior was said to be in the care of a charitable school and Annie Georgina travelling with a performing troupe or circus in France. Then, after the death of her firstborn, Annie's marriage, like those of Martha Tabram and Polly Nichols, ended in tatters. Police records indicate that her intemperate habits were to blame but John himself was a heavy drinker and the misfortunes of the children must have imposed strains upon the union. Whatever the cause, the couple lived apart for three or four years during which time Annie received an allowance of 10s. a week from her husband. In 1886 she was lodging at 30 Dorset Street, Spitalfields, with a man who made wire sieves, and for this reason was sometimes known as 'Mrs Sievey'. But the death of John Chapman and the loss of her allowance that same year robbed her of her remaining financial security.

Chapman died on 25 December 1886, at 1 Richmond Villas, Grove Road, Windsor. The cause of death was registered as cirrhosis of the liver, ascites and dropsy. He was only forty-four. One of Annie's friends during her last years was Amelia Palmer, a charwoman and the wife of a dock labourer named Henry Palmer. In testifying before the inquest into Annie's own death she spoke of the great effect that John Chapman's death seemed to have had upon Annie, emotionally as well as financially. The termination of her allowance, which came by postal order made payable at Commercial Road Post Office, was the first indication Annie received that something was wrong. She then learned, upon inquiry of one of John's relatives living in London, that her husband was dead. Annie cried as she told Amelia about it. And two years later Amelia remembered how she had often seemed downcast when speaking of her children and how 'since the death of her husband she has seemed to give way altogether.'

Very possibly the sieve maker's interest in Annie disappeared with her allowance. At any rate he left her and moved to Notting Hill soon after the death of John Chapman. Annie struggled on alone. At times she seems to have benefited from the charity of relatives. Her brother, Fountain Hamilton Smith, last saw her in Commercial Street a week or two before her death. She did not tell him where she was living but said that she was not doing anything and needed money for a lodging. Smith gave her 2s. On the last evening of her life she may also have borrowed money from other relatives at Vauxhall. Yet there must have been limits to such sponging. Amelia Palmer knew that Annie had a mother and sister living at Brompton but did not think that they were on friendly terms. 'I have never known her to stay with her relatives even for a night,' she informed the inquest.

Annie did crochet work, made antimacassars and sold flowers. On Fridays she would take what she had made to Stratford to sell. When sober she was industrious but she was overfond of liquor: 'I have seen her often the worse for drink,' said Amelia. She turned, too, ✓ to prostitution although, to judge by her photograph and police records, her appearance was unprepossessing. She was plump but only five feet tall. Her complexion was fair. Her hair was wavy and dark brown, her eyes blue. She had a large, thick nose, and two teeth were missing from her lower jaw.

About four months before her death Annie took up residence at Crossingham's lodging house, 35 Dorset Street, Spitalfields. Timothy Donovan, the deputy, remembered her as an inoffensive woman who never caused them any trouble and was on good terms with the other lodgers. Her main weakness was drink. Possibly her Stratford money was squandered on liquor. At least Donovan said that Annie was generally drunk on Saturdays.

Annie paid 8d. for a double bed. Her only regular visitor, however, was a man Donovan knew only as 'the pensioner'. In Annie's life 'the pensioner' is something of a mystery. If we are to believe the deputy he regularly came to the lodging house with Annie on Saturdays and stayed until the following Monday. More, he instructed Donovan to turn Annie away on any night that she tried to bring another man home with her. The pensioner, said Donovan, sometimes dressed like a dock labourer and at others had a gentlemanly appearance.

His real name was Ted Stanley. He lived at 1 Osborn Place, Osborn Street, Whitechapel, and he was not, in fact, a pensioner at all. In the inquest proceedings he is described as a bricklayer's labourer. We also know from police records that, on the night Polly Nichols was killed, Stanley was on duty at Fort Elson, Gosport, with the 2nd Brigade, Southern Division, Hants., Militia.

On 14 September 1888 Stanley made a statement at Commercial Street Police Station. Five days later he appeared as a witness at the inquest. Yet, he was scarcely forthcoming about his relationship with Annie. On the one hand, despite the repeated assertions of Timothy Donovan, he insisted that he had only visited Annie once or twice at the lodging house and absolutely denied telling Donovan to turn her away if she came with other men. On the other he admitted to having associated with her in other places and to having known her for about two years. Whatever the exact nature of their relationship Ted Stanley shunned any involvement once he knew that Annie was dead. On the day of the murder he turned up at the lodging house to verify a rumour he had heard from a shoeblack that she had been killed. Assured that the news was true, he turned and walked straight out without another word.

Annie must have heard and talked about the Whitechapel murders but, crushed by ill health and poverty, and frittering most of the little she had on drink, she found herself regularly back on the streets. To judge by the testimony of the doctor who performed the post-mortem examination she was tuberculous and, although plump, had suffered great privation. A week or more before her death she was involved in a fight. It was the only fracas Donovan could remember her in and the date and details are vague.

Annie's antagonist was Eliza Cooper, a hawker and fellow lodger at 35 Dorset Street. On 19 September she gave her version of the debacle to the inquest. The trouble started, explained Liza, on Saturday, 1 September. Annie brought Ted Stanley to the lodging house. When she began asking around for a piece of soap she was referred to Liza who loaned her one. Annie handed it to Stanley and he went out to get washed. Later that day Liza met Annie again and asked for the return of the soap. 'I will see you by and by' was the airy reply. On the following Tuesday the two women saw each other in the lodging house kitchen. Liza once more asked for her soap but Annie testily threw a halfpenny down on the table and said, 'Go and get a halfpennyworth of soap.' There was a quarrel which flared up again later in the day at the Britannia, on the corner of Dorset and Commercial Streets. On this occasion Annie slapped Liza's face and snapped: 'Think yourself lucky I did not do more.' Liza replied by striking Annie in the left eye and on the chest.

It is probable that, several weeks after the incident, Liza's memories of this sordid little squabble were already becoming confused. We may suspect, too, that she contrived to make herself the aggrieved party. Certainly, even if Annie was drunk, it is difficult to see in the vindictive, combative Annie of Liza's tale anything of the meek, inoffensive little woman of the other witnesses. John Evans, the nightwatchman at 35 Dorset Street, spoke at the inquest of the fight only two days after Annie's death. He confirmed the cause of it (a piece of soap) but said that it took place in the lodging house kitchen. In two particulars at least Eliza was mistaken. The fight cannot have taken place as late as 4 September. Ted Stanley noticed that Annie had a black eye on Sunday, 2 September, and the next day Annie showed her bruises to Amelia Palmer. Timothy Donovan, moreover, told the inquest that Annie was not at the lodging house during the week preceding her death. The best evidence that we have places the fight in the middle of the previous week. Donovan said that it occurred about Tuesday, 28 August, and that two days later Annie was sporting a black eye from the encounter. 'Tim, this is lovely, ain't it?' she chirped. John Evans deposed that the incident took place on 30 August. It is also clear that Annie sustained bruises to the chest and right, rather than left, temple, a point that will prove of some significance when we come to consider the post-mortem evidence.

In the week previous to her murder Annie was not at the lodging house. The only glimpses we get of her come from her friend Amelia Palmer. On Monday, 3 September, Amelia met her in Dorset Street and noticed a bruise on her right temple. 'How did you get that?' she asked. By way of reply Annie opened her dress. 'Yes,' she said, 'look at my chest.' And she showed Amelia a second bruise. Their talk passed from Annie's fight to other things. 'If my sister will send me the boots,' declared Annie, 'I shall go hopping [i.e. hop-picking].'

The next day Amelia saw Annie again near Spitalfields Church. Annie said that she felt no better and that she should go into the casual ward for a day or two. Amelia remarked that she looked very pale and asked if she had had anything to eat. 'No,' replied Annie, 'I haven't had a cup of tea today.' Amelia gave her 2d. to get some but told her not to spend it on rum.

Amelia last saw Annie alive on Friday, 7 September. At about 5.00 p.m. they met in Dorset Street. 'Aren't you going to Stratford today?' queried Amelia. 'I feel too ill to do anything,' said Annie. Some ten minutes later Amelia found her standing in the same spot. 'It's no use giving way,' Annie said, 'I must pull myself together and get some money or I shall have no lodgings.'

Earlier that same day, the last of Annie's life, she had turned up again at 35 Dorset Street. Between two and three in the afternoon she arrived at the lodging house and asked to be allowed to sit downstairs in the kitchen. Donovan asked her where she had been all week and she told him that she had been 'in the infirmary'.[2] Annie seems to have been coming and going for the rest of the day. Soon after midnight she came in saying that she had been to Vauxhall to see her sister. A fellow lodger told a newspaper that she went to 'get some money' and that her relatives gave her 5d.[3] If so it was quickly expended on drink. John Evans informed the inquest that upon her return she sent one of the lodgers for a pint of beer and then popped out again herself.

At about 1.30 or 1.45 a.m. on Saturday, 8 September, Annie was sitting in the kitchen, enjoying the warmth, eating potatoes and gossiping with the other lodgers. Donovan sent Evans to ask for her lodging money. Annie came up to the office. 'I haven't sufficient money for my bed,' she told the deputy, 'but don't let it. I shall not be long before I am in.' Donovan was scarcely sympathetic. 'You can find money for your beer,' he admonished her, 'and you can't find money for your bed.' But Annie was not dismayed. She would get the money. Leaving the office, she stood two or three minutes in the doorway. 'Never mind, Tim,' she repeated, 'I shall soon be back. Don't let the bed.' Evans, who had followed Annie upstairs now saw her off the premises. As she left the house, he told the inquest two days later, he watched her go. Not drunk but slightly the worse for drink, she walked through Little Paternoster Row into Brushfield Street and then turned towards Spitalfields Church. It was about 1.50 a.m.[4]

A little after six Annie's dead and mutilated body was discovered in the backyard of 29 Hanbury Street, Spitalfields, just three or four hundred yards away from her lodging.

No. 29 was a three-storeyed house on the north side of the street. Built for Spitalfields weavers, it had been converted into dwellings for the labouring poor after steam had banished the hand loom. By 1888 the toll of time was beginning to show on its facade. It was a dingy property flanked by equally dingy neighbours, on one side a dwelling house and on the other, its yellow paint peeling from its walls like skin disease, a mangling house. Yet a discerning observer might have detected remnants of pride about No. 29. A signboard above the street door proudly proclaimed in straggling white letters: 'Mrs A. Richardson, rough packing-case maker.' And the windows of the first floor front room, in which Mrs Richardson slept, were adorned with red curtains and filled with flowers.

At the time of the murder No. 29 was a veritable nest of living beings. Mrs Amelia Richardson, a widow, rented part of it and sublet some of the rooms. She slept with her fourteen-year-old grandson in the first floor front room and used two other rooms. The cellar in the backyard housed her packing case workshops. In the ground floor back room she did her cooking and held weekly prayer meetings. The front room on the ground floor was a cats' meat shop. The proprietress, Mrs Harriet Hardiman, slept in the shop with her sixteen-year-old son. Mr Waker, a maker of tennis boots, and his adult but mentally retarded son occupied the first floor back. The second floor front was tenanted by Mr Thompson, a carman, his wife and their adopted daughter. Two unmarried sisters who worked in a cigar factory lived in the back room on the same floor. The front room in the attic housed John Davis, another carman, together with his wife and three sons. While Mrs Sarah Cox, a 'little old lady' who Mrs Richardson maintained out of charity, occupied a back room in the attic. No less than seventeen persons thus resided permanently at No. 29. Others had legitimate business there. John Richardson, Amelia's son, and Francis Tyler, her hired hand, for example, both assisted her in her packing case business and used the cellar workshops.[5]

There must have been much coming and going and on market mornings at least the day began early. On Saturday, 8 September, the morning of the murder, Thompson went out for work at about 3.50. Mrs Richardson, dozing fitfully on the first floor, heard him leave and called out 'good morning' as he passed her room. Between 4.45 and 4.50 John Richardson visited the house on his way to work in Spitalfields Market. He called in to check on the security of the cellar. John Davis got up at 5.45 and went down to the backyard about a quarter of an hour later. And Francis Tyler, the hired help, should have started work at six. He was, however, frequently late. On the fatal Saturday he had to be sent for and didn't turn up until eight.

Intruders might also be found on the premises. By the shop door in Hanbury Street was a side door which gave access to the rest of the building from the street. It opened into a twenty or twenty-five foot passage. A staircase led to the upper floors and at the end of the passage was a back door giving access to the backyard. Most of the houses in the area, like No. 29, were let out in rooms and many of the tenants were market folk, leaving home early in the morning, some as early as one. It thus became the general practice to leave street and back doors unlocked for their convenience and the inevitable result was the regular appearance in these houses of trespassers. One morning Thompson challenged a man on the stairs of No. 29. 'I'm waiting for the market,' said the man. 'You've no right here, guv'nor,' replied Thompson. Prostitutes and their clients also used the premises. John Richardson told the inquest that he had found prostitutes and other strangers there at all hours of the night and had often turned them out.

In taking his victim into the backyard of No. 29, therefore, the murderer, perhaps unknowingly, exposed himself to some risk. Yet the regular traffic in and out of the house also facilitated his purpose.

For the permanent residents would scarcely have suspected anything amiss in the stealthy footsteps of the killer and his victim.

The backyard in which the body was found is of special interest to us. Although the house has long been demolished its appearance has been preserved in contemporary descriptions and drawings, in a few subsequent photographs, and in a rare piece of footage in that delightful if neglected James Mason film *The London Nobody Knows*. Three stone steps led from the back door down into the yard. It was perhaps five yards by four, in some places bare earth, in others roughly paved with flat or round stones. Close wooden palings, about five and a half feet high, fenced it off on both sides from the adjoining yards. Standing on the steps, an observer would have seen, three or three and a half feet to his left, the palings that separated the yard from that of No. 27. In the far left-hand corner, opposite the back door, was Mrs Richardson's woodshed. In the far right-hand corner was a privy. The entrance to the cellar, which contained Mrs Richardson's workshops, lay immediately to the right of the back door.

It was John Davis the carman who found Annie's body. He is described in the press as a small, elderly man with a decided stoop. He rented a room in the attic of No. 29, where he lived with his wife and three sons. For much of the night of 7–8 September Davis could not sleep. From three to five he lay awake and then he dozed until the clock at Spitalfields Church struck 5.45. That, and the light stealing through his large weaver's window, told him that it was time to bestir himself for another day's toil in Leadenhall Market. Davis and his wife got up. She made him a cup of tea and then he trudged downstairs to the backyard. Downstairs he noticed that the street door was wide open and thrown back against the wall. That was not unusual. The back door was closed. He opened it and stood at the top of the steps leading into the yard. The sight that met his casual glance shook him to his boots.

The body of a woman, sprawled upon its back, lay in the yard to his left, between the steps and the wooden fence adjoining No. 27. Her head was towards the house, her feet towards the woodshed, and Davis noticed that her skirts had been raised to her groin. He did not wait to investigate further. Hurrying through the passage, he stumbled out of the front door and into the street. There two packing case makers, James Green and James Kent, who worked for Joseph and Thomas Bayley of 23A Hanbury Street, were standing outside their workshop waiting for fellow workmen to arrive. And

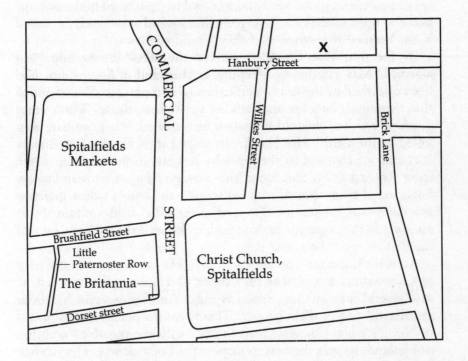

Hanbury Street and vicinity. ✕ marks No. 29, where the body
of Annie Chapman was discovered, at about 6.00 a.m. on 8
September 1888

there, passing through Hanbury Street on his way to work, was a
boxmaker named Henry John Holland. Their attention was arrested
by a wild-eyed old man who suddenly burst from the doorway of No.
29. 'Men,' he cried, 'come here!'

The workmen followed Davis back down the passage and gazed at
the body from the top of the yard steps. Davis, Kent and Green stood
nervously at the back door. Holland, by his own account, ventured
down into the yard itself but did not touch the body. Then they
dispersed to find a policeman. Kent seems to have been thoroughly
shaken by the experience. When he couldn't see a constable from
the front of the house he poured himself a brandy and then pottered
about his workshop in search of a piece of canvas to throw over the
body. By the time that he returned to No. 29 Inspector Chandler had

taken possession of the yard and a crowd had gathered in the passage and about the back door. 'Everyone that looked at the body,' recalled Kent, 'seemed frightened as if they would run away.'

By the time that Chandler arrived the whole house had been alarmed. Mrs Hardiman, sleeping in the ground floor shop, had been disturbed by the heavy traffic through the passage. She imagined that there must be a fire and sent her son to investigate. 'Don't upset yourself, mother,' he told her when he returned, 'it's a woman been killed in the yard!' Mrs Hardiman stayed in her room but Amelia Richardson, apprised of the news by her grandson, ventured down from the first floor. She found the passage clogged with spectators but none of them seemed inclined to view the body at close quarters for there was no one in the yard except the dead woman. Soon afterwards the inspector arrived and, as far as Amelia knew, he was the first to enter the yard.[6]

At 6.10 Inspector Joseph Chandler, H. Division, was on duty in Commercial Street near the corner of Hanbury Street when he saw several men running towards him. 'Another woman has been murdered,' one of them gasped. There was no one in the backyard of No. 29 when Chandler arrived and, with the possible exception of Holland, he was the first to inspect the body closely. The woman lay at the bottom and to the left of the steps leading into the yard, parallel with the fencing dividing the yards of Nos. 29 and 27. Her head was nearly two feet from the back wall of the house and six or nine inches from the steps. She was lying on her back, her left arm resting on her left breast, her right arm lying down her right side, her legs drawn up and her clothes thrown up above her knees. The handiwork of the murderer had been literally ghoulish. In terse language Chandler recorded the grisly sight for his superiors later in the day:

I at once proceeded to No. 29 Hanbury Street, and in the back yard found a woman lying on her back, dead, left arm resting on left breast, legs drawn up, abducted, small intestines and flap of the abdomen lying on right side, above right shoulder, attached by a cord with the rest of the intestines inside the body; two flaps of skin from the lower part of the abdomen lying in a large quantity of blood above the left shoulder; throat cut deeply from left and back in a jagged manner right around throat.[7]

The inspector at once sent for Dr George Bagster Phillips, the divisional police surgeon, and to the police station for further assistance and an ambulance. When the constables arrived he had the passage cleared. He also ensured that no one touched the body and covered it with a piece of sacking.

Dr Phillips arrived at 6.30. Then in his fifties, he had been the local divisional surgeon for many years. Walter Dew, who knew him well, remembered him as ultra old-fashioned in dress and personal appearance. 'He used to look,' wrote Dew, 'for all the world as though he had stepped out of a century-old painting.'[8] But his manners were charming, he was popular with the force and he knew his business. The doctor's inquest deposition of 13 September contains the fullest description of the appearance of Annie Chapman's body in the backyard of 29 Hanbury Street:

> I found the body of the deceased lying in the yard on her back, on the left hand of the steps that lead from the passage. The head was about 6 in. in front of the level of the bottom step, and the feet were towards a shed at the end of the yard. The left arm was across the left breast, and the legs were drawn up, the feet resting on the ground, and the knees turned outwards. The face was swollen and turned on the right side, and the tongue protruded between the front teeth, but not beyond the lips; it was much swollen. The small intestines and other portions were lying on the right side of the body on the ground above the right shoulder, but attached. There was a large quantity of blood, with a part of the stomach above the left shoulder ... The body was cold, except that there was a certain remaining heat, under the intestines, in the body. Stiffness of the limbs was not marked, but it was commencing. The throat was dissevered deeply. I noticed that the incision of the skin was jagged, and reached right round the neck.[9]

Phillips thought that the woman had been dead at least two hours, probably longer. He gave instructions for her to be removed and she was conveyed to the Whitechapel Mortuary on the police ambulance. The doctor and Chandler then made a careful search of the yard itself.

There were no signs of a struggle. On the back wall of the house, near where the woman's head had lain and about eighteen inches above the ground, were about six spots of blood. They varied in size from that of a sixpenny piece to that of a small point. There were also patches and smears of well clotted blood on the wooden palings, about fourteen inches from the ground. These too were close to the position of the head, immediately above the part where the blood had mainly flowed from the neck. Since there were no bloodstains in the passage and no others in the vicinity of the house, Dr Phillips was convinced that the murder had occurred in the yard.

A macabre discovery awaited them near the palings and close to where the feet of the dead woman had rested. It comprised a small piece of coarse muslin, a small-tooth comb and a pocket comb in a paper case. These articles appeared to have been the contents of the dead woman's pocket and Dr Phillips did not think that they had been casually cast to the ground. 'They had apparently been placed there in order,' he would tell the inquest, 'that is to say, *arranged* there.' Near the head position was a portion of an envelope containing two pills. The back of the envelope bore a seal and the words 'Sussex Regiment' embossed in blue. On the other side was a letter 'M' in handwriting and, lower down, 'Sp' as if someone had written 'Spitalfields.' The rest of the envelope was torn away. It bore no postage stamp but there was a postmark in red: 'London, Aug. 23, 1888.'

A few other articles were found about the yard – an empty nail box, a piece of flat steel and, about two feet from a water tap and saturated with water, a leather apron.[10]

Later in the morning Chandler visited the mortuary and examined the dead woman's clothing. If, as the inspector remembered, he arrived a few minutes after seven it is unlikely that anyone had had time to tamper with the clothes. Indeed, when he got there the body still lay on the ambulance and did not look as though it had been disturbed.

The main items were a black figured jacket that came down to the knees, a brown bodice, a black skirt and a pair of lace boots, all old and dirty. Chandler's evidence on the condition of the clothes, presented five days later to the inquest, was very loosely reported in the press but it is apparent that he discovered remarkably few bloodstains. The black jacket, which he found hooked at the top and buttoned down the front, was bloodstained about the neck, both inside and out, but otherwise bore only two or three spots of blood on the left arm. On the black skirt there was evidently only a little blood 'on the outside, at the back, as if she had been lying in it.' Chandler also mentions two bodices and two petticoats. The bodices were only stained about the neck and the petticoats were stained 'very little.' There were no traces of blood upon the stockings. The clothing was neither cut nor torn. But the woman wore a large pocket under her skirt, tied around her waist with strings, and this was torn, both down the front and at the side. It was empty.[11]

Dr Phillips conducted the post-mortem examination at the Whitechapel Mortuary that afternoon. The circumstances were difficult. When he arrived he was discomfited to discover that two nurses from the Whitechapel Union Infirmary had already stripped and partially washed the corpse and that it lay ready for him on the table. The mortuary itself was simply a shed belonging to the workhouse, lacking in proper facilities, and Robert Mann, the old keeper, a pauper inmate.

No report or post-mortem notes by Dr Phillips now exist. He presented his evidence, of course, to the inquest – on 13 and 19 September, but no official record of the inquest depositions has survived. For our knowledge of his findings, therefore, we must largely trust to press notices of the inquest and this is most unfortunate.

When Phillips first appeared before the inquest he was reluctant, as we shall see, to divulge all the details of his examination, especially with regard to the abdominal mutilations, and Coroner Baxter excused him for the time being from so doing. Upon his recall six days later the coroner obliged him to present the suppressed evidence in full but the press considered his remarks upon the abdominal injuries unfit for publication and deleted that part of his testimony from their reports. There is thus an important gap in the press coverage of the medical evidence. Curiously enough, however, the problem confronting the historian is not so much what the press refused to report as what it did print. The details of the abdominal mutilations can be accurately recovered from other sources. But for the rest of Phillips' testimony we are virtually dependent upon the newspapers and they edited it so arbitrarily, and reported it in such vague and ambiguous language, as to render parts of it almost unintelligible. Our reconstruction of Annie Chapman's injuries, then, must necessarily be provisional, pending the discovery of more exact evidence.[12]

The doctor discovered a bruise over the right temple and two bruises, each the size of a man's thumb, on the fore part of the top of the chest. He did not think that they were recent and he was quite right because Annie had sustained them in her fight with Eliza Cooper. He found more recent marks, however, on the face and about the sides of the jaw. Below the lower jaw on the left side, one and a half to two inches below the lobe of the ear, were three scratches. They ran in the opposite direction to the incisions in the throat. There were also evidently two recent bruises on the right side of the head and neck, one on the cheek and the other at a point corresponding with the scratches on the left side.

Phillips deduced from these that the woman had been seized by the chin before her throat had been cut. And the coroner's questions prompted him to express the view that she had been partially suffocated:

PHILLIPS: '... I am of opinion that the person who cut the deceased's throat took hold of her by the chin, and then commenced the incision from left to right.'
BAXTER: 'Could that be done so instantaneously that a person could not cry out?'
PHILLIPS: 'By pressure on the throat no doubt it would be possible.'
BAXTER: 'The thickening of the tongue would be one of the signs of suffocation?'
PHILLIPS: 'Yes. My impression is that she was partially strangled.'

There were the distinct marks of one or more rings on the proximal phalanx of the ring finger. An abrasion over the head of the proximal phalanx suggested that the killer had wrenched the rings from her finger.

The throat had been ferociously severed from left to right. The *Telegraph*, reporting Phillips' testimony on this point, stated that 'the incisions of the skin indicated that they had been made from the left side of the neck on a line with the angle of the jaw, carried entirely round and again in front of the neck, and ending at a point about midway between the jaw and the sternum or breast bone on the right hand.' This is difficult to interpret. It might be taken to mean that there were two cuts, one along the line of the jaw and completely encircling the throat, the other commencing at the front of the neck and terminating on the right side between the levels of the lower jaw and the breast bone. The doctor also intimated that the murderer had attempted and failed to cut off the woman's head. He discerned two distinct clean cuts on the left side of the spine, parallel to each other and half an inch apart. 'The muscular structures between the side processes of bone of the vertebrae,' he said, 'had an appearance as if an attempt had been made to separate the bones of the neck.'

Phillips held that the woman had been partially suffocated before death and that death had resulted from syncope, the sudden loss of blood supply to the brain caused by the severance of the throat. The abdominal mutilations, he contended, had been inflicted after death. Albeit the coroner compelled him, upon his recall, to describe the abdominal injuries the press censored the details. Fortunately this gap in the record can be filled from two other sources.

An unsigned piece in the *Lancet* of 29 September set down the gist of Dr Phillips' description of the injuries to the abdomen and indicated why he thought he had detected professional skill in their execution. It tells us that 'the abdomen had been entirely laid open; that the intestines, severed from their mesenteric attachments, had been lifted out of the body, and placed by the shoulder of the corpse; whilst from the pelvis the uterus and its appendages, with the upper portion of the vagina and the posterior two-thirds of the bladder, had been entirely removed. No trace of these parts could be found, and the incisions were cleanly cut, avoiding the rectum, and dividing the vagina low enough to avoid injury to the cervix uteri. Obviously the work was that of an expert – of one, at least, who had such knowledge of anatomical or pathological examinations as to be enabled to secure the pelvic organs with one sweep of a knife . . .' Chief Inspector Swanson also summarised the mutilations in his report of 19 October. 'Examination of the body,' he wrote, 'showed that the throat was severed deeply, incision jagged. Removed from, but attached to body, & placed above right shoulder were a flap of the wall of belly, the whole of the small intestines & attachments. Two other portions of wall of belly & "Pubes" were placed above left shoulder in a large quantity of blood . . . The following parts were missing:- part of belly wall including navel; the womb, the upper part of vagina & greater part of bladder.'

It was Phillips' opinion that the injuries to the throat and abdomen had probably been inflicted with the same knife. He told the inquest that it must have been a very sharp weapon, probably with a thin, narrow blade at least six to eight inches long. It was not a bayonet and the type of knife commonly used by cobblers and in the leather trades would not be long enough in the blade. A slaughterman's knife, however, well ground down, might fit the bill. Baxter asked whether it could have been such an instrument as a medical man might employ in post-mortem examinations. 'The ordinary post-mortem case,' replied Phillips, 'perhaps does not contain such a weapon.' Swanson credited the doctor with substantially the same views: 'The Dr gives it as his opinion . . . that the knife used was not an ordinary knife, but such as a small amputating knife, or a well ground slaughterman's knife, narrow & thin, sharp & blade of six to eight inches in length.'

Phillips thought that the murderer had demonstrated anatomical knowledge and surgical skill in extracting the viscera. 'There were indications of it,' he said on 13 September. 'My own impression is that anatomical knowledge was only less displayed or indicated in consequence of haste.' Six days later he reaffirmed this view: 'I myself could not have performed all the injuries I saw on that woman, and effect them, even without a struggle, [in] under a quarter of an hour. If I had done it in a deliberate way, such as would fall to the duties of a surgeon, it would probably have taken me the best part of an hour. The whole inference seems to me that the operation was performed to enable the perpetrator to obtain possession of these parts of the body.'

Hanbury Street lay within the jurisdiction of the Metropolitan Police's H Division. The divisional head of CID was Edmund Reid, who had investigated the Tabram murder, but he was now enjoying his annual leave and the conduct of the Chapman inquiry fell to Chandler and Detective Sergeants Thick and Leach.

The division was also anxious to secure Abberline's services. 'I would respectfully suggest,' wrote Acting Superintendent West on the day of the murder, 'that Inspector Abberline, Central, who is well acquainted with H Division, be deputed to take up this inquiry as I believe he is already engaged in the case of the Buck's Row murder which would appear to have been committed by the same person as the one in Hanbury Street.'[13] Abberline, in fact, had been instructed that very morning to assist the Chapman investigation.

West's view that the Buck's Row and Hanbury Street murders had been committed by the same man seems to have been general amongst the detectives investigating the crimes. Abberline certainly held to it and said so in his report of 19 September. And Inspector Helson of J Division, who had handled the Nichols investigation, evidently thought so too for he also actively assisted the H Division detectives working on the Chapman case.

The hunt for the Hanbury Street killer proved almost as frustratingly futile as had the previous investigations. Timothy Donovan and Fountain Smith quickly identified Annie's body but the police learned nothing of her history that suggested a serious suspect or a motive for her killing. The tenants at No. 29 were interviewed and their rooms were searched. Neither this, nor inquiries at adjoining houses, yielded a clue to the identity of the murderer. Detectives visited common lodging houses in the hope that someone might remember a man who entered after two on the morning of the murder and who behaved suspiciously or carried bloodstains on his face, hands or clothing. But these inquiries proved as fruitless as those amongst prostitutes and at local public houses.

Annie had been accustomed to wear brass rings on the third finger of her left hand. At the inquest Eliza Cooper spoke of three rings, which she said Annie had bought from a black man. Ted Stanley only remembered two. But when Annie's body had been found in Hanbury Street the rings were missing and an abrasion over the head of the proximal phalanx of the finger indicated that they had been wrenched off by force. Working on the assumption that the killer had mistaken them for gold rings, the police made inquiries at jewellers, pawnbrokers and other dealers throughout the area but met with no success.

Nor did the items found about the backyard yield a breakthrough. Dr Phillips did not think that the leather apron had any connection with the murder. It bore no traces of blood and did not look as if it had been recently unfolded. And so it proved, for Mrs Richardson told the inquest that the apron belonged to her son. Two days before the murder she had found it mildewed in the cellar and had put it under the water tap in the yard and left it there. Mrs Richardson also identified the nailbox and the piece of steel as her property.[14]

The police made a determined effort to trace the sender of the piece of torn envelope discovered near Annie's head. It bore the official stamp of the Royal Sussex Regiment and on 14 September Inspector Chandler visited the depot of the first battalion of the regiment at Farnborough to prosecute inquiries. There he learned that most of the men used the envelopes, which they could buy at the canteen, but none of them admitted to corresponding with anyone in Spitalfields and Chandler failed to match any of the signatures in the paybooks with the handwriting on the envelope. It became clear, moreover, that the sender of the envelope might not have been a soldier at all. The letter had been posted, not in the barracks, but at the nearby Lynchford Road Post Office. The postmasters there told Chandler that they stocked a supply of the envelopes and sold them to the general public!

An important development in the matter of the envelope occurred on 15 September. William Stevens, a painter and sometime lodger at 35 Dorset Street, turned up at Commercial Street Police Station and volunteered the information that he had seen Annie at the lodging house before she was turned out on the morning of her death. She said that she had been to the hospital and she had a bottle of medicine, a bottle of lotion and a box of pills with her. As she was handling the box it came to pieces. It had contained only two pills and Annie proceeded to wrap these in a piece of paper which she found on the kitchen floor by the fireplace. Stevens thought that the torn envelope bearing the stamp of the Royal Sussex Regiment and the paper picked up by Annie from the kitchen floor at 35 Dorset Street were identical.[15] It thus became apparent that the envelope had no connection whatever with the murderer and precious little with the victim.

In the light of these disappointments Chief Inspector Swanson's remark that the Chapman investigation 'did not supply the police with the slightest clue to the murderer' is perhaps understandable. And yet it is a harsh judgement. For the Chapman inquiry turned up three important witnesses. At the time, for reasons which will be explained shortly, the police never attached the significance to them that they deserved, but taken together their testimony reveals a good deal about the murderer and even, perhaps, a little about the murderer himself.

The first witness was John Richardson, Amelia's 37-year-old son. He lived at 2 John Street, Spitalfields, and worked as a porter in Spitalfields Market but he also assisted his mother with her packing case business at 29 Hanbury Street. Some time back the cellar at No. 29 had been broken into and a few tools stolen. Since then John had been in the habit of checking the cellar on market mornings and it was upon such an errand that he visited No. 29 between 4.45 and 4.50 on the morning of the murder.

The street door was closed. Richardson lifted the latch, walked through the passage and opened the yard door. But he did not walk out into the yard. One of his boots had been hurting a toe so he sat down on the middle step, his feet resting on the flags of the yard, and cut a piece of leather from the boot with a table knife. It was getting light and from the step he could see that the padlock on the cellar door was secure. Therefore, having tied up his boot, he left the house and went to the market. He had no need to close the yard door which closed itself (Coroner Baxter refers to it as a swing door) but he did shut the street door. While sitting on the step – about two minutes at the most – Richardson saw no body in the yard. Yet, as he explained to the inquest, 'I could not have failed to notice the deceased had she been lying there then.'[16]

The second witness was Mrs Elizabeth Long, the wife of a cart minder named James Long.

At about five that same morning she left her home at 32 Church Street to go to Spitalfields Market. It was about 5.30 as she walked westwards through Hanbury Street. She was sure of the time because she heard the clock of the Black Eagle Brewery, Brick Lane, strike the half hour just before she got to the street. A man and a woman were standing talking on the pavement near No. 29. How near it is impossible now to say because press reports of Mrs Long's inquest testimony do not agree. The *Telegraph* quotes her as saying that the couple were standing on the same side of the street as No. 29 and 'only a few yards nearer Brick Lane'. But *The Times*, which frequently reports inquest testimony erroneously, implies that they were actually outside the house, 'close against the shutters of No. 29.' Whatever, the woman had her back towards Spitalfields Market and hence faced Mrs Long as she approached, and the man's back was turned towards Mrs Long and Brick Lane. Mrs Long's evidence is crucial for she later visited the mortuary and positively identified Annie Chapman as the woman she had seen. Her companion was almost certainly the murderer.

At the inquest Mrs Long did her best to describe him:

BAXTER: 'Did you see the man's face?'
MRS LONG: 'I did not and could not recognize him again. He was, however, dark complexioned, and was wearing a brown deerstalker hat. I think he was wearing a dark coat but cannot be sure.'
BAXTER: 'Was he a man or a boy?'
MRS LONG: 'Oh, he was a man over forty, as far as I could tell.

He seemed to be a little taller than the deceased. He looked to
me like a foreigner, as well as I could make out.'
BAXTER: 'Was he a labourer or what?'
MRS LONG: 'He looked what I should call shabby genteel.'

Mrs Long heard the man ask 'Will you?' and the woman reply 'Yes.'
She then passed them and went on her way without looking back.

Mrs Long's description is recorded in police records in almost
identical terms: 'She only saw his back,' reported Chief Inspector
Swanson, 'and would be unable to know him again. She describes
him as apparently over 40 years of age. She did not see his face. He
appeared to be a little taller than the woman and in her opinion
looked like a foreigner. She thinks he had a dark coat on, but she
could not recognize him again.'[17]

Albert Cadosch, a carpenter living at No. 27 Hanbury Street, next
door to No. 29, was the last witness.

On the morning of the murder he got up at about 5.15 and went
into his backyard. By then it was about 5.20. A fence of wooden
palings, some five feet six inches high, divided the yard from that of
No. 29. Just as he was going back into the house he heard voices.
They were quite close, evidently in the backyard of No. 29, but the
only word Cadosch could catch was 'No.' He went indoors but three
or four minutes later returned to the yard. This time he heard another
noise from the yard of No. 29. It sounded like something falling
against the fence. The carpenter then left for work. When he passed
Spitalfields Church it was about 5.32.[18]

No further evidence on the Hanbury Street murder ever came to
light. With the clues that we have already assembled, however, we
can unravel some of the mysteries surrounding Annie's death.

Our sources depict her, on the last day of her life, as a pathetic
little woman in the last extremities of want. When Amelia Palmer
saw her in Dorset Street she was destitute. 'It is no use giving way,'
said Annie, 'I must pull myself together and get some money or I
shall have no lodgings.' Yet she did not, as was her wont, go to
Stratford. Indeed, if she had been ill in some infirmary it is more
than probable that she had made nothing to sell there. Instead she
went to Vauxhall to beg from one of her relatives. Annie returned to
her lodging house at 35 Dorset Street soon after midnight. Apparently
she had marshalled a few coppers but instead of using these to pay
for a bed she converted them into drink. It was a fatal moment of

weakness. For thus it was, that at about 1.50 a.m., she was turned into the street.

Annie had been drinking but she was not drunk and could walk in a straight line. Undoubtedly she banked upon raising her lodging money by prostitution. John Evans, the nightwatchman, saw her go through Little Paternoster Row into Brushfield Street and then turn towards Spitalfields Church. Four hours later she was dead.

We cannot know when or where Annie met her homicidal client. But there are some grounds for believing that she herself led him to the back yard of 29 Hanbury Street. The premises were regularly used by prostitutes. It was only three or four hundred yards away from her lodging house. And, for what it is worth, 29 was the number of Annie's regular bed at 35 Dorset Street.

The absence of blood in the passage, street and adjoining backyards led Phillips and Abberline to the conclusion that Annie had been slain where found. But when?

There is a serious conflict in the evidence on this point. When Dr Phillips saw Annie's body at 6.30 he judged that she had been killed at least two hours previously, i.e. not later than about 4.30. John Richardson, on the other hand, visited the yard between 4.45 and 4.50 and was positive that the body was not there then. Could he have missed it? Inspector Chandler was inclined to think that he had.

At about 6.45 on the fatal morning Chandler had talked to Richardson in the passage of No. 29. Upon that occasion the porter had told him about his early morning visit to the yard and had stated that he was sure that the woman had not then been lying there. But, according to Chandler, he had also said that 'he did not go down the steps.' The inspector surmised, therefore, that when Richardson had visited the yard he had merely opened the back door and stood on the top step. From such a position a downward glance to the right would quickly have determined that the padlock on the cellar was in place but Richardson's view of the left-hand side of the yard, where the body lay, might have been obscured by the back door, which opened outwards and swung to the left. Richardson, contended Chandler, had thus probably failed to see Annie's body.

Their faith in Dr Phillips, and Chandler's dismissal of Richardson, alike led the police to attach little significance to Mrs Long, who claimed to have seen Annie talking to a man near No. 29 at 5.30, or to Albert Cadosch, who thought he had heard voices from the backyard at about the same time. 'The evidence of Mrs Long, which appeared to be so important to the Coroner,' wrote Swanson, 'must be looked upon with some amount of doubt, which is to be regretted.'

It is time to appeal against this verdict of long standing and in doing so we are in good company since Coroner Baxter rejected it back in 1888.[19] In the first place the doctor's estimate of the time of death is far from conclusive. It was not based, as such judgements are today, on the internal body temperature of the deceased, taken rectally or from the liver, but upon an estimate from touch only of the external body temperature coupled with impressions as to how far rigor mortis had advanced. But there were several factors present in this case which would have contributed to rapid heat loss. The morning of 8 September was fairly cold. Annie's clothes had been thrown up to expose her legs and lower abdomen to the air. Her abdomen had been entirely laid open. And she had lost a great deal of blood. At the inquest Phillips himself qualified his estimate by acknowledging the existence of such imponderables and he may easily have underrated their significance. If he did Annie was killed after, not before, 4.30.

The crucial witness is Richardson. Chandler's understanding of his evidence seems to have been quite erroneous. When the porter testified before the inquest, just four days after the murder, he was adamant that, far from standing on the top step, he had walked down the steps and then sat down on the middle step to cut a piece of leather out of his boot. Working thus, it is inconceivable that he would not have seen the body if it had been there. 'You must have been quite close to where the body was found?' queried Baxter. 'Quite right, sir,' replied Richardson, 'if she had been there at the time I must have seen her.'

Richardson had nothing to hide. Under rigorous interrogation he stated his evidence clearly and unequivocally. It was consistent, furthermore, with what he had already told the press for as early as 10 September the *Telegraph* had noted: 'Richardson sat down on the steps to cut a piece of leather from his boot.' We have thus no reason to disbelieve him. It is possible that Chandler misunderstood him on the morning of the murder. Richardson is less likely to have said that he did not *go down the steps* than that he did not *go into the yard*. Such a statement would have been consistent with his inquest deposition in which he averred that although he sat down on the step he did not venture out into the yard itself. It should be borne in mind that when Richardson and Chandler met on 8 September the porter neither made a formal statement nor gave an exhaustive interview. Indeed, if Chandler was talking to Richardson in No. 29 at 6.45 and was at the mortuary in Old Montague Street at a few minutes past seven they might not have done more than exchange a few hurried words. In these circumstances the inspector could well have misconstrued Richardson's story.

In the light of Richardson's deposition the conclusion that Annie was killed at some time between 4.50 and 6.00 seems inescapable. Even Chandler, questioned at the inquest, conceded that if Richardson went down the steps he cannot have failed to see the body. Consequently the testimonies of Mrs Long and Albert Cadosch are very important indeed. Mrs Long saw Annie talking to a man in Hanbury Street at about 5.30. Cadosch, who lived at No. 27, got up at about 5.15. Before he went to work he twice visited his backyard. On the first occasion he thought he heard voices from the yard of No. 29 and on the second, three or four minutes later, he heard a noise like that of something falling against the fence. When Cadosch passed Spitalfields Church on his way to work it was 5.32. The experiences of these two witnesses are surely related and, given the vagaries of eyewitness evidence, the slight discrepancy in the times is not significant. We may thus place Annie's death at about 5.30.

Any reconstruction of the manner in which Annie met her death must take account of three facts. Firstly, although there were seventeen residents at No. 29, no less than five of them living in rooms overlooking the murder site, not one claimed to have heard any scream or cry. If, as Amelia Richardson told the papers[20], some of the residents at the back of the house had slept with their windows open, this circumstance is even more remarkable. Secondly, having examined the body twice, Dr Phillips was confident that he had detected signs of strangulation. One and a half to two inches below the lobe of Annie's left ear were three scratches and there was a corresponding bruise on the right side of the neck. The face was swollen, the tongue swollen and protruding. 'There could be little doubt that he first strangled or suffocated his victim,' reaffirmed the *Lancet* on 29 September, 'for not only were no cries heard, but the face, lips, and hands were livid as in asphyxia, and not blanched as they would be from loss of blood.' Finally, the victim's throat had been severed while she was lying on her back. The bloodstains demonstrate this beyond reasonable doubt. Annie was wearing an outside jacket, hooked at the top, buttoned down the front and so long that it reached down to her knees. Yet, apart from stains about the neck, the only traces of blood that it carried were two or three spots on the left arm. The relatively few bloodstains found in the yard were close to the ground and near Annie's head – about six small spots on the back wall of the house, perhaps eighteen inches above the ground, and patches on the wooden palings, about fourteen inches from the ground and immediately above the point where the blood had largely escaped from the neck.

The killer seems to have seized Annie by the chin. If he was standing talking to her – and Cadosch's testimony would suggest that he was – he gripped her with the right hand, his fingers producing the abrasions on the left side of the neck and his thumb the corresponding bruise on the right. By applying pressure to the throat he stifled any cry and throttled his victim, at least into insensibility. She was then lowered to the ground. At some point Annie may have fallen, or the murderer stumbled, against the fence. As she lay on the ground the killer deeply severed her throat in two cuts from left to right. If he knelt beside and to the right of the head, his back to the house, the knife would have been used in the right hand. The patches of blood on the fence, to the left of the head, and the spots on the left arm, which lay across the breast, may have been that which spurted from the wound as the murderer severed the left carotid artery. Dr Phillips believed that the abdominal injuries had been inflicted after death. The abdomen was laid open and the victim eviscerated. The small intestines were discovered above the right shoulder and part of the stomach above the left shoulder but the uterus, together with parts of the vagina and bladder, were taken away by the murderer. He wrenched the rings from the third finger of Annie's left hand and in throwing up her skirts discovered her pocket, attached by strings around the waist, and tore it open. The rings were never found but the contents of the pocket – a piece of muslin, a small-tooth comb and a pocket comb in a paper case – were discovered at Annie's feet. Dr Phillips' impression was that they had been carefully arranged there but their positions may have been quite fortuitous. The piece of envelope and the pills, which William Stevens had seen Annie place in her pocket, were found by the dead woman's head.

In at least one respect the Chapman killing was unique in the Whitechapel series. It was the only murder which was not committed during the hours of darkness. The sun rose at 5.23 and on this busy market morning there were already plenty of people about. Spitalfields Market had opened at five, at which time the western end of Hanbury Street had been clogged with market vehicles. When the killer and his victim entered the yard of No. 29, moreover, the house itself was rapidly coming to life. The carman Thompson had gone to work all of one and a half hours ago and Richardson had been in the yard within the last forty-five minutes. While the couple were still in the yard Cadosch visited the adjoining yard twice. And at 5.45, even as the murderer must have been completing his task, John Davis and his wife bestirred themselves. In slaughtering Annie when and where he did the murderer had thus taken an extraordinary risk. Yet his escape through the streets is scarcely less remarkable. There was a tap in the yard but the killer, perhaps fearful of capture, did not pause to wash the blood from his hands. We know this because Mrs Richardson saw a pan of clean water under the tap the evening before the murder and found it there, apparently undisturbed, in the morning. Emerging from No. 29, therefore, the murderer may well have been stained with gore. Secreted somewhere about his person was the murder weapon. And he must have had something in which to wrap or hold the pelvic organs he had just extracted from his freshly killed victim. But no one, in the grey dawn of that September morning, challenged or even seemed to notice him as he bore away his ghastly trophy.

On the question of the killer's identity the Chapman murder produced what appeared to be the first tangible clues. During the Tabram investigation a suspicion that the murderer had been a soldier had enjoyed very general acceptance. This view, as we have seen, had little to recommend it but as late as the Chapman inquiry echoes of it survived in the police investigation of the torn envelope and their search for Annie's 'pensioner'. In testifying that the murder weapon could not have been a bayonet Dr Phillips went some way to discrediting the theory in the public mind and we hear little more of it.

The doctor's testimony incriminated his own profession. He was not the first to point a finger in their general direction for Dr Llewellyn, at the Nichols inquest, had already credited the killer with 'some rough anatomical knowledge.' But Phillips spoke with much greater conviction. We do not know all the factors that influenced his conclusions. However, the fact that the uterus had been extracted intact, that the murderer had divided the vagina low enough to avoid damage to the cervix uteri, did suggest to Phillips that the murderer's object had been to secure this particular organ and that he knew how to recognize and excise it without injury. It is also evident – from the *Lancet*'s statement that the killer secured the pelvic organs 'with one sweep of a knife' and from Baxter's comment that there were 'no meaningless cuts' – that the random cuts or slashes present in the Tabram murder and in the later Eddowes and Kelly murders were absent in the Chapman case. 'The whole inference seems to me,' Phillips told the inquest, 'that the operation was performed to enable the perpetrator to obtain possession of these parts of the body.' And if that was the case then, in the doctor's opinion, the knowledge and skill of the murderer had been impressive given the haste in which he had been obliged to work. 'I myself could not have performed all the injuries I saw on that woman,' he said, 'and effect them, even without a struggle, [in] under a quarter of an hour.'

It is quite possible, of course, that the position of the lower cut severing Annie's uterus had been entirely fortuitous and that the absence of random mutilations simply reflected the killer's haste to escape from a perilous situation. Nevertheless, Dr Phillips had examined the victim's wounds and he had been a police surgeon for twenty-three years. His opinion commanded respect. Baxter was convinced and in his summing up on 26 September adverted to the killer's expertise in uncompromising terms: 'The body has not been dissected, but the injuries have been made by some one who had considerable anatomical skill and knowledge. There are no meaningless cuts. It was done by one who knew where to find what he wanted, what difficulties he would have to contend against, and how he should use his knife, so as to abstract the organ without injury to it. No unskilled person could have known where to find it, or have recognized it when it was found. For instance, no mere slaughterer of animals could have carried out these operations. It must have been some one accustomed to the post-mortem room.'[21]

Mrs Long's description of the man in the dark coat and brown deerstalker hat provided the further clue that the murderer may have been a foreigner. Jack Pizer, whose habit of abusing prostitutes had made him an obvious suspect, had already introduced that possibility but there had never been any genuine evidence linking him with the murders and, as we shall see, within days of the Chapman murder he was conclusively eliminated from police inquiries. The first valid evidence implicating a foreigner, then, came from Mrs Long and in so far as her testimony contained the first description ever given of a man who was plausibly the Whitechapel murderer it cannot be ignored.

We have three accounts of Mrs Long's experience. The most detailed is that contained in her inquest deposition of 19 September. We know from the newspapers, however, that she made her original statement to the police as early as 12 September and that she identified Annie's body on the same day. Unfortunately no copy of that first statement has survived though something of it has perhaps been preserved in the 19 October report of Chief Inspector Swanson, whose technique it was to synthesize and summarize the contents of earlier documents. Brief notices of Mrs Long's story were also circulated by the press on 12 and 13 September.[22]

Eyewitness testimony is at best treacherous. It can at least be said of Mrs Long that she reported the event while it was fresh in her memory and that a comparison of the different statements attributed to her suggests that her testimony remained consistent. Notwithstanding all which, the circumstances of Mrs Long's sighting oblige us to treat her evidence with caution. The couple did nothing to attract her attention and she passed them by without speaking to them. Worse, she did not see the man's face. Something – perhaps the sound of his voice or the darkness of his complexion – gave her the impression that he was a foreigner but it can have been no more than an impression and she was honest enough to admit that she would not be able to recognize him again.

Between adjournments of the Coroner's inquiry Annie's remains were buried. An outcast in life, she was virtually so in death. Fountain Smith, her brother, was a printer's warehouseman. When he testified at the inquest on 12 September his appearance was judged 'very respectable' by pressmen. But he seemed to want to have as little to do with the proceedings as possible and gave his evidence in so low a tone as to be 'all but inaudible two yards off.' If the press accounts of the funeral are to be believed the other relatives also judged themselves respectable. And conscious, perhaps, of their respectability they contrived to bury Annie with the utmost discretion.

The family paid the funeral expenses and kept all the arrangements a profound secret. Apart from themselves only the police and the undertaker, Harry Hawes of 19 Hunt Street, knew when it would take place. At seven on the morning of Friday, 14 September, a hearse was sent to the Whitechapel Mortuary. Quietly, expeditiously, the undertaker's men collected the body. It rested in an elm coffin draped in black. The coffin-plate read: 'Annie Chapman, died Sept. 8, 1888, aged 48 years.' Driven to Hunt Street, the hearse remained there until nine, when it set off for Manor Park Cemetery. There were no mourning coaches because the relatives, in order to avoid attracting attention, had arranged to meet the hearse at the cemetery. 'All the arrangements were carried out most satisfactorily,' noted the *Advertiser*, 'and there was no hitch of any kind.'[23]

Sadly the terrors, the passions, the recriminations evoked by the death of Dark Annie were not to be laid to rest as easily as her bones.

6

The Man in the Passage and other Chapman Murder Myths

DURING THE CENTURY that has elapsed since the Hanbury Street tragedy authors have told and retold the story with undiminished appetite. Unfortunately few of them bothered to adequately research the facts first. After studying the primary evidence and writing the previous chapter I read the accounts of the Chapman murder given in more than a score of supposedly factual Ripper books. Not one was free from error and most were literally riddled with them. The five pages of text that one centennial volume devoted to Annie contained at least twenty-eight errors. In the six-page account of another I counted no less than thirty-two! Some of these books were so grossly misleading as to merit dismissal to the fiction shelves.

The longevity of errors, once made, is quite remarkable. Back in 1928, for example, Leonard Matters wrote that John Davis, the market porter who discovered Annie's body, 'lived in the very room overlooking the backyard.' It was an error that would have been nailed by the most casual reading of the contemporary printed inquest testimony, for Amelia Richardson's deposition made it quite clear that Davis lived in the front attic, at the top of the house and overlooking Hanbury Street. But William Stewart, undeterred by anything as vulgar as fact, seized and elaborated upon Matters's statement. Davis, said Stewart, lived in a room 'just above the cellar and within a few feet of the spot where the body was discovered.' In this form the blunder survived at least until 1966, nearly forty years after Matters, when Robin Odell incorporated it into the revised edition of his book *Jack the Ripper in Fact and Fiction*. Similarly, Donald McCormick's gaffe that Annie's killer extracted one of her kidneys, published back in 1959, is still alive and well, as a glance at Peter Underwood's recent *Jack the Ripper: One Hundred Years of Mystery* will attest.[1]

Some fictions are almost as old as the murder itself. Repeated in book after book, they have marched relatively unscathed by research into our own day and have achieved the status of minor myths. Indeed, one might be forgiven for believing in the existence of an unspoken understanding amongst Ripperologists that once assertions have been committed to print they take the form of Holy Writ, that the oftener they are published the more authoritative they become, an attitude somewhat evocative of Lewis Carroll's lines in *The Hunting of the Snark*:

> Just the place for a Snark! I have said
>   it twice:
> That alone should encourage the crew.
> Just the place for a Snark! I have said
>   it thrice:
> What I tell you three times is true.

For far too long these myths have clouded our understanding of the character and background of the victim, the details of the crime, even the appearance of the murderer, and it is high time that they were categorically refuted.

Until 1939 no one doubted that Dark Annie had been a prostitute. Then William Stewart dismissed the belief that all the Ripper's victims were streetwalkers. Far from it, 'there is abundant proof that Annie Chapman and Mary Kelly were "one-man" women and that the former was able to support herself by artificial flower making and crochet work.' Inordinately proud of his discovery, Stewart adverted to it repeatedly. Thus, on a subsequent page, he tells us: 'Several witnesses stoutly denied that Chapman was a regular streetwalker. According to them she was comparatively respectable, and as an artificial flower maker and crochet worker she was capable of earning sufficient money to keep her off the streets.'[2]

Now, exploring the evidence for these assertions, we find that Stewart's 'abundant proof' and 'several witnesses' comes down to the inquest deposition of just one witness – Amelia Palmer. Amelia did, indeed, say that Annie was respectable. She never used bad language. Although often the worse for drink she was easily affected by liquor. And she was 'a very industrious, clever little woman in crochet and things of that kind.' But Amelia's testimony is open to the objection that she was obviously trying to say the best of a friend of five years' standing. Nor did she deny that Annie was a prostitute. In fact, under close interrogation she was obliged to concede that Annie had sometimes stayed out late and 'was not particular how she earned her living.'[3] Timothy Donovan, moreover, told the inquest that Annie often tried to bring men with her to the lodging house. Perhaps, however, we should not cavil too much at Stewart on this point. At least there was *some* basis for his contention which is more than can be said for many of his other statements.

More durable misconceptions, popularized by Donald McCormick, surround Annie's origins. 'Of all the Ripper's victims,' he wrote in 1959, 'she was the only woman with a respectable middle-class background. The fact that she had "known better days" did not endear her to some of the other prostitutes and she seems to have made a few enemies among them because of this . . . She had formerly lived at Windsor, where she was married to an Army pensioner, Fred Chapman, who was also a veterinary surgeon.'[4] Apart from Annie's residence at Windsor there is little or no truth in any of these statements but they continue to be repeated today and figure in two of the centennial studies.

Amelia Palmer's deposition, once again, is partly responsible for the misunderstandings. Amelia certainly did tell the inquest that Annie had been married to one Frederick Chapman, a Windsor veterinary surgeon, and this is possibly what Annie told her. But like many humble folk Annie seems to have been prone to romancing about her past as a means of enhancing her status in the eyes of present cronies. 'The other women in the lodging house,' noted the *Star*, 'say that from what she had said at different times Dark Annie was well connected. She used to do crochet work, and, from her conversation it was evident she was a woman of some education.'[5] Amelia's error was corrected on the second day of the inquest, however, when Fountain Smith, Annie's brother, explained that she had been married to a coachman named John Chapman. The notion that Chapman had been an army pensioner, also false, originally sprang from garbled news reports which confused him with Ted Stanley, the 'pensioner' who sometimes slept with Annie at 35 Dorset Street.

Research at St Catherine's House does not suggest that Annie was of middle-class origin. Her parents were married in Paddington on 22 February 1842. They were George Smith of Harrow Road and Ruth Chapman of Market Street. Smith is described on the marriage certificate as a private in the second battalion of Lifeguards. His father, Thomas Smith, was a shoemaker, and Ruth's father, William Chapman, belonged to the same trade. George never seems to have been promoted. On 25 February 1861, when his son Fountain Hamilton was born, he was still a private in the same regiment.

Before 1916 service in the army was always on a voluntary basis. In the mid-Victorian period the officer corps was dominated by a hierarchy of wealth, kinship and connection, but this was certainly not the case with the 'other ranks'. Indeed, the long period of enlistment (nominally for life between 1829 and 1847), low pay and harsh discipline and conditions of army life for the rank and file meant that 'going for a soldier' tended to be seen as an act of desperation or last resort. There were a few gentleman rankers but recruitment was primarily from the unemployed and least skilled sections of the working-class.[6] Our evidence suggests overwhelmingly, then, that Annie's father was of humble origin, a conclusion that is reinforced by the record of Annie's own marriage in 1869. By then George Smith was dead but his former occupation is noted on the certificate as 'servant'. Fountain Hamilton Smith, Annie's brother, was a printer's warehouseman in 1888.

The fact that Annie and her kin are recorded at respectable addresses is little indication of their social status since they were probably in service and living in the homes of their employers. In June 1873, for example, when Annie's second daughter was born, the family were living at 17 South Bruton Mews, Berkeley Square, off New Bond Street, and their presence there is seemingly explained by a news report of 1888[7] which states that John Chapman had once been the valet of a nobleman who lived in Bond Street and had been forced to resign his position because of Annie's dishonesty. We will encounter this situation again when we come to investigate the case of Elizabeth Stride, the next victim. Registered as a prostitute in her native Sweden, Elizabeth came to England in 1866 and found a place in the service of a gentleman living near Hyde Park. Three years later, when she married, her address was recorded as 67

Gower Street, unquestionably the residence of her employer at the time.

Annie, then, did not spring from middle-class stock, although her experiences in service may well have enabled her to ape the attitudes and mannerisms of the well-to-do with some success amongst her lodging house friends. There is no evidence whatsoever that such affectations made her unpopular. The inquest depositions of Timothy Donovan and John Evans, indeed, state otherwise. 'The deceased was always on very good terms with the other lodgers,' said Donovan, 'and the witness never had any trouble with her.'[8] The row with Eliza Cooper was the only one that Donovan could remember Annie being involved in. The cause? A bar of soap!

The most persistent myths about the murder itself concern Annie's neckerchief, her rings and the contents of her pocket. All originated in erroneous press reports.

On the day of the murder the *Star* told its readers that the killer had cut Annie's throat so fearfully that, thinking he had severed the head, he tied a handkerchief around the neck to stop it rolling away. This tale found its way into *The Times* two days later, into Walter Dew's reminiscences in 1938, into McCormick's influential *Identity of Jack the Ripper* in 1959 and most subsequent books. It is encouraging to see a number of studies (most recently those by Donald Rumbelow, Wilson & Odell, and Begg, Fido & Skinner) specifically refute the tale but it survives in several of the centennial studies, one of which added a grisly touch of its own: 'His [Dr Phillips'] nimble fingers untied the handkerchief around the neck, but he was unprepared for the result: as he fumbled with the knot the head rolled sideways, attached to the body by only a thin strip of skin.'[9] Apparently this writer forgot, or never knew, that the killer had failed to sever the spinal column.

The truth was that the handkerchief belonged to Annie and was tied about her neck *before* the killer placed his knife to her throat. Timothy Donovan recalled for the inquest that Annie had been wearing a white cotton handkerchief with a broad red border about her neck when she left his lodging house that night. It was folded 'three-corner ways' and was tied in front of the neck with a single knot.[10]

Reporters converged on 29 Hanbury Street like angry hornets on the morning of the murder. One of the earliest on the scene was Oswald Allen of the *Pall Mall Gazette* and his report, which appeared on the streets later in the day, carried the assertion that Annie's rings had been wrenched from her finger and placed at her feet. On the following Monday the *Daily Telegraph* printed another fable: 'There were also found two farthings polished brightly, and, according to some, these coins had been passed off as half-sovereigns upon the deceased by her murderer.' The farthings quickly passed into legend. Even two policeman later gave them credence. In 1889 Inspector Reid told a different murder inquiry that two farthings had been found on or about the body of Annie Chapman and in 1910 Major Henry Smith alleged in his memoirs that two polished farthings had been discovered in her pocket. Neither man, however, had personally investigated the Hanbury Street case. Reid had been on leave at the time and Smith, as Chief Superintendent of the City of London force, had no responsibility for the policing of Spitalfields.[11]

In succeeding years the rings and farthings became an obligatory part of the collection of items found at the feet of Annie's corpse. In 1928 Leonard Matters started the ball rolling: 'Another interesting fact in this case was that two brass rings which the woman wore were taken from her fingers, and the trumpery contents of her dress pocket – two or three coppers and odds and ends – were carefully laid out at her feet.' It will be noted that Matters did not mention the farthings and did not state that the rings were found at Annie's feet. But ten years later William Stewart went further. On one page he printed Allen's report, on another he asserted that two farthings had been amongst the items arrayed at the feet of the corpse. In 1959 Donald McCormick put Matters and Stewart together: 'Two brass rings, a few pennies and two farthings were neatly laid out in a row at the woman's feet.'[12] As set down by McCormick the story was reaffirmed in a whole bevy of major Ripper books: Cullen (1965), Odell (1966), Farson (1973), Rumbelow (1975 and revised edition 1987), Knight (1976) and Odell & Wilson (1987). Occasionally a renegade Ripperologist ventured a dissenting voice – Richard Whittington-Egan in 1975, Melvin Harris in 1987, Paul Begg in 1988 – but by this time the legend had almost assumed the status of an imperishable truth. In full or in part it appears in two of the most recent Ripper books: Paul Harrison, a serving police sergeant himself, has two brass rings and two new farthings at the feet of the corpse; Messrs Begg, Fido & Skinner, in their *Jack the Ripper A to Z*, content themselves with two farthings 'which may have been brightly polished.'[13]

In Stephen Knight's overheated imagination the rings and farthings were additional proof of his theory of a Masonic Ripper. According to this writer the clues pointing to such a conclusion were abundant in the Chapman murder. Annie had been divested of all metals such as rings and coins. So is a Mason before he is initiated to any degree. And brass is the sacred metal of the Masons because the Grand Master Hiram Abiff of Masonic legend was a worker in brass. He it was who supervised the moulding of the two hollow brass pillars commanding the entrance to Solomon's temple. When Annie's killer placed her brass rings at her feet, contends Knight, he did so because, side by side, they simulated the appearance of the two hollow brass pillars in cross-section! Then there were the mutilations. In Masonic myth Jubela, Jubelo and Jubelum, the three murderers of Hiram Abiff, were themselves killed 'by the breast being torn open and the heart and vitals taken out and thrown over the left shoulder.' This, said Knight, explained why Annie's intestines had been placed on her shoulder.[14]

The truth was very different. Neither rings nor farthings were found at Annie's feet and hers was certainly not a ritualized Masonic killing.

We have only four *authentic* eyewitness accounts of the appearance of the body in the backyard. The first, written on the same day, was contained in a confidential report of Inspector Chandler to his superiors. Then, four days later, James Kent, one of the men called in by John Davis, gave his highly coloured version to the coroner. Finally, Inspector Chandler and Dr Phillips both made depositions at the inquest on 13 September. Not one of these accounts mentions any rings or farthings placed by Annie's feet. The inquest depositions of Chandler and Phillips are very detailed and would unquestionably have recorded the presence of these articles had they been there but both men speak only of a piece of coarse muslin, a small-tooth comb and a pocket comb in a paper case. In addition to this evidence we have Abberline's report of 19 September in which he explicitly states that the rings had been missing when the body was found and that inquiries had been made at pawnbrokers and dealers throughout the district in the hope that the murderer had tried to pawn or sell them believing them to be gold.[15] The sum of the genuine evidence, then, is quite clear. The rings were not recovered and the only items discovered by the feet of the body were a muslin handkerchief and two combs.

Pressmen were not admitted to premises in which a murder had just been committed. And, except in the context of coroner's inquiries, they were not made privy to the details of police investigations. It cannot be emphasized too strongly, therefore, that however valuable the newspapers might be as sources of contemporary comment and for information on the public aspects of the subject like inquest hearings or street scenes they are not credible sources for the details of the crimes themselves and should not be used as such.

Knight's theory that several of the Ripper victims were mutilated in accordance with Masonic ritual received worldwide publicity. He – and those who have followed him – insist that the killer of Annie Chapman and Kate Eddowes, a later victim, consciously replicated the form of execution willed upon himself by Jubelo, in Masonic tradition one of the murderers of Hiram Abiff, the Masonic Grand Master and builder of Solomon's temple: 'O that my left breast had been torn open and my heart and vitals taken from thence and thrown over my left shoulder.'[16] This is not true. In the cases of both Chapman and Eddowes the intestines, not the heart and chest contents, were lifted out, and they were placed over the right, not the left, shoulder. One suspects that, in reality, this act had no especial significance. For if the killer was kneeling by the victim's right side and holding the knife in his right hand he would have lifted her entrails out in his left, and her right shoulder, immediately before him, would have been as convenient a place as any to deposit them so that he might proceed with the other abdominal mutilations.

The Masonic theory fares no better when applied to Mary Kelly, generally regarded as the Ripper's last and certainly his most extensively mutilated victim. Kelly's heart was, indeed, cut out but it was either taken away or, since the murderer maintained a fierce fire, burned by him. The other viscera and detached flesh were left in various places – under her head, by her right foot, between her feet, by her right or left side, and heaped on a bedside table, in short almost everywhere *except* over her left shoulder. Only by a shameless selection of evidence can the Masonic theory be invested with apparent credibility. Thus, for example, Melvyn Fairclough, attempting to resuscitate Knight's hypothesis as recently as 1991, points to the fact that Kelly's right thigh was denuded of skin and flesh. This, he assures us, is a Masonic allegory, 'a reminder of the initiation of a Master Mason when the candidate, in reference to his two previous initiations, says: "And my right leg bare". As he utters these words he has to roll up his trouser leg. With Kelly they rolled away the flesh.' Unfortunately, he neglects to explain, or even to mention, that Kelly's *left* thigh too was stripped of skin, fascia and muscles as far as the knee.

Knight's theory, in sum, was a colossus built on sand.

The speculations of Ripperologists have often taken us very far from the truth. Unfortunately, without ready access to the primary evidence it is very difficult for the reader with a genuine interest in the crimes to get back to the facts. The reported appearance of Annie's killer is a case in point.

My readers will already know that the only person who caught a glimpse of the murderer was Mrs Long, the market woman who saw him talking to Annie outside No. 29 at 5.30. Yet previous writers have claimed not one, but *three*, sightings of the killer. They can be summarized as follows:

2.00 a.m. A man seen entering the passage of No. 29.
5.00 a.m. A man and a woman seen talking outside No. 29 by Mrs Darrell.
5.30 a.m. A man and a woman seen talking outside No. 29 by Mrs Long.

The only genuine sighting in this list is the last. So whence the others?

The myth of Mrs Darrell was created by two factual errors. One was made by author Donald McCormick.[17] He discovered a reference to Mrs Darrell in the contemporary press, probably in the *Times* of 13 September 1888, but incorrectly copied the time of the sighting as 5.00 instead of 5.30. I have checked five news reports of Mrs Darrell's sighting.[18] All of them give the time 5.30. Now this, of course, was the time of Mrs Long's sighting and I am sure that with my discerning readers the penny will already have begun to drop. Mrs Darrell *was* Mrs Long.

The original source of the confusion must have been a mistake by one of the press agencies which botched the name of the witness but in every other respect reported her experience accurately. The details credited to Mrs Long in police records, and given by her to the coroner, are identical to those attributed in the press to Mrs Darrell. Even the words overheard by the witness – the man's laconic 'Will you?' and the woman's answer 'Yes' are the same in both. There is no doubt, then, that the many writers who have recorded Mrs Darrell's sighting have duplicated that of Mrs Long, another cautionary tale in the use of newspaper evidence.

The man in the passage is an even more mysterious character than Mrs Darrell. He first made his appearance in print two days after the murder in the *Daily Telegraph*:

> At eight o'clock last night the Scotland-yard authorities had come to a definite conclusion as to the description of the murderer of two, at least, of the hapless women found dead at the East-end, and the following is the official telegram despatched to every station throughout the metropolis and suburbs: 'Commercial-street, 8.20 p.m. – Description of a man wanted, who entered a passage of the house at which the murder was committed with a prostitute, at two a.m. the 8th. Aged thirty-seven, height 5 ft. 7 in., rather dark, beard and moustache; dress, short dark jacket, dark vest and trousers, black scarf and black felt hat; spoke with a foreign accent.'

A day later *The Times* proffered a slightly different version:

> The following official notice has been circulated throughout the metropolitan police district and all police-stations throughout the country: – 'Description of a man who entered a passage of the house at which the murder was committed. of a prostitute at 2 a.m. on the 8th. – Age 37; height, 5 ft. 7 in.; rather dark beard and moustache. Dress – shirt, dark jacket, dark vest and trousers, black scarf, and black felt hat. Spoke with a foreign accent.'[19]

This description of a suspect seen entering the passage of No. 29 at 2.00 a.m. cannot be reconciled with the evidence of Mrs Long, which places the murderer and his victim outside the house at 5.30, and Leonard Matters, the first important author on the murders, was frankly baffled by it. His successors have fared no better. 'I am inclined to believe that this description was entirely made up out of some policeman's head,' wrote a mystified Tom Cullen, 'for there is no record of any man's having been seen entering the passage of No. 29 Hanbury Street at 2.00 a.m. on the morning of the murder. Certainly no witness ever testified to this effect.'[20] Most writers on the case have quoted the description without understanding to whom it referred. A few have opted to avoid any reference to it at all. No one has satisfactorily explained it.

At the time the *News* speculated that the prostitute referred to in the police telegram was not Annie Chapman but one Emily Walter or Walton: 'That description applies, as well as can be gathered, to the man who gave the woman Emily Walton two brass medals, or bright farthings, as half-sovereigns when in a yard of one of the houses in Hanbury Street at 2 a.m. on Saturday morning, and who then began to ill-use the woman. The police attach importance to finding the man . . .'[21]

Emily's adventure is known to us only from newspaper reports. She told the police that early on the morning of the murder she had been accosted by a man in Spitalfields. Although he had presented her with two half-sovereigns, as she had supposed at the time, his manner had been violent and threatening. Eventually her screams had scared him off. Later Emily discovered that the 'half-sovereigns' were but brass medals. She evidently gave a description of the man to the police and conceivably this was the one circulated in the telegram. The earliest report of the Emily Walter affair, however, tends to cast doubt upon this explanation for it gives the time of her encounter as 2.30 not 2.00, and does not positively identify the house in which it allegedly took place as No. 29: 'It is said that this woman [Walter] did accompany the man, who seemed as if he would kill her, to a house in Hanbury Street, possibly No. 29, at 2.30 a.m.'[22] One also wonders whether the whole story of Emily Walter was a newspaper fiction. She was not called as a witness before the inquest and there is no official record of her in the police or Home Office files.

It will be noted that there are significant differences between the two published texts of the police telegram. The *Times* version suggests a much more likely solution to the mystery. It begins: 'Description of a man who entered a passage of the house at which the murder was committed of a prostitute at 2 a.m. on the 8th.'

Now, since Annie was killed at about 5.30 most students of the case have taken the time of two o'clock to relate to the man's entry into the passage. But two was an important time in the Chapman case. Abberline and Swanson both record it as the time at which Annie was turned out of the lodging house. Mrs Long did not volunteer her evidence until three days after the date of the telegram so when the police drafted it two o'clock was the last time at which Annie had been seen alive. It was for precisely this reason that detectives, visiting common lodging houses on the day of the murder, made inquiries about men who had entered after two. The first sentence of the telegram should therefore probably be amended thus: 'Description of a man who entered a passage of the house at which the murder was committed of a prostitute *after* 2 a.m. on the 8th.'

The whole sense of the sentence is now altered. The time and date are correct for the murder itself and no time or date is specified for the man's entry into the passage. The telegram simply records the description of a man seen (date and time not given) in the passage of the same house in which a prostitute was murdered after two on the morning of 8 September.

Having clarified the text of the telegram, we are in a position to solve the mystery. We know from police records that on the day of the murder they interviewed every occupant of No. 29. On that occasion Mrs Richardson surely told them about the trespasser Mr Thompson and herself had encountered on the premises about four weeks back. She referred to him again at the inquest:

CORONER: 'Did you ever see anyone in the passage?'
MRS RICHARDSON: 'Yes, about a month ago I heard a man on the stairs. I called Thompson, and the man said he was waiting for [the] market.'
CORONER: 'At what time was this?'
MRS RICHARDSON: 'Between half-past three and four o'clock.'[23]

The police would not have regarded this man as a serious suspect but they would have been anxious to trace him in order to eliminate him from their inquiries. And this was apparently the purpose of the telegram. The identification of the man in the passage with Mrs Richardson's trespasser would seem to be clinched by a statement which she gave to the *Daily Telegraph* as early as 8 or 9 September:

'The only possible clue that I can think of,' she said, 'is that Mr Thompson's wife met a man about a month ago lying on the stairs, about four o'clock in the morning. He spoke with a foreign accent. When asked what he was doing there he replied he was waiting to do a "doss" before the market opened. He slept on the stairs that night, and I believe on other nights also.'[24]

The police telegram, then, did not describe a man seen with Annie Chapman but one found skulking about No. 29 a month before the murder. As such it cannot seriously be advanced as a clue to Annie's killer. The detectives knew this perfectly well. Which is why Chief Inspector Swanson, reviewing the Chapman investigation on 19 October, recorded only *one* description of a suspect in connection with the murder – that of Mrs Long.[25]

Our demolition of these time-honoured shibboleths must not delude us into thinking that we have seen the last of them. They will continue to be trotted out by the idle and incompetent and facts, in any case, have never stood in the way of a sensational theory. The arrangement of Annie's pathetic belongings around the feet of her corpse struck William Stewart as a typically feminine gesture. And anxious to promote his own indictment of a demented midwife, he was not the man to question the truth of that neat array. Similarly, for Stephen Knight the rings and coins *had* to exist, if only to legitimize his fantasy of a Masonic murderer. 'Human kind,' sighed T. S. Eliot, 'cannot bear very much reality.' The century-old obsession with the Whitechapel murders might truly be cited as a vindication of his view. Jack the Ripper has been, and looks destined to remain, whatever writers, songsters and film-makers wish him to be.

None of which alters the fact that in the patient study and careful evaluation of our primary sources, the truth – or what survives of it – is there for those who seek it.

7

The Panic and the Police

ON SATURDAY, 8 SEPTEMBER, tidings of the fourth murder crackled out from Hanbury Street like a bushfire. They produced a run on the evening papers the like of which no newsagent for several miles around could remember. For when stocks sold out crowds waited outside the shops for fresh supplies to be brought in and customers successful in obtaining copies themselves became the centres of clamorous groups eager to hear the latest.

The press, by giving currency to inaccuracy and rumour, and by resort to the most sensational language imaginable, did much to promote alarm. On the day of the murder the *Star* prefixed a four-column notice of the tragedy with this bloodcurdling passage: 'London lies today under the spell of a great terror. A nameless reprobate – half beast, half man – is at large, who is daily gratifying his murderous instincts on the most miserable and defenceless classes of the community. There can be no shadow of a doubt now that our original theory was correct, and that the Whitechapel murderer, who has now four ... victims to his knife, is one man, and that man a murderous maniac. There is another Williams in our midst. Hideous malice deadly cunning, insatiable thirst for blood – all these are the marks of the mad homicide. The ghoul-like creature who stalks through the streets of London, stalking down his victim like a Pawnee Indian, is simply drunk with blood, and he will have more.' The quality papers were not exempt from such journalism. On Monday morning the *Telegraph* set the hearts of its dignified middle-class readers pounding with talk of a baleful prowler of the East End alleys, of 'beings who look like men, but are rather demons, vampires . . .'[1]

Whitechapel had stood firm in the face of three savage murders. But this fourth, coming so soon after the last, plunged the community into panic and hysteria. On Saturday evening thousands of people were out on the streets of the East End. 'Rumours of other murders were set afloat,' noted the *Observer*, 'and gained no small amount of credence, until East London became panic-stricken – for there is no other term to describe the aimless, frightened way in which the people paraded the crowded thoroughfares.'[2] The first three days after the murder witnessed extraordinary scenes in the vicinity of the crimes. Crowds gathered in Buck's Row and Hanbury Street outside both entrances to the mortuary, and about the police stations in Commercial Street, Leman Street and Bethnal Green. On Monday a *News* reporter encountered an immense throng of loafers in Hanbury Street. The upper storey windows on both sides of the street framed the faces of yet more spectators. 'Not a man could I see in any of those windows,' he wrote, 'only women, grown-up girls, and children. They had the air of people who thought their quarter of the world invested with a new importance.'[3]

Anger and indignation were the ruling passions of these crowds. With blind fury they turned upon anyone they fancied to blame for the tragedy. The newspapers record some half dozen such incidents for the weekend of the murder but details are garbled and untrustworthy. We will instance just one which seems to be related to a memory of Walter Dew.

In his memoirs, published in 1938, Dew devoted no less than six pages to the arrest of 'Squibby'. It was his most vivid memory of the Chapman murder. Squibby was a young villain. Covered from head to foot in tattoos, short but immensely strong, he engaged in regular battles with the police. 'Whenever this "charming" young fellow was arrested,' wrote Dew, 'it took six or eight policemen to get him to the station, and by the time he was brought in he was usually devoid of every stitch of clothing, and the policemen pretty well hors de combat.'[4] In short, Squibby was the complete Pocket Hercules.

Now, at the time of the Hanbury Street murder Squibby was wanted by the police. Some time previously he had been amusing himself by throwing bricks at a policeman and one badly aimed missile had struck and injured a child. Squibby had gone into hiding but the murder coaxed him out. Mingling with the crowds of sightseers, he made his way, on the morning of the murder, towards Hanbury Street. That morning Dew was one of many detectives taking statements in the neighbourhood. It was while standing talking to a fellow detective in Commercial Street that he espied Squibby. And at the same time Squibby saw and recognized the detectives.

In an instant he was off. Diving between the legs of a horse and crossing the road, Squibby raced like a hare up Commercial Street towards Aldgate. During the Whitechapel investigation detectives were permitted to carry truncheons and Dew and his colleague were thus armed. Immediately they gave chase to the fugitive, drawing their truncheons as they did so. The sight of a man fleeing from the neighbourhood of the murder with policemen at his heels whipped the crowds into a paroxysm of excitement. 'Jack the Ripper! Jack the Ripper! Lynch him!' they roared. Soon a frantic mob had joined in the pursuit. 'Behind us as I ran,' recalled Dew, 'I could hear the tramp of hundreds of feet.'

The detectives eventually cornered their quarry in a house in Flower and Dean Street. But although they anticipated a ferocious resistance they found Squibby a changed man. 'Instead of finding, as we expected, an animal of a man, foaming at the mouth and ready to fight to the last breath, his face was of a ghastly hue and he trembled violently.' He was, of course, petrified of the mob. And he had reason to be for the house was now in a state of siege. The rabble were calling out for his blood. Inside the detectives and their prisoner listened to their cries: 'Lynch him! Fetch him out! It's Jack the Ripper!'

Dew promised Squibby protection and their chances improved with the arrival of large reinforcements of uniformed police. Even then, however, the little man's ordeal was not over. When he was brought out of the house the crowd seemed to go mad and, making a concerted rush, nearly broke through the police cordon. When he was placed in a four-wheeled cab the mob set about the vehicle and its escort. More than once it was nearly overturned and eventually it had to be abandoned. And when he was lodged in Commercial Street Police Station the building was invested and repeatedly assaulted. From upper windows police inspectors tried to explain that their prisoner had nothing whatsoever to do with the murder and ultimately, although not until many hours later, the crowd began to quieten down and disperse.

After that desperate day Squibby's attitude to the police changed. Wrote Dew: 'Whenever he met me he never failed to thank me for "saving his life" and, as far as I know, he never again gave trouble to police officers whose duty it was to arrest him.'

In one respect at least Dew's fifty-year-old memory was confused. No one would have referred to the murderer as 'Jack the Ripper' as early as 8 September because at that time the dreaded nickname had not yet been invented. Undoubtedly too, the inspector used his imagination to pad out his recollections. But he explicitly stated that this incident took place on the morning of the Chapman murder and a study of contemporary newspapers certainly suggests that there is nothing inherently implausible about it. In fact it is typical of several incidents ascribed by the press to the first three days after the murder. One report, indeed, seems to refer to the same event.

On the evening of the 8th the *Star* reported that earlier in the day the police had arrested a man in Spitalfields. The arrest had precipitated a rumor that the murderer had been caught. 'In an instant the news spread like wildfire,' ran the report. 'From every street, from every court, from the market stands, from the public-houses, rushed forth men and women, all trying to get at the unfortunate captive, declaring he was "one of the gang", and they meant to lynch him. Thousands gathered, and the police and a private detective [plain-clothes detective] had all their work to prevent the man being torn to pieces.' The police succeeded in getting him inside the station and closing the doors against the mob. And the inspector in charge explained to a *Star* reporter that the man had been wanted for some time for an assault upon the police. 'The crowd sighed at hearing the news,' concluded the *Star*, 'but were not persuaded that the person in question had not something to do with the murder.'[5]

One aspect of the East End disturbances was particular sinister. The indignation of the community quickly developed anti-semitic overtones and on the day of the murder the crowds assembling in the streets began to threaten and abuse Jews. At that time there was no evidence of any kind to connect a Jew with the murders. How, then, might we explain the actions of the mobs?

The answer lies partly, of course, in the baseless press campaign against Leather Apron. Then, too, the crimes were unprecedented in English experience and in the minds of many bore a distinctly Continental stamp. 'It was repeatedly asserted,' said the *Observer*, reporting the attacks on Jews, 'that no Englishman could have perpetrated such a horrible crime as that of Hanbury Street, and that it must have been done by a Jew.'[6] Such notions were perhaps fortified by hazy folk memories of the medieval 'ritual murder' or 'blood libel' accusation against Jews, a superstition which held that the Jewish festival of Passover required a human sacrifice and that Jews abducted and ritually slaughtered unoffending Christians. Finally, the indictment of the Jews for the murders was acceptable to a swelling anti-alien if not anti-semitic sentiment in the East End. For it is important to understand that the crimes were enacted against a backdrop of mounting social tension in Whitechapel prompted by the rapid influx of destitute Jews after 1881. By the middle of the decade the sympathy that had first greeted these incoming victims of pogroms had started to crumble in favour of a climate of fear and suspicion sustained by job competition at a time of depression.

The outburst of Judaeophobia called forth by the death of Dark Annie immediately conjured up the spectre of serious anti-Jewish riots. 'It is so easy to inflame the popular mind when it is startled by hideous crime,' cried the *Jewish Chronicle*. 'There may soon be murders from panic to add to murders from lust of blood . . . A touch would fire the whole district in the mood in which it is now,' warned the *News*. It is difficult now to judge how realistic such fears were. But if Whitechapel was half the powder keg the *News* represented it to be it is scarcely surprising that Anglo-Jewry acted with haste to stamp out the match. One of its number dashed off a letter to the *Star*. No Jew, he insisted, could have committed the murders because Jews have a horror of blood traceable to the Bible: '"The blood is the life" is so perfectly and persistently before the Jews that they soak their butcher-meat in water before they will prepare it for cooking, and Jews have been seen to shrink from tasting the red juice that runs from a succulent beef-steak in process of cutting it.' Saturday, 15 September, was observed in the synagogues as the Day of Atonement. Adverting to the murders in his sermon at Bayswater, Dr Hermann Adler, the Acting Chief Rabbi, spoke to the same purpose. Although urging a need to humanize, civilize and Anglicize the impoverished Jewish refugees, he asserted that no Hebrew, native or alien, could be guilty of such atrocious and inhuman crimes.[7] It was partly a desire to exonerate the Jewish community from complicity in the murders, furthermore, that inspired prominent Jewish citizens to spearhead private efforts to bring the killer to justice. Samuel Montagu, the Jewish MP for the Whitechapel Division of Tower Hamlets, was the first to offer a reward for his capture and the Mile End Vigilance Committee, which quickly seconded his initiative, consisted largely of Jewish tradesmen.

Upon receiving news of the Hanbury Street tragedy, Montagu returned to the capital from Brighton. On 10 September he called on Acting Superintendent West of H Division and, offering a reward of £100 for the discovery and conviction of the criminal, authorized the police to print and distribute the posters at his expense. The police seem to have been disposed to help. At least A. C. Bruce, Assistant Commissioner, forwarded Montagu's proposal to the Home Office the same day and, in soliciting instructions, pointed out that Montagu was 'anxious that no time should be lost.' However, Edward Leigh-Pemberton's reply, dated 13 September, effectively terminated any police involvement in the matter. The practice of offering government rewards, it ran, had been discontinued some years ago because they had been found to produce more harm than good and, in the case of the Whitechapel murders, there was a special risk that a reward 'might hinder rather than promote the ends of justice.' Montagu was less than impressed. As he explained in a letter to Warren, the Home Secretary's view of rewards was 'not in accord with the general feeling on the subject.' In any case he was not apprised of the Home Office opposition to rewards until after his offer had been noticed by the press and by that time he felt honour-bound to abide by it.[8]

The Mile End Vigilance Committee, in which Jews were also prominent, was not the first nor the last organization of its kind to be inspired by the Whitechapel murders. The St Jude's committee, with its levies from Toynbee Hall, had already been operative for a month and others were to spring up in the aftermath of the double murder of 30 September. But it was the Mile End committee which dominated the contemporary news columns and, as we shall see, when its president received a human kidney through the post, apparently from the murderer himself, it ensured for itself a kind of immortality by commanding space in every book that would ever be written about Jack the Ripper.

The committee, sixteen strong, was appointed at a meeting of local tradesmen in Whitechapel on 10 September. Its president was George Akin Lusk of 1–3 Alderney Road, Mile End Road, a builder and contractor, a member of the Metropolitan Board of Works and a vestryman of the parish of Mile End Old Town.

The other leading committee members were the vice-president, John Cohen of 345 Commercial Road; the treasurer, Joseph Aarons of the Crown Tavern, 74 Mile End Road; and the honorary secretary, Mr B. Harris of 83 White Horse Lane.

These public-spirited citizens were grossly traduced in a recent television 'mini-series', which depicted them ceaselessly roaming the Whitechapel streets like vigilantes from the American frontier west, shouting, flourishing firebrands and hunting victims to string up in wild necktie parties. In reality the Mile End Vigilance Committee was nothing of the sort. Its purpose, as Aarons pointed out at a meeting of 15 September, was to strengthen the hands of the police by action on the part of the citizens. 'He wished it to be distinctly understood,' he said, 'that the Committee was in no way antagonistic to the police authorities, who were doing their best, as he believed they always did, to bring the culprits to justice.'[9] The methods employed by the committee to 'strengthen the hands of the police' were entirely pacific. At first they directed their efforts towards raising a reward fund. Later they organized patrols that, in the manner of present day neighbourhood watch schemes, reported to the police any suspicious circumstances observed.

On the morning of 11 September a notice, published by the committee in the form of handbills and posters, was being placarded in shop windows throughout Whitechapel, Mile End and Houndsditch. It began:

IMPORTANT NOTICE. – To the Tradesmen, Ratepayers, and Inhabitants Generally, of Whitechapel and District. – Finding that in spite of Murders being committed in our midst, and that the Murderer or Murderers are still at large, we the undersigned have formed ourselves into a Committee, and intend offering a substantial REWARD to anyone, Citizen, or otherwise, who shall give such information that will bring the Murderer or Murderers to Justice. A Committee of Gentlemen has already been formed to carry out the above object, and will meet every evening at nine o'clock, at Mr J. Aarons', the 'Crown', 74 Mile End Road, corner of Jubilee Street, and will be pleased to receive the assistance of the residents of the District . . .[10]

At first the committee seem to have been optimistic about building up a substantial reward fund. 'The movement has been warmly taken up by the inhabitants,' noted *The Times* on 11 September, 'and it is thought certain that a large sum will be subscribed within the next few days.' But by the end of the week it was becoming evident that raising the necessary cash would be no easy matter. On 15 September Mr M. Rogers told the committee that on many occasions, when he had approached people from whom he had expected donations of £5 or £10 without demur, he had found them unwilling to contribute because they considered it the duty of the Home Secretary to offer a reward. By 22 September the committee were beginning to complain that 'the people generally do not respond quickly to their appeal for funds.' And at the end of the month the fund still stood at no more than £60 or £70 and the committee were obliged to offer a preliminary reward of £50 only.[11]

It was in these circumstances that Mr Harris, the secretary, on 16 September solicited the help of the Home Secretary. He requested Matthews to augment their reward fund or state his reasons for declining to do so but Leigh-Pemberton, replying for the Home Office the next day, merely repeated that the practice of offering rewards had been discontinued because they tended to produce more harm than good. Disappointed, the committee wrote again on 24 September, inviting the Home Secretary to attend a meeting of their committee to explain his refusal of a reward. They had to wait several days for a reply that informed them only that Matthews was 'unable' to attend.[13]

On 27 September the committee switched to a new tack. Unable to elicit a satisfactory response out of Matthews, Mr Lusk addressed a petition to the Queen. He reminded Her Majesty that of the four murders that had been recently committed in the East End the last two at least had been the work of the same hand and that the 'ordinary means of detection had failed.' He felt that the killer would probably strike again and that the offer of a reward 'was absolutely necessary for securing Your Majesty's subjects from death at the hands of the above one undetected assassin.' Lusk took pains to point out that the Home Secretary's refusal to sanction a reward had already incurred hostile criticism from his vigilance committee, criticism that had been 're-echoed throughout Your Majesty's Dominions not only by Your Majesty's subjects at large but, with one or two exceptions, the entire press of Great Britain', and he therefore begged the Queen to direct that a government reward 'sufficient in amount to meet the peculiar exigencies of the case' be offered immediately. These efforts were to no avail. Lusk's answer, dated 6 October, came from the Home Office. The Home Secretary, explained Leigh-Pemberton, had laid the petition before the Queen and had also given directions that no effort or expense be spared to catch the murderer. But he had not felt able to advise the Queen that justice would be promoted by a departure from his previous decision.[13]

Notwithstanding the efforts of these worthies to apprehend the culprit it became evident on 19 September, when Mrs Long gave her evidence to the inquest, that the killer might indeed have been a foreigner. Here, despite all the disclaimers, was the first positive evidence that the murderer was a Jew and the prospect of anti-Jewish riots moved that much closer. By this time, fortunately, the excitement generated by the Chapman murder had subsided. But Sir Charles Warren recognized the danger and was deeply troubled by it.

A regular stream of stories and rumours, mostly unfounded, kept excitement at fever pitch the first few days after the murder. On the day of the crime there were tales of another body having been found at the back of the London Hospital and a woman told of a message chalked on the door of 29 Hanbury Street: 'This is the fourth. I will murder sixteen more and then give myself up.' To one story the police attached some significance. It was recounted by Mrs Fiddymont, wife of the proprietor of the Prince Albert at the corner of Brushfield and Steward Streets, and by two of her customers.

At seven on the morning of the murder Mrs Fiddymont was serving behind the bar and talking to a customer, Mrs Mary Chappell of 28 Steward Street. Suddenly a rough-looking man came into the middle compartment and asked for half a pint of ale. As she drew the ale Mrs Fiddymont studied the man in the mirror at the back of the bar and there was evidently something so frightening about him that she asked Mrs Chappell to stay. If the description given by the two women to the press was accurate there was no wonder.

His shirt was torn badly on the right shoulder. There was a narrow streak of blood under his right ear, parallel with the edge of his shirt. There were three or four small spots of blood on the back of his right hand and dried blood between his fingers. Above all, there was his look — 'so startling and terrifying.' The stranger wore a stiff brown hat drawn down over his eyes and when he saw Mrs Chappell watching him from the first compartment he turned his back to her and got the partition between them. Then he swallowed his ale at a gulp and left.

Joseph Taylor, a builder of 22 Steward Street, followed him as far as Half Moon Street, Bishopsgate, and described him later for the *Star*. He was a man of medium height, middle-aged or slightly older, with short sandy hair and a ginger moustache curling a little at the ends. He had faint hollows under his cheekbones. Taylor thought his dress 'shabby-genteel' – pepper-and-salt trousers of a villainous fit and a dark coat. His manner was nervous and frightened and he seemed disorientated, crossing Brushfield Street three times between the Prince Albert and Bishopsgate. The man walked rapidly with a peculiar springy stride. It was all Taylor could do to overtake him but when he did manage to come alongside the man glanced across at him. 'I assure you,' said Taylor, 'that his look was enough to frighten any woman. His eyes were wild-looking and staring. He held his coat together at the chin with both hands, the collar being buttoned up, and everything about his appearance was exceedingly strange.'14

The Prince Albert was only about four hundred yards from 29 Hanbury Street. Obviously, then, the police were interested in this tale of a man, bewildered and bloodstained, seen there on the morning of the murder. We know that detectives interviewed Mrs Fiddymont and her witnesses on the day of the occurrence. And later, as will be seen, Abberline tried to link the man with at least two suspects – William Henry Piggott and Jacob Isenschmid.

When darkness fell the indignation of the East End mobs gave way to terror. For several days after the murder the closing of the shops and the removal of the flaring lamps of the stalls precipitated a general stampede for home. After 12.30 the streets were all but deserted, abandoned to the possession of patrolling policemen. Some prostitutes fled from Whitechapel. Most people stayed indoors after dark and tradesmen did a roaring trade in locks. Within a week, it is said, most of the street doors of lodging houses in and about Hanbury Street had been newly fitted with locks and bona fide lodgers supplied with keys. There were those who could not even feel safe in their own homes. On Saturday 8th, when Mrs Mary Burridge, a dealer in floor cloth at 132 Blackfriars Road, was standing at her door reading the *Star*, she was so upset by the report of the murder that she retired to her kitchen and fell down in a fit. After briefly regaining consciousness two days later she died on Wednesday 12th.

No one could know for certain that only East End prostitutes were at risk and apprehension spread to all classes throughout the metropolis. A less tragic expression of it occurred at the White Hart Public House in Southampton Street, Camberwell, on the afternoon of 10 September. A 39-year-old labourer named John Brennan came into the pub. He was a man of 'a very rough and strange appearance' and his coat was torn up the back. Soon he began to talk about the murder in a loud voice. No, the police had not yet caught Leather Apron, he said. More, Leather Apron was a 'pal' of his and he had the very knife with which the deed had been done. In the East End he would probably have been mobbed. In Camberwell his boasts produced the opposite effect. Within no time at all the other customers were in the street, the landlady had locked herself in the bar-parlour and Brennan was in sole possession of the bar. But the arrival of a constable terminated the labourer's shenanigans and the next day he found himself before Camberwell Police Court. There Brennan, 'who treated the whole matter as a good joke', was ordered to enter into bail to keep the peace.[15]

The effects of the murder scare were still evident in the East End on Monday night. A central News Agency reporter, who visited Whitechapel that evening, depicted a general air of desolation.[16] Even in important throughfares like Commercial Street and Brick Lane the only prominent pedestrians were constables, patrolling silently past the little knots of homeless vagabonds that huddled in doorways. 'Other constables, whose "plain clothes" could not prevent their stalwart, well-drilled figures from betraying their calling,' wrote the journalist, 'paraded in couples, now and again emerging from some dimly lighted lane, and passing their uniformed comrades with an air of conscious ignorance.' Smaller thoroughfares like Flower and Dean Street appeared dark and unutterably forlorn, their gloom punctuated only at infrequent intervals by flickering gas jets, and almost everywhere there were caverns of Stygian blackness in narrow entries and areas of unlit waste ground.

But there was a sign that the worst of the panic was over. The Whitechapel Road had recovered its nerve. There groups of men and women chatted, joked and laughed boisterously upon the flagstones until long after one. And there prostitutes, driven by necessity to ply their trade at whatever risk, had reappeared. Young, noisy women, decked out in their finery, strutted or lounged at the brightly-lit crossroads. After one these began to disappear, leaving only the most desperate of their kind – the old, half-fed, impoverished drabs, to crawl about from lamp to lamp until the first signs of dawn.

Thereafter East End life began to return to its regular rhythms. Those who had feared to stir abroad after dark or who had not dared to stray from the lighted main throughfares began to move freely again. Those who had fled Whitechapel started to return. Even so, more than a week after the murder, a constable could tell Thames Police Court that the Bow Road was still being troubled by disorderly women whom the murders had driven out of Whitechapel. And, not merely in the East End but all over the metropolis, the calm was fragile. The discovery of a woman, drunk and suffering from a wound in the throat, in a by-way of Shepherd's Bush Road one night brought crowds flocking to the scene in the morning. When Ann Kelly, the 'victim', was treated at the West London Hospital it transpired that her wound was superficial and apparently self-inflicted. An assault upon another woman, Adelaide Rutter or Rogers, a few days later in Down Street, Piccadilly, triggered off another scare in the West End. 'The wildest rumors were flying about the West End this morning of a murder analogous to the Whitechapel tragedies being attempted,' said the *Star*. And as late as 19 September hostile mobs might still menace any suspicious-looking character. That night a policeman had to rescue a drunken cabinet-maker named Thomas Mills from a crowd in Wellington Row, Shoreditch. He found them pulling him about and shouting: 'We'll lynch him, he's Leather Apron!'[17]

There were people, of course, who sought to derive advantage from the tragedies. On the weekend of the murder the occupants of neighbouring houses in Hanbury Street did a brisk trade in charging sightseers a penny each to view the backyard of No. 29 from their own rear windows. The proprietor of a small waxworks in Whitechapel Road was just as quick off the mark. By daubing a few streaks of red paint on three old wax figures and by placarding three lurid pictures outside his premises he induced hundreds of passers-by to part with their pennies in order to view the 'George Yard, Buck's Row and 'Anbury Street wictims.' On the afternoon of Monday, 10 September, another opportunist – William McEvoy, a ship's fireman – was using the scare to cadge drinks at public houses in the area of Cable Street, St George's. His technique was to intimidate landlords by telling them that he had been locked up all day on suspicion of having committed the murder and then to demand liquor. Refusals were met with obscene language. Arrested, he struck a police constable at the station and the next day was sentenced at Thames Police Court to seven days' hard labour.[18]

In the meantime public journals and their correspondents maintained a spirited discussion about the motive for the murders and the nature of their perpetrator.

Dark Annie's pocket had been rifled and her rings wrenched from her finger. But robbery could not stand as a credible motive for crimes distinguished by 'a rage of cruelty, a fantastic brutality.' If Annie had been attacked by a common thief the abdominal mutilations would have been quite pointless since death had already resulted from the loss of blood at the throat.

So the press floundered about in search of a more adequate explanation. Was the killer a religious maniac bent upon the extirpation of sin by the slaying of whores? Or were his crimes actuated by revenge for some real or fancied injury suffered at their hands? Was he, perhaps, a member of some heathen sect that practised barbaric rites? Did he crave notoriety and seek to horrify the nation by acts of unexampled ferocity? Or was he simply a drunkard? The Reverend Lord Sidney Godolphin Osborne, a kindly if eccentric clergyman with a passion for writing letters to *The Times*, thought that he could detect the hand of a jealous woman in the affair.[19] But it was still the lunatic theory that led the field. Its most prestigious advocate was Dr L. Forbes Winslow, specialist in mental disorders, author of the *Handbook for Attendants on the Insane*, founder of the British Hospital for Mental Disorders and consultant in many of the principal criminal cases of the period. His contention was that homicidal mania was incurable but might be difficult to detect in that it sometimes lay dormant. Hence, when interviewed at Scotland Yard, he advised the detective department to call for returns from the various asylums so that the whereabouts of all such patients discharged by them as 'cured' might be ascertained.[20]

No serious challenge to the lunatic theory emerged until the end of the month. Then, on the last day of the Chapman inquest, Coroner Baxter introduced the possibility of an economic motive for the crimes.

The Nichols inquest was resumed on 17 September and adjourned to the 22nd, when it was concluded. The jury returned the only verdict possible – 'wilful murder against some person or persons unknown'. The Chapman inquest occupied five days in all – 10, 12, 13, 19 and 26 September. Again the coroner was Mr Wynne Baxter and the venue the Working Lads' Institute, Whitechapel

Road. Again, despite much valuable testimony, a verdict of 'wilful murder against some person or persons unknown' was recorded.

The proceedings in the Chapman case were enlivened by the intermittent sparring of Mr Baxter and Dr Phillips.

Phillips appeared before the court on the third day. He testified that death had occured from syncope, or heart failure, caused by the loss of blood from the throat. And that being the case he asked the coroner if he might be excused from giving details of the abdominal injuries. These, he pointed out, had been inflicted *after* death and were not necessary in order to understand the cause of death. Baxter demurred. 'The object of the inquiry,' he reminded the doctor, 'is not only to ascertain the cause of death, but the means by which it occurred. Any mutilation which took place afterwards may suggest the character of the man who did it.' However, in deference to Phillips' obvious reluctance to proceed, he postponed that part of his evidence until an adjourned sitting.

On 19 September Dr Phillips was recalled to conclude his testimony. Again he lodged a strong protest at having to reveal the details of the abdominal mutilations, alleging that to give publicity to this information would 'thwart the ends of justice'. But Baxter was not to be thwarted. Never before, he observed, had he heard of a request to keep back evidence at an inquest. And he swept aside Phillips' main argument: 'I delayed the evidence in question as long as possible because I understood you to say that there were reasons which you knew, but which I don't know, why that course was desirable in the interests of justice. It is now however nearly a fortnight since the death, and therefore justice has had some little time to avenge itself.' The court was cleared of women and newsboys and the unhappy doctor then proceeded to give evidence that the press considered unfit for publication.[21]

This dispute between Baxter and Phillips has been many times described but with little understanding of the issues involved.

Phillips was not party to an Establishment hush-up of any royal scandal. He was simply conforming to the code of practice that Howard Vincent had bequeathed to the CID, a code that required the utmost discretion on the part of police officials in all cases in which the identity of the culprit had not yet been established. It was a controversial policy then and has been generally abandoned by police authorities since. Yet, as we have seen, it rested upon important considerations.

Baxter had a weighty case too. In the first place he was obliged by law to take the whole of Dr Phillips' evidence for the Statute de Coronatore required coroners to inquire into the nature, character and size of every wound on a dead body and to enter the information on their rolls. The purpose of this requirement was to preserve the evidence of the crime. In the event of a suspect not being brought to trial until long after the date of the offence the only authoritative record of the injuries and marks found upon the body of the victim might be that in the inquest depositions. Similarly, as Baxter intimated at the Chapman inquest, it was important that the testimonies of all witnesses be fully entered in the records of the court so that their evidence might in future be turned up even if they themselves could no longer be traced. There was, finally, the question of publicity. Baxter believed – and most police officers today would probably endorse the view – that the publication of police knowledge furthered the process of detection by eliciting fresh information from the press and general public. And it was in justification of this belief that, on the last day of the Chapman inquiry, he presented the court with what appeared to be dramatic new evidence bearing upon the case.

Taking his lead from Dr Phillips, who had suggested at the previous sitting that the killer had slain Annie in order to secure a specimen of the uterus, Baxter told the court that the murderer need not necessarily have been a lunatic. For the doctor's testimony had elicited new evidence – evidence that pointed to the existence of a market for the organ in question:

> Within a few hours of the issue of the morning papers containing a report of the medical evidence given at the last sitting of the Court, I received a communication from an officer of one of our great medical schools, that they had information which might or might not have a distinct bearing on our inquiry. I attended at the first opportunity, and was told by the sub-curator of the Pathological Museum that some months ago an American had called on him, and asked him to procure a number of specimens of the organ that was missing in the deceased. He stated his willingness to give £20 for each, and explained that his object was to issue an actual specimen with each copy of a publication on which

he was then engaged. Although he was told that his wish was impossible to be complied with, he still urged his request. He desired them preserved, not in spirits of wine, the usual medium, but in glycerine, in order to preserve them in a flaccid condition, and he wished them sent to America direct. It is known that the request was repeated to another institution of a similar character. Now, is it not possible that the knowledge of this demand may have incited some abandoned wretch to possess himself of a specimen ... I need hardly say that I at once communicated my information to the Detective Department at Scotland yard.[22]

The coroner's solution to the mystery, quickly dubbed the 'Burke and Hare theory' by the newspapers, received a mixed reception. The press, itself bitterly opposed to the CID's secrecy policy, generally welcomed his contribution as a vindication of their own stand. 'The whole civilized world is concerned in bringing the murderer to justice,' declared *The Times*, 'and it cannot afford to be beaten in the attempt. The police will be expected to follow up with the keenest vigilance the valuable clue elicited through the coroner's inquest, and, since the lines of their investigation are plainly chalked out by information which they themselves failed to collect, it will be a signal disgrace if they do not succeed.'[23] The medical fraternity, on the other hand, predictably moved to refute it. James Risdon Bennett thus considered any insinuation of a Burke and Hare analogy a 'gross and unjustifiable calumny on the medical profession.' And he claimed that, either in Britain or America, there were ample facilities for procuring uteri in any number for legitimate research without recourse to crime.[24]

Baxter's integrity is not in doubt but it would be instructive to learn just how much truth there was in the information he was given. The press quickly received assurances from most of the main medical schools that no such application as that mentioned by Baxter had been made to them. There were, however, two important exceptions – the schools attached to the University College and Middlesex Hospitals. Spokesmen for these institutions refused to elucidate the matter. But, if a report in the *Telegraph* is to be credited, although intimating that some of the details of the story as it had been put out were inaccurate they 'indignantly repudiate the suggestion that it was a hoax or that the matter has no importance' and 'talk somewhat mysteriously about "the interests of justice" being imperilled by disclosure.'[25] This certainly suggests that there was some basis for the coroner's theory. Nevertheless, a week later the *British Medical Journal*, perhaps with the reputation of the profession in mind, did its best to bury the whole story:

> It is true that enquiries were made at one or two medical schools early last year by a foreign physician, who was spending some time in London, as to the possibility of securing certain parts of the body for the purpose of scientific investigation. No large sum, however, was offered. The person in question was a physician of the highest reputability and exceedingly well accredited to this country by the best authorities in his own, and he left London fully eighteen months ago. There was never any real foundation for the hypothesis, and the information communicated, which was not at all of the nature the public has been led to believe, was due to the erroneous interpretation by a minor official of a question which he had overheard and to which a negative reply was given. This theory may be dismissed, and is, we believe, no longer entertained by its author.[26]

We do not know whether Baxter adhered to his theory or not but it may be significant that he did not allude to it when conducting his inquest into the death of Elizabeth Stride, the next victim. Abberline remembered it and would revive it, in very curious circumstances, fifteen years later.

The Hanbury Street tragedy unleashed bitter recriminations against the Metropolitan Police from both press and public. Secondary writers have frequently taken press criticisms at face value. It should be understood, however, that the opposition and radical press quickly seized upon the murders as a weapon with which to embarrass the government by discrediting the Home Secretary and retaliate against the police for their anti-Irish Nationalist activities and stern policing of demonstrations by socialists and the unemployed. Much of their comment, then, was politically inspired and it is consequently hardly surprising that many of the specific accusations levelled against the police are demonstrably untrue. More ominous, perhaps, was the alienation of the Conservative press. The *East London Advertiser* denounced Warren as a 'martinet of apparently a somewhat inefficient type' who by militarizing the police, had made them neither good detectives nor good local guardians of life and property.

The *Daily Telegraph* acknowledged that under Sir Charles, an 'admirable commandant of gendarmerie', the uniformed branch was excellently organized but lamented that the want of an effective head of CID had reduced the detective service to an 'utterly hopeless and worthless condition.' Even The *Times* opened its columns to letters critical of the police.[27] Such comment, however inaccurate, reflected grave public disquiet over this fourth unsolved murder in months.

Unquestionably the CID's secrecy policy exacerbated the already strained relationship between press and police. Journalists, denied admittance to 29 Hanbury Street by stalwart constables and rebuffed at the police stations, were understandably frustrated. 'If the London police were as capable in other respects as they are in holding their peace,' one *Daily News* reporter tartly observed, 'no criminal in the realm would pass undetected.' For their part the police were particularly galled by the practice some newshounds adopted of following detectives about in the hope of discovering their informants. Calling at the Home Office on 18 and 19 September, Warren angrily denounced such antics. Neither Matthews, the Home Secretary, nor Sir Evelyn Ruggles-Brise, his private secretary, were there but an under-official promptly transmitted the Commissioner's complaint to Matthews:

> Sir Charles came to see me both yesterday & today about the Whitechapel Murders . . . He remarked to me very strongly upon the great hindrance, which is caused to the efforts of the Police, by the activity of Agents of Press Associations & Newspapers. These 'touts' follow the detectives wherever they go in search of clues, and then having interviewed persons, with whom the police have had conversation and from whom inquiries have [been] made, compile the paragraphs which fill the papers. This practice impedes the usefulness of detective investigation and moreover keeps alive the excitement in the district & elsewhere.[28]

Few of the columns of newsprint spawned by the Chapman murder displayed any recognition of the intractability of the detective problem confronting the police in Whitechapel. By now Abberline and his colleagues seem to have decided that they were dealing with a bold and cunning loner. He generally struck at night, in out-of-the-way places and so efficiently that his victims were unable to scream or cry out. In no case did he leave at the scene of his crime a weapon or any other object that might be traced back to him. And although he was not a random killer in that he exclusively targeted the prostitutes of Whitechapel and Spitalfields there was nothing to suggest a previous relationship with any of them. There was thus no accomplice that might betray him, no witness or clue that could identify him, no clear motive that might suggest a profitable avenue of investigation. Even today, with all the benefits of modern forensic science, the police find parallel cases very difficult to solve, the killers sometimes either remaining uncaught or being delivered into their hands by chance.

We know that the Hanbury Street tragedy immediately set the police casting about for some means of breaking the deadlock. One method they considered was the use of tracker dogs.

Historically the dogs chiefly employed in police work were bloodhounds. Their remarkable sense of smell enables them not only to follow trails up to two days old for many miles over difficult country but also to distinguish the scent of one individual from those of others, thus selecting the real miscreant from among innocent persons. Although dogs of this type have existed in the mountainous regions of Europe and Asia from time immemorial, the modern breed is thought to have been developed by the crossing of several strains – the St Hubert, talbot and old southern hounds. Before the Act of Union (1707) bloodhounds were used in border forays between England and Scotland. Scottish raiders, having attacked and pillaged English border towns, might find themselves pursued and cornered by retaliatory parties equipped with these dogs which were then known as 'slough' dogs. Later they found employment in police work but the use of bloodhounds was gradually discontinued during the nineteenth-century because, it is said, of their sinister name and undeserved ferocious reputation.

The East End murders revived interest in bloodhounds, and trials were suggested by 'A Whitechapel Workman' in the *Star* on 8 September, the day of the Chapman killing. The most persuasive advocate of the use of dogs, however, was J. H. Ashforth of Nottingham. In 1876 Ashforth had urged the Lancashire police to employ them in the case of William Fish and the dogs had brought evidence to light that had led to the conviction of the murderer. Now, on 12 September 1888, he addressed a reminder of that episode to Sir Charles Warren:

Some ten or twelve years ago a very dreadful murder was

committed upon a young girl at Blackburn in Lancashire. I wrote to the Chief Constable at Blackburn respectfully asking him to employ dogs in discovering the criminal, and he did so with the most complete success. The murderer was discovered by the dogs and executed.

The reason why I had such faith in the experiment was as follows. Some years ago one of my relatives had a dog, a clumber spaniel, who became very much attached to me. One day, walking with the dog in our market place along the most frequented pavement, the dog suddenly stopped and commenced to retrace the way I had come. Very much surprised, I followed the dog for about one hundred yards, and I saw him without hesitation enter a shop in which I found his mistress. Now, I thought a dog without training of any sort to pick up the scent of a person he knew upon a pavement traversed by hundreds, in the middle of the day, was so wonderful that I felt sure they would discover the crime at Blackburn and I was not disappointed.

I therefore respectfully suggest that you procure a couple of trained bloodhounds [and] keep them in the neighbourhood, and I fell sure that if they are upon the spot in an hour or two where a murder has been committed the dogs will ... run the culprit to earth, but secrecy is most imperative. If criminals are aware that the police use dogs for tracking, they will very likely try to adopt means for preventing them being effective.

When Annie Chapman was murdered the Metropolitan Police had no trained dogs to hand. Even had they possessed them their efficacy in a district like Whitechapel would at best have been doubtful. At 6.10 a.m., when the crime was reported to Inspector Chandler, the scent of the killer had probably already been obliterated by the market traffic which had then been heavy in Hanbury Street for more than an hour. Nevertheless, we know that soon after the murder, apparently within twenty-four hours, the police did consider the use of bloodhounds and consulted Dr Phillips about it. Phillips had opined, however, that dogs would be less likely to trace the murderer than the blood of the victim and the matter had been dropped. When Warren received Mr Ashforth's letter he sent a courteous acknowledgement but took no further action at this stage.[29]

On 13 September the *Star* gave publicity to the bizarre suggestion that Annie Chapman's eyes be photographed in the hope that the retinas would retain images of her murderer. This possibility, too, had already been considered by the police and put to Dr Phillips. 'I was asked about it very early in the inquiry,' the doctor told the inquest, 'and I gave my opinion that the operation would be useless, especially in this case.'

Probably springing from the development of photography in the first half of the century, the belief that the last image formed on the retinas of a dying person's eyes remained impressed upon them was invested with a spurious credibility by American press reports in the 1850s. In 1857 the *New York Observer*, citing the *Democratic Press*, noticed a series of experiments made in August of that year by Dr Pollock of Chicago. The doctor, examining the retinas of dead people's eyes, reputedly found 'in almost every instance . . . a clear, distinct, and marked impression.' Furthermore, according to the *Observer*, a Dr Sandford had examined one of the eyes of a recent murder victim and detected in the pupil 'the rude worn-away figure of a man with a light coat.' The myth achieved some currency through fiction, notably Villiers de l'Isle-Adam's 'Claire Lenoir' (1867) and, later, Kipling's 'At the end of the passage' (1890), and at the time of the Whitechapel murders was widely believed. In February 1888, on the eve of the crimes, the *British Journal of Photography* published a *New York Tribune* claim that a killer had been convicted in France on the strength of eyeball photography.

Even had the basis for this suggestion been sound, which it was not, the detailed photography of pupils would not then have been practicable and it is scarcely surprising that Phillips was incredulous. His dismissal of the idea is not quite the last we hear of it. For Matthews, in a letter of 5 October to Warren, asked whether any of the doctors had examined the eyes of Elizabeth Stride. We do not know what response, if any, Sir Charles made to this query. But Walter Dew's recollection, fifty years later, that attempts were made to photograph the eyes of Mary Kelly, the seventh victim, cannot be corroborated.[30]

With the police failure only too transparent it was to a large government reward that people increasingly looked for the unmasking of the killer. Warren, as we will discover, was by no means opposed to such an initiative but it was a measure only the Home Office could authorize and by 1888 it had set its face against the practice.

By the end of the seventeenth-century England had evolved two main forms of government reward – parliamentary rewards and advertised public or public rewards.

Parliamentary rewards were fixed statutory rewards paid upon the conviction of certain classes of offender. The earliest were authorized by an Act of 1692 which offered a reward of £40 for the arrest and successful prosecution of every highwayman. This Act was deemed successful and was followed, over a period, by a series of such Acts establishing similar rewards for other offences. There was some justification for parliamentary rewards at a time when the trouble and cost of apprehending and prosecuting a criminal was borne by private individuals, usually the victim of the offence and his relatives, but Acts of 1752 and 1818 empowered the courts to compensate prosecutors and with the emergence of a paid, professional police force in the nineteenth-century the task of arresting and prosecuting offenders fell in practice to the police. By this time, however, parliamentary rewards had already fallen into disrepute. Upon them a dubious class of 'thief-takers', who hunted down and prosecuted thieves for the sake of the rewards, had flourished. Corrupt and dishonest, they had been prone to the distortion and falsification of evidence in order to secure convictions. They were widely believed to have deliberately ignored the activities of young criminals until these had become sufficiently emboldened to commit offences which carried the maximum reward of £40. And, as the blood money conspiracy of 1754 demonstrated, they had sometimes prosecuted unwary youths whom they themselves had first inveigled into crime or framed. Parliamentary rewards were abolished in 1818.

Public rewards were announced by the government through proclamations and by advertisement. For most of the nineteenth-century the Home Office continued to sanction them sometimes in cases of serious crime like murder or for offences against the state. But in 1884, after a plot to dynamite the German Embassy and then frame an innocent person in order to collect the anticipated reward was uncovered, Sir William Harcourt, then Home Secretary, decided to discontinue them also.[31]

There were, then, some sound arguments against rewards, and in rejecting the regular calls for a government reward in the case of the Whitechapel murders Matthews was simply acting in accordance with the precedent established by Harcourt. Yet his apparent intransigence was greeted with dismay and anger throughout the East End. There were protests from the juries at both the Nichols and

Chapman inquests. At the former, on 17 September, the foreman bitterly complained that the last two victims would probably not have died if the government had published a reward after the George Yard murder. The Home Office had not acted, he intimated, because the victims were poor but 'these poor people have souls like anybody else.' Coroner Baxter remarked that the next victim might well be rich. 'If that should be,' replied the foreman caustically, 'then there *will* be a large reward.'[32] In the meantime private individuals and institutions were beginning to stump up a considerable sum. Samuel Montagu stood by his offer of £100. By the end of the month the Mile End Vigilance Committee had assembled £50. The outspoken foreman of the Nichols jury offered £25. And the proprietor of the *Illustrated Police News* pledged another £100.

Matthews, already an unpopular Minister, was scourged mercilessly by the press. The *Star* damned him as 'a feeble mountebank who would pose and simper over the brink of a volcano' while the *Telegraph*, which thought the government 'otherwise so capable and so popular', called repeatedly for his resignation. 'We have had enough of Mr Home Secretary Matthews,' it ranted on 19 September, 'who knows nothing, has heard nothing, and does not intend to do anything in matters concerning which he ought to be fully informed, and prepared to act with energy and despatch. It is high time that this helpless Minister should be promoted out of the way of some more competent man.'[33]

To some extent Matthews himself was to blame for this state of affairs. For although he had forcible reasons for resisting the popular clamour for a reward he evinced not the slightest disposition to explain them, even to the embattled representatives of a badly frightened community. For the rationale behind his inactivity we must turn to a Home Office minute of 11 September, prompted by Mr Montagu's proposal:

The H.O. rule is against offering rewards; and, even if exceptions to the rule are to be allowed, I think this case is the last in which it should be done. It is generally agreed that the Whitechapel murderer has no accomplices who could betray him. Any person, other than an accomplice, who possesses information, would be certain, in the present state of public feeling, to give it without prospect of reward. On the other hand the offer of a reward would be almost certain to produce *false* information.[34]

The Home Office were right about one thing at least. In the East End a general sense of outrage united the community against the killer and, reward or no, the public bestowed information upon Abberline and his team with largesse. It ushered into the police investigation a parade of lunatics, eccentrics, misfits and ne'er-do-wells whose behaviour or appearance had attracted attention to themselves. One arrest was particularly noteworthy.

At about nine on the morning of Monday, 10 September, three or four policemen entered Mulberry Street, Commercial Road East.[35] Their leader was an erect, fresh-complexioned man with dark hair and a heavy, drooping, light-brown moustache. He was Detective-Sergeant William Thick of H Division. There was an air of industry about Mulberry Street. It was a quarter mainly occupied by foreign workers in tailoring and boot and slipper-making and it was here that many of the stage shoes worn in London and Continental theatres were made. But Sergeant Thick's thoughts were far from the stage on this September morning. He went straight up to No. 22 and knocked on the door.

It was opened by a Polish Jew, a shoemaker of course, short, thickset and dark, with thinning black hair and a well-trained black moustache. The sergeant and the shoemaker knew each other at once. If we are to credit an interview which the latter gave later to a Press Association reporter his arrest was a dignified affair. Thick told him he was wanted. The shoemaker asked what for. 'You know what for,' replied Thick, 'you will have to come with me.' Secure in his innocence, the shoemaker was by no means disconcerted. 'Very well, sir,' he said, 'I'll go down to the station with you with the greatest of pleasure.' News reports tell of a more dramatic encounter. The sergeant, averred one, immediately clapped a hand upon his quarry and said, 'You are just the man I want.' While the little Jew, by the relation of another, turned deathly pale and exclaimed: 'Mother, he has got me!'

Sergeant Thick had good reason to be pleased with his catch because every policeman in the metropolis had been on the lookout for him for more than a week. He was John Pizer. He was Leather Apron.

8

The King of Elthorne Road

NO ONE COULD have walked the streets of London's East End that
September without finding his ears assailed on all sides by talk
of 'George Yard', 'Buck's Row', ''Anbury Street' – and 'Leather
Apron'. Street urchins mindlessly took up the theme. Two days after
the Chapman murder a *Daily News* reporter saw them stage a bogus
hue and cry outside Commercial Street Police Station. 'The murderer!
The murderer! Leather Apron's ketched!' they screamed to the crowd
of idlers there before scurrying off round the corner of the station
as if to the scene of this excitement. Echoes of those days survived
until comparatively recently in the memories of elderly folk. As late
as the 1950s a Mr Anderson, recalling his East End childhood for Dan
Farson, could tell how he and other youngsters used to pick on some
harmless old man and then, perhaps fifty strong, pursue him along
the street with raucous cries of 'Leather Apron!' He remembered, too,
that a local sweetshop started to make a new toffee called 'Leather
Apron Toffee.'[1]

Loafers were already standing about outside Leman Street Police
Station when Sergeant Thick arrived with his charge. Feeling against
Leather Apron ran so high that the police must have anticipated
trouble but there was probably little truth in a newspaper tale
of a large force of constables, with drawn staves, being held in
readiness at the station. Such preparations, by signalling the arrival
of an important detainee, would have drawn a huge throng about
the building and endangered both suspect and escort. Rather, by

walking into the station with Pizer as casually and nonchalantly as possible the sergeant seems to have banked upon the significance of the event being lost upon the bystanders. In this he was almost entirely successful. Pizer, noted the *Telegraph*, was 'led to Leman Street Police Station unperceived until close to the door of the station, when the cry was raised "Leather Apron!" and, as usual, there was a hostile demonstration.' By that time it was too late. Pizer was safely through the door. Outside the news of his arrest was soon being disseminated in broadsheet and special edition. One of the former summed up the mood of the day:

> They've captured Leather Apron now, if guilty you'll agree;
> He'll have to meet a murderer's doom, and hang upon a tree.[2]

At Leman Street Pizer made a statement accounting for his where-abouts on the crucial nights of 30–31 August and 7–8 September. According to his story, he was sleeping in a common lodging house called the 'Round House', in Holloway Road, when Polly Nichols was killed, and from Thursday, 6 September, until his arrest on Monday, 10 September, was sheltering with his relatives at 22 Mulberry Street, afraid to go out. The police, of course, sought to verify these assertions. Chief Inspector Swanson tells us that the first was 'fully corroborated and the date fixed by the proprietor [of the lodging house] who knows Pizer' and that the second was confirmed 'by several persons'.[3]

On Tuesday, 11 September, there was a new development. An identity parade was held in the station yard and Pizer was picked out by Emanuel Delbast Violenia, a half-Spaniard half-Bulgarian vagrant, as a man he had seen in Hanbury Street threatening to knife a woman early on the morning that Annie Chapman was killed. By the end of the day, however, the police were convinced that Violenia was lying. Press reports suggest that during a lengthy examination in the afternoon he contradicted himself 'over and over again' and that his 'anxiety' to view Annie's remains led detectives to suspect that his evidence had been inspired solely by a morbid curiosity to see the corpse.[4] Whatever, the police decided that there was no case against Pizer and at about 9.30 that night, after nearly two days in custody, he was released.

The next day Pizer appeared as a surprise witness during the resumed Chapman inquest at the Working Lads' Institute. It was clearly intended that he be provided with an opportunity to clear his name in public. Sergeant Thick, flashily dressed in a suit of loud checks, escorted him into the court and Pizer, after taking the oath in the Hebrew fashion, 'fell at once into an attitude of easy composure, which he maintained without moving a muscle through a tolerably long examination.' The *East London Observer* has left us with a forbidding, perhaps prejudiced, portrait of the man as he stood before Coroner Baxter:

> He was a man of about five feet four inches, with a dark-hued face, which was not altogether pleasant to look upon by reason of the grizzly black strips of hair, nearly an inch in length, which almost covered the face. The thin lips, too, had a cruel, sardonic kind of look, which was increased, if anything, by the drooping, dark moustache and side whiskers. His hair was short, smooth, and dark, intermingled with grey, and his head was slightly bald on the top. The head was large, and was fixed to the body by a thick, heavy-looking neck. Pizer wore a dark overcoat, brown trousers, and a brown and very much battered hat, and appeared somewhat splay-footed – at all events, he stood with his feet meeting at the heels, and then diverging almost at right angles. His evidence was given quietly and distinctly were it not for the thick, guttural foreign accent.

Pizer described his movements on the nights of the Buck's Row and Hanbury Street murders and Baxter told the court that his statements had been verified by the police. At one point during the examination Baxter touched upon the popular hostility that had imprisoned the little Jew in the house of his relatives from 6 to 10 September.

'Why were you remaining indoors?' he asked.
'Because my brother advised me.'
'You were the subject of suspicion, were you not?'
'I was the subject of a – false suspicion,' replied Pizer, speaking very distinctly and making an emphatic pause.
'It was not the best advice that could be given you,' commented Baxter.
'I will tell you why,' Pizer retorted immediately. 'I should have been torn to pieces!'

After his examination Pizer thanked the court and retired to the back benches. There, noted the *Advertiser*, he 'looked somewhat pale and worried after giving his evidence though throughout he was perfectly cool and collected. He displayed not the slightest symptoms of insanity, and chatted freely and affably with Sergeant Thick with whom he sat until the adjournment of the inquiry.' Perhaps he was worried about the large crowd gathered outside the institute. Certainly he was recognized at once and greeted with murmurs and muttering when he left the building but Sergeant Thick escorted him home. And with that, apart from some skirmishing in the libel courts and a complaint to Thames Magistrates' Court in October of continued persecution, this most famous of Whitechapel murder suspects disappears from the records of the case.[5]

Inspector Abberline told his superiors that the suspicions against Pizer had been 'conclusively' demonstrated to be groundless.[6] How far does the existing evidence justify this view?

Pizer was an unmarried man in his thirties. His relatives, who shared, of course, a natural disposition to protect him, insisted that he was sober, industrious and kind, and that, being ruptured, he was physically incapable of violence. He was 'not a man to commit murder,' his sister-in-law told the press, 'and she was accustomed to trust her children to his charge.' Since Pizer spent most of his time in common lodging houses, however, it is to be doubted whether his family at Mulberry Street knew very much about his activities. His stepmother conceded, according to one news report, that although he was always welcome when he came to visit them he was never asked where he had been. There is little doubt that Pizer *was* the man known locally as 'Leather Apron.' Sergeant Thick, who had known Pizer for eighteen years, and indeed Pizer himself, readily acknowledged that fact at the inquest. And although the allegations of his bullying prostitutes have never been substantiated there is certainly evidence to suggest that he was by no means the harmless put-upon he represented himself to be. On 7 July 1887 one John Pozer, almost certainly Pizer, was convicted at Thames Magistrates' Court of stabbing James Willis or Williams, a boot finisher, and was sentenced to six months imprisonment with hard labour. This incident occurred on the afternoon of the 6th. Willis was working at 42 Morgan Street when Pozer put his head through the window and complained: 'No wonder I can't get any work when you have got it all.' Then, when Willis went to the door to send him away,

Pozer lunged at his face with a shoemaker's knife. Throwing up a hand to shield himself, Willis received a wound in the back of the hand. A year later, on 4 August 1888, Pizer was charged at the same court with indecent assault. On this occasion, apparently, he was discharged, but for what reason is not recorded.[7]

However, none of this makes Pizer the Whitechapel murderer. It is important to understand that when the police detained him on 10 September they possessed no direct evidence of any kind linking him with the crimes. The first and only such evidence materialized the next day in the form of Emanuel Violenia and this witness, as we have seen, was very quickly discredited. The knives that were found at Mulberry Street do not constitute tangible evidence against Pizer for they were only such as might have been expected in the possession of a man of his trade. Furthermore, Pizer pleaded alibis for the last two murders. That for the night of 7–8 September, when Annie Chapman met her death, is hardly convincing. He swore that he never left 22 Mulberry Street between Thursday, 6 September, and the following Monday. This, according to Swanson, was corroborated by 'several persons'. But the only people who could have testified that Pizer stayed at home on the night of the murder were relatives anxious to shield him – his stepmother, his married brother and his sister-in-law. Pizer's alibi for the Nichols murder, on the other hand, is very strong. His claim to have been staying in a Holloway Road lodging house when Polly was killed was, again by Swanson's report, confirmed 'and the date fixed' by the proprietor. There is no reason to disbelieve the proprietor's testimony for the date could have been impressed upon his memory by some association with the dock fires which also occurred that night. Indeed, in his inquest deposition, Pizer specifically recalled seeing the glow in the sky caused by the fires and discussing it, at about 1.30 a.m., in Holloway Road with the lodging house keeper and two police constables.

There is one final consideration. After the Nichols murder Pizer was accused by public and press alike. Feeling ran so high against him that he feared for his life. One incident in particular seems to have terrified him. The details are obscure. Gabriel Pizer, John's brother, said that on Sunday, 2 September, some women pointed John out as Leather Apron in Spitalfields and called the attention of a policeman to him. The officer refused to take him in charge but Pizer 'was pursued by a howling crowd that had collected.' Sergeant Thick, interviewed by the *Star*, referred to the same incident when he said that Leather Apron had not been in a lodging house 'since the Sunday the woman denounced him in Whitechapel, and the police were bamboozled into letting him go.'[8] Whatever the truth of the matter, the episode so scared Pizer that he abandoned his regular haunts, the East End lodging houses, and fled, first to a lodging house in Peter Street, Westminster, and then to his relatives in Mulberry Street. Now, if for the sake of argument we assume that Pizer really did kill Polly Nichols, it is just not credible that he would have ventured out a week later, knowing full well that he was already suspected and that his life was in danger, and have murdered Annie Chapman off a busy Spitalfields thoroughfare in daylight.

Doubtless when the Ripperologists have tired of their black magicians and imaginary Russian doctors, their mad freemasons and erring royals, they will rediscover John Pizer and dress him up as a credible suspect. The fact is, however, that such evidence as has survived the wastage of a century provides no grounds upon which to challenge Abberline's judgement. We can only exonerate Leather Apron of any complicity in the Whitechapel murders.

Pizer was only one of several men detained by the police within three days of the Hanbury Street tragedy. Most of the police records have been lost and newspaper reports are vague and conflicting. But the *Star* tells us that at noon on Monday 10th no less than seven men were being held at different police stations, and a reading of this and other papers does not suggest that this was an exaggeration. Apart from Pizer, however, the only one of whom much was written was William Henry Piggott, a fifty-three-year-old ship's cook arrested in Gravesend on Sunday night.

One of Piggott's hands was injured but he is said to have initially drawn attention to himself in the Pope's Head Tavern by noisily expressing a hatred of women. After his arrest a paper parcel, which he had left at a local fish shop, was retrieved by the police and found to contain, amongst other items of clothing, a torn and bloodstained shirt. Piggott's explanation, apparently, was that he saw a woman fall down in a fit in Whitechapel at 4.30 on Saturday morning. He stooped to pick her up but she bit his hand and, in exasperation, he struck her. Then, seeing two policemen coming, he ran away.

Apprised by telegram of the arrest, Abberline went to Gravesend on Monday morning. Piggott's injured hand, bloody shirt and strange behaviour persuaded him that he might have found the man Mrs Fiddymont and others had seen in the Prince Albert public house on the morning of the murder. So he brought him up to London Bridge by train and from thence to Commercial Street by four-wheeled cab. Early in the afternoon the prisoner was placed in a line with other men and confronted, one by one, with the witnesses. Mrs Fiddymont and Joseph Taylor did not think Piggott was the man. Only Mrs Chappell picked him out and even she would not positively swear to him. Nevertheless, the police committed their suspect to the care of the Whitechapel Union Infirmary pending further inquiries.

By the end of the week the police were reported to have satisfied themselves that Piggott had nothing to do with the murders. 'His movements have been fully accounted for,' said *The Times* on 14 September, 'and he is no longer under surveillance.' The records of the Whitechapel Infirmary show that he was brought there by Sergeant Leach on 10 September, treated for delirium tremens, and discharged on 9 October 1888.[9]

The spate of detentions generated by the Chapman slaying seems to have come to an end on Monday 10th. After that date we know of no significant arrest for a week. Then, in two separate incidents in one night, the police encountered a very ugly customer indeed.

In the early hours of Tuesday, 18 September, a City constable, John Johnson, was on duty in the Minories. Suddenly he heard loud screams of 'Murder!' They came from a regular trouble spot called Three Kings' Court, an unlighted and walled-in yard about forty feet square, reached from the Minories by a gloomy alley that threaded its way between an empty house and a baker's shop. In the court PC Johnson found a man with a prostitute.

When the constable asked the man what he was doing there he received only the curt reply, 'Nothing.' But the prostitute was obviously very frightened. 'Oh, policeman,' she pleaded, 'do take me out of this!' The woman seemed too overcome to say more so Johnson got the couple out of the court, sent the man about his business and walked with the woman to the end of his beat. Now she was talking freely.

'Dear me,' she exclaimed, 'he frightened me very much when he pulled a big knife out!'

The import of her words must have struck Johnson with the force of a sledgehammer. 'Why didn't you tell me that at the time?' he angrily demanded.

'I was too much frightened.'

The constable quickly retraced his steps but by then the man had disappeared.

He was, in fact, a forty-year-old German hairdresser named Charles Ludwig and he was apprehended later the same night by a Metropolitan Police constable after a scrimmage at a coffee stall in Whitechapel High Street. Ludwig's victim on this occasion was Alexander Finlay or Freinberg, a youth who lived with his mother at 51 Leman Street and worked at an ice cream factory in Petticoat Lane. Finlay gave two contradictory accounts of the coffee stall affair, one to Thames Magistrates' Court and one to the press, both on the day of the occurrence. His court deposition was brief and to the point:

> Prosecutor [Finlay] said that at three o'clock on Tuesday morning he was standing at a coffee-stall in the Whitechapel Road, when Ludwig came up in a state of intoxication. The person in charge of the coffee-stall refused to serve him. Ludwig seemed much annoyed, and said to witness, 'What are you looking at?' He then pulled out a long-bladed knife, and threatened to stab witness with it. Ludwig followed him round the stall, and made several attempts to stab him, until witness threatened to knock a dish on his head. A constable came up, and he was then given into custody.

Finlay was more garrulous with representatives of the press. By this account Ludwig came to the stall at about five minutes past four and the trouble started when the stall-keeper served him with a cup of coffee and Ludwig only offered a halfpenny in payment. The German was well dressed and wore a frock coat and a tall hat. Dark, slightly built and about five feet six inches tall, he sported a grizzled moustache and beard. 'There is something the matter with one of his legs,' remembered Finlay, 'and he walks stiffly.' Noticing Finlay looking on, Ludwig suddenly rounded on the youth.

'What you looking at?' he demanded in broken English.

'I am doing no harm,' replied Finlay.

'Oh,' said Ludwig, 'you want something.' And so saying, he pulled out a long penknife and lunged at Finlay.

Eluding the drunken German, Finlay snatched a dish from the stall and prepared to hurl it at his head. But Ludwig retreated after his first rush and Finlay was content to call a nearby policeman.[10]

PC Gallagher 221H arrived at the stall to find Ludwig in a very excited state. On the way to Leman Street Police Station he dropped a long-bladed knife. It was a clasp-knife but the blade was extended. Upon being searched at the station Ludwig was also discovered to possess a razor and a long-bladed pair of scissors.

The circumstances in which Ludwig had been apprehended must have led police to wonder whether they had caught the Whitechapel murderer. Clearly he was seen as a serious suspect. On the day of his arrest he appeared at Thames Magistrates' Court charged only with being drunk and disorderly and with threatening to stab Finlay but the presiding magistrate, Mr Saunders, spoke of him as a dangerous man and he was remanded for a week. In succeeding days detectives diligently investigated his character and conduct and on 25 September, when he was again brought before the court, they were still not satisfied. At Abberline's request Saunders remanded the prisoner once more and, since Ludwig was professing to understand no English, granted the inspector leave to interview him with an interpreter so that his whereabouts on certain dates might be ascertained.

Notwithstanding the length of the Ludwig investigation no official records relating to it now survive and we must learn what we can of him from contemporary newspaper reports.[11] A recent immigrant, possibly from Hamburg, Ludwig was employed as a barber's assistant on 1 September by Mr C. A. Partridge of the Minories. Partridge engaged him at Richter's, a German club in Houndsditch, and found him a good workman if overfond of drink. After about a week Ludwig was permitted to sleep at the shop but on Sunday, 16 September, he moved out to lodge with a German tailor named Johannes in Church Street, Minories. Johannes, apparently, objected to Ludwig's dirty habits and on Monday morning told him to go.

Thus it was that Ludwig spent the night of 17–18 September wandering the streets. Wherever he went he created consternation. At about ten, already the worse for drink, he turned up at Richter's club. The manageress had him thrown out. Later he called at a Finsbury hotel. This was one of Ludwig's usual dives and he looked quite smart in his top hat. But producing a number of razors, he behaved so oddly that some of the inmates became frightened and, when the landlord told him he could not stay, 'was annoyed . . . and threw down the razors in a passion, swearing at the same time.' Ludwig left the hotel about one on Tuesday morning. It was not long after that that he took up with Elizabeth Burns, the prostitute PC Johnson rescued from his attentions in Three Kings' Court, and then, about three, he attacked Finlay in Whitechapel High Street. Both Johnson and Finlay noted that he had been drinking.

Ludwig's acquaintances reacted quite differently to talk that, after his arrest, linked him with the Whitechapel murders. Partridge, his employer, thought the idea quite ridiculous and expressed the view that Ludwig was too much of a coward to have committed the crimes. It would be difficult to imagine more cowardly acts than the Whitechapel atrocities but in any case, if the *Telegraph* is to be believed, Partridge's opinion was based upon little more than the fact that in a recent quarrel the hairdresser had struck his assistant on the nose and Ludwig had failed to retaliate.

The landlord of the hotel in Finsbury, on the other hand, told a newspaper correspondent that he had been suspicious of Ludwig ever since the Hanbury Street murder. The day after the tragedy (Sunday 9th) Ludwig, in a very dirty state and carrying a case of razors and a large pair of scissors, called at the hotel. He said that he had been out all night and asked to be allowed to wash. The landlord could not confirm a statement by one of his boarders that the German's hands were bloodstained but Ludwig did talk incessantly about the murder and when he offered to shave the landlord the latter very prudently refused. The landlord's portrait of Ludwig, moreover, depicts a very acceptable Whitechapel murderer: 'He is a most extraordinary man, is always in a bad temper, and grinds his teeth with rage at any little thing which puts him out. I believe he has some knowledge of anatomy, as he was for some time an assistant to some doctors in the German army, and helped to dissect bodies. He always carries some razors and a pair of scissors with him . . . From what he has said to me, I knew he was in the habit of associating with low women.'

As far as we are now able to judge there was a strong *prima facie* case for holding Ludwig. Admittedly the materials in the court depositions and newspapers contain nothing that directly implicates him in the murders. Certainly his alleged visit to the hotel in Finsbury to wash his hands – bloodstained or not – more than twenty-four hours after the Chapman murder did not prove anything. And there could not have been a sharper contrast between Ludwig's noisy, belligerent and clumsy progress of 17–18 September and the swift, silent and sure technique of the Whitechapel killer. Yet Ludwig was in many respects just the type of man the police should have been looking for. He was a foreigner and in age, height and complexion matched the details given by Mrs Long. If the Finsbury landlord is to be credited he even satisfied Dr Phillips' requirement of medical knowledge. Indeed it is possible that this was how he became a barber's assistant in the first place because on the Continent the barber also often functioned as the poor man's doctor. There were other circumstances, too, that must have made Ludwig seem a plausible suspect. He lived in the East End. He consorted with prostitutes. He carried a long-bladed knife (the possession of razors and scissors by a barber would not have been deemed significant). He was reluctant to account for his movements on the nights of the murders. He had a most volatile temper. And if Alexander Finlay's court deposition was true, if the barber pursued him round the stall and repeatedly tried to stab him, then Ludwig, at least under the influence of liquor, was potentially homicidal.

Ludwig's case could well serve as a cautionary tale for intending Ripperologists. The capacity of these amateur sleuths to delude themselves and their readers in futile attempts to incriminate men against whom not a jot of respectable evidence exists is apparently infinite. The case against Ludwig, at the height of the Hanbury Street scare, looked far blacker than almost any of those adduced in more recent years against other suspects. But he was *not* the Whitechapel murderer. For when the killer struck again, twice in the early hours of 30 September, Ludwig was still in police custody.[12]

'I cannot recall that my grandfather, General Sir Charles Warren, ever stated in writing his personal views on the identity of Jack the Ripper.' So wrote Watkin W. Williams, Warren's grandson, to author Tom Cullen.[13] And, as far as any final, considered judgement by Sir Charles is concerned, he seems to have been right. But, halfway through the murder hunt, the Commissioner did take up his pen – in response to an appeal for information by Matthews – and until now his letter has lain largely neglected in the Home Office files relating to the case.

About the middle of September the Home Secretary, evidently rattled by adverse press and public comment, sent a memorandum to Evelyn Ruggles-Brise, his secretary, directing him to solicit from Warren a progress report on the Whitechapel investigation. Ruggles-Brise was temporarily out of town but the note was sent on to Sir Charles by the Home Office on the morning of 19 September. Warren's reply was made the same day:

No progress has as yet been made in obtaining any definite clue to the Whitechapel murderers. A great number of clues have been examined & exhausted without finding anything suspicious.

A large staff of men are employed and every point is being examined which seems to offer any prospect of a discovery.

There are at present three cases of suspicion.

1. The lunatic Isensmith a Swiss arrested at Holloway who is now in an asylum at Bow & arrangements are being made to ascertain whether he is the man who was seen on the morning of the murder in a public house by Mrs Fiddymont.

2. A man called Puckeridge was released from an asylum on 4 August. He was educated as a surgeon & has threatened to rip people up with a long knife. He is being looked for but cannot be found as yet.

3. A brothel keeper who will not give her address or name writes to say that a man living in her house was seen with blood on him on morning of murder. She described his appearance & said where he might be seen. When the detectives came near him he bolted, got away & there is no clue to the writer of the letter.

All these three cases are being followed up & no doubt will be exhausted in a few days – the first seems a very suspicious case, but the man is at present a violent lunatic.[14]

Warren's first man was Jacob Isenschmid, an insane pork butcher, of whom more presently. The second man, however, is much more intriguing. For his release from an asylum occurred only three days before the George Yard murder and his alleged threat to 'rip people up' with a knife suggests that he was harbouring some grudge and hence may point to a motive. Yet, until the present writer identified Puckridge and published details about him in a recent number of *Ripperana*, nothing whatsoever was known about him.[15]

Sir Charles tells us that his suspect was released from an asylum on 4 August. Registers of patient admissions, kept by the Lunacy Commission, are preserved at the Public Record Office and that of admissions to Metropolitan licensed houses between 1886 and 1900 records that Oswald Puckridge was admitted to Hoxton House Lunatic Asylum on 6 January 1888 and discharged, 'relieved' but not cured, on the following 4 August. Hoxton House, at 50 & 52 Hoxton Street, Shoreditch, was primarily a private asylum for middle class patients. But it did accept paupers from boards of guardians and Puckridge was first entered in the register as a pauper. This, however, is struck out in faded red ink and, written against the correction in the same ink, is the annotation: 'Private 14 Jan. 1888.'[16] Research is continuing but it seems likely that no records of the asylum have survived for our period. Nevertheless, now that we have a name we can glean some basic biographical data about Puckridge from genealogical sources.

Oswald Puckridge was born to John and Philadelphia (née Holmes) Puckridge on 13 June 1838 at Burpham, near Arundel, in Sussex. The family are recorded there in the national census of 1841. John, a farmer, was then forty-five years old, exactly ten years older than his wife, and they had five children: Charlotte (11), Clara (7), Frederick (5), Oswald (3) and Arthur (1). Oswald married in the East End of London when he was thirty. His bride was Ellen Puddle, the daughter of Edward Puddle, a licensed victualler, and the ceremony was performed at the parish church of St Paul, Deptford, on 3 October 1868. On the marriage certificate Puckridge is described as a chemist resident in the same parish. Obviously his career subsequently entered into decline but whether the mental illness was a cause or consequence of his waning fortunes is not presently known. On 28 May 1900 he was admitted to the Holborn Workhouse in City Road from a men's lodging house at 34 St John's Lane, Clerkenwell. He died in the workhouse on 1 June. According to the death certificate he was then a general labourer and the cause of death was 'Broncho Pneumonia'.[17]

Lack of detail on Puckridge and the grounds upon which he was suspected make him a difficult suspect to assess. The police clearly gave his case some priority and if everything Warren tells us about him was true it is not difficult to see why. On the other hand, the Commissioner's comment that no 'definite clue' had been uncovered implies that the CID were not in possession of any hard evidence linking Puckridge with the crimes and, as Charles Ludwig has taught us, cases hung exclusively around characteristics like medical knowledge and insanity are inevitably inconclusive. There are, besides, other difficulties involved in charging Puckridge with the murders. His description of himself in 1868 as a chemist rather than a physician or surgeon suggests that his training may have been that of an apothecary and raises serious doubts about the nature and extent of his medical knowledge. Puckridge, furthermore, was fifty at the time of the murders. Admittedly, this is consistent with the statement of Mrs Long, who thought that the man she saw talking with Annie Chapman was over forty, but – as we will discover in later chapters

– it is in sharp conflict with the evidence of every other important witness who may have seen the killer. Their estimates of age range from twenty-eight to thirty-five. On this point, too, Mrs Long's testimony can almost certainly be discounted because she did not see her suspect's face. Finally, although most of the police records relating to the Whitechapel murders have been lost, it may still be significant that Puckridge's name does not reappear on the known record. And if he did not remain a suspect the probable reason is that, as Warren predicted, he was eventually traced and able to satisfactorily account for his movements on the nights of the murders. Puckridge is the most interesting suspect we have encountered so far. But unless he be incriminated by fresh evidence he must be exonerated.

Puckridge was by no means the only medical man investigated by the police after Dark Annie's murder. We know that Abberline and his team tried to trace three insane medical students who had attended London Hospital. Two were found, interviewed and eliminated from the inquiry. The third, the only one actually named in police records, was John Sanders of 20 Abercorn Place, Maida Vale. When a detective called at his home neighbours told him that the family had gone abroad but recent research has proved that Sanders was, in fact, then being held in an asylum in England. The son of an Indian Army surgeon, he entered London Hospital Medical College in 1879 and functioned as an out-patient dresser in 1880–1. Afterwards he became insane. By 1887 he was subject to attacks of violence, made unprovoked assaults on his friends and tyrannized over his household. The rest of his life was spent in various asylums. During the period of the murders he was confined at West Malling Place, a private asylum in Kent, and he died, aged thirty-nine, in the Heavitree Asylum, Exeter, in 1901.[18]

The memoirs of Major Henry Smith, Acting Commissioner of the City of London Police in 1888, are the source of yet another medical student story. Twenty years on, Smith recalled how, after the Chapman murder, he sent word to Sir Charles Warren that he had learned of a likely suspect. This man, wrote Smith, had all the requisite qualifications: 'He had been a medical student; he had been in a lunatic asylum; he spent all his time with women of loose character, whom he bilked by giving them polished farthings instead of sovereigns, two of these farthings having been found in the pocket of the murdered woman. Sir Charles failed to find him. I thought he was likely to be in Rupert Street, Haymarket. I sent up two men, and there he was; but, polished farthings and all, he proved an alibi without the shadow of doubt.'[19]

Although the two London Hospital students Abberline traced and the man Smith traced were all cleared it would be interesting to know who they were. Evidently Oswald Puckridge was *not* one of them. Admission registers of London Hospital Medical College students are extant and these demonstrate that no student named Puckridge was admitted between about 1850 and 1890. Smith's man lived in Rupert Street, in the parish of St James Piccadilly. But a search of the 1881 and 1891 censuses, and of local rate books from 1887 to 1890, does not reveal anyone by the name of Puckridge owning or occupying premises in the street.[20] So who were these mysterious students? Careful research suggests a possible identification of Smith's suspect.

We encounter him on 24 September in the columns of the *Star*:

Is It a Clue?

Some one representing himself as a detective called at a number of boarding establishments in Great Ormond Street on Saturday afternoon [22 September], making inquiries for a man by the name of Morford, who was supposed to have had lodgings in that street up to 10 Sept., but who since that time has mysteriously disappeared. At some of the places called at the detective said something about a letter having been received by the authorities which led to the idea that Morford might throw some light on the Whitechapel murders. He was described as a man who had been educated as a surgeon, but who had lost standing in the community through drink. It seems that attention was directed to him through a pawnbroker, who took several surgical instruments in pledge from him, and who afterwards had reason to suspect that he was not of sound mind. A shopkeeper in Great Ormond Street thought he knew the man who was being searched for, but as the detective had no address but 'Morford, Great Ormond Street', he was not able to make much progress without letting the whole neighbourhood know what he was about.

Contemporary rate books for Great Ormond Street do not identify 'Morford'. However, the *Medical Directory* for 1888 does list a John Orford as the Senior Resident Medical Officer at the Royal Free Hospital, in Gray's Inn Road, hard by. And in the same year one Henry Orford, a carman and contractor, was living at 40b Rupert Street. We cannot seriously identify Morford, the down-at-heel surgeon sought by police, with John or Henry Orford, the first an established and entirely respectable medical man, the second a 55-year-old carman. But given the comparative rarity of these names it is by no means improbable that John and Henry were related in some way or that the CID's suspect was kin to them.[21]

We know about a few other suspects at about this time. There was Edward McKenna, an itinerant pedlar arrested on 14 September. He was thought to be identical with men seen carrying knives in Flower and Dean and Heath Streets but was released after witnesses failed to recognize him. There was John Fitzgerald, a plasterer or bricklayer's labourer who confessed to the Chapman murder on 26 September. Within three days he had also been released, 'exhaustive inquiries having proved his statement to be entirely unfounded'. And there was 'Mary', a male hairdresser and known sex offender. The CID made inquiries about him of their counterparts in Bremen and were informed that he was serving a twelve months prison sentence in Oslebshausen. But without doubt the leading suspect at this stage of the hunt was Jacob Isenschmid, the 'mad butcher'.

'Although at present we are unable to procure any evidence to connect him with the murders,' wrote Abberline of Isenschmid on 18 September, 'he appears to be the most likely person that has come under our notice to have committed the crimes.' Warren obviously agreed. For a day later he accorded him pride of place on his list and singled him out as 'a very suspicious case'. Something of their optimism even seems to have reached the press. 'The detective officers who are engaged in the Whitechapel case', ran one report, 'are said to be more hopeful now than they have been before. It is stated they have some fresh information which encourages them to hope that before the week is over they will be able to solve the mystery.'[22]

Isenschmid, a Swiss of many years' residence in England, was first brought to the attention of the police by two doctors. Dr Cowan of 10 Landseer Road and Dr Crabb of Holloway Road called at Holloway Police Station on 11 September to point the finger of suspicion. Their grounds were slender enough. Isenschmid was a butcher, he was insane, and George Tyler, his landlord, had told them that he absented himself from his lodgings at nocturnal hours. Detective Inspector Styles, nevertheless, was bound to investigate.

Styles went first to Isenschmid's lodgings at 60 Mitford Road and talked to George Tyler. He told him that Isenschmid had taken lodgings at his house on 5 September and that on the night of the Hanbury Street murder he had come in at nine in the evening and gone out again at one the next morning. This was by no means unusual. In fact Isenschmid had gone out at one o'clock on four of the five working days he had spent at the house. But part of the doctors' allegations had been substantiated and Styles called next at 97 Duncombe Road. There he found Mary Isenschmid, the suspect's wife. She had not seen her husband since he had left home two months ago and did not know how he currently earned a living. She did say, however, that he was in the habit of carrying large butcher knives about with him. The inspector was sufficiently impressed by what he had heard to detail men to watch both addresses and to apprehend Isenschmid if he should turn up.

His diligence paid off. In the early hours of 12 September Isenschmid was arrested and taken to Holloway Police Station. Judged insane, he was sent to the Islington Workhouse and from thence, the same day, to Grove Hall Lunatic Asylum, Fairfield Road, Bow. Sergeant Thick, deputed by Abberline to investigate his case, examined the clothing in which he had been apprehended but could find no traces of bloodstains.

Fortunately a clutch of documents relating to Isenschmid has survived in the Metropolitan Police case papers and from these and other sources we can learn a good deal about him. At the time of his marriage to Mary Ann Joyce, the daughter of Richard Joyce, a farmer, in December 1867 he was a journeyman butcher and lived at 41 Bath Street, off the City Road. But afterwards he set up on his own account as a pork butcher at 59 Elthorne Road, Holloway. Sadly the business failed and he began to suffer recurring attacks of insanity.

No one seems to have been very sure what the cause of Isenschmid's problem was. His wife told Sergeant Thick that he became depressed after the failure of his business and the press that he had never been 'right in his head' since a fit in 1882 or 1883. Asylum records at different times attribute his attacks to drink and hereditary factors. While the *Star* traced their origin to an attack of sunstroke some years before 1888.

Whatever the cause of Isenschmid's malady, its symptoms could be frightening. According to the gossip scavenged in and about Elthorne Road by the *Star*, his behaviour during periods of insanity was frequently violent. He threatened to put people's 'lights out'. His landlord was cautioned several times against going near him. And, more ominously, he was continuously to be seen sharpening a long knife. The butcher also laboured under strange delusions. One of them was that everything belonged to him. Indeed, he styled himself 'the King of Elthorne Road'.

On 24 September 1887 he was admitted to Colney Hatch Lunatic Asylum. From his own observations Dr John Gray of the Islington Infirmary justified Isenschmid's committal on the grounds that he 'says he can build a church give him a shovel and cement . . . can lay 2000 bricks a day and mix his own mortar . . . says he shall be Member of Parliament soon [and] talks with great excitement & violence.' In addition, Mary Isenschmid had told him that her husband 'threatened to kill his wife and children, writes threatening letters to his neighbours saying he will fire their homes and throw vitriol over them, sometimes refuses food for days together [and] threatened to blow up the Queen with dynamite.' In the records of the asylum the illness is said to have been Isenschmid's first attack and to have been a month old upon his committal. On 2 December, only ten weeks after being admitted, he was discharged as cured.

The Isenschmids attempted a fresh start. They found a new home in Duncombe Road and Jacob a new job as a journeyman butcher with Mr Martell in Marylebone High Street. But at Whitsuntide 1888 he left this employment and began to behave as strangely as ever. Sometimes he lapsed into moods of sullen despondency, unwilling to bestir himself to do anything, even to wash. At others he sought solace in religion and sat reading the Bible for hours on end. But the book brought him no comfort. Mrs Isenschmid had seen him fling it across the room in exasperation and heard him lament that he must be 'a very wicked man if all the Bible says is true.' By July 1888 she had had enough. 'He got so bad,' she told the *Star*, 'that I got an order to have him put in the asylum again. A doctor came to see him and then he got suspicious. I told him the doctor was only the [pawn] broker's man but he said the broker's man wouldn't ask him how he was. He got afraid that he would be put in the asylum again, and ten weeks ago he ran away.'

Perhaps Isenschmid blamed his wife for driving him out of their home. Certainly Mary feared him. She confided in Sergeant Thick: 'I do not think my husband would injure anyone but me. I think he would kill me if he had the chance.' The *Star* also heard some disconcerting stories from the new tenant of Isenschmid's old shop in Elthorne Road. Isenschmid appeared there several times during July-September 1888. On one occasion he turned up at the shop with his butcher's apron on and his knife and steel hanging at his side. Holding up a bullock's tail, he announced that he had just slaughtered forty bullocks. On another he sent a load of bullocks' entrails to the shop at three o'clock in the morning.

Isenschmid's case is an instructive one. The fortuitous survival of police records enables us – for once – to penetrate the investigation and thinking that produced a leading suspect. And what they reveal is just how little *evidence* it took. For, notwithstanding Isenschmid's ferocious reputation, it is patently clear that the police had virtually no case against him.

Admittedly, as a butcher, he would have possessed crude anatomical knowledge. But such an argument could have been used to incriminate every slaughterman and butcher in the metropolis. He regularly left his lodgings at 1.00 a.m. But this was no more than thousands of working people in Victorian London were obliged to do. Isenschmid himself told the medical superintendent of Grove Hall that he got up early to go to the market where he bought sheeps' heads, kidneys and feet. These he took home, dressed and then sold to West End restaurants and coffee houses. 'That was the cause of him being up so early in the morning,' he said, 'and that was the only way open to him to get his livelihood.' He was mentally ill. And his Colney Hatch record does demonstrate that he was potentially dangerous. But although the police certainly knew that he had been in the asylum there is no evidence that they had any detailed knowledge of his record there. Mary Isenschmid, on the other hand, told Sergeant Thick: 'I do not think my husband would injure anyone but me.' Hardly proof that he was a homicidal maniac! The police even failed to establish a link between Isenschmid and Whitechapel. Mrs Isenschmid told them that Jacob used to frequent Mrs Geringher's public house in Wentworth Street, Whitechapel, but when Thick interviewed Mrs Geringher she denied all knowledge of the man.

One circumstance seems to have weighed particularly heavily with Abberline. He noted in his reports that Isenschmid's description tallied with that of the man seen by Mrs Fiddymont and others at the Prince Albert on the morning of the Chapman murder. Abberline was convinced that they were identical and, from what we know of

Isenschmid's appearance, he may have been right. A man in his early forties in 1888, he was about five feet seven inches tall, with ginger hair on head and face. Normally he was a powerfully built man but, as his wife told the press, since he had left home in July he had evidently been accustomed to walking about 'till he's nearly starved ... and he has got pinched in his appearance and much thinner.' Now all this is certainly consistent with Joseph Taylor's description of the Prince Albert man. Unfortunately, the only people who could have clinched the identification were Taylor, Mrs Fiddymont and Mary Chappell, and Dr Mickle, resident medical officer at Grove Hall, was so concerned about his patient's health that he declined to permit the witnesses to confront him. On 19 September, the date of our last police report on Isenschmid, the doctor was still obdurate and we do not know whether Mrs Fiddymont and her witnesses ever did identify the suspect. But, for the sake of argument, let us suppose that they did. What does it prove? Only that Isenschmid had been in the Prince Albert, about 400 yards from the murder site, at seven on the fatal morning. Bloodstains on a man of his trade could not possibly have been deemed significant.[23] And surely it is scarcely credible that one and a half hours after committing a murder the killer would have been sitting, in a bloodstained condition, drinking ale in a pub only yards away from the scene of his crime?

In the event Isenschmid was eventually exonerated. On 21 September the *Star* reported that his brother had satisfactorily accounted for his movements on the morning of the Chapman murder. This report is unconfirmed and, since Mary Isenschmid has left it on record that Jacob's relatives were all in Switzerland, probably untrue. But, like Ludwig, Isenschmid was cleared by the murderer himself. When he struck again the mad pork butcher was still confined at Grove Hall.[24]

The Yard's elevation of an innocent man to the position of chief suspect on such flimsy grounds is, at the very least, disturbing. Truly, as Abberline conceded on 18 September, they were never able 'to procure any evidence to connect him [Isenschmid] with the murders'. Yet one gets the distinct impression that if the real murderer had stopped killing after Hanbury Street poor, deranged Isenschmid, unheard and unconvicted, would have gone down in police record and memoir as the slayer of Martha Tabram, Polly Nichols and Annie Chapman. Why did detectives allow themselves to be misled so easily? Well, there were two important factors. One was that police inquiries – diligent though they were – uncovered so very little about the real killer that they were reduced to grasping at straws. The other was the public pressure upon the force to secure a conviction. Abberline himself, in a report of 19 September, let that particular cat out of the bag. There he suggests that the chief police surgeon or one of the divisional surgeons be requested to contact Dr Mickle in order to expedite arrangements for the witnesses to see Isenschmid because 'time is of the greatest importance in this case, not only with regard to the question of identity, but also for the purpose of allaying the strong public feeling that exists.' Such factors operated throughout the entire duration of the Whitechapel investigations. So when we come to consider the cases against the main suspects, at the end of our quest, we will do well to remember what we have learned here.

On 22 September *Punch* gave its readers 'A Detective's Diary À La Mode':

Monday. – Papers full of the latest tragedy. One of them suggested that the assassin was a man who wore a blue coat. Arrested three blue-coat wearers on suspicion.

Tuesday. – The blue coats proved innocent. Released. Evening journal threw out a hint that deed might have been perpetrated by a soldier. Found a small drummer-boy drunk and incapable. Conveyed him to the Station-house.

Wednesday. – Drummer-boy released. Letter of anonymous correspondent to daily journal declaring that the outrage could only have been committed by a sailor. Decoyed petty officer of Penny Steamboat on shore, and suddenly arrested him.

Thursday. – Petty officer allowed to go. Hint thrown out in the Correspondence columns that the crime might be traceable to a lunatic. Noticed an old gentleman purchasing a copy of *Maiwa's Revenge*. Seized him.

Friday. – Lunatic dispatched to an asylum. Anonymous letter received, denouncing local clergyman as the criminal. Took the reverend gentleman into custody.

Saturday. – Eminent ecclesiastic set at liberty with an apology. Ascertain in a periodical that it is thought just possible that the Police may have committed the crime themselves. At the call of duty, finished the week by arresting myself!

Baffled as the detectives undoubtedly were their search, of course, was by no means as arbitrary as that. The records of the Chapman inquiry are now very incomplete but in this chapter we have learned the names of nine new suspects – not many but perhaps enough to suggest the characteristics the police were looking for.

Insanity and medical knowledge appear to have been the most important. Notwithstanding Coroner Baxter's hypothesis of an economic motive the police were very interested in lunatics. Three suspects (Puckridge, Sanders and Isenschmid) out of nine had seen the inside of an asylum and at least another three (Piggott, Ludwig and Morford) were allegedly of unsound mind. Detectives also seem to have taken Dr Phillips' testimony to heart because not less than five suspects (Ludwig, Puckridge, Sanders, Morford and Isenschmid) had some pretensions to anatomical knowledge. The significance of these two factors in determining the direction of police inquiries is further reflected in the searches made by Abberline and Smith for the as yet unidentified insane medical students. Inevitably, the interest in medically qualified people led to men of middle-class origin being suspected and Puckridge, Sanders and Morford might be so described. Only three suspects (Ludwig, Mary and Isenschmid) were of Continental origin. Given the fact that Mrs Long had incriminated a foreigner this may seem a little surprising but the police remained uncertain about the value of her evidence because it could not be reconciled with Dr Phillips' estimate of the time of Annie Chapman's death.

A bright sunny September helped to banish the memory of the summer thunderstorms. And as the month wore on, too, the fear that had stalked the streets after the death of Dark Annie visibly receded. The police, including those in the City, into which the killer had not yet ventured, remained vigilant. But the majority of East Enders, quickly forgetful of terrors past, began to lose themselves once more in the struggle for economic survival. The murder of a woman at Birtley Fell near Gateshead on 22 September encouraged many of them to believe that the Whitechapel murderer had fled the capital.

Visiting Whitechapel Road one night in late September, a *Daily News* reporter found no sign of apprehension in the great thoroughfare.[25] There were the usual flaunting shops, noisy street traders, flaring gin-palaces, raucous entertainments and steaming cookshops. Crowds gathered here and there under the street lamps and stars to listen to the marvels of a new patent pill, to watch a busker 'beating out with a couple of quills what he takes apparently to be music from a sort of home-made dulcimer', to see a performing boy with no legs, to enjoy the spectacle of a street fight, to hear a trader extol the qualities of new trousers at 9s. 6d. a pair. 'A hundred people at least,' the reporter tells us, 'are clustered round the [trouser] salesman who descants hoarsely on the unrivalled qualities of his goods, and winds up by flinging a pair out into the crowd for closer inspection.'

Reminders of the tragedies there surely were. The proprietor of the waxworks, exhibiting outside his premises his 'horrible pictorial representations' of the murders, was still turning them to profitable account. And a newsvendor, standing with a bundle of papers under one arm, was exhorting passers-by to read the latest on the atrocities between alternate puffs at the half cigar he shared with a neighbouring shoeblack. But of the menace of the unknown killer there was now little trace.

Even away from the reassuring razzle-dazzle of Whitechapel Road, near the scenes of the very crimes themselves, the journalist found people heedless of the danger. On the spot where Polly Nichols had been done to death in Buck's Row he found a man grinding out 'Men of Harlech' on a piano organ. And in Hanbury Street he stopped an elderly pedestrian. 'There seems to be little apprehension of further mischief by this assassin at large?' he asked him. 'No, very little,' the old man replied. 'People, most of 'em, think he's gone to Gateshead.'

Just a few nights later, on 30 September, the murderer struck again. And this time he claimed two victims in less than an hour.

9

Double Event

ON THE SOUTH SIDE of Commercial Road was Berner Street. A thoroughfare of small two-storey slums in the parish of St George-in-the-East, its inhabitants – tailors, shoemakers and cigarette makers – were mostly Poles and Germans. On the west side of Berner Street, directly opposite a new London School Board building, was Dutfield's Yard. The name was no longer appropriate since Arthur Dutfield's business had moved to Pinchin Street but the two great wooden gates that guarded the entrance to the yard still proclaimed the connection in letters of white paint: 'W. Hindley, sack manufacturer, and A. Dutfield, van and cart builder.'

Inside the gates Dutfield's Yard was a narrow court flanked on the right by the International Working Men's Educational Club at 40 Berner Street and on the left by No. 42 and, behind that, a row of cottages. At the top of the yard were a store or workshop belonging to Hindley's sack manufactory and a disused stable.

The International Working Men's Educational Club was a Socialist club. Membership was open to working men of any nationality but it was mainly patronized by Russian and Polish Jews. Access to the premises could be gained by the front door in Berner Street or by a side or kitchen door in Dutfield's Yard. The most northerly of the big yard gates had a wicket for use when the main gates were closed. But they were frequently left open, even at night. 'In fact,' said a club member, 'it is very seldom that they are closed. It is customary for members of the club to go in by the side door to prevent knocking at the front.'[1]

On Saturday nights there were free discussions at the club and although the night of Saturday, 29 September, was wet and dismal some ninety to one hundred people crowded into the first-floor meeting room to debate 'why Jews should be Socialists.' Morris Eagle, a Russian Jew, took the chair. When the discussion ended, between 11.30 and 12.00, the bulk of the clientele went home but perhaps a few dozen members stayed. Most of these remained chatting or singing in the meeting room upstairs.

Outside, in the yard, it must have been dark. Mrs Diemschutz, the stewardess of the club, later told reporters that at about one the side door 'had been, and still was, half open, and from it the light from the gas jets in the kitchen was streaming out into the yard.' Light also came from the cottage windows, from the first-floor windows of the club and from a printing office at the back of the club where Philip Kranz, the editor of a Yiddish radical weekly *Der Arbeter Fraint* (*The Worker's Friend*), was still reading in his room. But no lamp shone in the yard itself. And the illumination from the upper storey of the club fell not so much upon the court below as upon the cottages opposite. Furthermore, whatever benefits the club's side door, the cottages and the printing office conferred farther up the yard, they did little to penetrate the gloom immediately within the gates. Here, for a distance of some eighteen feet from the street, anyone entering the yard had to pass between the dead walls of Nos. 40 and 42. Here, after sunset, the darkness was almost absolute.

Although dark Dutfield's Yard was by no means unfrequented. We know the names of three members of the club who visited it between midnight and one that night.[2] Others probably came and went unrecorded.

About ten minutes past midnight William West popped out of the club by the side door to take some literature to the printing office where he worked farther up the yard. Returning, he glanced towards the gates and noticed that they were open. But he saw nothing suspicious there. Then he re-entered the club, again using the side door, called his brother and set off home. They left by the Berner Street door at about 12.15 a.m.

Joseph Lave, a printer and photographer visiting London from the United States, had temporary lodgings at the club. 'I was in the club yard this morning about twenty minutes to one,' he would tell a reporter later in the day. 'I came out first at half-past twelve to get a breath of fresh air. I passed out into the street, but did not see anything unusual. The district appeared to me to be quiet. I remained out until twenty minutes to one, and during that time no one came into the yard. I should have seen anybody moving about there.'

After the Saturday night debate Morris Eagle, the chairman, escorted his lady friend home. At about 12.40 he returned. When he tried the street door he found it closed so he walked round the side into Dutfield's Yard. The gates were thrown wide open. As soon as he passed through the gateway he could hear, from the open first-floor windows of the club, the strains of a friend singing in Russian. Entering by the side door, he went upstairs and joined in. Just twenty minutes later the huddled body of a woman was discovered lying by the wall of the club between the gates and the side door. Yet Eagle, walking that same ground, had seen nothing. Nor did he remember noticing anyone in the yard. His testimony is good evidence that at 12.40 the crime had not yet been committed. The site of the murder was in the passage between Nos. 40 and 42, where it was too dark to enable Eagle to swear positively at the inquest that the body had *not* been there. But the corpse would be found lying obliquely across the pathway, both face and feet very close to the right-hand wall, and had it been there at 12.40 Eagle, passing up the yard, would very likely have brushed against it, if not have actually stumbled over it. 'I naturally walked on the right side [of the path],' he explained, 'that being the side on which the club door was.'[3]

At 1.00 a.m. on Sunday, 30 September, a man driving a two-wheeled barrow harnessed to a pony approached Dutfield's Yard.[4] The driver was a Russian Jew named Louis Diemschutz. He was the steward of the International Working Men's Educational Club and he lived on the premises with his wife, who assisted him in the management. In addition to being the club steward Diemschutz was a hawker of cheap jewellery and every Saturday he took wares to sell in the market at Westow Hill, Crystal Palace. Now, after the day's trading, he had come to deposit his unsold stock at the club before stabling his pony in George Yard, Cable Street.

The steward noticed nothing untoward as he turned into the gateway. He heard no cry, he saw no one about and certainly there was nothing unusual in the fact that both gates were wide open. Yet, as he drove into the yard, his pony shied to the left. Peering down to the right, Diemschutz thought that he could discern a dark object on the ground by the club wall but it was too dark for him to see

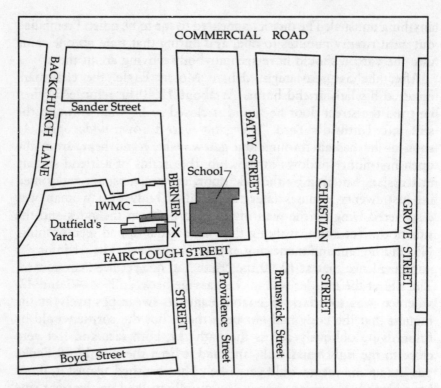

*Berner Street and its vicinity. × marks the place where Elizabeth Stride's
body was discovered, at 1 a.m. on Sunday, 30 September 1888*

what it was. He prodded it and tried to lift it with the handle of his
whip. Then he jumped down from his barrow and struck a match. It
was windy but before his feeble flame was extinguished the steward
could make out the shape of a prone figure. And the dim outline of
a dress told him that the figure was that of a woman.

Diemschutz's first concern was for his wife. Perhaps he thought it was
she lying there. Or perhaps, as he would tell the press, 'all I did was to
run indoors and ask where my missis was because she is of weak constitution, and I did not want to frighten her.' Whatever the reason, leaving
his pony at the side door, he dashed into the club and enquired for his
wife. He found her, safe in the company of some of the members in
the ground-floor dining room, and then stammered: 'There's a woman
lying in the yard but I cannot say whether she's drunk or dead.'

Having procured a candle and reinforcements in the form of Isaac

Kozebrodski, a young tailor machinist, Diemschutz ventured back into the yard. Even before they reached the body they could see blood. Mrs Diemschutz followed them but only as far as the kitchen door. 'Just by the door,' she later explained to journalists, 'I saw a pool of blood, and when my husband struck a light I noticed a dark heap lying under the wall. I at once recognized it as the body of a woman, while, to add to my horror, I saw a stream of blood trickling down [i.e. up] the yard and terminating in the pool I had first noticed. She was lying on her back with her head against the wall, and the face looked ghastly. I screamed out in fright, and the members of the club hearing my cries rushed downstairs in a body out into the yard.'

Diemschutz and Kozebrodski made no attempt to disturb the body. Instead they immediately set off in search of a policeman. Turning right at the gates and then left into Fairclough Street, they raced with pounding hearts, shouting 'Police!' at the tops of their voices, as far as Grove Street. But no constable did they descry and there they turned back. On the way to Grove Street they had passed a horse-keeper by the name of Edward Spooner.

Spooner was standing with a woman outside the Beehive Tavern, at the corner of Christian and Fairclough Streets, when he saw the two Jews running and 'hallooing out "Murder" and "Police"'. They passed him but stopped at Grove Street and came back. Intrigued to discover what all the fuss was about, Spooner accosted them. And when they told him that another woman had been murdered he returned with them to Dutfield's Yard. Upon reaching the yard they found a small crowd already clustered around the body. Someone struck a match and Spooner bent down and lifted up the dead woman's chin. It was just warm and he noticed blood still flowing from her throat and running up the yard towards the side door of the club. When the horse-keeper lifted the woman's chin Louis Diemschutz, looking on, saw for the first time the terrible wound in her throat. 'I could see that her throat was fearfully cut,' he told the press some hours later. 'There was a great gash in it over two inches wide.'

At the time of Diemschutz's discovery of the body most of the members remaining on the club premises were still upstairs singing. But when someone came up to tell them that there was a dead woman in the yard Morris Eagle for one tumbled pell-mell down the stairs and out at the side door. 'I went down in a second and struck a match,' he would tell the inquest. Notwithstanding his alacrity, Eagle took very little cognizance of the appearance of the body. As he explained it later to a representative of the press, 'I did not notice the appearance of the woman because the sight of the blood upset me and I could not look at it.' He it was, however, who informed the police. For whereas Diemschutz had turned southwards from the gateway towards Fairclough Street Eagle sped in the opposite direction. And in Commercial Road he encountered PC Henry Lamb 252H and a brother constable.

Lamb's beat in Commercial Road took him past the end of Berner Street. He had last passed it only six or seven minutes earlier. And it was between Christian and Batty Streets on his way back that he first saw two men shouting and running towards him from the direction of Berner Street. They were Morris Eagle and a companion. He advanced to meet them. 'Come on,' they cried, 'there has been another murder.' Followed by another constable fresh from a fixed point duty in Commercial Road, Lamb ran to the scene of the crime.

There was a crowd there and when he turned his lantern on the body the bystanders eagerly pressed forward to see. 'I begged them to keep back,' Lamb told the inquest, 'otherwise they might have their clothes soiled with blood and thus get into trouble.'

Kneeling down, he placed his hand against the woman's face. It was slightly warm. Then he felt her wrist but could detect no movement of the pulse. Lamb was uncertain as to whether blood was still flowing from the wound in the throat but he did note that the blood which had run towards the club door was still in a liquid state. That on the ground near to the woman's neck was slightly congealed. There were no signs of a struggle and the woman's clothes did not appear to have been disturbed. Only the soles of her boots were visible from beneath her voluminous skirts. 'She looked,' said Lamb, 'as if she had been laid quietly down.'

PC Lamb lost no time in summoning assistance. He sent his fellow constable for the nearest doctor and despatched the energetic Morris Eagle to Leman Street Police Station. The best evidence on the appearance of the fifth victim as she lay dead in Dutfield's Yard comes from the medical witnesses.[5]

It was about ten minutes past one when Lamb's colleague called at 100 Commercial Road, the residence of Dr Frederick William Blackwell. The doctor had to be roused from his bed but while he struggled into his clothes his assistant, Edward Johnston, accompanied the policeman to Berner Street. Johnston felt the body and 'found all warm except the hands, which were quite cold.' By this time, however, the wound in the woman's throat had stopped bleeding and the stream of blood that had flowed up the yard had clotted. He found very little blood left in the vicinity of the neck.

Dr Blackwell consulted his watch as he arrived on the scene. It was 1.16 a.m. By the light of a policeman's lantern he made a remarkably detailed examination of the body and two days later reported his findings at the inquest:

The deceased was lying on her left side obliquely across the passage, her face looking towards the right wall. Her legs were drawn up, her feet close against the wall of the right side of the passage. Her head was resting beyond the carriage-wheel rut, the neck lying over the rut. Her feet were three yards from the gateway. Her dress was unfastened at the neck. The neck and chest were quite warm, as were also the legs, and the face was slightly warm. The hands were cold. The right hand was open and on the chest, and was smeared with blood. The left hand, lying on the ground, was partially closed, and contained a small packet of cachous wrapped in tissue paper. There were no rings, nor marks of rings, on her hands. The appearance of the face was quite placid. The mouth was slightly open. The deceased had round her neck a check silk scarf, the bow of which was turned to the left and pulled very tight. In the neck there was a long incision which exactly corresponded with the lower border of the scarf. The border was slightly frayed, as if by a sharp knife. The incision in the neck commenced on the left side, $2^{1}/2$ inches below the angle of the jaw, and almost in a direct line with it, nearly severing the vessels on that side, cutting the windpipe completely in two, and terminating on the opposite side $1^{1}/2$ inches below the angle of the right jaw, but without severing the vessels on that side. I could not ascertain whether the bloody hand had been moved. The blood was running down the gutter into the drain in the opposite direction from the feet. There was about 1 lb. of clotted blood close by the body, and a stream all the way from there to the back door of the club.'

It should be noted that the woman's clothing had not been disturbed by her killer. Dr Blackwell indeed discovered that her dress had been unfastened at the neck but this had been done by his assistant Edward Johnston during his brief inspection of the body.

In the meantime Dr Phillips, the divisional police surgeon, had been summoned to Leman Street and sent on from there to Dutfield's Yard. When he got there Chief Inspector West and Inspector Charles Pinhorn were in possession of the body. The record of his examination, dictated on the spot to Pinhorn, largely corroborates that of Dr Blackwell. It was presented to the inquest by Phillips on 3 October:

> The body was lying on its left side, face turned toward the wall, head toward the yard, feet toward the street, left arm extended from elbow, which held a packet of cachous in her hand. Similar ones were in the gutter. I took them from her hand, and handed them to Dr Blackwell. The right arm was lying over the body, and the back of the hand and wrist had on them clotted blood. The legs were drawn up, the feet close to the wall, the body still warm, the face warm, the hands cold, the legs quite warm, a silk handkerchief round the throat, slightly torn (so is my note, but I since find it is cut) . . . This corresponded to the right angle of the jaw; the throat was deeply gashed, and an abrasion of the skin about an inch and a quarter diameter, apparently slightly stained with blood, was under the right clavicle.[6]

On a minor point of fact the medicos were in conflict. The victim died clutching a packet of cachous (small aromatic sweetmeats, sucked to sweeten the breath) in her left hand. On 3 October Dr Phillips told the inquest that he released them from her hand and passed them to Dr Blackwell. But Blackwell, recalled before the inquiry two days later, swore:

> I removed the cachous from the left hand of the deceased, which was nearly open. The packet was lodged between the thumb and the first finger, and was partially hidden from view. It was I who spilt them in removing them from the hand. My impression is that the hand gradually relaxed while the woman was dying, she dying in a fainting condition from the loss of blood.

Both doctors examined the area about the body as well as the available light permitted. There was a patch of blood on the ground to the left of the neck. From this a stream had run along the gutter to within a few inches of the side door of the club. But Blackwell could find no spots of blood on the dead woman's clothes or on the wall of the club. And although he saw other traces on the ground he thought that these had been trodden about on the boots of bystanders. Phillips agreed: 'I could trace none [blood spots] except that which I considered had been transplanted – if I may use the term – from the original flow from the neck.'

Precisely when did the woman die? Dr Blackwell noted that her hands were cold. But he detected some warmth in her face, and her neck, chest and legs were quite warm. The fact that the clothes were not wet with rain also indicated that she had not been lying in the yard long. On the other hand there were factors present conducive to a slow loss of body heat. The victim would have bled to death comparatively slowly because only the vessels on the left side of the neck had been cut and even then the carotid artery had not been completely severed. Furthermore, the night itself had been very mild. It was Blackwell's opinion, nevertheless, that when he arrived in the yard the woman could not have been dead 'more than twenty minutes, at the most half an hour.' We know that Blackwell reached Dutfield's Yard at 1.16. He was saying, then, that the murder took place after 12.46 and very possibly after 12.56 a.m.

Dr Phillips informed the inquest that the woman had been alive 'within an hour' of his own arrival at the scene of the crime. Since existing versions of his testimony neglect to tell us when that was, however, his statement is difficult to interpret. Blackwell thought that Phillips arrived between twenty and thirty minutes after himself. If so Dr Phillips' evidence places the time of death after 12.36–12.46 a.m.

While Johnston was examining the body PC Lamb had the yard gates closed and posted a man at the wicket. He then made a cursory investigation of the club premises, turning his light on the hands and clothes of inmates and searching rooms. Finding nothing suspicious, he next turned his attention to the cottages across the way. The tenants had retired for the night. Lamb found them in a state of undress and very frightened. We do not know the details of his exploration of these cottages but under the circumstances it was almost certainly perfunctory. 'I told them [the tenants] there was "nothing much the matter",' he said at the inquest, 'as I did not wish to scare them more.' The constable's preliminary searches also evidently took in Hindley's store and two waterclosets in the yard. When he returned from his perambulations he found West and Phillips with the body.

Perhaps because Dutfield's Yard was easily sealed off the police occupied it for some hours. The onlookers that had gathered there were detained until they had been identified and searched by the police and examined for bloodstains by Dr Phillips. The body itself was eventually removed to St George's Mortuary, Cable Street, and at 5.30 PC Albert Collins washed the last vestiges of gore from the yard. No weapon, no clue to the murderer, had been found.

By then the real centre of the night's events had long since moved, some three-quarters of a mile and twelve minutes' walk away, to a small, stone-cobbled square, just within the eastern boundary of the City of London.

Behind Mitre Street, off Aldgate, is Mitre Square. About twenty-four yards square, it was accounted a 'respectable' place, largely comprised of business premises, and was, during business hours, extensively used. But, although close to the junction of Fenchurch Street, Leadenhall Street and Aldgate, Mitre Square was ill-lit and almost deserted after dark. Only two lamps directly illuminated the square itself. A lamp post stood in the northwestern part of it and a 'lantern lamp' was affixed to the wall at the entrance of Church Passage, in the eastern corner. The silence of the square after nightfall reflected the relative seclusion of its location and the fact that it could boast but an insignificant resident population, the few houses that existed there, mostly dilapidated and empty, crouching in the shadow of tall warehouses that dominated Mitre Square on every side. 'This particular square,' wrote a journalist, 'is as dull and lonely a spot as can be found anywhere in London.'[7]

Ironically the only private residents of Mitre Square at its moment of notoriety were a City policeman – PC Richard Pearce 922 – and his family. They lived at No. 3, one of two tenements in the western corner of the square, sandwiched between the warehouses of Walter Williams & Co. and Kearley & Tongue. The adjacent house was an empty, tumble-down slum with broken windows. These were the only dwelling houses that actually faced into the square. In the southern corner of Mitre Square, fronting upon Mitre Street, was a row of four further houses. Their back windows overlooked the square but no less than three of the houses were empty and the fourth, the shop of Mr Taylor, a picture-frame maker, at the end of the row, was customarily locked-up and unoccupied at nights.

Some of the warehouses did contain caretakers or watchmen. In the southeast part of the square, between the row of empty houses and

Horner & Company's warehouses was a private yard. It belonged to Messrs Heydemann & Co., general merchants, of 5 Mitre Street, and the second and third floor back windows of their premises, behind the yard, commanded an uninterrupted view of the southern and western parts of Mitre Square. George Clapp, the resident caretaker, slept with his wife in a back room on the second floor. The only other resident in Heydemann's premises was an old nurse who attended Mrs Clapp. She slept in a room on the third floor. Across the square from Heydemann's, in the premises of Kearley & Tongue, wholesale grocers, a watchman, George James Morris, started work at 7.00 p.m.

There were three approaches to Mitre Square – one carriageway and two narrow foot passages. The carriageway led into the square from Mitre Street, passing between Mr Taylor's shop on the right and the Walter Williams & Co. warehouse on the left. At the eastern corner of the square was Church Passage. It communicated with Duke Street. The other passage ran from St James' Place ('the Orange Market') to the northern point of Mitre Square.

At about 1.44 a.m., just three-quarters of an hour after the Dutfield's Yard discovery, PC Edward Watkins 881 of the City Police approached Mitre Square from Mitre Street. All was quiet. George Clapp and his wife had been in bed since about 11.00 and PC Pearce since 12.30. They were now sleeping soundly. George Morris, Kearley & Tongue's watchman, was cleaning the offices on the ground floor of their counting house block. PC Watkins' beat normally took him about twelve or fourteen minutes to patrol. When he had last explored Mitre Square, at about 1.30, it had been deserted. And so, as he stepped into the square, it seemed now. There was no sound but that of his own footsteps. Yet, turning right into the southern corner of the square, the constable beheld in the beam of the lantern fixed in his belt one of the most gruesome sights he had witnessed in seventeen years of police work.

Four days later, before the coroner, Watkins described what he had found in the tersest language: 'I next came in at 1.44. I turned to the right. I saw the body of a woman lying there on her back with her feet facing the square [and] her clothes up above her waist. I saw her throat was cut and her bowels protruding. The stomach was ripped up. She was laying in a pool of blood.' To the representatives of the press the constable was a

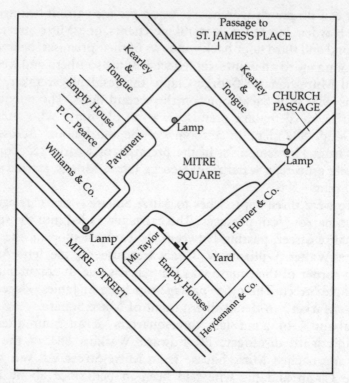

Mitre Square. × *marks the spot where the body of Catherine Eddowes was discovered, at 1.44 a.m. on Sunday, 30 September 1888*

little more expansive. 'She was ripped up like a pig in the market,' he told the *Star*, '. . . I have been in the force a long while, but I never saw such a sight.' *The Daily News* carried his most detailed account:

> I came round [to Mitre Square] again at 1.45, and entering the square from Mitre Street, on the right-hand side, I turned sharp round to the right, and flashing my light, I saw the body in front of me. The clothes were pushed right up to her breast, and the stomach was laid bare, with a dreadful gash from the pit of the stomach to the breast. On examining the body I found the entrails cut out and laid round the throat, which had an awful gash in it, extending from ear to ear. In fact, the head was nearly severed from the body. Blood was everywhere to be seen. It was difficult

to discern the injuries to the face for the quantity of blood which covered it . . . The murderer had inserted the knife just under the left eye, and, drawing it under the nose, cut the nose completely from the face, at the same time inflicting a dreadful gash down the right cheek to the angle of the jawbone. The nose was laid over on the cheek. A more dreadful sight I never saw; it quite knocked me over.

PC Watkins at once ran across the square to Kearley & Tongue's. Finding the door ajar, he pushed it open and hailed the watchman. Inside George Morris was sweeping the steps down towards the door. As he remembered it, the door behind him was knocked or pushed and he turned round, opened it wide and discovered the constable. 'For God's sake, mate,' gasped Watkins, 'come to my assistance.' Morris was a Metropolitan Police pensioner himself. Getting his lamp, he followed Watkins outside. 'What's the matter?' he demanded. 'Oh dear,' replied Watkins, 'there's another woman cut up to pieces!'

Watkins showed Morris the body and then, mounting guard over it, sent him off to bring more help. The watchman dashed out into Mitre Street and then into Aldgate. There, blowing his whistle furiously, he attracted the attention of Police Constables James Harvey and James Thomas Holland.

The news reached Inspector Edward Collard at Bishopsgate Street Police Station at 1.55. Telegraphing it to HQ and sending a constable for Dr Frederick Gordon Brown, the City Police Surgeon, at 17 Finsbury Circus, Collard set out for the scene of the crime. When he arrived, at two or three minutes past two, he found a doctor as well as several policemen already there. Dr George William Sequeira of 34 Jewry Street, Aldgate, had been called out by PC Holland at 1.55. He would tell the inquest later that the woman had not been dead for more than fifteen minutes before he saw her. But neither Sequeira nor anyone else touched the body until the arrival of Dr Gordon Brown.[8]

The dead woman lay on the pavement in the southern corner of Mitre Square, her head perhaps eighteen inches from the wall and railings that enclosed the rear and yard of Heydemann's premises, her feet towards the carriageway out of Mitre Street. A 'coal plate', immediately to the left of the victim's head, guarded the entrance to a coal chute, and an arched grating, to the left of her legs, admitted light to the cellar of the empty house next to Mr Taylor's shop. The back wall of the house was parallel with, and several feet to the left of, the body. A later generation would damn the spot as 'Jack the Ripper's Corner'. Back in 1888, on the eve of the murder, it had no such sinister repute but it was the darkest corner in the square and a favourite place for prostitutes and their clients. The lamp-post was sixty-five feet away. And, since the corner of Mr Taylor's shop interposed between the murder site and a 'lantern lamp' on the corner of the Walter Williams & Co. warehouse in Mitre Street, the spot was plunged into shadow after lighting-up time.

Dr Frederick Gordon Brown reached Mitre Square at about 2.18 and we are indebted to him for almost all of our scene-of-crime information. He found the dead woman stretched out upon her back. Her throat had been cut and her abdomen ripped open. Her intestines had been lifted out and placed over her right shoulder and one detached portion of intestine, perhaps two feet long, had been placed between her body and her left arm. Her face had been savagely mutilated. The doctor took careful notes and four days later made this report to the inquest:

> The body was on its back; the head turned to left shoulder; the arms by the side[s] of the body as if they had fallen there, both palms upwards, the fingers slightly bent; a thimble was lying off the finger on the right side; the clothes drawn up above the abdomen; the thighs were naked; left leg extended in a line with the body; the abdomen was exposed; right leg bent at the thigh and knee; the bonnet was at the back of the head; great disfigurement of face; the throat cut across; below the cut was a neckerchief; the upper part of the dress was pulled open a little way; the abdomen was all exposed; the intestines were drawn out to a large extent and placed over the right shoulder; they were smeared over with some feculent matter; a piece of about 2 feet was quite detached from the body and placed between the body and the left arm, apparently by design; the lobe and auricle of the right ear was cut obliquely through; there was a quantity of clotted blood on the pavement on the left side of the neck, round the shoulder and upper part of arm, and fluid blood coloured serum which had flowed under the neck to the right shoulder, the pavement sloping in that direction; body was quite warm; no death stiffening had taken place; she must have been dead most likely within the half hour; we looked for superficial bruises and saw none; no blood on the skin of the abdomen or secretion of any kind on the thighs; no

spurting of blood on the bricks or pavement around; no marks of blood below the middle of the body; several buttons were found in the clotted blood after the body was removed; there was no blood on the front of the clothes; there were no traces of recent connection.[9]

The appearance of the body in Mitre Square was also depicted by Brown in a pencil sketch he made upon the spot. This sketch, long lost, was one of several discovered in 1966 by Sam Hardy in the basement of the London Hospital and published by Professor Francis Camps in the *London Hospital Gazette*.[10]

There may be a slight discrepancy between the evidence of Dr Brown and that of Inspector Collard. Brown stated that several buttons were found in the clotted blood, which was near the left side of the neck and about the left shoulder and upper arm, and that a thimble was discovered near the right hand. In his inquest testimony, however, Collard swore that Sergeant Jones picked up three small black buttons ('generally used for women's boots'), a small metal button, a common metal thimble and a small mustard tin containing two pawn tickets, all by the left side of the body. The inspector recorded two other important details. The dead woman was not in possession of any money and there was no evidence that she had put up a struggle.

After he had examined it, Dr Brown gave instructions for the body to be taken to the City Mortuary in Golden Lane. By then Mitre Square had become the centre of a frantic police investigation. In 1888, as now, the City of London had its own police force, responsible to the corporation. Its Commissioner, Sir James Fraser, was on leave at the end of September and, in any case, ripe for retirement. So the search for the Mitre Square killer was directed by Major (late Lieutenant Colonel Sir) Henry Smith, the Acting Commissioner, and Inspector James McWilliam, head of the City Detective Department.

On the night of the murder Smith was roused from his bed at Cloak Lane Police Station. He recalled that awakening vividly in his memoirs, published in 1910:

The night of Saturday, September 29, found me tossing about in my bed at Cloak Lane Station, close to the river and adjoining

Southwark Bridge. There was a railway goods depot in front, and a furrier's premises behind my rooms; the lane was cause-wayed, heavy vans were going constantly in and out, and the sickening smell from the furrier's skins was always present. You could not open the windows, and to sleep was an impossibility. Suddenly the bell at my head rang violently. 'What is it?' I asked, putting my ear to the tube. 'Another murder, sir, this time in the City.' Jumping up, I was dressed and in the street in a couple of minutes. A hansom – to me a detestable vehicle – was at the door, and into it I jumped, as time was of the utmost consequence. This invention of the devil claims to be safe. It is neither safe nor pleasant ... Licensed to carry two, it did not take me long to discover that a 15-stone Superinten-dent inside with me, and three detectives hanging on behind, added neither to its comfort nor to its safety. Although we rolled like a 'seventy-four' in a gale, we got to our destination – Mitre Square – without an upset, where I found a small group of my men standing round the mutilated remains of a woman.[11]

When Inspector McWilliam heard the news he went first to the City Detective Office at 26 Old Jewry. Arriving at 3.45, he wired the news to Scotland Yard and then set out for Mitre Square via Bishopsgate Street Police Station. Major Smith, Inspector Collard, Detective Superintendent Alfred Foster and others of his colleagues were already at the scene when he reached the square.

Although the previous murders had all taken place within White-chapel and Spitalfields, the City Police had by no means remained complacent. The Tabram and Nichols murders in August had caused Smith to instruct his detective department to employ extra men in plain clothes to patrol the eastern fringes of the City, maintain a close watch on prostitutes and account for every man and woman seen out together after dark. In his memoirs the major claimed to have employed nearly one third of his total force upon such duties and fondly pictured them sitting on doorsteps, smoking pipes, loafing about pubs and gossiping with all and sundry in the September sunshine. 'It was subversive of discipline,' he conceded, 'but I had them well supervised by senior officers.'[12] At the very moment that the hapless woman in Mitre Square was being murdered and mutilated, indeed, three City detectives – Outram, Halse and Marriott – were searching the passages of houses only a few streets away. At about 1.58, when they received tidings of the murder, these detectives were on the corner of Houndsditch and Aldgate High Street.[13]

Tragically the elaborate precautions taken by the City Police proved insufficient to save the woman found dead in Mitre Square. Major Smith was undoubtedly galled at the failure of his strategy. But he was also beginning to understand something of the ruthless efficiency of the man he was up against. In no crime was this demonstrated more clearly than in this killing in the City.

The murderer had passed through Mitre Square like some invisible phantom. PC Watkins, whose beat took in the square, found it deserted at about 1.30. On returning, just fourteen or fifteen minutes later, he discovered the body but even then saw no one and heard nothing suspicious as he entered the square. Watkins entered and left Mitre Square by Mitre Street. At about 1.41 or 1.42 another patrolling constable, PC James Harvey 964, reached (but did not, apparently, enter) Mitre Square from the opposite direction – through Duke Street and Church Passage. This was several minutes before Watkins found the body but yet, as Harvey assured the inquest, 'I saw no one [and] I heard no cry or noise.' A third City policeman, PC Pearce, actually lived in Mitre Square. From the window of their house at No. 3 he and his wife might have witnessed the murder but they both slept throughout the entire incident. George Morris, the watchman at Kearley & Tongue's offices, had been a Metropolitan Police constable. When alerted to the atrocity by Watkins he was working only about two yards inside Kearley & Tongue's front door and the door itself had been ajar for perhaps two minutes. According to a statement he made in the *Star*, Morris 'had gone to the front door to look out into the square two moments before Watkins called to him.' Notwithstanding all which he, too, knew nothing of what had occurred. Finally there was George Clapp, the caretaker who slept at the back of Heydemann's, overlooking the murder site. 'During the night I heard no sound or any noise of any kind,' Clapp told the coroner. Indeed, he had not learned of the murder until between five and six the next morning and by then the Mitre Square victim was lying in Golden Lane Mortuary.[14]

In less than fifteen minutes, then, the murderer inveigled his victim into Mitre Square, killed her, mutilated her and made good his escape, taking – as it would soon transpire – the woman's left kidney and womb with him, all virtually under the noses of four serving or ex-policemen!

George Morris, at least, made no excuse. 'The strangest part of the whole thing,' he explained to the press later in the day, 'is that I heard no sound. As a rule I can hear the footstep of the policeman as he passes by every quarter of an hour, so the woman could not have uttered any cry without my detecting it. It was only last night I made the remark to some policemen that I wished the butcher would come round Mitre Square, and I would soon give him a doing, and here, to be sure, he has come, and I was perfectly ignorant of it.'15

Having failed to prevent the murder the City Police moved swiftly to apprehend the murderer before he could go to ground or leave the district. It was at best a long chance for there was every possibility that the killer escaped across the City boundary within the ten minutes it took for the news of the Mitre Square tragedy to reach Bishopsgate Street Police Station. No one could be absolutely certain, however, that the Mitre Square and Whitechapel murderers were one and the same man. And even if he was it was by no means out of the question that he operated out of a base in the City.

The earliest detectives on the scene were Detective Sergeant Robert Outram and Detective Constables Daniel Halse and Edward Marriott. They had been searching the passages of houses in the neighbourhood and were on the corner of Houndsditch and Aldgate High Street when, at about two minutes to two, they first received intimation that their presence was needed in Mitre Square. When they got there and realized that a murder had been committed they set out at once in different directions to look for suspects. In the light of subsequent events the proceedings of one of the three – Daniel Halse – are important. He described them at the inquest: 'I gave instructions to have the neighbourhood searched and every man examined. I went by Middlesex Street into Wentworth Street, where I stopped 2 men who gave satisfactory accounts of themselves. I came through Goulston Street at 20 past 2 and then went back to Mitre Square.' Inspector McWilliam, upon his arrival at the square, also ordered immediate searches of neighbouring streets and lodging houses. Several men were stopped and searched but without any tangible result.16

By three in the morning two major murder investigations were thus going on simultaneously, one based upon Berner Street and in the hands of the Metropolitan Police, the other centred upon Mitre Square and the responsibility of the City force. But the night had still one more surprise in store for the embattled officers. For at 2.55 a

Metropolitan Police constable made a discovery that switched the centre of attention once more, this time back from Mitre Square to Whitechapel.

PC Alfred Long 254A had been temporarily drafted from A Division (Westminster) to serve in Whitechapel. There, on duty in Goulston Street at about 2.55, he found a piece of a woman's apron, wet with blood, lying in the entry leading to the staircase of Nos. 108–119 Wentworth Model Dwellings. The constable immediately started to cast about for other signs of blood. There were none. But on the right-hand side of the open doorway to the entry, just above the apron, he saw something else. Written in white chalk on the fascia of black bricks edging the doorway were the words:

> The Juwes are
> The men That
> Will not
> be Blamed
> for nothing.

Long made no inquiries of the tenants in the building but he did search the staircases. He found no traces of blood or recent footmarks. Then, leaving the constable from the adjoining beat to guard the writing and observe anyone leaving or entering the premises, he took the piece of bloodstained apron and handed it in to the duty inspector at Commercial Street Police Station. When he arrived at Commercial Street it was about 3.05 or 3.10 a.m.[17]

Soon there were City as well as Metropolitan officers gathering at Wentworth Model Dwellings. The precise sequence of events is imperfectly documented but a report of Long's discoveries seems to have reached the City Police in Mitre Square and Detective Constables Halse and Hunt evidently went to the Metropolitan station at Leman Street to make inquiries. From there they were directed to Goulston Street. Having ascertained the situation at Wentworth Model Dwellings, Halse stayed to guard the chalked message while Hunt returned to Mitre Square to report and receive further instructions. When Hunt got back to the square he found that Inspector McWilliam had arrived. McWilliam listened to Hunt's report. Then he gave instructions for the chalk message to be photographed and ordered Hunt, in the meantime, to return to Wentworth Model Dwellings and assist Halse in making a search of the tenements there.[18]

The search was duly executed. As Halse later apprised the coroner, 'when Hunt returned an enquiry was made at every tenement of the building but we could gain no tidings of anyone going in likely to be the murderer.' But no photographs of the chalk message would be taken. For, in what was to prove his most controversial intervention in the Whitechapel investigations, Sir Charles Warren ordered the writing to be wiped away before a photographer arrived.

To Sir Charles alone is generally attributed the decision to obliterate the writing. He made the final decision and unhesitatingly accepted full responsibility for it but contemporary documents make it quite plain that it originated in a proposal of Superintendent Thomas Arnold of H Division. The news from Berner Street brought Warren to Commercial and Leman Street police stations in the early hours of 30 September. When he arrived at Leman Street, shortly before five, Arnold briefed him on the two murders and the discoveries in Goulston Street. The superintendent proposed that the writing be obliterated. Indeed he had already sent an inspector to Wentworth Model Dwellings with a sponge and instructions to await his arrival. But Warren considered it 'desirable that I should decide this matter myself, as it was one involving so great a responsibility whether any action was taken or not', and decided to call at Goulston Street on his way to Berner Street.

Why should Superintendent Arnold, in whose division four out of the six murders had been committed, advocate the destruction of an important clue? And why should Warren, whom the public would hold directly responsible for any failure to catch the murderer, entertain such a proposal for a moment? For more than a century Warren has been mocked and vilified over this matter and it is high time that he and Arnold were allowed to speak for themselves. Their cases are set out in reports for the Home Office dated 6 November 1888.[19]

First, Superintendent Arnold:

. . . knowing that, in consequence of a suspicion having fallen upon a Jew named John Pizer alias 'Leather Apron' having committed a murder in Hanbury Street a short time previously, a strong feeling existed against the Jews generally, and as the building upon which the writing was found was situated in the midst of a locality inhabited principally by that sect, I was apprehensive that if the writing were left it would be the means of causing a

riot and therefore considered it desirable that it should be removed
... Had only a portion of the writing been removed the context
would have remained.'

Arnold's dilemma on the night of the double murder is thus laid
bare. He appreciated the possibility that the writing might yield a clue.
But he also remembered the anti-semitic outburst that had disgraced
Whitechapel after Dark Annie's murder. And he dreaded what the
consequences might be in the morning if the chalk message, with its
overt incrimination of the Jews, became public property at a time
when the East End was reeling with the shock of two new murders.

As Sir Charles was being driven to Goulston Street he would have
been pondering Arnold's proposal. He was not obliged to accept it,
of course, but the superintendent knew far more about conditions
in Whitechapel than he did and Warren would have accorded his
opinion very great weight. Sir Charles' report takes up the story:

I . . . went down to Goulston Street . . . before going to the scene
of the murder: it was just getting light, the public would be in the
streets in a few minutes, in a neighbourhood very much crowded
on Sunday mornings by Jewish vendors and Christian purchasers
from all parts of London.

There were several police around the spot when I arrived, both
Metropolitan and City.

The writing was on the jamb of the open archway or doorway
visible to anybody in the street and could not be covered up without
danger of the covering being torn off at once.

A discussion took place whether the writing could be left
covered up or otherwise or whether any portion of it could be
left for an hour until it could be photographed; but after taking
into consideration the excited state of the population in London
generally at the time, the strong feeling which had been excited
against the Jews, and the fact that in a short time there would be
a large concourse of the people in the streets, and having before
me the report that if it was left there the house was likely to be
wrecked (in which from my own observation I entirely concurred)
I considered it desirable to obliterate the writing at once, having
taken a copy . . .

I do not hesitate myself to say that if that writing had been
left there would have been an onslaught upon the Jews, property
would have been wrecked, and lives would probably have been

lost; and I was much gratified with the promptitude with which Superintendent Arnold was prepared to act in the matter if I had not been there.

When Warren decided to obliterate the writing only Daniel Halse, the City detective, protested. He wanted it to remain, at least until Major Smith had seen it, and suggested a compromise in which only the top line ('The Juwes are') would be rubbed out. But it was getting light, the area was already beginning to come to life with costermongers preparing for the Petticoat Lane market, and in Metropolitan Police territory Warren's word was final. According to Constable Long, who was present, the chalk message was wiped off at about 5.30.[20]

There was still the piece of bloodstained apron that Long had found in the entry beneath the writing. It had been surrendered to Dr Phillips. Inspector McWilliam was at Golden Lane Mortuary when it was compared to the apron worn by the Mitre Square victim. About one half of the dead woman's apron had been severed by a clean cut. And the piece retrieved by Long fitted exactly. Dr Brown's testimony on the apron, part of his inquest deposition of 4 October, leaves no room for doubt that after murdering the woman in Mitre Square the killer escaped across the City boundary into Whitechapel: 'My attention was called to the apron [found on the body]. It was the corner of the apron with a string attached. The blood spots were of recent origin. I have seen a portion of an apron produced by Dr Phillips and stated to have been found in Goulston Street ... I fitted the piece of apron which had a new piece of material on it which had been evidently sewn on to the piece I have, the seams of the borders of the two actually corresponding. Some blood and apparently faecal matter was found on the portion found in Goulston Street.'[21]

The escape had been almost as remarkable as the murder. Major Smith's well-known description, however, is quite erroneous. 'There is no man living,' he wrote in 1910, 'who knows as much of those murders as I do; and before going farther I must admit that, though within five minutes of the perpetrator one night, and with a very fair description of him besides, he completely beat me and every police officer in London; and I have no more idea now where he lived than I had twenty years ago.' There is, unfortunately, no known occasion on which the major was within five minutes of the killer. He did visit

Mitre Square. But the earliest senior police officer on the scene of the crime was Inspector Collard and even he was eighteen or nineteen minutes behind PC Watkins' discovery of the body. It seems likely that Smith would also have visited the Goulston Street site although there is no actual record of it. If he did the visit undoubtedly occurred after 5.30, when the chalk message was removed. The only possible justification for Smith's curious claim to have been 'within five minutes' of the murderer lies, therefore, in just two sentences of his reminiscences: 'In Dorset Street, with extraordinary audacity, he [the murderer] washed them [his hands] at a sink up a close, not more than six yards from the street. I arrived there in time to see the bloodstained water.' This episode, however, cannot be corroborated from any other source. Furthermore, even if Smith's recollection of it was accurate there was no way of knowing that the bloodstained water in Dorset Street had any connection with the murders. Smith's claim to have been armed with a 'very fair description' of the killer is equally misleading. As we will discover, the City Police did find a witness – Joseph Lawende, a commercial traveller – who may have seen the Mitre Square murderer, but his evidence was turned up by Inspector Collard's subsequent house-to-house inquiries in the area and was not available on the night of the double killing.[22]

The murderer's escape was remarkable nonetheless. It would have been less so had he fled into Whitechapel immediately after the Mitre Square atrocity, before the City Police had been alerted, but this does not seem to have been the case. PC Long, whose beat embraced Goulston Street, patrolled it at about 2.20. Although he passed the spot where he would afterwards find the apron he was positive that it had not been there then. And Daniel Halse, who passed by the same spot at about the same time in pursuit of the criminal, also failed to notice anything. They might have missed it, of course, but if their testimony is to be depended upon the apron was deposited at Wentworth Model Dwellings some time between 2.20 and 2.55, as much as thirty-six to seventy-one minutes after Watkins discovered the body in Mitre Square. The murderer could have reached Goulston Street in five minutes from the square so where he was, and what he was doing, during the intervening time is a mystery. Whatever the cause of his delay, the killer evidently slipped unseen out of the City at a time when its officers had already become active in his pursuit and, again unseen, into a Whitechapel already alerted by the Berner Street murder. Not only that, but he paused long enough in Goulston Street to leave a calling card!

In his memoirs Major Smith concluded his account of the double murder thus: 'I wandered round my station-houses, hoping I might find someone brought in, and finally got to bed at 6 a.m., after a very harassing night, completely defeated.' Inspector McWilliam, in a report for the Home Office, tells how he visited the City Mortuary and then returned to the Detective Office and wired the Mitre Square victim's description to all divisions and to the Metropolitan Police. 'Additional officers had then arrived,' he wrote, 'and they were sent out in various directions to make enquiry.' To no purpose. And Sir Charles? From Goulston Street he drove to the site of the murder in Dutfield's Yard, and from there, with Superintendent Arnold, to the City Police headquarters in Old Jewry. There, at about seven, he explained his reasons for ordering the obliteration of the writing at Wentworth Model Dwellings. If he anticipated support for his decision, however, he was disappointed. McWilliam thought that he had made a mistake and told him so. And Warren's action rankled with Major Smith so much that, twenty-two years later, the major could still write of it as a 'fatal mistake', an 'unpardonable blunder.'[23]

When the sun rose on Sunday, 30 September, the new day thus found the police baffled and bickering. Nothing was as apparent as their defeat.

10

Long Liz

THE BERNER STREET VICTIM, like Martha Tabram and Annie Chapman before her, had been killed within the jurisdiction of the Metropolitan Police's H Division. At 1.25 a.m. on Sunday, 30 September, a telegram bearing the news of the tragedy reached Detective Inspector Edmund Reid at Commercial Street Police Station. Twenty minutes later he was at the scene of the crime. Chief Inspector West, Inspector Pinhorn and several sergeants and constables were already there. Doctors Blackwell and Phillips were with the body.

The police did what they could. Dutfield's Yard and the adjoining buildings were thoroughly searched several times. And a crowd of twenty-eight bystanders that had been shut in the yard by PC Lamb were detained. Some of them were tenants of the cottages in the yard, some members of the International Working Men's Club, others merely passers-by drawn to the scene by the promise of excitement. They were interrogated, their names and addresses taken and their pockets searched. Then, before they were allowed to go, the doctors inspected their hands and clothes for traces of blood. These activities yielded no clue whatsoever to the mystery. Later in the day, acting under instructions from Inspector Abberline, detectives were extending the scope of their investigations to the extent of house-to-house inquiries in Berner Street.

Reid, in the meantime, had set about the task of identifying the victim. At St George's Mortuary, where the body had been taken at about 4.30 a.m., he examined the dead woman and made careful notes upon her appearance. Her age, he guessed, might be about forty-two. She was five feet two inches in height. Her hair was dark-brown and curly, her complexion pale. Reid lifted an eyelid. Her eyes were light grey. Parting her lips, he discovered that her upper front teeth were missing. The woman's clothes consisted of a long black jacket trimmed with black fur, an old black skirt, a dark-brown velvet bodice, two light serge petticoats, a white chemise, a pair of white stockings, a pair of side-spring boots and a black crape bonnet. The jacket was decorated by a single red rose, backed by a maidenhair fern.

The inspector found nothing among the victim's belongings that offered any clue to her identity. Her jacket pocket contained but two pocket handkerchiefs, a thimble and a piece of wool on a card. The description, however, was communicated by wire to all police stations.[1]

Identifying the dead woman and unravelling something of her history proved no straightforward task. Almost immediately police inquiries were bedevilled by the intrusion of Mrs Mary Malcolm. Mrs Malcolm was the wife of a tailor and lived at 50 Eagle Street, Red Lion Square, Holborn. On Monday, 1 October, she identified the body as that of her sister, Mrs Elizabeth Watts.

Mrs Malcolm had a very strange story to tell. She said that her sister, who lived in East End lodging houses, had been in the habit of coming to her for assistance for the past five years. They met every Saturday afternoon at four, at the corner of Chancery Lane, and Mrs Malcolm always gave her sister two shillings for her lodgings. But on Saturday, 29 September, the day before the murder, Mrs Watts did not come. Mary, who waited in vain from half past three to five, was troubled. Her sister had not missed a meeting for nearly three years. At twenty minutes past one the next morning Mrs Malcolm was lying in bed. It was then that she had a presentiment that some disaster had befallen her sister: 'About 1.20 on Sunday morning I was lying on my bed when I felt a kind of pressure on my breast, and then I felt three kisses on my cheek. I also heard the kisses, and they were quite distinct.' When, later in the day, she heard that another murder had been committed about that time, it seemed to Mrs Malcolm that her worst fears had been confirmed. She walked into Whitechapel, made inquiries at a police station and was directed to St George's Mortuary.

On Tuesday, 2 October, Mrs Malcolm assured the inquest that

the deceased was undoubtedly Elizabeth Watts. She also gave her sister a very dubious character indeed. Her husband had sent her back to her mother because he had caught her misbehaving with a porter. She had once left a naked baby, the product of an illicit affair with a policeman, on Mrs Malcolm's doorstep. And she had been several times taken into custody for being drunk and disorderly. The coroner asked Mrs Malcolm what her sister did for a livelihood. She replied curtly: 'I had my doubts.' Notwithstanding all this, Mary was apparently genuinely distressed by the loss of her sister. One newspaper commented that she seemed 'deeply affected' as she gave her evidence. Upon several occasions during the examination she burst into tears.

The police can hardly have been impressed by Mary Malcolm's fanciful tale of a presentiment. The credibility of her evidence, furthermore, was seriously undermined by her vacillation at the mortuary. When she first saw the body on the Sunday she could not identify it. Before the coroner, she gave various explanations of her failure. At one point she ascribed it to the fact that she saw the body in gaslight, between nine and ten at night. At another she said that she had been unsure because the body did not exhibit a crippled foot. Mrs Watts, she stated, had 'a hollowness in her right foot, caused by its being run over.' Whatever, on Monday she came back to the mortuary, twice, and this time she made a positive identification. Not, be it noted, because she recognized her sister in the dead woman's face but from a small black mark on one of her legs. It was, she explained, an adder bite. As children they had been rolling down a hill when an adder had bitten Mary on the left hand and her sister on the leg.

Neither the police nor the coroner were happy with Mary Malcolm's identification. And their misgivings were eventually vindicated when the real Elizabeth Watts, now Mrs Elizabeth Stokes, turned up, with an appropriately crippled foot, alive if not well. Married to a brickmaker and living at 5 Charles Street, Tottenham, Mrs Stokes said that she had not seen her sister Mary for years. On 23 October she inveighed bitterly against Mrs Malcolm at the inquest. 'Her evidence was infamy and lies,' she cried heatedly, 'and I am sorry that I have a sister who can tell such dreadful falsehoods.' By then, of course, Mary Malcolm had wasted a great deal of police time.[2]

Despite such distractions the detectives did succeed in establishing the true identity of the victim. She was a Swedish woman named

Elizabeth Stride and her last address had been a common lodging house at 32 Flower and Dean Street. But no one, not even Michael Kidney, with whom she had lived for three years, seemed to know much of her past beyond what she herself had told them. And therein the police encountered another difficulty – for Elizabeth Stride had been gifted with an imagination every bit as lively as that of Mrs Malcolm.

Her principal fantasy was inspired by the loss of the *Princess Alice* in 1878. This tragedy, described by *The Times* as 'one of the most fearful disasters of modern times', has now been almost entirely forgotten. On 3 September 1878 a pleasure steamer, *Princess Alice*, collided in the Thames with a steam collier, *Bywell Castle*, and sank with the loss of between 600 and 700 lives. Elizabeth Stride gave out that her husband and two of her children had been drowned in the *Princess Alice*. She had saved herself by climbing a rope. But during that frantic scramble for life a man clambering up the rope ahead of her had slipped and acciden- tally kicked her in the face, knocking out her front teeth and stoving in the whole or part of the roof of her mouth. Elizabeth seems to have told this story to anyone who would listen – to Sven Olsson, clerk of the Swedish Church in Prince's Square, to Michael Kidney, the waterside labourer who lived with her, to Elizabeth Tanner and Thomas Bates, the deputy and watch- man respectively of the lodging house at 32 Flower and Dean Street, to Charles Preston, a fellow lodger there, and doubtless to many another lost to record. Yet there was not a word of truth in it.

The story was dismissed by a Greenwich correspondent of the *Daily News*:

Mr C. J. Carttar, late coroner for West Kent, held an inquiry, extending over six weeks, on the bodies of 527 persons drowned by the disaster, at the Town Hall, Woolwich, the majority of whom were identified, and caused an alphabetical list of those identified, above 500, to be made by his clerk. An inspection of the list, which is in the possession of Mr E. A. Carttar, the present coroner, and son of the late coroner, does not disclose the name of Stride. Whole families were drowned, but the only instance of a father and two children being drowned where the children were under the age of 12 years was in the case of an accountant named Bell, aged 38, his two sons being aged respectively 10 and 7 years. It is true that Mr Lewis, the Essex coroner, held inquests on a few of the bodies cast ashore in Essex, but it is extremely improbable that the three bodies of Mr Stride and his two children were cast ashore on that side of the river, or that they were all driven out to sea and lost.[3]

Wynne Baxter, the coroner at the Stride inquest, also pointed out that although a subscription had been raised to assist the bereaved relatives of the *Princess Alice* dead no person by the name of Stride ever applied for relief from the fund. Elizabeth's upper front teeth were missing. But as for her assertion that the roof of her mouth had been injured during the disaster, that was easily disproved. On 5 October Dr Phillips, who had examined the mouth of the dead woman specifically to verify this point, reported to the inquest that he could not find 'any injury to or absence of any part of either the hard or the soft palate.'[4]

The truth, when Inspector Reid unearthed it, turned out to be a dull substitute for Elizabeth's colourful tale. John Thomas Stride, her husband, survived the *Princess Alice* disaster by six years. He died in 1884, an impoverished resident of the Poplar Union Workhouse. It is probable, although we cannot know, that Elizabeth concocted her story to conceal a failed marriage and to elicit sympathy from the Swedish Church or such others as she dared approach for assistance.

Disregarding the red herrings and piecing together what the police discovered in 1888 and what subsequent researchers have been able to learn since, we can now reconstruct the broad outline of Elizabeth Stride's life accurately.[5]

Her maiden name was Elisabeth Gustafsdotter. The daughter of Gustaf Ericsson, a farmer, and his wife Beata Carlsdotter, she was born on 27 November 1843 in the parish of Torslanda, north of Gothenburg. Their farm was called Stora (meaning Big) Tumlehed. On 14 October 1860, when Elizabeth was nearly seventeen, she took out a certificate of altered residence from the parish of Torslanda and moved to that of Carl Johan in Gothenburg. She found work there as a domestic in the service of Lars Fredrik Olofsson, a workman, but soon moved on, taking out a new certificate to the Cathedral parish in Gothenburg on 2 February 1862. Elizabeth still gave her occupation as that of a domestic but this time her place of work is not known.

In March 1865 the police of Gothenburg registered her as a prostitute. Subsequent register entries tell us that she was a girl of slight build with brown hair, blue eyes, a straight nose and an oval face, that in October 1865 she was living in Philgaten in Östra Haga, a suburb of Gothenburg, and that she was twice treated in the special hospital, Kurhuset, for venereal diseases. On 21 April 1865 Elizabeth gave birth to a still-born girl. Nearly a year later, on 7 February 1866, she took out a new certificate of altered residence from the Cathedral parish to the Swedish parish in London. The certificate states that she could read tolerably well but possessed only a poor understanding of the Bible and catechism.[6]

Why did Elizabeth come to England? According to Michael Kidney's inquest deposition, she told him at one time that she first came to see the country and at another that she had come in the service of a family. This is not good evidence but it is the best we have and there is possibly some truth in both of Elizabeth's explanations. Certainly they are not incompatible. Kidney understood, moreover, that at one time she was in domestic service with a gentleman living near Hyde Park.

On 10 July 1866 she was registered as an unmarried woman at the Swedish Church in Prince's Square, St George-in-the East. Three years later she married. The bridegroom was a carpenter named John Thomas Stride and the service was performed by William Powell in the parish church of St Giles-in-the Fields on 7 March 1869. Elizabeth is described on the marriage certificate as Elizabeth Gustifson, spinster, the daughter of Augustus Gustifson, labourer. At the time of the marriage Stride was living at 21 Munster Street, Regent's Park, and Elizabeth at 67 Gower Street.

Almost nothing is known about their marriage. Elizabeth later told Michael Kidney that she had borne nine children but this statement has never been corroborated. However, we do know that when Walter Stride, John's nephew, last saw the couple, soon after the marriage, they were ensconced in East India Dock Road, Poplar. And Kelly's trade directory for 1870 lists John Thomas Stride as the keeper of a coffee room in Upper North Street, Poplar. In 1872 his business moved to 178 Poplar High Street and there it remained until taken over by John Dale in 1875.

At some point Elizabeth's marriage broke down. We cannot tell why or when. But at the inquest Sven Olsson, clerk of the Swedish Church, recalled that 'she told me about the time the *Princess Alice* went down that her husband was drowned in that vessel.' She was then in 'very poor' circumstances and about that time Olsson gave her some assistance. Indeed, he believed that the Church had assisted her even before they had heard of the death of her husband. Now in 1878 John Stride was very much alive. The fact that Elizabeth was accepting charity and giving out that he was dead, however, most strongly suggests that the couple had separated. The other evidence we have supports such a conclusion. On 21 March 1877 Elizabeth was an inmate of the Poplar Workhouse. From 28 December 1881 to 4 January 1882 she was treated in the Whitechapel Infirmary for bronchitis. Discharged from the infirmary, she went straight into the workhouse. Then, from 1882, she lodged on and off at a common lodging house at 32 Flower and Dean Street. This was still two years before John Stride's death. He died in the Sick Asylum at Bromley on 24 October 1884. The cause of death is given on the death certificate as 'morbus cordis' (heart disease).

Elizabeth spent her last three years with a waterside labourer named Michael Kidney. Their address is of some import. For press versions of Kidney's inquest testimony give it as 38 Dorset Street and this has led some writers, most notably Stephen Knight, to suppose a connection between Elizabeth Stride and two other victims, Annie Chapman and Mary Jane Kelly, who lived in Dorset Street. But Kidney was misreported. In a statement to the Central News he explained that he lived with Elizabeth 'at 35 Devonshire Street down to five months ago, when they moved to No. 36 in the same street.' That Devonshire Street, close to the river where Kidney worked, was the correct address is substantiated by other evidence. In May 1886, when applying for relief from the Swedish Church, Elizabeth gave her address as Devonshire Street, Commercial Road, and Catherine Lane, who lodged with Elizabeth at 32 Flower and Dean Street in 1888, also heard her say that she had once lived in Devonshire Street.[7] On Elizabeth herself Kidney's inquest testimony cannot be said to be very revealing, but he did say that she was in the habit of occasionally going away on her own: 'During the three years I have known her she has been away from me about five months altogether . . . It was drink that made her go . . . She always came back again. I think she liked me better than any other man.'

From 1882 Elizabeth was an occasional lodger at 32 Flower and Dean Street. She seems to have been generally well-liked there and was known affectionately as 'Long Liz'. Elizabeth Tanner, the deputy, remembered her as a quiet, sober woman. And a Central News reporter, after interviewing her lodging house cronies, gave her a similar character: 'According to her associates, she was of calm temperament, rarely quarrelling with anyone; in fact, she was so good-natured that she would 'do a good turn for anyone'. Her occupation was that of a charwoman.'[8] Notwithstanding such golden opinions Elizabeth was well known at Thames Magistrates' Court. In the two years before her death she appeared there frequently for being drunk and disorderly, sometimes with obscene language.

Unless her funds were being squandered on drink Long Liz may only have been an occasional prostitute. This was certainly the view of Thomas Bates, the watchman at No. 32. 'Lor' bless you,' he told one reporter, 'when she could get no work she had to do the best she could for her living, but a neater and a cleaner woman never lived!' Kidney gave her money and she sometimes earned a little by sewing or charring. Elizabeth Tanner saw her frequently during the last three months. 'She told me,' Mrs Tanner deposed at the inquest, 'that she was at work among the Jews.' If all else failed Elizabeth could and did throw herself upon the charity of the Swedish Church. We know from its records that she applied for and received financial assistance from them on 20 and 23 May 1886 and on 15 and 20 September 1888.

The movements of Elizabeth Stride during the week before her death are obscure. Catherine Lane said that she turned up at 32 Flower and Dean Street on Thursday, 27 September, saying that she had had words with the man she had been living with. The man, Michael Kidney, told a different story. He said that he had last seen Elizabeth in Commercial Street on the Tuesday. At that time they were on friendly terms and when he got home after work he fully expected her to be there. But although she had been home she had gone out again and returned but once – in his absence the next day – to collect a few belongings. This story of a sudden and unexplained departure does not ring true. It is very likely that there was a quarrel. There had been others. In April 1887 Elizabeth had charged Kidney with assault but had then failed to appear at Thames Magistrates' Court to prosecute.[9] Kidney was obviously anxious to deny a new argument with his paramour lest he be suspected of her murder but there is little reason to doubt his statement that he did not see her after Tuesday. Mrs Tanner and

Catherine Lane testified that Elizabeth arrived at their lodging house on Thursday. They seem, however, to have been mistaken. Thomas Bates, the watchman, said she arrived on the Tuesday and, besides, we have evidence from a most unexpected witness that Elizabeth was at No. 32 at least as early as Wednesday, 26 September.

Dr Thomas Barnardo, in a letter to the *Times*, said that on that day he had visited No. 32 in order to elicit from the residents their opinions upon a scheme he had devised 'by which children at all events could be saved from the contamination of the common lodging houses and the streets.' Talking to them in the kitchen, he found the women and girls 'thoroughly frightened' by the recent murders. One poor creature, who had apparently been drinking, cried bitterly: 'We're all up to no good, and no one cares what becomes of us. Perhaps some of us will be killed next!' They were prophetic words indeed, for Barnardo later viewed the remains of Elizabeth Stride at the mortuary. 'I at once recognized her,' he wrote, 'as one of those who stood around me in the kitchen of the common lodging house on the occasion of my visit last Wednesday week.'[10]

According to Mrs Tanner, the deputy, Elizabeth spent the nights of Thursday and Friday at her house. On Saturday morning she cleaned two rooms and Mrs Tanner paid her sixpence. The last time the deputy saw her alive was at about 6.30 on Saturday evening. They drank together at the Queen's Head in Commercial Street and then walked back to the lodging house. Elizabeth went into the kitchen. Mrs Tanner, who went to another part of the house, did not see her again until she was called upon to identify her body.

At least two lodgers saw Elizabeth in the kitchen between six and seven. Charles Preston, a barber, noticed that she was dressed to go out. She asked him to lend her his clothes brush but he had mislaid it. At that time there was no flower in her jacket. The charwoman Catherine Lane saw Elizabeth leave the kitchen. She remembered that Elizabeth had given her a large piece of green velvet to keep for her until she came back. 'I know deceased had sixpence when she left,' said Mrs Lane. 'She showed it to me, stating that the deputy had given it to her.'

Elizabeth did not say where she was going. Nor did she intimate when she might be back. It is possible that she intended to return to the lodging house for the night. Admittedly she had not paid Mrs Tanner for a bed on Saturday night but, as Charles Preston pointed out, the lodgers sometimes did not pay their money until just before going to bed.

Inquiries into the background of a murder victim are usually productive of some clue pointing to the identity of the killer. This is because in the majority of cases murderer and victim are known to each other. By the fifth Whitechapel investigation, however, it must have become apparent that this type of information was not going to elucidate this particular series of crimes. Chief Inspector Swanson, writing his summary report on the Stride murder, did not deem what the police had learned about the victim's past even worthy of recapitulation. 'It may be shortly stated,' he noted gloomily, 'that the inquiry into her history did not disclose the slightest pretext for a motive on behalf of friends or associates or anybody who had known her.'[11]

The post-mortem examination commenced on 1 October at St George's Mortuary.[12] In several respects public criticism during and after the Chapman inquiry seems to have forced the police to sharpen up their procedures. Medical men, for example, had lamented the lack of a second medical opinion at the inquiry. It is perhaps significant then that two surgeons – Phillips and Blackwell – conducted the autopsy upon the body of Elizabeth Stride. Blackwell consented to perform the dissection while Phillips took notes. For part of the time Dr Reigate and Blackwell's assistant, Edward Johnston, were also present. In this case, too, the body was stripped by the doctors themselves.

They found a long gash in Stride's throat. Dr Phillips described it for the benefit of the inquest on 3 October:

Cut on neck; taking it from left to right there is a clean cut incision 6 inches in length, incision commencing two and a half inches in a straight line below the angle of the jaw. Three-quarters of an inch over undivided muscle then becoming deeper, about an inch dividing sheath and the vessels, ascending a little, and then grazing the muscle outside the cartilages on the left side of the neck, the cut being very clean, but indicating a slight direction downwards through resistance of the denser tissue and cartilages. The carotid artery on the left side, and the other vessels contained in the sheath were all cut through save the posterior portion of the carotid to about a line or [of?] 1–12th of an inch in extent, which prevented the separation of the upper and lower portion of the artery. The cut through the tissues on the right side of the cartilages are more superficially cut, and the cut tails off to about two inches below the right angle of the jaw. It is evident that the haemorrhage, which probably will be found to be the cause of death, was caused through the partial severance of the left carotid artery.

There were no other cuts, no signs of gagging, no marks about the head and neck to indicate strangulation. An abrasion that Phillips at first thought he could detect on the right side of the neck, below the angle of the jaw, proved to be nothing of the kind. When it was washed the mark disappeared and the skin was found to be uninjured. There were, however, bluish discolourations over both shoulders. They were under the collar-bones and in front of the chest. These were neither bruises nor abrasions but pressure marks, apparently caused by the pressure of two hands upon the shoulders. One point will be of some interest to us later on. The lower lobe of the left ear was torn, as if by the forcible removal or wearing through of an ear-ring, but this was an old wound, now thoroughly healed.

The doctor agreed that the cause of death had been haemorrhage resulting from the partial severance of the left carotid artery and the division of the windpipe.

We have a few comments from Dr Blackwell on the murderer's technique. On the day of the crime he told the press that 'it does not follow that the murderer would be bespattered with blood, for as he is sufficiently cunning in other things he could contrive to avoid coming in contact with the blood by reaching well forward.' Two days later he told the inquest that he thought the killer had probably caught hold of Stride's silk scarf, which was found tight and knotted, and had pulled her backwards before cutting her throat. The throat had not been cut while she was standing up: 'the throat might have been cut as she was falling, or when she was on the ground. The blood would have spurted about if the act had been committed while she was standing up.'

On 5 October Dr Phillips gave the inquiry his reconstruction of what had occurred. It was his contention that the murderer had seized his victim by the shoulders and placed her on the ground. From a position on her right side he had then cut her throat from left to right. This injury might have been inflicted in just two seconds. The murderer would not necessarily have been bloodstained because 'the commencement of the wound and the injury to the vessels would be away from him, and the stream of blood – for stream it was – would be directed away from him, and towards the gutter in the yard.'

A single incision in the neck provided little basis, of course, for pronouncements upon the degree of anatomical knowledge displayed by the killer. But both doctors seem to have believed at least that he knew what he was doing. Interviewed by the press, Blackwell spoke of a man 'who is accustomed to use a heavy knife.' And the injury to the left carotid artery prompted Phillips to remark at the inquest that 'in this case, as in some others, there seems to have been some knowledge where to cut the throat to cause a fatal result.'

The doctors also gave evidence relating to a knife that had been found on a doorstep in Whitechapel Road on Monday morning. It was the type of instrument commonly used in chandler shops and known as a slicing knife. The blade was long – perhaps nine or ten inches – and rounded at the tip. Blackwell and Phillips agreed that although the knife could conceivably have inflicted the injury to Elizabeth Stride it was most unlikely to have been the murder weapon. 'It appears to me,' Blackwell told the coroner, 'that a murderer, in using a round-pointed instrument, would seriously handicap himself, as he would be only able to use it in one particular way.' Phillips conceded that there was nothing to indicate that the killer had employed a sharp-pointed weapon. But, taking into account the relative positions of the murderer, the victim and the incision, he considered it improbable that such a long-bladed knife as that found in Whitechapel Road had been used. In his opinion a short knife, like a shoemaker's well ground down, could have made the cut.

By contrast with the previous murders the killing of Elizabeth Stride produced a bumper crop of witnesses who claimed to have seen the victim in company with a man shortly before her death. Two of them, PC William Smith 452H and Israel Schwartz, came forward with what appeared to be vital information.

PC Smith's beat, a long, circular one that took him 25-30 minutes to patrol, embraced Berner Street. He was there at 12.30 or 12.35 on the morning of the murder and passed a man and a woman standing talking on the pavement, a few yards away from where the body was later discovered but on the opposite side of the street. The woman was wearing a red rose in her coat. PC Smith saw her face and subsequently identified the body as that of the same woman. The man was about five feet seven or eight inches tall and had a 'respectable' appearance. Smith did not take much notice of his face. However, he later described him as about twenty-eight years old, of dark complexion, with a small dark moustache. He wore a hard felt deerstalker hat of dark colour, a white collar and tie, and a black diagonal cutaway coat, and he carried in one hand a parcel wrapped up in newspaper. It was about eighteen inches long and six to eight inches broad. Both the man and the woman appeared to be sober but the constable did not overhear any of their conversation.[13]

PC Smith was a good witness. As a policeman on duty he was probably more observant than most and although a relatively young man (twenty-six) had notched up more than five years' experience in the force. The testimony of the second witness, Israel Schwartz, is possibly of even greater significance. Alone of the witnesses called forth by this terrible series of crimes, Schwartz may actually have seen a murder taking place. More than that, with its possible implication of two men, his evidence cautions us against embracing too readily the conventional wisdom that the killings were the work of a lone psychopath.

Schwartz volunteered his information at Leman Street Police Station on the evening of Sunday, 30 September. No copy of the original statement has survived. Its substance, however, has been preserved for us in Chief Inspector Swanson's synthesis of the Stride evidence, written on 19 October:

12.45 a.m. 30th. Israel Schwartz of 22 Helen [i.e. Ellen] Street, Backchurch Lane, stated that at that hour on turning into Berner St from Commercial Road & had got as far as the gateway where the murder was committed he saw a man stop & speak to a woman, who was standing in the gateway. The man tried to pull the woman into the street, but he turned her round &

threw her down on the footway & the woman screamed three times, but not very loudly. On crossing to the opposite side of the street, he saw a second man standing lighting his pipe. The man who threw the woman down called out apparently to the man on the opposite side of the road 'Lipski' & then Schwartz walked away, but finding that he was followed by the second man he ran as far as the railway arch but the man did not follow so far.

Schwartz cannot say whether the two men were together or known to each other. Upon being taken to the Mortuary Schwartz identified the body as that of the woman he had seen & he thus describes the first man who threw the woman down: – age about 30, height 5 ft. 5 in., complexion fair, hair dark, small brown moustache, full face, broad shouldered; dress, dark jacket & trousers, black cap with peak, had nothing in his hands.

Second man, age 35, height 5 ft. 11 in., complexion fresh, hair light brown, moustache brown; dress, dark overcoat, old black hard felt hat wide brim, had a clay pipe in his hand.[14]

The police obviously took Schwartz seriously. They circulated his description of the first man on the front page of *The Police Gazette* on 19 October. And Swanson, as he tells us in his summary report on the Stride murder, even preferred Schwartz's testimony to that of PC Smith, if only because his sighting was closer to the time of the murder: 'If Schwartz is to be believed, and the police report of his statement casts no doubt upon it, it follows if they [Smith and Schwartz] are describing different men that the man Schwartz saw & described is the more probable of the two to be the murderer, for a quarter of an hour afterwards the body is found murdered.' Why, then, did the police not produce Schwartz as a witness at the inquest? Unfortunately we have no information that can answer that question. A possible explanation is that, as in the case of the writing in Goulston Street, they deliberately suppressed his evidence because it seemed to implicate the Jews, but there are others. Perhaps they considered his testimony so important that they wished to keep the details secret. Perhaps Schwartz, for reasons best known to himself, did not want to appear. Did he, like Pearly Poll, absent himself from his lodgings? Or, quite simply, did he fall ill? We can speculate, but we do not know.

If the police hoped to enshroud Schwartz in secrecy their intentions were almost immediately thwarted by one of the *Star*'s newshounds. On 1 October, just one day after the murder, this paper put out its own version of the story:

Information which may be important was given to the Leman Street police late yesterday afternoon by an Hungarian concerning this murder. This foreigner was well dressed, and had the appearance of being in the theatrical line. He could not speak a word of English, but came to the police station accompanied by a friend, who acted as an interpreter. He gave his name and address, but the police have not disclosed them.

A *Star* man, however, got wind of his call, and ran him to earth in Backchurch Lane. The reporter's Hungarian was quite as imperfect as the foreigner's English, but an interpreter was at hand, and the man's story was retold just as he had given it to the police. It is, in fact, to the effect that he saw the whole thing.

It seems that he had gone out for the day, and his wife had expected to move, during his absence, from their lodgings in Berner Street to others in Backchurch Lane. When he came homewards about a quarter before one he first walked down Berner Street to see if his wife had moved. As he turned the corner from Commercial Road he noticed some distance in front of him a man walking as if partially intoxicated. He walked on behind him, and presently he noticed a woman standing in the entrance to the alley way where the body was afterwards found. The half-tipsy man halted and spoke to her. The Hungarian saw him put his hand on her shoulder and push her back into the passage, but, feeling rather timid of getting mixed up in quarrels, he crossed to the other side of the street. Before he had gone many yards, however, he heard the sound of a quarrel, and turned back to learn what was the matter, but just as he stepped from the kerb a second man came out of the doorway of the public house a few doors off, and shouting out some sort of warning to the man who was with the woman, rushed forward as if to attack the intruder. The Hungarian states positively that he saw a knife in this second man's hand, but he waited to see no more. He fled incontinently, to his new lodgings.

He described the man with the woman as about 30 years of age, rather stoutly built, and wearing a brown moustache. He was dressed respectably in dark clothes and felt hat. The man who came at him with a knife he also describes, but not in detail. He says he was taller than the other, but not so stout, and that his moustaches were red. Both men seem to belong to the same grade of society.

The police have arrested one man answering the description the Hungarian furnishes. This prisoner has not been charged, but is held for inquiries to be made. The truth of the man's statement is not wholly accepted.'[15]

House-to-house inquiries in the neighbourhood of Berner Street produced two other witnesses – William Marshall and James Brown. The sightings of these witnesses, unlike those by Smith and Schwartz, were neither mentioned by Swanson in his summary report nor published in the *Police Gazette*. Clearly the Yard did not accord them the same importance. But both men made depositions at the inquest and we have no reason to doubt their honesty.

William Marshall lived at 64 Berner Street and worked as a labourer in an indigo warehouse. At about 11.45 on Saturday night, loafing in his doorway, he saw a man and a woman standing talking quietly on the pavement, 'opposite No. 58 [Berner Street], between Fairclough Street and Boyd Street.' This was three doors to the north of Marshall's house. Marshall saw the man kissing the woman and overheard a snatch of their conversation. The man said: 'You would say anything but your prayers.' The woman laughed. They stood there for about ten minutes and then began to walk unhurriedly in Marshall's direction, passing him and continuing southwards towards Ellen Street. Neither of them appeared to be the worse for drink.

Marshall did not think that the woman was wearing a flower in her coat. The next day, however, he was taken to the mortuary and identified the deceased as the woman he had seen. At the inquest on 5 October Mr Baxter, the coroner, pressed him hard for a description of the man:

BAXTER: 'Did you notice how he was dressed?'
MARSHALL: 'In a black cutaway coat and dark trousers.'
BAXTER: 'Was he young or old?'
MARSHALL: 'Middle-aged he seemed to be.'
BAXTER: 'Was he wearing a hat?'
MARSHALL: 'No, a cap.'
BAXTER: 'What sort of a cap?'
MARSHALL: 'A round cap, with a small peak. It was something like what a sailor would wear.'

BAXTER: 'What height was he?'
MARSHALL: 'About 5 ft. 6 in.'
BAXTER: 'Was he thin or stout?'
MARSHALL: 'Rather stout.'
BAXTER: 'Did he look well dressed?'
MARSHALL: 'Decently dressed.'
BAXTER: 'What class of man did he appear to be?'
MARSHALL: 'I should say he was in business, and did nothing like hard [meaning manual] work.'
BAXTER: 'Not like a dock labourer?'
MARSHALL: 'No.'
BAXTER: 'Nor a sailor?'
MARSHALL: 'No.'
BAXTER: 'Nor a butcher?'
MARSHALL: 'No.'
BAXTER: 'A clerk?'
MARSHALL: 'He had more the appearance of a clerk.'
BAXTER: 'Is that the best suggestion you can make?'
MARSHALL: 'It is.'
BAXTER: 'You did not see his face. Had he any whiskers?'
MARSHALL: 'I cannot say. I do not think he had.'
BAXTER: 'Was he wearing gloves?'
MARSHALL: 'No.'
BAXTER: 'Was he carrying a stick or umbrella in his hands?'
MARSHALL: 'He had nothing in his hands that I am aware of.'
BAXTER: 'Different people talk in a different tone and in a different way. Did his voice give you the idea of a clerk?'
MARSHALL: 'Yes, he was mild speaking.'
BAXTER: 'Did he speak like an educated man?'
MARSHALL: 'I thought so.'[16]

Marshall's evidence is intriguing because the man he described was similar in appearance to those seen by PC Smith and Israel Schwatz. All three witnesses could easily have observed the same man. The value of the labourer's testimony, unfortunately, was reduced by his failure to get a good look at the man's face. Where the couple were first standing, by No. 58, it was too dark for Marshall to see the man's face distinctly. The nearest gas lamp, he explained, was 'at the corner, about twenty feet off.' Later, when the two set out in the direction of Ellen Street, they were walking towards Marshall and into the ambit of a lamp at the corner of

Boyd Street. But they walked in the middle of the road and, as they passed Marshall, the man was looking towards the woman: 'he [the man] was looking towards the woman, and had his arm round her neck.' Unquestionably the main objection to Marshall's evidence as far as the police were concerned, however, was the time of his sighting. It took place at about 11.45, one hour and fifteen minutes before the murder was discovered, and although Marshall's man might indeed have been the killer a prostitute like Elizabeth Stride could have accosted, or have been accosted by, several men in the ensuing hour.

The testimony of James Brown, a dock labourer, of 35 Fairclough Street, is more problematical. At about 12.45 on Sunday morning Brown was returning from a chandler's shop at the junction of Fairclough and Berner Streets to his home when he saw a man and a woman standing at the corner of the board school. The woman was facing the man and standing with her back to the wall. The man was bending over her, his arm resting on the wall above her head. As he passed them Brown heard the woman say: 'Not tonight, some other night.' The man's height was about five feet seven inches and he was wearing a dark overcoat, so long that it nearly came down to his heels. Brown did not think that either of the two were drunk.[17]

It will be noted that the Schwartz and Brown sightings were supposed to have occurred at the same time – 12.45 a.m. This means that one of the witnesses must have been mistaken in the time or that they had observed different people. The question of times will be considered later. Here it is enough to say that one if not both of the witnesses could certainly have been in error. Brown's timing, for example, does not seem to have been much more than intelligent guesswork. He arrived home that night at 12.10 a.m. and not long after that went to the chandler's to get something for his supper. He thought that he was there about three or four minutes but, as he admitted at the inquest, 'I did not look at any clock at the chandler's shop.' On his way home with his victuals he saw the couple by the school. And home again, he had nearly finished his supper when terrified cries of 'Murder!' and 'Police!' from the street first alerted him to the tragedy. It was Diemschutz and Kozebrodski pounding eastwards along Fairclough Street in futile quest of a policeman. Brown said that this had occurred about fifteen minutes after he had got back from the shop.

A mistake of minutes on the part of just one witness would

reconcile the statements of Schwartz and Brown on that score. But Brown's descriptions of the man and woman he saw raise grave doubts as to whether he can have been talking about the same people observed by William Marshall, PC Smith or Israel Schwartz.

Brown saw Elizabeth Stride's body at the mortuary. He was 'almost certain', he told the inquest, that this was the same woman he had seen by the school. One wonders. Elizabeth had been wearing dark clothes on the night of her death – a black jacket trimmed with black fur, a black skirt and a black crape bonnet. The only splash of colour about her had been that solitary red rose and maidenhair fern, prominently displayed on the breast of her jacket. PC Smith had seen them there at 12.35. But ten minutes later Brown missed these obvious items. 'Did you notice any flower in her dress?' queried the coroner. 'No,' replied Brown. And later he added: 'I saw nothing light in colour about either of them.'

Brown's description of the woman's companion is very vague indeed. He gave no details whatsoever about the man's face and if the suspect was wearing any headgear at all Brown did not see, or could not remember, anything of it. The few particulars the labourer did swear to accord ill with the statements of other witnesses. Perhaps the most distinctive feature of the man's appearance was a long, dark overcoat 'which came very nearly down to his heels.' This detail cannot possibly be reconciled with Marshall's talk of a small, black, cutaway coat, with Smith's description of a black diagonal cutaway coat, or with Schwartz's reference to a dark 'jacket'. The height of Brown's man – five feet seven inches – is consistent with the descriptions proffered by the other witnesses but the build is not. Brown's man was of average build. Schwartz, on the other hand, described Elizabeth's assailant as a broad-shouldered man. And William Marshall, who saw Elizabeth with a man at about 11.45, thought that he appeared 'rather stout'.[18]

At this date the truth can no longer be recovered. There remains, however, a distinct possibility that the labourer Brown did not see Elizabeth Stride. PC Smith told the inquest that very few prostitutes were accustomed to solicit in Berner Street. But there *was* a second couple in the vicinity at the time of the murder. Mrs Fanny Mortimer of 36 Berner Street saw them and mentioned them in a statement to the press on the day of the tragedy: 'A young man and his sweetheart were standing at the corner of the street, about 20 yards away, before and after the time the woman must have been murdered, but they told me they did not hear a sound.' What was evidently the same pair were alluded to again in a news report. 'A young girl had been standing in a bisecting thoroughfare not fifty yards from the spot where the body was found,' it ran. 'She had, she said, been standing there for about twenty minutes, talking with her sweetheart, but neither of them heard any unusual noises.'[19] The board school, at the corner of which Brown saw his couple, was at the junction of Berner and Fairclough Streets.

Before leaving the Berner Street murder we will need to consider some of the questions arising out of the evidence.

The time of the murder can be established with reasonable certainty. At about 12.40 Morris Eagle, passing over the spot where the body would later be found, noticed nothing. At one Louis Diemschutz discovered the body. All the indications are that it had not been there long. Edward Spooner, one of the early arrivals on the scene, distinctly saw blood still flowing from the wound in the dead woman's throat. By 1.16, when Dr Blackwell saw the body, the bleeding had stopped. Elizabeth's neck, chest and legs, however, were still quite warm and her face slightly so. Blackwell thought that she must have been murdered after 12.46 and possibly after 12.56. Elizabeth died, then, not long before Diemschutz's barrow clattered into the yard. Indeed, the steward's approach might well have disturbed the murderer at his grisly task.

The evidence we possess suggests that Dr Phillips' reconstruction of the murder was correct. He opined that the victim had been placed upon the ground and that her killer, working from a position on her right side, had then cut her throat from left to right. There is no doubt that Elizabeth's throat was cut while she was lying down for the wound to the left carotid artery and other vessels had bled out upon the ground a few inches to the left of her neck. From this pool, blood had flowed along the gutter towards the side door of the club. No other traces of blood were discovered except for a few stains on Elizabeth's right hand and wrist. Equally, the close proximity of the body to the club wall seems to preclude any possibility of the murderer working from a position on the victim's left. Elizabeth was found huddled up, her face, knees and feet close to the wall. Diemschutz told the inquest that the body was only about a foot from the wall, PC Lamb that her face was not more than five or six inches distant from it.

This reconstruction does, however, pose problems. We cannot

believe that Elizabeth would have voluntarily lain down in Dutfield's Yard. Earlier that evening there had been heavy rain and the passage between Nos. 40 and 42 had evidently been transformed into a muddy channel. Elizabeth's body was discovered lying on its left side and the left side of her head, hair and coat were well plastered with mud.[20] Dr Phillips, taking his cue from the pressure marks over Elizabeth's shoulders, reasoned that she had been seized by the shoulders and 'placed' on the ground. Since she was lying on her left side, head up the yard, one must presume that at the moment of the fatal attack she was facing the wall of the club and that the murderer then pressed her down to his left. But if Elizabeth was forced or thrown down, why were there no signs of a struggle? 'She looked as if she had been laid quietly down,' said PC Lamb. Why did she die still clutching her packet of cachous in her left hand? In the event of a struggle is it not likely that Elizabeth would have dropped these items, either to defend herself or as she flung her arms out to break her fall? Most puzzling of all, if Elizabeth was attacked and forced down, why did no one hear her cries? At the time Morris Eagle was singing upstairs in the International Working Men's Club. Despite the music, he felt that he would have heard a scream from the yard if there had been one. The windows were open but Eagle heard nothing. Downstairs, Mrs Diemschutz was busy about the kitchen and dining room. The day after the murder she told the press that although the side door of the club, close to the kitchen, had been half open, she had not heard anything suspicious whatsoever: 'I am positive I did not hear any screams or sound of any kind. Even the singing on the floor above would not have prevented me from hearing had there been any. In the yard itself all was as silent as the grave.' Mrs Mortimer of 36 Berner Street, standing at the door of her house 'nearly the whole time' between 12.30 and 1.00, heard no noise. And Diemschutz himself, trundling into the yard at one, noticed nothing suspicious at all until his pony shied.[21]

We just do not know enough to resolve these riddles. A possibility that Elizabeth was drunk or had been drugged is apparently dismissed by Dr Phillips' testimony that there was no trace of malt liquor in her stomach and 'no perceptible trace of any anaesthetic or narcotic.'[22] In the Tabram, Nichols and Chapman cases clear signs of strangulation indicated a likely explanation for the absence of cries but these do not seem to have been present in Elizabeth's case. As Mr Baxter pointed out in his summing-up, 'there were no marks of gagging, no bruises on the face.'[23] Elizabeth's scarf, the bow of which Dr Blackwell found turned to the left and pulled very tight, may present us with a solution. Blackwell thought that the murderer had pulled his victim backwards by catching hold of her scarf. Even this promising circumstance, however, has but a doubtful bearing on the problem. The killer, for example, could have jerked the scarf tight when his victim was already on the ground, simply in order to expose her throat to the knife. None of this speculation precludes the possibility that Elizabeth did call out and that her cries were lost in the strains of the singing from the club.

The Berner Street evidence raises an even more intriguing question. Was Elizabeth's killer responsible for any of the other Whitechapel murders? Since 1965 it has been fashionable for Ripperologists to name Elizabeth Stride as the third victim of Jack the Ripper, Nichols and Chapman being seen as the first and second. In fact, there is a very strong case for regarding Martha Tabram as the first Ripper victim and at least a plausible one for discounting Elizabeth Stride altogether.

On the face of it the arguments for excluding Elizabeth from the reckoning are formidable. There were, as we have noted, no obvious signs of strangulation. There were no abdominal mutilations. Although Elizabeth's throat had been cut there was, as Dr Phillips told the inquest, a 'very great dissimilarity' between that wound and those which had nearly decapitated Dark Annie. Annie's throat had been severed all round down to the vertebral column. Furthermore, the vertebral bones had been marked by two sharp cuts and there had been an evident attempt to separate the bones. The cut in Elizabeth Stride's throat was neither as deep nor as extensive. It left the vessels on the right side of the neck untouched and the left carotid artery only partially severed. 'The wound was inflicted,' said Dr Phillips at one point, 'by drawing the knife across the throat.'[24] The doctor's testimony on the weapon used in the Stride murder also cautions us against any glib association of this crime with the slaying of Annie Chapman. In his judgement Annie's injuries had been inflicted with a knife having a blade at least six to eight inches long. He did not believe, however, that a long-bladed weapon had been used on Elizabeth Stride. In this case a short knife, like those employed by shoemakers, could have been the murder weapon.

Because of these factors there must always be an element of doubt about the Stride case. On the evidence as it now stands, however, it seems probable that she was indeed struck down by the slayer of Polly Nichols and Annie Chapman. The case for discounting Elizabeth as a Ripper victim is not as weighty as it first appears. The differences between her injuries and those inflicted upon Polly Nichols and Annie Chapman do not oblige us to take the view that she was slain by another hand. The less extensive wounding of the throat and total absence of abdominal mutilations in her case may only mean that her killer was disturbed and scared off before he could complete his task. Again, the fact that Annie Chapman and Elizabeth Stride may have been mutilated with different knives proves nothing. Even if we knew for certain that a single killer was responsible for all the murders we would not be entitled to assume that he invariably used the same weapon. In this context it is nevertheless worthy of note that Dr Llewellyn, who carried out the post-mortem examination of Polly Nichols, thought that her injuries had been inflicted, not with an exceptionally long-bladed knife, but with a pointed one that had a stout back, perhaps a cork-cutter's or shoemaker's knife. This appears to have been just such a weapon as was later used upon Elizabeth Stride. In many respects the Stride murder was very like its predecessors. Tabram, Nichols, Chapman and Stride were all prostitutes, silently slaughtered in dark or unfrequented byways of the East End. More than that, in the last three cases the victims had all had their throats cut from left to right while they were lying upon the ground.

Dutfield's Yard was a cul-de-sac. A visitor had only two means of egress: he might, like William West, pass through the premises of the International Working Men's Club, or go through the main gateway. Whether the murderer could have availed himself of the first option is doubtful for at 12.40 on the fatal night Morris Eagle had tried the club's street door and had found it locked, at least to someone on the outside. More probably the killer escaped through the main gates.

Mrs Mortimer, who was standing at the door of No. 36 for much of the time between 12.30 and 1.00, saw no one leave Dutfield's Yard before one, and Louis Diemschutz, approaching the yard at one, noticed no one running away. The murderer, then, could still have been there when the steward turned into the gateway. If so he retreated farther into the yard and awaited his chance, slipping out when Diemschutz dashed into the club to raise the alarm or vanishing into the crowd of onlookers that gathered in minutes around the body. It was not until after 1.10, while Edward Johnston,

Dr Blackwell's assistant, was examining the dead women, that PC Lamb closed the main gates.

Which route did the killer take from Berner Street? The answer to this question, curiously enough, may just be found in an uncorroborated newspaper report. For the day after the murder the *Star* printed this item: 'From two different sources we have the story that a man, when passing through Church Lane at about half past one, saw a man sitting on a doorstep and wiping his hands. As everyone is on the look-out for the murderer the man looked at the stranger with a certain amount of suspicion, whereupon he tried to conceal his face. He is described as a man who wore a short jacket and a sailor's hat.'[25]

Compare this description with those derived from Marshall and Schwartz. Marshall's man wore a small black cutaway (as opposed to a frock) coat and a round, peaked cap, 'something like what a sailor would wear.' And the man Schwartz saw attacking the woman was dressed in a dark jacket and trousers and a black cap with a peak. Compare it, too, with a description of the supposed Mitre Square murderer, procured by the City Police from a commercial traveller named Joseph Lawende. Lawende's suspect wore a loose pepper-and-salt jacket and a grey cloth cap with a peak and he had the 'appearance of a sailor.' The fascinating thing about the Church Lane report is that it appeared before any of these other descriptions had been published. Only a version of PC Smith's description, with references to a black diagonal coat and hard felt hat, was then in circulation.[26] Furthermore, Church Lane might logically have been traversed by anyone walking from Berner Street to Mitre Square.

Driven out of Dutfield's Yard, the killer's first priority would have been to put distance between himself and the scene of his crime. If he turned northwards along Berner Street he would probably not have felt safe until he reached Commercial Road. But then a new danger would have presented itself. He could not remain in Commercial Road, let alone hazard Whitechapel High Street, with bloodstained hands, for both thoroughfares were well-lighted and populous on Saturday nights, even after one. Church Lane, a relatively secluded byway running from Commercial Road to the High Street, could thus have proved a tempting haven to clean up. This done, he would have passed from thence into Whitechapel High Street, the main artery into Aldgate. If the Church Lane report did describe a genuine sighting of the murderer, however, the estimated time (about 1.30) was at least ten minutes too late.

Hitherto this report has been neglected by students of the Ripper crimes. There are, indeed, good reasons for passing it by now. After all, the two independent sources alluded to in the *Star* cannot be identified and no substantiation for the story exists. Nevertheless, it is difficult to escape the feeling that this was a rare occasion upon which the press turned up a clue the police would have done well to follow up.

Finally, what can we learn from the evidence of the eyewitnesses who claimed to have seen Elizabeth with a man? The man seen by William Marshall at 11.45 was very like those observed by PC Smith at 12.35 and Israel Schwartz at 12.45. All three descriptions might well refer to one and the same man. If they do, and if he was the killer, he exposed himself to great risk in hanging about the area with his intended victim for over an hour. More, Dutfield's Yard was a hazardous spot in which to commit murder. Although gloomy it was frequented at night by the inhabitants of the cottages as well as by members of the club, and it was a cul-de-sac which could and very nearly did become a trap in the event of discovery.

The most important witness, if he was telling the truth, was Schwartz. As the closest in time to the discovery of the body he was the most likely to have seen the murderer. Above and beyond that, however, his evidence challenged the popular assumptions then being made about this series of crimes. For, on the face of it, he incriminated not one man, but two, not Jews but Gentiles.

Before considering the implications of Schwartz's evidence we had best remind ourselves that there is a real possibility that his sighting had nothing to do with the murders. Admittedly he claimed to have seen an assault near the entry of Dutfield's Yard at 12.45, about the time Elizabeth must have been attacked, but most witnesses to the events of that night were vague in the matter of times. Diemschutz seems to have given the inquest something better than a guess when he said that he returned home at one, noticing the time 'at the baker's shop at the corner of Berner Street.'[27] And Dr Blackwell was presumably accurate when he swore that he was called out at 1.10 because he at least had a watch. But few of the other principal witnesses seem to have had any means of verifying the time. Even PC Lamb and Edward Johnston, Blackwell's assistant, admitted at the inquest that they did not carry watches. Edward Spooner, the horse-keeper whom Diemschutz brought back to the yard instead of a policeman, thought that he reached the scene of the crime at about 12.35, half an hour earlier than could have been the case, but then, as Spooner explained before the coroner, 'the only means I had of fixing the time was by the closing of the public houses.' Matthew Packer, a greengrocer of whom much more later, also used closing time at the pubs to estimate the time at which he had put up the shutters of his shop at 44 Berner Street. Similar imprecision is to be found in the depositions of witnesses at the inquest into the death of Catharine Eddowes, the woman murdered in Mitre Square on the same night. 'I can only speak with certainty as to time,' said PC Harvey, 'with regard to the post-office clock.'[28]

Schwartz's time, then, was not necessarily correct. Furthermore, altercations such as that he described seem to have been commonplace in the area. Baxter asked PC Lamb, whose beat in Commercial Road took him past the end of Berner Street, whether he had seen anything suspicious that night. The constable's reply is revealing: 'I did not at any time. There were squabbles and rows in the streets, but nothing more.'[29] Berner Street itself was the subject of conflicting testimony. PC Smith said that very few prostitutes were to be seen there. William West, Morris Eagle and Louis Diemschutz, stalwarts of the International Working Men's Club and hence doubtless anxious to dissociate it from all scandalous imputation, denied that the club yard was regularly used by prostitutes. Nevertheless, West did concede at the inquest that he had once seen a couple chatting by the yard gates and that he had sometimes noticed low men and women standing about and talking to each other in Fairclough Street close by. Some Berner Street residents, moreover, certainly did regard the club and its yard as a troublespot. 'I do not think the yard bears a very good character at night,' said Barnett Kentorrich of No. 38, 'but I do not interfere with any of the people about here. I know that the gate is not kept fastened.' The reaction of several residents to the alarm occasioned by the finding of the body is instructive. Charles Letchford of No. 30 told the press that he had taken no notice because 'disturbances are very frequent at the club and I thought it was only another row' and Mrs Mortimer of No. 36 similarly attributed the commotion to 'another row at the Socialists' Club close by.'[30]

If Schwartz was out just fifteen minutes in his reckoning, if the incident he saw took place, not at 12.45 but, say, at 12.30, then the significance of his statement is greatly reduced. We do not know that he was mistaken but it will always be on the cards that he was witness to nothing more than a street brawl.

Despite these reservations we have in Schwartz a witness – and a witness the police believed – who claimed to have seen a woman attacked at the time and place of a known murder. Not only that, but we have a witness who identified the dead woman as the victim of the attack he saw. His is crucial evidence and we cannot ignore it.

We may be wrong in thinking of Jack the Ripper as just one man. For Schwartz compels us to take very seriously the possibility that he was really two. The Hungarian certainly saw two men at the scene of the crime that night. Were they, in fact, confederates? Schwartz's impression at the time was that they were. In his statement to the police he said that the first man, the one attacking the woman, 'called out apparently to the man on the opposite side of the road "Lipski".' Schwartz then walked away but, 'finding that he was followed by the second man', started to run. He ran as far as the railway arch 'but the man did not follow so far.' Quite clearly Schwartz was under the impression that the murderer had alerted his accomplice to Schwartz's presence and that the accomplice, the second man, was seeing him off.

But a badly frightened man is not a good observer. Later, safe in the police station and under Abberline's patient cross-examination, Schwartz could not be absolutely certain that the two men had been acting together.

'Schwartz cannot say,' runs Swanson's digest of the original report, 'whether the two men were together or known to each other.' Schwartz's first impression may have been mistaken. Perhaps, like Schwartz, the second man was simply an innocent passer-by. And perhaps, like Schwartz, he took fright at what he was seeing and fled in the same direction. We do not know. However, to judge by the interview Schwartz later gave to the *Star*, the Hungarian remained true to his first instinct. The newspaper evidently dressed the story up to make it a more exciting read but the connection between the two men was reaffirmed. In this version the second man, perceiving Schwartz, called out a warning to the murderer and then rushed forward, knife in hand, 'as if to attack the intruder [i.e. Schwartz]'. Schwartz, once again, precipitately fled.

Schwartz's story is also quite strong evidence that the murderer was not a Jew. Since the Home Office made precisely the opposite deduction from it, though, this statement calls for explanation.

Schwartz thought at the time that when Stride's attacker shouted 'Lipski' he was addressing his accomplice across the road. Lipski was a familiar Jewish name throughout the East End because of the trial and execution of Israel Lipski, a Polish Jew, for the murder of Miriam Angel in 1887. The Home Office favoured the view, therefore, that the murderer probably had an accomplice named Lipski and that both were Jews.

On 24 October, in response to a call for 'a report of all the measures which have been taken for the detection of the perpetrator of the Whitechapel Murders and of the results', Warren forwarded to the Home Office copies of Chief Inspector Swanson's summary reports on the murders. In the margin of the Stride report, against the passage relating to Schwartz, Godfrey Lushington, Permanent Under-Secretary at the Home Office, wrote: 'The use of "Lipski" increases my belief that the murderer was a Jew.' And on 27 October Matthews himself minuted the papers: 'The statement of Schwartz that a man, who was in the company of Elizabeth Stride 15 minutes before she was found dead, & who threw her down, addressed a companion (?) as "Lipski" seems to furnish a clue which ought to be followed up. The number of "Lipskis" in Whitechapel must be limited. If one of them were identified by Schwartz it might lead to something of importance.'[31]

Abberline's own interpretation of Schwartz's observations, however, was very different. We owe its committal to paper to the Home Secretary's continued interest in the affair. Matthews' queries on Swanson's reports were transmitted to Warren on 29 October. 'It does not appear,' one of them ran, 'whether the man [murderer] used the word "Lipski" as a mere ejaculation, meaning in mockery "I am going to 'Lipski' the woman", or whether he was calling to a man across the road by his proper name. In the latter case . . . the murderer must have an acquaintance in Whitechapel named Lipski. Mr Matthews . . . will be glad if he can be furnished with a report as to any investigations made to trace the man "Lipski".'[32]

Abberline was consulted by his superiors for material with which to furnish a reply to this missive and his report, dated 1 November 1888, has survived. It reads in part:

I beg to report that since a Jew named Lipski was hanged for the murder of a Jewess in 1887 the name has very frequently been used by persons as a mere ejaculation by way of endeavouring to insult the Jew to whom it has been addressed, and as Schwartz has a strong Jewish appearance I am of opinion it was addressed to him as he stopped to look at the man he saw apparently illusing the deceased woman.

I questioned Israel Schwartz very closely at the time he made the statement as to whom the man addressed when he called Lipski, but he was unable to say.

There was only one other person to be seen in the street, and that was a man on the opposite side of the road in the act of lighting his pipe.

Schwartz being a foreigner and unable to speak English became alarmed and ran away. The man whom he saw lighting his pipe also ran in the same direction as himself, but whether this man was running after him or not he could not tell. He might have been alarmed the same as himself and ran away.

. . . Inquiries have also been made in the neighbourhood but no person named Lipski could be found.[33]

This report, marrying personal knowledge of the witness with an intimate understanding of conditions in Whitechapel, is such a document as only Abberline could have written, and as one of very few that enable us to see inside the head of this fine detective is quite fascinating. The inspector knew that the name Lipski had become an insult, spat in the faces of Jews in the East End, and he noted Schwartz's 'strong Jewish appearance'. His deduction, therefore, was that when Stride's attacker shouted 'Lipski!' he was not addressing an accomplice by name, as Lushington and Matthews both assumed, but directing an anti-semitic taunt at Schwartz himself. The import of Abberline's interpretation is clear – the murderer was probably an East Ender and almost certainly *not* a Jew.[34]

There is, though, a third possible interpretation of Schwartz's evidence. It is an attractive one because it preserves Schwartz's original feeling that 'Lipski' was shouted to an accomplice while, at the same time, suggesting a solution to other unexplained riddles of the 'double event'. Referring to accomplices by false names in front of witnesses was just as obvious a ploy to Victorian villains as it is to their counterparts today. So if the murderer *did* call an accomplice 'Lipski' it was perhaps because he intended Schwartz to *think* that this was the man's real name and that both he and the murderer were Jews. We may be dealing, then, with a deliberate subterfuge designed to incriminate the Jews, crude certainly, but good enough to hoodwink the Home Office and perhaps only one of several such ploys practised by the murderer that night. A plan to fix the blame on the Jews would explain, for example, why the murderer killed Elizabeth in Dutfield's Yard, by the door of the International Working Men's Educational Club, a club largely patronized by Jewish immigrants, and why, in order to accomplish that object, he might have been prepared to loiter about the street with his chosen victim for more than an hour, observing the movements of PC Smith and awaiting his chance. No other murder in the series took place to the south of the Aldgate-Whitechapel Road thoroughfare.

Such a design could explain, too, that cryptic message left in chalk in a doorway in Goulston Street, just above a piece of the Mitre Square victim's bloodstained apron: 'The Juwes are the men that will not be blamed for nothing.'

11

False Leads

No account of the Stride killing would be complete without reference to Matthew Packer and Mrs Mortimer. Both witnesses were, and indeed still are, commonly believed to have seen the murderer. And both, in their different ways, contributed immeasurably to the mythology surrounding Jack the Ripper.

Matthew Packer was a greengrocer and fruiterer, trading from a barrow and from his small shop at 44 Berner Street, two doors south of the International Working Men's Educational Club. Police records describe him only as an elderly man. The reporter who interviewed him for the *Evening News* said that he was quiet and intelligent, that he and his wife were 'both a little past the prime of life and . . . known as respectable hard-working people.'

The first detective to encounter Packer was Sergeant Stephen White of H Division, one of two officers detailed by Abberline on Sunday, 30 September, the day of the murder, to make house-to-house inquiries in Berner Street. We know that he was supplied with a special notebook in which to record his findings. This, alas, has disappeared. So our only record of White's first interview with Packer is contained in a report written by the sergeant on 4 October:

About 9 a.m. [30 September] I called at 44 Berner Street, and saw Matthew Packer, fruiterer in a small way of business. I asked him what time he closed his shop on the previous night. He replied 'Half past twelve, in consequence of the rain it was no good for me to keep open'. I asked him if he saw anything of a man or woman going into Dutfield's Yard, or saw anyone standing about the street about the time he was closing his shop. He replied 'No I saw no one standing about neither did I see anyone go up the yard. I never saw anything suspicious or heard the slightest noise. And knew nothing about the murder until I heard of it this morning.'

I also saw Mrs. Packer, Sarah Harrison and Harry Douglas residing in the same house but none of them could give the slightest information respecting the matter.[1]

If the police imagined that they had done with Packer they were very much mistaken. For by 2 October, just two days later, the greengrocer was telling a quite different story to Messrs Grand and Batchelor of 283 Strand, two private detectives in the employ of the Mile End Vigilance Committee. He now insisted that at about 11.45 on the night of the murder he had sold half a pound of black grapes to a man and a woman standing outside his shop in Berner Street and that this couple had afterwards loitered about the street for more than half an hour. 'The man,' said Packer, 'was middle-aged, perhaps 35 years; about five feet seven inches in height; was stout, square-built; wore a wideawake hat and dark clothes; had the appearance of a clerk; had a rough voice and a quick, sharp way of talking.'[2]

Further inquiries by Grand and Batchelor apparently tended to substantiate this story. Two sisters, Mrs Rosenfield and Miss Eva Harstein of 14 Berner Street, told them that early on the Sunday morning they had noticed a grape-stalk, stained with blood, in Dutfield's Yard, close to where the body had been found. Reasoning that the police could have washed the stalk down the drain when they cleaned up the yard, Grand and Batchelor then visited Dutfield's Yard to search the sink. There, amidst a heap of heterogeneous filth, they are said to have discovered a grape-stalk.

The *Evening News* got wind of this development. And on the evening of 3 October one of its reporters called at 44 Berner Street to hear the full story from the lips of the man 'who spoke to the murderer'. Packer's tale, as set forth in this interview, is worth recounting at length.

For most of Saturday, 29 September, Packer was out with his barrow. But he didn't do much business and, 'as the night came on wet', decided to go home and take his wife's place serving in the shop. At some time between 11.30 and midnight a man and a woman walked up Berner Street from the direction of Ellen Street and stopped outside his window to look at the fruit.

The man looked about 30–35 years of age, was of medium height and had rather a dark complexion. He wore a black coat and a black, soft, felt hat. 'He looked to me,' explained Packer, 'like a clerk or something of that sort. I am certain he wasn't what I should call a working man or anything like us folks that live around here.' His companion was middle-aged. She wore dark clothes and was carrying a white flower in her hand.

After the couple had stood there for about a minute the man stepped forward and said: 'I say, old man, how do you sell your grapes?'

'Sixpence a pound the black 'uns, sir,' replied Packer, 'and four pence a pound the white 'uns.'

The man turned to the woman. 'Which will you have, my dear, black or white? You shall have whichever you like best.' The woman chose the black. 'Give us half a pound of the black ones, then,' ordered the man. Packer thought that he sounded educated. He had 'a loud, sharp sort of voice, and a quick commanding way with him.'

There was no need for the couple to come into the shop. It had a half window in front and most of Packer's dealings were carried on through the lower part of the window case in which his fruit was exposed for sale. He put the grapes into a paper bag and handed them out to the man.

For a minute or two the man and woman stood near the entrance of Dutfield's Yard. Then they crossed the road and, for more than half an hour, stood across the way from the shop. 'Why,' Packer exclaimed to his wife, 'them people must be a couple o' fools to stand out there in the rain eating the grapes they bought here, when they might just as well have had shelter!' They were still there when the Packers went to bed. Packer couldn't remember exactly when that was but thought that it 'must have been past midnight a little bit, for the public houses were shut up.'[3]

The *Evening News* concluded its article with a sally at the police. 'Well, Mr Packer,' the reporter is made to observe, 'I suppose the police came at once to ask you and your wife what you knew about the affair, as soon as ever the body was discovered?'

'The police?' echoed Packer. 'No. THEY HAVEN'T ASKED ME A WORD ABOUT IT YET!!!' He then went on to explain that although a plain-clothes officer had come to the shop a day after the murder in order to look over the backyard no policeman had yet questioned him about what he might know of the tragedy.

When the *Evening News* story was published on 4 October the police were understandably bewildered. Inspector Moore immediately sent Sergeant White to talk to Packer again and to take him to the mortuary to see if he could recognize Elizabeth Stride. White's efforts, however, were consistently thwarted by the private detectives. First he went to Packer's shop but Mrs Packer told him that two detectives had already collected her husband and taken him to the mortuary. On his way there the sergeant met Packer, with one of his escorts, coming back.

'Where have you been?' asked White.

'This detective asked me to go to see if I could identify the woman,' said Packer.

'Have you done so?'

'Yes' replied Packer. 'I believe she bought some grapes at my shop about 12 o'clock on Saturday.'

Soon they were joined by the second detective. White then asked them what they were doing with Packer. They said that they were detectives and when the sergeant asked to see their authority added that they were private detectives. One of them produced a card from his pocket book but would not allow White to touch it. Eventually they 'induced' Packer to go away with them.

Later in the day White again visited Packer in his shop. But while he was talking with him the same two men drove up in a hansom cab. This time they said that they were taking Packer to Scotland Yard to see Sir Charles Warren and persuaded him to go off in the cab with them.[4] The antics of Grand and Batchelor, however frustrating for the police, were apparently well intended. Certainly they delivered Packer to Scotland Yard. There he was examined by Warren personally. The grocer's statement written in Sir Charles' hand, is dated 4 October:

On Sat. night [29 September] about 11 p.m., a young man from 25–30, about 5 [feet] 7 [inches], with long black coat buttoned up, soft felt hat, kind of Yankee hat, rather broad shoulders, rather quick in speaking, rough voice. I sold him ½ pound black grapes, 3d. A woman came up with him from Back Church end (the lower end of street). She was dressed in black frock & jacket, fur round bottom of jacket, a black crape bonnet, she was playing with a flower like a geranium white outside & red inside. I identify the woman at the St. George's Mortuary as the one I saw that night.

They passed by as though they were going up [to] Commercial Road, but instead of going up they crossed to the other side of the road to the Board School, & were there for about ½ an hour till I should say 11.30, talking to one another. I then shut up my shutters. Before they passed over opposite to my shop, they went near to the club for a few minutes apparently listening to the music. I saw no more of them after I shut up my shutters.

I put the man down as a young clerk. He had a frock coat on – no gloves. He was about 1½ inches or 2 or 3 inches – a little bit higher than she was.[5]

On 6 October the *Daily Telegraph* published a new Packer account. It contained a few more details about his suspect's appearance. He was described as a square-built man, about five feet seven inches tall and perhaps thirty years of age. His hair was black, his complexion dark, his face full and alert-looking. He had no moustache. Wearing a long black coat and a soft felt hat, the man struck Packer as being more like a clerk than a workman. He spoke in a quick, sharp manner. What distinguished the *Telegraph*'s article, however, was its attempt to go beyond words.

The journalist responsible for the article was J. Hall Richardson. 'In accordance with the general description furnished to the police by Packer and others,' he explained, 'a number of sketches were prepared, portraying men of different nationalities, ages and ranks of life.' The sketches had been submitted to Packer and – according to Richardson – he had unhesitatingly picked out a picture of a man without a moustache and wearing a soft felt or American hat as most resembling the man he had seen. His choice was one of two woodcut sketches published in the article under the caption: 'SKETCH PORTRAITS OF THE SUPPOSED MURDERER.'[6] The difficulty for the police in all this was that, for reasons we will presently notice, they were unhappy about the accuracy and relevance of Packer's evidence. Fearing, therefore, that Richardson's initiative would mislead rather than inform the public, they issued a notice in the *Police Gazette* disavowing the sketches as 'not authorized by Police.' And, at the same time, they published as a corrective the descriptions furnished by PC Smith, Israel Schwartz and Joseph Lawende, though suppressing the names of these witnesses.[7]

What value is to be placed on Packer's evidence? Perhaps he was telling the truth. Perhaps, when White questioned him on the morning of the murder, Packer had not yet made a connection in his mind between the couple who bought the grapes and the crime. Perhaps he did not do so until the next day, when the press carried statements alleging that grapes had been found in one of the dead woman's hands. Perhaps. Certainly, to judge by the number of latter-day Ripperologists who trawl up the grocer's story to sustain their own theories, his evidence is still very widely believed.

Assuming for the moment that Packer *was* an honest witness, how does his information fit in with that of the other witnesses? Well, his man was very like the one seen by James Brown at 12.45. Both Packer and Brown described a man of about five feet seven, wearing a long dark coat, standing with a woman by the board school. The only recorded difference between them – Packer's suspect is said to have been square-built and Brown's of average build – is less significant than the sum of the like factors. It is thus tempting to link these two and to speculate whether the differences between the reported times of the witnesses could have been produced by the obvious imprecision of both. However, in several respects (in the absence of a moustache and in the wearing of a long frock coat rather than a short/cutaway coat and of a wideawake, soft felt or Yankee hat rather than a peaked hat or cap) Packer's man is impossible to identify with those described by PC Smith and Israel Schwartz. An obvious explanation of this difficulty is that Stride got rid of the man with the long coat seen by Packer and Brown and accosted or was accosted by her murderer, the man in the peaked cap, almost immediately afterwards. Indeed, the words James Brown overheard testify to some kind of rejection of the man in the long coat by the woman. 'Not tonight,' she said, 'some other night.' The stumbling block to this tidy little reconstruction of events is William Marshall. For Marshall deposed to having seen Stride with a man strikingly similar to those described by Smith and Schwartz as early as 11.45. This raises once again the possibility that Packer and Brown may have seen a different couple altogether. We have already noted the presence in the vicinity of at least one other couple before and after the time of the murder.

Overwhelmingly, though, the available evidence suggests that Packer was not an honest witness.

There is a serious discrepancy between his narratives on times. According to the statement he made to Sir Charles Warren, he sold the grapes at about 11 o'clock and closed his shutters, leaving the couple standing by the school, at about 11.30. But the other accounts all place the whole episode an hour later. The time that the man and woman came to the shop is given by Grand and Batchelor as about 11.45, by the *Evening News* as between 11.30 and 12.00, by Sergeant White as about 12.00 and by Richardson as about 11.30. The couple were standing across the road for perhaps half an hour after that and were still there when Packer closed up and went to bed. Packer told White that he closed at 12.30 because of the rain. Grand and Batchelor understood that he had last seen the couple, as he was preparing to close, at 12.10 or 12.15, and that he had estimated the time 'by the fact that the public houses had been closed.' And the *Evening News* got the same story: 'I couldn't say exactly, but it must have been past midnight a little bit, for the public houses were shut up.' In all fairness it should be said that witnesses are characteristically vague on times and that, Warren apart, those given by Packer are broadly consistent. It is possible that the Commissioner simply misunderstood his informant.

More damaging is Packer's readiness to modify details in his story in order to accommodate fresh knowledge or movements in popular opinion. It is noticeable, for example, how Packer's suspect shed years during the course of the grocer's four narratives. In the statement procured by Grand and Batchelor the man was said to have been middle-aged, perhaps 35, and in the *Evening News* interview about 30–35. Packer told Warren, however, that the suspect was a young man, aged between 25 and 30. And Richardson understood, too, that the man's age was 'not more than thirty'. Inevitably one suspects that this rejuvenation of Packer's man had something to do with the release of PC Smith's description to the press. For the constable's account, describing a man aged 28, was being circulated in the newspapers from 1 October.[8]

Even more revealing is this extract from the *Evening News* interview:

'Did you observe anything peculiar about his voice or manner, as he spoke to you?'

'He spoke like an educated man, but he had a loud, sharp sort of voice, and a quick commanding way with him.'

'But did he speak like an Englishman or more in this style?' I asked, imitating as well as I could the Yankee twang.

'Yes, now that you mention it, there *was* a sound of that sort about it,' was the instantaneous reply.

The notion that an American might have been involved had been fostered by Baxter's story of the American seeking specimens of the uterus and by the alleged Americanisms of the first Jack the Ripper letter, to be discussed in a later chapter, and it is remarkable how easily Packer fell in with the reporter's suggestion. Packer's description of his suspect's headgear is also instructive in this context. He told Grand and Batchelor that the man was wearing a wideawake hat and the *Evening News* that it was a black, soft, felt hat. After the *News* interview Packer's terminology changed. Warren was told of a 'soft felt . . . kind of Yankee hat', Richardson of a soft felt or American hat.

Finally, there are definite suggestions in the Packer evidence that his story owed less to personal knowledge and observation than it did to contemporary press reports. Thus, in at least two instances, we can catch him out incorporating details from earlier newspaper accounts which were subsequently shown to be incorrect. One is the alleged colour of Elizabeth Stride's flower. On 2 October Edward Spooner told the inquest that he saw a red and white flower pinned to the dead woman's coat. This was an error for PC Smith, who saw Elizabeth at 12.35, later deposed to a red rose in her coat, and Inspector Reid, who examined the body specifically in order to compile a description, only inventoried a red rose and maidenhair fern. It is probable, then, that when Packer spoke of the woman carrying a white or white and red flower in her hand, his comment was inspired, not by actual observation, but by press reports of Spooner's testimony.

Even more important to the credibility of Packer's story are the grapes.

On Monday, 1 October, the *Daily News* carried statements by Louis Diemschutz, Isaac Kozebrodski and Fanny Mortimer, all alleging that the dead woman had been found clutching a packet of sweetmeats in one hand and a bunch of grapes in the other.[9] Now, a packet of cachous was most certainly discovered in Elizabeth's left hand. But the detail about the grapes appears to have been a baseless fiction. At the inquest the doctors were interrogated on this very point.

Dr Phillips deposed: 'Neither in the hands nor about the body of the deceased did I find any grapes, or connection with them. I am convinced that the deceased had not swallowed either the skin or seed of a grape within many hours of her death.' Dr Blackwell was equally emphatic:

'Did you perceive any grapes near the body in the yard?'

'No.'

'Did you hear any person say that they had seen grapes there?'

'I did not.'[10]

We do not know how the press conducted their interviews with Diemschutz, Kozebrodski and Mrs Mortimer but one of these witnesses – the only one summoned before the coroner – testified differently at the inquest. According to Louis Diemschutz's press statement, supposedly made on the day of the murder, Stride's hands 'were clenched, and when the doctor opened them I saw that she had been holding grapes in one hand and sweetmeats in the other.' The very next day, however, Baxter asked Diemschutz: 'Did you notice her hands?' And Diemschutz replied: 'I did not notice what position her hands were in.'[11]

It is very doubtful if any grapes were seen in Dutfield's Yard but the printing of such a falsehood could well have given Packer ideas.

We are left with the inescapable feeling that when Packer told Sergeant White that he had seen no one 'standing about' on the night of the murder he was speaking the truth and that his story of selling grapes to a strange couple was an afterthought, cobbled together with the aid of newspaper and local gossip. The Yard reached a similar conclusion for Chief Inspector Swanson, reporting on the matter later that month, wrote that Packer had 'unfortunately made different statements so that . . . any statement he made would be rendered almost valueless as evidence.'[12] This may be why he was never summoned to appear before the Stride inquest as a witness.

But why *should* Packer seek to deceive the police? It is possible that the fantasy was designed to enhance this modest grocer's status amongst his neighbours by providing him with a key role in the drama, by enrolling him in the company of the few who had 'seen the murderer'. A much more likely explanation, however, will be found in the sudden escalation in the scale of the reward money prompted by the double murder. On 30 September Packer told White that he had seen nothing suspicious. Two days later, when Grand and Batchelor were conducting their investigations, he had changed his mind. But in the interval fresh rewards, including one of £500 from the Corporation of London, had increased fivefold the total sum on offer for information leading to the arrest and conviction of the killer. The money probably provided the spur, the story about grapes being found in Elizabeth's dead hand, published on 1 October, the substance for Packer's tale. On the night of 1–2 October, lured by the rewards, amateur sleuths appeared in force on the streets of the East End. And the next day, sensing a new spirit abroad, the *Star* spoke of others 'who turn in descriptions on the chance of coming near enough the mark to claim a portion of the reward if the man should be caught, just as one buys a ticket in a lottery.'[13] This prescient columnist seems to have hit the nail right on the head. For by then there seems little doubt that Packer, too, had joined the gold rush.

Packer continued to regale the press with stories. On 27 October, while standing with his barrow at the junction of Greenfield Street and Commercial Road, he supposedly saw the murderer again. The man gave Packer 'a most vicious look' but, when the grocer sent someone to find a policeman, escaped by jumping on a tram bound for Blackwall. According to yet a third tale, a man who came to his shop on 13 November to buy rabbits told him that he believed his own cousin to be the murderer.[14] By this time, however, even the press offices had begun to weary of Packer and soon he slipped back into the obscurity from whence he came.

Unlike Matthew Packer, Mrs Fanny Mortimer was not a romancer. But unwittingly she bestowed upon the growing legend of the Whitechapel killer one of its most potent symbols. Mrs Mortimer lived at 36 Berner Street, two doors from the scene of the tragedy, and for most of the critical half hour between 12.30 and 1.00 on the fatal morning was standing at the door of her house. What she saw and heard has been greatly misrepresented by twentieth-century authors.

Walter Dew, writing in 1938, told his readers of a man, aged about 30, dressed in black and carrying a small, shiny black bag, whom Mrs Mortimer saw stealing furtively out of Dutfield's Yard just before Diemschutz's pony and cart turned into the gate. It was more than probable, wrote Dew dramatically, that she was 'the only person ever to see the Ripper in the vicinity of one of his crimes.' Twenty years later Donald McCormick quoted what purported to be the actual words of Mrs Mortimer's contemporary statement. This related how she heard a suspicious noise from the direction of the International Working Men's Educational Club: 'It wasn't like an argument, though there was something like a stifled cry, or an angry voice. Then there was a bump; it must have been the body falling . . . Before I could properly tell what it was I saw a young man carrying a black shiny bag, walking very fast down the street. He looked up at the club, then went round the corner by the Board School.'[15] Since Dew and McCormick are amongst the Ripperologists' favourite cribs it is scarcely surprising that Mrs Mortimer continues to figure in the literature as one of those likely to have seen Jack the Ripper. But the truth was very different.

Mrs Mortimer's original statement, made on the day of the murder, can be found in the *Daily News* of 1 October. It contains no references to stifled cries or the thuds of falling bodies. Indeed, she categorically states that until Diemschutz raised the alarm she had heard nothing. 'There was certainly no noise made,' she said, 'and I did not observe anyone enter the gates.' She did see a man with a black bag but her statement makes it quite clear that he came, not from Dutfield's Yard, but from Commercial Road: 'the only man whom I had seen pass through the street previously [before one] was a young man carrying a black shiny bag, who walked very fast down the street from the Commercial Road. He looked up at the club, and then went round the corner by the Board School . . . If a man had come out of the yard before one o'clock I must [i.e. would] have seen him.'

There is nothing here to suggest that the man with the black bag was anything other than an innocent passer-by. But a day or so after Mrs Mortimer had made her statement he voluntarily presented himself at Leman Street Police Station to clear himself of any possible suspicion. He was Leon Goldstein of 22 Christian Street, a member of the International Working Men's Club. He had left a coffee house in Spectacle Alley only a short time before Mrs Mortimer had seen him. And his bag had contained empty cigarette boxes.[16]

Goldstein must be dismissed from our investigation. Nevertheless, his brief appearance in the drama had consequences far more reaching than he or anyone else can have imagined. Mrs Mortimer's statement was widely broadcast in the press and soon everyone seemed to know that a man with a black bag had been seen near the scene of the Berner Street murder. Perhaps because it reinforced the view given currency by Dr Phillips at the Chapman inquest that the killer might be a doctor, the bag lodged in popular imagination.

So that, even today, in legend Jack the Ripper is as inseparable from his black bag as Davy Crockett from his coonskin cap or Long John Silver from his parrot.

12

'Don't Fear for Me!'

THE IDENTIFICATION OF the Mitre Square victim, lying dead in the city Mortuary, proved a simpler task for the City Police than that of Elizabeth Stride for their Metropolitan counterparts.

At first there seemed little enough to go on. The dead woman looked about forty. She was thin and about five feet in height. She had dark auburn hair and hazel eyes.

Her clothes were old and dirty. The main items were a black straw bonnet trimmed with green and black velvet and black beads; a neckerchief of red gauze silk; a black cloth jacket with imitation fur edging around the collar and fur edging around the sleeves; a dark-green chintz skirt, patterned in Michaelmas daisies and golden lilies, with three flounces; a man's white vest [i.e. waistcoat]; a brown linsey dress bodice with a black velvet collar and brown metal buttons down the front; a pair of brown ribbed stockings, mended at the feet in white; a pair of men's laced boots; and a piece of old white apron. She wore no drawers or stays but there were plenty of undergarments: a grey stuff petticoat, a very old dark-green alpaca skirt, a very old ragged blue skirt and a white calico chemise.

The quantity and condition of the woman's clothing, and the nature of her belongings, stamped her as a vagrant or, at best, a frequenter of common lodging houses. Her belongings consisted of a large white handkerchief, one blue striped bedticking pocket and two unbleached calico pockets, a white cotton pocket-handkerchief, twelve pieces of white rag, a piece of white coarse linen, a piece of blue and white shirting, two small blue bedticking bags, two short clay pipes, one tin box containing tea and another containing sugar, one piece of flannel and six pieces of soap, a small tooth comb, a white-handled table-knife, a metal tea-spoon, a red leather cigarette case with white metal fittings, an empty tin match-box, a piece of red flannel containing pins and needles, and a ball of hemp.[1]

An examination of the body and its effects yielded possible leads. There was a tattoo (the initials 'T.C.') in blue ink on the dead woman's left forearm. And there was the mustard tin picked up by Sergeant Jones from beside the body. It contained two pawntickets. One was for a man's flannel shirt, pledged in the name of Emily Burrell, 52 White's Row, on 31 August for 9d. The other was for a pair of men's boots, pledged in the name of Jane Kelly, 6 Dorset Street, on 28 September for 2s. 6d. Both items had been pledged at the shop of Joseph Jones, 31 Church Street, Spitalfields.[2] When the police tried to trace these women they discovered that the addresses given were fictitious. In White's Row, Spitalfields, there was no No. 52. And at 6 Dorset Street no one by the name of Jane Kelly was known to the occupants. But it was the publicity accorded these leads by the press that succeeded in identifying the dead woman. For on the evening of Tuesday, 2 October, a middle-aged labourer walked into Bishopsgate Street Police Station and said that he thought he knew her. His name was John Kelly.[3] The deceased, he said, was Kate Conway alias Kelly, a woman he had been living with for seven years at Cooney's lodging house at 55 Flower and Dean Street.

Kate's real name was Catharine Eddowes and in some ways she was the most likeable of all the murderer's victims. Mrs Eliza Gold, her married sister, spoke of her as a "regular jolly sort", and Frederick Wilkinson, the deputy at Cooney's, where Kate regularly stayed, knew her as a "very jolly woman, always singing." In 1888 friends in Kate's native Wolverhampton still remembered her. To them she was an "intelligent, scholarly woman, but of fiery temperament." Her history, quarried from contemporary records, is set down here in full for the first time.[4]

Kate's parents, George and Catharine (née Evans) Eddowes, were married at Bushbury, near Wolverhampton, on 13 August 1832. They were a young couple. George, a tinplate worker, was twenty-one, his bride only sixteen.[5] Catharine would bear George eleven children. The earliest were Alfred (born 1833 or 1834), Harriet (1834), Emma (1835), Eliza (1837) and Elizabeth (1838 or 1839).

In 1841, when the household was recorded in the national census, it was ensconced at Graisley Green, Wolverhampton, amidst a community of tinplate workers. And it was there, on 14 April 1842, that Kate was born. Her birth certificate renders her name Catharine, like that of her mother, but no matter. To her family she was known by the nickname 'Chick', to John Kelly and the friends of her later life simply as 'Kate'.

The early 1840s were years of prosperity for the tinplate industry in Wolverhampton. But despite this George Eddowes, in search of a better future for his burgeoning brood, took the family to London not long after Kate's birth. In December 1844, when the second son, Thomas, was born, they were living at 4 Baden Place, Bermondsey, in what is now the Borough of Southwark. Soon there were even more mouths to feed – George (1846), Sarah Ann (1850) and Mary (1852). The 1851 census found them at 35 West Street, Nelson Street, in Bermondsey. Harriet and Emma, the oldest girls, were not listed with the others. Since neither had yet married it is probable that they were in domestic service and living in the houses of their employers. Alfred, the oldest boy, was recorded as an idiot. Eliza was a domestic servant. And Elizabeth, Kate, Thomas and George were still at school.

Kate's schooling is a bit of a mystery. Press reports of 1888 aver that she was educated at Dowgate Charity School but Neal Shelden, a modern scholar, opts for St John's Charity School in Potters Fields, Tooley Street. The first is unlikely because Dowgate is in the City of London, on the north side of the river. The school in Potters Fields, a charity school for girls for the parish of St John, Horselydown, was merged with St Olave's Grammar School in 1899. Unfortunately, only one admissions register, covering 1842–7, survives. Neither this, nor the minutes up to 1857, which list all applicants, contain Kate's name.

The prosperity for which George Eddowes laboured eluded him. Not only that, but tragedy struck the family in the mid 1850s. Their last child, William, was born at 7 Winters Square, Bermondsey, in July 1854, and died there of 'convulsions' within five months. Worse, Catharine Eddowes died of phthisis, or tuberculosis of the lungs, at the same address on 17 November 1855. This last calamity dispersed the household.

Harriet and Emma were already in domestic service but some of the younger children were placed in the Bermondsey Workhouse and Industrial School. Kate should have fared better. Emma wrote to an aunt, Mrs Elizabeth Eddowes, who still lived in Wolverhampton, and persuaded her to take Kate to live with her. Mrs Eddowes is listed, together with her husband William, a tinplate worker, and three children, at 17 Bilston Street, Wolverhampton, in the 1851 census. Sadly Kate did not settle. Only a few months after the youngster had returned to Wolverhampton Mrs Eddowes wrote to Emma and told her that Kate had robbed her employer and run away to Birmingham, where she was living with an uncle in Bagot Street. The uncle, too, is listed in the 1851 census. He was a shoemaker named Thomas Eddowes and he lived at No. 7, Court 5, Bagot Street, with his wife Rosanah and children Jane, Thomas and Mary. But Kate didn't stay long with him either. It was in Birmingham a few years later that she met and fell in love with Thomas Conway and the couple decided to live together. Kate was then only about sixteen years old.

Almost nothing is known about Conway. Even his correct name is in doubt. From about 1873 he was drawing an army pension by virtue of service in the 18th Royal Irish Regiment, in which, as the police discovered, he had enlisted under the name of Thomas Quinn. During his later years he supplemented his pension by working as a hawker. Kate's life with Conway is also very shadowy. They never married. But they lived together for more than twenty years and produced three children. On 3 August 1885 Annie, the oldest, married Louis Philips, a lamp-black packer, in Southwark. Annie was then twenty years of age. Kate's other children, both boys, were born in about 1868 and 1873. Conway tattooed his initials, 'T. C.', on Kate's left forearm.

It was with Conway that Kate returned to London and it was there that they eventually separated in 1880 or 1881. Kate's sister Elizabeth blamed Conway for the failure of the relationship. 'My sister left Conway because he treated her badly,' she said. 'He did not drink regularly, but when he drew his pension they went out together and it generally ended in his beating her.' Emma, the sister who had tried to provide for Kate after their mother's death, heard about the beatings too. But she felt that Kate's own drinking was the root of the problem: 'On the whole, I believe they lived happily together; but there were occasional quarrels between them, owing to my sister's habit of excessive drinking. She has been seen with her face frightfully disfigured [i.e. beaten] . . . I fancy he [Conway] must have left her in consequence of her drinking habits.' Annie Philips, testifying before the inquest, corroborated Emma's fancy.

She explained that her father was a teetotaller, that he lived on bad terms with Kate because she drank. 'He left deceased between 7 and 8 years ago,' said Annie, 'entirely on account of her drinking habits.'

In 1881 Kate met John Kelly in the common lodging house at 55 Flower and Dean Street. He was to be her companion and this her home for most of the rest of her life. Three days after Kate's death Kelly told the *Star* how their friendship started: 'It is nigh on to seven years since I met Kate, and it was in this very lodging house I first set eyes on her. We got throwed together a good bit, and the result was that we made a regular bargain. We have lived here ever since, as the people here will tell you, and have never left here except when we've gone to the country together hopping. I don't pretend that she was my wife. She was not.'

Kate's friends and acquaintances insisted that she was not a prostitute. During the winters she worked as a charwoman for the Jews or hawked trifles about the streets. Kelly picked up labouring jobs in the markets. For the greater part of the summers they tramped the countryside together, hop-picking, fruit-picking or hay-making. 'She would never do anything wrong,' said Eliza, Kate's sister, 'I cannot imagine what she was doing in Mitre Square.' John Kelly told the inquest that although Kate sometimes drank to excess she did not solicit. When they were together, he maintained, she regularly came home about eight or nine at night. And Frederick Wilkinson, the lodging house deputy, spoke well of Kate and Kelly when he appeared before the coroner. They were, by his account, pretty regular in paying their rents. They lived on good terms with each other. They did, admittedly, sometimes quarrel when Kate had been drinking but that was not often and he had never seen Kelly drunk. Kate herself was generally in bed between nine and ten and Wilkinson had never known or heard of her 'being intimate with anyone but Kelly'.

Such protestations carry little conviction. Eliza was perhaps unwilling to speak ill of a sister. Kelly would have been anxious to scotch any suggestion that he lived off Kate's immoral earnings and Wilkinson that he ran a disreputable house. Besides which it would presumably have been very difficult for anyone to talk of the faults of the murder victims in a community still grieving their loss. Kate probably did indulge in some casual prostitution. Certainly her indigent lifestyle distanced her from her relatives.

After the break with Thomas Conway she kept in touch with Annie

Philips, her daughter, for some time. Indeed, in 1886, she nursed Annie during her confinement. But soon after that Annie moved from King Street, Bermondsey, without leaving a forwarding address and at the time of the murder she had not seen Kate for two years. It is possible that Annie's flit had been deliberately designed to give her mother the slip because Kate had frequently pestered her for money. Certainly Annie admitted at the inquest that the addresses of her two brothers had been withheld from Kate to prevent her scrounging from them. However, a story Eliza told the press suggests otherwise. 'It's rather strange,' she said, 'one of them [Kate's children], the girl that's married [Annie], came to me last week and asked me if I had seen anything of her mother. She said it was a very long time since she had seen her. But it was a long time since I had, too, and I told her so.'

At least three of Kate's sisters had settled in London. In 1888 Eliza Gold, now widowed, was living at 6 Thrawl Street, Spitalfields, and Mrs Elizabeth Fisher, another sister, was living at 33 Hackliffe Street, Greenwich. Emma, now Emma Jones and married to a packer, lived at 20 Bridgewater Place, Aldersgate Street. Neither Eliza nor Emma got on with Kate. Eliza told the press that they were not on the best of terms and that she had not seen Kate much more than once or twice since she had been cohabiting with Kelly. At the inquest she said that she had not seen her for three or four weeks although that may have been because Kate was away hop-picking. Emma admitted in her press statement that she had not been on good terms with Kate for many years because 'she led a life that was not to my liking.' They met but rarely. Perhaps, upon such occasions, Kate's displays of remorse were intended to elicit Emma's sympathy and hence tap her purse. Or perhaps Kate looked at her sister and saw – but for a wasted life – what she herself might have become. Whatever the cause, when Kate came to visit her, recalled Emma, she 'used always to cry when she saw me, and say, "I wish I was like you".'

Nevertheless, Kate seems to have found a loyal consort in John Kelly. Little of their precarious life together has come down to us but occasional glimpses of them may be had in the stark records of the Whitechapel Workhouse Infirmary. Kelly was admitted on 31 December 1886 for rheumatism and discharged to the workhouse on 24 January 1887. Kate was treated at the infirmary for a 'burn of foot' from 14 to 20 June 1887. She was admitted under the name of Kate Conway and her religion was noted as Roman Catholic. Then, on 24 November 1887, Kelly was readmitted suffering from frost-bite. He was discharged on 28 December 1887. On all of these occasions Kate and Kelly were admitted to the infirmary from 55 Flower and Dean Street.[6]

The autumn of 1888 found them hop-picking at Hunton, near Maidstone, in Kent. According to the *Star*, Kelly remembered it this way:

We went hopping together mostly every year. We went down this year as usual. We didn't get on any too well, and started to hoof it home. We came along in company with another man and woman who had worked in the same fields, but who parted with us to go to Chatham when we turned off towards Maidstone. The woman said to Kate, 'I have got a pawnticket for a flannel shirt. I wish you'd take it, since you're going up to town. It is only in for 9d., and it may fit your old man.' So Kate took it and we trudged along. It was in at Jones's, Church Street, in the name of Emily Burrell.

Walter Besant's romantic portrait of hop-picking depicts the roads to London after the season as being 'strewn with the old boots discarded by the hoppers when they bought new ones on their way home.'[7] At Maidstone our couple certainly had enough money for Kelly to buy a pair of boots from Mr Arthur Pash in the High Street and for Kate to invest in a jacket from a shop nearby, but by the time they got back to London, on Thursday, 27 September, they were flat broke. That night they slept in the casual ward at Shoe Lane.

On Friday they woke up destitute. Kelly managed to earn sixpence 'at a job' but this was not enough to buy them a double bed for the night at Cooney's (single beds were priced at 4d. per night, doubles at 8d.). 'Here, Kate,' said Kelly, 'you take 4d. and go to the lodging house and I'll go to Mile End [casual ward].' Kate would not hear of it. 'No,' she replied, 'you go and have a bed and I will go to the casual ward.' She had her way. That night Kelly stayed at Cooney's and Kate went to the casual ward at Mile End, where she would have to perform some menial task such as picking oakum in return for shelter.

They teamed up again at eight the next morning, Saturday, 29 September, the last day of Kate's life. Kelly looked ruefully at his new boots. 'We'll pop [pawn] the boots,' he announced, 'and have a bite to eat anyway.' 'Oh, no, don't do that,' protested Kate, but this time Kelly insisted on having his way. Kate took the boots to Jones' shop at 31 Church Street and was paid 2s. 6d. Kelly waited at the door in his bare feet. After buying tea and sugar they had enough left over for breakfast and ate it in the kitchen at Cooney's. It was their last meal together. Kelly then resolved to try his luck in the markets, Kate to go to her daughter in King Street to see what she could do. When they parted in Houndsditch at about two that afternoon John Kelly was worried about his partner. He reminded her of the murders and begged her to return home early. Kate promised to be back no later than four. Her parting words, as Kelly remembered them four days later, were: 'Don't you fear for me. I'll take care of myself and I shan't fall into his hands.'[8]

Kate did not see her daughter that Saturday. Annie, indeed, had left King Street since Kate had last visited her there. In the summer of 1887 she seems to have been living at 15 Anchor Street, Southwark Park, and at the time of the Mitre Square murder her address was 12 Dilston Grove, Southwark Park Road. Yet – somewhere, somehow – Kate found money. For when we glimpse her next, at 8.30 that evening, she was helplessly drunk in Aldgate High Street.

At that time a crowd outside No. 29 in the High Street attracted the attention of PC Louis Robinson 931. Pushing his way to its centre he found a woman lying drunk on the pavement. The constable picked her up and leaned her against the shutters of No. 29 but she slipped sideways. Then, summoning PC George Simmonds 959 to his assistance, he managed to get her to Bishopsgate Street Police Station. James Byfield, the station sergeant, remembered the woman being brought in, supported between two constables, at about 8.45. She smelt strongly of drink. When they enquired her name she replied: 'Nothing.'

The woman was placed in a police cell to sleep it off. That night PC George Hutt 968, who came on duty at 9.45, visited the prisoner several times. At 11.45 he found her out of her stupor and singing to herself. And at 12.30 she asked him when she would be allowed to go. 'Shortly,' replied Hutt. 'I am capable of taking care of myself now,' she said.

Twenty-five minutes after that Sergeant Byfield told Hutt to see if any of the prisoners were fit to be discharged and Hutt, judging the woman to have sobered up, unlocked her cell and escorted her back to the office. As he did so she asked him what time it was.

'Too late for you to get any more drink,' he replied.

'Well,' she insisted, 'what time is it?'

'Just on one.'

'I shall get a damned fine hiding when I get home then.'

'And serve you right,' Hutt retorted. 'You have no right to get drunk.'

In the office she gave her name and address as Mary Ann Kelly of 6 Fashion Street, Spitalfields, and was discharged. 'This way, missus,' said Hutt, pushing open a swing door. It admitted her to the passage leading to the street door and as she reached the street door Hutt called: 'Please pull it to.' 'All right,' replied the woman, 'good night, old cock.' A moment later she had passed through the door, pulled it almost closed, and turned left towards Houndsditch. Mitre Square was just eight minutes' walk away.[9]

Much later PC Robinson would identify the Mitre Square victim as the drunk he had taken into custody in Aldgate High Street. But full identification had to wait upon John Kelly. The extent of his personal tragedy may, perhaps, be gauged from part of the interview he gave the *Star* on 3 October:

When she [Kate] did not come home at night I didn't worry, for I thought her daughter might have asked her to stay over Sunday with her. So on Sunday morning I wandered round in the crowds that had been gathered by the talk about the two fresh murders. I stood and looked at the very spot where my poor old gal had laid with her body all cut to pieces and I never knew it. I never thought of her in connection with it, for I thought she was safe at her daughter's. Yesterday morning [2 October] I began to be worried a bit, but I did not guess the truth until after I had come back from another bad day in the market. I came in here [Cooney's] and asked for Kate, she had not been in. I sat down on that bench by the table and carelessly picked up a *Star* paper. I read down the page a bit, and my eye caught the name of 'Burrill'. It looked familiar, but I didn't think where I had seen it until I came to the word 'pawnticket'. Then it came over me all at once. The tin box, the two pawntickets, the one for that flannel shirt, and the other for my boots. But could Kate have lost them? I read a little further. 'The woman had the letters T. C., in India ink, on her arm.' Man, you could have knocked me down with a feather! It was my Kate, and no other. I don't know how I braced up to go to the police, but I did. They took me down to see the body, and I knew it was her. I knew it before I saw it, and I knew her for all the way she was cut ... I never knew if she went to her daughter's at all. I only wish to God she had, for we had lived together a long while and never had a quarrel.

Although a study of the full interview does suggest that Kelly furnished the bulk of the information in this account the words were probably the *Star*'s as much as his. There were, moreover, inaccuracies and misrepresentations. Most importantly, the interview leaves us with the impression that Kelly knew nothing of Kate's imprisonment at Bishopsgate Street. This was not the case. At the inquest he told the court that two women had told him that Kate had been locked up at the police station and that he 'made sure she would be out on Sunday morning.' And Frederick Wilkinson, the lodging house deputy, testified that he had asked Kelly where Kate was when the labourer came in on Saturday night. 'I have heard she's been locked up' was Kelly's reply.[10] Plainly, then, the reason that Kelly was not immediately concerned for Kate was that he believed her to have been safely under lock and key at the time of the murders. However, when questioned by the *Star* he did not like to admit that Kate had been arrested drunk and tried to protect her by saying that he thought she was at her daughter's.

Whatever the detail there is no doubt that Kelly called at Bishopsgate Street late on Tuesday, 2 October. He was convinced that the dead woman was Kate and, taken to the mortuary, identified her at once. Press reports concur that he was 'very much affected'. The next morning he helped detectives locate Mrs Gold, Kate's sister, in Thrawl Street. Conducted to the City Mortuary, Eliza confirmed Kelly's identification of the body. 'I never dreamed that she would come to such an end as this,' she told reporters that night, 'and I can't get over it.'[11]

The autopsy upon Kate's body was performed by Dr Brown at the City Mortuary on the afternoon of Sunday, 30 September. Present were Dr Sequeira, who had been the first medical man on the scene of the crime, Dr William Sedgwick Saunders, the City's Public Analyst, and Dr Phillips.

As in the Nichols and Chapman murders, the victim's throat had been deeply severed from left to right. Dr Brown's inquest deposition reads:

The throat was cut across to the extent of about 6 or 7 inches. A superficial cut commenced about an inch and 1/2 below the lobe and about 2½ inches below behind the left ear and extended across the throat to about 3 inches below the lobe of the right ear. The big muscle across the throat was divided through on the left side. The large vessels on the left side of the neck were severed. The larynx was severed below the vocal cord. All the deep structures were severed to the bone, the knife marking intervertebral cartilages. The sheath of the vessels on the right side was just opened. The carotid artery had a fine hole opening. The internal jugular vein was opened an inch and a half, not divided. The blood vessels contained clot. All these injuries were performed by a sharp instrument like a knife and pointed.[12]

It was Brown's opinion that the murderer had first cut the woman's throat, that death had been occasioned by the escape of blood from the left common carotid artery, and that the other mutilations had been inflicted after death.

The most extensive mutilation had been to the abdomen, which had been ripped open upwards in a great jagged wound extending from the pubes to the breastbone. The left kidney and part of the womb had been cut out and taken away. Press reports of Dr Brown's inquest deposition suppressed this part of his testimony altogether but the official transcript in the coroner's papers records it in detail:

We examined the abdomen. The front walls were laid open from the breast bone to the pubes. The cut commenced opposite the ensiform cartilage. The incision went upwards, not penetrating the skin that was over the sternum. It then divided the ensiform cartilage. The knife must have cut obliquely at the expense of the front surface of that cartilage.

Behind this the liver was stabbed as if by the point of a sharp instrument. Below this was another incision into the liver of about 2½ inches, and below this the left lobe of the liver was slit through by a vertical cut. 2 cuts were shewn by a jagging of the skin on the left side.

The abdominal walls were divided in the middle line to within 1/4 of an inch of the navel. The cut then took a horizontal course for two inches and a half towards right side. It then divided round the navel on the left side and made a parallel incision to the former horizontal incision, leaving the navel on a tongue of skin. Attached to the navel was 2½ inches of the lower part of the rectus muscle on the left side of the abdomen. The incision then took an oblique direction to the right and was shelving. The incision went down the right side of the vagina and rectum for half an inch behind the rectum.

There was a stab of about an inch on the left groin. This was done by a pointed instrument. Below this was a cut of 3 inches going through all tissues making a wound of the perineum about the same extent.

An inch below the crease of the thigh was a cut extending from the anterior spine of the ilium obliquely down the inner side of the left thigh and separating the left labium, forming a flap of skin up to the groin. The left rectus muscle was not detached.

There was a flap of skin formed from the right thigh attaching the right labium and extending up to the spine of the ilium. The muscles on the right side inserted into the Poupart's ligament were cut through.

The skin was retracted through the whole of the cut in the abdomen, but the vessels were not clotted. Nor had there been any appreciable bleeding from the vessel. I draw the conclusion that the cut was made after death, and there would not be much blood on the murderer. The cut was made by someone on right side of body, kneeling below the middle of the body . . .

The intestines had been detached to a large extent from the mesentery. About 2 feet of the colon was cut away. The sigmoid flexure was invaginated into the rectum very tightly.

Right kidney pale, bloodless, with slight congestion of the base of the pyramids.

There was a cut from the upper part of the slit on the under surface of the liver to the left side, and another cut at right angles to this, which were about an inch and a half deep and $2^{1}/2$ inches long. Liver itself was healthy.

The gall bladder contained bile. The pancreas was cut but not through on the left side of the spinal column. $3^{1}/2$ inches of the lower border of the spleen by $1/2$ an inch was attached only to the peritoneum.

The peritoneal lining was cut through on the left side and the left kidney carefully taken out and removed. The left renal artery was cut through. I should say that someone who knew the position of the kidney must have done it. The lining membrane over the uterus was cut through. The womb was cut through horizontally, leaving a stump of $3/4$ of an inch. The rest of the womb had been taken away with some of the ligaments. The vagina and cervix of the womb was uninjured.

The bladder was healthy and uninjured, and contained 3 or 4 ounces of water. There was a tongue-like cut through the anterior wall of the abdominal aorta. The other organs were healthy. There were no indications of connection.

Brown could suggest no reason for the removal of the left kidney and womb. These parts, he said, would be 'of no use for any professional purpose.'

For the first time in this series of crimes the murderer mutilated his victim's face. According to Brown, the

face was very much mutilated. There was a cut about 1/4 of an inch through the lower left eyelid dividing the structures completely through. The upper eyelid on that side, there was a scratch through the skin on the left upper eyelid near to the angle of the nose. The right eyelid was cut through to about 1/2 an inch. There was a deep cut over the bridge of the nose extending from the left border of the nasal bone down near to the angle of the jaw on the right side across the cheek. This cut went into the bone and divided all the structures of the cheek except the mucous membrane of the mouth. The tip of the nose was quite detached from the nose by an oblique cut from the bottom of the nasal bone to where the wings of the nose join on to the face. A cut from this divided the upper lip and extended through the substance of the gum over the right upper lateral incisor tooth. About 1/2 an inch from the top of the nose was another oblique cut. There was a cut on the right angle of the mouth, as if by the cut of a point of a knife. The cut extended an inch and a half parallel with lower lip. There was on each side of cheek a cut which peeled up the skin forming a triangular flap about an inch and a half. On the left cheek there were 2 abrasions of the epithelium. There was a little mud on left cheek. 2 slight abrasions of the epithelium under the left ear.

Photographs were taken of Kate's body before and after post-mortem stitching but her wounds were most clearly depicted in two sketches made by Frederick William Foster, an architect and surveyor, at the City Mortuary on the morning of the murder. One of them depicted the injuries to the face and head. It recorded the detail that the lobe of Kate's right ear had been cut off. This wound, which will prove of some significance to us later, was not described in Brown's autopsy report although he did note that when the body was stripped at the mortuary 'a piece of deceased's ear dropped from the clothing.'[13]

From all that he had seen Dr Brown concluded that the mutilations had all been inflicted by one man on the spot where the body had been found. There was a current theory that Kate had been murdered somewhere else and then dumped in Mitre Square but the doctor did not agree. 'The blood on the left side [of the neck] was clotted,' he said, 'and must have fallen at the time the throat was cut.' That clotted blood, and the absence of bloodstains on the front of her jacket and bodice, proved that Kate's throat had been severed while she was lying on her back. The murderer, at least when inflicting the abdominal injuries, had been kneeling on the right side, and below the middle, of the body. In Brown's opinion he had performed the mutilations to the face and abdomen with a sharp, pointed knife. From the abdominal injuries the doctor judged that the blade of this weapon must have been at least six inches long.[14]

In the case of Annie Chapman the murderer had removed the womb intact but in that of Kate Eddowes a stump of about three quarters of an inch had been left in the body. Despite this, Dr Brown concluded that Kate's killer, too, must have possessed both anatomical knowledge and surgical skill. He based his case primarily upon the careful extraction of the left kidney: 'I should say that someone who knew the position of the kidney must have done it ... I believe the perpetrator of the act must have had considerable knowledge of the position of the organs in the abdominal cavity and the way of removing them ... It required a great deal of knowledge to have removed the kidney and to know where it was placed. Such a knowledge might be possessed by someone in the habit of cutting up animals.'[15] According to a press version of his testimony, Brown explained to the court that the removal of the kidney would have required 'a good deal of knowledge as to its position, because it is apt to be overlooked, being covered by a membrane.'[16]

It is worth reiterating – given some of the eccentric interpretations of Brown's evidence put about in recent years – that the doctor attributed surgical skill as well as anatomical knowledge to the killer. His references to the left kidney being 'carefully taken out and removed' and to the murderer possessing knowledge of the position of the organs and of 'the way of removing them' demonstrate this. The point is more explicitly made in some of the newspaper transcripts of his deposition. The *Daily Telegraph* quoted him thus: 'The way in which the kidney was cut out showed that it was done by somebody who knew what he was about.' And the *Daily News* thus: 'The left kidney had been carefully taken out in such a manner as to show that it had been done by somebody who not only knew its anatomical position, but knew how to remove it.' More, in an early interview, Brown told a *Star* reporter that the murderer 'had some knowledge of how to use a knife.'[17]

Brown did not believe, however, that the *degree* of knowledge and skill displayed would only have been possessed by a medical man. A slaughterman, for example, would have known enough to have inflicted the injuries.

What of the other medicos?

Implicit in Brown's view was the belief that the murderer had deliberately sought out the kidney. Sequeira and Saunders do not seem to have been so sure. Perhaps they wondered whether he could have come across the organ fortuitously and cut it out without understanding what it was. Anyway, they both told the inquest that they did not think that the killer had had designs on any particular organ and that he did not seem to have been possessed of 'great anatomical skill.'[18] The wording is unfortunate because it has led some writers to assert, incorrectly, that these doctors testified to a *total* absence of skill on the part of the killer. In fact, if they were endorsing Brown (and they both explicitly said that they were), they meant that the killer possessed an elementary degree of skill rather than none at all. That this was Sequeira's intended meaning is confirmed by an interview he gave to the *Star*. He told its reporter that the atrocity had been performed quickly. 'By an expert, do you think?' queried the reporter. 'No, not by an expert,' explained Sequeira, 'but by a man who was not altogether ignorant of the use of the knife.'[19]

Dr Phillips made no report to the inquest but his position seems to have been very close to those of Sequeira and Saunders. A report of Chief Inspector Swanson gives us the most detailed précis of Phillips' view:

The surgeon, Dr Brown, called by the City Police, and Dr Phillips, who had been called by the Metropolitan Police in the cases of Hanbury Street and Berner Street, having made a post-mortem examination of the body, reported that there were missing the left kidney and the uterus, and that the mutilation so far gave no evidence of anatomical knowledge in the sense that it evidenced the hand of a qualified surgeon, so that the police could narrow their enquiries into certain classes of persons. On the other hand, as in the Metropolitan Police cases, the medical evidence showed that the murder could have been committed by a person who had been a hunter, a butcher, a slaughterman, as well as a student in surgery or a properly qualified surgeon.

In other words, although the murder *might* have been committed by a qualified surgeon the degree of expertise *actually displayed* could also have been possessed by a hunter, butcher, slaughterman or medical student. Phillips saw less evidence of medical expertise in the Eddowes murder than in that of Annie Chapman and for this reason was inclined to the belief that these crimes had been done by different men.[20]

While the doctors were thus learning something about Kate's killer in the post-mortem room the detectives were finding out a little more by knocking on doors. Searches of Mitre Square and neighbourhood lodging houses, launched soon after the discovery of Kate's body, had availed them nothing. But a house-to-house inquiry in the vicinity of the square turned up two Jews who saw a woman who might have been Kate in the forty-five minutes between her discharge from Bishopsgate Street and the discovery of her body by PC Watkins. Furthermore, the woman was talking to a man, and if she was indeed Kate her companion was almost certainly the murderer.[21]

The witnesses were Joseph Lawende, a commercial traveller, of 79 Fenchurch Street, and Joseph Hyam Levy, a butcher, of 1 Hutchinson Street, Aldgate. On the evening of Saturday, 29 September, these men, together with Harry Harris, a Jewish furniture dealer, went to the Imperial Club at 16–17 Duke Street. It rained that night so they stayed on there until 1.30 the next morning. Then they prepared to go. At the inquest Lawende said that they left the building at about 1.35. Levy put the time at 1.33 or 1.34.

As they left the club they saw a man and a woman standing at the corner of Church Passage, about fifteen or sixteen feet away. 'Look there,' Levy said to Harris, 'I don't like going home by myself when I see those characters about.' But however unsavoury the couple might have appeared there seemed nothing noteworthy about them.

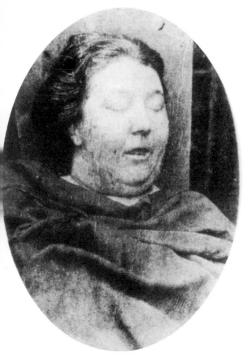

1. Martha Tabram   2. George Yard Buildings

3. Commercial Street Police Station. The fourth storey was added in 1906

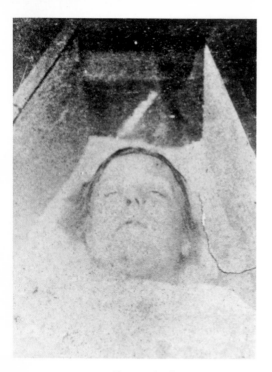

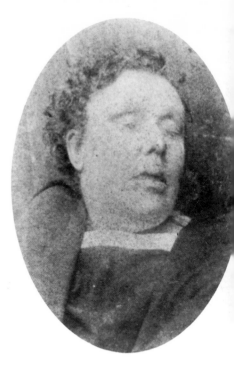

4. Polly Nichols

5. Annie Chapman

6. Hanbury Street, looking East, c. 1918–20

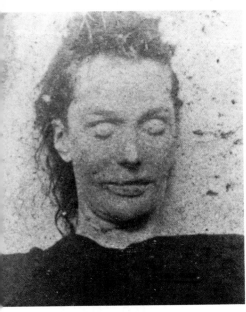

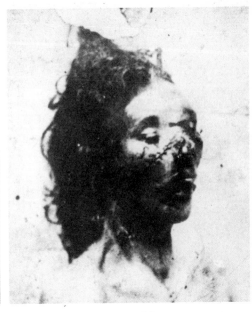

7. Liz Stride

8. Kate Eddowes

9. Mitre Square, c. 1925, showing murder site, rear of Mr
Taylor's shop and carriageway into Mitre Street

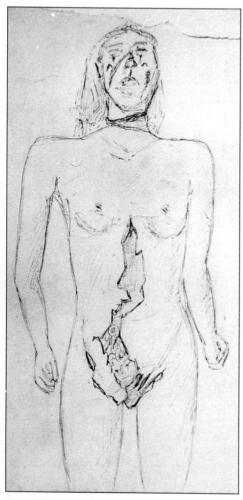

10. Kate Eddowes: mortuary sketch by
Frederick Foster

11. John Kelly

12. Michael Ostrog

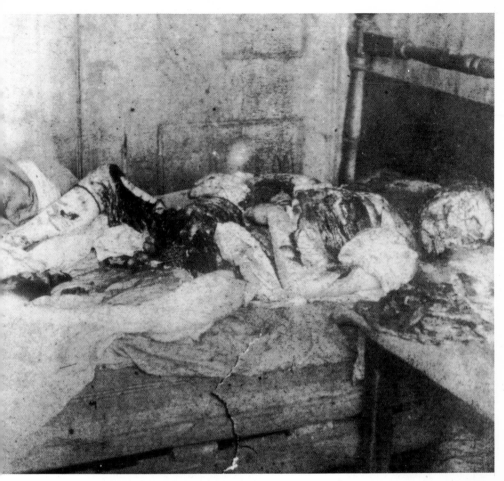

13. Body of Mary Kelly, as discovered in Miller's Court

14. John McCarthy

15. Thomas Bowyer

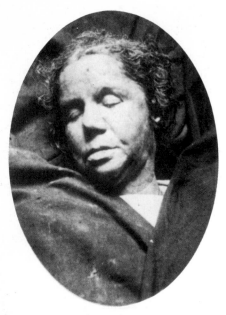

16. Alice McKenzie

17. Frances Coles

18. Tom Sadler

19. Swallow Gardens

20. Montague John Druitt   21. Frederick Deeming

22. Colney Hatch Asylum, where Aaron Kosminski was
detained in 1891

23. George Chapman with Bessie Taylor

24. Chapman's shop at 126 Cable Street (abandoned premises, centre) photographed in 1943. He lived and worked at this address in the autumn of 1888

And this, together with the fact that they were standing in a badly lighted spot, may explain why Levy's recollection of them was so vague: 'I passed on, taking no further notice of them. The man, I should say, was about three inches taller than the woman. I cannot give any description of either of them.'

Lawende, walking a little apart from his companions, was nearer to the couple. He saw more. The woman was short and wearing a black jacket and bonnet. She stood facing the man, one hand resting upon his chest. Lawende only saw her back. There was no quarrel in progress. Rather the couple appeared to be talking very quietly and Lawende could not hear what was being said.

Lawende saw the man too but the official transcript of his inquest deposition records only that he was taller than the woman and wore a cloth cap with a cloth peak. Press versions of the testimony, however, add the detail that 'the man looked rather rough and shabby'[22] and reveal that the full description was suppressed at the request of Henry Crawford, the City Solicitor, who was attending the hearing on behalf of the police. Fortunately this deficiency in the record can be redressed from other sources. Lawende's description of the man was fully published in the *Police Gazette* of 19 October 1888:

> At 1.35 a.m., 30th September, with Catherine Eddows, in Church Passage, leading to Mitre Square, where she was found murdered at 1.45 a.m., same date – A MAN, age 30, height 5 ft. 7 or 8 in., complexion fair, moustache fair, medium build; dress, pepper-and-salt colour loose jacket, grey cloth cap with peak of same material, reddish neckerchief tied in knot; appearance of a sailor.

On the same date Chief Inspector Swanson attributed precisely the same details to Lawende in his report on the Stride murder.[23]

Much later some remarkable claims would be made in relation to Lawende's sighting so it is important here to note that he did not see his suspect well enough to feel confident that he would be able to recognize him again. Our sources make this absolutely clear. On 11 October, only eleven days after the event, Lawende told the inquest: 'I doubt whether I should know him again.' At the end of the same month Inspector McWilliam reported to the Home Office that 'Mr Lewend (sic), who was nearest to the man & woman & saw most of them, says he does not think he should know the man again.' On 6 November, also writing for the Home Office, Swanson similarly asserted that 'the other two [Levy and Harris] took but little notice and state that they could not identify the man or woman, and even Mr Lawende states that he could not identify the man.' Although Major Smith's memoirs may recall Lawende's description inaccurately they also corroborate the commercial traveller's diffidence: 'The description of the man given me by the German [Lawende] was as follows: Young, about the middle height, with a small fair moustache, dressed in something like navy serge, and with a deerstalker's cap – that is, a cap with a peak both fore and aft. I think the German spoke the truth, because I could not "lead" him in any way. "You will easily recognize him, then," I said. "Oh no!" he replied; "I only had a short look at him."'[24]

Lawende and his friends walked down Duke Street into Aldgate, leaving the couple still talking at the corner of Church Passage.

A weakness of Lawende's testimony is that he did not see the woman's face. It is possible that she was not Kate Eddowes although when Lawende was permitted to examine Kate's clothing at the police station he expressed the opinion that they were identical to those worn by the woman he saw. Church Passage, moreover, led directly into Mitre Square where Kate was found dead just nine minutes after Lawende's sighting.

Many minor mysteries surround the Eddowes murder. To begin with there are several unanswered questions concerning Kate's conduct on the day of her death. When John Kelly last saw her, on Saturday afternoon in Houndsditch, he was quite sure that she was destitute and sober, and she gave him to understand that she was going to her daughter's in King Street, Bermondsey, to see what she could scrounge. Whether she went there or not we do not know but if she did she did not find her daughter because Annie left King Street two years previously without leaving a forwarding address. Where Kate went, who she saw and what she did our sources do not tell. Somewhere, however, she acquired enough money to drink herself into a stupor. More important, we know nothing of Kate's movements between 1.00 a.m., when she was discharged from Bishopsgate Street, and 1.35 a.m., when she was seen, apparently soliciting, in the entry of Church Passage in Duke Street. She had spent her former earnings on drink and may have been making her way to the casual ward at Mile End. If so she was not averse to exploiting any opportunity that presented itself along the way to earn a few coppers. Perhaps she aspired to raise sufficient to pay for a bed at Cooney's or to make her peace with Kelly. 'I shall get a damned fine hiding when I get home,' she had told PC Hutt.

A yet more intriguing question concerns Kate. The City Police seem to have seriously considered the possibility that her presence in Mitre Square had not been entirely fortuitous, that she had, in fact, kept a pre-arranged appointment there with the man who slew her.[25] The rationale for this view was that since no policeman observed Kate and her killer walking *together* towards Mitre Square – and the City Police were under instructions to keep men and women out together under close surveillance – they may have made their separate ways there as to a pre-arranged rendezvous. Support for such a contention might be read into Kate's anxiety for an early discharge from the police station and into her insistent inquiry of PC Hutt about the time. More, the appointment theory could tie in neatly with this tantalizing item from the *East London Observer* of 13 October:

A reporter gleaned some curious information from the Casual Ward Superintendent of Mile End, regarding Kate Eddowes, the Mitre Square victim. She was formerly well-known in the casual wards there, but had disappeared for a considerable time until the Friday preceding her murder. Asking the woman where she had been in the interval, the superintendent was met with the reply that she had been in the country 'hopping'. 'But,' added the woman, 'I have come back to earn the reward offered for the apprehension of the Whitechapel murderer. I think I know him.' 'Mind he doesn't murder you too,' replied the superintendent jocularly. 'Oh, no fear of that,' was the remark made by Kate Eddowes as she left. Within four and twenty hours afterwards she was a mutilated corpse.

This snippet is one of those scraps of evidence that surface occasionally to challenge our conventional view of the Whitechapel killings. But however intriguing, as it stands it is nothing more than a piece of unsupported hearsay. It may even be less than that because the parting exchange alleged between Kate and the casual ward superintendent is so like that between Kate and John Kelly that it is tempting to see the *Observer*'s tale simply as a piece of dishonest reporting drawing upon confused memories of Kelly's various press statements. That no police officer observed Kate and her killer wending their way together towards Mitre Square proves nothing. The fact is that they *were* apparently seen – by Lawende in Duke Street – and it is entirely possible that they had just met there. No, at present there is little reason to suppose that the penniless waif who was 'always singing' met Jack the Ripper by anything but a desperately unlucky chance.

Thanks to the survival of the Brown and Foster sketches and of the official inquest record the Mitre Square murder is more satisfactorily documented than any other crime in the series. Nevertheless, analysis of this material leaves us with a problem already familiar from three previous cases.

Brown decided that loss of blood, resulting from the cutting of the left carotid artery, had been the cause of death. When Kate's throat had been cut, however, she was already lying on the ground. Why? Surely she would not voluntarily have lain down in the wet (the back of her jacket was found covered in dirt as well as blood) but there were no signs of a struggle, nothing to indicate that she had been forced down, and no one had heard a cry.

Questioned by the coroner, the medicos could offer nothing like a convincing explanation for that absence of a cry. 'The throat had been so instantly severed that no noise could have been emitted,' said Brown. 'I account for the absence of noise as the death must have been so instantaneous after the severance of the windpipe and the blood vessels,' chimed Sequeira. All of which neglects to explain why Kate didn't cry out as she was being put down, *before* her throat was cut. Could she have been poisoned or drugged? If so the traces escaped Dr Saunders' analysis of her stomach contents. 'I carefully examined the stomach and its contents,' he reported, 'more particularly for poisons of the narcotic class, with negative results, there not being the faintest trace of these or any other poison.'

The absence of any scream or cry suggests, once again, the possibility that the victim had been strangled before her throat had been cut. Such a hypothesis finds support in the comparatively small spillage of blood. When the murderer severed Kate's throat blood did not spurt out over the front of her clothes. The left carotid artery bled out onto the pavement on the left side of the neck and Brown found a pool of clotted blood there at 2.18 a.m. Because of the slope of the pavement some of it had trickled under the neck to form a fluid patch about the right shoulder. Blood had also accumulated under Kate's back and the backs of her jacket, vest and bodice were all badly stained. This pattern of staining, for reasons already noticed, is consistent with the view that her throat was cut after death.[26]

The theory that Kate's mutilations were Masonic in character has been refuted elsewhere. Nevertheless, in her case, as in that of Annie Chapman, there does seem to have been some eerie ritualistic element. Dr Brown found a piece of the intestine, about two feet long, placed between the body and the left arm, 'apparently by design'. And there were matching cuts on each of Kate's cheeks, peeling up the skin to form triangular flaps of skin, and corresponding nicks to her eyelids.

Brown seems to have been more impressed than his colleagues by the murderer's medical expertise but the doctors concurred in the view that his handiwork had evidenced *some* degree of skill. Recent medical experts have disagreed with each other. After studying Foster's sketch of Kate's abdominal injuries and police photographs, the pathologist Francis Camps concluded that the murderer may have had some elementary anatomical knowledge but little if any surgical skill. 'Far from being the work of a skilled surgeon,' he said, 'any surgeon who operated in this manner would have been struck off the Medical Register.' Quite so. But Nick Warren, a practising surgeon, contends from personal experience that because the kidney is so difficult to expose from the front of the body the killer must have possessed some anatomical experience.[27] It should be borne in mind, too, that the mutilations were performed in exceptionally difficult circumstances. In Mitre Square the murderer worked at great speed, in constant danger of discovery, and in the darkest corner of the square, deep in the shadow cast by Mr Taylor's shop.

He was undoubtedly a fast worker, just how fast will become immediately apparent to anyone who cares to consider the matter of times. The killer was seen with his victim in the entry of Church Passage soon after 1.30 by the three men leaving the Imperial Club. The precise time was fixed by Lawende, one of the three, at about 1.35. and by Levy, a companion, at 1.33 or 1.34. We can be reasonably confident in these times because the witnesses checked the club clock before they left the building and Lawende, in addition, owned a watch. Murderer and victim must have passed through Church Passage and into Mitre Square very soon after Lawende's party had gone. At 1.44 or 1.45, just ten minutes after the Church Passage sighting, PC Watkins found Kate's body.

The testimony of PC James Harvey is problematical. If his deposition is to be credited, Harvey walked through Church Passage and looked into the square at about 1.41 or 1.42 but detected nothing untoward. 'I saw no one, I heard no cry or noise,' he said. Perhaps the murderer was still there, crouching unseen in the shadow of Taylor's shop. Or perhaps – it might have been possible, though only just – he had already slain Kate and left by Mitre Street or St James' Place. Neither of these possibilities seem very likely and inevitably one wonders about Harvey. His timing may well have been awry. It was, as he conceded himself, not much better than guesswork: 'I passed the post office clock between 1 and 2 minutes to the half hour . . . I can only speak with certainty as to time with regard to the post office clock.'[28] When the murder occurred Harvey had served twelve years in the City Police. Within another year he would be dismissed from the force for reasons as yet unknown.

Whatever view we take of Harvey's claim, the killer worked with ruthless speed and efficiency. Dr Sequeira thought that the murder would have taken about three minutes but Brown told the inquest that the injuries he had seen could not have been inflicted in less than five. Even so, after cutting the throat and mutilating the abdomen, the killer had obviously had enough time in hand to indulge in further gratuitous cutting and slashing to the face.

One further clue, albeit small, is afforded by the medical evidence. Professor James Cameron, a specialist in forensic medicine, recently deduced from the medical sketches and photographs that Kate's murderer had been right-handed, 'as the incision drags to the right, as would happen, and is deeper as more viscera is exposed.'[29] Precisely the same inference can be made from Dr Brown's comments that the abdomen was laid open upwards by a man kneeling at the prostrate victim's right side. For it would have been difficult if not impossible for anyone to have worked left-handed from such a position.

On the face of it there is no more baffling aspect of the whole Mitre Square mystery than the murderer's escape from the City. If Constables Halse and Long were correct and the piece of apron which the killer deposited in Goulston Street was not there at about 2.20 this is especially the case. For, since the apron was not found until 2.55, we are left with the possibility that the murderer loitered for an hour or more on the fringes of the City before making good his escape. The capacity of the culprit to elude patrolling policemen perplexed Walter Dew, then a young Metropolitan detective attached to H Division. Half a century later he noted the precautions that had been taken by both forces before the double murder and marvelled that 'the Ripper, or any other human being, could have penetrated that area and got away again . . . It seemed as though the fiend set out deliberately to prove that he could defeat every effort to capture him.'[30]

Remarkable the escape certainly was – but not inexplicable. Although the murderer's clothes may have been bloodstained the area through which he passed abounded in slaughterhouses. There was, for example, a Jewish abattoir in Aldgate High Street, hard by Mitre Square. Consequently the sight of slaughtermen on the streets at night in bloodstained aprons or overalls was presumably a familiar one. But more importantly, we are almost certainly wrong in imagining the murderer fleeing the scene of his crime reeking with blood. An examination of Kate's clothing demonstrated that some of the cuts had been made through the clothes, which would have afforded the murderer some protection against bloodstaining. Furthermore, if the mutilations were inflicted after Kate had already been strangled the spillage of blood would have been relatively slight. The abdominal injuries were certainly inflicted after death and, as Brown noted, occasioned little appreciable bleeding. A greater effusion of blood flowed from the left carotid artery. But by kneeling on the right side of the body, and turning the victim's head to the left as he severed her throat, the murderer could have directed the flow towards the ground and away from him. Mud found on Kate's left cheek does suggest that her head had been held in this way. Whatever, neither Brown nor Sequeira thought that the murderer need necessarily have been bespattered with blood.

The police should not be judged too harshly for allowing the killer to slip through their clutches. The City force, it is true, had been put on standing alert by Major Smith but they had been enjoined to watch prostitutes and couples rather than single men. Then, too, we are not treating of an age of panda cars and radio communication. We do not know how quickly the news from Mitre Square reached the various patrolling constables and plain clothes men in and about the City. The experience of Halse, Outram and Marriott proves that some at least had heard something of the tragedy within fifteen minutes of PC Watkins' discovery but even after they knew, a man with a plausible tale would have given them no cause for detaining him unless he was bloodstained or behaving in an obviously suspicious manner. In addition, the police on duty that night had virtually no idea what their quarry looked like. The only description that they might have read or been told about – that from Elizabeth Long – had emanated from a witness who had not even seen the suspect's face. When Inspector McWilliam arrived on the scene of the crime he ordered immediate searches of streets and lodging houses in the vicinity. It must then, however, have been about four or later and by that time the bird had long since flown.

Much of the discussion surrounding the Eddowes murder has inevitably centred upon the cryptic message chalked in the entry of Wentworth Dwellings in Goulston Street: 'The Juwes (Juews?) are the men that will not be blamed for nothing.' Why did Sir Charles order it wiped away before it could be photographed? What did it mean? And to what extent was its obliteration by the Metropolitan Police, in Smith's phrase, an 'unpardonable blunder'? We have already dealt with the first of these questions and the answer to the last partly hinges upon our response to the second.

The trouble with the chalk message is that, like many clues relating to these murders, we can document its existence but do not know enough to interpret its meaning. There are at least three permissible interpretations of this particular clue. All three are feasible, not one capable of proof.

The first is that the writing was not the work of the murderer at all. It was attributed to him only because of its proximity to the discarded piece of Eddowes apron. But suppose the killer happened to throw the apron, quite fortuitously, down by an existing piece of graffiti? In such a case we would be utterly wrong in according to the writing any significance whatsoever. Walter Dew was inclined to endorse this approach to the problem. Why, he asked, should the murderer 'fool around chalking things on walls when his life was imperilled by every minute he loitered?' He might, of course, have been right. Chief Inspector Swanson referred to the writing as 'blurred', which suggests that it might have been old. Constable Halse, on the other hand, saw it and thought it looked recent. And Chief Inspector Henry Moore and Sir Robert Anderson are both on record as having explicitly stated their belief that the message was written by the murderer.[31] The position of the writing, just above the bloodstained piece of Kate's apron, and the unlikelihood of any overtly anti-semitic message surviving long in chalk in an entry principally used by Jews, oblige us to take it seriously.

Both of the remaining interpretations assume that the killer was its author.

One interpretation would take the scribe at his word. It may seem strange that a Jewish killer should so publicly direct suspicion towards his co-religionists and, hence, to himself, but, as Dew himself conceded, 'murderers do foolish things.' It is by no means impossible that the chalk message was the defiant gesture of a deranged Jew, euphoric from bloody 'triumphs' in Dutfield's Yard and Mitre Square. When the message became public property it was widely proclaimed that the spelling 'Juwes' or 'Juewes' unmistakably incriminated a Jew. 'The language of the Jews in the East End,' said the *Pall Mall Gazette* of 12 October, 'is a hybrid dialect, known as Yiddish, and their mode of spelling the word Jews would be "Juwes". This the police consider a strong indication that the crime was committed by one of the numerous foreigners by whom the East End is infested.' Warren, in fact, did not believe that the killer was a Jew. But the newspaper stories prompted him to take the matter of the spelling up with Hermann Adler, the Acting Chief Rabbi. On 13 October Adler replied: 'I was deeply pained by the statements that appeared in several papers today . . . that in the Yiddish dialect the word Jews is spelled "Juewes". This is not a fact. The equivalent in the Judao-German (Yiddish) jargon is "Yidden". I do not know of any dialect or language in which "Jews" is spelled "Juewes".' Such was Sir Charles' fear of anti-semitic disturbances that, on the strength of Adler's letter, he issued a statement to the press in which he explicitly refuted the claim that 'Juwes' was the Yiddish spelling of Jews.[32]

It was not the second but the third interpretation that was most favoured at Scotland Yard and Old Jewry. This read the chalk message as a deliberate subterfuge, designed to incriminate the Jews and throw the police off the track of the real murderer. Thus, in his report on the Eddowes murder Swanson noted the fact that the writing was on the wall of 'a common stairs leading to a number of tenements occupied almost exclusively by Jews' and asserted that its purport was 'to throw blame upon the Jews'. Warren, in a minute of 13 October, declared that he could not understand the crimes 'being done by a Socialist because the last murders were evidently done by someone desiring to bring discredit on the Jews & Socialists or Jewish Socialists'. Similarly, on 6 November, he told the Home Office that the message was 'evidently written with the intention of inflaming the public mind against the Jews'. And however critical Major Smith might be of Sir Charles' eradication of the clue he concurred in the Commissioner's reading of it. Its probable intent, he wrote in his memoirs, was 'to throw the police off the scent, to divert suspicion from the Gentiles and throw it upon the Jews'.[33] The implication of this reasoning is obvious – the murderer himself was *not* a Jew.

Although it seems likely that the graffito was written by the murderer it yields little clue to his identity. Warren, writing to Lushington on 10 October, could not make much of it: 'The idiom does not appear to me to be either English, French or German, but it might possibly be that of an Irishman speaking a foreign language. It seems to be the idiom of Spain or Italy.' The spelling 'Juwes', however, may simply reflect local dialect. According to A. G. B. Atkinson's study of the parish of St Botolph Aldgate, published a decade after the murders, Jewry Street was long known in the area as Poor Jewry or 'Pouere Juwery'.[34]

Advocates of the Masonic conspiracy theory cite 'Juwes' as proof that the murderer was a Freemason. This assertion is based upon an erroneous belief, promulgated by Stephen Knight, Melvyn Fairclough and others, that 'Juwes' was a Masonic term by which Jubela, Jubelo and Jubelum were collectively known. In fact this was simply not the case. By 1888 the three murderers of Hiram Abiff had not been part of British Masonic ritual for more than seventy years, and although they had survived in American ritual in neither country had they ever been called, officially or colloquially, the 'Juwes'. 'It is a mystery,' wrote Paul Begg, one of the most dependable modern students of the case, 'why anyone ever thought that "Juwes" was a Masonic word.'[35]

Few of those who have pondered the events of 30 September have doubted that both murders were the work of the same killer. As we have noted in a previous chapter, some doubt about the relationship of the Stride killing to the rest of the series will always remain but there are at least two compelling arguments in favour of linking her death with that of Kate Eddowes. First, the technique by which the victims' throats were cut was virtually identical. The throat of each victim was severed from left to right while she was lying on the ground. And in both cases the left carotid artery suffered far more damage than the right. The cut in Elizabeth's throat partially severed the left carotid but left the vessels on the right side of the neck untouched. In Kate's case the left carotid was completely severed and the right sustained only a 'fine hole opening'. Second, a comparison of the description furnished by Lawende with those provided by Marshall, Smith and Schwartz of men seen with Liz Stride reveals several points of similarity. The likeness between Lawende's man and Schwartz's man is especially marked. Admittedly Lawende's man was of medium build and appeared rather 'rough and shabby' whereas Schwartz's was broad shouldered and respectably dressed. But both men looked about thirty. Both were of fair complexion and medium height. Both sported small moustaches. And both wore jackets and caps with peaks. It is perhaps needless to add that the most important difference between the Stride and Eddowes murders – the absence of abdominal and facial mutilations in the former – is plausibly explained by Diemschutz's disturbance of Stride's killer. Dr Blackwell, Inspector McWilliam and Major Smith all declared that the same man claimed both victims. The only known dissentient was Dr Phillips.[36]

If, as seems probable, the same man did commit both crimes he must have been possessed of reckless daring. For, having nearly been trapped in a cul-de-sac with the body of his first victim, he walked into the City to claim a second within the hour, and then, knowing full well that the Metropolitan Police must have been alerted by the first murder, returned to Whitechapel carrying knife and gruesome mementoes of Mitre Square with him. If this scenario is correct – and it probably is – Martin Friedland's suggestion that the murders were carefully contrived 'to throw as much suspicion as possible on the Jewish community' deserves better than it has received from later commentators.[37] The murder of Elizabeth Stride next to the International Working Men's Educational Club, the apparent hailing of an accomplice by the name 'Lipski', the murder of Kate Eddowes close to another club (the Imperial) frequented by Jews, and the message 'The Juwes are the men that will not be blamed for nothing' chalked in the entry of a house of Jewish tenements – these signify little by themselves but, taken together, begin to make a persuasive case.

There is no credible evidence from Mitre Square that the murderer was assisted by an accomplice. This does not prove that there was no accomplice, only that one was not noticed, for the role of such a man might plausibly have been to loiter at a distance from the actual killer, watching for signs of danger and ready to intervene only if the murderer looked as though he might be caught red-handed. I say no *credible* evidence because there is James Blenkingsop:

James Blenkingsop, who was on duty as a watchman in St James's Place (leading to the square), where some street improvements are taking place, states that about half-past one a respectably-dressed man came up to him and said, "Have you seen a man and a woman go through here?" "I didn't take any notice," returned Blenkingsop. "I have seen some people pass".[38]

This newspaper tale is not corroborated in any of the official documentation now extant. Even if it is not a complete fiction there is no proof that the man Blenkingsop claimed to have seen had any connection with the murderer. Indeed, given the possibility that the estimated time was wrong, it is conceivable that he was a plain-clothes detective, investigating the crime soon after it had occurred.

A day after the double event Londoners opened their morning papers to read of yet more horrors. They were told that several days before the latest atrocities the Central News had received a letter from someone who claimed to be the Whitechapel murderer. The writer declared himself to be 'down on whores', promised further killings and signed his letter with a name that would live in history and become a synonym for sexual serial murder the world over – Jack the Ripper.

13

Letters from Hell

NEWSMEN RECOGNIZED THE EXISTENCE of a multiple murderer in Whitechapel soon after the Nichols murder of 31 August, but it was not until after the double killing a month later that the assassin because generally known as 'Jack the Ripper'. In the interval people spoke of him only as 'the Whitechapel murderer' or 'Leather Apron'.

It is now well known that the name 'Jack the Ripper' was coined by the author of a pseudonymous letter received by the Central News Agency on 27 September. The sources of this scribe's inspiration, however, still invite speculation.

'Jack' is as obvious a name as anyone could have chosen and we need really seek no explanation of it. Nevertheless, William Stewart's suggestion that this particular use of 'Jack' may have been inspired by the frequency of the name amongst criminal celebrities of the past[1] has found favour with students who believe the author of the original Jack the Ripper letter to have been a young man steeped in penny dreadful literature. Stewart may just have a point because the most celebrated criminal in the 19th century was the burglar and prisonbreaker Jack Sheppard. Sheppard died at Tyburn in 1724 but his reputation was revived in 1839 in a best-selling romance by William Harrison Ainsworth and for the rest of the century his short but spectacular career continued to inspire romances, chapbooks and plays. Indeed, such was the vogue for Jack Sheppard on the stage that for many years anxious Lord Chamberlains, fearful of the alleged pernicious influences of such dramas upon public morals, refused to license plays under that name. This did nothing to check the legend, however, and as late as 1885 Nellie Farren enjoyed rapturous applause at the Gaiety impersonating Jack in Yardley and Stephens' hit burlesque *Little Jack Sheppard*. Another penny dreadful hero of the period was the 18th century highwayman John Rann, better known as 'Sixteen String Jack' from his habit of decorating the knees of his breeches with silk strings. A little of Rann's fame still persisted in the Ripper's day and devotees of *Peter Pan*, J. M. Barrie's 'terrible masterpiece', will probably know that Barrie, growing up in the 1870s, was dubbed 'Sixteen String Jack' by one of his schoolmates because of his taste for blood and thunder literature. Closer in spirit to the Ripper than these engaging rogues was 'Spring Heeled Jack'. This was the popular name of a miscreant who, in a variety of bizarre disguises, assaulted and terrified women and children in the environs of London in 1837–38. Spring Heeled Jack was neither identified nor caught but he entered folklore as a bogy man and his name was used by exasperated mothers well into the Ripper's time to scare fractious offspring into better behaviour.

It is thus possible that the name Jack would have subconsciously suggested itself to a man well versed in cheap crime literature. The word 'Ripper' was, of course, derived from the murderer's technique of laying open the abdomens of his victims. It was a term that had been used in connection with these crimes ever since the death of Polly Nichols, the first victim to sustain this particular injury. Polly was at first thought to have been the victim of a 'High Rip' gang that levied blackmail upon street-walkers. The early newspaper gossip about Leather Apron credited him with threatening to 'rip up' Widow Annie. And Warren, commenting on the suspect Puckridge for the Home Office on 19 September, related how he had threatened to 'rip people up' with a long knife.

The letter to the Central News was not the first purporting to come from the murderer and it was far from being the last. But as the first signed Jack the Ripper and the one that inspired almost all the others it was perhaps the most important. The Central News Ltd of 5 New Bridge Street received it on 27 September. It was written in red ink and read as follows:

25 Sept: 1888.

Dear Boss
             I keep on hearing the police
have caught me but they wont fix
me just yet. I have laughed when

they look so clever and talk about
being on the <u>right</u> track. That joke
about Leather Apron gave me real
fits. I am down on whores and
I shant quit ripping them till I
do get buckled. Grand work the last
job was. I gave the lady no time to
squeal. How can they catch me now.
I love my work and want to start
again. You will soon hear of me
with my funny little games. I
saved some of the proper <u>red</u> stuff in
a ginger beer bottle over the last job
to write with but it went thick
like glue and I cant use it. Red
ink is fit enough I hope <u>ha. ha</u>.
The next job I do I shall clip
the lady's ears off and send to the
police officers just for jolly wouldnt
you. Keep this letter back till I
do a bit more work then give
it out straight. My knife's so nice
and sharp I want to get to work
right away if I get a chance.
Good luck.
　　　　　Yours truly
　　　　　Jack the Ripper
Dont mind me giving the trade name

wasnt good enough
to post this before
I got all the red
ink off my hands
curse it.
No luck yet. They
say I'm a doctor
now <u>ha ha</u>

The envelope was addressed to 'The Boss, Central News Office,

London City.' It bore a London East Central postmark dated 27 September. The editor's instinct was to treat the whole matter as a hoax and he delayed two days before transmitting the letter to Chief Constable Williamson at the Yard. 'The enclosed was sent the Central News two days ago,' he explained, '& was treated as a joke.'

'You will soon hear of me with my funny little games.' Remembering that line, the police must have looked hard at the letter again when, the night after it reached them, Liz Stride and Kate Eddowes were cruelly murdered in the East End. Then, by the first post on Monday morning, a day after the killings, the Central News received a second communication. It was a postcard, apparently bloodstained. There was no date but there was a 'LONDON. E.' postmark dated 1 October. Couched in the same mocking tones and written in the same hand as the letter, it read:

> I wasnt codding
> dear old Boss when
> I gave you the tip.
> youll hear about
> saucy Jackys work
> tomorrow double
> event this time
> number one squealed
> a bit couldnt
> finish straight
> off. had not time
> to get ears for
> police thanks for
> keeping last letter
> back till I got
> to work again.
> Jack the Ripper[2]

The Metropolitan Police, to whom both letter and postcard passed, now took them seriously enough to launch a determined attempt to trace the scribe. On this occasion the assistance of the public was speedily enlisted. Preparing facsimiles of letter and card, the police published them in a poster of 3 October requesting anyone who recognized the handwriting to contact them. It was placarded outside every police station. At the same time facsimiles were sent to the press and on 4 October several papers published them in full or in part.

Perhaps the most important result of all this publicity was that it gave the murderer a name. From the Yard's point of view the other results were disastrous. For although the publicity did nothing to unmask the the killer, or even the letter writer, it did inspire a host of imitative pranksters to deluge police and press in a tide of bogus Ripper letters. They all had to be read and, where possible, followed up, and they wasted a great deal of police time.

The much depleted Metropolitan Police case papers still contain hundreds of letters purportedly written by the Whitechapel murderer. Many, many others were sent to the City Police, to newspapers and to private businesses and individuals.[3] A reading of those extant reveals only one that merits serious consideration along with the first letter and postcard. This was a very nasty little communication addressed to George Lusk of 1 Alderney Road, Mile End, the new chairman of the Mile End Vigilance Committee.[4]

On the evening of Tuesday, 16 October, Lusk received through the post a small parcel wrapped in brown paper. The next night he mentioned it at a meeting of the vigilance committee at the Crown in Mile End Road. Joseph Aarons, the treasurer, told the press how Lusk approached him in a 'state of considerable excitement'. Aarons asked what the matter was. 'I suppose you will laugh at what I am going to tell you,' said Lusk, 'but you must know that I had a little parcel come to me on Tuesday evening, and to my surprise it contains half a kidney and a letter from Jack the Ripper.' Aarons did laugh. Someone, he told the chairman jocularly, was trying to frighten him. But Lusk was visibly shaken. 'It is no laughing matter to me,' he grumbled. It was already late. So Aarons suggested that they let the matter rest until the morning when he and some of the other members would call round to inspect the package.

At about 9.30 the next morning, 18 October, Aarons, together with Mr B. Harris, the secretary, and Messrs Reeves and Lawton, two of the committee members, called upon the chairman at his home in Alderney Road. Lusk opened his desk and took out a small cardboard box. It was about 3^1/$_2$ inches square. 'Throw it away,' he said, handing it to them, 'I hate the sight of it!' They opened the box.

Inside was one half of a kidney, divided longitudinally. It stank. There was also a letter:

> From hell
> Mr Lusk
>   Sor
>   I send you half the
> Kidne I took from one women
> prasarved it for you tother piece I
> fried and ate it was very nise I
> may send you the bloody knif that
> took it out if you only wate a whil
> longer
>   signed   Catch me when
>   you can
>   Mishter Lusk[5]

Aarons felt sure he was not looking at a sheep's kidney and he proposed that they take it to the surgery of Dr Frederick Wiles at 56 Mile End Road. The doctor wasn't in but his assistant, Mr F. S. Reed, was. Reed opined that the kidney was human and had been preserved in spirits of wine. But, to make sure, he popped over to the London Hospital and submitted the kidney to Dr Thomas Horrocks Openshaw, Curator of the Pathological Museum, for examination under the microscope.

Openshaw's alleged findings have influenced everyone who has ever written about the kidney. According to Aarons, when Reed returned he told them that Openshaw had said that the kidney 'belonged to a female, that it was part of the left kidney, and that the woman had been in the habit of drinking. He should think that the person had died about the same time the Mitre Square murder was committed.' This account is generally supported by a Press Association report, compiled from 'inquiries made at Mile End' and published on 19 October. Openshaw pronounced the kidney, it said, to be 'a portion of a human kidney – a "ginny" kidney – that is to say, one that had belonged to a person who had drunk heavily. He was further of opinion that it was the organ of a woman of about forty-five years of age, and that it had been taken from the body within the last three weeks.' Interviewed the same day for the *Star*, though, Openshaw himself repudiated most of what had been published: 'Dr Openshaw told a *Star* reporter today that after having examined the piece of kidney under the microscope he was of opinion that it was half of a left human kidney. He couldn't say, however, whether it was that of a woman, nor how long ago it had been removed from the body, as it had been preserved in spirits.'[6]

Whatever Lusk's party were given to understand about Openshaw's views they heard enough to convince them that the police had to be told. Without further ado they took the parcel to Leman Street and placed it in the hands of Inspector Abberline. The Metropolitan Police, in their turn, sent it to their City colleagues and the kidney was examined by Dr Gordon Brown, the City Police surgeon. His report, although crucial to any assessment of the importance of Mr Lusk's parcel, has not survived and all we know of it comes secondhand or worse from Chief Inspector Swanson and Major Smith.

Swanson's information probably came from Inspector McWilliam. On 6 November he told the Home Office that 'the result of the combined medical opinion they [the City Police] have taken upon it, is, that it is the kidney of a human adult, not charged with a fluid, as it would have been in the case of a body handed over for purposes of dissection to an hospital, but rather as it would be in a case where it was taken from the body not so destined.'[7]

Smith's account was published more than twenty years later: 'I made over the kidney to the police surgeon, instructing him to consult with the most eminent men in the profession, and send me a report without delay. I give the substance of it. The renal artery is about three inches long. Two inches remained in the corpse, one inch was attached to the kidney. The kidney left in the corpse was in an advanced stage of Bright's Disease; the kidney sent me was in an exactly similar state. But what was of far more importance, Mr Sutton, one of the senior surgeons of the London Hospital, whom Gordon Brown asked to meet him and another practitioner in consultation, and who was one of the greatest authorities living on the kidney and its diseases, said he would pledge his reputation that the kidney submitted to them had been put in spirits within a few hours of its removal from the body – thus effectually disposing of all hoaxes in connection with it. The body of anyone done to death by violence is not taken direct to the dissecting-room, but must await an inquest, never held before the following day at the soonest.'[8]

The wrapping in which the parcel had arrived bore two penny stamps and a postmark. Except for the letters OND (a vestige of 'LONDON') the postmark was too indistinct to be read. Nevertheless, the Post Office is said to have expressed an opinion that the package was posted in the Eastern or the East Central district.[9] There were arguments in favour of both. Items travelling from one district to another usually bore the postmark of both districts. Lusk's package, however, had only been franked once and this indicated that it had been posted in the district in which it had been received, i.e. the Eastern district. On the other hand, the package was too large to have been dropped into an ordinary post-box. It was thus suggested that it had been posted at the Lombard or Gracechurch Street office, in the East Central district, for there the receptacles were of unusually wide dimensions.

A possible lead on the sender of the parcel came from Miss Emily Marsh, whose father traded in leather at 218 Jubilee Street, Mile End Road.

Shortly after one on Monday, 15 October, she was minding her father's shop when a tall man dressed in clerical costume came in. He referred to a vigilance committee reward bill posted up in the window and asked Emily for the address of Mr Lusk, mentioned in the bill as the president of the committee. Emily advised him to see Mr Aarons, the treasurer, who lived at the corner of Jubilee Street and Mile End Road, just thirty yards away, but the man said he did not want to go there. She then produced a newspaper. It gave Mr Lusk's address as Alderney Road, Globe Road, and she offered it to the stranger. But he declined to take it. Instead he told Emily to 'read it out' and proceeded to write in his pocket-book, all the time keeping his head down. Later, after thanking her for the information, he left the shop. Something about the stranger's furtive manner and appearance worried Emily so much that she sent John Cormack, the shop boy, after him to see that all was right.

A description of the man, apparently based upon the observations of Emily, John Cormack and Mr Marsh, who turned up in time to encounter him on the pavement outside the shop, was published by the *Telegraph*: 'The stranger is described as a man of some forty-five years of age, fully six feet in height, and slimly built. He wore a soft felt black hat, drawn over his forehead, a stand-up collar, and a very long black single-breasted overcoat, with a Prussian or clerical collar partly turned up. His face was of a sallow type, and he had a dark beard and moustache. The man spoke with what was taken to be an Irish accent.'[10]

Was this the man who posted the kidney? Well, he inquired

after Lusk's address on the 15th, the day before the kidney was delivered. Emily's newspaper, moreover, printed the address simply as Alderney Road, Globe Road. No number in Alderney Road was given. And the address on the parcel Lusk received likewise contained no house number. The spelling of some of the words in the letter, too, is interesting. For the rendition of 'Sir' as 'Sor', of 'er' as 'ar' in 'prasarved' and of 's' as 'sh' in 'Mishter' could suggest a writer with an Irish accent. It is thus possible that Lusk's correspondent and Emily's tall stranger *were* identical. But the fact that Lusk had been the recipient of several hoax letters obliges us to regard it as no more than a possibility.

The important question is whether any one of the three communications we have noticed was actually written by the murderer. The first two – the letter and postcard signed Jack the Ripper – were in the same handwriting and should be considered together.

Leonard Matters and William Stewart, the first modern Ripperologists, both dismissed these documents as hoaxes. But Donald McCormick, writing in 1959, thought differently. He drew attention to the letter writer's promise, on 25 September, to clip the victim's ears off 'the next job I do' and interpreted the injuries to Stride's left and Eddowes' right ear as abortive attempts to redeem that promise. McCormick also assumed that the postcard was written and posted on 30 September. This, as he pointed out, was a Sunday and no report of the murders would appear in the dailies until the next morning. Yet the writer of the postcard not only knew of the 'double event' but, in McCormick's view, mentioned details only the murderer could have known. 'Unless Jack the Ripper was the killer,' he asked, 'how could he have known that Elizabeth Stride had 'squealed a bit' . . . or that an attempt had been made to clip off the ears?'[11]

McCormick's view of the matter held sway for more than fifteen years. During that time every major writer on the case – Odell, Cullen, Farson and Rumbelow – lent their weight to the belief that the murderer had penned the communications to the Central News and had thereby coined his own *nom de guerre*. Then, in 1975, Richard Whittington-Egan and Stephen Knight sowed seeds of doubt. Whittington-Egan did not believe that the postcard had shown any foreknowledge of the double murder at all. It was, he reminded his readers, postmarked 1 October, which meant that it could have been posted on the Monday, after details of the murders had been splashed across the columns of the morning papers. Knight, after checking with the records department of the Post Office, endorsed this conclusion. He revealed that there were Sunday collections from post-boxes in 1888 and that any letter collected on a Sunday would have been stamped with that date. The Jack the Ripper postcard, however, was franked 'OC 1', not 'SP 30', and that proved, as far as Knight was concerned, that it had to have been posted on the Monday.[12]

The ranks of the Ripperologists have since been in total disarray on the subject. Some, like Colin Wilson, Robin Odell and Paul Harrison, have continued to identify the Central News Agency's correspondent with the murderer. Others, notably Martin Fido, Melvin Harris and Paul Begg, have followed Whittington-Egan and Knight in denouncing him as a fraud.

At this date it is not possible to establish the exact date on which the postcard was mailed. For even if further research into Post Office procedures could verify Stephen Knight's findings they would not preclude a Sunday posting after the last collection time. My own feeling is that the postcard *was* written and posted on Sunday, 30 September, the day of the murders. The wording of the card certainly suggests that this was the case: 'Youll hear about saucy Jackys work tomorrow [i.e. in Monday morning's papers].' And a Sunday posting would seem consistent with the understanding of the press that the card was delivered with the first post on Monday morning.[13]

The argument over posting dates, however, rests upon an entirely false assumption — that if the card was mailed on Sunday 30th it displayed some foreknowledge of the details of the double murder. In truth neither card nor preceding letter contain anything whatsoever to justify a belief that they were written by the murderer. This conclusion holds good whether the card was posted on Sunday *or* Monday and the preoccupation with the date is a red herring that has diverted attention from the critical study of the content of the communications for far too long.

All three claims usually made on behalf of the Jack the Ripper letter and postcard are easily refuted.

First, the matter of the ears. 'The next job I do,' boasted the letter writer, 'I shall clip the ladys ears off and send to the police officers just for jolly.' The threat was not carried out and after the double murder the postcard explained: 'had not time to get ears for police.' Now, it has been alleged that attempts were indeed made to remove the ears of Liz Stride and Kate Eddowes, and this 'fact' has been repeatedly adduced to authenticate the correspondence. Unfortunately for the argument the medical records tell a different story. Dr Gordon Brown, examining Kate's body in Mitre Square, did discover that the lobe of her right ear had been severed. But one detached ear lobe does not constitute evidence of an attempt to remove both ears and, given the extensive mutilation to Kate's face and head, can scarcely be deemed significant. If the murderer had really wanted to cut off Kate's ears he would have done so. There was certainly time enough, as the intricate cuts to her eyelids and cheeks attest. In the case of Liz Stride the murderer inflicted no injury whatsoever to the victim's ears. There was, it is true, a tear on the lower lobe of her left ear. But this was not a recent injury. It was, as Dr Phillips made clear at the inquest, an old wound, apparently caused by the forcible removal of an ear-ring, and now healed.

The second claim is that the postcard displayed foreknowledge of the Stride and Eddowes killings by referring to a 'double event' in advance of Monday's press reports. Even if we suppose that the postcard *was* written on Sunday 30th, this contention is, quite frankly, absurd. Innumerable people knew of the murders on the Sunday and could have alluded to them in conversation or correspondence. Within hours of the discovery of the bodies the news was being circulated by word of mouth throughout the district. Even some editions of the Sunday papers managed to catch the story. 'Successive editions of the Sunday papers were getting a marvellous sale yesterday,' commented Monday morning's *Daily News*, 'and the contents were being devoured with the utmost eagerness.' The *Telegraph* described the state of 'almost frantic excitement' that prevailed throughout the East End on the fatal Sunday. 'Thousands of people visited both Mitre Square and Berner Street, and journals containing details of the crimes were bought up by crowds of men and women in Whitechapel, Stepney, and Spitalfields.'14 Curiously, despite the scrutiny to which the postmark has been subjected, no one seems to have pointed out that the card was posted in the Eastern district, where the double murder was common knowledge on Sunday as well as Monday. Pressmen swarmed around the murder sites throughout Sunday. Trawling for copy for next morning's papers, they, in particular, would have acquired a detailed knowledge of the crimes, a fact which, as we will see, might not be without significance.

Finally, it is regularly claimed that the postcard's statement that 'number one [Stride] squealed a bit' is proof of the killer's authorship because only the murderer could have known such a detail. This argument, of course, assumes that the information given about Stride was correct. We cannot be certain that it was. There were several witnesses in and about Dutfield's Yard at the time of the murder. Only one (Israel Schwartz) swore to hearing screams. Others, like Morris Eagle, Mrs Diemschutz and Mrs Mortimer, were close enough to the scene of the crime to hear cries but heard nothing. Perhaps Elizabeth did 'squeal a bit'. Perhaps her screams were drowned in the singing from the International Working Men's Club. But even if this were so it is the kind of detail a hoaxer could easily have invented and stood a good chance of getting right. It might also have been possible for the postcard writer, if he were a pressman, to have learned the detail from Schwartz. We know for certain that one journalist successfully tracked him down to his lodgings in Backchurch Lane, either on Sunday evening or Monday morning, and procured an interview from him. This interview was published too late to influence the postcard[15] and, in any case, did not mention Elizabeth's screams, but since one newshound found Schwartz it was clearly possible for others to do so.

In short there is no reason to believe that the Jack the Ripper letter and postcard were anything more than hoaxes. This was Warren's view at the time. 'At present,' he told Lushington on 10 October 1888, 'I think the whole thing a hoax but we are bound to try and ascertain the writer in any case.' Many years later some detectives even insisted that they knew the identity of the hoaxer. Anderson categorically asserted in 1910 that the letter was the creation of an 'enterprising London journalist'. He was tempted, he added, to reveal his name, provided his publishers would accept responsibility in the event of a libel action, but demurred because 'no public benefit would result from such a course, and the traditions of my old department would suffer.' In annotating his copy of Anderson's book, Ex-Chief Inspector Swanson also maintained that '*head* officers of CID' at Scotland Yard knew the identity of the journalist.[16]

Unfortunately the claims of Anderson and Swanson are probably unjustified. I do not doubt that they had a specific name in mind. But Anderson's concern over a possible libel suit suggests that he knew very well that he could not substantiate his allegation at law and new evidence from the Metropolitan Police case papers casts further doubt upon it.

On 14 October 1896, eight years after the first letters, a fresh Jack the Ripper letter was received through the post at Commercial Street

Police Station. 'Dear Boss,' it began, 'you will be surprised to find that this comes from yours as of old Jack the Ripper. Ha Ha. If my old friend Mr Warren is dead you can read it. You might remember me if you try and think a little. Ha Ha . . .' Much in the same vein followed, liberally sprinkled with words and phrases cribbed from the original communications but not in the same handwriting. The writer explained that he had just come back from abroad and was ready to resume his work, and he concluded with an enigmatic reference to the writing found in Goulston Street: '"The Jewes are people that are blamed for nothing." Ha Ha. have you heard this before.' It was signed 'yours truly, Jack the Ripper.'

One of many crude imitations of the original, the letter concerns us less than the police reaction to it. From Commercial Street it was forwarded to Scotland Yard. There, on 15 October, Melville Macnaghten, then Chief Constable, minuted the covering note: 'This is not, I think, the handwriting of our original correspondent – but it is not a bad imitation. Will you get out the old letters & compare?' Chief Inspector Henry Moore undertook the comparison. His report, dated 18 October, has not been published before:

I beg to report having carefully perused all the old 'Jack the Ripper' letters and fail to find any similarity of handwriting in any of them, with the exception of the two well remembered communications which were sent to the 'Central News' Office; one a letter, dated 25th September 1888, and the other a postcard, bearing the postmark 1st October 1888 . . .

On comparing the handwriting of the present letter with [the] handwriting of that document, I find many similarities in the formation of letters. For instance the y's, t's, and w's are very much the same. Then there are several words which appear in both documents; viz:– Dear Boss; ha ha (although in the present letter the capital H is used instead of the small one); and in speaking of the murders he describes them as his 'work' or the last 'job'; and if I get a (or the) chance; then there are the words 'yours truly' and – the Ripper (the latter on postcard) are very much alike. Besides there are the finger smears.

Considering the lapse of time, it would be interesting to know how the present writer was able to use the words 'The Jewes are people that are blamed for nothing'; as it will be remembered that they are practically the same words that were written in chalk, undoubtedly by the murderer, on the wall at Goulston

St., Whitechapel, on the night of 30th September, 1888, after the murders of Mrs Stride and Mrs Eddows; and the word Jews was spelt on that occasion precisely as it is now.

Although these similarities strangely exist between the documents, I am of opinion that the present writer is not the original correspondent who prepared the letters to the Central News; as if it had been I should have thought he would have again addressed it to the same Press Agency; and not to Commercial Street Police Station.

In conclusion I beg to observe that I do not attach any importance to this communication.

Swanson wrote a capital A in the margin against Moore's last sentence. Then he endorsed the report: 'In my opinion the handwritings are not the same. I agree as at A.'[17]

These documents prove that, eight years after the original enquiry, the CID still did not know who had written the original Jack the Ripper letter and postcard. For had they possessed such information Moore's exercise would have been quite pointless. As late as 1914, furthermore, Sir Melville Macnaghten, freshly retired from ten years as *the* head of the CID, would only own to a *suspicion* as to the hoaxer: 'In this ghastly production I have always thought I could discern the stained forefinger of the journalist – indeed, a year later, I had shrewd suspicions as to the actual author! But whoever did pen the gruesome stuff, it is certain to my mind that it was not the mad miscreant who had committed the murders.'[18]

In asserting a conclusive identification of the hoaxer Anderson's memoirs went beyond the truth. This should caution us as to their worth as historical evidence. And later, when we come to consider Sir Robert's extraordinary claims in relation to one of the major murder suspects, we will need to read them with a generous pinch of salt.

Nevertheless, police intuition that the letter and postcard had been penned by an irresponsible journalist was probably correct. Telltale signs pointing to such a conclusion abound in the communications themselves. Although all question-marks and most apostrophes are omitted in the letter the overall impression it conveys is that it was the work of an educated man trying to appear less so. The handwriting and general layout are neat and careful. Capital letters and full stops are properly employed. And, despite the presence of words that would sorely have tested a semi-literate man[19], there is not one spelling mistake. The fact that the communications were sent, not to Scotland

Yard, but to the Central News, suggests, moreover, that the hoaxer knew exactly where to go in order to achieve maximum publicity for his creations. Lastly we come back to the postmarks. It may be significant that the letter was posted in the East Central district. For it embraced the Fleet Street/Farringdon Road area, where many of the main newspaper offices were situated. The postcard bore an Eastern district postmark and could easily have been written and mailed by a young reporter investigating the double murder. In 1966 a writer in *Crime and Detection* claimed that in 1931 an ex-*Star* reporter named Best confessed to him that he and a provincial colleague had written all the Jack the Ripper letters using a pen known as a 'Waverley Nib', deliberately battered to achieve an impression of semi-literacy and 'National School' training.[20] Best's claim to have written all the letters is ridiculous. That he wrote some, to 'keep the business alive' as he said, is possible but assertions made so long after the event must be treated with extreme caution.

The 'From hell' letter sent to George Lusk, backed by Openshaw's and Brown's findings on the kidney, has been accepted as authentic by most students of the Whitechapel murders. It could have been written by the killer. But the case is by no means conclusive.

In the first place the results of Openshaw's examination of the kidney on 18 October were obviously misreported. On average a woman's kidney is smaller and lighter than a man's but the difference is small and it would have been extremely difficult for him to have determined from a portion of kidney whether the organ had been extracted from a man or a woman.

Bright's Disease was originally thought to have been caused by overindulgence in 'ardent spirits' such as gin. However, the term 'ginny kidney', attributed to Openshaw, is now known to be meaningless since the kidneys are not injured by alcohol.

The first accounts of Openshaw's findings come to us through so many intermediaries that it would, indeed, be surprising if they *were* reliable. When directly interviewed by representatives of the press on 19 October the doctor repudiated almost every pronouncement that had been attributed to him.[21] He did reiterate his belief that the organ was part of a left human kidney. But that is about the only view we can confidently ascribe to him.

It is enough to set up an intriguing poser. The left kidney was cut out of Kate Eddowes' body in Mitre Square on 30 September. So was the kidney received by George Lusk sixteen days later, also a portion of a left human kidney, sent by the murderer? Or did someone else, learning from the inquest revelations of 4 October that Kate's left kidney was missing, perpetrate a disgusting hoax? Contemporary opinion was divided. Dr Saunders, the City's Public Analyst, thought the Lusk kidney a practical joke, a 'student's antic'. Major Smith did not.

Let us consider the facts.

Openshaw decided that the postal kidney was part of a left human kidney, Brown that it was the kidney of a human adult. These claims are not unreasonable. As Nick Warren has recently explained, it should have been possible in 1888 for professional medical men to distinguish a human kidney from those of common domestic animals on morphological grounds. And since a kidney may shrink by up to 1 cm. in length between the ages of thirty and seventy, it may also have been possible for them to have determined whether the kidney had been taken from an adult. It should be noted, however, that kidneys afflicted by Bright's Disease, as this is said to have been, are pathologically contracted anyway.

Could the kidney have been sent by a medical student as a prank? Perhaps it could. But there is an important objection to this theory. Bodies delivered to hospitals for dissection were charged with preserving fluid (formalin). The organ received by Lusk had not been treated in this way. It had been preserved in spirit.

Major Smith mentions two circumstances which seem to link the postal kidney specifically with Kate's murder. The right renal artery is generally about three inches long, the left a little less but not shorter than two and a half inches. Now, Smith tells us that about two inches of left renal artery remained in Kate's body and that only about one inch was attached to the postal kidney. Moreover, according to Smith, the right kidney left in Kate's body had been found in an advanced stage of Bright's Disease and the left kidney sent to Lusk was in 'an exactly similar state'.

One hesitates to take Smith at his word. His book, written so long after the event, is inevitably unreliable. And a press statement by Dr Brown, discovered by Stewart Evans, casts real doubt upon his account of the kidney. In his statement Brown would not confirm that the postal kidney was part of a left kidney and contended that it had not been immersed in spirit for more than a week. Furthermore, he asserted that no portion of renal artery adhered to the postal kidney because the organ had been 'trimmed up'.

If accurately reported this statement effectively refutes Smith. But therein lies the rub. Is it accurately reported? Contemporary newspapers are frequently as misleading as later police memoirs. And it is certainly possible to find press support for Smith. A *Daily Telegraph* report of 20 October 1888, for example, says: 'it is asserted that only a small portion of the renal artery adheres to the kidney, while in the case of the Mitre Square victim a large portion of this artery adhered to the body.'

On the matter of Bright's Disease time has vindicated Smith. Dr Sedgwick Saunders, quoted by the *Evening News* in October 1888, flatly contradicts him in saying that 'the right kidney of the woman Eddowes was perfectly normal in its structure and healthy, and by parity of reasoning, you would not get much disease in the left.' But Dr Brown's recently discovered inquest deposition proves that Smith was right and Saunders wrong. Brown told the inquest that Kate's right kidney was 'pale, bloodless, with slight congestion of the base of the pyramids'. These symptoms, as Nick Warren points out, unquestionably do indicate Bright's Disease.[22]

In the end the evidence fails to persuade either way. The postal kidney could have been genuine. On the other hand we cannot *prove* that it had not been extracted from some other person recently autopsied. Experts continue to disagree and the jury is still out.

If the kidney really was Kate's the accompanying letter was written by her murderer. Yet, although the subject of several amusing exercises in graphology, it has inspired only one detailed study by a serious handwriting expert – that by Thomas Mann, a charter member of the World Association of Document Examiners.[23]

Mann's most important conclusion is that the author of the Lusk letter was a semi-literate person. The script exhibits a cramped style of writing – vertical strokes are retraced, letters are crowded together, often very little space separates one word from another. It is a product of finger movement rather than forearm or whole-arm movement. With finger movement letters are formed almost entirely by the action of the thumb and the first and second fingers. It is a method of writing that permits only slight lateral freedom and is characteristic of the semi-literate, of those who have not the assured command of the pen and easy arm motion of the practised penman. Other telltale signs indicate a semi-literate author. Numerous ink blots attest to someone little concerned with legibility and clarity and relatively unskilled in the use of his writing instrument. There is no punctuation.

'Kidne', occurring in the middle of a sentence, is capitalized while 'it', beginning the sentence 'it was very nise', is not. Separate ideas are run together ungrammatically. The sentence 'prasarved it for you' is incomplete. 'Catch me when you can' should probably be 'Catch me if you can.' And more than one seventh of the words in the letter are spelled incorrectly.

There are, admittedly, some indications of rudimentary learning. By no means all the spelling errors are phonetic. The words 'knif' and 'whil' prove that the writer had sufficient education to know of the silent k and h. And conversely, he could not phonetically have arrived at the correct spelling of a word like 'piece'. The setting out of the letter, too, suggests some formal training in writing because it generally follows the correct form as taught in copybooks of the period. Notwithstanding such indications, however, Mann does not believe that the writer was an educated person disguising his handwriting so as to appear semi-literate.

Disguised writing is necessarily slowly drawn. Only by writing so slowly that one is consciously in control of each stroke of the pen is it possible to prevent one's natural, idiosyncratic characteristics from appearing in the script. But, Mann tells us, such conscious attention to the process of writing is almost always detectable: 'The strokes of slowly drawn writing become tremulous in appearance; they lose the clean-cut edges of quickly written lines. Furthermore, a stroke normally produced by one quick motion may, in drawn writing, be composed of several distinct movement impulses – i.e., minute changes of direction will be noticeable in a stroke which could appear firm if it were written with normal speed.' After a careful examination of the Lusk script, Mann believes that it was written more slowly than average handwriting. Difficulty in moving the pen is not surprising in finger movement and the generally heavy pressure exerted by the writer of the Lusk letter may also indicate a relatively slow speed. However, apart from a few exceptions (for example, in the tails of 'hell' and 'nise'), the pen strokes do not, in Mann's judgement, exhibit the halting or hesitating quality characteristic of deliberate disguise. Occasionally, indeed, the writing displays evidence of having been so rapid that the ink track failed to register, as in the e of 'Kidne' and the L, u and s of 'Lusk' at the end of the letter. A disguised hand, finally, is almost certain to be inconsistent with itself in its features or qualities. This is not true of the Lusk script. Throughout it exhibits many subtle idiosyncrasies which are habitually repeated. Mann details no less than twenty-six of them. 'All elements considered,' he writes, 'the indices of speed and internal consistency in the script do not support the hypothesis of generally disguised handwriting; and, on the other hand, these indications do accord with the hypothesis of a semi-literate penman.'

So much for the handwriting. What about nationality and dialect? Well, it is certainly worthy of note, given the debate about whether the murderer was a foreigner or not, that the author of the Lusk letter was probably of British origin. The abbreviation 'Mr', written with the r raised above the line, is a peculiarity of English handwriting, and 'tother', used as a contraction of 'the other', was common to Scotland, Ireland, England and America. More specifically, the words 'prasarved' and 'Mishter' may reflect a Cockney dialect because William Matthews, in his study *Cockney Past and Present*, produces evidence to show that in Cockney speech 'er' was commonly pronounced 'ar' as in 'clerk' until late in the 19th century and that 'sh' was widely substituted for 's'. The possibility of an Irish author has already been mooted.[24]

The Lusk letter may have been written by the murderer, it may not. Given our present state of knowledge we can only keep an open mind on the subject.

Sue Iremonger, a member of the World Association of Document Examiners, is at present engaged in a fresh study of the Ripper letters. She believes a communication of 6 October to be in the same hand as the 'Dear Boss' letter and does not think either of them could have been produced by Best's flattened Waverley nib. The results of her research will be fascinating. However, despite some published claims to the contrary[25] it should be remembered that only the Lusk letter can be directly linked – and that but tenuously – to the murderer. For this reason comparisons between the handwriting in the Ripper correspondence and that of some suspect or other are almost invariably futile. Yet Ripperologists, eager to invest their fantasies with a veneer of credibility, will continue to make them. Besides which the idea of the Ripper brazenly taunting his enemies with insolent jibes and lines of sleazy doggerel is just too good for fictioneers to relinquish. At the beginning of its second century the myth of the murderer-scribe is probably too firmly entrenched in popular legend to be touched by anything written here. As Arthur Koestler, the wise Hungarian writer and essayist, understood only too well, 'nothing is more sad than the death of an illusion.'

14

In the Shadow of the Ripper

'WE HEAR STARTLING NEWS of abounding sin in this great city. Oh God, put an end to this, and grant that we may hear no more of such deeds. Let Thy gospel permeate the city, and let not monsters in human shape escape Thee.'[1] Such was the earnest prayer of Mr Spurgeon at the Metropolitan Tabernacle on the morning of Sunday, 30 September 1888, only hours after the bodies of Liz Stride and Kate Eddowes had been found in the East End.

The news of the double killing was already sweeping through the metropolis. By eleven that same morning, one reporter tells us, it seemed 'as if the entire population of the East End was out of doors.'[2] Both murder sites had been cordoned off by police but thousands of ghoulish sightseers choked the approaches to Mitre Square and congregated outside Dutfield's Yard. At one time Berner Street resembled a sea of heads from end to end. Windows overlooking the sites were thrown open and seats at them openly sold and eagerly sought. On the fringes of the crowds costermongers, selling edibles from bread and fish to fruit, sweets and nuts, and newsvendors, proclaiming the latest particulars, did spectacular trade. And because many East Enders were illiterate or unable to understand English fascinated audiences clustered round anyone fortunate enough to have procured a paper and willing to read aloud the news of the hour.

Mitre Square and Berner Street continued to attract crowds for several days. The same hysterical scenes that had been witnessed after Dark Annie's murder were re-enacted and, as the excitement subsided, the same terrors were re-awakened. In the East End, after dark, they emptied all but the most illuminated and populous thoroughfares. It is probable that, given the circumstances, some lodging house deputies allowed regular customers to stay even if they did not possess their doss money. But many women were, as was the custom, mercilessly turned out into the streets. Some of these fled westwards to better-lit quarters of the metropolis. Others sought shelter in the casual wards and both in the City and throughout the East End boards of guardians noted substantial increases in female admissions during the first two weeks in October. But even on the first few nights after the double murder, when the panic was at its height and temperatures plummeted to freezing, groups of these miserable and forlorn-looking creatures might still be seen in the darkness and cold, touting at street corners or under the glare of lamps, or huddling in doorways to screen their ill-clad bodies from the biting wind. Their plight was summed up by one of their number, rebuked after accosting a rescue officer near Shoreditch Church: 'Good heavens! What *are* we to do? At one o'clock last night Mother Morris came down into the kitchen, and she says, "Now then, you girls who haven't got your doss money – out you go," and all of them as hadn't got enough was forced to turn out and go into the streets shuddering at every shadow, and expecting every minute to be murdered. What *are* we to do?' Some of these women, more spirited than their comrades, were determined to go down fighting. 'Afraid? No. I'm armed. Look here,' one told a reporter, pulling a knife out of her pocket. 'I'm not the only one armed. There's plenty more carry knives now.'[3]

A noticeable reduction in the number of prostitutes out after dark was not the only effect of the murders. Respectable women, even men, began to shun the East End. There was a rumour that emigrants, en route for the West, were refusing to be located in Whitechapel. And traders complained of a loss of business. On 3 October Mr R. Rycroft told a meeting of the parish vestry of St Mary, Whitechapel, that trade had fallen off in the district by nearly 50 per cent during the past month. Presumably the problem was exacerbated in the middle of October when parts of the metropolis, including the East End, were enveloped in a dense, smoke-laden fog. About that time more than 200 Whitechapel traders, through Samuel Montagu, memorialized the Home Secretary for an increase in the number of police in the district. 'The universal feeling prevalent in our midst,' they declared, 'is that the Government no longer ensures the security of life and property in East London and that, in consequence, respectable people fear to go out shopping, thus depriving us of our means of livelihood.'[4]

This atmosphere of fear and suspicion was heightened by the antics of irresponsible simpletons who delighted in impersonating the Ripper by brandishing knives in the faces of defenceless women. There was a spate of such incidents in the aftermath of the double murder. One victim was Mrs Sewell, a cleaner, of 2 Pole Street, Stepney Green. On the night of 4 October, while walking to a temperance meeting at the Great Assembly Hall in Mile End Road, she was scared by a man who came up behind her, suddenly and noiselessly, in dark Redman's Road. She turned round sharp and confronted him. 'Did I frighten you, missus?' he inquired. Of course he had, but striving to calm her pounding heart and control the tremor in her voice, Mrs Sewell assumed her boldest expression and told him that he had not. The man was tall and bearded. He wore a brown overcoat and a felt hat and was accompanied by a white dog. And he held something that glittered up against his sleeve. At this moment a young man came up and the bearded stranger made off, 'very quickly and silently . . . I could hardly hear his feet.' 'Did you see what he had, missus?' asked the young man. Mrs Sewell hadn't, so the young man told her. 'That was a knife,' he said, 'and the blade was a foot long.'[5]

Inevitably, perhaps, the terror claimed victims beyond the mutilated dead. On 17 September a young butcher named Hennell cut his own throat at the house of his parents, 76 Enfield Buildings, Ashford Street, in Hoxton. He had, it was said, 'repeatedly expressed the fear that they "were after him for the Whitechapel murder".' Sarah Goody, a forty-year-old needlewoman committed to an asylum by Thames Magistrates' Court a month later, was haunted by a similar delusion. In her fantasies she was being followed about London by murderers and these spectres of the imagination had so terrified her that she could neither eat nor sleep. On 10 October Mrs Sodeaux, the wife of a silk weaver, hanged herself from the stair banisters of No. 65 Hanbury Street, not far from the Chapman murder house. This poor woman had been depressed and, it was reported, had become 'greatly agitated' since the murders. Truly there seemed no end to the tragedies that autumn and the ripples of fear spread wide from Whitechapel. In Kilkeel, County Down, a certain Miss Milligan, just twenty-one years of age, died, supposedly from the effects of shock, a fortnight after a knife-wielding practical joker pounced out at her declaring himself to be Jack the Ripper.[6]

Such tragedies did nothing to deter entrepreneurs large and small from exploiting the commercial possibilities of the situation. Newspapers enjoyed massive sales and broadsheets, some in verse and sung by hawkers to popular tunes, appeared in almost every street. The crowds of sightseers played host to swarms of parasites: omnibus and cab companies that shunted them about Whitechapel, costermongers who plied them with eatables, householders who rented them seats at windows overlooking the fatal spots, even the committee of the International Working Men's Club which charged them a small fee for admission to its premises. On 6 October a pavement artist attracted immense crowds in Whitechapel Road with his graphic delineations of the murders. And a *Daily News* correspondent, doing a round of the hiring fairs in the Midlands that month, found entertainments inspired by the atrocities at every one. A penny at one such bought three shies at a door with the object of bringing out Jack the Ripper or 'one of them from Whitechapel'. In the heart of the murder district there was profit in fear. One woman did a brisk trade in swordsticks. 'Here you are, now,' she would cry, carrying about an armful, 'sixpence for a swordstick. That's the sort to do for 'em!'

Overwhelmingly, though, East Enders united in sympathy for the slain. The educated and propertied classes expressed it via the correspondence columns of the press, in renewed calls and schemes for social reform, the labouring and destitute poor by turning out *en masse* to honour their dead. 'Long Liz', far from her native Sweden, was quietly buried in a pauper's grave in East London Cemetery on Saturday, 6 October. But on the following Monday the funeral of Kate Eddowes generated some of the excitement and emotion of a state occasion.

At about 1.30 p.m. the *cortège* left the mortuary in Golden Lane. First, in an open hearse, Kate's body, ensconced in a handsome coffin of elm bearing a plate inscribed in letters of gold. Then, in a mourning coach, the chief mourners, all neatly attired in black. They included John Kelly and four of Kate's sisters – Harriet, Emma, Eliza and Elizabeth. And bringing up the rear in a brougham, representatives of the national and local press. To all which one unconfirmed report added mention of a bevy of women, mostly dressed 'in a style not at all befitting the occasion' and riding in a large wagon. If they existed they were almost certainly Kate's old comrades from Flower and Dean Street, clothed in the only habiliments they had.

The crowds of spectators, swollen by workers taking their dinner-hour, were prodigious. In the vicinity of the mortuary they filled the windows and clambered about the roofs of adjoining buildings as well as choked the route of the procession. 'Never, perhaps, has Golden Lane and the precincts of the mortuary presented a more animated appearance,' noted the *Observer*. 'The footway was lined on either side of the road with persons who were packed in rows five deep, the front row extending into the roadway. Manifestations of sympathy were everywhere visible, many among the crowd uncovering their heads as the hearse passed.' With police clearing a way, the *cortège* rumbled slowly along Old, Great Eastern and Commercial Streets and turned into Whitechapel High Street. There, lining the route on both sides as far as St Mary's Church, was another dense crowd. The *Observer* again: 'The sympathy shown here was more marked than at any other point of the route, the majority of the women having no covering to their heads, whilst a number of rough-looking labouring men removed their caps as the body passed.'

Shortly before 3.30 Kate's body reached its final resting place – the City of London Cemetery at Ilford. Hundreds more people, many of the women carrying infants in their arms, gathered about the grave to see her buried. In the chapel and at the graveside the service was performed by the Rev T. Dunscombe, the cemetery chaplain. The City authorities, who owned the burial ground, remitted the usual fees and George Hawkes, vestryman and undertaker of St Luke's, paid the funeral expenses.[7]

The community united, too, in a cry for retribution, a cry quickly taken up by broadsheet hacks who vied with each other in devising suitable fates for the murderer:

'as anyone seen him, can you tell us where he is,
If you meet him you must take away his knife,
Then give him to the women, they'll spoil his pretty fiz,
And I wouldn't give him twopence for his life.

Now at night when you're undressed and about to go to rest
Just see that he ain't underneath the bed
If he is you mustn't shout but politely drag him out
And with your poker tap him on the head.

But before the Ripper could be punished he had to be caught. And the inquest proceedings provided few grounds for optimism that that was about to happen.

On 4 October the inquest into the death of Kate Eddowes commenced at the City Mortuary in Golden Lane before Samuel Frederick Langham, the City Coroner. It was adjourned to the 11th but Langham did not consider it necessary to prolong the inquiry further in the hope of procuring more evidence and at the end of the second day advised the jury to return their verdict and leave the matter in the hands of the police. Since Langham assured them that the medical evidence proved that only one man could have been implicated, the jury returned a verdict of wilful murder against some *person* unknown. Obviously the public were greatly disappointed in the result and the *Daily News* spoke for most when it complained: 'Practically the world knows nothing more of this crime than it did on the morning when it was first announced. We have some details about the victim, few or none about the murderer. The "person unknown" has every right to his designation.'[8] Wynne Baxter, who opened the Stride inquest at the vestry hall of St George-in-the-East in Cable Street on 1 October, was a man of a very different stamp to Langham. As was his wont, his examination of the witnesses was nigh exhaustive, his summing-up meticulous. The inquiry was adjourned no less than four times. But it made no difference. Terminating the proceedings on 23 October, Baxter felt obliged to acknowledge his sorrow that the time of the court had not succeeded in unmasking the killer and his jury then returned the usual verdict of wilful murder by some person or persons unknown.

The failure of the police to catch the Ripper fuelled a fierce clamour for a government reward. Kate Eddowes had died in the City and on 1 October, upon the recommendation of Colonel Sir James Fraser, Commissioner of the City Police, the Lord Mayor authorized a reward of £500 for anyone who could provide information leading to the discovery and conviction of her murderer.[9] Repeated attempts to persuade Henry Matthews to follow suit were spearheaded by the Mile End Vigilance Committee.

Hoping that the double murder had wrought a change of heart at the Home Office, Mr B. Harris, the committee secretary, wrote on 30 September requesting Matthews to reconsider their former application for a reward. Three days later the Home Office penned its reply: the Secretary of State saw no reason to alter his previous decision. Undaunted, the committee tried again on 7 October. This time George Lusk, the president, called not only for a substantial government reward but also for a free pardon to any accomplice who would inform against the killer. And he pointed out 'that the present series of murders is absolutely unique in the annals of crime, that the cunning, astuteness and determination of the murderer has hitherto been, and may possibly still continue to be, more than a match for Scotland Yard and the Old Jewry combined, and that all ordinary means of detection have failed.' It was all to no avail. Once again the offer of a reward was rejected outright. And although that of a pardon received strong support from Sir Charles Warren all the Home Office would promise was to keep the matter under review.[10]

Other bodies were similarly rebuffed. On 1 October Harry Marks, editor of the *Financial News*, sent Matthews a cheque for £300 on behalf of some of his readers, requesting him to offer the money in the name of the government for the discovery of the murderer. The cheque was promptly returned. Again, Sir Alfred Kirby, Colonel of the Tower Hamlets Battalion, Royal Engineers, offered £100 on behalf of his officers as well as the services of up to fifty members of his corps. Both gestures were politely declined.

Bewildered and exasperated by the Home Secretary's obduracy, private donors went where Matthews feared to tread and by 2 October it was being reported that £1,200 already awaited anyone who could put a name to the Ripper.[11]

The Mile End Vigilance Committee did more than lobby and collect subscriptions for a reward. Dissatisfied with the degree of protection afforded by the police, it inaugurated a system of amateur patrols. Picked men from the ranks of the unemployed patrolled the streets of the East End from shortly before midnight to between four and five the next morning. Each man was assigned a particular beat, equipped with a police whistle, a stout stick and a pair of galoshes, and paid a modest wage by the committee. The committee met nightly at nine in an upstairs room of the Crown, Mile End Road, and when the house closed at 12.30 members themselves took to the streets to inspect and supplement the patrols. To advise them in the organization and supervision of all this amateur police work the committee hired the services of Grand & Batchelor, a private detective agency in the Strand.

To judge from news reports it was at midnight on Wednesday, 3 October, that the patrols of the Mile End Vigilance Committee first trooped into the streets. This committee largely consisted of small tradesmen. Its members included a builder, a cigar manufacturer, a tailor, a picture-frame maker, a licensed victualler and an actor. But soon its patrols were being reinforced by those of the Working Men's Vigilance Committee. Little is known about this organization. Apparently a child of the waterfront trade unions, it held meetings at the Three Nuns, Aldgate, and is said to have established fifty-seven patrols by 9 October.[12]

It was all beyond doubt a most praiseworthy effort. But was it productive of any good? Grand & Batchelor did the Whitechapel investigation no service when they unearthed the charlatan Matthew Packer. In one sense, too, vigilance committee patrols made life harder rather than easier for the regular police. For the constable on the beat was now confronted with more strange men on the streets at night than ever before and it must, at least in the early days of the patrols, have been a full-time job checking out their credentials. This was certainly Inspector Dew's view of the matter, and although his comments perhaps reflect the contempt of the professional for the amateur there is some support for it in contemporary news reports. Thus, a week after the double murder, the *Daily News* commented that 'in several instances some of the plain clothes [police] men who were strange to the neighbourhood were watched by members of the Vigilance Committee, while they in their turn came under the scrutiny of the detectives.'[13] On the other hand the Mile End committee at least regularly passed on information about suspicious characters and the state of the streets to the police and the increased surveillance of the district, to which the private patrols contributed, may well have acted upon the Ripper as a deterrent. It would be nearly six weeks before he struck again and then it would be in the squalid back room of a house, not on the open streets.

Inevitably the double murder lashed the press into fresh volleys of vituperation against the Metropolitan Police and its masters. Matthews' refusal to sanction a government reward was condemned on all sides. The *Daily Telegraph*, so representative of Conservative opinion, denounced the Home Secretary as a 'helpless, heedless, useless figure' while the radical *Star* accused him of 'philandering with pot-house Tories at Birmingham while God's poor are being slaughtered wholesale in London.' 'We do not ask what is the duty of the Home Secretary,' said the *Pall Mall Gazette* scathingly, 'because whatever it is he will not do it.' Criticism of the police, too, transcended political alignments. The *Star* predictably damned the entire force as 'rotten to the core.' But even Conservative journals castigated the CID. The *Daily Telegraph* fumed about the 'notorious and shameful shortcomings of the Detective Department, or rather of the botched-up makeshift which does duty for a Detective Department at Scotland Yard' and the *East London Advertiser* considered that there was 'no detective force in the proper sense of the word in London at all.'[14]. It was widely believed that under Warren the energies, resources and organization of the police had been subverted from the prevention and detection of crime to the politically motivated containment of outcast London. A huge placard, exhibited at a meeting of the unemployed in Hyde Park on 2 October, summed it all up: 'The Whitechapel Murders. Where are the Police? Looking after the Unemployed!'

Part of the trouble was that police secrecy made it impossible for press or public to judge how adequately the force *was* discharging its responsibilities. Sir Charles Warren, replying on 3 October to a plea from the Whitechapel District Board of Works for improved policing of the area, assured the board that 'every nerve' was being strained to detect the murderer. But, he added, 'you will agree with me that it is not desirable that I should enter into particulars as to what the police are doing in the matter. It is most important for good results that our proceedings should not be published.'[15] Curiously, newspaper reporters often contrasted the silence and churlishness of Metropolitan officers with the courtesy and co-operation of their counterparts in the City. Yet both forces embraced the secrecy principle. Thus when Joseph Lawende was called before the Eddowes inquest on 11 October, his description of the suspect was suppressed at the express wish of Henry Crawford, City Solicitor, appearing on behalf of the City Police. In 1888 such tactics effectively blindfolded the press. Now, a century after the crimes, confidential Home Office and Metropolitan Police files have been opened and we can see that despite the ultimate failure of the Ripper hunt a great deal was done.

One of Warren's first actions after the double killing was to draft extra men into the district. These were transferred temporarily from duties in other divisions. One of them was Frederick Porter Wensley, then a uniformed constable of but nine months' standing in the Lambeth Division, later to rise to the rank of Chief Constable of CID. In his book, *Detective Days*, published more than forty years later, Wensley recalled his Whitechapel interlude: 'In common with hundreds of others I was drafted there and we patrolled the streets – usually in pairs – without any tangible result. We did, however, rather anticipate a great commercial invention. To our clumsy regulation boots we nailed strips of rubber, usually bits of old bicycle tires, and so ensured some measure of silence when walking.'[16]

There were no policewomen in the Metropolitan Police before World War I. Back in 1888, therefore, it was commonly suggested in the press that detectives might successfully entrap the Ripper if they perambulated the streets dressed as women. At that time police recruits were all five feet seven inches in height or over so this idea would not have been as easy to implement as it sounded. Nevertheless, we know of at least one detective who *did* don female disguise. He was Detective Sergeant Robinson of G Division and his activities have come down to us because he became embroiled in a melée with a pair of pugnacious cab-washers in Phoenix Place, St Pancras.

Investigating a rumour that the Ripper was in the neighbourhood, Robinson proceeded to Phoenix Place where, between twelve and one on the morning of 9 October, he was with Detective-Sergeant Mather, one Henry Doncaster and several Italians, watching a man who 'was in company with a woman under circumstances of great suspicion'. Robinson was disguised in female clothing. At this point the watchers themselves came under the notice of William Jarvis and James Phillips, two cab-washers from a nearby cabyard, and they evidently concluded that the strangers were up to no good.

What happened next depends upon which party one believes. According to Robinson, the cab-washers accosted him in an intimidating manner.

'What are you messing about here for?' demanded Jarvis.

Robinson took off his woman's hat. 'I am a police officer,' he said.

'Oh, you are cats and dogs, are you?' replied Jarvis. And with that he threw a punch at the detective.

Then, when Robinson grasped him by the coat, Jarvis pulled a knife.

Jarvis and Phillips told a different story. By their account, they asked Robinson's party what they were doing near the cabs and Robinson told them to mind their own business and thrust Jarvis away by putting a fist against his chin.

Whatever the origins of the dispute, a fierce struggle ensued during which Robinson was stabbed over the left eye and on the bridge of the nose, Doncaster was stabbed in the face and had his jaw dislocated, and Jarvis was cracked across the head with Robinson's truncheon. Jarvis' cries for assistance – 'Come on, George, cats and dogs!' – brought several other men from the cabyard, armed with pitchforks and other implements. But they made no attempt to use their weapons and, after police reinforcements had come up, Jarvis and Phillips were taken into custody.

The combatants made a sorry sight when they came before Clerkenwell Police Court later in the day, the cab-washers accused of cutting and wounding Detective-Sergeant Robinson. Robinson appeared with surgical straps around his left eye, Doncaster and Jarvis with their heads bound in bloodstained bandages. Robinson contended that he had struck at the hand with which Jarvis had been holding his knife but had missed and struck his head. However, pressed by Mr Ricketts, the prisoners' solicitor, he conceded that after he had been stabbed he didn't care whether he hit Jarvis on the hand or the head. The prisoners were remanded for a week and then committed for trial and released on bail. At the end of the month they were tried at the Middlesex Sessions of the Peace for assaulting police in the execution of their duty. Phillips was acquitted but Jarvis was convicted and sentenced to six weeks' imprisonment with hard labour.[17]

The influx into Whitechapel of plain clothes detectives, with or without women's clothes, must have presented something of a problem to patrolling constables. The night after the murders PC Ludwig, patrolling between Cannon Street Road and Back Church Lane, encountered a very strange figure indeed, its height and masculine stride ill-befitting its shabby raiment as a woman of the town.

'Stop!' cried the constable. 'You're a man, aren't you? I can see that you are.'

The figure confessed that it was.

'Are you one of us?' queried Ludwig.

No, the man explained, he was not a detective but a reporter who had disguised himself as a prostitute the better to root out copy on the murders.

Ludwig eyed him dubiously and then conducted him to Leman Street Police Station. There, however, his story was verified and he was allowed to go.[18]

Although there was always a chance that the murderer might be taken red-handed attempting another crime, the drafting in of extra men was designed primarily as a short-term, preventative measure. Detection of the criminal required more offensive operations and, in the days immediately after the Stride murder, the Metropolitan Police conducted extensive inquiries and searches throughout Whitechapel.

One was the inevitable visitation of common lodging houses and over 2,000 lodgers were interviewed. By this stage, though, it was commonly believed that if the killer had resorted to such an establishment he would not have escaped notice and that it was more likely that he lived with relatives or in private lodgings. So, in order to solicit information from landlords and their tenants, some 80,000 handbills[19] were printed and distributed in the area:

POLICE NOTICE
TO THE OCCUPIER.

On the mornings of Friday, 31st August, Saturday 8th, and Sunday, 30th September, 1888, Women were murdered in or near Whitechapel, supposed by some one residing in the immediate neighbourhood. Should you know of any person to whom suspicion is attached, you are earnestly requested to communicate at once with the nearest Police Station.

Metropolitan Police Office, 30th September, 1888.

Critics doubted the efficacy of this bill, pointing out that it contained no promise of a reward for information leading to the arrest of the killer and that, printed in English, it was incomprehensible to large numbers of the immigrant population, a fact not without significance if it was held that the murderer was a foreigner being sheltered by compatriots.

But other searches were in hand too. Seventy-six butchers and slaughterers were visited by police and the characters of their employees inquired into. The Thames Police investigated sailors working aboard vessels in the docks or on the river. Inquiries were mounted into Asiatics living in London and into the reputed presence of Greek gipsies in the capital. The latter were cleared of suspicion when it was learned that they had not been in London at the times of the murders. Similarly, three cowboys attached to the

American Exhibition were traced and satisfactorily accounted for their whereabouts at the critical times. If the newspapers are to be credited the net was cast wider still, taking in hospitals, workhouses, prisons and vacant buildings.[20]

Sir John Whittaker Ellis, a former Lord Mayor of London, wrote to Matthews on 3 October with an idea for a bolder initiative. He suggested that the police draw a half-mile cordon around the centre of Whitechapel and search every house within it. 'It is a strong thing to do,' he admitted, 'but I should think such occasion never before arose.' A better word than 'strong' would have been 'illegal' because the police had no authority to forcibly enter and search anyone's home without a warrant from a magistrate.

Warren baulked at the prospect. He felt that if the search failed to unearth the killer it was sure to be roundly condemned, and worried that such an unlawful step might succeed in uniting the Socialists to resist the operation, endangering the lives of his constables and exposing them, in the event of damage to property or injury to civilians, to dire legal consequences. Writing to Ruggles-Brise, Matthews' private secretary, on 4 October, Sir Charles declared himself 'quite prepared to take the responsibility of adopting the most drastic or arbitrary measures that the Secretary of State can name which would further the securing of the murderer, however illegal they may be, provided HM Government will support me.' But he doubted whether it was worth risking riot and loss of life in order 'to *search* for one murderer whose whereabouts is not known.' The next day Matthews replied with a more practicable alternative. Could not the police, he suggested, take all the houses in a given area 'which appear suspicious upon the best inquiry your detectives can make', search those for which the permission of the owners or occupiers could be procured and then apply to a magistrate for search warrants to enter the rest? The flaw in his plan, of course, was that since the police didn't know where the killer might be hiding they would have found it next to impossible to show plausible grounds for the granting of a warrant to search any particular house. That suggested by Matthews – that it was possible 'the murderer may be there' – could have been applied to almost any habitation in the metropolis! The Home Secretary did appreciate the difficulty. 'If search warrants are refused,' he wrote, 'you can only keep the houses under observation.'[21]

In the end it was decided to confine the search to those premises within a given area for which the consent of the occupier could be obtained and by 13 October the operation was under way. Embracing some of the worst slums of Whitechapel and Spitalfields, the area of the search was bounded by Lamb Street, Commercial Street, the Great Eastern Railway and Buxton Street on the north and Whitechapel Road on the south, by the City boundary on the west and Albert Street, Dunk Street, Chicksand Street and Great Garden Street on the east. There, for the best part of a week, plain clothes officers went from house to house, seeking admission to every room, looking under beds, peering into cupboards, inspecting knives, interviewing landlords and their lodgers. Mrs Andleman of 7 Spelman Street regaled the *Star* with her story of the search:

I came home from work yesterday, and as soon as I opened the street door, two men came up and said, 'Do you live in this front room?' 'Yes,' I said. 'We want to have a look at it.' 'Who are you, and what do you want?' 'We are police officers, and we have come to look for the murderer.' 'Do you think I keep the murderer here, or do you suggest that I associate with him?' I replied. They answered that it was their duty to inspect the rooms. I showed them into my room. They looked under the bed, and asked me to open the cupboards. I opened a small cupboard, where I keep plates and things. It is not more than two feet wide and about one in depth. They made an inspection of that also. 'Do you think,' I said, 'that it is possible for a man, or even a child, to be hidden in that small place?' They made no answer, and walked out. Then they went next door and inspected those premises.

Mrs Andleman obviously resented the intrusion and, in the East End, it would have been astonishing had there been no animosity shown towards the police. There must have been those who refused them entry. But Warren's fears of widespread obstruction happily proved unfounded. For such was the desire of the community to rid itself of the murderer that almost everywhere the police found occupiers more than happy to co-operate with them. Our evidence is virtually unanimous on this point. 'With few exceptions,' said Warren on the 17th, 'the inhabitants of all classes and creeds have freely fallen in with the proposal, and have materially assisted the officers engaged in carrying it out.' Dr Anderson, the new head of CID, in a confidential minute written six days later, agreed: 'the public generally and especially the inhabitants of the East End have shown a marked desire to assist in every way, even at some sacrifice to themselves, as for example in permitting their houses to be searched.' And so did the press: 'The greatest good feeling prevails towards the police, and noticeably in the most squalid dwellings the police had no difficulty in getting information.'

The search was completed on 18 October. It did not unmask the murderer. Nor did its failure to do so demonstrate that he did not live in the area designated for the search. In a permissive undertaking such as this anyone who really had something to hide might easily have denied the police access to their property, and although Chief Inspector Swanson reported that the exceptions were not such as to warrant suspicion the CID had no means of being certain of that. Indeed, the police knew so little about their quarry that they might well have interviewed him without suspecting him in the least. However, if the search did something to appease the public's clamour for action it fulfilled what was arguably one of its main objectives.[22]

Unquestionably the most famous and misunderstood initiative of the Metropolitan Police was the experiment with bloodhounds. Misunderstood, because Ripperologists have foisted three tenacious myths upon the public: that the bloodhound trials were Warren's pet project, that they were discredited when the dogs got lost in a fog on Tooting Common, and that the fiasco made Sir Charles the laughing stock of London. Now the truth was very different. Warren undertook the experiment at the suggestion of the Home Office, and the Home Office simply responded to advice daily urged upon the police by public and press. The Tooting Common episode, so beloved of Ripperologists, was a complete fiction. And far from the trials heaping ridicule upon the Commissioner's head, they were generally welcomed by public and press and both continued to repose great faith in the hounds long after they had been returned to their owner. Indeed, some went so far as to attribute the Ripper's inactivity during October to the well-publicized presence of the dogs in London.

The suggestion that bloodhounds might be used to track the killer, first heard after the Hanbury Street murder, was at once raised again in the wake of the double event. On 1 October a *Times* editorial reminded its readers that in 1876 the murderer William Fish had been detected with the help of a bloodhound. Noticing this editorial, Percy Lindley, a breeder of bloodhounds at York Hill, Loughton, in Essex, wasted no time in writing to *The Times* to extol the virtues of the breed. 'As a breeder of bloodhounds, and knowing their power,' he said, 'I have little doubt that, had a hound been put upon the scent of the murderer while fresh, it might have done what the police have failed in.' Lindley suggested that a couple of trained dogs be kept at one of the police stations in Whitechapel, ready for immediate use in the event of another murder, and it was his letter that launched the Metropolitan Police experiment. For when it was printed in *The Times* on 2 October it was spotted by the Home Office and promptly transmitted by them to Sir Charles Warren.[23]

Wise after the event, Sir Melville Macnaghten and Ex-Chief Inspector Dew later wrote disparagingly of the experiment, but in 1888 even the experts were divided on the potential value of bloodhounds for police work in the East End. H. M. Mackusick of Merstham in Surrey, boasting the largest kennel of bloodhounds in existence, agreed with Percy Lindley and declared that 'ten well-trained bloodhounds would be of more use than a hundred constables in ferreting out criminals who have left no trace beyond the fact of their presence behind them.' Edwin Brough, a breeder from Wyndyate near Scarborough, was less hopeful. Brough admired the bloodhound. It could, he asserted, hunt 'a lighter scent than any other hound, and when properly trained will stick to the line of the hunted man, although it may have been crossed by others.' But he doubted whether there were in England dogs sufficiently well trained to work in the crowded streets of Whitechapel. 'Unless laid on [the scent] at once,' he warned, 'the chances are that the hound might hit off the wrong trail.'[24]

Neither Warren nor Matthews was unaware of the problems. Indeed, in a letter to Percy Lindley, Warren queried how a dog could be expected to track the killer without a vestige of his clothing or trace of his blood, especially 'on a London pavement where people have been walking all the evening [and] there may be scores of scents almost as keen as those of the murderer.' But given the contradictory advice on offer their decision to attempt the experiment can only be commended. On 5 October Warren requested authority from the Home Secretary to expend £50 in the present financial year and £100 per annum thereafter in keeping trained bloodhounds in London. This would be irrespective of any 'expenses which may occur in the special use of bloodhounds at the present moment.' Matthews trod warily. He decided to sanction one payment of £50 only, to be spent on the use of dogs in the present emergency, but declined to commit himself to a permanent annual charge unless the venture could demonstrate that bloodhounds could be usefully employed in the metropolis without danger to the public.[25] Warren had already made inquiries of several dog breeders. As a result, on Saturday, 6 October, Edwin Brough arrived in London with Barnaby and Burgho, two of his finest animals.

At seven on Monday morning the trials began in Regent's Park. Although the ground was thickly coated in hoar frost the hounds performed well, successfully tracking a man who had been given a fifteen-minute start for nearly a mile. That night they were tried again, this time in Hyde Park. It was dark and the dogs were worked on a leash but once more they were successful in performing their allotted task. Next morning, 9 October, further trials were held in the presence of Sir Charles Warren. In all, half a dozen runs were made, the Commissioner himself acting the part of the hunted man on two occasions. Again the results were encouraging. In every instance the bloodhounds hunted complete strangers and occasionally the trail was deliberately crossed to deceive them. Whenever this happened the dogs were checked, but only temporarily, for one or other of them, casting around, invariably picked up the trail again. 'In consequence of the coldness of the scent,' reported the Central News, 'the hounds worked very slowly, but they demonstrated the possibility of tracking complete strangers on to whose trail they had been laid. The Chief Commissioner seemed pleased with the result of the trials, though he did not express any definite opinion on the subject to those present.' Warren's caution was justified. We are not told the venue of the third trial but it was, like the others, in one of the London parks. Therein lay the problem. For however impressively the dogs might work on grass and across country there could be no certainty that they could repeat their success in Whitechapel.[26] Nevertheless, Sir Charles thought they were worth a try and instructions were issued that, in the event of another murder, the body must not be touched until the dogs had been put on the scent.

The Tooting Common episode, which is said to have discredited the whole experiment, is a myth. It sprang from a false news report of 19 October: 'It is stated that Sir Charles Warren's bloodhounds were out for practice at Tooting yesterday morning and were lost. Telegrams have been despatched to all the Metropolitan Police stations stating that, if seen anywhere, information is to be immediately sent to

Scotland Yard.' The truth was less dramatic. On 18 October a sheep was killed on the common and local police wired to London for the loan of the dogs. Unfortunately neither animal was available. Burgho had already been returned to Scarborough. And Barnaby was out being practised by Mr Taunton, a friend of Edwin Brough, at Hemel Hempstead. Some comment that the hounds did not arrive in Tooting when sent for must have been made and noised abroad. This, blown up as only a journalist knows how, was the sole basis for the press story.[27]

However, at the end of the month the project did founder – in misunderstandings between Warren and Brough. Warren was under the impression that Brough had public-spiritedly loaned his dogs to the CID free of charge. Which is why, when seeking finance from Matthews, he had included no estimate of the cost of 'the special use of bloodhounds at the present moment' in his application. Public-spirited Brough may have been. But he knew the value of his animals and anticipated that the police would either purchase them or pay hire charges and insure them against accidents.

After the trials in the London parks Brough returned to Scarborough, leaving Barnaby and Burgho in the care of his friend, Mr Taunton of 8 Doughty Street, while negotiations continued with the police. When he failed to get firm assurances from Sir Charles he took steps to repossess both dogs. Burgho, sent to participate in a show at Brighton, was thereafter never returned to police use. And Barnaby remained in London only a little longer. About the end of October Taunton received a telegram from Leman Street Police Station, requesting the use of the dog. 'It was then shortly after noon,' he recalled later, 'and I took Barnaby at once. On arriving at the station I was told by the superintendent that a burglary had been committed about 5 o'clock that morning in Commercial Street, and I was asked to attempt to track the thief by means of the dog. The police admitted that since the burglary they had been all over the premises. I pointed out the stupidity of expecting a dog to accomplish anything under such circumstances and after such a length of time had been allowed to elapse, and took the animal home.'[28] This incident proved the last straw for Brough. The police had not offered to buy Barnaby. They had paid nothing for his hire. And, although there might be a danger that villains would try to poison the dog if they learned he was being used to track burglars, there had been no pledge that the police would pay compensation. So, without further ado,

Brough reclaimed his second dog. Hence, from the end of October, there were no trained police bloodhounds in the metropolis.

Warren obviously wanted the experiment to proceed. Writing to the Home Office on 23 October, he applied for an additional sum of £50 to be expended in the current financial year. This would enable him, he explained, to insure Barnaby against accident while in police service, to pay his hire charges until the end of March 1889, and to buy a puppy. The puppy would then be trained with Barnaby and, when the latter was returned to his owner, take his place.[29] To judge by the minutes scribbled on Sir Charles' application, the Home Office was willing to sanction this further expenditure. Evidently, though, Brough took the dog back before any action could be taken.

Even had the dogs been laid on the scent at once it is improbable that they could have achieved anything amidst the multifarious trades, traffic and smells of the East End. The whole affair did provide Radical hacks with another opportunity to lampoon the Establishment. But the Radicals did not speak for the metropolis, or even for the impoverished masses whom they propagandized for recruits. Most newspapers – even, perhaps especially, the *Star* – supported experiments with tracker dogs. So, too, did the public. Thus, when Mary Kelly was murdered on 9 November, many bemoaned the fact that hounds were no longer available to trace the Ripper. 'Amongst the populace,' said the *Telegraph*, 'there was very widespread disappointment that bloodhounds had not been at once employed in the effort to track the criminal. The belief had prevailed throughout the district that the dogs were ready to be let loose at the first notice of a murder having been committed, and the public had come to possess greater confidence in their wonderful canine instincts and sagacity than in all Sir Charles Warren's machinery of detection. They even attributed the fact that more than a month had passed since the last revolting outrage to the fear which it was thought had been inspired by the intimation that these detectives of nature would be employed.'[30]

Other measures were discussed at high level and either rejected or shelved. The most contentious was that of a government reward. There were important arguments against large rewards. In particular, while such an offer would be unlikely to produce fresh information about a murderer who probably operated alone, it might well encourage unscrupulous people to concoct false evidence against an innocent man purely for the sake of the reward.[31] But Matthews' stubborn refusal to countenance a government reward had little to do with such altruistic considerations.

In rejecting the first applications of Walter & Son, Samuel Montagu and the Mile End Vigilance Committee, he simply followed a precedent set by his predecessor, Sir William Harcourt, in 1884. Presumably he acted upon the advice of his civil servants, probably without giving the matter much personal thought. The outcry unleashed upon him by the double murder, however, caused him to rue his early complacency. Unfortunately, having publicly refused rewards several times by then, he did not feel able to go back on those decisions without discrediting himself altogether. As he explained on 5 October in a private letter to Evelyn Ruggles-Brise, his secretary:

I have never myself shared to the full extent the HO prejudice against rewards; nor have I thought Harcourt's reasoning on the subject at all conclusive. I am disposed to regret now that in the first instance I did not sacrifice to popular feeling and offer a considerable reward. But in as much as I did yield to the official view and refuse to make an offer and subsequently repeated that refusal, I feel that my hands are tied ... I feel very strongly that to make such an offer now, after what has passed, so far from conciliating public opinion ... would cover me with ridicule and contempt – as having given way to popular pressure – with nothing to justify or call for a change, which would of itself be the strongest condemnation of my previous action.

Warren's position was different. Consulted by the Home Secretary on 3 October, he said that although a government reward might do something to appease public opinion it was unnecessary from a police point of view because £500 had already been offered by the City authorities. All this must have been music to Matthews' ears. But two days later the Commissioner had had second thoughts. Popular agitation for decisive action had not diminished. The CID was doggedly pursuing every lead it had but seemed no closer to a solution of the mystery. And it was beginning to look as if the City reward had been insufficient to produce results. So Warren called at the Home Office and told Ruggles-Brise that he had come round to the view that a large government reward might, after all, succeed in detecting the murderer. Matthews, fearful that a change of policy would damage him irreparably, was embarrassed and furious at Sir

Charles' endorsement of a reward. 'Anybody can offer a reward and it is the first idea of ignorant people,' he fumed in his letter to Ruggles-Brise. 'But more is expected of the CID. Sir C. W. will not save himself, or put himself right with the public, by merely suggesting that. His conversation with you looks as if he wanted to hedge at my expense.'

In succeeding days the Home Secretary and his Commissioner fenced inconclusively. Matthews understood that he might eventually be forced to bow to public opinion and offer a reward and he knew that if that day came his political survival might depend upon his ability to show good cause for his change of tack. Perhaps there was such cause – in the incompetence of the police. Matthews, again, to Ruggles-Brise:

> If Sir C. W. felt able to write to me officially that the police had exhausted every means at their command – that they had not only failed, but had no expectation of succeeding in tracing the murderer – and that therefore, as a last resort, he felt bound to suggest recourse to an expedient which experience proves to be unsatisfactory and even mischievous, namely the offer of a reward – I might act on such a letter – provided I might make it public.

Such a letter, of course, would have freed Matthews from the hook only by gaffing Warren. Nevertheless, on 7 October, intimating his willingness to review his policy on rewards, Matthews solicited from Warren written answers to three questions. The first was a cynical ploy, designed to trap the Commissioner on paper so that he might be saddled with the responsibility for any future Home Office climb-down: 'Is it your opinion that the police & the CID have now exhausted all the means within their power of discovering the criminal, & have not only failed, but have no reasonable prospect of succeeding in any moderate time?' Sir Charles was too wily a bird to be thus ensnared and when he replied, ten days later, he gave Matthews nothing that could be used against him: 'To this I have to reply, NO. I think we have hardly begun: it often takes many months to discover a criminal.'

For his part Warren discomfited the Home Secretary with repeated written advice in favour of a reward. Thus, on 6 October, he urged Matthews to offer a free pardon to any of the killer's accomplices who would inform, together with a government reward of £5,000, and hinted darkly that 'if other murders of a similar nature take place shortly . . . the omission of the offer of a reward on the part of the government may exercise a very serious effect upon the stability of the government itself.' Worse, if questions were to be asked in parliament, Warren wanted Matthews to say that the Commissioner of Police was of the opinion that a government reward should have been offered.

It was all very sad. A Home Secretary – once, perhaps, open-minded, now an embattled partisan – resisting the offer of a reward for the worst of reasons, to save his own skin, and determined, if he should be forced to yield, that the Commissioner of Police would take the blame. And a Commissioner of Police, looking to such a reward for the rescue of his floundering CID, and intent on the Home Secretary shouldering the blame for *not* issuing one. On 13 October *Moonshine*, a strong Tory journal, carried a cartoon captioned 'A Question of Resignation.' In it Matthews and Warren are depicted glaring at each other, eyeball to eyeball, across a desk strewn with news reports and petitions relating to the murders. 'Why don't you resign?' urges Matthews. 'Why don't *you* resign?' growls Warren. In the background stands the long suffering figure of Lord Salisbury, the Prime Minister. 'Why don't they *both* resign,' he sighs in an aside. Unhappily there was more truth in that cartoon than any of *Moonshine's* readers could have guessed.[32]

Another possibility, urged upon the Home Office by both Warren and Lusk, was the offer of a pardon to any accomplice of the murderer who would betray him to the police. Matthews was willing to consider this proposal. It would not have been as open to abuse as that of a reward and since he had not already refused a pardon he could act on the suggestion without loss of face. The main objection was the absence of credible evidence that the murderer had an accomplice. Curiously, when Warren wrote in support of Lusk's proposal on 9 October he made no mention of Israel Schwartz's story. He did, however, refer to an anonymous letter. It had reached the Yard that very day and the writer, who claimed to be an accomplice of the killer, was asking for a free pardon. Warren told the Home Office that he was attempting to contact the writer through an advertisement in a journal but conceded that the letter was probably a hoax, the police having received 'scores of hoaxing letters'. It would be interesting to know more about this intriguing episode. Eight days later, in a note to Charles Murdoch, principal clerk at the Home

Office, Warren referred to it again: 'The alleged accomplice did not turn up & it looks like a hoax: but a communication has come in from another source which looks more genuine. We have not tested it yet.'[33]

On 12 October George Lusk was told that the Home Office was keeping the offer of a pardon under review. But the decline of public interest towards the end of the month signalled a waning in the government's determination to grapple with the Whitechapel problem. It was also well understood at Whitehall that another murder might occur at any moment. If that happened the beleaguered Home Secretary would be faced with an outcry for action greater than anything he had yet endured. It would be well to keep measures in reserve to meet that emergency. So the reward and pardon questions were quietly shelved.

The prize for the silliest proposals must go to Dr Robert Anderson, the new head of CID. His absence during the crisis had by no means gone unnoticed by the press. 'The chief official who is responsible for the detection of the murderer,' carped the *Pall Mall Gazette*, 'is as invisible to Londoners as the murderer himself. You may seek Dr Anderson in Scotland Yard, you may look for him in Whitehall Place, but you will not find him ... Dr Anderson, with all the arduous duties of his office still to learn, is preparing himself for his apprenticeship by taking a pleasant holiday in Switzerland.' In response to an urgent appeal from Matthews, Anderson returned to London on or soon after 5 October. No doubt he was briefed by Chief Inspector Swanson. And, according to his memoirs, he spent the day of his return and half the following night in 'reinvestigating the whole case'. The next day he joined Matthews and Warren in conference:

'We hold you responsible to find the murderer,' was Mr Matthews' greeting to me. My answer was to decline the responsibility. 'I hold myself responsible,' I said, 'to take all legitimate means to find him.' But I went on to say that the measures I found in operation were, in my opinion, wholly indefensible and scandalous; for these wretched women were plying their trade under definite Police protection. Let the Police of that district, I urged, receive orders to arrest every known 'street woman' found on the prowl after midnight, or else let us warn them that the Police will not protect them. Though the former course would have been merciful to the very small class of women affected by it, it was deemed too drastic, and I fell back on the second.'

These measures were frankly absurd. The suggestion that all prostitutes found 'on the prowl' after midnight could be arrested was utterly unworkable. A police report prepared that same month estimated the number of known brothels in H Division at 62, the number of common lodging houses at 233 (accommodating about 8,530 people), and the number of prostitutes at about 1,200! Anderson's second proposal implied, moreover, that these women enjoyed the option of ready accommodation. In fact, had he read the Nichols and Chapman evidence more carefully, he would have known that many prostitutes were forced to ply their trade in order to earn their fourpenny doss, that if they did not do so they would be obliged to walk the streets all night.[34]

While their superiors pondered fresh initiatives, Abberline and his colleagues struggled to process the mass of information coming in from the general public. Some idea of the scale of their labours can be gleaned from Swanson's report on the Stride murder. Writing on 19 October, he said that about eighty people had been detained at Metropolitan Police stations and that the movements of more than three hundred others, about whom communications had been received by the police, had been investigated. 'There are now,' he concluded, '994 dockets besides police reports.'[35]

Walter Dew's reflections on the Ripper hunt conjured up painful memories of long hours on duty, sleepless nights, loss of appetite and nausea inspired by the sight of butcher's shops. Abberline, co-ordinating Metropolitan Police inquiries in the East End, had even greater cause to remember it. The public were so eager to help the police, especially after the City reward offer, that he and his team were deluged with statements, all of which had to be recorded and followed up. In all they made out 1,600 sets of papers about their investigations. When he came off duty Abberline would patrol the Whitechapel streets until four or five in the morning instead of going home. Then, having driven home, he would sometimes discover, just as he was about to flop exhausted into bed, that he would be summoned by telegraph back to Whitechapel, there to interrogate some lunatic or suspect whom the inspector in charge would not take the responsibility of questioning. Not surprisingly, he nearly broke down under the strain.[36]

The search for Kate Eddowes' killer was the responsibility of the City Police. Unfortunately, apart from a collection of letters to them from members of the public, now preserved at the Corporation of London Records Office, no files relating to the investigation appear to have come down to us and we know next to nothing about it. Searches similar to those undertaken by the Metropolitan force were conducted. We know, for example, that McWilliam sent officers to all the lunatic asylums in London to inquire after patients recently admitted or discharged. And, when a correspondent wrote to direct the attention of the City Police to the possibility of the murderer being a Jewish slaughterman, Major Smith drafted a reply on the back of his letter thus: 'Thank him for the suggestion and say we have accounted for the times of all the butchers and slaughterers.'[37]

Tragically, all this effort brought police no nearer to the Ripper. On 13 October Warren was mooting the possibility that the crimes had been committed by a secret society. Eleven days later, transmitting Swanson's summary reports on the murders to the Home Office, he confessed that although 'very numerous and searching enquiries' had been made, no 'tangible result' had been achieved. And Dr Anderson, in a minute dated 23 October, admitted that despite five successive killings the CID had not unearthed 'the slightest clue of any kind.'[38] Although hundreds of men fell under suspicion between the double murder and that of Mary Jane Kelly in November the names of but a handful are given in the surviving evidence. During the research for this book I recorded those of nine who made false confessions and seven other suspects. Only one – Michael Ostrog, dealt with in a later chapter – is of any significance.

Popular speculation about the killer's identity was rife. On one point there was widespread agreement – that such a monster could not possibly be an Englishman. This notion naturally produced accusations against all manner of foreigners and soon found expression in broadsheet doggerel:

> In famous London City, in eighteen eighty-eight,
> Four beastly cruel murders have been done . . .

began one, and continued:

> Some say it was old Nick himself,
> Or else a Russian Jew.
> Some say it was a 'cannibal' from the

Isle of Kickaiboo.
Some say it must be Bashi-Bazouks,
Or else it's the Chinese
Come over to Whitechapel to commit
Such crimes as these.

Some theorists thought the Ripper a Jewish immigrant. One former resident of India assured *The Times* that the mutilations were 'peculiarly Eastern', typical of those practised by the criminal classes there to express hatred and contempt, and predicted that the killer would prove a Lascar primed with opium, bhang or gin. But Americans were perhaps the favourite suspects.

Coroner Baxter's story of the American seeking specimens of the womb had not been forgotten and during succeeding weeks circumstances conspired to strengthen rather than weaken the American connection in the public mind. First, an American newspaper, the Atlanta *Constitution*, suggested a link between the Whitechapel slayings and a series of brutal and unsolved murders of negro women in Texas about three years earlier. The Texas killings had abruptly ceased. So had their perpetrator taken refuge in England? This theory was wired to the *Daily News* by its New York correspondent and was soon all over London. Then, neither press nor public were slow to detect Americanisms in 'Jack the Ripper's' notorious letter to the Central News Agency. In reproducing a facsimile of the handwriting on 4 October, the *Daily Telegraph* hazarded the view that the writer was 'probably an American or an Englishman who has mixed with our cousins on the other side of the Atlantic' because 'Boss', 'Fix me', 'shan't quit' and 'right away' were American forms of expression. As far as many amateur sleuths were concerned Matthew Packer clinched the matter. For by 5 October he was telling anyone who would listen that he had seen a man, wearing a soft felt or American hat and speaking with a Yankee twang, buy grapes for Elizabeth Stride less than two hours before she was murdered. Inevitably suspicious Yankees began to feature in a welter of newspaper tales and East Enders started to look askance at every American they met. Even the police, who knew that the Central News letter was of doubtful authenticity and that Packer was unreliable, went so far as to question three cowboys working at the American Exhibition in London.[39]

While some armchair detectives concentrated on the Ripper's

nationality others attempted to identify his occupation. The fact that four of the crimes had been committed in the early hours of a Friday, Saturday or Sunday prompted a suggestion that the murderer might be a sailor. 'Waterside', writing to the *Telegraph* on 1 October, was one of the first to advocate this theory. He pointed out that steamers plying between London and the outports or the Continent left the river every Sunday morning and returned during the week, a circumstance which could explain the timing of the murders as well as the Ripper's mysterious disappearances. However, Doctors Llewellyn, Phillips and Brown all testified to the anatomical knowledge and/or surgical skill of the murderer so the most commonly indicted occupational groups were naturally those possessing such expertise – slaughtermen and butchers, medical students, physicians and surgeons, even midwives. Once lodged in popular consciousness, suspicion against the medical profession was hardened by other factors: perhaps by the proximity of the London Hospital in Whitechapel Road to the murder sites, certainly by the stories from the night of the double murder about a man with a black bag.

There were two important black bag stories. One, from Mrs Mortimer, has been dealt with already. The other, from Albert Backert of 13 Newnham Street, told of a stranger who plied Backert with questions about local prostitutes at the Three Nuns, Aldgate, about an hour before Liz Stride was killed. This man, like the one Mrs Mortimer saw in Berner Street at about the time of the murder, carried a shiny black bag.[40] Leon Goldstein, Mrs Mortimer's man, proved to have been an innocent passer-by. And there is no evidence to link the man from the Three Nuns with the crimes or with Goldstein. Nevertheless, the stories received widespread publicity and, in their turn, generated more tales of suspicious characters with black bags. Soon the mere ownership of such an article was enough to excite suspicion. This is not to say that there were not some very eccentric bag owners.

At about 3.30 on the morning of 9 October a police constable, investigating a rumour that Jack the Ripper was going about Covent Garden Market threatening people, found George Henderson, a man of 'rather singular appearance', wandering aimlessly to and fro, carrying a black bag and acting very oddly. The constable took him to a police station where he was searched and found to possess no less than 54 pawn tickets. Later in the day Henderson was brought before Bow Street Magistrates' Court and charged with suspicious loitering but he was able to produce witnesses to his character and was discharged. Even more peculiar was Simeon Oliphant, the 67-year-old engineer who went into King Street Police Station on 16 October and complained of the loss of a black bag. After making a rambling statement to the desk sergeant he offered to cut off the sergeant's head and replace it on his shoulders 'in such a manner that he would be able to talk . . . as if it had never been removed'! When he appeared at Bow Street he claimed that he could prove by mathematical calculations that every man and woman was equal to God. Not surprisingly, Justice Vaughan made an order for his removal to the workhouse as a lunatic.[41]

The problem of motive was, if anything, even more baffling than that of identity. Even Baxter's 'Burke and Hare' theory, which for about a week had seemed to offer some sort of tangible clue, was reduced to an irrelevance by Brown's testimony at the Eddowes inquest. A simple desire to procure a specimen of the uterus could not explain the wanton cuts to Kate's head and body, and although an attempt to extract the uterus had been made it had been performed so clumsily that part of the organ had been left in the corpse. By contrast Kate's left kidney had been carefully excised. Various alternative explanations of the crimes were aired in the press. Perhaps the most bizarre, implying that they were the work of a gang of German thieves, traced their origin to an old German superstition that potential victims of robbery could be sent into a deep slumber by subjection to the light of a candle fashioned from the uterus and other female organs!

Increasingly there was an emerging consensus among medical men that the murderer must be insane, even if the nature of his insanity could only be guessed at. Dr L. Forbes Winslow, interviewed for the Central News on 1 October, remained steadfast to the view he had championed almost from the beginning – that the killer was a 'homicidal monomaniac of infinite cunning.' Other medical men were now openly falling in behind him. Sir James Risdon Bennett saw the Ripper as a homicidal maniac suffering under some erotic delusion. And Dr Edgar Sheppard, agreeing that he was probably insane, wondered whether he might also be 'an earnest religionist with a delusion that he has a mission from above to extirpate vice by assassination.' Doctors directly involved in the police investigation are known to have held similar views. Dr Blackwell and Dr Gordon

Brown both publicly stated their belief that the murderer was a lunatic.[42]

The police, for all their undoubted diligence, knew little more about the Ripper than the general public. Indeed, it is fascinating to note how they investigated the same suggestions and leads highlighted in the press – Asiatics and cowboys, sailors, slaughtermen and doctors, lunatics and opium addicts, carefully leaving no stone unturned but finding nothing to elucidate the mystery.

Extra policing in the district was maintained. But as autumn faded into winter the rigour of nightly vigils and the improbability of effecting a capture sapped the determination of the amateur patrols and they began to disappear from the streets. On the last day of October the Mile End Vigilance Committee was obliged to make a fresh appeal for funds, owning sadly that because of 'the outlay entailed by their work' they felt unable to continue their efforts without further subscriptions.[43]

By then complacency was even beginning to infect those at risk from the unknown killer. Walter Dew was continually amazed by the hardiness of the Whitechapel whores. If they ventured out at all immediately after a murder, he remembered, it was generally in terror-stricken groups. But as the days passed without further incident the groups dwindled to pairs and the pairs to lone streetwalkers. With the fatalism of the hopeless some even learned to joke about their plight and as Dew passed them in the street would call, 'I'm the next for Jack!'

One of the women Dew knew by sight was Mary Jane Kelly. 'Often I had seen her parading along Commercial Street, between Flower and Dean Street and Aldgate, or along Whitechapel Road,' he wrote a half-century later. 'She was usually in the company of two or three of her kind, fairly neatly dressed and invariably wearing a clean white apron, but no hat.'[44] Mary may have been apprehensive about the murders. At least, we know that she used to ask Joe Barnett, the man who lived with her at 13 Miller's Court in Dorset Street, to read her the news about them. But whatever her fears, she was soliciting on the streets by the end of October. Her rent was several weeks in arrears, Barnett was out of work, and young and quite attractive, Mary probably found no shortage of clients. Besides, the Ripper had been inactive for more than a month.

Events in Whitechapel were relentlessly sweeping to a bloody and grotesque climax.

15

'I want to go to the Lord Mayor's Show'

APART FROM THE occasional stable or chandler's shop, Dorset Street, Spitalfields, in 1888, was almost entirely occupied by common lodging houses offering beds at fourpence and sixpence a night. Several narrow courts, largely inhabited by prostitutes, led off Dorset Street. One such, on the north side of the street, was Miller's Court. A stone-flagged passage, three feet wide and twenty feet long, gave access to the court, a small paved yard upon which faced some half dozen mean houses.

Mary Jane Kelly, a young Irish prostitute, rented a ground-floor room in Miller's Court. But she did not lodge in any of the half dozen houses we have noticed. The house in which Mary lived actually fronted on Dorset Street. Indeed her room had once been the back parlour of No. 26, but the house had been let out in furnished rooms and Mary's, partitioned off from the rest of the house, commanded a rent of 4s. 6d. a week. The only entrance to the room, designated No. 13, was in Miller's Court, the second door on the right from Dorset Street. Its only two windows also looked out into the court. In the smallest window, that nearest the door, two panes of glass were broken.

No. 13 was perhaps the most public habitation in Miller's Court. At the opposite side of the court its doorway could be observed from a small window at the back of John McCarthy's shop (27 Dorset Street) and from the windows of at least three of the succeeding tenements up the court, and at night the traffic in and out of Mary's room was illuminated in the yellow shade of a gas lamp, located almost directly opposite her door. Yet few residents of the court seem to have known much about Mary Jane Kelly or to have been more than passing acquaintances.

She was, they well knew, occasionally drunk. At such times she was noisy, 'spreeish' and given to singing Irish songs. She was probably the 'Mary Jane Kelley', aged twenty-two, who was fined 2s. 6d. at Thames Magistrates' Court on 19 September 1888 for being drunk and disorderly[1] and it was during a drunken quarrel with Joe Barnett, the man who lived with her, that she broke the window of her room. In general, however, Mary was a quiet woman with few serious relationships. Of Joe Barnett she was genuinely fond. Sometimes she visited another friend, a prostitute as herself, in the Elephant and Castle district. But the name of only one close female friend – that of Maria Harvey, a laundress who came to live at New Court in Dorset Street a day or two before Mary's death – can be reliably established and at the subsequent inquest only Barnett could tell the coroner anything of Mary's history.

Her story, as Barnett had it from Mary herself, is simply told. She was born in Limerick (whether the county or the town is not stated) but the family moved to Wales when she was very young. Her father, John Kelly, became a foreman at an ironworks, either in Carmarthenshire or Carnarvonshire, and Mary married a collier named Davis or Davies when she was about sixteen. A mine explosion, which killed her husband two or three years later, ended that part of her life. In 1884, when Mary was about twenty-one, she came to London. She found work in a West End brothel and so engaged one of the clientele there that he asked her to accompany him to France. It was not, apparently, a happy experience and after only two weeks abroad Mary returned to London. In the East End she attracted several paramours and, when not being supported by one of them, made a living by prostitution. At one time she was living with a man named Morganstone near the Commercial Gas Works, Stepney, at another with a mason's plasterer named Joe Flemming in Bethnal Green Road.[2]

The only corroboration of any of this comes from a long news report of 12 November. By this account Mary entered the service of a French lady living in Knightsbridge when she first came to London. While with this lady she led a 'degraded life' but drove about in a carriage and made several trips to Paris. Later she found her way to the East End. There she stayed first with Mrs Buki in St George's Street,

Ratcliff Highway. On one occasion both women went back to the French lady's house to demand Mary's box containing numerous costly dresses. From 1885 to 1886 or 1887 Mary lodged at the house of Mrs Carthy at Breezer's Hill, Pennington Street. According to Mrs Elizabeth Phoenix of 157 Bow Common Lane, Burdett Road, in Bow, Mrs Carthy's sister, Mary was very quarrelsome and abusive when drunk but 'one of the most decent and nicest girls you could meet' when sober. Mrs Carthy herself said that Mary eventually left her house 'to live with a man who was apparently in the building trade, and who she (Mrs Carthy) believed would have married her.'[3]

Presumably the man in the building trade was Joe Flemming, the plasterer also mentioned by Barnett. It is obvious that an especially close relationship once existed between Mary and Flemming. Barnett tells us that Mary was very fond of him. Mrs Carthy believed that Flemming would have married Mary. And Mary told Julia Venturney, a German charwoman who lodged opposite her in Miller's Court, that a man called Joe continued to visit her after she had taken up with Barnett. But we know next to nothing about this or any other of Mary's early relationships. Our sources, too, leave important questions unanswered. Why did Mary leave Wales for London? What was the truth behind the stories of the West End brothel and that mysterious jaunt to France? And why was a girl of Mary's youth and apparent good looks precipitated so swiftly into the desperate squalor of the East End lodging house? Ripperologists have pondered such questions for decades. We can reap a harvest of speculation and theory from their labours. But they are no substitute for facts.

Mary's life acquires sharper focus after her meeting with Joe Barnett in Commercial Street in 1887. At that time she was living at Cooley's lodging house in Thrawl Street.[4] Barnett, a steady respectable Irish cockney, worked as a market porter at Billingsgate. The two struck up an immediate friendship. Over a drink they arranged to meet again the next day and on that second meeting agreed to live together. At first the couple took lodgings in George Street. From there they moved to Little Paternoster Row, Dorset Street, and from there, evicted for getting drunk and failing to pay their rent, to Brick Lane. At the beginning of 1888 they rented 13 Miller's Court from John McCarthy, the owner of a chandler's shop at 27 Dorset Street.

Neither the horrendous scene-of-crime photographs taken by the police nor the fanciful sketches of the illustrated papers help us to visualize Mary's appearance. But she was young and evidently quite attractive. Mrs Phoenix said that she was about '5 feet 7 inches in height, and of rather stout build, with blue eyes and a very fine head of hair, which reached nearly to her waist.' Some of Mary's neighbours in Dorset Street have also left us word portraits of her. To Elizabeth Prater, lodging in a room directly over Mary's, she was 'tall and pretty, and as fair as a lily', a very pleasant girl who 'seemed to be on good terms with everybody'. To Caroline Maxwell, living in Dorset Street across the way from Miller's Court, 'a pleasant little woman, rather stout, fair complexion, and rather pale . . . she spoke with a kind of impediment.'5 The only durable result of her French connection seems to have been the affectation of the name Marie Jeanette Kelly.

Mary lived at Miller's Court with Joe Barnett until 30 October, when Barnett walked out after a quarrel. He had been out of work for several months, the couple had fallen behind in their rent and Mary had returned to prostitution. Her trade had occasioned differences between the two. 'I have heard him say that he did not like her going out on the streets,' Julia Venturney, a neighbour, told the police, 'he frequently gave her money, he was very kind to her, he said he would not live with her while she led that course of life.'6 But Mary's compassion was the immediate cause of their separation. Always big-hearted, she invited a homeless prostitute to share their room at Miller's Court.7 Barnett suffered the intrusion two or three nights and then remonstrated and left.

Barnett found shelter in a common lodging house in New Street, Bishopsgate, but he and Mary remained friends. On the evening of Thursday, 8 November, he visited her at Miller's Court and told her that he was very sorry he had no work and could not give her any money. The terror that had gripped the East End that autumn had touched Mary as it had every other prostitute. In Dorset Street, within a few yards of the entrance to Miller's Court, a bill proclaiming the *Illustrated Police News* £100 reward offer hung precariously from a wall. And several times Mary had asked Barnett to read to her from the newspapers about the murders. But when they parted that Thursday night, perhaps about eight, neither could possibly have anticipated the disaster that was about to engulf them. It was the last time Barnett saw Mary alive. And when he would look upon her, dead and mangled in Shoreditch Mortuary, he would recognize her only by her hair and eyes.8

Friday, 9 November 1888. The day of the Lord Mayor's Show. The day when the Right Honourable James Whitehead, the new Lord

Mayor, would drive in state, amidst all the pomp and pageantry the wealthiest city in the kingdom could devise, to the Royal Courts of Justice in the Strand for his oath of office. Mary would have enjoyed the festivities. Apparently she had been looking forward to it. 'I hope it will be a fine day tomorrow,' she had told Mrs Prater on Thursday morning, 'as I want to go to the Lord Mayor's Show.'[9]

John McCarthy, Mary's landlord, had other things on his mind. At 10.45 on Friday morning he was in his shop at 27 Dorset Street and checking his books with concern. He was not a hard man but he had already allowed Mary to clock up 29s. in rent arrears. So, calling Thomas Bowyer, his shop assistant, he sent him round to her room to see if she could pay the money. Perhaps he thought they might catch her before she disappeared to see the Lord Mayor's procession.[10]

Bowyer knocked twice at the door of No. 13. Each time there was no answer. He stepped round the corner to the broken window and, reaching inside, pulled aside the curtain. A first glance into the room revealed two lumps of flesh on the bedside table. A second discovered Mary's bloody and mutilated corpse lying on the bed itself. It was enough for poor Bowyer. He fled precipitately back to the shop. 'Governor,' he stammered, 'I knocked at the door and could not make anyone answer. I looked through the window and saw a lot of blood.' Such words, in the East End that autumn, presaged horrific murder, and filled with forebodings McCarthy returned with Bowyer to No. 13. There the sight which greeted the landlord when he looked through the window was even more stomach-turning than he had prepared himself for. The bedside table was covered with what looked like pieces of flesh and the body on the bed resembled that of a butchered beast. White-faced and shaken, he turned to Bowyer. 'Go at once to the police station,' he said, 'and fetch someone here.'

At Commercial Street Bowyer found Inspector Walter Beck on duty. Chatting with him was Walter Dew, the young detective who, fifty years later, recalled for us Bowyer's dramatic entrance. A youth, his eyes bulging out of his head, burst panting into the station. For a time he was so overcome with fright as to be unable to utter a single intelligible word. But at last he managed to babble something: 'Another one. Jack the Ripper. Awful. Jack McCarthy sent me.'[11] Soon they were hearing the tale from McCarthy himself who, having recovered his composure, had hurried after his assistant. 'Come along, Dew,' said the inspector, donning his hat and coat, and they set out together with Bowyer and McCarthy for the scene of the

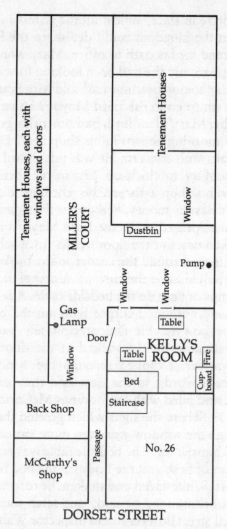

Miller's Court and Mary Jane Kelly's room

crime. They arrived at Miller's Court at or soon after eleven. 'The room was pointed out to me,' recalled Dew. 'I tried the door. It would not yield. So I moved to the window, over which, on the inside, an old coat was hanging to act as a curtain and to block the draught from the hole in the glass. Inspector Beck pushed the coat to one side and peered through the aperture. A moment later he staggered back with his face as white as a sheet. 'For God's sake, Dew,' he cried. 'Don't look.' I ignored the order, and took my place at the window. When my eyes had become accustomed to the dim light I saw a sight which I shall never forget to my dying day.'

Miller's Court was soon bustling with police personnel. Dr George Bagster Phillips, the divisional police surgeon, arrived at 11.15. Abberline was there by 11.30. Both must share some responsibility for the ensuing fiasco. The door of Mary's room was locked but, incredibly, no attempt was made to force it until 1.30 in the afternoon. Although Phillips was primarily responsible for the delay the testimony he gave three days later at the inquest cannot be said to be very illuminating on the point. There he described how, having looked through the broken window and ascertained that Mary was beyond help, he decided that 'probably it was advisable that no entrance should be made into the room at that time.' It was left to Abberline, who had charge of the case, to explain this bizarre decision to the inquest: 'I had an intimation from Inspector Beck that the dogs had been sent for [and] Dr Phillips asked me not to force the door but to test the dogs if they were coming.'[12] The dogs, as we now know, were no longer available, and in the two and a half hours after eleven the police did little more than seal off Miller's Court, accumulate statements from local residents and get in a photographer to photograph the corpse. At 1.30 Superintendent Arnold arrived. He brought the news that the order for the bloodhounds had been countermanded and gave immediate instructions for the door to be forced. John McCarthy then broke it open with a pickaxe. It was an unfortunate beginning to the investigation. Even the violence visited upon the offending door was unnecessary. Joe Barnett later told Abberline that the key had been missing for some time. The door had a spring lock that fastened automatically when it was pulled to but the catch could easily be moved back from the outside by reaching through the broken window!

The little room was cluttered. As the door was pushed open it banged against the bedside table. A moment later Abberline and his team were inside. The sight that met their eyes was one to haunt dreams.

Sparsely furnished, the room was nevertheless so small that there was very little space in which to move around. It was about twelve or fifteen feet square. The bedside table, against which the door had knocked, was close to the left-hand side of an ancient wooden bedstead and the right-hand side of the bedstead was close up against the wooden partition which sealed Mary's room off from the rest of the house. The only other furnishings were another old table, a chair or two, a cupboard, a disused washstand and a fireplace. The grate contained the ashes of a large fire. There was little attempt at decoration. A cheap print, 'The Fisherman's Widow', hung over the fireplace. But the floorboards were bare and filthy and although the walls themselves were papered the pattern was barely discernible beneath the dirt.

Mary's body, grotesquely mutilated, lay on the bed, two-thirds over towards the left-hand edge, that nearest the door. The first person through the door was Dr Phillips. From Phillips, above all others, we might have expected an authentic report about the condition of the body but he tells us almost nothing. Certainly he spoke at the inquest three days later. On that occasion, however, he deliberately suppressed the details of Mary's injuries. The immediate cause of death, he said, was the severance of the right carotid artery. From the blood-saturated condition of the palliasse, pillow and sheet at the top right-hand corner of the bed, and from the large quantity of blood found under the bedstead there, he deduced that she had been moved from the right-hand side of the bed after receiving her death wound.[13]

Phillips' silence ensured that for a century little authentic scene-of-crime information was known about what was perhaps the Ripper's last and most gruesome murder. Then, in 1987, a set of long-lost medical notes made by Dr Thomas Bond, who had worked with Phillips at Miller's Court and during the subsequent post-mortem, came to light among a bundle of documents posted anonymously to Scotland Yard. These notes, written on 10 November 1888, after the post-mortem, blow to bits the untrustworthy news reports and the fictional flourishes of Ripperologists that have served to bridge the gap in the documentation for so many years.

Dr Bond had been sucked into the Ripper investigation as early as 25 October, when Anderson had written to him requesting him to review the medical evidence given at the inquests and to hazard an opinion respecting the killer's alleged anatomical knowledge. 'In dealing with the Whitechapel murders,' the Assistant Commissioner had explained, 'the difficulties of conducting the inquiry are largely increased by reason of our having no reliable opinion for our guidance as to the amount of surgical skill and anatomical knowledge probably possessed by the murderer or murderers.'[14] Anderson looked to Bond for such guidance and, on the face of it, there were few more qualified to give it. For in addition to conducting the post-mortem examination in the celebrated Whitehall torso case at the beginning of October[15] he had twenty-one years' experience as police surgeon to A Division.

When the Kelly murder occurred Bond had already studied police notes on the Buck's Row, Hanbury Street, Berner Street and Mitre Square outrages. And at two on the afternoon of 9 November he turned up at Miller's Court to conduct his personal examination of the latest victim. His notes, written the next day, tell us what he saw:

> The body was lying naked in the middle of the bed, the shoulders flat, but the axis of the body inclined to the left side of the bed. The head was turned on the left cheek. The left arm was close to the body with the forearm flexed at a right angle & lying across the abdomen, the right arm was slightly abducted from the body & rested on the mattress, the elbow bent & the forearm supine with the fingers clenched. The legs were wide apart, the left thigh at right angles to the trunk & the right forming an obtuse angle with the pubes.
>
> The whole of the surface of the abdomen & thighs was removed & the abdominal cavity emptied of its viscera. The breasts were cut off, the arms mutilated by several jagged wounds & the face hacked beyond recognition of the features & the tissues of the neck were severed all round down to the bone. The viscera were found in various parts viz: the uterus & kidneys with one breast under the head, the other breast by the right foot, the liver between the feet, the intestines by the right side & the spleen by the left side of the body.
>
> The flaps removed from the abdomen & thighs were on a [bedside] table.
>
> The bed clothing at the right corner was saturated with blood, & on the floor beneath was a pool of blood covering about 2 feet square. The wall by the right side of the bed & in a line with the neck was marked by blood which had struck it in a number of separate splashes.[16]

Bond's statement that Mary's body was found naked was contradicted by Phillips' inquest testimony that she was clad in a linen under garment. Phillips was right because in a surviving police photograph of the scene a puffed sleeve of the garment is clearly visible about the top of Mary's left arm. One possible explanation of the discrepancy is that most of the under garment had been cut away from the body in the process of mutilation.

From the moment the police and their surgeons descended upon Miller's Court the local residents became little more than helpless bystanders to the drama being enacted in their midst. The few who saw inside the butcher's shambles that was No. 13 were left numb with shock. One was Elizabeth Prater. Her husband, a boot machinist named William Prater, had deserted her five years since and she now earned a living by prostitution and lodged alone in No. 20 Miller's Court, above Mary's room. 'I'm a woman myself,' she sobbed to a *Star* reporter on the day of the murder, 'and I've got to sleep in that place tonight right over where it happened.' Mrs Prater had good cause to know what had happened. A pump stood in the court near No. 13 and Mrs Prater took advantage of a trip for water to peep through the window of Mary's room. 'I could bear to look at it only for a second,' she said, 'but I can never forget the sight of it if I live to be a hundred.'[17]

John McCarthy, who had forced the door, was among the first to enter No. 13. 'The sight we saw,' he said later in the day, 'I cannot drive away from my mind. It looked more like the work of a devil than of a man. The poor woman's body was lying on the bed, undressed. She had been completely disembowelled, and her entrails had been taken out and placed on the table. It was those that I had seen when I looked through the window and took to be lumps of flesh. The woman's nose had been cut off, and her face gashed and mutilated so that she was quite beyond recognition. Both her breasts too had been cut clean away and placed by the side of her liver and other entrails on the table. I had heard a great deal about the Whitechapel murders, but I declare to God I had never expected to see such a sight as this. The body was, of course, covered with blood, and so was the bed. The whole scene is more than I can describe. I hope I may never see such a sight again.'[18]

Tidings of the murder soon swept through the crowded courts and alleys of the East End. 'Women rushed about the streets,' said one report, 'telling their neighbours the news, and giving utterance in angry voices to expressions of rage and indignation.'[19] As the Lord Mayor's procession swung into Fleet Street from Ludgate Circus the news burst upon the crowds lining the route there. Soon spectators were deserting the show in thousands and converging upon Dorset Street. Cordons of police at each end denied them access but the entrances from Bell Lane and Commercial Street became choked by crowds of excited, frightened-looking people.

At about four o'clock a one-horse carrier's cart with a tarpaulin cover was driven into Dorset Street and halted opposite Miller's Court. A long shell or coffin, scratched and dirty with use, was taken from the cart and carried into No. 13. The surgeons had completed their preliminary examination of the remains. The news that the body was about to be removed produced a great rush of people from the courts leading out of Dorset Street and a determined push against the police cordon at the Commercial Street end. 'The crowd, which pressed round the van [cart], was of the humblest class,' ran the *Times* report, 'but the demeanour of the poor people was all that could be desired. Ragged caps were doffed and slatternly-looking women shed tears as the shell, covered with a ragged-looking cloth, was placed in the van.'[20]

After the remains had been driven to Shoreditch Mortuary the windows of No. 13 were boarded up and the door padlocked. The cordons at the ends of the street were withdrawn but although crowds of idlers roved through Dorset Street all evening there was nothing for them to see since two stalwart constables vigilantly guarded the passage into Miller's Court.

In Whitehall the news of the latest murder was greeted with dismay. When Beck saw Mary's mutilated corpse through the broken window he lost no time in apprising Commercial Street by fast-running constables and from there the news was promptly relayed by telegraph to Scotland Yard. Warren dashed off a brief note to Lushington. 'I have to acquaint you, for the information of the Secretary of State,' he wrote, 'that information has just been received that a mutilated dead body of a woman is reported to have been found this morning inside a room in a house (No. 26) in Dorset Street, Spitalfields.' The matter, he added, had been entrusted to Anderson. Messages then flew back and forth. The Home Office telephoned Warren. They wanted to be informed as soon as possible of any further news. And, after personally inspecting the scene of the murder, Anderson telephoned the Home Office. A scribbled note of his message still survives in the Home Office papers: 'Body is believed to be that of a prostitute terribly muti [sic] much mutilated. Dr Bond is at present engaged in making his examination but his report has not yet been received. Full report cannot be furnished until medical officers have completed enquiry.'[21]

On Saturday morning the police returned eagerly to their investigation of the crime. Abberline was back at Miller's Court, exploring the ashes cold in the grate of Mary's room. It had been a large fire, so fierce that it had melted the spout of the kettle, but the only clues his search turned up were a few remnants of women's clothing. A *Times* report assures us that they were a piece of burnt velvet, presumed to be the remains of a jacket, and the charred rim and wirework of a woman's felt hat. Press versions of Abberline's inquest testimony speak of the remnants of a skirt and the brim of a hat.[22] What had been the purpose of this blaze? To destroy something? Abberline did not think so. He discovered but one piece of candle in the room and decided that the Ripper had been compelled to burn clothes in order to provide the light by which he mutilated his victim.

That same morning Doctors Phillips, Bond and Gordon Brown carried out a post-mortem examination at the mortuary. Press notices of their labours are brief and unreliable and leave the question as to whether any parts of the body were missing unresolved. Indeed, on the matter of missing organs, they performed a complete *volte-face*. The earliest reports of the autopsy insisted that after Phillips had 'fitted' the dismembered portions of Mary's anatomy into their proper places all the organs had been fully accounted for. By the beginning of the following week, however, the same papers were confidently asserting the contrary. Thus, on 13 November, the *Daily Telegraph*: 'We are enabled to state, on good authority, that notwithstanding all that has been said to the contrary, a portion of the bodily organs was missing.'[23] To discerning members of the public the behaviour of the medicos would have proved a better guide. For on Saturday afternoon, only hours after the post-mortem had been terminated, Phillips and Dr Roderick Macdonald, the district coroner, went to the scene of the crime and, having sifted the ashes from the grate through a sieve, proceeded to inspect the residue for traces of burnt human remains. Obviously Mary's corpse had not been restored complete.

In providing us with our first accurate account of the autopsy findings, Dr Thomas Bond's newly discovered post-mortem notes finally settle this long standing controversy.[24] They make harrowing reading. But they are an important part of the record.

Mary's throat had been cut with such ferocity that the tissues had been severed right down to the spinal column and the fifth and sixth vertebrae had been deeply notched by the knife. The air passage had been cut at the lower part of the larynx through the cricoid cartilage.

There were terrible mutilations to the face: 'The face was gashed in all directions, the nose, cheeks, eyebrows & ears being partly removed. The lips were blanched & cut by several incisions running obliquely down to the chin. There were also numerous cuts extending irregularly across all the features.'

But the injuries inflicted upon Mary's torso and limbs exceeded in bestiality anything the Ripper had yet done. Dr Bond wrote:

> Both breasts were removed by more or less circular incisions, the muscles down to the ribs being attached to the breasts. The intercostals between the 4th, 5th & 6th ribs were cut & the contents of the thorax visible through the openings.
>
> The skin & tissues of the abdomen from the costal arch to the pubes were removed in three large flaps. The right thigh was denuded in front to the bone, the flap of skin including the external organs of generation & part of the right buttock. The left thigh was stripped of skin, fascia & muscles as far as the knee.
>
> The left calf showed a long gash through skin & tissues to the deep muscles & reaching from the knee to 5 in. above the ankle.
>
> Both arms & forearms had extensive & jagged wounds.
>
> The right thumb showed a small superficial incision about 1 in. long, with extravasation of blood in the skin & there were several abrasions on the back of the hand & forearm showing the same condition.
>
> On opening the thorax it was found that the right lung was minimally adherent by old firm adhesions. The lower part of the lung was broken & torn away.
>
> The left lung was intact; it was adherent at the apex & there were a few adhesions over the side. In the substances of the lung were several nodules of consolidation.
>
> The pericardium was open below & the heart absent.

Mary's heart had obviously been cut out and could not be found but Bond does not venture an opinion as to whether the murderer had burned it or had carried it away. For what they are worth – and upon such matters they are worth very little – the newspaper reports aver that no traces of human remains were discovered in the ashes of the fire.

The doctors found partly digested food, consisting of fish and potatoes, in the abdominal cavity. Similar food was discovered in the remains of the stomach attached to the intestines.

The post-mortem over with, Bond felt able to respond to Anderson's plea for guidance on the degree of medical expertise displayed by the murderer. And, in a general report penned for the Assistant

Commissioner later in the day, he set down his conclusions on this and other aspects of the case.[25] His remarks embraced the Nichols, Chapman, Stride and Eddowes murders, police notes relating to which he had read, as well as that of Mary Kelly.

Bond was sure that all five women had been slain by the same hand. The throats of the first four appeared to have been cut from left to right. In Mary's case extensive mutilations made it impossible to tell in which direction the fatal cut had been made but, like the others, her throat had been cut first for splashes of arterial blood were found on the wall close to where her head must have been lying.

In no case had any sign of a struggle been discovered. It thus appeared to the doctor that the attacks were 'probably so sudden and made in such a position that the women could neither resist nor cry out.' The victims were probably lying down when murdered. As noted by Phillips, the sheet at the top right-hand corner of Mary's bed was bloody and badly cut. The explanation that occurred to Bond was that Mary's face might have been covered with the sheet at the time the attack was made. In the first four cases the murderer must have attacked from the right side of the victim. In the case of Mary Kelly this would have been impossible because there would not have been room for him between the wooden petition and the bed. He must therefore have attacked her from in front or from the left. Although Bond did not think that the murderer need necessarily have been 'deluged' with blood, he did believe that his hands and arms must have been covered in it and that parts of his clothing must have been stained.

The mutilations of Nichols, Chapman, Eddowes and Kelly, said the doctor, were 'all of the same character.' They were inflicted with a strong knife, very sharp, pointed at the top, about an inch in width and at least six inches long. 'It may have been a clasp knife, a butcher's knife or a surgeon's knife,' he speculated, '[but] I think it was no doubt a straight knife.'

On the important question of the killer's medical expertise Bond provided Anderson with a categoric reply. The murderer was a man of physical strength and 'great coolness and daring.' But, as far as Bond was concerned, he possessed no anatomical knowledge: 'In each case the mutilation was inflicted by a person who had no scientific nor anatomical knowledge. In my opinion he does not even possess the technical knowledge of a butcher or horse slaughterer or any person accustomed to cut up dead animals.'

Of more immediate interest to Abberline, struggling to unravel the mysteries of Miller's Court, would have been the answer to a different question. When did Mary die? But on this point Dr Bond was less sure of his ground:

In the Dorset Street case the body was lying on the bed at the time of my visit, 2 o'clock, quite naked and mutilated . . . Rigor Mortis had set in, but increased during the progress of the examination. From this it is difficult to say with any degree of certainty the exact time that had elapsed since death as the period varies from 6 to 12 hours before rigidity sets in. The body was comparatively cold at 2 o'clock and the remains of a recently taken meal were found in the stomach and scattered about over the intestines. It is, therefore, pretty certain that the woman must have been dead about 12 hours and the partly digested food would indicate that death took place about 3 or 4 hours after the food was taken, so one or two o'clock in the morning would be the probable time of the murder.

The most dramatic development of Saturday 10th was the intervention of the government. A Cabinet Council held at the Foreign Office decided that Mr Matthews should stand firm on his refusal of a reward and instead agreed to countenance the offer of a free pardon to any accomplice of the murderer of Mary Kelly who would betray him into the hands of the police. Lushington accordingly authorized Warren to issue the following notice, which appeared in the press and outside police stations:

MURDER. – PARDON. – Whereas on November 8 or 9, in Miller Court, Dorset Street, Spitalfields, Mary Janet [sic] Kelly was murdered by some person or persons unknown: the Secretary of State will advise the grant of Her Majesty's gracious pardon to any accomplice, not being a person who contrived or actually committed the murder, who shall give such information and evidence as shall lead to the discovery and conviction of the person or persons who committed the murder.
CHARLES WARREN, the Commissioner of Police
of the Metropolis.
Metropolitan Police Office, 4 Whitehall Place,
S.W., Nov. 10, 1888.[26]

It would be naive to believe that the Cabinet expected to detect the Ripper by this intervention. Their decision was immediately challenged in the Commons. W. A. Hunter, the Member for Aberdeen North, asked on 12 November whether the Home Secretary had considered extending the pardon to the killer's accomplices in the earlier murders, especially since 'in the case of the first murder, committed last Christmas [Emma Smith], according to the dying testimony of the woman, several persons were concerned in the murder.' Matthews declined to answer at that time. When Hunter repeated his question eleven days later, however, he attempted to project a facade of omniscience and replied that he would be quite prepared to extend the pardon if he had any evidence that such a decision might be fruitful. But, he pointed out, 'in the case of Kelly there were certain circumstances which were wanting in the earlier cases, and which made it more probable that there were other persons who, at any rate after the crime, had assisted the murderer.'[27]

Matthews' explanation of the rationale of the pardon offer is, quite frankly, unbelievable. In at least two of the earlier murders, that of Emma Smith, which was apparently perpetrated by three men, and that of Liz Stride, for which Israel Schwartz had accused two, there *had* been evidence of accomplices. The Home Secretary was not ignorant of these facts. Hunter himself had drawn his attention to the first instance and Warren had sent him a detailed report on the Stride murder on 24 October. In the case of Mary Kelly, on the other hand, there was no evidence whatsoever that more than one man had been involved and Dr Bond had said so in his report. So what was the real purpose of the Cabinet's hasty, ill-judged action? Simply that the latest murder threatened to deluge the Home Secretary in a tidal wave of public anger and recrimination and it was deemed imperative that he do something, however futile, to appease the outcry. Having argued so forcefully against rewards in the past, Matthews could scarcely endorse them now and retain credibility. But a pardon . . . It was, then, an empty gesture, a sop to public opinion, prompted not by wisdom but by fear.

The inquest was held on Monday, 12 November. The murder had been committed in Spitalfields and the body had been deposited in Shoreditch Mortuary. So the proceedings were conducted, not by Wynne Baxter, but by Dr Roderick Macdonald, Coroner for the North Eastern District of Middlesex. The venue was Shoreditch Town Hall.

There was great public excitement. All day curious sightseers rambled up and down Dorset Street. They were prevented from entering Miller's Court, still guarded by two constables, but a crowd collected outside the court and maintained a permanent vigil. At Shoreditch Town Hall, where the inquest got under way at 11.00 a.m., large numbers of people had to be shut out. When the crush outside threatened to overwhelm the coroner's officer, trying to hold the door, the door was locked and an inspector stationed there. By that time the inquest room was packed.

After the jurors had been sworn they were conducted by Abberline to the mortuary to view the body and then to Miller's Court to see the murder room. Mary's corpse had been stitched together and coffined. Only her face was visible, her mutilated body lying concealed beneath a dirty grey cloth. 'The eyes were the only vestiges of humanity,' commented the *Pall Mall Gazette*. 'The rest [of the face] was so scored and slashed that it was impossible to say where the flesh began and the cuts ended.'[28] It was close on twelve before any evidence was taken. The jury learned something about Mary from Joe Barnett. Thomas Bowyer and John McCarthy told them how her body had been discovered on Friday morning. And depositions bearing upon her final hours were contributed by half a dozen residents of Dorset Street and Miller's Court. But those anticipating a feast of gory revelations were profoundly disappointed. Dr Phillips spoke only briefly about the medical aspects of the case. Indeed, beyond his assertion that death had been caused by the severance of the right carotid artery he told the jury virtually nothing. And no question was put to him as to the details of the extensive mutilations or as to whether any organs were still missing. From Beck and Abberline, whose testimonies wound up the day's proceedings, they heard little more about the police investigation.

However frustrating to the modern historian, the attitude of Phillips and the police was, of course, understandable. Their view was that the work of the police might be hindered by the immediate publication of the full details. Dr Macdonald, himself a police surgeon (to the Metropolitan Police's K Division), recognized the logic of their case and told the jury that he was only going to take the preliminary portion of Phillips' evidence, the remainder of which could be more fully given at the adjourned inquiry. The inquiry, in the event, was not to be adjourned. After Abberline had made his deposition Macdonald terminated the day's proceedings. In doing so he advised the jury that it would be sufficient for them to ascertain the cause of death only, leaving other matters in the hands of the police, and he asked them if they had already heard enough evidence to enable them to reach a verdict. The foreman, having consulted his colleagues, affirmed that they had. They returned a verdict of 'wilful murder against some person or persons unknown'.

During the days immediately after the Miller's Court outrage East Enders were witness to frantic police activity. But, from the first, the press expressed little confidence in their success. 'It is quite clear,' thundered the *Star*, 'that nothing can be expected from the police, and that we may have 20 murders, as well as seven or eight, without their doing a single thing or making a single effort which will be fruitful for the public good.' Even *The Times* was beginning to despair of the CID: 'The murders, so cunningly continued, are carried out with a completeness which altogether baffles investigators. Not a trace is left of the murderer, and there is no purpose in the crime to afford the slightest clue, such as would be afforded in other crimes almost without exception. All that the police can hope is that some accidental circumstance will lead to a trace which may be followed to a successful conclusion.'[29]

Admirable as *The Times*' exposition of the problem was, we must challenge its assumption that the Ripper had left absolutely no new clues to his identity. Clues in the form of tangible objects there were certainly none. No weapon had been discovered. A pipe found by the police in No. 13 turned out to belong to Joe Barnett and a man's black overcoat to have been left there by Mary's friend Maria Harvey. But there was no shortage of witnesses who saw Mary on the night of the murder. Several of them even claimed to have seen her in the company of strange men.

It is time for us to examine the evidence of these witnesses, to explore the last few hours of Mary Jane Kelly's life, to probe the dark secrets of Miller's Court on that cold November night a century ago.

16

'Oh! Murder!'

OUR SEARCH FOR THE FACTS about the murder of Mary Kelly must discount the unsupported tattle of the Victorian press. Even when important witnesses were seen by reporters, interviews were often conducted so sloppily and edited and published so hastily that the words of witnesses appear to have been quite misconstrued.

Take, for example, the John McCarthy statement printed by the *Daily News* on 10 November. It was made on the day of the murder and contains this intriguing passage: 'At eleven o'clock last night she [Kelly] was seen in the Britannia public house, at the corner of this thoroughfare [Dorset Street], with a young man with a dark moustache. She was then intoxicated. The young man appeared to be very respectable and well dressed.' Who was McCarthy's informant? He does not say. But a sighting of Mary with a man on the night of her death would have been an observation of the greatest importance so it is difficult to understand why McCarthy made absolutely no reference to the incident in his statement to the police or in his testimony before the coroner.

A report from the *Western Mail*, published in Paul Begg's book, seems at first glance to provide a plausible solution to this mystery – McCarthy's informant was his assistant, Thomas Bowyer, and the observation had been made, not on Thursday night but on Wednesday, more than a day before the murder. The report reads: 'Harry Bowyer states that on Wednesday night he saw a man speaking to Kelly who resembled the description given by the fruiterer of the supposed Berner Street murderer. He was, perhaps, 27 or 28 and had a dark moustache and very peculiar eyes. His appearance was rather smart and attention was drawn to him by [his] showing very white cuffs and a rather long white collar, the ends of which came down in front over a black coat. He did not carry a bag.'[1] Sadly even this tidy solution will not do. For Bowyer's inquest deposition proves that he saw Mary Kelly *neither* on Wednesday night *nor* on Thursday night. Replying to a specific question from the inquest jury, Bowyer said: 'I last saw deceased alive on Wednesday afternoon in the court [Miller's Court].'[2]

If the incident alluded to in McCarthy's press statement happened at all the informant was not Bowyer or it had predated the murder by several days. In either case the story, as it stands, is worthless as evidence. This is not to say that newspapers do not yield occasional gems and we will have occasion to be thankful to them when we encounter George Hutchinson. But unless, as in that case, we can corroborate them from police or coroner's file, press statements of witnesses should be used with great caution and news reports – when they treat of the details of the murders and murder investigations – altogether discounted. Fortunately authentic evidence of the Kelly case does exist and if we are to find any answers to our questions we must seek them there.

Nine local residents appeared to give evidence at the inquest on 12 November. The records of coroners' inquests held for the North Eastern District of Middlesex still survive. And the papers relating to this case[3] contain, not only an official record of the depositions made at the inquest, but copies of the original statements made by the nine witnesses to the police three days earlier. The statements are all dated 9 November and all but one are in the handwriting of Inspector Abberline.

Taken together the depositions and statements of these witnesses constitute our main source of documentary evidence relating to the murder. They furnish invaluable insights. Nevertheless, full of comings and goings, suspicious characters and contradictory testimony, they are often frustrating to use. And the light they shed upon the events of that night is but a fitful one. By it we can drive the shadows from Miller's Court for brief intervals, but they lurk in the corners, and as regularly as our light falters they close around us again to envelop us in impenetrable gloom.

Maria Harvey, our first witness, was a laundress. She was also one of Mary Kelly's closest friends. Indeed, on the nights of 5 and 6 November Mary had put Maria up in No. 13. Although Maria had since found a room of her own, at 3 New Court, Dorset Street, the two women enjoyed each other's company. So Maria spent the whole afternoon of Thursday 8 November with Mary and was still there when Joe Barnett called early in the evening.

After Barnett's arrival, however, she left. Maria must have known about her friend's recent quarrel with Barnett but she seems to have felt no apprehension in leaving them alone together. 'They seemed,' she would tell the police next day, 'to be on the best of terms.' The laundress left some clothes in No. 13 – a man's black overcoat, two men's cotton shirts, a boy's shirt, a girl's white petticoat, a black crepe bonnet with black strings and a pawn ticket for a shawl. The next time she saw the overcoat it was in the custody of the police. Abberline had a special interest, of course, in identifying this item. It is possible that the other garments were consumed in the flames of the Ripper's fire but the silence of our sources respecting them does not preclude the possibility that they were also found by the police in the room.[4]

In the statements Maria Harvey and Joe Barnett gave to the police on 9 November there is a slight discrepancy on the matter of times. Maria said that she left Mary at 6.55, when Barnett arrived. Barnett averred that he visited Mary between seven and eight and that he stayed until eight o'clock. At the inquest he said that he called on Mary between 7.30 and 7.45 and stayed about fifteen minutes.[5] Whatever the precise time of Barnett's visit, his was, as we have seen, a friendly call. But he could give Mary no money and that helps to explain why, later in the evening, she ventured out into the streets.

When Barnett saw her last Mary was quite sober. Four hours later, when Mary Ann Cox encountered her in Dorset Street, she was intoxicated and with a stranger. Mrs Cox, described by the Star as 'a wretched looking specimen of East End womanhood', was a thirty-one-year-old widow who supported herself by prostitution. She lived at 5 Miller's Court, the last house on the left at the top of the court, and had known Mary about eight or nine months.

That Thursday night Mrs Cox had been soliciting in Commercial Street. But there was a chill in the autumn air and she decided to pop home and warm herself up before trying her luck on the streets once more. It was about 11.45 when she turned into Dorset Street. There she saw Mary walking in front of her with a man. The young

Irish prostitute wore a red knitted 'crossover' about her shoulders and a linsey frock, but neither hat nor bonnet. She had had far too much to drink. The couple turned into Miller's Court just ahead of Mrs Cox. When the widow entered the court they were going into Mary's room. 'Good night, Mary Jane,' called Mrs Cox. 'She was very drunk,' the widow told the police, 'and could scarcely answer me, but said good night.'

Mary's client is of great interest to us. Mrs Cox, who saw him in the light of the gas lamp opposite the door of No. 13, gave two descriptions. Her statement to the police, made on the day of the murder, reads: 'the man was carrying a quart can of beer . . . was about 36 years old, about 5 ft. 5 in. high, complexion fresh and I believe he had blotches on his face, small side whiskers, and a thick carrotty moustache, dressed in shabby dark clothes, dark overcoat and black felt hat.' Three days later she told the inquest of 'a short stout man shabbily dressed . . . he had a longish coat very shabby dark and a pot of ale in his hand, he had a hard billy cock black hat on, he had a blotchy face and a full carrotty mustache his chin was clean.'

As Mrs Cox went into her own room she heard Mary singing 'A violet I plucked from Mother's grave when a boy.' Soon after midnight the widow went out again. When she returned, at about one o'clock, there was a light in Mary's room and she was still singing. Mrs Cox warmed her hands and ventured out again shortly after one. At three she was back. There was then no light in No. 13 and all was quiet.

Mrs Cox did not go out again but she could not sleep. It rained hard that night. Occasionally, through the drumming of the rain, she heard the heavy tread of men entering or leaving the court. 'I heard men going in and out, several go in and out,' she told the inquest. 'I heard someone go out at a quarter to six. I do not know what house he went out of [as] I heard no door shut.'[6]

Neither Mary Cox nor Julia Venturney, the German charwoman in No. 1, heard anything suspicious or alarming during the night. But two other witnesses did. One of them was Elizabeth Prater, who lodged in Room 20 in 26 Dorset Street, above Mary's room.

On this particular night she retired at about 1.30 a.m. She barricaded her door with a couple of tables, lay down to rest and, having drunk heavily, at once fell fast asleep. Two or three hours later she was suddenly awake. It had been her kitten, clambering across her neck, which had disturbed her slumbers. But just then she heard screams of 'Murder!' Unfortunately neither upon the time of the screams nor upon their nature is Mrs Prater's evidence consistent. In both her statement to the police and her inquest testimony she estimated the time at about 3.30 to 4.00 a.m. But at the inquest she reflected further: 'I noticed the lodging house light was out, so it was after 4 probably.' And while she spoke to the police of 'screams of murder about two or three times in a female voice' she told the inquest jury of but one cry of 'Oh! Murder!', faint but seemingly close at hand. It is nevertheless apparent that she was unperturbed. 'I did not take much notice of the cries,' Mrs Prater explained to the police, 'as I frequently hear such cries from the back of the lodging house where the windows look into Miller's Court.' Dismissing the incident from her mind, she went back to sleep.

Up and about at 5.30, Mrs Prater walked to the Ten Bells at the corner of Commercial and Church (present Fournier) Streets for a tot of rum. There was no one about in Miller's Court but she saw two or three carmen harnessing their horses in Dorset Street. When she returned to her lodging she went back to bed and slept until eleven.[7]

Elizabeth Prater's befuddled tale of screams in the night would command scant consideration were it not for the corroboratory testimony of the laundress Sarah Lewis. Sarah lived at 24 Great Pearl Street in Spitalfields, but in the early hours of Friday, 9 November, after a quarrel with her husband, she came to stay with her friends the Keylers at No. 2 Miller's Court. For the real beginning of Sarah's story, however, we must go back two days to the evening of Wednesday the 7th, to her encounter with a sinister stranger in Bethnal Green Road.

At 8 o'clock that evening the laundress was walking along Bethnal Green Road with a female friend when a man, who had already passed them by, turned back to speak. A middle-aged man, perhaps forty years old, he was short of stature, pale-faced and sported a small black moustache. His short black coat and 'pepper and salt' trousers were partly concealed by a long brown overcoat. He wore a high round hat and carried a black bag some nine or twelve inches long. The man wanted one of the women – he did not mind which one – to follow him. Both of them refused and he went away, but he was soon back. This time, promising to treat them, he tried to inveigle Sarah and her friend into a narrow passage, but his appearance and persistence had now seriously alarmed the women and they held back. 'What are you frightened of?' he asked, putting down his bag. When he undid and reached for something beneath his coat the women ran without looking back.

Between two and three o'clock on Friday morning Sarah went to stay with the Keylers. As she passed Christ Church, Spitalfields, she looked at the clock. It was 2.30 a.m. Despite the lateness of the hour there were still people about. And in Commercial Street, near the Britannia, Sarah saw the stranger who had accosted her on Wednesday night. On this occasion he had no overcoat but he wore the same trousers, short coat and high hat. And he carried the same black bag. Somewhat shaken, Sarah hurried past and then looked back. But the man was preoccupied talking to another woman and made no attempt to stop her. When she reached the corner of Dorset Street Mrs Lewis looked back at the man again.

In Dorset Street, opposite Miller's Court, was a lodging house. As Sarah entered the court she noticed, standing alone by the lodging house, yet another man. In her statement to the police Sarah said that she could give no description of this man but at the inquest, three days later, her memory had improved: 'He was not tall, but stout, had on a wideawake black hat, I did not notice his clothes. Another young man with a woman passed along. The man standing in the street was looking up the court as if waiting for someone to come out.'

At the Keylers' Mrs Lewis hardly slept. She dozed in a chair until 3.30 and then sat awake until nearly five. Just before four o'clock the silence was shattered by a single loud scream of 'Murder!' It sounded like the cry of a young woman not far distant but Sarah did not even trouble to look out of the window. Such cries were common in Whitechapel. Her estimate of the time of the scream, nevertheless, is probably preferable to that of Mrs Prater for she seems to have been more fully awake. She thus heard the clock strike 3.30.[8]

Did Elizabeth Prater and Sarah Lewis hear Mary's last terrified scream? If the testimony of another witness, Mrs Caroline Maxwell of 14 Dorset Street, is to be credited they did not. For Mrs Maxwell insisted that she saw and spoke to Mary at the corner of Miller's Court at about 8.30 on Friday morning.

'What brings you up so early?' asked Mrs Maxwell.

'I have the horrors of drink upon me,' Mary replied, 'as I have been drinking for some days past.'

'Why don't you go to Mrs Ringer's[9] and have half a pint of beer?'

Mary pointed to some vomit in the roadway. 'I have been there and had it,' she said, 'but I have brought it all up again.'

Some thirty minutes later Mrs Maxwell saw her again although only at a distance. Mary was wearing a dark skirt, black velvet bodice and maroon shawl, and she was talking to a man outside the Britannia.[10]

The statements and depositions in the coroner's papers contain nothing further to our purpose. But we have already learned something very important from them – the probable time of Mary's death. Admittedly our witnesses offer conflicting testimony on this point. On the one hand Elizabeth Prater and Sarah Lewis both attested to a cry of 'Murder!' just before 4.00 a.m. And on the other Mrs Caroline Maxwell was emphatic that she saw Mary as late as 8.30 and 9.00. A moment's consideration of the medical evidence, however, will enable us to decide the issue between them.

When Dr Bond saw the body at two in the afternoon rigor mortis was beginning to set in. If this normally occurred, as he explained, six to twelve hours after death, Mary died at some time between two and eight in the morning. But the body was comparatively cold so Bond opted for an early time, about 1.00 or 2.00 a.m. It is possible, however, that Mary's body lost heat more rapidly than is usual and that she was killed at a later hour than two. Such, indeed, seems to have been the view of Dr Phillips. Unfortunately we have no official report from him and he made no reference at the inquest to the time of death. But *The Times* appeared to reflect his views in the following paragraph: 'the opinion of Dr George Bagster Phillips, the divisional surgeon of the H Division, [is] that when he was called to the deceased (at a quarter to 11) she had been dead some five or six hours. There is no doubt that the body of a person who, to use Dr Phillips's own words, was "cut all to pieces" would get cold far more quickly than that of one who had died simply from the cutting of the throat; and the room would have been very cold, as there were two broken panes of glass in the windows. Again, the body being entirely uncovered would very quickly get cold.'[11] Phillips was, in fact, called out at about eleven and arrived at Miller's Court fifteen minutes later. If his opinion was correctly reported, therefore, the doctor believed the murder to have been committed at about 5.00 or 6.00 a.m. This estimate, though, is possibly *too* late because Phillips does not seem to have taken into consideration the heat of the Ripper's fierce fire. A time of death between the estimates of Bond and Phillips would thus seem reasonable.

It will be readily apparent that the testimony of Elizabeth Prater and Sarah Lewis is consistent with the medical evidence and that of Caroline Maxwell is not. The scream of 'Murder!' heard by Prater and Lewis was close at hand and sounded like that of a young woman. Sarah even told the inquest that it seemed to come from the direction of Mary's room. It is difficult to avoid the conclusion that both women disregarded what was Mary's last desperate cry for help. Bond, it is true, told Anderson that the attack was probably so sudden and 'made in such a position' that Mary could neither resist nor cry out. But his comment may have been prompted partly by an erroneous belief that no one had heard a cry and is, in any case, in conflict with some of his other findings. The autopsy revealed that Mary had sustained a small incision to her right thumb and abrasions to the back of her hand and forearm and these indicate that she attempted some kind of defence.

The testimony of Mrs Maxwell is an unanswered riddle. Was she lying, drunk, or simply mistaken? On the first occasion she supposedly saw Mary, at 8.30, they conversed across the street. On the second Mary was standing about twenty-five yards away. At either distance Mrs Maxwell should have been able to recognize Mary and it seems more likely that she confused the date than the person. Whatever the answer, all we can say for certain is that her testimony was wrong.

What of the Ripper himself? The coroner's papers, alas, probably tell us nothing about him. The stories of the witnesses certainly abound in dubious characters. The man Mrs Maxwell thought she saw talking to Mary at nine, if he ever existed, is exonerated. But there are plenty of others – the short, stout man with the blotchy face and carrotty moustache seen by Mrs Cox, the man with the black bag and the high hat, the man with the wideawake black hat Sarah Lewis saw lurking opposite the entrance of Miller's Court and looking up the court 'as if waiting for someone to come out', and the young man seen with a woman by Sarah in Dorset Street. It should be remembered, though, that the fact that strange men, with or without women, were seen about Dorset Street in the nocturnal hours is of no significance in itself. The street consisted almost entirely of common lodging houses. That at 14 Dorset Street, where Mrs Maxwell's husband was deputy, alone could accommodate 244 people. And, as we have already noted, the street and its courts harboured prostitutes galore. It was thus by no means unusual to encounter men and prostitutes in the street in the early hours of the morning.

The only suspect these witnesses refer to against whom a case can be made is the man with the carrotty moustache because he was actually seen to enter No. 13 with Mary Kelly. Even the case against him, however, is extremely weak. It was about 11.45 p.m. when Mrs Cox followed them into Miller's Court, no less than four hours before the probable time of the murder and far too early for us to assume that he was the killer. Mary was a prostitute. She was, moreover, in financial trouble. Her rent arrears stood at 29s. and Thomas Bowyer's call the next morning may not have been unanticipated. Quite possibly she feared eviction. When Joe Barnett's visit on Thursday evening proved barren of succour she took to the streets. She procured one client, the man Mrs Cox saw at 11.45, and in the ensuing four hours, impelled by necessity, she could easily have procured another. Indeed, there is crucial eyewitness evidence that she did precisely that.

The witness was George Hutchinson, a casual labourer then living at the Victoria Working Men's Home in Commercial Street. His name will not be found in the coroner's papers for the simple reason that he did not appear at the inquest. This was not, as some have recently alleged, because his evidence was deliberately suppressed, but because at the time of the inquest neither the police nor the coroner knew anything of him.

It was not until six in the evening of Monday, 12 November, after the inquest had been concluded, that Hutchinson walked into Commercial Street Police Station and made his statement. This document, still preserved in the records of the Metropolitan Police, merits quotation in full:

About 2 a.m. 9th I was coming by Thrawl Street, Commercial Street, and just before I got to Flower and Dean Street I met the murdered woman Kelly and she said to me Hutchinson will you lend me sixpence. I said I can't I have spent all my money going down to Romford. She said good morning I must go and find some money. She went away towards Thrawl Street. A man coming in the opposite direction to Kelly tapped her on the shoulder and said something to her. They both burst out laughing. I heard her say alright to him and the man said you will be alright for what I have told you. He then placed his right hand around her shoulders. He also had a kind of a small parcel in his left hand with a kind of a strap round it. I stood against the lamp of the Queen's Head Public House and watched him. They both then came past me and the man hung down his head with his hat over his eyes. I stooped down and looked him in the face. He looked at me stern. They both went into Dorset Street. I followed them. They both stood at the corner of the court for about 3 minutes. He said something to her. She said alright my dear come along you will be comfortable. He then placed his arm on her shoulder and gave her a kiss. She said she had lost her handkerchief. He then pulled his handkerchief a red one out and gave it to her. They both then went up the court together. I then went to the court to see if I could see them but could not. I stood there for about three quarters of an hour to see if they came out. They did not so I went away.

Description: age about 34 or 35, height 5 ft. 6, complexion pale, dark eyes and eye lashes, slight moustache curled up each end and hair dark, very surley looking; dress, long dark coat, collar and cuffs trimmed astracan and a dark jacket under, light waistcoat, dark trousers, dark felt hat turned down in the middle, button boots and gaiters with white buttons, wore a very thick gold chain, white linen collar, black tie with horse shoe pin, respectable appearance, walked very sharp, Jewish appearance. Can be identified.[12]

Hutchinson has been widely described by students of the case as the witness most likely to have met Jack the Ripper. Fortunate it is for us, then, that he was sniffed out by the newshounds as quickly as Israel Schwartz had been before him. On 13 November, just one day after his appearance at Commercial Street, he gave the press a fuller statement than that preserved in the police file.

By this account Hutchinson was in Romford, Essex, on Thursday the 8th. We are not told why. However, tramping back to London, he reached Whitechapel Road early on Friday morning. When he passed St Mary's Church it was between ten and five minutes to two. He turned north into Commercial Street. Walking into Spitalfields, he passed a man standing at the corner of Thrawl Street and then, approaching Flower and Dean Street, met Mary Kelly. 'Kelly did not seem to me to be drunk,' remembered Hutchinson, 'but was a little bit spreeish.'

'Mr Hutchinson,' she asked, 'can you lend me sixpence?'

'I cannot,' replied Hutchinson, 'as I am spent out going down to Romford.'

'I must go and look for some money,' said Mary.

She walked off towards Thrawl Street and there she met the man Hutchinson had already seen standing at the corner. He went up to her, put his hand on her shoulder and said something. Hutchinson did not hear the words but the couple both burst into laughter. The man then again placed his hand on Mary's shoulder and they began to walk slowly in Hutchinson's direction. Hutchinson himself walked on until he reached the corner of Fashion Street, where he loitered by the public house. The man with Kelly wore a soft felt hat 'drawn down somewhat over his eyes'. As the couple passed him Hutchinson ducked down to see his face and the man 'turned and looked at me very sternly'.

They crossed the street and turned into Dorset Street. Hutchinson followed them as far as the corner and from there watched them stand for about three minutes at the entrance of Miller's Court. 'I have lost my handkerchief,' Mary was saying loudly. The man pulled a red one out of his pocket and gave it to her. They both then went into Miller's Court.

Hutchinson's efforts to learn more were persistent but fruitless. When he ventured up the court himself he saw no light in the house and heard no noise. And although he stood about the entrance of Miller's Court for about forty-five minutes the couple did not reappear. 'When I left the corner of Miller's Court,' he told the press, 'the clock struck three o'clock.'

The labourer's press statement contained a more elaborate description of the suspect than had been set down in his statement to the police:

The man was about 5 ft. 6 in. in height, and 34 or 35 years of age, with dark complexion and dark moustache, turned up at the ends. He was wearing a long dark coat, trimmed with astrachan, a white collar, with black necktie, in which was affixed a horseshoe pin. He wore a pair of dark 'spats' with light buttons over button boots, and displayed from his waistcoat a massive gold chain. His watch chain had a big seal, with a red stone, hanging from it. He had a heavy moustache curled up and dark eyes and bushy eyebrows. He had no side whiskers, and his chin was clean shaven. He looked like a foreigner . . . The man I saw did not look as though he would attack another one [i.e. man]. He carried a small parcel in his hand about 8 in. long, and it had a strap round it. He had it tightly grasped in his left hand. It looked as though it was covered with dark American cloth. He carried in his right hand, which he laid upon the woman's shoulder, a pair of brown kid gloves. One thing I noticed, and that was that he walked very softly. I believe that he lives in the neighbourhood, and I fancied that I saw him in Petticoat Lane on Sunday morning, but I was not certain.[13]

This information clears the man with the carrotty moustache seen by Mrs Cox. And it answers some of the questions raised by Sarah Lewis' testimony. The man in the black wideawake hat, whom Sarah saw about 2.30 looking up Miller's Court 'as if waiting for someone to come out', was probably Hutchinson since by his account he stood outside the court from about 2.15 to 3.00 for precisely that purpose. The man with the black bag and the young man with the woman, both reported by Sarah, are likewise cleared. At 2.30, when she saw them, Mary was already in No. 13 with her new client and Hutchinson was upon his lone vigil outside.

All this, of course, assumes that Hutchinson's story was true. But was it? No other witness who claimed to have seen a suspect with one of the murder victims swore to such a wealth of detail or spoke with such confidence. The last three words of the labourer's statement to the police must have fired Abberline with hope: 'Can be identified.' It was a claim Hutchinson repeated to the press. 'I could swear to the man anywhere,' he said. That, sadly, is part of the problem. Hutchinson sound just too good to be true.

Only once, by the lamp of the Queen's Head, did Hutchinson get a good look at Mary's companion close up. For most of the time, in dim gaslit streets, he watched from a discreet distance. Yet we are asked to believe that he could describe the man with a precision worthy of Sherlock Holmes, in detail that would have been quite beyond a casual observer even in daylight. Hutchinson's account raises other disturbing questions. If he really did see a man with Mary Kelly on the fatal night why did he wait more than three days after the murder to tell the police? And if he thought he saw the same man again at Petticoat Lane Market on the following Sunday why did he not follow him again or, at the very least, find a constable?

By this time some of my readers may feel that Hutchinson's

statements belong in the waste paper basket with Packer's. But the labourer is not to be dismissed as easily as the greengrocer. Two circumstances in particular speak strongly in his favour. The first is the remarkable consistency between his two statements. They each contain information not to be found in the other but there are only two actual discrepancies of fact between them. In his statement to the police Hutchinson said that Mary's client had a *pale* complexion and a *slight* moustache turned up at the ends. To the press he described a man of *dark* complexion with a '*heavy* moustache curled up'. Given the length of the statements, however, these small discrepancies are not significant. Far more impressive are the numerous points of corroboration (at least forty) between the two accounts. This consistency in two statements made on different days to different parties certainly suggests that the labourer's story was not a total invention.

A yet more telling circumstance supports Hutchinson. Abberline, an experienced and outstanding detective, interrogated him on the 12th – and believed him. In forwarding the statement to the Yard that same night the inspector made his view perfectly clear: 'An important statement has been made by a man named George Hutchinson which I forward herewith. I have interrogated him this evening, and I am of opinion his statement is true.'[14]

If Hutchinson was telling the truth he cannot have been a casual or disinterested observer. His statements, indeed, prove that he was not. For he evinced the keenest interest in Mary and her client, loitering by the Queen's Head to get a close look, shadowing them to Miller's Court and standing the best part of an hour outside on a cold night waiting for them to come out. Hutchinson told Abberline that his curiosity had been aroused by seeing such a well-dressed man in Mary's company but this explanation is too thin. Inevitably, one suspects that he shared some undisclosed relationship with Mary. All we know for certain, however, is what he told the inspector – that he had known her about three years and had occasionally given her a few shillings.

A relationship of some kind with Mary Kelly might help to explain why Hutchinson was so slow to come forward after the murder. In his press interview he said that he had first told a policeman on Sunday 11th, the day before he reported to Commercial Street, but there is no corroboration of this in police records. Even if it were so he still delayed more than two days. Possibly he feared being implicated in the crime. After all, by his own admission, he had spoken to Mary and followed her to Miller's Court on the night she was killed, and he had no companion to confirm that his role in the events of that night had been an innocent one. There was, too, a danger that someone who had seen him skulking about there might accuse him and pick him out at a police identity parade. If it should transpire then that he knew more about Mary than he cared to admit he would have had some serious explaining to do. Perhaps, like Ted Stanley, the 'pensioner' in Annie Chapman's life, George Hutchinson's first instinct was simply not to get involved.

As we will discover, Hutchinson would prove to be a lasting influence on Abberline. Presumably he had a forthright manner and responded well to questions. Abberline must have reflected too, of course, that Hutchinson had volunteered his statement even though it placed him at Miller's Court about the time of the murder. Whatever the inspector's reasons for believing in him, he at once backed his judgement with action. Attaching two detectives to Hutchinson, he sent them out that very night to perambulate the East End with him in the hope that he might spot the man again. They trudged the streets fruitlessly until three the next morning and later on the 13th were out searching again.

At this point the last important dispute between police and press occurred. Although circulating their description of Hutchinson's suspect to police stations, the CID had hoped to keep it out of the newspapers while they searched for the wanted man. But, as we have seen, on the 13th Hutchinson was found and interviewed by the press and the next day his story was gracing the columns of both morning and evening journals. This publicity may, of course, have been beneficial. It may have elicited helpful information from the public. We cannot tell because the police records have almost all been lost. But the CID view at the time seems to have been that it blighted Abberline's efforts to trace the suspect by alerting him to the hunt and perhaps encouraging him to change his appearance.

While Abberline was searching high and low for a foreigner in an astrakhan trimmed coat the body of the latest victim rested at the mortuary attached to St Leonard's Church, Shoreditch. The funeral took place on Monday 19 November. There was much public sympathy for Mary. No relatives came forward but Henry Wilton, verger of St Leonard's, was determined that she would not lie in a pauper's grave and bore the entire cost of the funeral.

At noon the church bell began to toll. It was as a signal to the residents of the neighbourhood and they gathered in a solemn crowd, several thousand strong, about the main gate of the church. When the coffin, borne on the shoulders of four men, appeared at the gate scenes of great emotion erupted amongst the crowd. Men stood bare-headed. Women, who predominated in this multitude, cried 'God forgive her!', their faces wet with tears. As the coffin was placed in an open car people closed around it, jostling and struggling to touch it. 'The sight,' wrote the *Advertiser*'s reporter, 'was quite remarkable, and the emotion natural and unconstrained.'[15]

Shortly after 12.30 the funeral procession set off. It was headed, at a very slow pace, by the open car drawn by two horses. The coffin was fully exposed to view. Of polished elm and oak, with metal mounts, it bore a coffin-plate with the terse inscription: 'Marie Jeanette Kelly, died 9th Nov. 1888, aged 25 years.' Upon the coffin rested two crowns of artificial flowers and a cross made up of heart's-ease. After the car came two mourning coaches, one containing three, the other five mourners. Mary, far from home, had few real friends. At her funeral even the mourners – one a representative from McCarthy's, most of the others women who had testified at the inquest – were mainly casual acquaintances. But Joe Barnett was there. And so too surely, although the press did not mention her by name, was Maria Harvey.

When the procession moved off the entire crowd appeared to set off simultaneously in attendance, blocking the thoroughfare and stopping the traffic. Only with the greatest difficulty were the police able to clear a passage for the *cortège* through the mass of carts, vans and tramcars. But at length the little procession made its way along the Hackney Road to St Patrick's Roman Catholic Cemetery at Leytonstone.

And there, beneath a cloudy and unsettled sky, the tortured remains of the girl from Limerick were committed to the earth.

17

The End of the Terror

ON THURSDAY, 15 NOVEMBER, a week after the Miller's Court horror, an indignant resident of Pembroke Square in the West End addressed a furious letter to the *Daily Telegraph*.

'Can nothing be done,' he fumed, 'to prevent a set of hoarse ruffians coming nightly about our suburban squares and streets, yelling at the tops of their hideous voices, "Special Edition" – "Whitechapel" – "Murder" – "Another of 'em!" – "Mutilation" – "Special Edition!" – "Beautiful – Awful – Murder!" and so on, and nearly frightening the lives out of all the sensitive women and children in the neighbourhood? Last evening (Wednesday), for instance, these awful words were bawled out about nine o'clock in a quiet part of Kensington; and a lady who was supping with us was so greatly distressed by these hideous bellowings that she was absolutely too unnerved to return home save in a cab, because she would have to walk about a hundred or two yards down a quiet street at the other end of her journey by omnibus. Now, I venture to ask, Sir, is it not monstrous that the police do not protect us from such a flagrant and ghastly nuisance?'[1]

The Ripper never ventured west of Mitre Square. His victims were prostitutes all. Yet, as this letter neatly illustrates, he instilled fear into the hearts of women all over London.

In the East End the latest murder produced scenes of indescribable panic. At night the streets were abandoned to the patrolling police-man and the amateur detective. During the day noisy, excited crowds milled about the scene of carnage and struck out in helpless rage at any they fancied to blame.

There were a spate of incidents in which men had to be rescued from violent mobs. Some were drunks or eccentrics who courted disaster by shouting 'I am Jack the Ripper!' in public places. But any display of innocent curiosity, especially by a respectably dressed man, might attract ugly crowds. On the day of the murder a young Somerset House clerk, taking a holiday to celebrate the Lord Mayor's Show and the birthday of the Prince of Wales, went to Dorset Street to see the scene of the murder. There he enquired anxiously of the sightseers whether the bloodhounds had arrived. Concern was mistaken for fear. And when the clerk walked away up Commercial Street, he became aware of three men dogging his steps. He quickened his pace. They quickened theirs. Soon it was obvious that some strange kind of pursuit was in progress and passers-by happily fell in with the crowd. The clerk, increasingly rattled by the swelling throng marching in his tracks, broke into a run. It was the signal for a wild and clamorous chase. Eventually the terrified fugitive was pursued into Bishopsgate, where he gave himself into the custody of a policeman and was escorted hurriedly to the safety of a police station.

Abroad the Miller's Court murder was making headlines around the world. In Paris it was discussed as keenly as if it had been perpetrated on the Boulevards. 'The smell of blood was still in the air,' wrote a correspondent of an afternoon in the French capital, 'and wherever you turned the talk was almost sure to be about murder ... Jack the Ripper looms in the imagination as a more fearful scourge of humanity than Cardillac, the secret assassin in Hoffmann's tale.' In Austria the tragedy became the sensation of the hour and accounts from the London papers were reproduced almost *in extenso* by the Viennese press. And in America, too, the papers carried full accounts and editors combed their backfiles in vain for parallel atrocities. 'Nothing in the history of American crime,' declared a New York correspondent, 'can, for special and particular horror, be said to outmatch the East End butcheries.'[2]

At home it snapped the patience of the Queen. Victoria seems to have followed events in Whitechapel from the first. After the double murder she had telephoned the Home Office to express her shock and ask for information. Now, a day after Miller's Court, she dashed off a telegram to her Prime Minister. 'This new most ghastly murder,' she said, 'shows the absolute necessity for some very decided action. All these courts must be lit, and our detectives improved. They are not what they should be.' Three days on she was priming Matthews with suggestions. Had the cattle and passenger boats been searched? Had any investigation been made as to the number of single men occupying rooms to themselves? And was there sufficient surveillance at night? 'These are some of the questions that occur to the Queen on reading the accounts of this horrible crime.'[3]

The most dramatic development at Scotland Yard was the resignation of Sir Charles Warren. When it was announced in the Commons it was greeted with lusty cheers from the Opposition benches. The radical press had a field day. Whitechapel, they crowed, had revenged them for Trafalgar Square.

Today the Commissioner's sudden fall still confuses Ripperologists. Some attribute it directly to police failure in Whitechapel. Others insist that the events were entirely unconnected.

The immediate cause was an article Sir Charles wrote for *Murray's Magazine* on the administration of the Metropolitan Police.[4] Now, in 1879 a Home Office ruling had forbidden officers connected with the department from publishing anything relating to the department without the sanction of the Home Secretary. So on 8 November Matthews wrote to Warren, drawing his attention to the ruling and requesting his future compliance with it. Sir Charles was furious. In his reply, penned the same day, he declined to accept the Home Secretary's instruction and tendered his resignation. If he had been told that such a rule applied to the police, he declared, he would never have accepted the post of Commissioner in the first place, for it enabled anyone to traduce the force without according him a right of reply. He even went on to question the authority of the Home Secretary under the statutes to issue orders for the police.

The article itself was of little consequence. But Matthews could not tolerate such a flagrant display of independence on the part of the Commissioner and he accepted his resignation with alacrity.

None of this, it is true, sprang directly out of the Ripper affair. But the murderer was casting a long shadow and it would be wrong to exonerate him of all blame in producing the impasse that had developed between the Home Secretary and his Commissioner of Police. The police were under daily attack for their inability to catch the Ripper. And it was partly for this reason that Sir Charles insisted so fiercely on the right to speak out in defence of his men.

There is little doubt, furthermore, that Matthews and Warren could have resolved their difficulty over the 1879 ruling had a reasonable working relationship existed between the two men. Sadly, though, by November 1888 their relationship had become one of mutual distrust. It was an atmosphere of suspicion to which their fencing over the Ripper investigation had contributed no small measure.

Some writers have contended that Warren's resignation on 8 November left the police leaderless at a critical time and that this was in some way responsible for their delay in breaking into Mary Kelly's room the following morning. This is not correct. Although the Commissioner tendered his resignation on the 8th he continued to perform his duties for some time after that. His resignation was not officially accepted until 10 November and it was not until 27 November that a successor was appointed. As Matthews told the Commons on the 26th, Warren had 'not yet been relieved from the responsibility of the office, and, therefore, properly continues to discharge its functions.'[5] He was succeeded by James Monro, the ex-head of CID with whom he had quarrelled so bitterly early in the year.

In the meantime detectives relentlessly pursued their inquiries into the winter. Very few serious suspects seem to have come to light.

A typical inquiry began in Mile End on the morning of 17 November. At 10.30 that morning Harriet Rowe, a married woman, was sitting alone in her parlour in Buxton Street when a man, a complete stranger, opened the door and walked in. She asked him what he wanted. But all he did was grin at her. Badly frightened, Mrs Rowe ran to the window to attract help and the man then quickly left the house. When Mrs Rowe followed him outside she found him talking to PC Imhoff 211H and asking directions to Fenchurch Street Post Office. The distraught woman told Imhoff what had happened and he took the stranger into custody.

The man proved to be Nikaner Benelius, a Swedish traveller who lodged in Great Eastern Street, Shoreditch. Brought before Worship Street Magistrates' Court later in the day, he was charged only with entering a dwelling house for an unlawful purpose and with refusing to give any account of himself. But it is obvious that he was suspected of complicity in the Whitechapel murders. Detective Sergeant Dew told the court that he had been arrested under circumstances which justified 'the fullest inquiries' and that he had been previously questioned in connection with the Berner

Street murder. The court remanded him so that an investigation could be made.

Benelius' behaviour does not seem to have been exactly normal. His landlord, for example, said that he sometimes preached in the streets and acted 'very strangely'. But there is no reason to believe that he was homicidal. He made no aggressive move against Mrs Rowe and when he was searched at the police station no weapon was found on him. Benelius himself insisted that he only went into Mrs Rowe's house to ask the way to Fenchurch Street and, since she admitted leaving her street door open, his explanation is likely to have been correct. We do not know the details of the police inquiry. However, Inspector Reid is said to have told the *Star* within two days of Benelius' arrest that his innocence of any hand in the murders had been fully established.[6]

The case of the unfortunate Swede illustrates the kind of mis-understanding that could occur when women lived in terror of every shadow. Press reports describe Benelius as a 'man of decidedly foreign appearance, with a moustache' so it is also possible that he was partly suspected because of a resemblance to George Hutchinson's foreigner. If so, he was by no means the only one. In December one Joseph Denny, clad in a long, astrakhan-trimmed coat, was brought in for questioning after being seen accosting women. When subsequent inquiries cleared him, too, he was released from custody.

The story of Mr Galloway, a clerk employed in the City, suggests that some policemen may have been rather too preoccupied with the image of the dark continental.

In the early hours of Wednesday, 14 November, Galloway was walking home along Whitechapel Road when he encountered a man very like the one Mrs Cox had seen with Mary Kelly. 'The man had a very frightened appearance, and glared at me as he passed,' Galloway remembered. 'He was short, stout, about 35 to 40 years of age. His moustache, not a particularly heavy one, was of a carrotty colour, and his face blotchy through drink and dissipation. He wore a long, dirty brown overcoat, and altogether presented a most villainous appearance.' Galloway followed the man into Commercial Street, where his quarry unsuccessfully tried to accost a woman and then, near Thrawl Street, appeared disconcerted by the sudden appearance of a policeman. For a moment it looked as though the man would turn back or cross the road in order to avoid the constable, but in the end he recovered himself and went on. Galloway stopped the constable and, pointing out the man, told him that he resembled the one reported by Mrs Cox. 'The constable,' said Galloway, 'declined to arrest the man, saying that he was looking for a man of a very different appearance.'[7]

Despite Galloway, there is sufficient evidence to prove that the police brought in all manner of suspects in the weeks following Mary Kelly's murder. The trouble was that they knew next to nothing about the man they were seeking and were simply overwhelmed by the size of the task confronting them. A *Times* report, which gives every sign of having originated from within the CID, set out their predicament:

> Since the murders in Berner Street, St George's, and Mitre Square, Aldgate, on September 30, Detective-Inspectors Reid, Moore and Nairn, and Sergeants Thicke, Godley, M'Carthy and Pearce have been constantly engaged, under the direction of Inspector Abberline (Scotland Yard), in prosecuting inquiries, but, unfortunately, up to the present time without any practical result. As an instance of the magnitude of their labours, each officer has had, on an average, during the last six weeks to make some 30 separate inquiries weekly, and these have had to be made in different portions of the metropolis and suburbs. Since the two above-mentioned murders no fewer than 1,400 letters relating to the tragedies have been received by the police, and although the greater portion of these gratuitous communications were found to be of a trivial and even ridiculous character, still each one was thoroughly investigated. On Saturday [10 November] many more letters were received, and these are now being inquired into. The detective officers, who are now subjected to a great amount of harassing work, complain that the authorities do not allow them sufficient means with which to carry on their investigation.[8]

Throughout that long winter police and amateur patrols braved the weather to plod the streets of Whitechapel after dark. By spring, with no recurrence of the atrocities, they had been disbanded.

In February 1889 the Toynbee Hall students, out as part of the St Jude's Vigilance Committee effort, finally gave up, 'unable to bear the long hours and exposure involved in patrol work.'[9]

Special plain clothes police patrols in H and J Divisions went at much the same time. From 7 December 1888 Monro procured an extra allowance of one shilling a day for 1 inspector, 9 sergeants and 126 constables employed in these patrols. The men had been transferred from the uniformed ranks. They did continuous night duty and many, sent from other divisions, were working at some distance from their homes. On 26 January 1889 Monro told the Home Office that he was 'gradually reducing the number of men employed on this duty as quickly as it is safe to do so'. And by 15 March the duty had ceased. A better idea of the duration and size of the plain clothes patrols can be gleaned from figures Monro sent to the Home Office in 1889. From these it appears that they were first established in September 1888, probably after the Chapman murder, and that 27 men were then employed in the duty. In October, after the double event, the number was increased to 89, and in November, following the Kelly murder, again to 143. During December the patrols were maintained at the same strength. But in 1889 they were phased out. In January the number was cut to 102 and in February to 47. After that the patrols were disbanded.[10]

The termination of plain clothes patrols should not be mistaken for proof that the police knew that the Ripper had died or been locked in some prison or asylum. Finance was a factor. The Receiver for the Metropolitan Police District was worried about the 'great expense' of the extra allowance and anxious to impose limits upon the charge. But the main reason for the ending of the patrols was the absence of fresh outrages. As we shall see, when the death of Alice McKenzie in July 1889 suggested that the Ripper may have resumed his activities the patrols were immediately re-established. It should also be remembered that our evidence relates almost exclusively to plain clothes patrols. Extra uniformed police had also been drafted into Whitechapel from other divisions but we know very little about them. We do know, however, that when the plain clothes patrols were disbanded at least 34 uniformed police, originally detailed for duty in Trafalgar Square, were continued in Whitechapel and that they were still there in the summer of 1889.

For several years the spectre of Jack the Ripper continued to haunt East London. There were regular news stories. And almost invariably unsolved murders were popularly attributed to him. Of the latter, however, only two were truly similar in character to the 1888 atrocities. These were the killings of Alice McKenzie in 1889 and Frances Coles in 1891.

Alice McKenzie was a freckle-faced woman of some forty years. A native of Peterborough, she had lived in the East End for at least fourteen years, sharing the last six or seven of them with a labourer named John McCormack.

In 1889 their home was a common lodging house at 52 Gun Street, Spitalfields. Friends insisted that Alice paid her way by charring. The police regarded her as a prostitute and she is certainly known to have frequently gone out at night. There were other vices. She sometimes drank to excess and was an inveterate pipe smoker.

On the afternoon of 16 July 1889, after working his early morning shift, McCormack returned to the lodging house in Gun Street. Before going to bed he gave Alice 1s. 8d. to pay for their doss and other necessities. But Alice didn't pay the money. They had quarrelled and McCormack's words had upset her. She went out drinking and he never saw her alive again.[11]

Her movements for the rest of the day are sketchy. At about 7.10 p.m. she took George Dixon, a blind boy, into a public house near the Royal Cambridge Music Hall. He heard her asking someone to stand her a drink and a man reply: 'Yes'. After a few minutes Alice took the boy back to 52 Gun Street and left him there. Elizabeth Ryder, the lodging house deputy, saw her at about 8.30. At that time Alice, who was 'more or less drunk', left the house without speaking to Mrs Ryder. The last firm sighting of Alice placed her in Brick Lane at about 11.40. The witness was a friend named Margaret Franklin. Margaret was sitting with two friends, Catherine Hughes and Sarah Mahoney, on the step of a barber's shop at the Brick Lane end of Flower and Dean Street, when Alice passed them, walking hurriedly down the lane toward Whitechapel. Margaret asked her how she was but Alice would not tarry. 'All right,' she replied, 'I can't stop now.' She was not wearing a bonnet but had a light coloured shawl wrapped about her shoulders.[12]

At 12.15 that night PC Joseph Allen 423H stopped under a street lamp in Castle Alley, off Whitechapel High Street, to eat a snack. The alley was deserted. As he left it, about five minutes later, another constable entered it on patrol. He was PC Walter Andrews 272H. Andrews remained in Castle Alley for two or three minutes. Like Allen, he saw no one else there. But Andrews' beat brought him back to the alley at about 12.50. And on this occasion, only a few feet away from the lamp under which Allen had taken his snack, he found Alice McKenzie lying dead on the pavement. Blood was flowing from wounds in the left side of her neck and her skirts had been turned up, exposing a mutilated abdomen. When the police later removed the body they found underneath it an old clay pipe of the type referred to in lodging houses as a 'nose warmer' and a bronze farthing.

Alice was killed in the alley between 12.25 and 12.50. Probably before 12.45 because at about that time it started to rain and the ground beneath the body was found to be dry. No one heard a noise or scream. Sarah Smith, manageress of the Whitechapel Baths and Washhouses, backing upon Castle Alley, went to bed between 12.15 and 12.30. The window of her bedroom, though closed, overlooked the fatal spot. Sarah sat awake reading in bed. She was still awake when PC Andrews blew his whistle. Yet she had heard nothing suspicious outside. Alice's killer was never identified.[13]

Was Alice a victim of Jack the Ripper? There is some reason to think so. Alice, like her now famous predecessors, died when her left carotid artery was severed. As in those cases the cut was made from left to right while she was lying on the ground. And, like them, she suffered abdominal injuries after death. In many of the 1888 murders doctors thought they could detect a degree of anatomical knowledge and/or surgical skill. This was also true of the McKenzie killing. In his medical report Dr Phillips, who performed the post-mortem examination, stated that the injuries to the throat had been perpetrated by someone who 'knew the position of the vessels, at any rate where to cut with reference to causing speedy death.'[14]

If the Ripper did kill Alice McKenzie, however, he departed in some respects from the modus operandi of the canonical murders.

His mature technique had been to sever the throat all round down to the spinal column. There were two jagged wounds in the left side of Alice's neck. But these did not extend to any greater length than four inches and left the air passages undivided. Indeed, Dr Bond, who saw Alice's body the day after the autopsy, wrote of them as two 'stabs', the knife then being 'carried forward in the same skin wound'. Bruises high on Alice's chest suggested that the killer had held her down with one hand and inflicted the cuts with the other.

The abdominal wounds, too, were untypical of the Ripper's handiwork. Alice, to be sure, suffered numerous wounds to the abdomen but the majority were no more than scratches. The most serious was a seven-inch cut on the right side. But even this only divided the skin and subcutaneous tissues. It neither opened the abdominal cavity nor injured the muscular structure.

The 1888 evidence indicated that the Ripper was right-handed.

Alice's abdominal wounds, on the other hand, suggested that her murderer might have been left-handed. Phillips detected five superficial marks on the left side of her abdomen. They had been produced, he thought, by the pressure of a right thumb and fingers, and he deduced that the killer had applied pressure to the stomach with his right hand, perhaps to facilitate the introduction of the knife under the tight clothing, and then mutilated the abdomen with left-handed cuts. True, Bond disagreed. When Phillips showed him the marks he saw 'no sufficient reason to entertain this opinion.' Instead he speculated that Alice's murderer had lifted her clothes with his left hand and inflicted the abdominal injuries with his right. It should be borne in mind, however, that Bond did not inspect the body until the 18th, the day after the post mortem, and by then some of the wounds had been so disturbed that Phillips felt it necessary to accompany him to point out their original appearance. By then, too, the body had begun to decompose.

Both doctors agreed that the wounds had been inflicted with a sharp-pointed weapon. Phillips contended that it had been a smaller weapon than 'the one used in most of the cases that have come under my observation' in the Whitechapel series. Bond was more cautious. He could not, he said, form any opinion on the width or length of the blade, but he did acknowledge that the cuts could have been done with a short knife.

Clearly Alice could have fallen foul of the Ripper. Opinion at the time was divided. The doctors, of course, could not agree. Phillips did not believe the Ripper was involved because Alice's wounds were not as severe and the cut on her stomach 'not so direct' as in previous cases. Bond, writing to Anderson on 18 July, demurred: 'I see in this murder evidence of similar design to the former Whitechapel murders, viz. sudden onslaught on the prostrate woman, the throat skilfully & resolutely cut with subsequent mutilation, each mutilation indicating sexual thoughts & a desire to mutilate the abdomen & sexual organs. I am of opinion that the murder was performed by the same person who committed the former series of Whitechapel murders.' Anderson himself was on leave when Alice was murdered and it was Monro who turned out at three on the fatal morning to investigate the crime on the spot. Years later Anderson claimed that the killing was an 'ordinary murder . . . not the work of a sexual maniac'. But this was not the view Monro sent to the Home Office after his visit to Castle Alley. 'I am inclined to believe,' he said, '[that the murderer] is identical with the notorious "Jack the Ripper" of last year.' The importance Monro attached to the latest development, moreover, may be gauged by his actions. On the day of the murder he re-established plain clothes patrols in Whitechapel, deploying 3 sergeants and 39 constables in the duty, and increased the uniformed strength in the district with an extra 22 men.[15]

Two months later the scare deepened when the headless and legless torso of a woman was found under a railway arch in Pinchin Street, south of Commercial Road. After careful consideration of the medical evidence, Phillips, Monro and Swanson all concluded that this crime was not linked with the Ripper series.[16] Nevertheless, plain clothes patrols in Whitechapel were strengthened and Monro immediately called for another 100 men for temporary duty in the district.

There was no repetition of the outrages and in April 1890 plain-clothes patrols were finally withdrawn. Nearly a year later, in the cold February of 1891, the last real Ripper scare occurred.

Frances Coles was the prettiest of all the Whitechapel murder victims. The daughter of a former bootmaker, she was twenty-six, about five feet tall and had brown hair and eyes.[17]

Her descent into drink and prostitution is as mysterious as that of Mary Jane Kelly. In 1891 her father, James William Coles, was a 'feeble old man' in the Bermondsey Workhouse, Tanner Street, and her sister, Mary Ann Coles, a single and entirely respectable lady living at 32 Ware Street, Kingsland Road. Frances, too, once held a respectable if humble position at a wholesale chemist's in the Minories, where her work involved 'capsuling' or 'stoppering bottles'. Frances said that she could earn from six to seven shillings a week. But she didn't like the work. It hardened the skin of her knuckles and she complained to her sister that they had become very painful.

Frances seems to have slipped into prostitution when she was only eighteen. In 1891 James Murray, one of her clients, told police that she had been living in doss houses in the Commercial Street area and soliciting in Whitechapel, Shoreditch and Bow for some eight years. When he first met her she had been staying at Wilmot's lodging house at 18 Thrawl Street.

Frances did her best to keep it all from her family. On Boxing Day 1890 she visited her sister for tea. Frances gave her to understand that she was still working at the chemist's and living with an elderly lady in Richard Street, Commercial Road. Perhaps Mary Ann knew or sensed the truth. She noticed that Frances 'was very poor, and looked very dirty'. Sometimes she smelt of drink. Frances regularly visited their father at the workhouse and used to take him to church on Sundays. As late as Friday, 6 February 1891, when he saw his daughter last, the old man thought she was living in Richard Street. He seems to have known that she had left the chemist but not how she was earning her living. Frances promised to call on him again a week on Sunday. It was an appointment she never kept.

Enter James Thomas Sadler, ship's fireman, fifty-three years old, estranged from his wife and belligerent in his cups.

On 11 February Sadler was discharged from his ship, S.S. *Fez*, and made his way into Commercial Street. He had been a former client of Frances Coles. So when they saw each other in the Princess Alice public house they teamed up again. They slept together that night at a common lodging house at 8 White's Row, Spitalfields, and spent much of the next day drinking at various pubs in the area. Sadler gave Frances 2s. 6d. and between 7.00 and 8.00 p.m. on the 12th she bought a new black crape hat at a millinery shop, 25 Nottingham Street, Bethnal Green. Peter Hawkes, who served Frances, remembered that she was 'three sheets in the wind' (i.e. drunk).

At some time during the evening Frances quarrelled with Sadler. Apparently Sadler was knocked down and robbed in Thrawl Street. 'I was then penniless,' he told police later, 'and I had a row with Frances for I thought she might have helped me when I was down.' It is to be doubted whether Frances, in her intoxicated condition, was capable of helping herself let alone Sadler. No matter, the two went their separate ways.

Frances returned to the lodging house in White's Row, where she sat on a bench in the kitchen, rested her head in her arms on the table and promptly fell into a drunken stupor. Some time after that Sadler came back. He was drunk. Worse, his face was bleeding, his clothes smothered in dust and he was spoiling for a fight. 'I have been robbed,' he told the lodgers, 'and if I knew who had done it I would do for them.' Neither Sadler nor Frances had their lodging money. Charles Guiver, the watchman, helped Sadler to clean up in the yard and then, with great difficulty, persuaded him to leave. Later, when Frances woke up, she left too. Witnesses were to dispute the times. Guiver thought that Sadler left just before midnight, Frances between 1.30 and 1.45 a.m. But as Samuel Harris, one of the lodgers, remembered it,

Sadler left at about 12.30 and Frances only three or four minutes after that.

Frances was seen at about 1.30 in Shuttleworth's eating house in Wentworth Street. She was alone and asked for three halfpenceworth of mutton and some bread and ate the food in the corner. She stayed for about fifteen minutes. Joseph Hassell, who worked there, asked her to leave three times. But Frances had nowhere to go. 'Mind your own business!' she told him. Finally, at about 1.45, he put her out and she turned in the direction of Brick Lane.

2.15 a.m., Friday, 13 February 1891. PC Ernest Thompson 240H was patrolling his beat westwards along Chamber Street. Leman Street Police Station was only minutes away but PC Thompson must have been nervous. He had been in the force for less than two months and this was his first night on the beat alone. It was a night that would haunt him for the rest of his short life.

As he made his way along the street the constable heard, in the darkness ahead of him, the retreating, unhurried footsteps of a man. The man was too far away to see but he seemed to be walking in the same direction as Thompson, towards Mansell Street. Thompson paid it no attention. But then, turning left into Swallow Gardens, a short passage that led under a dismal railway arch into Royal Mint Street, he saw something lying in the middle of the roadway under the arch. When he shone his lamp on it he discovered that it was a woman. Blood was flowing from her throat. And, as Thompson stood horrified, he saw her open and shut one eye. In an instant the constable was blowing frantically on his whistle. The latest victim was Frances Coles. She died there under the arch, before a doctor could arrive.

Frances may have been thrown down violently because there were wounds to the back of her head. Certainly Dr Phillips, who performed the autopsy, and Dr F. J. Oxley, the first medical man on the scene in Swallow Gardens, agreed that her throat had been cut while she was lying on the ground. Phillips concluded that the murderer had held Frances' head back by the chin with his left hand and cut her throat with a knife held in his right. The knife had been passed three times across the throat – from left to right, right to left and then left to right again. The killer had worked from the right side of the body and it had been tilted in such a way as to suggest that he had tried to avoid becoming bloodstained. Frances' clothes were found in perfect order and there were no abdominal mutilations. Phillips did not think that the attacker had demonstrated any skill and he did not believe that he was the perpetrator of the 1888 murders. Dr Oxley told the inquest that although there was but one incision of the skin there must have been two wounds because the larynx had been opened in two places. He thought that they had been made by someone standing in front of the fallen woman.

The police quickly found a suspect in Tom Sadler. He knew and had quarrelled with the dead woman. Then, at about three on the fatal morning, less than an hour after PC Thompson's discovery in Swallow Gardens, Sadler returned to the lodging house in White's Row and asked to be allowed to sit in the kitchen. Again he was bloodstained and again he claimed to have been set upon and robbed, this time in Ratcliff Highway. Sarah Fleming, the deputy, noticed that he was so drunk that he could scarcely stand or speak intelligibly. She turned him away. 'You are a very hard-hearted woman,' he grumbled. 'I have been robbed of my money, of my tackle and half a chain.' Duncan Campbell, a seaman at the Sailor's Home in Wells Street, told an even more incriminating story. He said that at about 10.15 the same morning a man had sold him a knife for a shilling and a piece of tobacco. He identified Sadler as the man.

At Thames Magistrates' Court on 16 February Sadler was charged with the murder of Frances Coles and remanded pending further investigations. Detectives were cock-a-hoop. They seemed to have the murderer of Frances Coles. Might they have Jack the Ripper as well? Careful inquiries were set afoot into Sadler's whereabouts at the times of the other Whitechapel murders.

It was a false dawn. The case against Sadler soon fell apart. Ample witnesses were discovered to testify that Sadler had not been with Frances in the hours immediately preceding her death. In particular, they proved that the fireman's story of a second beating that night had been true. At between 1.15 and 1.50 he got into a fight with some dock labourers outside the gates of St Katharine Dock, a scrimmage that left him bleeding profusely from a wound in the scalp. And the knife? Well, Dr Phillips did not think that the murder weapon had been a very sharp knife. But even so, it is exceedingly doubtful if the knife sold to Duncan Campbell could have done the business. Thomas Robinson, a marine stores dealer to whom Campbell sold the knife, found it so blunt that he had to sharpen it before he could use it at supper. Dr Oxley saw the knife *after* it had been sharpened. Yes, it could have been used by the murderer in its present condition, he said, but 'if it were much blunter . . . it could not have produced the wound.' There is a further point. The murderer of Frances Coles displayed some presence of mind. Would Sadler, in his besotted condition, have been capable of carrying out the deed? Witnesses who saw him that morning leave us in no doubt of his incapacity. Sergeant Edwards saw Sadler outside the Royal Mint only fifteen minutes before Frances died. He said that he was 'decidedly drunk' and weaving about on the pavement. And Sarah Fleming, an hour later, found him scarcely able to stand. Let Dr Oxley have the last word: 'If a man were incapably drunk and the knife blunt I don't think he could have produced the wound . . . If a man were swaying about I don't think he could control the muscles of his hand and arm sufficiently to cause the wound.'

Wynne Baxter, presiding at the inquest into Frances' death, carefully presented the evidence. His jurors were not impressed by the case against Sadler and on 27 February returned a verdict of murder against some person or persons unknown. Four days after that all proceedings against him in Thames Magistrates' Court were dropped. As Sadler left the court his cab was loudly cheered by the crowds standing outside.

It was the right decision. We know that as late as 1894 Melville Macnaghten, Chief Constable of the CID, still suspected Sadler. But the contemporary evidence – and there is plenty of it – contains little to justify his view.

Attempts to link Sadler with the 1888 murders foundered the moment his voyages were documented. On 17 August 1888 he signed on at Gravesend for a voyage to the Mediterranean in the *Winestead*. This vessel did not return to London until 1 October and Sadler was discharged on this date. In other words, when Polly Nichols, Annie Chapman, Liz Stride and Kate Eddowes met their deaths, the fireman was safely at sea.

Friday, 13 February. Unlucky for Tom Sadler, most assuredly for Frances Coles, but also for PC Thompson, alone on night duty for the first time. Those footsteps in the dark troubled him. If he had given pursuit could he have caught the murderer? Could he have captured Jack the Ripper? It was, and is, useless to speculate. For Thompson remained with Frances and, in truth, he could do no other. Police standing orders, tightened up after the 1888 atrocities, required a constable finding a murder victim to summon assistance and remain on the site. In any case Frances was still alive when Thompson appeared and he could not possibly have abandoned her.

Yet the events of that night remained with the young constable. Frederick P. Wensley, who would rise from the ranks to become Chief Constable of CID, knew Thompson. 'I fancy that the lost opportunity preyed on Thompson's mind,' he wrote, 'for I heard him refer to it in despondent terms more than once, and he seemed to regard the incident as presaging some evil fate for himself.'[18] The forebodings proved true. In 1900 Thompson was stabbed to death when he intervened to prevent a disturbance at a coffee stall in Commercial Road.

Perhaps the Ripper hunters sensed that they were actors in a historic drama. For despite frustration and failure an undoubted camaraderie grew amongst them. Still preserved at Bramshill Police Staff College is a walking stick presented to Abberline by the detectives who worked on the case with him. Similarly, the Metropolitan Police History Museum holds a pipe presented to Inspector Nearn. It is inscribed: 'Souvenir to James Nearn, Whitechapel Murders, 1888, from six brother officers.'

The Metropolitan Police file on the murders was closed in 1892. We do not know what, if any, significance is to be attached to the date. Abberline, the Yard's principal authority on the case, retired from the force in 1892 so it may simply be, as Donald Rumbelow has suggested, that the file was closed at the same time. Certainly it does not reflect a solution to the mysteries. For some years afterwards the police kept a weather-eye open for likely suspects. Thus, when William Grant Grainger, yet another ship's fireman, was arrested for stabbing a woman in Spitalfields in February 1895, police tried hard to establish his whereabouts at the dates of the Ripper murders. They were not even able to prove his presence in London in 1888.[19]

There were no Ripper-type murders after 1891. The Ripper, for whatever reason, had gone. But his crimes were the stuff of legend and would not be forgotten. Around them a century of claim and counter-claim, discussion and debate, fictioneering and fraud, had already begun.

18

Murderer of Strangers

READERS WHO HAVE stayed the distance now know as much about the Jack the Ripper murders as history can tell. It is time for us to stop and take stock of what we have learned. The answers to many of the questions commonly asked about the case are already within our grasp. On other matters the historical record is silent.

There were nine killings in the series. How many are likely to have been slain by the same hand, that of the man we now call Jack the Ripper? Popular report at the time credited him with all nine. But detectives and surgeons who worked on the case held widely divergent views.

At the extremes Inspector Reid attributed all nine murders to the Ripper and Superintendent Arnold felt that he was responsible for no more than four, apparently those of Polly Nichols, Annie Chapman, Liz Stride and Mary Kelly.[1] Possibly Arnold was influenced by the views of Dr Phillips. Phillips, who performed or attended the last six post-mortems in the series, is known to have discounted Alice McKenzie and Frances Coles as Ripper victims and to have entertained serious doubts about Kate Eddowes. 'After careful & long deliberation,' he wrote in 1889, 'I cannot satisfy myself, on purely anatomical & professional grounds, that the perpetrator of all the Whitechapel murders is one man. I am on the contrary impelled to a contrary conclusion in this, noting the mode of procedure & the character of the mutilations & judging of motive in connection with the latter.'[2]

In the opinion of Sir Melville Macnaghten the Ripper slew five victims – Polly Nichols, Annie Chapman, Liz Stride, Kate Eddowes and Mary Kelly. Inspector Abberline and Sir Robert Anderson both opted for a tally of six by adding Martha Tabram to Macnaghten's names. Walter Dew believed that these six women were 'definite' Ripper victims. But he made the total seven because he felt that Emma Smith had been the Ripper's first victim.[3]

Dr Bond personally examined the wounds inflicted upon Mary Kelly and Alice McKenzie and studied medical notes relating to four of the earlier victims (Nichols, Chapman, Stride and Eddowes). In his view all these six had been killed by the same man.

Obviously there was no contemporary consensus. We must look at the evidence and make up our own minds.

A careful sifting of the facts suggests that, despite Dr Phillips, we are pretty safe in ascribing at least four victims to Jack the Ripper – Polly Nichols, Annie Chapman, Kate Eddowes and Mary Kelly. To that number Martha Tabram and Liz Stride should probably be added.

The only reason for discounting Martha is the nature of her injuries. For as far as we know her throat was not cut nor was any attempt made to disembowel her. The actual degree of mutilation she sustained is uncertain because of lack of precise information. My friend Jon Ogan, a much respected authority on the Whitechapel murders, sees evidence of similar motivation on the part of her killer as in the subsequent crimes. Martha's clothes were turned up to reveal the lower torso but Dr Killeen did not believe that sexual intercourse had taken place. So Jon contends that the murderer displaced the clothing in order to mutilate the corpse and finds support for his view in the cut, three inches long and one inch deep, in Martha's lower abdomen. This is certainly an interesting hypothesis. But although Martha sustained thirty-nine wounds the three-inch cut seems to have been the only one in the lower torso and cannot be said to bear comparison with those inflicted upon Polly Nichols, the next victim. Martha's injuries, moreover, suggest that she was subjected to a less organized and disciplined attack than those that followed. It is arguable, given the large number of wounds and use of two weapons, that she was slain by more than one assailant. If that was the case then Privates Leary and Law have got to be prime suspects.

Nevertheless, bearing in mind that this was the first murder, the departures from the Ripper's mature modus operandi are not necessarily significant. It is a mistake to think that a killer's technique will invariably remain the same. Experience and circumstance alike prompt development and change. The techniques of some serial murderers are known to have varied much more dramatically than is suggested by Martha's case. David Berkowitz, the 'Son of Sam' killer who terrorized New York in the seventies, only reverted to the revolver after an unsuccessful and particularly gruesome attempt to knife a girl to death. Peter Kürten, the Düsseldorf vampire of 1929–30, exchanged knife for hammer in a deliberate attempt to confuse the police. And Peter Sutcliffe strangled his twelfth victim, Marguerite Walls, with a ligature in 1980, mainly, as he claimed at his trial, to escape the stigma of his nickname, the 'Yorkshire Ripper'.

In time and place, type of victim, the sudden, silent onslaught, the signs of strangulation, the multiple stab wounds, the absence of weapons or clues left at the murder scene, above all in the frenzied character of the attack, in virtually every other respect, the Tabram murder is kin to its successors.

Macnaghten discounted Martha on grounds which are now known to have been largely erroneous. Abberline, Anderson, Reid and Dew, on the other hand, all included her among the Ripper victims. This, indeed, seems to have been a general police view in 1888. We know that suspects detained after the Chapman murder were also questioned as to their movements on the dates of the Tabram and Nichols atrocities. And when Matthews called for a report on the murders in October 1888 he was sent briefs dealing with the Tabram, Nichols, Chapman, Stride and Eddowes killings.

The case for supposing Martha Tabram to have been a victim of Jack the Ripper is thus very strong. Of recent writers only Sean Day and Jon Ogan have cared to espouse it.[4] But on balance the present evidence suggests that they are right.

There are also doubts about Liz Stride. Her injuries, like those of Martha Tabram, were dissimilar to those of the four certain victims. The evidence has been discussed earlier and need not detain us here. Most of the difficulties are resolved if we accept that the murderer was disturbed by Diemschutz rattling up with his pony and barrow and, all circumstances considered, it appears probable that Liz, too, fell victim to the same man.

The remaining possibilities are Emma Smith, Alice McKenzie and Frances Coles. We can discount Emma Smith. Contemporary sources prove that she was set upon by three ruffians, and although she was badly beaten and sexually assaulted her assailants did not, apparently, intend murder. After the attack Emma walked home. She died in hospital the next day.

It is undoubtedly possible that the Ripper slew both Alice McKenzie and Frances Coles. Their injuries were similar, though not identical, to those of the canonical victims. The differences, however, may be more significant than the similarities, because by then the Ripper's technique had become all too well-known. As police court records attest, the 1888 atrocities inspired a spate of imitative attacks. And there will always be a suspicion in the cases of Alice and Frances that they fell victim to copycat killers.

So how many women did Jack the Ripper strike down? There is no simple answer. In a sentence: at least four, probably six, just possibly eight.

It is unlikely, though, that the career of Jack the Ripper was launched in George Yard Buildings or Buck's Row. Earlier attacks by the same man almost certainly occurred. Two such possibilities are documented in this book – the non-fatal knife attacks on Annie Millwood and Ada Wilson in the spring of 1888.

The attack on Ada Wilson seems to have been the outcome of a robbery which badly misfired and took place at Mile End, well to the east of the Ripper's known range. It is best discounted. That on Annie Millwood is a different proposition entirely. Annie lived in White's Row, very close to George Yard, and since she was a widow may well have been supporting herself by prostitution. Apparently she was the victim of an unprovoked attack by a stranger and sustained 'numerous' stab wounds in the legs and lower body. This incident, like many of the Ripper's known atrocities, took place on a weekend.

If Annie was attacked by the George Yard murderer, and there is every chance that she was, we may, at last, be beginning to document the evolution of Jack the Ripper: a casual, botched attack on Annie Millwood in Spitalfields in February, the ferocious but disorganized slaying of Martha Tabram in George Yard in August and, finally, the emergence of the killer's mature modus operandi, that which would earn him his terrible sobriquet, in Buck's Row three weeks later.

We know much more about the victims today than the police did at the time. They were not the broken-down harridans, mostly in their forties but looking 'nearer sixty', of popular legend. Two, Mary Kelly and Frances Coles, were attractive young women in their mid-twenties. The rest were middle-aged but few looked their years. Indeed, it is interesting that police and press estimates of age, based on appearance, consistently misjudged their ages by making them younger than they are now known to have been. In some cases the difference was considerable. A reporter who saw the body of Polly Nichols said that her features were those of 'a woman of about thirty or thirty-five years.'[5] She was forty-three. The official police description of Kate Eddowes described her as about forty. She was well over forty-six.

Children of decent working-class parents, virtually all the women had slipped into destitution through failed marriages and drink.

The inquest testimony respecting them is frequently misleading. Time and time again we are told that they were quiet and inoffensive, sober and industrious, that they kept regular hours and did not walk the streets. We are entitled to take such protestations with a pinch of salt.

The men who cohabited with these women did not wish to be accused of living from the fruits of prostitution. Lodging house keepers could scarcely admit that their tenants were other than models of propriety without incurring charges of running disorderly houses and having their licenses revoked. And no one, at that time of popular outrage over the murders, could have found it easy to speak ill of the dead. Charity was the mood of the hour and the women of the streets knew it. 'The people speak so kind and sympathisin' about the women he has killed,' one told the *Pall Mall Gazette*, 'and I'd not object to being ripped up by him to be talked about so nice after I'm dead.'[6]

In a district of low incomes, unemployment and housing shortages, women bereft of male support fared badly. For the types of work commonly offered – charring, washing and hawking – supply far exceeded demand. Inevitably, prostitution became an instrument of survival. All the Ripper's victims were regular or casual prostitutes. In the awesome surroundings of the coroner's court their friends felt constrained to suppress the fact. But in the kitchens of the lodging houses it was another matter. Here, amidst communities which pirouetted regularly on the edge of disaster, the prostitute incurred little opprobrium. As Thomas Bates, the watchman, said of Liz Stride: 'Lor' bless you, when she could get no work she had to do the best she could for her living, but a neater and a cleaner woman never lived!'[7]

Stephen Knight, in his book *Jack the Ripper: The Final Solution*, argued that the Ripper victims knew each other. If this were true it would suggest that the murderer was known to them also, that the killings were not random.

Knight pointed out that although the bodies were discovered in different parts of Whitechapel, Spitalfields and Aldgate, the women all *lived* in one tiny part of Spitalfields.[8]

His data are by no means always valid. He tells us, for example, that Liz Stride and Michael Kidney lived at 35 Dorset Street, where Annie Chapman is known to have stayed, but this is not correct. When Liz was with Kidney they were living at 35 Devonshire Street, off Commercial Road. Still, Knight's observation was basically sound. At the times of their deaths all the victims were living in the small cluster of squalid streets about Flower and Dean Street in Spitalfields. Three were in Flower and Dean Street itself, Liz Stride at No. 32, Kate Eddowes at No. 55, and Polly Nichols either at No. 55 or No. 56. Another two were in nearby Dorset Street. Annie Chapman regularly stayed at No. 35. And Mary Kelly lodged at 13 Miller's Court, which was part of No. 26. The other victims lived in lodging houses in George Street (Tabram), Gun Street (McKenzie) and White's Row (Coles).

Unfortunately, we cannot infer any personal relationships from these addresses. The fact is that the Flower and Dean Street area was notorious throughout the East End as the lodging house quarter. Its cheap beds attracted the indigent from all parts of East London. In 1888 a report of the London City Mission claimed that there were forty lodging houses in the area accommodating some 4000 souls.[9]

The history of the victim is usually crucial in a murder case. This is because the killer nearly always turns out to be a relative, friend or acquaintance of the deceased. But our research into the lives of the Whitechapel murder victims has uncovered no link between a major suspect and any of the dead women. Nor has it suggested any convincing new suspect. At present there is nothing to indicate that Jack the Ripper was anything but that most elusive of criminals, the murderer of strangers.

A great deal of printer's ink has been spilled in speculation about the Ripper's modus operandi. The evidence assembled in this book enables us to reconstruct its mature form with some confidence.

It is probable that the victims accosted or were accosted by the murderer in thoroughfares like Whitechapel Road and Commercial

Street, and that they then conducted him themselves to the secluded spots where they were slain. This was certainly the case with Mary Kelly, who died in her own room in Miller's Court. And it was probably true of the others. Martha Tabram is known to have serviced another client in George Yard just three hours before she was killed there. Annie Chapman met her death in the backyard of 29 Hanbury Street and there is reason to believe that she led her killer there. The house is known to have been a resort of prostitutes, it was within a few hundred yards of Annie's lodging house at 35 Dorset Street and 29 was also the number of Annie's regular bed in the lodging house. Buck's Row, Dutfield's Yard and the dark corner of Mitre Square were also frequently used by prostitutes.

In these wet and muddy streets sexual intercourse would normally have been performed against a wall or fence. Alone with her client in a dark and sheltered spot, the woman stood with her back to the wall and raised her skirts. In such a place and such a position she was completely vulnerable to attack. And before she could utter a cry, the Ripper seized her by the throat. He strangled her, at least into insensibility, and lowered her to the ground with her head towards his left.

A number of circumstances indicate that the murderer strangled his victims before resorting to the knife. In most cases no screams were heard. We also know that the women were lying on their backs when their throats were cut and that there was relatively little spillage of blood. The wounds bled out on the ground beside or under the neck, much of the blood accumulating beneath the body and being soaked up by the back of the clothes. Then, in some cases, direct evidence of strangulation was recorded of the bodies. Martha Tabram was found with her hands clenched and her face swollen and distorted. Polly Nichols had a bruise on one side of the neck and an abrasion on the other. Her face was discoloured and her tongue slightly lacerated. Annie Chapman's face was livid and swollen, her tongue swollen and protruding. She, too, had marks on the neck, a bruise on the right side and several scratches in the corresponding position on the left. They were, thought Dr Phillips, the impressions of the murderer's right thumb and fingers.

The throats of the prostrate women were severed from left to right down to the spinal column. Typically the Ripper worked from the right side of the victim. In at least four cases (Nichols, Chapman, Stride and Eddowes) the close proximity of the left side to a gate, fence or wall probably precluded any attack from that quarter. But by kneeling to the right of the victim's head while cutting the throat the Ripper also ensured that the flow of blood from the left carotid artery was directed away from himself.

The abdominal mutilations were inflicted after death. In 1903 Inspector Reid insisted that the Ripper never took away any bodily parts from his victims.[10] But this is a good example of how grievously our memories can deceive us. In truth three women were served thus. Annie Chapman's uterus, together with parts of her vagina and bladder, were carried off by the murderer. In the case of Kate Eddowes it was the uterus and left kidney. And Mary Kelly's heart was cut out and never recovered.

In no case did the murderer leave a weapon or other clue at the scene of the crime.

Sitting quietly in retirement at his home on the Sussex coast, Walter Dew often reflected on these most gruesome murders. What puzzled the old detective most was the Ripper's ability to evade vigilant police patrols. 'I was on the spot, actively engaged throughout the whole series of crimes,' he reminds us in his memoirs. 'I ought to know something about it. Yet I have to confess I am as mystified now as I was then by the man's amazing elusiveness.'[11]

Dew and his colleagues were blamed and denigrated for their failure at the time. The charges are still thoughtlessly bandied about by amateur criminologists today. But it is a harsh judgement. If all the historical circumstances are taken into account it is not difficult to understand why the Ripper remained uncaught.

By retiring with the Ripper into secluded byways where they were unlikely to be seen the victims themselves greatly facilitated his crimes. Even at the height of the panic, when prostitutes fled the district or sought shelter in casual wards, the most desperate of their kind might still be seen soliciting for the price of a doss or a drink. A fatalism born of despair possessed such women. Chief Inspector Moore, interviewed in 1889, understood their plight only too well: 'I tell many of them to go home, but they say they have no home, and when I try to frighten them and speak of the danger they run they'll laugh and say, "Oh, I know what you mean. I ain't afraid of him. It's the Ripper or the bridge with me. What's the odds?" And it's true; that's the worst of it.'[12]

The Ripper's escapes from the scenes of his crimes are surprising but not inexplicable. No one knew what he looked like. And although he may well have been bloodstained there is no reason to depict him scuttling through the streets in clothes that were saturated with blood. In fact, his modus operandi suggests otherwise. We know that the Ripper severed the throats of his victims from the opposite side of the head to the first escape of arterial blood. It is probable, too, that the victims were first strangled. Certainly the abdominal mutilations were inflicted after death. These circumstances all point to the likelihood of the killer remaining very little bloodstained. Then the character of the district worked to his advantage. A warren of dark, evil-smelling courts, alleys and yards, it was impossibly complex for any police force to patrol adequately. The murderer may even have effected escapes through private houses. For, as we learned in the case of Hanbury Street, many tenements in the area were never locked. Any fugitive could duck in by the front door and leave by the back.

The police investigation ultimately failed because the Victorian CID were simply not equipped to deal with 'motiveless' murders of this kind. Inquiries into the histories of the victims afforded no clues. Traditional methods of detection, resting heavily upon rewards and informants, were almost useless in a hunt for a lone killer. Even in our own day, with all the advantages of fingerprinting, the biochemical analysis of blood, DNA fingerprinting and psychological profiling, the capture of such offenders is often a matter of luck. Back in 1888 the luck always ran with the Ripper.

Paul Begg, Martin Fido and Keith Skinner, in their *Jack the Ripper A to Z*, one of relatively few sane books on the case, contend that the police investigation was 'professional and competent'.[13] Bearing in mind that we must judge the police by the standards of their own time, not by those of our own day, I would not wish to dissent from that view. Indeed, the dedication and diligence of the investigation on the ground is worthy of admiration.

Nevertheless, in one respect the criticisms of the Victorian press were probably justified. The *Telegraph* spoke at the time of a lack of imagination in the detective department, and a study of the Whitechapel crimes certainly does suggest a want of innovative spirit at the Yard. For detectives not only failed to exploit fully the advantages of photography, the one important aid to detection then available, but they evinced no disposition, in the midst of the most important murder hunt of the century, to explore new methods of criminal investigation.

The potential of the popular press, then beginning to come into its own on the strength of Education Acts of 1870, 1876 and 1880, went largely unrecognized. CID policy on the press has already been explained. It rested upon some sound principles. But there can be little doubt that, on balance, the possibilities of this increasingly influential institution were undervalued. Opportunities were lost. To take just one example, although police rightly repudiated the sketches Richardson showed to Packer and published after the double murder, why was it beyond them to couple a professional artist with one or more reliable witnesses of their own in order to produce a more accurate impression of the murderer?

Most telling is the absence of any reference to fingerprinting in the Whitechapel murder files, even though the pioneers of this technique had been trying to promote their discoveries for over a decade. Herschel, who had employed fingerprinting as a means of identification in India, had advocated its use in a letter to the Registrar General as early as 1877, and Faulds, who had discussed fingerprint classification in *Nature* in 1880, had been trying to interest a suspicious Scotland Yard in the method since 1886. The subject came up again in the midst of the Ripper hunt. Learning that the Jack the Ripper postcard bore a bloody thumbprint, Mr Frederick Jago, a correspondent of the *Times*, observed that the 'surface markings on no two thumbs are alike' and urged that the thumbs of suspects be compared through a microscope with the print on the card.[14]

One might reasonably have expected this most baffling of murder mysteries to have called forth advances in the techniques of criminal detection. 1888 did prompt some police soul-searching. Standing Orders on the discovery of murdered bodies were tightened up after the Nichols murder and post-mortem examinations were conducted in the presence of more than one surgeon after that of Annie Chapman. But there was little genuine reappraisal of police methods. And what there was looked back, to tracker dogs, pardons and rewards, not ahead, to photography and fingerprinting.

What of the Ripper himself? Well, historical records tell us a good deal about him.

First, are we dealing with one man or two?

Cases of *folie à deux*, a madness shared by two people, are relatively uncommon in the annals of serial murder but they do occur. Perhaps the most notable recent examples were Kenneth Bianchi and Angelo Buono, the 'Hillside Stranglers' who raped and murdered a dozen girls in California in the late 1970s.

The only tangible evidence that Jack the Ripper had an accomplice comes from Israel Schwartz. As he told it, the man he saw attacking Liz Stride in Berner Street called out 'Lipski!', apparently to a second man across the way, who then saw Schwartz off. Unfortunately, although the substance of this story may well be true the correct interpretation of the facts observed is greatly in doubt. Did the murderer call out to the second man, for example, or to Schwartz himself? And was the second man really an accomplice? Or was he, like Schwartz, a scared bystander who hurriedly left the scene to escape involvement? Under interrogation even Schwartz was not certain.

No other witness is known to have seen a murder victim in the company of more than one man immediately preceding the crime. The nearest to it is Sarah Lewis. She saw a man loitering outside Miller's Court on the night Mary Kelly was killed. A short, stout man, who wore a black wideawake hat and was looking up the court 'as if waiting for someone to come out.' This man may, of course, have been an accomplice, on watch outside while his confederate slew Mary in No. 13. However, there is nothing conclusive to connect him with the murder. And a more reasonable explanation is that he was George Hutchinson, the labourer, for by his own account Hutchinson was waiting outside Miller's Court at precisely this time.

Certainly the Ripper may have had an accomplice, someone whose function it was to stand at a distance and warn him of impending danger. But, intriguing as the 'two man' theory of the murders undoubtedly is, it must at present be set aside. Typically this type of offender works alone and the evidence for the second man in the case is altogether too flimsy.

Our study of the facts enables us to tear away at least part of the murderer's mask.

Three out of the six probable Ripper murders, those of Annie Chapman, Liz Stride and Kate Eddowes, took place at weekends. Another two occurred on public holidays. Martha Tabram died on the night of August Bank Holiday, Mary Kelly on the morning of the Lord Mayor's Show. All six were committed between the hours of midnight and six a.m. We can infer, then, that the murderer was probably in regular work and free of family accountability, i.e., that he was single.

The statements of witnesses who gave descriptions of men seen with one or other of the victims are invaluable but must be used with care. Some, like Mrs Long, were good witnesses but only had a partial view of the suspect. Others, like Packer, appear to have been dishonest. Several reported sightings too far ahead of the crime for us to presume a likelihood that they saw the murderer.

A study of the best (Long, Smith, Schwartz, Lawende, Levy and Hutchinson) suggests that the murderer was a white male of average or below average height in his twenties or thirties. The man Lawende saw with Kate Eddowes was reportedly 'rather rough and shabby'. But three witnesses – Mrs Long, PC Smith and Israel Schwartz – described men of 'shabby-genteel' or 'respectable' appearance. And Hutchinson's suspect looked positively affluent. John Douglas of the FBI Behavioral Science Unit has suggested that the killer may have intentionally dressed up to persuade potential victims that he had money and thus relieve himself of the task of initiating contact with them.[15] Whatever, the evidence is that we will not find our man amongst the labouring classes or indigent poor.

Two of the six victims (Tabram and Nichols) were killed in Whitechapel, two (Chapman and Kelly) in Spitalfields, one (Stride) in St George's-in-the-East and one (Eddowes) in the City. But all of the murder sites are within a single square mile.

This close grouping of the killings, together with the killer's apparent familiarity with the district, undoubtedly suggests that he was a local man. Can we, then, as Professor Canter suggests, plot the murder sites on a map and simply plump for some central spot within the area circumscribed by the sites as the likely location of his home?[16] Frustratingly, we cannot.

The Ripper's earliest crimes are certainly likely to have been close to home. The trouble is that the historical data does not permit us to say what his earliest crimes were. As already noted, the Tabram murder was probably predated by other offences. These may have been rapes or unsuccessful attacks, or even crimes that were not sex-related. The point is that by the time the Ripper turned to murder he may already have become a relatively experienced and confident criminal, striking further afield to minimize the chances of being recognized. Whitechapel and Spitalfields, with their large populations of needy prostitutes, would have been rich hunting grounds for such a miscreant.

I strongly believe that the Ripper lived in the East End but I would not wish to hazard any closer location than that. The only real information we have is that after killing Kate Eddowes in

Mitre Square, at the western margin of the murder district, he doubled back into Whitechapel, leaving a portion of Kate's apron in Goulston Street.

The police made repeated inquiries at common lodging houses in the neighbourhood of the murders. This is understandable because every victim except Mary Kelly had lived in one of these places.

It is not impossible that the murderer found boltholes in them. Very little notice was taken of men inquiring for beds during the night. At the Eddowes inquest Frederick Wilkinson, the deputy from 55 Flower and Dean Street, said that when men came for lodgings he entered the number of the bed in his book but not the man's name. Pressed, he conceded that he sometimes lodged over 100 people at a time and that if the beds were paid for boarders were 'asked no questions'.[17] It may even have been possible for a bloodstained man to clean up in a common lodging house. It was the practice in these establishments for men to use a common washing place. Water, once used, was thrown down the sink by the lodger using it.

It is unlikely, however, that a man of respectable appearance, a man in regular work, would have needed to resort to a common lodging house. In all probability the Ripper lived in private lodgings or with relatives. The police themselves eventually seem to have come to this conclusion. This is why, after the double murder, they distributed handbills to householders and made a house-to-house search of parts of Whitechapel and Spitalfields. When he retired in 1892 Abberline commented that he did not think that the killer would be found lurking in a 'dosser's' kitchen.[18]

Modern writers frequently allege that the Ripper was left-handed or ambidextrous. Our best evidence indicates that neither statement is true. His modus operandi, as reconstructed from contemporary records and outlined in this chapter, implies that he was right-handed. Professor Cameron's deductions in the case of Kate Eddowes confirm this conclusion.

Did the murderer possess any anatomical knowledge or surgical skill? This question has been fiercely debated by Ripperologists for decades.

The medical evidence given in police reports and inquest depositions has been fully set down in this book. From it we know that although the doctors and surgeons who examined one or more of the 'canonical' victims (Nichols, Chapman, Stride, Eddowes and Kelly) disagreed about the *extent* of the murderer's expertise almost all attested to some degree of knowledge or skill. The sole dissentient was Dr Bond. But even his attitude was ambivalent. Examining Mary Kelly's injuries, he concluded that her killer had demonstrated no anatomical knowledge. Yet, only eight months later, he attributed Alice McKenzie's death to the same man, partly on the grounds that her throat had been 'skilfully & resolutely cut'. Doctors Phillips and Gordon Brown, in their post-mortem examinations of Annie Chapman and Kate Eddowes respectively, thought they could detect a great deal of expertise, both anatomical knowledge and surgical skill, in the mutilations.

Modern opinion has too often been the servant of pet identity theories. For many years Professor Francis Camps' views have held sway amongst serious students of the case. The professor decided, largely on the strength of sketches and photographs of Kate Eddowes, that the Ripper possessed little if any medical expertise.[19] However, this judgement was made at a time when Ripper research was in a very primitive state. Since then much detailed medical evidence relating to the murders has come to light. Camps ignored, too, the conditions in which the murderer had worked – at great speed, in poor light and in constant danger of detection.

For an up-to-date view I turned to an acknowledged expert in the field – Nick Warren. As a practising surgeon and a Fellow of the Royal College of Surgeons of both England and Edinburgh, he is well qualified to assess the medical evidence, and as a keen criminologist and the editor of *Ripperana*, the specialist's quarterly, he is conversant with all aspects of the case.

Nick raises doubts about the validity of Dr Bond's judgement. Bond had been instructed by the Home Office to investigate the 'Thames Torso' murders. From 1887 to 1889 the dismembered remains of four women were recovered along and near the Thames. Three of them were fully decapitated and the heads were never found. Now, the beheadings in these cases suggested to Bond that their perpetrator possessed anatomical skills. So when he considered the Ripper evidence and noted that the murderer had apparently tried and failed to decapitate two of his victims, Annie Chapman and Mary Kelly, he put him down as an unskilled operator. Unfortunately, modern experience suggests that Bond's assumption that only skeletal dismemberment required 'anatomical skill' is a false one.

Nick believes that the Ripper's attempt to separate the vertebrae of Annie Chapman's neck and his pelvic dissection of this victim indicate anatomical knowledge. He believes, too, that the removal of the left kidney in the case of Kate Eddowes evidenced definite anatomical knowledge and surgical skill. For it required both to extract the organ, as the Ripper did, through the vascular pedicle from the front. It lay embedded in fat, behind the peritoneum and overlain by the stomach, spleen, colon and jejunum.[20]

In a district of high immigration and rising social tension it was perhaps inevitable that the murders should be blamed upon a foreigner.

It was a view even found at Whitehall. Godfrey Lushington, Permanent Under-Secretary at the Home Office, saw evidence of Jewish guilt in the message left by the murderer in Goulston Street on the night of the double murder. 'It seems to me,' he wrote on 13 October, 'that the last murder [Eddowes] was done by a Jew who boasted of it.' Later, when he read a police report of Israel Schwartz's statement, he assumed that the man Schwartz saw had addressed an accomplice by his proper name of 'Lipski' and noted in the margin: 'The use of "Lipski" increases my belief that the murderer was a Jew.'[21]

It is not as simple as that. 'Lipski!' was a taunt commonly applied to Jews in the East End and it was Abberline's belief that Schwartz's suspect had used it against Schwartz himself. Even if he did address an accomplice by the name it is quite likely to have been a trick, designed to fool Schwartz into thinking that the murderers were Jews. Indeed, the evidence from the double event frequently suggests crude attempts to incriminate the Jews. The police certainly interpreted the Goulston Street graffito, left at the entrance of a tenement largely inhabited by Jews, as such. And the fact that Long Liz was murdered outside a club patronized by Jewish socialists suggests the same possibility.

The only tangible evidence that the murderer was a foreigner came from Mrs Long and George Hutchinson. Mrs Long thought that the man she saw with Annie Chapman was a foreigner. However, her evidence doesn't really count because she only saw the suspect's back. Hutchinson's does. He said that the man he saw going into Miller's Court with Mary Kelly looked like a Jew. It persuaded Abberline. In 1903 he told a reporter that in his opinion the murderer was 'a foreign-looking man'.[22] But Hutchinson's evidence is not above question. And it is always possible that Mary got rid of the man he saw and picked up another client shortly before her death.

It may be significant that none of the other witnesses indicated that they had seen men of foreign appearance.[23] Attempts to correlate the dates of the murders with sacred days in the Jewish calendar have also been unsuccessful.[24]

Jack the Ripper may have been a foreigner. We must bear this possibility in mind. But the historical evidence is far too fragmentary and contradictory to prove it.

On some aspects of the case the historical record tell us little. Perhaps the most important is motive. No significant link between the victims has been established. Robbery cannot explain the slaughter of destitutes. And we cannot even infer a grudge against prostitutes because these women were obvious and easy targets for anyone with murder and mutilation in mind. The Jack the Ripper crimes are now generally described as sex murders. Despite the tag sex does not seem to be the primary motivation for many such offenders. But the roots of their behaviour are complicated and contentious and this is no place to speculate upon them. Whether the Ripper was driven by fear and hatred of women, whether he suffered from ego-frustration and craved recognition and esteem, or whether he was simply a sexual sadist, these are matters upon which history cannot enlighten us.

Equally mysterious is the killer's disappearance.

Serial killers rarely take their own lives. Yet many writers have found suicide a likely explanation for the termination of the Ripper crimes. It is usually buttressed by the assertion that they became progressively more ferocious, the inference being that the killer's brain gave way altogether after Miller's Court. This is misleading. Martha Tabram, the probable *first* victim, died in a frenzied attack. And the extent of the mutilations of the others reflected the time at the disposal of the murderer more than anything else. Nichols and Stride escaped relatively lightly because in their cases the killer seems to have been disturbed and driven off. Mary Kelly was the most extensively mutilated victim. But then she was killed in her own home, where the Ripper had the time and safety to indulge himself.

There are other feasible solutions to the riddle. The murderer may have been imprisoned for an unconnected offence or confined in an asylum. He may have emigrated. Or, perhaps after a police interview, he may simply have stopped killing for fear of detection. Serial murderers do sometimes lie dormant for extended periods. After murdering thirteen women from June 1962 to January 1964, Albert DeSalvo, the Boston strangler, lost his compulsion to kill and reverted to simple rape. Colin Wilson and Donald Seaman, in their book *The Serial Killers*, instance the further case of *Il Mostro*, the 'Monster of Florence', who killed sixteen people between 1968 and 1985. There was a gap of six years between his first double murder in 1968 and his second in 1974 and seven years between that event and the third double killing in 1981.[25]

So who was Jack the Ripper?

Previous writers have almost always tailored the facts to suit a theory. We will proceed from the opposite direction. It is time for us to reassess the main police suspects. But in doing so we must keep the historical facts ever before us.

We are looking for a white male of average or less than average height in his twenties or thirties, a man of respectable appearance who lived in the neighbourhood of the crimes, probably in private lodgings or with relatives. The dates of the murders indicate that he was in regular work, the times that he was single. He was probably right-handed and possessed a degree of anatomical knowledge and surgical skill. He may have been a foreigner. I do not claim that a single one of these contentions is beyond challenge. I do believe that if the real killer is ever identified most of them will prove to have been correct.

But enough, let's get to the suspects!

19

Found in The Thames:
Montague John Druitt

'AS A CHILD I often thought that if some fairy offered me three wishes, the first thing I would ask would be the identity of Jack the Ripper; the thought that it might remain a mystery forever was intolerable.'[1] So wrote Colin Wilson, bestselling author of *The Outsider*, but all of us who have ever been intrigued by this most baffling of mysteries will recognize the feeling. Driven by a strange, compelling need to know the truth, we find it hard to accept that written proof of the Ripper's identity probably never existed.

In that respect Tom Cullen, who wrote the first important book on the Ripper, was no different from the rest of us. Cullen endorsed Sir Melville Macnaghten's identification of the killer with a man whose body was taken out of the Thames in December 1888. But he would not agree with Macnaghten that 'the truth . . . will never be known, and did indeed, at one time lie at the bottom of the Thames.' No, argued Cullen, 'in all likelihood the truth is locked up in a steel filing cabinet at Scotland Yard; or perhaps it lies buried in some musty attic among letters that have long since been forgotten, photographs that have faded, the lock of hair that is mouldy with age.'[2]

Stories surface fairly regularly to torment the ardent student of the crimes with visions of some final, conclusive proof, usually lost or irretrievable, and therefore just beyond his grasp. One of the latest comes from Christopher Monro, a grandson of James Monro, Warren's successor as Chief Commissioner of the Metropolitan

Police. According to Christopher, Monro set down his views on the Whitechapel murders in 'highly private memoranda' which passed, upon his death in 1920, to his eldest son Charles. Charles Monro died in his sixties about 1929. A year or two before his death, however, he confided to his brother Douglas (Christopher's father) that he still had the papers but didn't know whether he should destroy them or not. Monro's theory about Jack the Ripper, said Charles, was a 'very hot potato' and Monro had kept it a close secret, even from his wife. Douglas, who died in 1958, made no attempt to learn from Charles the identity of Monro's suspect. Instead, he urged him: 'Burn the stuff, Charlie, burn it and try to forget it!'[3]

In following up this intriguing story Martin Howells and Keith Skinner contacted several of Monro's other living descendants. No one knew anything of the papers mentioned by Christopher but one of them did produce, from the back of a cupboard in an Edinburgh suburb, Monro's handwritten memoirs, written for the benefit of his children in 1903. To serious students of police history this document must represent a veritable gem. But, as Howells and Skinner discovered when they were permitted to see it, it contains no reference to the murders.

Despite this and other stories of documents once extant final, irrefutable proof of the murderer's identity has consistently eluded us. The experience of Howells and Skinner is, indeed, very much par for the course in Ripper research. A similar fate befell Donald Rumbelow's efforts to trace the surviving papers of Chief Inspector Abberline. His heart must have leaped when, in the records of the Hampshire Genealogical Society, he unearthed a scrapbook of the inspector's press cuttings interspersed throughout with his handwritten notations. Once again, however, there was nothing, not even a press cutting, on the Ripper crimes.[4]

Our century-old obsession with this case has wrung the reminiscences of senior police officers dry of every conceivable shade of meaning. It has repeatedly plundered the archives of Scotland Yard for relevant names. It has sucked into the quest living descendants of policemen and suspects alike. Sometimes, as in the instances we have noted, it has uncovered valuable incidental materials. But it has not put a name to Jack the Ripper. Where anything at all bearing upon the killer's identity has come to light it has proved at best inconclusive, at worst downright fraudulent. In this context those who hunt the Ripper are vaguely reminiscent of the Spanish conquistadores, those foolhardy adventurers of four centuries ago who, driven by shimmering visions of El Dorado, Cibola or Quivira, cut their way through steaming jungles or toiled across burning deserts to find at their journey's end, not the riches for which their souls longed, but clusters of dirt villages or desolate plains.

Although no one was ever brought to trial for any of the White-chapel crimes, claims that the identity of the killer was known, or at least strongly suspected, by the police are almost as old as the murders themselves. Unquestionably the best known story of this kind maintains that in the opinion of the CID the Ripper was a man who committed suicide by throwing himself into the Thames soon after the Miller's Court murder. The person who did more than anyone else to broadcast this tale was the journalist and author George R. Sims.

Under the pseudonym 'Dagonet' Sims wrote a regular piece for *The Referee* in which he frequently adverted to the suicide in the Thames. Thus, in July 1902, he assured his readers that during the course of their inquiries the police reduced the number of suspects to seven and then, 'by a further exhaustive inquiry', to just three. They were 'about to fit these three people's movements in with the dates of the various murders when the one and only genuine Jack saved further trouble by being found drowned in the Thames, into which he had flung himself, a raving lunatic, after the last and most appalling mutilation of the whole series. But prior to this discovery the name of the man found drowned was bracketed with two others as a possible Jack, and the police were in search of him alive when they found him dead.' Returning to the theme a year later, Sims wrote that 'no one who saw the victim of Miller's Court as she was found ever doubted that the deed was that of a man in the last stage of a terrible form of insanity ... A little more than a month later the body of the man suspected by the chiefs at the Yard, and by his own friends, who were in communication with the Yard, was found in the Thames. The body had been in the water about a month. I am betraying no confidence in making this statement, because it has been published by an official who had an opportunity of seeing the Home Office Report, Major Arthur Griffiths, one of her late Majesty's inspectors of prisons.' If Sims is to be believed the case was closed. He never admitted to any doubt in the matter. 'Jack the Ripper was known, was identified, and is dead,' he declared in 1903. 'Let him rest.'[5]

Major Arthur Griffiths, writing in *Mysteries of Police and Crime* in 1898, was much more circumspect. 'The outside public,' he began, 'may think that the identity of . . . Jack the Ripper was never revealed. So far as actual knowledge goes, this is undoubtedly true. But the police, after the last murder, had brought their investigations to the point of strongly suspecting several persons, all of them known to be homicidal lunatics, and against three of these they held very plausible and reasonable grounds of suspicion.'

✳ He described but did not name the three suspects. One, a known lunatic, was a Polish Jew. He was at large in Whitechapel at the time of the murders and was afterwards committed to an asylum. Another was an insane Russian doctor. Formerly a convict, both in Siberia and England, he was accustomed to carry surgical knives and other instruments about with him and, during the period of the murders, 'was in hiding, or, at least, his whereabouts were never exactly known.' The cases against these men, although based on 'certain colourable facts', were weak. Against the third suspect, however, 'the suspicion . . . was stronger, and there was every reason to believe that his own friends entertained grave doubts about him.' This man was also a doctor. He was insane or 'on the borderland of insanity'. He disappeared after the Miller's Court murder. And his body was found floating in the Thames on the last day of the year. 'It is at least a strong presumption,' concluded Griffiths guardedly, 'that Jack the Ripper died or was put under restraint after the Miller's Court affair, which ended this series of crimes.'[6]

The police files were closed to the public. So there – for more than sixty years – the story of the drowned doctor rested.

Then, in 1959, the curtain of secrecy that had veiled the Thames suicide for so long was at last torn aside. The man who did it was Dan Farson, the journalist and television presenter, but it was all an unlooked for accident. At the time Farson was staying with Lady Rose McLaren in North Wales and he happened to mention that he was in the midst of preparing a television investigation on the mystery of Jack the Ripper. 'That's an extraordinary coincidence,' said Lady McLaren. She explained that they were going to visit her mother-in-law, the Dowager Lady Aberconway, that very afternoon. And Lady Aberconway was a daughter of Sir Melville Macnaghten, who had been the Assistant Commissioner in charge of the CID from 1903 to 1913.

'A few hours later at Maenan Hall,' Farson afterwards recalled, 'I explained my interest to Christabel Aberconway and she was kind enough to give me her father's private notes which she had copied out soon after his death. At the time I hardly realized the discovery that lay in my hands . . .'[7] What Farson was holding, in fact, was a copy of a draft report prepared by Macnaghten as Chief Constable of the CID in 1894. It was this draft that Griffiths had copied from in 1898 and to which Sims had alluded in 1903. It contained details, with names, of three men against whom the police held 'very reasonable suspicion' and it is still one of the most important documents that we possess on the identity of Jack the Ripper.

Farson's programmes were transmitted by Associated Rediffusion in the series *Farson's Guide to the British* in November 1959. Once he had been given the name of the man who had committed suicide it was, of course, a relatively simple matter for Farson to turn up his death certificate at Somerset House. It was displayed on the television screen but, in deference to a request of Lady Aberconway, Farson blanked out the name. He released only the suspect's initials, M. J. D. It was a futile gesture for once the Macnaghten notes had been publicized on television there was little possibility of keeping their full contents a secret for long. Indeed, in a letter to *The New Statesman* of 7 November 1959, Lady Aberconway herself drew attention to the existence of her father's notes. Tom Cullen published the full text – insofar as it treated of the three main suspects – in 1965. His text also followed Lady Aberconway's copy of Sir Melville's draft. Then the official copy of Macnaghten's final report, which had all the while been slumbering undisturbed amongst the closed case papers at Scotland Yard, was also released. Robin Odell published the relevant section of this document in 1966.[8] There are significant differences between the Aberconway and official versions. So, before examining their contents, we will need to understand the relationship between the two.

Melville Macnaghten joined the Metropolitan Police as Assistant Chief Constable of the CID in June 1889, too late to participate in the Ripper inquiry. It was said of him, indeed, that he owned to only two disappointments in his life. One was that he was turned out of the Eton Eleven before a match with Harrow and the other was that he became a detective six months after the Ripper committed suicide and 'never had a go at that fascinating individual'.[9] In 1890 he was promoted to Chief Constable and in 1903 to Assistant Commissioner in charge of CID, an office he held for ten years. He was knighted in 1908 and died in 1921.

On 13 February 1894 a series of sensational articles began in the *Sun* identifying the Ripper with a certain Thomas Cutbush. The *Sun*'s suspect had been arraigned at the London County Sessions in 1891 on charges of maliciously wounding one girl and attempting to wound another, and he had been pronounced insane and sentenced to be detained during Her Majesty's pleasure. But he was not the Whitechapel murderer and the whole purpose of Macnaghten's report was to refute the *Sun*'s claims. The official report is marked 'confidential' and dated 23 February 1894. No associated papers have survived. It seems probable, nonetheless, that it was prepared upon the instructions of the Chief Commissioner in response to an appeal for information from the Home Office respecting the statements being broadcast in the *Sun*.

The document held by Macnaghten's descendants has been several times discussed[10] and there is no need to enter into the full ramifications of its history here. It appears to have been Macnaghten's original draft and it passed, after Lady Macnaghten's death in 1929, to Julia Donner, their eldest daughter. In 1950 Philip Loftus apparently saw it in the possession of Gerald Melville Donner, Julia's son. Although, twenty-two years later, Loftus retained only the haziest impressions as to the document's contents, he did remember that it was 'in Sir Melville's handwriting on official paper, rather untidy and in the nature of rough jottings.'[11] Gerald died in India in 1968 and the present whereabouts of the draft are not known. By a lucky chance, however, the text was preserved by Christabel Aberconway, Julia Donner's younger sister, for Christabel made a copy of her father's notes, evidently in the early 1930s. It was this copy that was made available to Farson and Cullen.

Well, what does Sir Melville tell us? The relevant section of Lady Aberconway's copy of the draft reads:

A much more rational and *workable* theory, to my way of thinking, is that the rippers brain gave way altogether after his awful glut in Millers Court and that he then committed suicide, or, as a *less* likely alternative, was found to be so helplessly insane by his relatives, that they, suspecting the worst, had him confined in some Lunatic Asylum.

No one ever saw the Whitechapel murderer (unless possibly it was the City P. C. who was on a beat near Mitre Square) and no proof could in any way ever be brought against anyone, although very many homicidal maniacs were at one time, or another, *suspected*. I enumerate the cases of 3 men against whom Police held very reasonable suspicion. Personally, after much careful & deliberate consideration, I am inclined to exonerate the last 2, but I have always held strong opinions regarding no 1., and the more I think the matter over, the stronger do these opinions become. The *truth*, however, will never be known, and did indeed, at one time lie at the bottom of the Thames, if my conjections [sic] be correct.

No. 1 Mr M. J. Druitt a doctor of about 41 years of age & of fairly good family, who disappeared at the time of the Miller's Court murder, and whose body was found floating in the Thames on 31st Dec: i.e. 7 weeks after the said murder. The body was said to have been in the water for a month, *or more* – on it was found a season ticket between Blackheath & London. From private information I have little doubt but that his own family suspected this man of being the Whitechapel murderer; it was *alleged* that he was sexually insane.

No 2. Kosminski, a Polish Jew, who lived in the very heart of the district where the murders were committed. He had become insane owing to many years indulgence in solitary vices. He had a great hatred of women, with strong homicidal tendencies. He was (and I believe still is) detained in a lunatic asylum about March 1889. This man in appearance strongly resembled the individual seen by the City P.C. near Mitre Square.

No: 3. Michael Ostrog, a mad Russian doctor & a convict & unquestionably a homicidal maniac. This man was said to have been habitually cruel to women, & for a long time was known to have carried about with him surgical knives & other instruments; his antecedents were of the very worst & his whereabouts at the time of the Whitechapel murders could never be satisfactorily accounted for. He is still alive.[12]

The corresponding passage of the final report, preserved in the Scotland Yard files at the Public Record Office, reads:

A much more rational theory is that the murderer's brain gave way altogether after his awful glut in Miller's Court, and that he immediately committed suicide, or, as a possible alternative, was found to be so hopelessly mad by his relations, that he was by them confined in some asylum.

No one ever saw the Whitechapel murderer: many homicidal maniacs were suspected, but no shadow of proof could be thrown on any one. I may mention the cases of 3 men, any one of whom would have been more likely than Cutbush to have committed this series of murders:-

✳   (1) A Mr M. J. Druitt, said to be a doctor & of good family, who disappeared at the time of the Miller's Court murder, & whose body (which was said to have been upwards of a month in the water) was found in the Thames on 31st December – or about 7 weeks after that murder. He was sexually insane and from private information I have little doubt but that his own family believed him to have been the murderer.

(2) Kosminski, a Polish Jew, & resident in Whitechapel. This man became insane owing to many years indulgence in solitary vices. He had a great hatred of women, specially of the prostitute class, & had strong homicidal tendencies; he was removed to a lunatic asylum about March 1889. There were many circumstances connected with this man which made him a strong 'suspect'.

(3) Michael Ostrog, a Russian doctor, and a convict, who was subsequently detained in a lunatic asylum as a homicidal maniac. This man's antecedents were of the worst possible type, and his whereabouts at the time of the murders could never be ascertained.[13]

M. J. Druitt was Sir Melville's principal suspect. Since 1959 he has inspired a great deal of research and today we probably know much more about him than the police did at the time. The details of his career have been published many times[14] so a brief summary will suffice here.

Montague John Druitt, the second son of a surgeon, William Druitt of Wimborne in Dorset, was born on 15 August 1857. He was educated at Winchester and New College, Oxford, and graduated in 1880 with a third class honours degree in classics.

Upon leaving university, Druitt took a teaching post at a boarding school at 9 Eliot Place, Blackheath. This establishment prepared boys for the universities, the army and the professions. Its headmaster, George Valentine, lost little time in introducing Druitt to the local elite. In 1881 he proposed his new master for membership of the Blackheath Hockey Club and in the same year Druitt began to play for the Morden Cricket Club of Blackheath.

A year later Druitt embarked on a second career in the law. On

17 May 1882 he was admitted to the Inner Temple. He financed his studies by borrowing against a £500 legacy of his father and, on 29 April 1885, was called to the Bar. The Law List entry for 1886 states that Druitt was of the Western Circuit and the Winchester Sessions. In 1887 he was recorded as a special pleader for the Western Circuit and Hampshire, Portsmouth and Southampton Assizes.

Druitt's last years were marred by tragedy. His father died of a heart attack in 1885 and his mother, Ann (née Harvey) Druitt, subsequently slipped into mental illness and was admitted to the Brooke Asylum in Clapton in July 1888. Yet by that time Druitt himself seems to have been financially secure. He taught at a respected private school and his work as a special pleader was lucrative – at least he left an estate worth £2,600, more than can be accounted for by his father's bequest, a posthumous inheritance of £1,083 from his mother and his earnings as a teacher. His social standing, moreover, was considerable. When Morden Cricket Club merged in 1885 with the Blackheath Cricket, Football and Lawn Tennis Co. Druitt became a director, being appointed treasurer and honorary secretary. His fellow directors included Rowland Hill, one of England's most renowned rugby footballers, Dr Lennard Stokes, a distinguished sportsman and captain of the England rugby team, and R. H. Poland, a wealthy fur broker. In 1883 Druitt was nominated for membership of the MCC by C. R. Seymour, an Old Harrovian and barrister who played for MCC and Hampshire and who would become a Wiltshire and Hampshire JP, and by the celebrated cricketer Vernon Royle, then a Hertfordshire curate and assistant master at Elstree School. He was elected on 26 May 1884 and his subscriptions were fully paid up at the time of his death. In both the MCC Candidates' and Members' Books Druitt's address is recorded as 9 Eliot Place, Blackheath.

Druitt's suicide at the end of 1888 must, therefore, have come as a profound shock to many of his acquaintances. Commenting upon it, the *Southern Guardian* of 5 January 1889 noted that he was 'well known and much respected in the neighbourhood. He was a barrister of bright talent, he had a promising future before him, and his untimely end is deeply deplored.'

Druitt's body was found floating in the Thames off Thorneycroft's Wharf, Chiswick, by Henry Winslade, a waterman out in his boat, at about one o'clock p.m. on Monday, 31 December 1888. He brought the body ashore and notified the police. PC George Moulson 216T, who searched the dead man, found that he was fully dressed except for a hat and collar. His possessions included £2 17s. 2d. in cash; two cheques on the London and Provincial Bank, one for £50, the other for £16; a first-class season ticket from Blackheath to London on the South Eastern Railway; the second half of a return ticket, Hammersmith to Charing Cross, dated 1 December; a silver watch and a gold chain with a spade-guinea attached; a pair of kid gloves and a white handkerchief. The body was rather decomposed and had obviously been in the water for some time but there were no marks of injury upon it. In each pocket of the top coat PC Moulson discovered four large stones. Although there were no other papers or letters on the body, the cheques must have carried Druitt's name. William Druitt, a Bournemouth solicitor and Montague's elder brother, was eventually contacted and subsequently identified the corpse.[15]

What blackness of the soul induced Montague Druitt to take his life we cannot tell. We do know that he was discharging his social duties at least as late as 19 November because on that day the minutes of a Blackheath Cricket, Football and Lawn Tennis Co. board meeting record that he proposed that 'an acre of land be taken behind the grand stand at a similar proportionate rent to that paid for the present land.' But the only evidence directly bearing upon the cause of his suicide was presented at the inquest. It was held before Dr Thomas Diplock at the Lamb Tap, Chiswick, on Wednesday, 2 January 1889, and concluded that Druitt took his own life whilst of unsound mind. Unfortunately the coroner's papers have not survived. Our knowledge of the testimony given, therefore, rests almost entirely upon a report in the *Acton, Chiswick, and Turnham Green Gazette* of 5 January. The key witness was William Druitt:

William H. Druitt said he lived at Bournemouth, and that he was a solicitor. The deceased was his brother, who was 31 last birthday. He was a barrister-at-law, and an assistant master in a school at Blackheath. He had stayed with witness at Bournemouth for a night towards the end of October. Witness heard from a friend on the 11th of December that deceased had not been heard of at his chambers for more than a week. Witness then went to London to make inquiries, and at Blackheath he found that deceased had got into serious trouble at the school, and had been dismissed. That was on the 30th of December. Witness had deceased's things searched where he resided, and found a paper addressed to him (produced). The Coroner read the letter, which was to this effect: – 'Since Friday I felt I was going to be like mother, and the best thing for me was to die.' Witness, continuing, said deceased had never made any attempt on his life before. His mother became insane in July last. He had no other relative.

The main difficulty in the interpretation of this extract is the ambiguous reporting of the date 30 December. For careful study of the passage will demonstrate that the date can be read either as that upon which Druitt lost his job or as that upon which William made inquiries at the school. Probably the first meaning was intended because if one of Montague's friends was sufficiently concerned to apprise William of his disappearance as early as 11 December it is unlikely that William would have procrastinated for another three weeks before making inquiries. If 30 December is meant to be the date of Montague's dismissal, however, it is incorrect, for by that time his body had been in the river for the best part of a month. One explanation of this difficulty would be that 30 December is, in fact, a misprint for 30 November.

A date of 30 November for Druitt's dismissal makes sense. We do not know when he threw himself into the river. A death date of 4 December, exactly one week before William learned of his disappearance, is inscribed upon his tombstone. According to William's story, however, he was told on 11 December that Montague had been missing for *more* than a week and a suicide date of 1 December, the date of the unused return ticket from Hammersmith to Charing Cross, is more likely. Perhaps, then, Druitt was dismissed from the school on Friday, 30 November, and committed suicide the next day. Such a reconstruction would be consistent with his alleged suicide note, presumably penned on the day of his death, to the effect: 'Since Friday I felt that I was going to be like mother, and the best thing for me was to die.'

It is possible – although there is no evidence of it – that the cheques found on the body were written by George Valentine in settlement of Druitt's teaching salary. We do not know why he was dismissed. Some writers have suggested that he was a homosexual, that his offence was molesting his young charges, but this is mere conjecture. Whatever the reason, by itself the dismissal is not likely to have prompted Druitt's suicide. He was still a qualified barrister and, with his social connections, might have acquired another teaching post. To a personality already disturbed, however, it could have proved the final straw. In this context it is important to note that depression and suicidal urges blighted the lives of several members of the Druitt clan and may have been inherited traits linked with diabetes. Ann Druitt, Montague's mother, who died at the Manor House Asylum in Chiswick in 1890, suffered from depression and paranoid delusions and once tried to kill herself by taking an overdose of laudanum. Ann's mother had committed suicide whilst insane and her sister had also once suffered from mental illness and had attempted suicide. Montague's niece, the daughter of his sister Edith, told Dan Farson in 1973 about a strong streak of melancholia in the family. His eldest sister, Georgiana Elizabeth, for example, had committed suicide by jumping from an attic window when she was an old woman.

What is conspicuously absent from this portrait of the ill-fated barrister is the existence of any verifiable links with the Jack the Ripper murders or even with Whitechapel. So just how serious a suspect is Druitt?

The main, indeed the only, reason why Druitt stands high on the list of suspects is because Macnaghten held a strong conviction that he was the Ripper. Writing the official version of his report, he cautiously mentioned Druitt only as one of three men, 'any one of whom would have been more likely than Cutbush to have committed this series of murders.' But there is no doubt that privately he believed Druitt to have been the killer. 'Personally, after much careful & deliberate consideration,' he tells us in the draft, 'I am inclined to exonerate the last 2 [Kosminski and Ostrog], but I have always held strong opinions regarding no. 1, and the more I think the matter over, the stronger do these opinions become.' Twenty years later, in his autobiography, he affirmed his belief that the 'individual who held up London in terror resided with his own people; that he absented himself from home at certain times, and that he committed suicide on or about the 10th of November 1888.'[16]

Macnaghten did not join the force until the summer of 1889. His views, however, are not easily discounted for he had access to the files and, more important, to the officers who had investigated the murders. Furthermore, inquiries continued intermittently until 1895 and two of Sir Melville's names – Druitt and Kosminski – did not become suspects until after he had taken up his post at the Yard. Macnaghten made this plain in relation to Druitt in his autobiography: 'Although ... the Whitechapel murderer, in all probability, put an end to himself soon after the Dorset Street affair in November 1888, certain facts, pointing to this conclusion, were not in possession of the police till some years after I became a detective officer.'[17]

Nevertheless, it is much easier to demonstrate that Macnaghten thought Druitt was the Ripper than it is to explain why. The only *evidence* to which he alludes is mentioned in the enigmatic statement that 'from private information I have little doubt but that his own family believed him to have been the murderer.' Writers who promote the Druitt theory usually contend that the source was one of Montague's relations – his brother William is the conventional choice – but in truth we know neither the source nor the nature of Macnaghten's information. And we are never likely to know. For Macnaghten, interviewed by the *Daily Mail* in 1913, claimed that although he had 'a very clear idea' who the Ripper was and how he committed suicide he would never reveal what he knew. 'I have destroyed all my documents,' he said, 'and there is now no record of the secret information which came into my possession at one time or another.'[18]

A careful study of Macnaghten's writings on the Ripper suggests that his accusation of Druitt owed as much to his 'theory' of the murders as to anything he may specifically have heard about the suspect. He attributed just five killings to Jack the Ripper, the first that of Polly Nichols, the last that of Mary Kelly, and was greatly impressed by the fact that the extent of the mutilations generally increased throughout this series. It reflected, in Macnaghten's view, less the circumstances in which the individual murders had been committed than the deteriorating mental state of the killer. He was a sexual maniac and such a man, in the grip of a progressively worsening condition, could scarcely have abstained from killing after the Miller's Court affair. Rather, contended Macnaghten, it was far more likely that 'after his awful glut on this occasion, his brain gave way altogether and he committed suicide; otherwise the murders would not have ceased.'[19] These views certainly help to explain why Sir Melville found Druitt such a plausible suspect and the argument is as potent today as it was then. Many latter-day students of the case undoubtedly find the drowned barrister so intriguing precisely because his death would furnish us with a tidy explanation of the increased ferocity and abrupt termination of the killings. A good, recent example of such thinking came from the late Professor Francis Camps, the eminent pathologist. Writing a foreword to Dan Farson's book, Camps asserted that the crimes 'increased in the degree of mutilation, each one being worse than the last' and that 'murders of this type only stop when the murderer is either dead or incarcerated.' As for Druitt, the professor told Farson 'this is the type of person you're looking for. He wouldn't have stopped had he lived.'[20]

No police officer other than Macnaghten ever accused Druitt[21] so we must examine his position very carefully. And the harder we do that the less tenable it appears to be.

First, the 'evidence'. 'From private information,' Sir Melville wrote, 'I have little doubt but that his own family believed him to have been the murderer.' Now, Druittists have contended that this cryptic statement proves that the family's alleged suspicions about Montague were divulged to the police by one of their number. However, close scrutiny of the wording affords no grounds for any such belief. Macnaghten's use of the phrase 'I have little doubt' indicates that he was not *absolutely certain* that Druitt's family suspected him. The suggestion of uncertainty is telling. It implies most strongly that the informant was *not* one of Druitt's immediate family and that Macnaghten was relaying suspicions garnered, at best, at second hand. Common sense, too, suggests that Druitt's close kin are unlikely to have been the source of Macnaghten's information. For if they really did suspect Montague they are hardly likely, once he was dead, to have broadcast their fears to the police or anyone else. Such an action would only have exposed them to the risk of unnecessary distress and embarrassment. There is the further point that had Macnaghten's source been a close relative of Druitt he would have been able to furnish him with accurate biographical data about the dead man. But, as we will presently discover, many of the things Macnaghten wrote about Druitt are now known to have been wrong.

Attempts to identify the informant must of necessity be speculative. He may have been a distant relative of Montague or a family acquaintance. We do know that there were tenuous links between the Macnaghten and Druitt clans. Sir Melville's father, the last chairman of the East India Company, appointed Druitt's aunt's brother to the board in 1855. And Walter Boultbee, who worked at the Yard as private secretary to Macnaghten's friend and patron James Monro, married Ellen Baker, niece of Alfred Mayo, a friend and distant relative of Thomas Druitt, in 1885. It is now exceedingly unlikely that we will ever discover the precise nature and source of Macnaghten's information. Nevertheless, it does not seem to have been better than secondhand and may well have been mere hearsay.

Whatever the source, suspicion alone carries little weight. During the murder scare any abnormal behaviour was apt to invoke a charge that the disturbed or eccentric individual was Jack the Ripper and innumerable innocents fell under suspicion. As the *Times* observed, 'it seems at times as if every person in the streets were suspicious of everyone else he met, and as if it were a race between them who could first inform against his neighbour.'[22]

Macnaghten's interpretation of the murder evidence is no more persuasive than his 'private information' about Druitt. There is little to substantiate his view that the mutilation of the victims evidenced changes in the disposition or mental state of the murderer. As explained in the previous chapter, the extent of the injuries inflicted seems to have been directly related to the amount of time at the disposal of the killer. More, Macnaghten's contention that they progressively increased throughout the series is only true if the Tabram and Stride slayings are excluded from the toll. There are good grounds, however, for including both. And if Martha Tabram is included as a Ripper victim Macnaghten's argument collapses completely for this first killing was as ferocious as anything that followed it. The notion endorsed by Macnaghten and Camps that sexual serial killers cannot abstain from murder has never been more than an unverified assumption. More recent experience, as already noted, seems to demonstrate the contrary. Even if it were true the abrupt termination of the Ripper killings might be explained by any number of scenarios other than suicide – by the incarceration of the murderer in asylum or prison, by his emigration, or by his death from accident or natural causes. Despite the dramatic increase of such crimes in recent decades, both here and in the United States, no major offender is known to have committed suicide.

In the end, though, it is Macnaghten's readiness to accuse Druitt without verifying even basic facts about him that most discredits his case. For it is quickly apparent from Sir Melville's writings that he knew almost nothing about his suspect. Macnaghten believed that Druitt resided with his own people and absented himself from home at certain times. MCC records and Druitt's involvement in

Blackheath's sporting activities, on the other hand, alike suggest that he lived at his school at 9 Eliot Place, possibly as senior resident master. Macnaghten thought that Druitt committed suicide 'on or about the 10th of November'. This was three weeks too early. The correct date was probably 1 December. Certainly it cannot have been sooner. Macnaghten asserted that Druitt was about forty-one years old at the time of his death. In fact he was thirty-one. Above all, Macnaghten wrote of him as a doctor. His true professions were those of schoolmaster and barrister.

Recognizing the fragility of the case against Druitt, later writers have tried hard to unearth more credible evidence against him. No one has succeeded.

Donald Rumbelow wondered whether Montague might have been one of the three insane medical students investigated by the police after the Hanbury Street murder. Macnaghten tells us, however, that Druitt only became a suspect some years after he himself had joined the force in 1889. And although Druitt may have contemplated a medical career at one time he had never been a student at the London Hospital. The three suspected students had all attended this institution but a search of the student registers there by Howells & Skinner did not discover Druitt's name.[23]

One of the most indefatigable Druittists was Dan Farson. When preparing his television programmes in 1959 he made an appeal for information on the Ripper from the public which elicited a deluge of replies. One correspondent, a Mr A. Knowles, told him that he had once seen a document in Australia entitled 'The East End Murderer – I knew him.' After many years Mr Knowles' memory was understandably vague but he apparently recalled that the document had been written by a Lionel Druitt, Drewett or Drewery and that it had been privately printed by a Mr Fell of Dandenong in 1890. The significance of Knowles' letter was seemingly enhanced by the revelations of another correspondent – Maurice Gould of Bexleyheath. Gould had been in Australia from 1925 to 1932 and there he had encountered not one, but two, men who claimed to know the identity of Jack the Ripper. One of them was a freelance journalist named Edward MacNamara. MacNamara claimed that a man called Druitt, who had once lodged with a Mr W. G. Fell of Dandenong, had left Fell papers proving the Ripper's identity. Somehow MacNamara had gained possession of them but, according to Gould, he 'would not part with [the papers] unless he received a considerable sum, £500 I think, which I had not got in those days.' The second man, McCarritty or McGarritty, was sixty when Gould met him in 1930: 'I lost track of him in a little place called, I think, Koo-Wee-Rup, near Lang-Lang, where Fell, also an Englishman, at times looked after him.'[24]

These tales do not inspire confidence. The contents of Knowles' letter cannot now be verified because Dan Farson's dossier of letters and papers, containing the original, was stolen from Television House during the time he was working on his programmes.[25] And as it stands Gould's story is, quite frankly, unbelievable, for if MacNamara had the Druitt papers why did he not publish their secrets himself? In any case both informants, thinking back over many years, would unquestionably have been extremely confused over dates and other details. Yet Farson, knowing that Lionel Druitt, Montague's cousin, had emigrated to Australia in 1886, was tantalized by these clues and soon found an opportunity to pursue his search for Jack the Ripper in the land of the Southern Cross.

With Alan Dower, a 'laconic and rather tough' special correspondent of the Melbourne *Truth*, he drove into Western Gippsland, southeast of Melbourne, in 1961. The results were disappointing. The places certainly existed. They found Koo-Wee-Rup and Lang-Lang. But of 'The East End Murderer' there was not a trace. 'At Lang-Lang I saw the end in sight,' recalled Farson, 'when I heard of a storekeeper called Fell – but when I met him he said he was no relation of the Fell who printed the document.' The last echo of the story was heard at the nearby town of Drouin. There Farson met the elderly Miss Stevens who remembered Dr Lionel Druitt and said that he had practised there in 1903. 'Someone in Victoria can still finally solve the riddle of Jack the Ripper,' Dower concluded. 'British TV investigator Dan Farson and I are sure of this having travelled 250 miles through West Gippsland this week seeking documents and records that would provide the few missing clues.'

Subsequent research has not justified this optimism. Many attempts to trace 'The East End Murderer' have been made in Australian libraries, newspaper files and archives but without result. No one by the name of Fell is known to have lived in Dandenong in 1890 and in that year Dr Lionel Druitt definitely began to practise in St Arnaud, Victoria. It is just possible that Knowles saw the unrelated Jack the Ripper story that appeared in a supplement to the *St Arnaud Mercury* of 29 November 1890. But a more likely explanation is that Knowles' date of 1890 is wrong and that both he and Gould were transmitting hazy memories of the Deeming affair of 1892.

Frederick Deeming was executed in Australia on 23 May 1892 for the murder of his wife Emily Mather. Following his arrest newspaper gossip, both there and in Britain, linked him with the Whitechapel murders. The London *Globe*, for example, printed the claim of an East End dressmaker that Deeming, using the name Lawson, had been in London on the night that Stride and Eddowes had been killed, and this story was splashed across the Melbourne *Evening Standard* of 8 April 1892 under the headline: 'JACK THE RIPPER: DEEMING AT ALDGATE ON THE NIGHT OF THE WHITECHAPEL MURDERS.' Another rumour, denied by Richard S. Haynes, Deeming's lawyer, averred that he had actually confessed to some of the Whitechapel crimes. Deeming was a multiple murderer. Before emigrating to Australia in 1891 he murdered a former wife and four children and entombed their bodies beneath the floor of Dinham Villa, a cottage he rented at Rainhill in Lancashire. But he was not the Ripper. Notwithstanding the tales of the press the best evidence we have places Deeming in South Africa in the autumn of 1888.[26]

That the Knowles and Gould stories were inspired by Deeming is suggested by a similarity of names. Shortly after his arrival in Melbourne Deeming assumed the alias of Druin or Drewen. He rented a house in the Melbourne suburb of Windsor, through which the main Dandenong Road ran. And his third fiancée – who may have been his intended next victim – was Kate Rounse*fell*. In the case of Gould the Deeming origin of the story was proved beyond reasonable doubt when, in 1986, Martin Howells and Keith Skinner traced and re-interviewed Dan Farson's old informant. Gould's new account was only marginally more convincing than the original yarn but he did now disclose that his conversation with Edward MacNamara about Jack the Ripper had taken place within the context of a discussion of the Deeming case. Gould, then eighteen, had met MacNamara in a famous Melbourne pub called Young's. Their talk had passed from Deeming to Jack the Ripper, at which point MacNamara had fished 'two or three handwritten sheets' out of his pocket. These Gould had taken to be the Ripper's confession.

The researches of Howells and Skinner, incidentally, demonstrate how treacherous reminiscent evidence can be. Maurice Gould told Dan Farson that the original owner of the Ripper papers had been a Mr W. G. Fell of Dandenong. Howells and Skinner, however, eventually learned from Australian researcher John Ruffels that W. G. Fell had in reality been the name of a storekeeper who had employed Gould back in 1930. By writing his former employer into the tale Gould seriously misled Farson. Farson, indeed, met W. G. Fell without realizing it for he was the very same Mr Fell with whom Farson and Dower had spoken of Jack the Ripper at Lang-Lang in 1961!

The Australian connection, in short, was a colossal red herring drawn across the trail by fading memories and tall tales. Its failure throws us back upon Macnaghten and leaves the case against Druitt seriously flawed by a lack of tangible evidence. What is left? Well, Professor Camps insisted that Druitt was the *type* of man we should be looking for. So, in the light of what we now know about both the murderer and Druitt, how far does Sir Melville's suspect fit the bill?

There is no simple answer. For example, it might be supposed that Druitt's professions of schoolmaster and barrister disqualify him as a suspect because of his lack of medical knowledge but he is by no means as ill a fit in this respect as many of the other suspects on offer. Although the Ripper probably did possess some degree of medical knowledge it is impossible to say how much. After studying the medical sketches of Kate Eddowes' injuries, Professor Camps was convinced that the killer had been no surgeon. He continued: 'One should then consider other people who might have surgical knowledge but be, as it were, in the early stages of medical knowledge, and might have . . . the opportunity of access to books.'[27] This could well be a perfect description of Druitt. Intelligent and educated, he was raised in an environment of medical men and medical books. His father (William), uncle (Robert) and cousin (Lionel) were all doctors and Montague may well at one time have contemplated such a career for himself.

There are, nonetheless, considerable difficulties in identifying Druitt with the Ripper.

We know little about Druitt's appearance. What we have accords with descriptions of the murderer in some particulars but not in others. Druitt became thirty-one in August 1888. Of the five most important witnesses who gave descriptions of men seen in the company of one or other of the murder victims only one – Elizabeth Long – gave an estimate of age inconsistent with this. She thought that the man she saw talking with Annie Chapman in

Hanbury Street was over forty. But she acknowledged that she did not see his face and the other witnesses all gave estimates very close to Druitt's known age: PC Smith (twenty-eight), Israel Schwartz (thirty), Joseph Lawende (thirty) and George Hutchinson (thirty-four or five). A photograph of Druitt shows him sporting a small moustache. Three of the key witnesses mention such a moustache, although Smith said it was dark, Schwartz brown and Lawende fair. And Druitt sprang from the professional class. His body, when recovered from the river, was said to have been well-dressed. Admittedly, the man Lawende saw with Kate Eddowes had the appearance of a sailor. But the other important witnesses spoke of a 'shabby genteel' (Long), respectable (Smith and Schwartz) or even prosperous-looking (Hutchinson) man. On the other hand Druitt's build does not accord well with the Ripper evidence. Photographs depict Druitt as a slender, even gaunt, man. Only two of the chief Ripper witnesses mention build. Lawende, however, described a man of medium build while Schwartz spoke of a rather stout, broad shouldered figure. Then two if not three of the witnesses indicated a foreigner. Elizabeth Long's suspect 'looked like a foreigner', George Hutchinson saw a man of 'Jewish' appearance and, as we shall see, Joseph Lawende evidently later identified a Polish Jew.

Even less is known of Druitt's personality than of his appearance. His school record suggests a self-confident, competitive spirit. At Winchester he was a prominent member of the debating society. Many of his topics were political. In one debate he praised Gladstone as the 'only redeeming point' in the Liberal Party, in another he denounced Bismarck's influence as 'morally and socially a curse to the world', and in his final appearance he defended the record of his own generation against those of its predecessors. 'The old theory of government was "man is made for States",' he contended. 'Is it not a vast improvement that States should be made for man, as they are now?' Druitt's passion for sport, especially cricket, blossomed at an early age. In 1876 he won a place in the Winchester First Eleven and while still at Oxford became a member of the influential Kingston Park and Dorset County Cricket Club, the principal club side in his native county. The sporting evidence depicts a man with considerable strength in his arms and wrists. He excelled at Fives, which is played with the bare hands rather than with a bat, and won the Double Fives and Single Fives titles at both Winchester and Oxford. On 9 March 1875 he came third in a 'throwing the cricket ball' event at

Winchester with a throw of more than ninety-two yards. All this suggests that Druitt would have possessed the strength, confidence and presence of mind necessary to have committed the murders. But there is nothing to corroborate Macnaghten's claim that he was sexually insane and no evidence of attacks on women or any act of violence whatsoever.

Furthermore, the Ripper knew and probably lived in the East End. Druitt, as far as we can tell, had no connection with it. Dan Farson, discovering the fact that Lionel Druitt, Montague's cousin, assisted Dr Thomas Thyne at 140 Minories in 1879, suggested that Montague may have visited Lionel at the surgery there. Unfortunately for this line of speculation there is no evidence that the cousins were particularly close. Montague was born and bred in Dorset; Lionel was born in London and raised at 39a Curzon Street, Mayfair. Additionally, Lionel's sojourn in the Minories seems to have been of the most temporary kind. In both 1878 and 1880 the *Medical Register* and the *Medical Directory* record him at 8 Strathmore Gardens, Kensington. Montague, of course, was still a student at Oxford when Lionel was assisting Dr Thyne. Martin Howells and Keith Skinner wondered whether Druitt could have walked through Whitechapel on his way to visit his mother after her committal to the Brooke Asylum in Clapton in July 1888. This hypothesis is not entirely implausible in that the asylum was less than two miles northeast of Whitechapel. It does, however, ignore the facts that Druitt seems to have normally travelled by train and that Ann Druitt, after only two months at the asylum, was transferred on leave of absence to an establishment in Brighton, where she remained until 1890. There is thus no provable or even probable link between Druitt and the murder district.[28]

Did Druitt, then, have a known base from which he might have made murderous forays into the East End? MCC records, which give his address throughout as 9 Eliot Place, Blackheath, suggest that he was a resident master at George Valentine's school. But the absence of an all-night train service between London and Blackheath makes it difficult to believe that the Ripper could have operated out of a base there. In 1888 the latest train calling at Blackheath left London Bridge Station at 12.25 a.m., the earliest Cannon Street Station at 5.10 a.m. The approximate times of the six murders in the autumn of 1888 were 2.30, 3.40, 5.30, 1.00, 1.44 and just before 4.00 a.m. On the nights of the Tabram and Stride and Eddowes killings at least, therefore, a Blackheath murderer would have had perilous hours to survive before catching a homeward-bound train and might necessarily have had recourse to a common lodging house. Although not impossible such conduct would have incurred considerable risks, especially, perhaps, for a well-dressed stranger.

Appreciating this difficulty, Tom Cullen argued that Druitt's chambers at 9 King's Bench Walk, near Victoria Embankment, were the Ripper's lair. We know from the Law Lists of 1886–7 that Druitt did retain chambers at this address, and these would have been within walking distance of the East End. However, the Ripper's known movements on the night of the double murder are very damaging to this hypothesis. After cutting down Elizabeth Stride in Dutfield's Yard before one, he walked westwards to Mitre Square in the City, where, between 1.30 and 1.45, he killed and mutilated Kate Eddowes. Now, if his base had been in King's Bench Walk the murderer would then have continued westwards, away from the police activity stirred up by his crimes and towards the safety of his chambers. Instead, he turned in the *opposite* direction, plunging deeper into the East End and leaving a blood-stained piece of Kate's apron in Goulston Street to the northeast.

Finally, Druitt's known cricket fixtures for August and September 1888 cast real doubt upon whether he can have committed three of the murders. Martha Tabram died on Tuesday, 7 August. But on 3 and 4 August, the previous Friday and Saturday, Druitt played for Bournemouth against the touring Parsees at Dean Park, Bournemouth, and on 10 and 11 August, the succeeding Friday and Saturday, he was at Dean Park again, this time playing for the Gentlemen of Dorset in a match against Bournemouth. It is entirely possible, therefore, that when Martha Tabram was butchered Druitt was on the south coast, perhaps staying with his brother William. Indeed, one wonders whether he spent any of the school vacation that summer in London. For on 22 August a Druitt played for Bournemouth against Sir William Bathurst's XI at Salisbury and on 1 September, the day after Polly Nichols was killed, Montague is positively known to have played for Canford, Dorset, against Wimborne at Canford. By 8 September, the date of the Hanbury Street murder, Druitt had returned to the capital. At 11.30 that same morning he played for the Blackheath Cricket Club against the Brothers Christopherson on the Rectory Field at Blackheath. Druitt could have killed Annie Chapman. It would have been possible for him to have murdered her in Spitalfields at 5.30 and then to have caught a train to Blackheath and to have washed, changed and breakfasted in time to turn out on the Rectory Field by 11.30. Nevertheless, it must be conceded that bearing in mind the probability that Annie's killer had been prowling the East End streets for most of the night such a scenario does seem distinctly unlikely.[29]

Nothing we have learned categorically rules Druitt out of the picture. Still, the absence of hard evidence against him, coupled with the objections we have noted, compels us to regard him us an improbable suspect.

Those who have championed the Druitt theory will doubtless continue to do so in the belief that credible evidence must once have existed against him even if it doesn't now. They will remind us of Macnaghten's destroyed papers. And they will point out that the bulk of the Yard files have also been lost. My own feeling is that if all the relevant records had survived we would be very disappointed in their content. As explained, there are good grounds for believing that Macnaghten heard secondhand suspicions at the very best, put about when such suspicions against men of unsound mind were commonplace. It is noteworthy, too, that in both versions of the 1894 report the only evidence to which Macnaghten alludes is designated 'private information'. This surely implies that no *official* inquiry into Druitt's alleged connection with the murders was made or, if it was, no incriminating evidence was uncovered. In this context there is one last, very important, piece of testimony. It comes from the Scotland Yard detective most intimately involved in the Ripper hunt – Chief Inspector Frederick G. Abberline.

Interviewed for the *Pall Mall Gazette* in 1903, Abberline firmly rebutted any suggestion that the CID knew for certain that the murderer was dead. 'You can state most emphatically,' he said, 'that Scotland Yard is really no wiser on the subject than it was fifteen years ago. It is simple nonsense to talk of the police having proof that the man is dead. I am, and always have been, in the closest touch with Scotland Yard, and it would have been next to impossible for me not to have known all about it. Besides, the authorities would have been only too glad to make an end of such a mystery, if only for their own credit.' To prove his point he produced recent documentary evidence which, according to the *Gazette*'s man who saw it, 'put the ignorance of Scotland Yard as to the perpetrator beyond the shadow of a doubt.' The journalist ventured to draw Abberline's attention to

George R. Sims' claims. 'Yes,' the detective replied, 'I know all about that story. But what does it amount to? Simply this. Soon after the last murder in Whitechapel the body of a young doctor was found in the Thames, but there is absolutely nothing beyond the fact that he was found at that time to incriminate him. A report was made to the Home Office about the matter, but that it was "considered final and conclusive" is going altogether beyond the truth.'[30]

If Druitt was not the killer can a credible case be made out against No. 2 or No. 3 on Macnaghten's list? No. 2, the Polish Jew named by Sir Melville as Kosminski, is of particular interest to us. For no less an authority than Sir Robert Anderson, Assistant Commissioner in charge of CID at the time of the murders, categorically asserted – and on more than one occasion – that he was Jack the Ripper.

20

Caged in an Asylum: Aaron Kosminski

IT WAS ONCE SAID of Sir Melville Macnaghten that his head was 'crammed full with official secrets'. The description might have been applied with even greater justification to his predecessor, Sir Robert Anderson. For when he retired and accepted a knighthood from a grateful King Edward VII in 1901 he had notched up twenty years in gathering and processing intelligence on Fenian activities for the Home Office and another thirteen as Assistant Commissioner of the Metropolitan Police in charge of CID. Anderson's was a retirement punctuated by only infrequent references to the Jack the Ripper murders. But the few he made have given rise to immense speculation.

Readers of his book *Criminals and Crime* (1907) were told that the identities of the murderer and of the author of the infamous letter to the Central News had both been established. There Anderson categorically asserted that the killer had been 'safely caged in an asylum' and that the 'Jack the Ripper' letter had been penned by an 'enterprising journalist'. No names were given, no proof cited, but three years later Sir Robert fed more details to the public.

His memoirs, 'The Lighter Side of My Official Life', were then being serialized in *Blackwood's Magazine*. Part VI (March 1910) contained some remarkable revelations:

> One did not need to be a Sherlock Holmes to discover that the criminal was a sexual maniac of a virulent type; that he was living

in the immediate vicinity of the scenes of the murders; and that, if
he was not living absolutely alone, his people knew of his guilt,
and refused to give him up to justice. During my absence abroad
the Police had made a house-to-house search for him, investigating
the case of every man in the district whose circumstances were such
that he could go and come and get rid of his blood-stains in secret.
And the conclusion we came to was that he and his people were
low-class Jews, for it is a remarkable fact that people of that
class in the East End will not give up one of their number to
Gentile justice.

And the result proved that our diagnosis was right on every
point. For I may say at once that 'undiscovered murders' are rare
in London, and the 'Jack-the-Ripper' crimes are not within that
category. And if the Police here had powers such as the French
Police possess, the murderer would have been brought to justice.
Scotland Yard can boast that not even the subordinate officers of
the department will tell tales out of school, and it would ill become
me to violate the unwritten rule of the service. The subject will come
up again, and I will only add here that the 'Jack-the-Ripper' letter
which is preserved in the Police Museum at New Scotland Yard
is the creation of an enterprising London journalist.

A footnote added:

Having regard to the interest attaching to this case, I should almost
be tempted to disclose the identity of the murderer and of the
pressman who wrote the letter above referred to, provided that
the publishers would accept all responsibility in view of a possible
libel action. But no public benefit would result from such a course,
and the traditions of my old department would suffer. I will only
add that when the individual whom we suspected was caged in
an asylum, the only person who had ever had a good view of
the murderer at once identified him, but when he learned that the
suspect was a fellow-Jew he declined to swear to him.

When the memoirs were published in book form later in the year
a few modifications were made to this passage. The reference to
'low-class Jews' was expanded to 'certain low-class Polish Jews'. And
the footnote was rewritten and incorporated into the main text:

Having regard to the interest attaching to this case, I am almost tempted to disclose the identity of the murderer and of the pressman who wrote the letter above referred to. But no public benefit would result from such a course, and the traditions of my old department would suffer. I will merely add that the only person who had ever had a good view of the murderer unhesitatingly identified the suspect the instant he was confronted with him; but he refused to give evidence against him.

In saying that he was a Polish Jew I am merely stating a definitely ascertained fact. And my words are meant to specify race, not religion. For it would outrage all religious sentiment to talk of the religion of a loathsome creature whose utterly unmentionable vices reduced him to a lower level than that of the brute.

Finally, in the introduction he wrote to H. L. Adam's *The Police Encyclopaedia* (1920), Anderson reaffirmed his belief that the Ripper case had been solved: 'Despite the lucubrations of many an amateur "Sherlock Holmes", there was no doubt whatever as to the identity of the criminal, and if our London "detectives" possessed the powers, and might have recourse to the methods, of Foreign Police Forces, he would have been brought to justice.'[1]

For another half-century nothing more was known about Anderson's low-class Polish Jew. But in 1959 his identity was revealed by Dan Farson's discovery of Lady Aberconway's copy of Macnaghten's draft report of 1894. According to the draft the second suspect against whom the police had reasonable grounds for suspicion was:

No 2. Kosminski, a Polish Jew, who lived in the very heart of the district where the murders were committed. He had become insane owing to many years indulgence in solitary vices. He had a great hatred of women, with strong homicidal tendencies. He was (and I believe still is) detained in a lunatic asylum about March 1889. This man in appearance strongly resembled the individual seen by the City PC near Mitre Square.

The official version, in the Scotland Yard case papers, is briefer:

(2) Kosminski, a Polish Jew, & resident in Whitechapel. This man became insane owing to many years indulgence in solitary vices. He had a great hatred of women, specially of the prostitute class, & had strong homicidal tendencies; he was removed to a

lunatic asylum about March 1889. There were many circumstances connected with this man which made him a strong 'suspect'.[2]

A last police fragment concerning Kosminski came to light at the height of the publicity surrounding the centenary of the murders. Chief Inspector Donald Sutherland Swanson died in 1924. In 1980 or 1981, upon the death of his unmarried daughter, some of his books and papers passed to James Swanson of Peaslake in Surrey, her nephew and the chief inspector's grandson. Among his new acquisitions James found a copy of Anderson's memoirs, annotated in pencil by Chief Inspector Swanson himself. At the bottom of page 138, on which Anderson had asserted that the murderer had been identified but that the witness had refused to give evidence, Swanson had written:

because the suspect was *also a Jew* and also because his evidence would convict the suspect, and witness would be the means of murderer being hanged which he did not wish to be left on his mind.

In the margin he continued:

And after this identification which suspect knew, no other murder of this kind took place in London.

On the back end-paper of the book Swanson had added a further note:

Continuing from page 138, after the suspect had been identified at the Seaside Home where he had been sent by us with difficulty in order to subject him to identification, and he knew he was identified. On suspect's return to his brother's house in Whitechapel he was watched by police (City CID) by day & night. In a very short time the suspect with his hands tied behind his back, he was sent to Stepney Workhouse and then to Colney Hatch and died shortly afterwards – Kosminski was the suspect – DSS

In 1987, when James Swanson revealed the existence of this evidence to the *Daily Telegraph*, the paper trumpeted its scoop on the front page under the caption 'WHITECHAPEL MURDERS:

SENSATIONAL NEW EVIDENCE'. Inside it published a special report by Charles Nevin. But Paul Begg was the first to print the Swanson marginalia in full, in his book *Jack the Ripper: The Uncensored Facts*, in 1988.[3]

Macnaghten and Swanson give us the name of Anderson's suspect: Kosminski. The first author to attempt to follow up these leads was Martin Fido, whose book, *The Crimes, Detection and Death of Jack the Ripper*, was published in 1987. I can find little to say in favour of his theory that David Cohen, a lunatic found wandering at large in December 1888, was the murderer. But Fido is to be congratulated upon his explorations into asylum records at a time when their importance was generally unrecognized and his discovery of Aaron Kosminski in the archives of Colney Hatch Asylum was a find of major importance.

Fido published some details from Kosminski's Colney Hatch record.[4] By no means do they tell the complete story. However, when I set out to learn more I quickly discovered that searching Kosminski out in workhouse and asylum records would be no straightforward task. Medical records of individual patients in public asylums are closed to public access for 100 years. Fortunately, after I had explained that my purpose was to write an accurate and objective history, the hospitals in which Kosminski was treated graciously permitted me to examine all relevant files. As a result what survives of Kosminski's story can be told in full for the first time. The records demonstrate that the memories of our police informants were faulty even on the most basic facts. For Kosminski was not committed to Colney Hatch in 1889 but in 1891. And far from dying shortly afterwards, he lived for another twenty-eight years.

The records of Mile End Old Town Workhouse show that Aaron Kosminski, an unmarried Jewish hairdresser, was admitted to the workhouse on Saturday, 12 July 1890, from 3 Sion Square, the home of Wolf Kosminski, his brother. He was able-bodied but insane. Three days later he was discharged into Wolf's care. On Wednesday, 4 February 1891, Aaron was re-admitted, this time from 16 Greenfield Street. On 6 February he was examined at the workhouse by Dr Edmund King Houchin of 23 High Street, Stepney. The doctor concluded that Aaron was of unsound mind 'and a proper person to be taken charge of and detained under care and treatment' so Henry Chambers, a JP for the County of London, accordingly made an order committing him to the county lunatic asylum at Colney Hatch. Aaron was discharged from the workhouse to Colney Hatch on 7 February. There is a slight discrepancy in the workhouse records as to Kosminski's age. In July 1890 the year of his birth is noted as 1865, in February 1891 as 1864. On both occasions the informant was Wolf Kosminski.

Today the only documents in the records of the Mile End Old Town Board of Guardians which actually shed light on Kosminski's mental state are the medical certificate and the committal order made out on 6 February by Houchin and Chambers respectively.

The medical certificate sets out the grounds for Dr Houchin's opinion of insanity. It rested partly upon his personal examination of Kosminski: 'He declares that he is guided & his movements altogether controlled by an instinct that informs his mind; he says that he knows the movements of all mankind; he refuses food from others because he is told to do so and eats out of the gutter for the same reason.' But in addition Jacob Cohen of 51 Carter Lane, St Paul's, had informed Houchin that Kosminski 'goes about the streets and picks up bits of bread out of the gutter & eats them, he drinks water from the tap & he refuses food at the hands of others. He took up a knife & threatened the life of his sister. He says that he is ill and his cure consists in refusing food. He is melancholic, practises self-abuse. He is very dirty and will not be washed. He has not attempted any kind of work for years.'

On the reverse of the committal order some particulars about Kosminski, prepared by Maurice Whitfield, Relieving Officer for the Western District of Mile End Old Town, were recorded for the benefit of the receiving doctors at Colney Hatch. They tell us that none of Aaron's close relatives were known to have suffered from insanity and that the cause of his illness was unknown. His first attack had occurred at the age of twenty-five and he had been treated at the Mile End Old Town Workhouse in July 1890. The present attack had lasted six months. It is particularly significant that, despite Jacob Cohen's mention of a knife threat, Whitfield's statement explicitly asserted that Kosminski was not suicidal or dangerous to other people.[5]

The records of Colney Hatch confirm that Kosminski was admitted to the asylum on 7 February 1891. On the day he came Mr F. Bryan, one of the assistant medical officers, reported that he was clean and of fair bodily health. Kosminski was held at Colney Hatch for the next three years and his progress there was documented in brief case notes made two or three times a year. At first doctors found him difficult to deal with because of his obedience to his guiding 'instinct'. This, they thought, was probably aural hallucination (i.e. he was hearing voices). Whatever, Kosminski's 'instinct' forbade him to wash and notes of 10 February and 21 April 1891 tell us that he was objecting to weekly baths. By January 1892 his habits were cleanly. But the doctors failed to cure him of another symptom mentioned in Houchin's medical certificate – a refusal to work. Between 21 April 1891, when he was described as 'incoherent, apathetic, unoccupied', and 18 September 1893, when we are told that he was 'never employed', all but one case note referred to his unwillingness to work. Kosminski's general health remained satisfactory but his mental condition seems to have deteriorated. Although tending to be reticent and morose, he could answer questions fairly when first admitted. In November 1892, however, he was only speaking German. And two months later it was noted that he was suffering from chronic mania and that his intelligence was impaired. As late as September 1893 he could still answer questions about himself. But on 13 April 1894, just six days before he was discharged to Leavesden Asylum near Watford, he was described tersely as 'demented & incoherent'.

Of particular interest to us is any disposition Kosminski may have exhibited towards violence. Our evidence is pretty conclusive on this point.

When Kosminski first came to Colney Hatch the information provided about him by Whitfield was dutifully copied into the male patients' casebook. But as a result of their experiences with the patient and, presumably, regular contact with his relatives, the staff at the asylum subsequently made alterations in red ink to some of these entries. We thus find the cause of Kosminski's illness altered in the casebook from 'unknown' to 'self-abuse' and the duration of the present attack corrected from six months to six years. Obviously, though, the doctors learned nothing to persuade them that Kosminski was a homicidal patient. For Whitfield's statement that he was not dangerous to others was allowed to stand unamended.

The case notes strongly suggest that their assessment was right. Nine notes in all cover the three years Kosminski remained at Colney Hatch. Only one, dated 9 January 1892, explicitly mentioned violence: 'Incoherent; at times excited & violent – a few days ago he took up a chair, and attempted to strike the charge attendant;

apathetic as a rule, and refuses to occupy himself in any way; habits cleanly; health fair'. Another, entered on 18 January 1893, recorded that at times he was 'noisy, excited & incoherent'. It is apparent, then, that Kosminski could be excitable. But more frequently he was described as quiet, apathetic or indolent. And there is no evidence of malice or cunning.

One last piece of evidence on Kosminski's behaviour at Colney Hatch exists. On 18 April 1894, a day before he was discharged to Leavesden, a statement giving brief details about him for the receiving doctors was signed by William J. Seward, the Medical Superintendent at Colney Hatch. In it Seward reiterated Whitfield's assessment that Kosminski was neither suicidal nor dangerous to others and commented simply: 'Incoherent; usually quiet; health fair.'[6]

Leavesden was an asylum for adult imbeciles established in 1870. And on 19 April 1894 W. Thacker, Clerk to the Board of Guardians, Mile End Old Town, signed an order for Kosminski's admission there as a 'chronic harmless lunatic, idiot or imbecile'. The order named his mother, Mrs Kosminski of 63 New Street, New Road, Whitechapel, as his nearest known relative.

Leavesden was Kosminski's home for the remaining twenty-five years of his life. No case notes before 1910 appear to have survived. But from that date eight entries afford us glimpses of his behaviour. Two (1 April and 16 July 1914) noted that he was excitable and 'troublesome' at times, one (17 February 1915) that he was occasionally 'very excitable' and another (2 February 1916) that he could be 'very obstinate'. None referred to him as a violent patient or as one that represented any risk to staff or other patients. Clean, but untidy and slovenly in his habits, he did no work and seemed unable to respond rationally to the simplest questions. This last point is mentioned in all but two of the eight case notes. 'Patient is morose in manner. No sensible reply can be got by questions. He mutters incoherently.' So ran a typical entry in January 1913. 'Patient merely mutters when asked questions,' another reported in February 1915. From four entries between 1 April 1914 and 2 February 1916 we learn that Kosminski was hearing voices and seeing things that were not there. By the latter date he had become a sad shell of a man, dull and vacant, and locked in a secret world of his own: 'Patient does not know his age or how long he has been here. He has hallucinations of sight & hearing & is at times very obstinate. Untidy but clean, does no work.'

Of Kosminski's general health we know a little more. Dr Henry Case, Medical Superintendent at Leavesden, informed Thacker upon Kosminski's arrival at his asylum in 1894 that his bodily condition was 'impaired'. Detailed medical records after 1910 note that it ranged from weak to good and record such mundane facts as Kosminski sustaining a cut over the left eye from an encounter with a wash-house tap in November 1915 and being twice put to bed with swollen feet in January and February 1919. It was in 1918, however, that his general health seems to have entered into terminal decline. On 26 May he was put to bed suffering from diarrhoea and 'passing loose motions with blood & mucus'. Eight days later, his diarrhoea having ceased, he was ordered up by Dr Reese. In May 1918, too, his weight fell below seven stone. In May 1915 it had exceeded seven stone eight pounds. By February 1919, the last time he was weighed, it stood at six stone twelve pounds. It is from such arid medical data that we must of necessity reconstruct the last days of the man Sir Robert Anderson insisted was Jack the Ripper. From late February 1919 Kosminski was more or less permanently bedridden with erysipelas. On 13 March it was reported that his right hip had 'broken down'. On 22 March he was very noisy but took little nourishment. The next day he again took little nourishment and appeared 'very low'. Then, at five minutes past five on the morning of 24 March 1919, he died at the asylum in the presence of S. Bennett, the night attendant. There was a sore on his left hip and leg. Some of Kosminski's symptoms suggest that he may have been suffering from cancer but the male patients' medical journal and Kosminski's death certificate both record the cause of death as gangrene of the left leg.[7]

To judge by Anderson's comment that there was 'no doubt whatever as to the identity of the criminal' one would think the case against Aaron Kosminski cut and dried. In one respect, certainly, Kosminski was unique among major Whitechapel murder suspects – he was the only one against whom any direct evidence linking him with the crimes was ever adduced. That evidence, of course, was the positive identification of a witness mentioned both by Anderson and Swanson and the credibility of the case against the Polish Jew rests almost entirely upon it.

So who was the witness? Neither Anderson nor Swanson tell us his name but there are sufficient clues in the police evidence for us to determine his identity with reasonable certainty.

First, we have Macnaghten's comment in the draft version of his 1894 report that 'this man [Kosminski] in appearance strongly resembled the individual seen by the City PC near Mitre Square'. Now, as we have seen, Macnaghten's draft and official report are factually weak. This particular statement is quite erroneous for despite Major Smith's orders that couples be kept under close observation no City policeman saw the Ripper with his victim near Mitre Square and this led to speculation in the force that they might have met there by prior appointment.[8] The Mitre Square witness, in fact, was Joseph Lawende, the commercial traveller who saw a man with a woman who may have been Kate Eddowes at the entrance of Church Passage, leading into Mitre Square, ten minutes before Kate's body was discovered in the square itself. Macnaghten's 'City PC' was undoubtedly a hazy memory of PC William Smith. Smith, however, was a Metropolitan, not a City, constable, and he reported seeing a man with Liz Stride in Berner Street, not one with Kate Eddowes near Mitre Square. In short Macnaghten confused two separate sightings made on the night of the double murder: those of PC Smith in Berner Street at about 12.35 and Joseph Lawende near Mitre Square an hour later.

It may seem difficult to believe that a senior police officer could have botched his facts as badly as this. But Macnaghten's report shows every indication of having been largely compiled from memory. In the last chapter we noted several errors in his account of Druitt and that of Kosminski is similarly flawed by its assertion that this suspect had been committed to an asylum about March 1889. The correct date was February 1891. There are also errors in Macnaghten's remarks on the Tabram, Chapman and Stride murders. The last is particularly revealing in that, like the reference to the City PC, it seems to have arisen from a transposition of the events surrounding the Berner Street and Mitre Square killings. Macnaghten's draft avers that Stride's killer was disturbed when 'three Jews drove up to an Anarchist Club in Berners Street'. Now the Berner Street killer might very well have been disturbed but if he was it was by just *one* Jew – Louis Diemschutz, the steward of the International Working Men's Club, who drove his barrow into Dutfield's Yard, next to the club, within minutes of the time Long Liz must have been killed. Macnaghten's reference to *three* Jews, then, was probably inspired by the story of Joseph Lawende, Joseph Hyam Levy and Harry Harris, the three Jews who, upon leaving the

Imperial Club in Duke Street later that same night, chanced upon the couple subsequently believed to have been the Ripper and Kate Eddowes. Haste and a disposition to trust too much in the memory are the causes of the Chief Constable's lapses. 'I never kept a diary, nor even possessed a notebook,' he confessed in his autobiography in 1914, 'so that, in what I write, I must trust to my memory, and to my memory alone.'[9]

If there is any truth at all in Macnaghten's statement the witness who identified Kosminski was *either* PC Smith *or* Joseph Lawende. Other clues, though, clearly rule Smith out. Both Anderson and Swanson were emphatic that the witness was a Jew. And Swanson's revelation that it was the City CID who watched Wolf Kosminski's house points unmistakably at Lawende. In 1890 Wolf was living in Sion Square at the north end of Mulberry Street. It was on the other side of Commercial Road from, and nearly opposite to, Berner Street, and was well within the jurisdiction of the Metropolitan Police. So why was the surveillance being undertaken by the City force? There seems only one plausible explanation. The witness who had identified Kosminski was Lawende so the police were seeking to charge the suspect with the murder of Kate Eddowes in Mitre Square. Since the investigation of this crime, the only one in the series which occurred in the City, was the responsibility of the City detectives they had, of necessity, to be involved in the inquiry.

If the witness was a Jew the only alternative to Lawende is Israel Schwartz. But Schwartz does not fit the bill anything like as well. If Schwartz was the witness then Macnaghten was completely wrong and the City Police would have had no business trespassing into Metropolitan Police territory in order to watch a man suspected of a crime (the Berner Street murder) committed within the jurisdiction of the Metropolitan force. Furthermore, if the man Schwartz claimed to have seen attacking Stride in Berner Street really did call out 'Lipski!' he is unlikely to have been, as Kosminski unquestionably was, a Jew.

The witness mentioned by Anderson and Swanson was almost certainly Lawende and it is upon his identification of Kosminski that the case against the Polish Jew largely hinges. This single piece of positive evidence at once marks Kosminski out as a more likely suspect than Druitt but in other ways, too, he sounds a more plausible Whitechapel murderer than the ill-starred barrister.

His known addresses in Sion Square and Greenfield Street were within walking distance of all the murder sites. Additionally, a killer making his way there from Mitre Square could have traversed Goulston Street, where the bloodstained portion of Kate's apron was found. Evidence of a violent disposition, lacking altogether in the case of Druitt, is there for all to read in Kosminski's record. He was said by Jacob Cohen to have threatened his sister with a knife. When he was conveyed to Mile End Old Town Workhouse the authorities are said by Swanson to have felt obliged to restrain him by tying his hands behind his back. And in Colney Hatch he attacked an attendant with a chair. In his personal appearance, too, Kosminski arguably displayed some of the characteristics reported by witnesses of the Whitechapel killer. Mrs Long spoke of a man of 'shabby genteel' appearance. Three witnesses (Marshall, Smith and Schwartz) described one who was respectably or decently dressed. One (Marshall) said that the man he saw reminded him of a clerk rather than a manual worker. A hairdresser like Kosminski would scarcely have been an affluent man but he would not have been accustomed to dress like a labourer. 'Shabby genteel', 'decent' and 'respectable'. These terms do not seem inappropriate ones to describe the general appearance of a poor immigrant barber. Then, of course, two important witnesses (Mrs Long and George Hutchinson) explicitly reported a man of foreign or Jewish appearance.

So have we found Jack the Ripper?

Well, there is no doubt that at the moment informed opinion regards Kosminski as the leading suspect. In *The Secret Identity of Jack the Ripper*, an American TV documentary broadcast in 1988, a panel of experts including Scotland Yard's Bill Waddell unanimously chose Kosminski as the most likely murderer from a list of five admittedly ill-chosen candidates. And Begg, Fido & Skinner, in their influential *Jack the Ripper A to Z* (1991) contend that nothing Anderson wrote about his suspect has been 'shown to be false', that the documentary case against Kosminski is 'very strong indeed' and that it is research into Kosminski which will most likely lead to the identification of Jack the Ripper 'if it has not done so already'. Such comments led at least one reviewer to observe that the answer to the mystery seemed 'tantalizingly close'. Unfortunately it isn't. For the facts established in the present work about Kosminski and the Ripper prove that there is no credible evidence against the Jewish hairdresser, that there are important objections to attempts to identify him with the Ripper and that Anderson, the 'rock' upon which these accusations have been founded, is repeatedly and demonstrably inaccurate and misleading.

We had better start with that crucial identification of Kosminski by Lawende.

Just how incriminating this identification was depends upon the answers to three questions. When did it take place? Under what circumstances? And how confident was Lawende in the result? We do not have the information to furnish precise answers but the little that we do know, or can deduce, sheds great doubt upon the worth of Lawende's evidence.

The important clue to the date of the identification is Swanson's statement that it took place at the 'Seaside Home'. This is a reference to the Convalescent Police Seaside Home at 51 Clarendon Villas, West Brighton, officially opened by the Countess of Chichester in March 1890, and its use proves that the identification was made between March 1890 and 4 February 1891, when Kosminski was last committed to the workhouse. If Swanson is to be believed we can narrow it down still further. For his statement that Kosminski was committed to the workhouse, and from thence to Colney Hatch, 'in a very short time' after his return strongly suggests that we should place the identification nearer the latter than the former date. The upshot of all this is clear; Lawende did not identify Kosminski until two years or more after his original sighting.

It is difficult to understand why it was considered necessary to take Kosminski to the Seaside Home unless it was to escape the attentions of the London press. The venue, however, does give cause for disquiet concerning the circumstances of the identification. Was Kosminski picked out from a line-up, as he would have been, for example, at Leman or Commercial Street, or were suspect and witness, as Anderson perhaps implies, simply confronted with each other? The last method would have ensured a measure of secrecy but the value of any identification made under such circumstances would have been extremely doubtful. Victorian detectives do not appear to have been consistent in their approach to the identification of suspects. The line-up, as in the case of John Pizer, may have been usual, but circumstance sometimes dictated variations in the routine. In the Lipski case of 1887 Charles Moore was taken to the London Hospital to see if he could identify Lipski, then a patient, as the man to whom he had sold a bottle of nitric acid on the morning of the murder. He picked Lipski out but doubts about the validity of his identification were not settled during the trial when Moore admitted that before he had been allowed into the ward one police officer had already told him that he would most likely find his customer there and, worse, that although he was permitted to walk from bed to bed and look at the various patients Lipski had been the only one guarded by a policeman! The argument did not cease with Lipski's conviction. Inspector Final insisted that the constable guarding Lipski was 'a young man in plain clothes, and not brash like a constable', and that the identification was 'not open to exception'. A hospital nurse, on the other hand, contended that when Moore, Final and Detective Sergeant Thick came into the ward they 'were all together and, it seemed to me, went altogether direct to the foot of Lipski's bed.'[10]

Anderson claimed that his witness 'unhesitatingly' identified Kosminski 'the instant he was confronted with him'. But when we look at the circumstances of Lawende's original sighting of 1888 it is impossible to understand how this could have been so. He saw the Ripper, if indeed it was the Ripper, at 1.35 on the night of the double murder, 29–30 September 1888. The distance between them was not great, perhaps fifteen or sixteen feet, but the observation was a fleeting one, Lawende neither spoke to nor took especial interest in the man, and it was dark. More important, at a time when the incident was still fresh in his mind Lawende insisted repeatedly that he would not be able to recognize the man again. The contemporary records leave us in absolutely no doubt of it. 'I doubt whether I should know him again,' Lawende told the Eddowes inquest on 11 October 1888, less than two weeks after the sighting. He told the police the same thing. We know because Inspector McWilliam and Chief Inspector Swanson in their reports of 27 October and 6 November 1888 both explicitly said so. And Major Smith, writing in his memoirs of 1910, remembered it the same way. 'I could not "lead" him [Lawende] in any way. "You will easily recognize him, then," I said. "Oh no!" he replied; "I only had a short look at him".'[11]

It should now be clear why Lawende's identification of Kosminski cannot possibly be considered a conclusive or even persuasive piece of evidence. Anderson's book is seriously misleading on this point. He is expecting us to believe that Lawende, who saw the murderer but once, fleetingly and in a dimly lit street, and who admitted within two weeks that he would not be able to recognize him again, made a cast-iron identification of the culprit more than two years later! The notion, of course, is quite unacceptable and inevitably one wonders what pressures were brought to bear upon Lawende and why, despite them, he ultimately refused to give evidence against the suspect. Anderson and Swanson have it that he backed out when he learned that the suspect was a fellow Jew. Perhaps. But why, if the identification was sound, could not Lawende have been served with a subpoena compelling him to testify? One cannot help but speculate that Lawende was less sure of his identification than the police wanted him to be and that, when he discovered that they had no other evidence against Kosminski, his misgivings overwhelmed him. If so he was right to withdraw. His identification would not have stood up in court for a moment.

Nowhere does Anderson so much as hint that the witness who identified his suspect was used on any other occasion. Yet we have evidence that he was – twice.

In February 1891, after Kosminski had been lodged in Colney Hatch, Tom Sadler, the suspect in the Coles case, was put in a line-up to see if Lawende could identify him. He couldn't. But then, in the spring of 1895 the CID came up with another Ripper suspect in the person of William Grant Grainger. The *Pall Mall Gazette*, reporting their inquiries, says: 'there is one person whom the police believe to have actually seen the Whitechapel murderer with a woman a few minutes before that woman's dissected body was found in the street. That person is stated to have identified Grainger as the man he then saw. But obviously identification after so cursory a glance, and after the lapse of so long an interval, could not be reliable.'[12]

It would be fascinating to know who this witness was. For if the police considered Lawende an honest witness and were in touch with him as late as 1890–1 it is by no means unlikely that they were able to use him again in 1895. Indeed, careful scrutiny of the *Gazette* report indicates that the 1895 witness probably *was* Lawende. Mrs Long and Mary Cox can be ruled out because the witness was a man. Hutchinson is eliminated by the reference to the victim being found in the street. The best candidates, then, are PC Smith, Israel Schwartz and Joseph Lawende. But if the victim was 'dissected', as the *Gazette* says, we can discount the first two. They saw Liz Stride and her body, as is well-known, was not mutilated. All this leaves Kate Eddowes the victim and Lawende, once again, the witness.

It would be wrong to make too much of unsubstantiated news reports. Time and the loss of police records have buried the truth, probably forever. Nevertheless, the fact that Lawende was confronted with witnesses after he had identified Kosminski demonstrates that the first identification was anything but conclusive. And at the very least it is food for thought that he may have identified different men at different times. If it can be proved that Lawende did identify Grainger in 1895 his previous identification of Kosminski will be completely discredited.

Besides all this, the facts we have established on Kosminski raise serious difficulties for those who would identify him with the Ripper.

Take the question of his appearance. The little we know about this is soon said. His weight, recorded in May 1915, was only seven stone eight pounds and ten ounces, which suggests that he was small and slight of stature (he was said to have been in good bodily health as late as 1916). In 1888 he was twenty-three or twenty-four years old. He was a Polish Jew. And he was a hairdresser. Now it is true that these details are consistent with *some* of the observations reported by witnesses who may have seen the killer but, on the whole, what we know about Kosminski does not match their descriptions particularly well.

Our best witnesses concur that the murderer was of average or below average height. This fits our data on Kosminski. Build, however, is a problem. Only two important witnesses mention build. Lawende said that the man he saw was of medium build, which could fit Kosminski, but Schwartz described a stout, broad-shouldered man, which doesn't sound like him at all. Age is very difficult to estimate. Nevertheless the witnesses consistently described men who looked older than Kosminski is known to have been. And although two of the key witnesses did, indeed, accuse a foreigner neither can be said to have described Kosminski. He could fit Mrs Long's description of a 'shabby genteel' foreigner but not her estimate of age – over forty. George Hutchinson's man looked Jewish. But in this case Kosminski is seemingly ruled out both by the man's age (thirty-four or five) and by his obviously prosperous appearance. It might justifiably be argued the Mrs Long be discounted on age because she did not see her suspect's face. Hutchinson's middle-aged 'toff', however, would seem a world away from Anderson's young 'low-class' Polish barber. The other important witnesses (Smith, Schwartz and Lawende) did not indicate at the time that they had seen foreigners.

Although Kosminski's earnings as a hairdresser would not have enabled him to tog himself out like Hutchinson's man they might, as we have said, have financed the shabby genteel or respectable appearance reported by Long, Smith and Schwartz. There is, though, a real problem here in the case against Kosminski: we cannot be certain that he was working at hairdressing or anything else in 1888.

Among the symptoms of Kosminski's mental illness was a refusal to work and wash. We do not know when these particular symptoms first manifested themselves. In February 1891 Maurice Whitfield stated that Kosminski's first attack of insanity had occurred in 1890 and that the present attack had lasted six months. These details were entered in the male patients' casebook at Colney Hatch. But at some time during Kosminski's stay at the asylum the entry recording the duration of the present attack at time of admission was altered in the casebook from six months to six years and six years is also the period specified in the male admissions register. In other words Kosminski may have been exhibiting symptoms of mental illness since 1885. Jacob Cohen's statement in February 1891 certainly indicates that refusal to work had been a long-standing characteristic of his behaviour: 'He has not attempted any kind of work for years.' It is entirely on the cards, then, that in 1888 Kosminski was already dirty, dishevelled and out of work. In this condition his appearance would be irreconcilable with the descriptions given by Long, Smith or Schwartz, to say nothing of Hutchinson, and his circumstances would not square with our deduction, suggested by the dates and times of the murders, that the killer was in regular work.[13]

Kosminski's known acts of violence no more qualify him for the role of Jack the Ripper than his physical appearance. Certainly they fall far short of proving Macnaghten's claim that he was a homicidal lunatic with a deep hatred of women. His altercation with his (or Cohen's) sister, in which he is said to have menaced her with a knife, can hardly be considered significant by itself in the light of the great amount of domestic violence evidenced weekly in the Victorian police courts. And the workhouse and asylum records are very revealing. In 1891, when Kosminski was committed to Colney Hatch, Maurice Whitfield, the Relieving Officer at Mile End, explicitly stated that he was not considered dangerous to other people. Three years later, upon Kosminski's discharge from Colney Hatch to Leavesden, William Seward, Medical Superintendent at Colney Hatch, did the same. As late as 1910 the records of Leavesden Asylum were reiterating this belief. Clearly the authorities in these institutions never knew that their patient had been suspected of the Whitechapel murders and, notwithstanding the incident of the chair, nothing in his behaviour while under their care gave them reason to believe that he had homicidal tendencies. Typically he languished indolent and apathetic.

Then, again, we have no evidence that Kosminski possessed even an elementary degree of anatomical knowledge. This point would not, perhaps, have troubled Anderson because he was much influenced by Dr Bond, and Bond, in his report of 10 November 1888, asserted unequivocally that the murderer did not possess anatomical knowledge. Unfortunately Bond's opinion was not shared by any other medical expert who saw the wounds inflicted by the Ripper and whose judgement is on record. The rest seem to have subscribed to *some* degree of expertise, with Phillips and Brown attributing a great deal to the killers of Annie Chapman and Kate Eddowes respectively. Anderson's suspect thus retains credibility only if we are prepared to select the evidence that can be used to incriminate him and discount what remains.

Finally, whereas Druitt's death might explain the cessation of the crimes so neatly, Kosminski's incarceration took place more than two years after the Miller's Court murder. If Kosminski was the killer, therefore, we have to accept that after committing five if not six murders in three months he quietly went to ground and remained inactive for another two years three months. If we add Alice McKenzie to the Ripper's toll it still leaves us with a period of nineteen months between the last murder and Kosminski's committal to Colney Hatch to account for. It is by no means impossible that the Ripper remained at large and refrained from murder in order to avoid detection. But does Kosminski, foraging for bread in the gutter, drinking water from taps, dirty, unwilling if not unable to work and listening to his voices, sound like the type of man with the necessary cunning and discipline to have done so? Lawende's identification, it should be noted, cannot satisfactorily account for Kosminski's inactivity because, according to Swanson, it occurred only 'a very short time' before the committal to Colney Hatch.

If only because of Lawende we have to take Kosminski seriously. Nevertheless, the more we have discovered about this sad and pathetic suspect the less plausible the case against him has appeared. Its central strut – mentioned by Anderson, Swanson and Macnaghten – was the alleged identification but this, for all the reasons we have discussed, cannot possibly be regarded as satisfactory. What else the police had upon Kosminski it is impossible now to say. But to judge by the vagueness, even falsity, of the other circumstances alleged against him it was not very much. Macnaghten's claim that Kosminski had strong homicidal tendencies is not substantiated at all by the medical record. And Swanson's that the murders ceased *with* Kosminski's identification is patently untrue. On the present evidence the case against Kosminski is so extraordinarily flimsy that we have simply no alternative but to exonerate him.

Sir Robert Anderson thought otherwise – and said so in no uncertain terms. 'There was no doubt whatever as to the identity of the criminal' – '"undiscovered murders" are rare in London, and the "Jack-the-Ripper" crimes are not within that category' – 'in saying that he was a Polish Jew I am merely stating a definitely ascertained fact.' This is not the language of compromise. So our dismissal of Anderson's suspect inevitably raises questions about the worth of his writings as a source of historical information.

In accounts written long after the event lapses of memory are only to be expected. Anderson makes his fair share of such slips. His memoirs state, for example, that the police undertook their house-to-house search during his absence abroad. In truth it was conducted after his return to London. Again, he is inconsistent about the date of his return. Anderson's book tells us that, having decided to spend the last week of his holiday in Paris, he arrived in the French capital on the night of the double murder, and that, when the next day's post brought an urgent summons from Matthews to return to London, he complied. A letter he wrote to one of the daily papers in April 1910, however, maintains that he was actually on his way home from Paris the night Stride and Eddowes were slain.[14] The interesting thing about these memories is that neither was accurate. Contemporary documents prove that Anderson did not return to duty until nearly a week after the double murder.

Reminiscent accounts suffer, too, from the natural tendency of their authors to interpret the past in ways advantageous to themselves. And it is in the interpretation of his memories, rather than in simple errors of fact or chronology, that Anderson most misleads later students of the Ripper case. His book foisted five important myths upon them when it contended that:

(1) his policy of warning prostitutes that the police would not protect

them ended street murders in the Jack the Ripper series after the double event;

(2) the house-to-house inquiry led the police to believe that the Ripper was a low-class Polish Jew;

(3) subsequently Kosminski was identified by 'the only person who had ever had a good view of the murderer';

(4) although the witness refused to testify against Kosminski the identification was conclusive and solved the case;

(5) the identity of the writer of the original Jack the Ripper letter was conclusively established as that of a London journalist whom Anderson could name.

From contemporary and other evidence, every one of these contentions can be categorically refuted.

In his book Anderson explains that when he returned to London after the double murder he initiated a policy of warning prostitutes that the police would not protect them. He continues: 'However the fact may be explained, it is a fact that no other street murder occurred in the "Jack-the-Ripper" series. The last and most horrible of that maniac's crimes was committed in a house in Miller's Court on the 9th of November.'[15] The inference of these words is plain. Anderson is trying to suggest that his policy put an end to street murders by scaring Whitechapel whores off the streets.

The truth is that many of these women were compelled to solicit in the streets in order to raise money for their beds in common lodging houses. Admittedly, the terror unleashed by the double murder did temporarily diminish the number seen out at night as some sought refuge in casual wards and others fled to safer parts of the metropolis. But resilience the Whitechapel sisterhood had in abundance. And by the end of October they were back on the pavements of the East End. Mary Kelly herself picked up at least two clients in this way on the night she was killed. And as far as her murderer was concerned the fact that she turned out to possess a room of her own to which she could take him was probably an unlooked for bonus. It is impossible to find contemporary evidence that Anderson's heartless and politically impracticable proposal was ever implemented by the police let alone that it drove the prostitutes from the streets. The official response to the double murder was to afford them increased protection by drafting extra men into the murder district and maintaining them there throughout the crisis.

This subject is not directly linked with Kosminski. But the fact that Anderson was capable of interpreting events so perversely in order to claim credit for himself surely cautions us against accepting his other statements.

The house-to-house inquiry was completed on or about 18 October 1888. It did not persuade the police that the murders had been committed by a Jew. Indirect evidence to this effect is contained in reports Warren and Swanson prepared for the Home Office as late as 6 November. Both officers interpreted the chalked message left in Goulston Street – 'the Juwes are the men that will not be blamed for nothing' – as a deliberate subterfuge on the part of the murderer to throw the blame for his crimes upon the Jews. And the fact that they subscribed to this view implies, of course, that neither of them believed that the murderer himself was a Jew. Perhaps the clearest evidence that the house-to-house search did not incriminate the Jews, though, is furnished by a CID minute directed to Warren on 23 October, at least five days *after* the search. It mentioned the co-operation of the people of the East End, especially in permitting their homes to be searched, and acknowledged that, despite five successive murders, the CID were without 'the slightest clue of any kind'. The author of this frank admission of failure? None other than Anderson himself![16] No, for credible evidence that the Ripper may have been a Jew the police had to wait for George Hutchinson.

Anderson's statement that the witness who identified Kosminski was the 'only person who had ever had a good view of the murderer' is absurd. The witness, as I have demonstrated, was probably Lawende. But there were at least four other witnesses who were as likely to have seen the killer as he. And the evidence of three of them – Smith, Schwartz and Hutchinson – was arguably preferable. Although it is generally supposed that Lawende saw the Ripper talking with Kate Eddowes his evidence is open to the objection that since he did not see the woman's face he could not positively identify her as the Mitre Square victim. This type of criticism cannot fairly be levelled at the other three. Smith and Schwartz both identified Liz Stride's body as that of a woman they had seen in the company of a man in Berner Street shortly before the murder there, and Hutchinson, who described a man with Mary Kelly on the night of the Miller's Court murder, had known Mary for years. These witnesses enjoyed other advantages over Lawende. As a patrolling policeman, Smith was possibly a more careful observer. The great advantage of Schwartz's evidence was that the man he described had actually been seen attacking Stride. And Hutchinson took such an unusual and persistent interest in Mary Kelly's client as to enable him to describe the suspect in exceptional detail. Lawende, then, was merely one of five important witnesses and probably not the best at that. Nevertheless, he was the one who identified Kosminski and as such acquired special significance in the mind of Sir Robert Anderson, anxious as he was in his twilight years to believe that in this Polish Jew he had tracked down the murderer.

Incidentally, it is worth noting that back in 1888 neither Swanson, who synthesized the reports coming in from Abberline and the divisions, nor Anderson, who primarily drew upon Swanson, were in the best position to assess the relative values of the witnesses. It is to be doubted whether they saw, let alone interviewed, a single one of them. Abberline, who did interrogate them, who looked them in the eye, seems to have been particularly impressed by Hutchinson.

I have already shown that Lawende's identification of Kosminski cannot possibly have been conclusive. It is equally apparent that it was not *generally* regarded as such among those best qualified to judge.

Melville Macnaghten succeeded to the post of Chief Constable of the CID, the second highest office in the department, in 1890. If he was not himself a party to the Kosminski inquiry he must have been familiar with its findings. Yet, drafting his report of 1894, he explicitly exonerated Kosminski and opted for Druitt. Twenty years later, notwithstanding everything Anderson had written, Macnaghten's belief in Druitt's guilt remained unshaken and he reiterated it in his book *Days of My Years.*

Frederick George Abberline attained the rank of Chief Detective Inspector on 22 December 1890. His special knowledge of the East End, and of the Ripper investigation in particular, qualified him above all others to lead the Kosminski inquiry and although we have no documentary proof that he did it must be regarded as a strong probability. In any event, had conclusive evidence of Kosminski's guilt been procured it is inconceivable that Abberline would not have known about it. The two interviews he gave to the *Pall Mall Gazette* in March 1903 thus contain a formidable rebuttal of Anderson's assertions. 'You must understand,' the detective told the *Gazette* on 23 March, 'that we have never believed all those stories about Jack the Ripper being dead, or that he was a lunatic, or anything of that kind.' A week later he was even more categoric. 'You can state most emphatically,' he said, 'that Scotland Yard is really no wiser on the subject than it was fifteen years ago.' Warming to his theme, he refuted the Druitt theory, dismissed as 'another idle story' a rumour that the poisoner Thomas Neill Cream had been the Ripper and, in the following remarks, *may* have referred to Kosminski: 'I know that it has been stated in several quarters that "Jack the Ripper" was a man who died in a lunatic asylum a few years ago, but there is nothing at all of a tangible nature to support such a theory.' Abberline showed the reporter recent documentary evidence which proved that the case had never been solved and concluded in language as trenchant as any Anderson would later employ: 'No; the identity of the diabolical individual has yet to be established, notwithstanding the people who have produced these rumours and who pretend to know the state of the official mind.'[17]

Although Macnaghten and Abberline clearly did not share Anderson's view of Kosminski neither are known to have ever been personally critical of their ex-chief. When Anderson's memoirs were serialized in *Blackwood's*, however, they provoked an immediate and scathing riposte from Sir Henry Smith. Anderson's claim that the East End Jews protected the murderer as one of their own was denounced by Smith as a 'reckless accusation'. 'Surely,' he wrote, 'Sir Robert cannot believe that while the Jews ... were entering into this conspiracy to defeat the ends of justice, there was no one among them with sufficient knowledge of the criminal law to warn them of the risks they were running.' The latter were then considerable for in murder cases accessories after the fact were liable to penal servitude for life. Smith concluded his diatribe by recommending Anderson to read *Bleak House* and the Bible. Why? 'In the former book,' he explained, 'Mademoiselle Hortense, to divert suspicion from herself, writes "Lady Deadlock, Murderess" – with what result Inspector Bucket tells us. In the latter, Daniel interprets the writing on the wall which brought things to a crisis at Belshazzar's Feast.'[18] What Smith was saying, of course, was that if Anderson had correctly interpreted the Goulston Street writing as an attempt to throw the police off the scent of the real culprit he would have known that Jack the Ripper could not have been a Jew. There is more than a hint of personal and professional rivalry in Smith's account but his views cannot be dismissed lightly. We know from Swanson that the City CID actively participated in the Kosminski inquiry and by then

Smith had already succeeded Sir James Fraser as Commissioner of the City Police.

Macnaghten, Abberline and Smith. These men must have known the truth about Kosminski. Had the Ripper case been solved they would presumably have been only too glad to say so. So by disassociating themselves from Anderson on this point they demonstrated that his claim to have definitively identified the murderer was simply addle-headed nonsense. They were not alone. Thomas Arnold, interviewed upon his retirement as Superintendent of H Division in 1893, spoke of the Whitechapel murders as unsolved. Edmund Reid, who served in H Division as Head of CID between 1887 and 1896, clearly thought that Frances Coles, killed *after* Kosminski's committal to Colney Hatch, was the last victim of Jack the Ripper. In 1903 he dismissed Macnaghten's draft account of the three suspects, as served up by Griffiths, as 'full of inaccuracies'. And, after mooting a different theory of his own, John Littlechild, Head of the Special (Irish) Branch at the time of the murders, pointedly told George R. Sims in a personal letter of 1913 that Anderson 'only *"thought he knew"*.'[19]

Chief Inspector Swanson, a strong authority on the case, did endorse Anderson. Swanson enjoyed a particularly close friendship with Sir Robert, transmitting greetings to his 'dear former master' every Christmas until Anderson's death in 1918. Loyalty and a deep sense of personal obligation may have coloured his judgement. It is also possible that the Kosminski theory originated with Swanson rather than Anderson. If so Swanson's known comments suggest that he would have argued it with greater caution.[20] No matter, Anderson's claim that the case was solved by the unmasking of Kosminski cannot possibly be reconciled with the fact that inquiries continued until at least as late as 1895, with Macnaghten's assertion, in his official report of 1894, that 'many homicidal maniacs were suspected, but no shadow of proof could be thrown on any one', or with the undoubted fact that on the identity of the Whitechapel killer senior police officers continued to contradict each other in print well into the next century.

Anderson's contention that the identity of Jack the penman was *positively* established as that of a London journalist is equally untenable. I have dealt with this matter elsewhere[21] and need not reiterate the arguments but documentary evidence from the Scotland Yard files is there adduced which proves that as late as 1896, eight years after the murders, the police still did not know who had written the original letter and post card.

Anderson's memoirs do not seem to have enjoyed a high contemporary reputation. Winston Churchill, then Home Secretary, read them while they were being serialized in *Blackwood's* to determine whether Anderson should forfeit his police pension because of his disclosures of confidential information. He decided that to deprive Sir Robert of his pension would be to attach 'far too much importance to the articles and to their author' but noted that the articles did Anderson little credit. In particular he hit the nail right on the head when he told the Commons in April 1910 that the memoirs seemed 'to be written in a spirit of gross boastfulness . . . in the style of "How Bill Adams Won the Battle of Waterloo." The writer has been so anxious to show how important he was, how invariably he was right, and how much more he could tell if only his mouth was not what he was pleased to call closed.'[22] There is no doubt that the section on the Ripper crimes was very misleading indeed and Anderson may have made at least one other blunder when he implied that James Monro had sanctioned the 'Parnellism and Crime' articles he had written for the *Times* in 1887. Monro denied it: 'No such authority was asked by Mr Anderson, and none was given to him by me . . . A long time afterwards Mr Anderson informed me that he had written one or more of the articles, and I felt much annoyed.'[23]

None of this entitles us to dismiss Sir Robert as an arrant liar. A competent police chief, he was valued and respected by many of his colleagues, and he did not invent Kosminski. Why, then, did he write so misleadingly about him? We can but speculate. That irritating sense of self-importance detected by Churchill suggests part, but only part, of the answer. I incline to the belief that Anderson's errors of interpretation stemmed not from a wilful intent to deceive but from wishful thinking, that what he was doing was interpreting his memories of Kosminski in exactly the same way that Warren and Abberline had interpreted their clues on Jacob Isenschmid in 1888. They had found themselves propelling the mad pork butcher in the direction of the gallows because of the public clamour for a conviction. The pressures upon Anderson, though different, were productive of similar results.

By 1910 the Ripper murders had slipped into history. In writing their reminiscences, however, public servants naturally have no wish to depict themselves as fools or failures. And a man of Anderson's self-conceit would have found it especially difficult to concede a blow to his personal and professional pride as ignominious as the CID's inability to detect the Whitechapel killer. After all, this was the man who had recklessly boasted, after Polly Nichols' death, that he could personally unravel the mystery 'in a few days' provided he could devote his undivided attention to it.

It is not unreasonable to suppose that Anderson was also deeply galled by public criticism over the Ripper affair. Certainly he fumed – and not without reason – at the jibes of amateur sleuths like Dr Winslow, who freely dispensed blame and advice and pretended that they knew more than the police. About one such, Edward K. Larkins, Anderson wrote in 1893: 'Mr Larkins is a troublesome busybody whose vagaries on the subject of the Whitechapel murders have cost this department, the Public Prosecutor and the Foreign Office a great deal of trouble ... it is a mere waste of time attempting to deal with him on this subject.' And the same brand of derisive exasperation surfaced in his 1910 reminiscences. 'When the stolid English go in for a scare,' he observed tartly, 'they take leave of all moderation and common sense. If nonsense were solid, the nonsense that was talked and written about those murders would sink a *Dreadnought*.'[24]

Troubled by deafness and an increasing sense of isolation, his days occupied in quiet contemplation of the scriptures, his nights plagued by the attacks of 'blue devils', Sir Robert lived out his retirement at his home at 39 Linden Gardens, Hyde Park. He must sometimes have reflected there upon those hectic days at the Yard. And when he did it would doubtless have given him comfort to think, that whatever the world might say, he had laid the Ripper by the heels. Over the years, with the selective and faulty memory characteristic of advancing age, he came to believe it.

In supporting him, Swanson exhibited that same capacity for self-deception. 'After this [Kosminski's] identification which suspect knew,' he wrote, 'no other murder of this kind took place in London.' He had conveniently forgotten, of course, about the Ripper-type slaying of poor Frances Coles in February 1891, only six days after Kosminski had been 'caged' in his asylum. And if it be objected that Swanson was subscribing to the conventional view that Mary Kelly had been the Ripper's last victim, surely he should have made it clear that the crimes had ended, not *with* Kosminski's identification, but two years *before* it.

None of this mattered. Anderson and Swanson had come to inhabit a world of wish-dreams. And together they transformed a harmless imbecile, sheltering within the walls of Leavesden, into the most infamous murderer of modern times.

21

The Mad Russian: Michael Ostrog

THE THIRD MAN, named by Macnaghten as Michael Ostrog, was a thief and confidence trickster accustomed to living under numerous aliases.

In his draft report Macnaghten wrote:

> No: 3. Michael Ostrog, a mad Russian doctor & a convict & unquestionably a homicidal maniac. This man was said to have been habitually cruel to women, & for a long time was known to have carried about with him surgical knives & other instruments; his antecedents were of the very worst & his whereabouts at the time of the Whitechapel murders could never be satisfactorily accounted for. He is still alive.

The official version, preserved in the Scotland Yard files, is just two sentences long:

> (3) Michael Ostrog, a Russian doctor, and a convict, who was subsequently detained in a lunatic asylum as a homicidal maniac. This man's antecedents were of the worst possible type, and his whereabouts at the time of the murders could never be ascertained.[1]

Until recently nothing else was known about Ostrog, which is a mystery in itself because at the time of the Ripper murders the

Metropolitan Police publicized their interest in him in *The Police Gazette*, an obvious source for any student of the Whitechapel crimes. Six years ago, when I came to investigate the double murder, the *Gazette*'s notice of Ostrog was one of the first items I discovered and it led me to explore his long and colourful career in other contemporary records. In 1991, in the midst of this research, Paul Begg, Martin Fido and Keith Skinner, having discovered Ostrog independently, published a brief sketch of him in their book, *The Jack the Ripper A to Z*, and concluded that he was 'a plausible historical suspect'. Although accurate as far as it went their account left much unsaid. In particular, it failed to explain why Ostrog became a suspect in the first place and to notice the obvious weaknesses in the case against him. Weaknesses which, far from leaving him a 'plausible' suspect, come close to ruling him out of the reckoning altogether.

Ostrog's story has not been told in detail before. So first, just what do historical documents tell us about this elusive Russian?

We first hear of him in Oxford in 1863.

At the beginning of the year there was a spate of mysterious robberies at the university. Watches, purses, coats, indeed all manner of portable items, disappeared from the chapel, from college rooms and even from the dining hall. The police were called in and the thief turned out to be Ostrog, then representing himself to be Max Kaife Gosslar, a 27-year-old German student.

On 11 February he stole an opera glass and case at Oriel College from Charles Leir. Arrested at Cambridge six days later, he was returned to Oxford and tried for this offence at the county assize on 3 March. He pleaded guilty and was sentenced to ten months' hard labour in the House of Correction. A second indictment stood against Ostrog. This was for stealing a dressing case, two coats, a cape, a pair of trousers, a pair of silver cufflinks and a handkerchief from the Reverend George Price at New College, also on 11 February. But because he had admitted the first offence the second indictment was not proceeded with. Ostrog is described as a labourer in these indictments but this was conventional where the accused's occupation was at all uncertain.[2]

Shortly after his release Ostrog appeared at Bishop's Stortford. There he posed as Count Sobieski, the son of a fallen Polish nobleman, who had escaped from Warsaw after being sentenced, like his father, to end his days in Siberia. His melancholy story and well-bred and amiable manners won numerous friends.

To one tradesman he displayed all the money he had – one shilling and eight pence – and explained that he was in need of a hotel room, 'not grand' because his means were so precarious, but clean. The tradesman left his business to introduce the 'Polish count' personally to the landlord of the Coach and Horses, an adjoining hostelry. At the Coach and Horses Ostrog dined on the choicest fare the house could provide and was allocated the best spare bed. Better yet, the next morning the landlord told him that there was 'nothing to pay' and gave him a hearty shake of the hand, leaving in his palm a piece of gold to help him on the road. Another dupe, a professional gentleman, invited Ostrog to stay at his home. For four days he lived there as the 'star of the house'. And when he left the gentleman loaned him two or three sovereigns and went with him to the railway station to procure for him a first-class ticket for Cambridge.

At Cambridge he obtained money under false pretences from several of the undergraduates. One was Herbert Draper of Magdalene College. Ostrog came to his rooms and introduced himself as Max Sobieski, a Russian Pole of good family. Having escaped from the Russian authorities, he had, he said, just arrived in England from Amsterdam and had tramped penniless from Ipswich to Cambridge. He accounted for his knowledge of the language by explaining that he had been taught by an English governess when young. And so plausibly did he spin his heartrending yarn that Draper gave him a sovereign.

When Ostrog returned to Bishop's Stortford his friends found him a good deal wealthier than when he had left. Nevertheless, attending church one Sunday, he prevailed upon one of them to lend him a piece of silver so that he might contribute to the church restoration fund as a 'charitable Christian'.

Doubtless in hopes of further pickings, Ostrog then went back to Cambridge. It was a mistake. For while he had been absent at Bishop's Stortford Draper had begun to suspect him and had confided with Police Superintendent Turrall. When Ostrog's train pulled into the station at Cambridge the Russian found to his dismay that the superintendent was there waiting for him. On 2 February 1864 Ostrog was prosecuted as a rogue and a vagabond at Cambridge Police Court and sentenced to three months' imprisonment. Confronted by Draper in court, he protested: 'Did I not ask you only to *lend* the sovereign?' 'Whether you did or not,' replied Draper, 'I never expected to see it again.'[3]

The following summer an unrepentant Ostrog visited Tunbridge Wells. In the guise of Count Sobieski, a son of the late King of Poland, he claimed that he had been exiled by the Russian government because of his political beliefs. Young, tall and well-dressed, he would wander gloomily about, asking the band on the Parade to play the Polish national anthem or, whenever anyone would listen, reciting the wrongs and sufferings he had endured in the cause of his native land. Again, many were taken in. Gifts of money and property were bestowed upon him. It is even said that ladies became enamoured of the 'distinguished young exile'.

He was not so lucky in Tormoham, Devonshire, where he stole a silver-plated tankard from William Angleis on 16 December and obtained a sovereign, £2 in silver and a five-franc-piece from John Windeyer by false pretences three days later. Indicted under the names of Mutters Ostrogoc and John Sobieski at the Devonshire Quarter Sessions of January 1865, he pleaded guilty to both indictments and was sentenced to four months' imprisonment with hard labour for each offence.[4]

In the autumn of 1865 he appeared in Gloucestershire. A bundle of depositions relating to his activities there have survived in the county records and these enable us to reconstruct his progress in full.[5]

Calling himself Knuth Ostin, he turned up at the house of the Reverend Edward Brice of Newnham on 2 October. Let Brice take up the story:

> He said he called upon me as the clergyman of the parish as he was not known to anyone, that he had walked all the way from Chepstow that morning, that he was quite overcome with fatigue in consequence and that he had no means to procure refreshment or shelter. He said that he was a Swede and that he had been educated in the University of Heidelberg and that he had come away suddenly to escape the consequences of a duel. He said he came through Paris and arrived by a sailing vessel at Bristol. I sent for Mr. Lubbren who is a German and himself and Mr. Lubbren conversed in German and we found that he was a gentleman and highly educated and were induced to believe that his representations were correct.

Ostrog appeared destitute. Yet he persuaded Brice that he shortly expected to receive money from his mother, from a Miss Bourke at Bishop's Stortford and from various other people. The gullible clergyman believed every word of it and referred him to the Victoria Hotel in Newnham. More, he went there himself and bade George Hawkins, the landlord, make Ostrog comfortable until such time as the money should arrive.

Ostrog lodged at the Victoria for two weeks. He told Hawkins that Brice would pay the bills and Hawkins never questioned it. The landlord even loaned his guest £2 5s. 0d. of his own money on the understanding that Ostrog would use it to bring his luggage over from Torquay and make some small donations to the poor. Of the value of his luggage Ostrog spoke glowingly. Hawkins heard him speak of a portmanteau containing gold watches and other valuables. And Charlotte Averill, the barmaid, must have been simply overwhelmed when Ostrog casually informed her that his portmanteau was 'as long as the sofa in the bar', that the bar itself would not hold all his luggage!

The luggage never materialized. Worse, when the matter of Ostrog's bill was taken up with Reverend Brice the indignant clergyman refused to pay. Sergeant James Scott of the Newnham police arrested Ostrog on 23 October and he was lodged in Gloucester Gaol the next day. The gaol register gives his age as twenty-nine and his height as five feet ten and three-quarter inches. His complexion was dark and his hair and eyes brown. In January 1866 Ostrog was tried at the Gloucestershire Quarter Sessions for obtaining food, lodgings and money worth £7 14s. 0d. under false pretences from George Hawkins. He had a narrow escape. The evidence was judged insufficient and he was acquitted.

Soon after this escapade Ostrog turned up in Kent using the names Bertrand Ashley and Ashley Nabokoff. On 19 March 1866 he called at the house of Esther Carpenter in Maidstone under pretence of wishing to speak to a clergyman who lived there and stole a gold watch and other articles. The next day he took lodgings at the Globe Inn, Chatham. There he posed as a Polish exile once more and succeeded in ingratiating himself with the local gentry. One of these was Thomas Ayrton White of the military service at Chatham. When Ostrog visited him on 13 April White unwittingly showed him a gold cross attached to a watch-chain and then left the room. He was only out about five minutes. But the next morning he discovered that the cross had gone. At the end of April Ostrog left the Globe, taking a couple of books belonging to James Burch, the landlord, and took new lodgings at the Bull Inn, Rochester.

As in Tunbridge Wells he made attachments with women. Esther Brenchley of Rochester would testify that he was in the habit of calling at her house for a glass of ale. On 14 April he gave her a gold cross suspiciously like the one Thomas White had lost. He wanted, he said, to give her something 'in remembrance of him'. He was accompanied by a woman, too, when he took lodgings at the Bull. Because he left this establishment without settling his account George Wilson, the landlord, opened his portmanteau and there found the books stolen from the Globe.

Ostrog was brought to trial at the Kent Summer Assize in Maidstone in July 1866. A mixed jury of foreigners and Englishmen acquitted him of stealing the cross but convicted him of the theft of James Burch's books and the robbery of Esther Carpenter. These offences were no worse than those he had committed elsewhere. But the judge knew of his previous convictions and was determined to teach him a sharp lesson. He sentenced him to seven years' penal servitude for each offence, the sentences to run concurrently. Ostrog, reported the local paper, 'appeared astonished at the severity of the sentence but walked away with a firm step.'[6]

Unfortunately, Ostrog's penal servitude record has not survived. All we know is that in 1872 he was transferred to Chatham Prison and that he was released from there on licence on 23 May 1873.[7] He was soon up to his old tricks.

On 3 July 1873 he visited Woolwich barracks. There he gained access to the quarters of Captain F. W. Milner and stole a silver soap dish, a shaving pot, a glass toothbrush dish with a silver top and eleven studs worth, in all, about £5. But his greatest depredations were at Eton College. Four days after the Woolwich theft Ostrog took lodgings at the South Western Railway Hotel in Windsor. His gentlemanly appearance and plausible manner soon won him acceptance into polite society and his tales of misfortune elicited widespread sympathy. This time he passed himself off as a surgeon of the Russian navy or Imperial Guard who had been forced to flee his country after killing a man in a duel in St Petersburg. It was from Windsor that he made his visits to Eton.

He pilfered several items from the boys' apartments there. On 15 July he stole a silver cup valued at £4 10s. out of the room of Alfred Cooke. And on 28 September two silver cups and a coat, together worth £30, from that of John Ellison. Oscar Browning, one of the assistant masters, fell for his stories to the extent of giving him money and lending him books. Ostrog decamped with nearly a dozen books from his library. The titles are instructive. They included Smith's *Dictionary of Biography and Mythology*, Smith's *Dictionary of Geography*, a Spanish dictionary, a work by Darwin and a book of Latin quotations and indicate that Ostrog's pretensions to a good upbringing and superior education were not entirely unjustified.

In September he was in London, duping Dr Watkins O'Connor of Osnaburgh Terrace, Portland Road, with the same stories. He even inveigled O'Connor into pawning the cup he had stolen from Alfred Cooke. It was, he assured the doctor, a prize he had won at 'a boat race on the Neva' and he had erased the names from it to avoid discovery by the Russian detectives.

Ostrog was eventually arrested in October at the Fox and Goose Inn, Burton-on-Trent, by Police Superintendent Thomas Oswald. The incident is unique in Ostrog's record because it is the only one in which he is known to have resorted to violence. Oswald said later that he found his quarry in the dining room:

> Fearing the prisoner [Ostrog] would give some trouble witness [Oswald] threw the knives and forks to another part of the room, and showed him the *Police Gazette*, and charged him with stealing a silver cup at Eton. Prisoner replied that he had never been to Eton in his life, that he was a Swedish doctor and had visited Burton to see the breweries. He was taken into custody and had to be forced into a cab. On alighting at the police station he pulled a revolver out of his pocket, but witness seized it and turned it against him. The weapon had eight chambers and was loaded. He took the prisoner to Windsor and handed him over to the police there.[8]

Ostrog was tried at the Buckinghamshire Quarter Sessions held at Aylesbury in January 1874. Convicted of stealing Browning's books and of receiving, but not stealing, Cooke's silver cup, he received a sentence of ten years' penal servitude and seven years' police supervision. Given the relative pettiness of his crimes it was a hard sentence. But by then Ostrog seems to have given way to resignation and despair. 'I am sick of my life,' he protested at one point. 'Why do you go into the different charges? Why not give me my sentence and let me go? That is all I crave.' At another, addressing the Duke of Buckingham, who presided at the trial, he declared that he 'had taken poison and endeavoured to starve himself to death to no purpose, so that he did not care what became of himself.'

Ostrog was very much an oddity. The *Buckinghamshire Advertiser*, recording his conviction in 1874, put it well:

> Ostrog is no ordinary offender, but a man in the prime of life, with a clever head, a good education and polished manners, who would be certain to succeed in almost any honest line of life to which he might devote himself, but who, nevertheless, is an inveterate criminal. With natural and acquired abilities such as few men possess, and having before his eyes a warning in the shape of seven years' penal servitude to which he had been sentenced at Maidstone for felony, he nevertheless risked his liberty and forfeited a position which he had obtained in respectable society, by pilfering a few books and a silver cup, worth to him about £5. The case is altogether a psychological puzzle. It is impossible to gauge the mental condition of a man of such intellectual and personal advantages, who would run the risk of ten years' penal servitude for such a miserable stake.[9]

Ostrog spent the next decade in various government prisons but no detailed record now seems to exist. From Aylesbury Gaol, where he had been held during the trial period, he was sent to Pentonville. Received there on 28 January, he was discharged to Millbank just three days later. Ostrog was held at Millbank from 2 February to 11 September 1874. On the last date he was transferred to Portland Prison and he was still there in 1876 when our records fail. Prison registers describe him as a surgeon and forty years of age at the time of his conviction. His religion is given as Roman Catholic. Although his behaviour is often noted as good it is clear that he could sometimes be troublesome. While at Millbank his name was twice entered in the misconduct book and the Governor of Portland Prison, too, occasionally refers to him being punished in his journals.[10]

On 28 August 1883 Ostrog was released on licence. Within two months he was wanted by the Metropolitan Police for failing to report to them regularly. They circulated his description in the *Police Gazette* and from it we learn that he was five feet eleven inches tall, had dark-brown hair, grey eyes and a dark complexion, and bore flogging marks on his back. He was considered to be fifty years of age.[11]

We glimpse no more of Ostrog for four years. Then, on 19 July

1887, we find him at his old trade. At about four in the afternoon George Bigge, a cadet at the Royal Military Academy, Woolwich, was lying on his bed resting a sprained ankle. The door opened and Ostrog, wearing india-rubber sports shoes, stealthily entered the room. Not noticing Bigge, whose bed was behind the door, he took a metal tankard from the mantelpiece, put it in his bag and went out. Crippled as he was, Bigge followed him and knocked him down. Ostrog abandoned his bag and hat and made off across Woolwich Common. Bigge could pursue him no further. But several other cadets did. And PC Frank Mulvey, on duty on the common at the time, saw the chase and joined in. After running about a mile the constable met some of the cadets, with Ostrog under guard, coming back. 'I know I have made a mistake,' Ostrog told Mulvey. 'I am a gentleman. Don't press the charge on account of my family, not on account of myself.'

Ostrog, indeed, appears to have been terrified of another long prison sentence. While being taken to the police station he either took poison or pretended to have done so and had to be taken to the Miller Hospital in Greenwich until well enough to go before a magistrate. Then, when being conducted to gaol on remand, he tried to throw himself under a train and nearly dragged a boy to whom he had been handcuffed with him.

These desperate measures availed him little. On 9 August Justice Marsham of Woolwich Police Court committed him to Newgate for trial at the Central Criminal Court. And there, in September, he was convicted under the name of Claude Cayton for stealing the tankard, valued at ten shillings, and sentenced to six months' imprisonment with hard labour.

During his various court appearances Ostrog displayed signs of insanity. PC Mulvey didn't believe them genuine. 'He was quite sane then [when apprehended],' he told the Central Criminal Court, 'but now he is putting it on.' Dr Herbert Hillier agreed: 'I was called to see the prisoner at the police station. He showed no signs of insanity then. I saw him again a week afterwards and he was behaving the same as he is now. He is merely shamming.' Nevertheless, on 26 September, Ostrog was certified insane. And four days later he was transferred from Wandsworth Prison to the Surrey County Lunatic Asylum in Tooting. In the admission register he is recorded as a Jewish surgeon. Having served his sentence, he was discharged 'recovered' on 10 March 1888.[12]

It is not quite the last we hear of him. For on 26 October 1888, in the midst of the Ripper affair, his description was published in the *Police Gazette* once more for failing to report. This notice described Ostrog as a Polish Jew and said that he was about fifty-five years of age and 'generally dressed in a semi-clerical suit'. It concluded with the words: 'Special attention is called to this dangerous man.'

The *Gazette*'s notice proves that the police were seeking Ostrog at the time of the Whitechapel murders. Were the two events connected? Almost certainly.

It is true that the notice does not mention the murders. But since the police never appear to have possessed any tangible evidence to link Ostrog with the crimes, and since they were probably anxious that their inquiries maintain a low profile, this is scarcely surprising. It is also true that convicts under police supervision were routinely described in the *Gazette* for failure to report. But why, if Ostrog had failed to report, did the police delay more than seven months after his release to advertise their interest in him? And why did they direct 'special attention' to a man convicted of nothing more serious than the theft of a metal tankard?

It is highly probable that it *was* the Ripper scare that gave urgency to the need to locate Ostrog. For Macnaghten has it that attempts to establish Ostrog's whereabouts were linked to the Ripper case, and the timing of the *Gazette*'s notice is surely significant – three weeks after the double event, when the police were under the fiercest pressure to detect the culprit, and hard on the heels of systematic inquiries about patients discharged from lunatic asylums.

Ostrog, then, was the only one of Macnaghten's three names who actually fell under suspicion before the murders had run their course. Why was he suspected?

The answer to that question is relatively obvious once the state of police knowledge in the aftermath of the double murder is borne in mind. By then two police surgeons – Phillips and Gordon Brown – had testified to a considerable degree of surgical skill and anatomical knowledge on the part of the murderer. And the indiscriminate nature of the injuries inflicted upon Kate Eddowes had strengthened the hand of those who contended that the culprit would prove a lunatic. Sir James Risdon Bennett, President of the Royal College of Physicians, and Doctors L. Forbes Winslow, Edgar Sheppard, Frederick William Blackwell and Gordon Brown had all pointed the finger at a lunatic killer within days of the double murder.

Faced with such an impressive array of expert opinion, the police inevitably continued to accord much priority to suspects in possession of anatomical knowledge and to lunatics. There were detailed inquiries at hospitals and amongst butchers and slaughtermen at this time. Even more significant, at least for any consideration of Ostrog, there were visits to asylums.

Soon after the Chapman murder Dr Winslow had been interviewed at Scotland Yard and had urged the Metropolitan Police to call for returns of lunatics recently escaped or discharged from asylums. Perhaps, when the Eddowes killing brought the City Police into the hunt, he tendered them the same advice. On 2 October, just two days after the murder, he sent the following telegram to Sir James Fraser, Commissioner of the City force: 'My services are placed at your disposal.'[13] We do not know the outcome of Winslow's attempted intervention. But there is no doubt that the City Police did make such inquiries. For Inspector McWilliam, in his report of 27 October, told the Home Office that he had 'sent officers to all the lunatic asylums in London to make enquiry respecting persons recently admitted or discharged: many persons being of opinion that these crimes are of too revolting a character to have been committed by a sane person.'[14]

Walter Dew, writing in 1938, retained vivid memories of an even wider search by the Metropolitan Police. 'One of the strongest inferences to be deduced from the crimes,' he said, 'was that the man we were hunting was probably a sexual maniac. This angle of investigation was pursued relentlessly. Inquiries were made at asylums all over the country, including the Criminal Lunatic Asylum at Broadmoor, with the object of discovering whether a homicidal lunatic had been released as cured about the time the Ripper crimes commenced.'[15] Unfortunately, Dew's memory cannot be precisely dated and Chief Inspector Swanson's summary reports on the murders curiously make no reference to inquiries at lunatic asylums. The CID were, nevertheless, fully aware of City Police efforts in the area. On 9 October Warren wrote to Fraser proposing daily conferences between Metropolitan and City detectives to avoid 'our working doubly over the same ground.' These were evidently established. At the beginning of November Swanson noted that the inquiries 'of the City Police are merged into those of the Metropolitan Police, each force cordially communicating to the other daily the nature and subject of their enquiries.'[16]

Against the background of these investigations it should be clear why Ostrog fell under suspicion. His pretensions to medical knowledge, his discharge from an asylum less than six months before the murders began, and his long criminal record marked him out as an obvious possibility for detectives to check out. Doubtless there were other similar names on their list. But after his discharge from the Surrey asylum, Ostrog could not be traced and the police could not, therefore, eliminate him from their inquiries. It was for this reason, and because the Ripper crimes were never conclusively brought home to anyone else, that his name survived on police files as a possible suspect.

Some writers assume that the police must have possessed tangible evidence against Ostrog. This is a naive view. Consider Macnaghten's comments. From them we can reasonably infer that the CID did not have any hard evidence linking Ostrog with the murders. Had they such information Macnaghten, in a confidential report, would surely have said so. Instead he was reduced to the citation of alleged aspects of Ostrog's personality and criminal past – he was said to be habitually cruel to women, he sometimes carried surgical knives and instruments about with him, etc. – in order to justify his inclusion as a suspect. Still more telling, Macnaghten explicitly admitted that Ostrog's whereabouts at the time of the murders 'could never be ascertained'. This means, in short, that the police held no satisfactory evidence to connect Ostrog with Whitechapel, let alone the murders, in the autumn of 1888.

We are now presented with a final, crucial question? Is Ostrog, in the light of what we now know, likely to have been Jack the Ripper? Without a doubt the answer has got to be: No.

First, since Ostrog was an incorrigible liar and confidence trickster even the qualities that brought him under suspicion – his medical knowledge and insanity – cannot be taken for granted. His claims to have been a former surgeon need have had no greater substance than that to have been an exiled son of the King of Poland. It is interesting, too, that his mental illness manifested itself suddenly in 1887. At this time Ostrog was in custody for the theft of George Bigge's tankard and the police were convinced that his odd behaviour was part of a ploy for lenient treatment in court. Since Ostrog passed himself off regularly as a medical man (his aliases included Dr Bonge and Dr Grant) it is quite likely that he did possess some degree of medical knowledge. However, before we can seriously accuse him of the Whitechapel murders it is important that further research clarifies such points. About one aspect of the Russian's character there is no doubt. Well-educated and genteel, he displayed a remarkable capacity for deception. Such a quality could unquestionably have served the Ripper well in reassuring potential victims and, if necessary, hoodwinking police constables who stopped him while he was making his escape. Nevertheless, possible medical expertise, a short detention in a lunatic asylum and a talent for confidence trickery are far from adequate grounds for supposing that Ostrog was the murderer.

Macnaghten undoubtedly did consider Ostrog a serious suspect in the Ripper case as late as 1894. But our evidence demonstrates that almost everything he wrote about him was misleading if not completely wrong.

We have covered every one of Ostrog's criminal convictions. He cozened people out of money and goods by telling hard luck stories. He stole valuables when their owners weren't looking. And he didn't return his library books. Not a record to be proud of, certainly, but far from being one 'of the worst possible type', as Macnaghten would have us believe. Macnaghten tells us, too, that Ostrog was 'unquestionably a homicidal maniac' and was 'said to have been habitually cruel to women'. But his criminal record does not substantiate either of these claims. In 1873, resisting arrest and the probability of a long prison sentence, Ostrog menaced Superintendent Oswald with a revolver, but neither his general behaviour nor the manner of his crimes suggest anything like a propensity to violence. There is no record of any attempt by him to attack or molest a woman. Macnaghten's assertion that Ostrog sometimes carried surgical knives and other instruments about with him may well be equally misleading. For in the context of a report about the Ripper murders the natural inference is that these items were being carried about with intent to murder and mutilate. In fact, as a glance at Ostrog's career will attest, he repeatedly posed as a surgeon or doctor, and a doctor's bag, complete with instruments, would have been a basic prop to any such disguise.

The most serious objection to Ostrog as a Ripper candidate – and to my mind it is near conclusive – is that his known appearance just cannot be reconciled with the descriptions supplied by witnesses who saw the murderer with one or other of his victims.

These witnesses, as we have seen, indicate that the Ripper was a man in his twenties or thirties. Now, Ostrog's age in 1888 is uncertain. The Russian was as dishonest about his age as he was about almost everything else and contemporary documents credit him with at least eight different birth dates ranging from 1833 to 1848. However, our last record – the *Police Gazette* of 26 October 1888 – reports his age as fifty-five and a surviving photograph, probably taken in 1883, depicts a man who could have been even older. It shows a man with a receding hairline, a lined face and sunken cheeks, a man who might conceivably be in his fifties, even in his sixties, but a man who could never have been consistently mistaken for one of twenty-eight to thirty-five.

We may not know Ostrog's precise age in 1888 but we do know that he was a tall man. Police sources record his height as five feet eleven inches. This was well above the average for men at a time when people were generally smaller than they are today. John Beddoe, in his survey of 1870, estimated the average height of adult Englishmen at between five feet six inches and five feet seven inches, an estimate that is perhaps too generous in that his research was heavily reliant upon data derived from military recruits. And in 1888 Mr A. E. Knowles, an ex-Pinkerton detective, suggested that the CID be reinforced by a team of civilian detectives, no taller than five feet seven because 'a person over that stature attracts attention.'[17]

At five feet eleven Ostrog would have been only too conspicuous. Yet our witnesses are broadly consistent in describing the Ripper as a man of average or below average height. Especially revealing, perhaps, is the testimony of those who explicitly compared his height to that of a victim. Both Annie Chapman and Kate Eddowes are known to have been only about five feet tall. Ostrog would have towered almost a foot above either of them. Yet Mrs Long, who saw Annie with a man in Hanbury Street only minutes before the time she must have been murdered, thought that the man stood only 'a little taller' than Annie. And Joseph Hyam Levy, Lawende's companion on the night of the double murder, thought that the man they saw talking with a woman (probably Kate) near Mitre Square was only 'about 3 inches taller than the woman.'[18]

Although Ostrog is the least plausible of Macnaghten's three names there is no shirking the fact that a credible case cannot be made against a single one of them.

Ever since Dan Farson turned up the Chief Constable's report more than thirty years ago it has dominated serious discussion of the identity of Jack the Ripper. With very few exceptions students have assumed that Macnaghten reflected the official view of the CID and that his choices were considered ones, the result of a careful weeding-out process. It is now clear that these assumptions were unsound.

There was no consensus within the CID about the Ripper's identity. Indeed, recorded opinions of officers who worked on the case reveal widespread disagreement on the point. Macnaghten's comments, moreover, seem to have owed as much to his personal theorizing as to the views of his colleagues. Only one of his three names is known to have been seriously suspected by anyone else. There is no doubt, too, that Macnaghten was ill-informed, both about the crimes and about the men he accused. We know far more about Druitt, Kosminski and Ostrog now than he did then, and what we know strongly suggests that all three were innocent. Macnaghten was right to refute the *Sun*'s preposterous claims about Thomas Cutbush. But in advancing alternatives he grasped at straws.

Inspector Abberline, the man at the heart of the Whitechapel investigation, would have none of Macnaghten's names. 'You can state most emphatically,' he said in 1903, 'that Scotland Yard is really no wiser on the subject than it was fifteen years ago.'

By then, however, the inspector was beginning to develop theories of his own.

22

'You've got Jack the Ripper
at last!': George Chapman

WITHOUT A DOUBT Chief Inspector Frederick George Abberline has become the most celebrated of all the detectives that hunted Jack the Ripper.

This may be an historical injustice but Abberline was by no means just another officer on the case. He was marked out by outstanding ability. When he retired from the Metropolitan Police in 1892 he had received no less than eighty-four commendations and awards, close, he thought, to a record, and for another twelve years he earned fresh laurels as a private inquiry agent, accepting in 1898 the European agency of the world-famous Pinkerton organization.

It is probable that he possessed, moreover, a more intimate knowledge of the Whitechapel murders than any other officer in the Metropolitan Police. Donald Swanson, it is true, amassed a vast knowledge by processing the reports sent in to headquarters. But it was Abberline who co-ordinated the divisional investigations on the ground, searching murder sites for clues, interrogating witnesses and suspects, following up the multitudinous leads proffered by the public, turning out daily, and sometimes nightly too, to supervise his staff or to patrol the streets of Whitechapel. His was a knowledge that could not be acquired from behind a desk. It was, if not unique, extraordinarily comprehensive, backed by fourteen years' experience in Whitechapel, nearly ten of them as local head of CID.

Recent writers, anxious to promote theories suggested in the writings of Macnaghten or Anderson, have sometimes found it necessary to disparage Abberline's knowledge or contribution to the case. His pivotal importance in the Ripper inquiry, however, is well illustrated by the Yard's response to Matthews' query about the witness Israel Schwartz.

Perusing a report on the Berner Street murder, Matthews wondered whether the man Schwartz claimed to have seen attacking Liz Stride used the word 'Lipski!' as 'a mere ejaculation, meaning in mockery "I am going to 'Lipski' the woman"' or whether he was calling to 'a man [an accomplice] across the road by his proper name.' This query was transmitted to Warren on 29 October 1888 and the Commissioner duly passed it on to Anderson.

But neither Anderson nor Swanson were capable of making such judgements. Swanson's knowledge of the murders was encyclopaedic but mainly confined to what he had read in incoming reports, a serious limitation reflected, for example, in such comments as 'if Schwartz is to be believed, and the police report of his statement casts no doubt upon it . . .' Inevitably the Home Secretary's query was referred to Abberline, the officer who had interrogated Schwartz and who had followed up the leads he presented. In his reply Abberline expressed the view that the man Schwartz saw attacking a woman in Berner Street had shouted 'Lipski!' at Schwartz himself. For Schwartz had a strong Jewish appearance and in the East End the name Lipski had become an epithet applied to Jews after the conviction of Israel Lipski, a Polish Jew, for murder in 1887. Abberline's interpretation of Schwartz's evidence was adopted by the Yard. On 5 November it was incorporated virtually unchanged into a draft reply to the Home Office, prepared by Anderson, and the next day was sent to the Under Secretary of State there by Warren.[1]

There was thus no more authoritative voice on the Whitechapel murders than that of Abberline. Indeed, it is even possible, as Donald Rumbelow has suggested, that the file on these crimes was officially closed in 1892 because that was the year when Abberline, the investigating officer, retired.

For this reason the recent discovery by Martin Howells and Keith Skinner of two interviews the detective gave to the *Pall Mall Gazette* in 1903[2] is more important than those two authors realized. Howells and Skinner were primarily interested in Druitt. And certainly Abberline's dismissals of Druitt and others were well worth finding. But the central thrust and principle value of the

Gazette interviews lies in Abberline's indictment of an altogether different suspect – George Chapman, the Polish multiple murderer hanged in 1903.

Sixty years ago Hargrave L. Adam carefully documented the Chapman case for the Notable British Trials series. At that time, however, the official records were closed to public access. When I began to investigate the story for myself I soon learned that since then many important documents have disappeared. Nevertheless, a wealth of Chapman material still does exist – in the records of Southwark Coroner's Court, the Central Criminal Court, the Home Office and elsewhere. Studiously ignored by all previous writers on both Jack the Ripper and Chapman, they have been searched for the present work and enable us to bring the figure of the sinister Pole into sharper focus.[3]

Chapman's real name was Severin Klosowski. The son of a carpenter, he was born in the village of Nagornak, Poland, in 1865. In 1880 his parents apprenticed him to Moshko Rappaport, Senior Surgeon in Zvolen, and he faithfully served his apprenticeship until 1885, when he went to Warsaw armed with a certificate signed by Rappaport to the effect that he was 'diligent, of exemplary conduct, and studied with zeal the science of surgery'. An eyewitness testified that during his apprenticeship Klosowski had rendered 'very skilful assistance to patients – i.e., in cupping by means of glasses, leeches, and other assistance comprised in the science of surgery', which suggests, perhaps, that his training didn't amount to much. Nevertheless, for two more years he worked in Poland as an assistant-surgeon or *feldscher* and during the last quarter of 1885 attended a practical course in surgery at the Praga Hospital, Warsaw.

We know from a receipt for hospital fees paid by Chapman at Warsaw that he was still in Poland in February 1887. But soon after that he emigrated to London.

Chapman's movements in the East End are central to any consideration of the claim that he was Jack the Ripper. In 1887 or early the following year he took a position as assistant hairdresser in the shop of Abraham Radin at 70 West India Dock Road. He stayed in this job about five months. During that time Mrs Radin's eldest son fell ill and Chapman helped to nurse him.[4]

We next find him running a hairdresser's shop of his own at 126 Cable Street, St George's-in-the-East. He is listed at this address in the *Post Office London Directory* of 1889 so was probably living there in the autumn of 1888 when the Ripper murders occurred.

In October 1889 Chapman married a Polish woman named Lucy Baderski. The ceremony was performed in accordance with the rites of the German Roman Catholics. At this time he was still in Cable Street. But in 1890 Wolff Levisohn, a traveller in hairdresser's appliances, met him in a barber's shop in the basement of the White Hart public house, 89 Whitechapel High Street.

Levisohn gave evidence against Chapman at Southwark Police Court in January 1903. According to his testimony, Chapman was calling himself Ludwig Zagowski in 1890 and speaking a mixture of Polish and Yiddish. At first he worked as an assistant at the shop under the White Hart. He may have been lodging with his employer but Levisohn did not think so. 'I believe prisoner [Chapman] was living in Greenfield Street near Commercial Road,' he said, '[but] I never visited him there.' However, by September 1890, when Lucy bore Chapman a son, he had become the proprietor of the shop and had taken her to live there.

What did Chapman look like in the autumn of 1888? Of medium height, he had blue eyes and dark hair and was nearly twenty-three years old. In his later years he sported a formidable moustache turned up at the ends. Whether this was so in 1888 it is impossible now to say. But by 1890 he had already begun to cultivate a taste for fastidious dressing, complete with black coat, patent boots and high hat. Thus, when Levisohn saw him in the dock at Southwark, he is credited with the outburst: 'There he sits! That is his description. He has not altered from the day he came to England; he has not even a grey hair. Always the same – same la-di-da, 'igh 'at and umbrella.'[5]

The baby son, Wladyslaw or Wohystaw Klosowski, died of 'pneumonia asthenia' on 3 March 1891. Chapman and Lucy were then living at 2 Tewkesbury Buildings, Whitechapel. They were still there a month later when the national census of 1891 was taken. But soon after that they emigrated to New York. Their names have not yet been traced on surviving passenger lists[6] but it seems likely that it was the loss of their son that triggered their decision and that they made the passage in April 1891.

Chapman eventually established himself in a barber's shop in Jersey City. There the couple quarrelled. The rift is said to have been caused by Chapman's attentions to other women but no details are preserved. Whatever it was, Chapman attacked Lucy with a knife and Lucy, pregnant and terrified, returned to London without him in February

1892. She found refuge with her sister at 26 Scarborough Street, Whitechapel, and her second child, Cecilia, was born there on 15 May. Then, about a fortnight after that, Chapman reappeared in the East End.

A reunion with Lucy was short-lived. In 1893 Chapman found a new consort. Her name was Annie Chapman (not to be confused with the Ripper victim of the same name) and they met in Haddin's hairdresser shop at 5 West Green Road, South Tottenham, where Chapman himself then worked as an assistant. For about a year they lived together. But towards the end of 1894 Chapman brought another woman home with him and insisted that she share their lodging. This *ménage à trois* fell apart when Annie walked out some weeks later. By that time, however, she was pregnant, and in January or February 1895 she was obliged to seek Chapman out to tell him and solicit his support. 'When I told him I was going to have a baby,' Annie recalled eight years later, 'he did not take much notice.' Even so Annie fared much better than any of Chapman's other 'wives'. And from her the barber's assistant borrowed the name by which he would become notorious. He never admitted to being Severin Klosowski again.

Later in 1895 Chapman obtained a situation as assistant in William Wenzel's barber shop at 7 Church Lane, Leytonstone. While at Leytonstone he lodged at the house of John Ward in Forest Road and it was probably there that he first made the acquaintance of Mrs Mary Isabella Spink, a married woman living apart from her husband, for Mrs Spink was a lodger in the same house. The lodgers were soon conducting an indiscreet affair and Ward had occasion to upbraid Chapman about it.

'My wife has seen you kissing Mrs Spink,' he began. 'We cannot allow that sort of thing to go on in the house.'

'It's all right, Mr Ward,' replied Chapman, 'we are going to get married about Sunday week.'

When the day came, Sunday 27 October 1895, Chapman and Spink left the house early in the morning. Chapman, who posed as a Jew (he was, in fact, a Roman Catholic), told the Wards that they were going to Whitechapel to get married. They returned that night and Chapman, ushering Mrs Spink into the presence of the Wards, said: 'Allow me to present you to my wife.' Mrs Ward asked to see the certificate but Chapman waved her away. 'Oh,' he said, 'our laws are different to your laws.'

Wherever Chapman went that day he did not marry Mrs Spink

because the marriage registers at St Catherine's House contain no record of such a ceremony. Nevertheless, it was a subterfuge Chapman would employ successfully time and again.

Mary Spink seems to have been almost mesmerized by Chapman. She cohabited with him, entered into a bogus marriage with him and, amazingly, made the proceeds of a £500 legacy over to him. With part of the money he took the lease of a barber's shop in George Street, Hastings, in 1896.

The Chapmans prospered in Hastings. Mary lathered the customers and, while George shaved them, entertained the clientele by playing a piano installed in the front of the shop. The popularity of these 'musical shaves' was such that Chapman was able to buy a sailing boat. He named her the 'Mosquito' and, although his nautical adventures were confined to short cruises along the coast, boasted to his customers that he would sail her to Boulogne. Behind the facade, however, all was not well in the Chapman household.

Mrs Annie Helsdown, who lodged in the same house as the Chapmans in Hill Street, occasionally heard Mary cry out. Sometimes Mary's face bore the marks of blows and on at least one occasion she showed Annie marks around her throat.[7] More ominous still, Chapman began to pay court to Alice Penfold, a domestic servant, telling her that he was a single man and the manager of a pianoforte shop. On 3 April 1897 he walked into the shop of William Davidson, a chemist in the High Street, and purchased one ounce of tartar-emetic.

Tartar-emetic, a white powder soluble in water, contains antimony. With his knowledge of medicine Chapman had plumped upon what, from a murderer's point of view, was in many respects an ideal poison. For antimony is colourless, odourless, practically tasteless and, in the form of tartar-emetic, easily soluble in water. Furthermore, in Chapman's time its properties were little known, even to many physicians, so that it might be administered by the poisoner in relative safety in cases where the use of arsenic or strychnine would have been foolhardy. Given in a large dose antimony is likely to cause vomiting and be expelled. For this reason Chapman opted to torture Mary Spink to death with comparatively small doses repeated over time. Unfortunately for him there was one effect of the poison of which even he seems to have been unaware. Administered during the lifetime of a victim it preserves the body from decomposition long after death. Chapman had made a fatal mistake.

In 1897 Chapman returned to London and took the lease of

the Prince of Wales public house in Bartholomew Square, off the City Road. There a transformation in Mary's health took place. Formerly rather stout, fresh-complexioned and strong, she was now tormented by violent stomach pains, spewed green vomit, suffered from diarrhoea and grew emaciated and exhausted. A physician, Dr J. F. Rodgers, was called in to attend her but it was Chapman who prepared and administered the medicines prescribed. By Christmas Mary was close to death.

Neither Elizabeth Waymark nor Martha Doubleday, who nursed Mary, were impressed by Chapman's concern. Elizabeth remembered that on Christmas Day, the last day, she sent downstairs several times for Chapman: 'At first he did not come up, and when he did she [Mary] said to him, "Do kiss me". She put her arms out for him to bend over to kiss her but he did not do so. The last time I sent for him just before she died he did not come up in time. I prepared the body for burial. It was a mere skeleton.'

When Martha Doubleday realized that Mary's life was slipping away she, too, alerted Chapman. 'Chapman,' she cried, 'come up quickly! Your wife is dying!' By the time Chapman got there Mary was dead. He stood at her bedside, looked down at her body and said 'Polly, Polly, speak!' Then he went into the next room and cried. After that he went downstairs and opened the pub. 'You are never going to open the house today?' Martha protested. 'Yes, I am,' said Chapman.

Dr Rodgers certified the cause of death as phthisis.

A few months after Mary's death Chapman advertised for a barmaid and engaged former restaurant manageress Bessie Taylor. Then history repeated itself. As in the case of Mary Spink there was a bogus marriage. There was the same abuse by Chapman. According to Elizabeth Painter, Bessie's longtime friend, Chapman shouted and threw things at Bessie and on one occasion threatened her with a revolver.[8] After three years Bessie succumbed to the same wasting illness.

During that final illness Mrs Painter visited Bessie almost every evening at the Monument public house in Union Street, Southwark, which Chapman had leased from the Bridge House Estates Committee. Although overtly attentive to Bessie's needs Chapman was wont to indulge in callous jests at Mrs Painter's expense. Sometimes, when she came into the house and asked how Bessie was, he would tell her: 'Your friend is dead.' Then, when Mrs Painter went upstairs, she would find Bessie alive. On 7 February 1901 Bessie seemed better and Mrs Painter didn't call again until the 14th. On that occasion, however, she found Chapman in the bar parlour. He said that Bessie was 'much about the same'. But when Mrs Painter went up she found that Bessie had died the previous day.

Dr James Stoker certified the cause of death as intestinal obstruction, vomiting and exhaustion.

In August 1901 Chapman hired eighteen-year-old Maud Marsh as his new barmaid at the Monument. Soon he persuaded her to collude with him in the now well-rehearsed ritual of the bogus marriage, a stratagem that seems to have completely deceived Maud's parents, and before Christmas they were ensconced as man and wife at the Crown, 213 Borough High Street. Maud was to be his last victim.

By the summer of 1902 Chapman had tired of his young 'bride'. In June he engaged one Florence Rayner as a barmaid. As she frankly admitted later, Florence did not find her employer's repeated amorous advances unwelcome but she baulked when he asked her to go to America with him. 'No, you have your wife downstairs,' she reminded him, 'and you don't want me.' Chapman snapped his fingers. 'Oh, I'd give her that,' he said, 'and she would be no more Mrs Chapman.'

There is also evidence of Chapman's violence towards Maud. On one occasion, out on a tramride down Streatham Hill with her married sister, Mrs Louisa Morris, Maud burst into tears when it became apparent that she would get home late. In comforting her sister, Louisa learned that she lived in fear of Chapman. 'You don't know what he is,' said Maud and she told of how he had sometimes beaten her.

'Well,' asked Louisa, 'has he hit you then?'

'Yes, more than once,' replied Maud.

'How did he hit you?'

'He held my hair and banged my head.'

'Didn't you pay him back?'

'Yes, I kicked him.'[9]

On 22 October Maud died as wretchedly as her predecessors. But by then the toils were closing fast around the sadistic Pole.

Dr Stoker, who attended Maud, was as bewildered by her symptoms as he had been by those of Bessie Taylor. This time, however, the victim's relatives insisted on a second opinion. Maud's father called in Dr Francis Grapel, the family doctor from Croydon. And Grapel became the first medical man in the whole Chapman saga to suspect foul play. Tragically, he failed to act quickly enough to save Maud's life.

On 21 October, after examining Maud and consulting with Stoker, Grapel concluded that the girl was suffering from some acute irritant poison. It even crossed his mind on his way home that she might be the victim of repeated doses of arsenic. But he naturally hesitated to raise what would have been a cry of attempted murder and the next day, before he could return to London and confer with Stoker again, he learned that Maud was dead. Nevertheless, prompted by Grapel's diagnosis, Stoker refused a death certificate and submitted Maud's stomach and its contents to Richard Bodmer, the consulting chemist to the Clinical Research Association. And Bodmer found both arsenic and antimony in the stomach. It was, in fact, the antimony that had done the business, the negligible quantity of arsenic having been introduced into the woman's body only as an impurity in the antimony. When Dr Thomas Stevenson, a Home Office analyst, conducted the post-mortem examination of Maud's body he discovered that her stomach, bowels, liver, kidneys and brain alone contained 7.24 grains of metallic antimony.

Now it was that justice reached out from the grave to claim Chapman. Any hopes he may have cherished that Maud's death might be written off as a tragic accident were dashed when the bodies of Bessie Taylor and Mary Spink were exhumed in November and December 1902. Antimony acts to preserve the body. Although Bessie's corpse was covered with a mouldy growth it seemed otherwise fresh. And an even greater surprise awaited Stevenson's team when they raised the lid of Mary's coffin. Mary had been five years in the ground but when Elizabeth Waymark gazed upon her face she recognized it instantly. 'She looked as if she had only been buried about nine months,' said Elizabeth. 'The only difference was that her hair had grown a little longer on the forehead. The face was perfect.' Significant quantities of metallic antimony were traced in the remains of both women.

Tried and convicted of the murder of Maud Marsh, Chapman went to the scaffold in Wandsworth Prison on 7 April 1903.

Saturday, 25 October 1902, was the day on which the Coronation Procession of King Edward VII passed through the streets of London. It was also the day that Inspector George Godley went to the Crown in Borough High Street and arrested George Chapman. At that time Godley thought he was dealing with nothing more spectacular than a one-off wife murder, tragic certainly, but by no means out of the ordinary. However, as detectives untangled the web of deceit and homicide that was Chapman's past it became clear that they had stumbled across a very dark horse indeed.

Here was a man who had passed under at least four names (Severin Klosowski, Ludwig Zagowski, George Chapman and 'Smith'), two nationalities (for after 1892 he commonly posed as an American) and two faiths (Roman Catholic and Jewish), a man who had slain not one, but three 'wives', and a man who had not scrupled to add arson and perjury to his crimes. Police inquiries demonstrated, for example, that in 1901, when Chapman's lease of the Monument was nearing expiry, he had deliberately attempted to burn the property down in order to lodge a claim against the insurance company. And, worse, that at the Newington Sessions of June 1902 he had falsely prosecuted Alfred Clark and Matilda Gilmor for conspiracy to defraud him of £700. On that occasion Chapman alleged that he had paid Clark and Gilmor the money on the security of share certificates which later turned out to be worthless. Clark was convicted and sentenced to three years' penal servitude. But when Godley arrested Chapman in October he found banknotes at the Crown with serial numbers that matched some of those Chapman, only four months earlier, had sworn he had paid to Clark and Gilmor. What the Pole hoped to gain by fabricating his dastardly charge is not clear but upon Godley's discovery the Home Office ordered Clark's immediate release from Portland Prison.

Not surprisingly, by this time the police seem to have formed the opinion that Chapman was capable of almost any villainy. Were there other skeletons rattling about in his cupboard? Only Chapman himself knew and, even after sentence of death, he said nothing. Sometimes, from his cell at Wandsworth, he proclaimed his innocence. For the rest of the time he languished restless, moody and silent. After the failure of his appeal to the Home Secretary he had to be carefully watched because it was thought that he contemplated suicide.

What Chapman knew died with him. But there were those who wondered even then whether this man of mystery harboured a still more terrible secret than any that had yet been uncovered.

Chapman's name does not appear on Macnaghten's list of major Ripper suspects for the reason that in 1894, when the Chief Constable drafted his report, the police knew nothing about him. Nevertheless, there is no doubt that in 1903 he did become a leading suspect.

Inspector Godley, the man who headed the Chapman inquiry, knew a great deal about the Whitechapel murders. Indeed, when he retired in 1908, the *Police Review* claimed that his knowledge of the crimes was perhaps 'as complete as that of any officer concerned'. That, probably, was an exaggeration. But Godley had been actively involved in the Ripper hunt. We have already encountered him, a detective sergeant from J Division, working on the Nichols murder. Later his name frequently appears in the Ripper evidence. In September 1888 he was credited with making inquiries about one suspect living not far from Buck's Row. And he is known to have arrested others in the following October and December.[10]

As he prepared his case against George Chapman in 1903 Godley was struck by the similarities between Chapman and the Ripper and considered the possibility that they were one and the same man. Unfortunately, the Metropolitan Police file on Chapman, which might have been expected to shed light upon his inquiries, no longer survives. But they were noticed briefly in the *Daily Chronicle* on 23 March 1903:

> The police officers who have been engaged in tracing Klosowski's movements in connection with the three murders with which he was charged, are forming some rather startling theories as to the antecedent history of the criminal. These theories are connected with the Whitechapel murders which startled the world some fifteen years ago, and were attributed to 'Jack the Ripper'. The police have found that at the time of the first two murders Klosowski was undoubtedly occupying a lodging in George Yard, Whitechapel Road, where the first murder was committed. Moreover, he always carried a black bag and wore a 'P. and O.' cap. The man who was 'wanted' in connection with the Whitechapel murders always wore a 'P. and O.' cap, and carried a black bag, according to the tale of some of the women who escaped him. In pursuing their investigations into the movements of Klosowski, the London detectives have found that he went to New Jersey City soon after the Whitechapel atrocities ceased, and that he opened a barber's shop there.
>
> It will be remembered that soon after the murders ceased in London crimes of a similar character were committed in America. Klosowski's real wife, Lucy Klosowski, who was present in the Central Criminal Court last week, has made a startling statement as to what occurred in the New Jersey shop. She states that on one occasion, when she had had a quarrel with her husband, he held

her down on the bed, and pressed his face against her mouth to
keep her from screaming. At that moment a customer entered the
shop immediately in front of the room, and Klosowski got up to
attend him. The woman chanced to see a handle protruding from
underneath the pillow. She found, to her horror, that it was a sharp
and formidable knife, which she promptly hid. Later, Klosowski
deliberately told her that he meant to have cut her head off, and
pointed to a place in the room where he meant to have buried her.
She said, 'But the neighbours would have asked where I had gone
to.' 'Oh,' retorted Klosowski, calmly, 'I should simply have told
them that you had gone back to New York.'

In the light of these and other definite statements, the police
have considerable doubt whether the full extent of the criminality
of Klosowski has been nearly revealed by the recent investigations,
remarkable as they were in their extent.

Lucy Klosowski was Lucy Baderski and the incident referred to in
this report was the assault which caused her to return to England
without Chapman in 1892. I have discovered no other detailed
account of it. After Chapman's arrest in 1902 Detective Sergeant
Arthur Neil, working with Godley, traced Lucy and she picked her
husband out at an identity parade. As Neil remembered it in his
autobiography, Forty Years of Man-Hunting, published in 1932,
Lucy identified Chapman without hesitation. 'I don't know this
woman,' he protested. 'Ah, Severino, don't say that!' she exclaimed.
'You remember the time you nearly killed me in Jersey City!'[11]
Presumably, at about that time, Lucy made a statement to the police
about the incident but if she did it has gone missing with the rest of
the Metropolitan Police file on Chapman.

Intrigued by the theory expounded in the Chronicle, a reporter for
the Pall Mall Gazette called on Abberline for expert comment. He
found the great detective developing an identical hypothesis of his
own. His views on Chapman are given here in full for the first time
since 1903:

Should Klosowski, the wretched man now lying under sentence
of death for wife-poisoning, go to the scaffold without a 'last
dying speech and confession', a great mystery may for ever remain
unsolved, but the conviction that Chapman and Jack the Ripper
were one and the same person will not in the least be weakened in
the mind of the man who is, perhaps, better qualified than anyone

else in this country to express an opinion in the matter. We allude to Mr. F. G. Abberline, formerly Chief Detective Inspector of Scotland Yard, the official who had full charge of the criminal investigations at the time of the terrible murders in Whitechapel.

When a representative of the *Pall Mall Gazette* called on Mr. Abberline yesterday and asked for his views on the startling theory set up by one of the morning papers, the retired detective said: 'What an extraordinary thing it is that you should just have called upon me now. I had just commenced, not knowing anything about the report in the newspaper, to write to the Assistant Commissioner of Police, Mr. Macnaghten, to say how strongly I was impressed with the opinion that Chapman was also the author of the Whitechapel murders. Your appearance saves me the trouble. I intended to write on Friday, but a fall in the garden, injuring my hand and shoulder, prevented my doing so until today.'

Mr. Abberline had already covered a page and a half of foolscap, and was surrounded with a sheaf of documents and newspaper cuttings dealing with the ghastly outrages of 1888.

'I have been so struck with the remarkable coincidences in the two series of murders', he continued, 'that I have not been able to think of anything else for several days past – not, in fact, since the Attorney-General made his opening statement at the recent trial, and traced the antecedents of Chapman before he came to this country in 1888. Since then the idea has taken full possession of me, and everything fits in and dovetails so well that I cannot help feeling that this is the man we struggled so hard to capture fifteen years ago . . .

'As I say,' went on the criminal expert, 'there are a score of things which make one believe that Chapman is the man; and you must understand that we have never believed all those stories about Jack the Ripper being dead, or that he was a lunatic, or anything of that kind. For instance, the date of the arrival in England coincides with the beginning of the series of murders in Whitechapel; there is a coincidence also in the fact that the murders ceased in London when Chapman went to America, while similar murders began to be perpetrated in America after he landed there. The fact that he studied medicine and surgery in Russia before he came over here is well established, and it is curious to note that the first series of murders was the work of an expert surgeon, while the recent poisoning cases were proved to be done by a man with more than an elementary knowledge of medicine. The story told by Chapman's wife of the attempt to murder her with a long knife while in America is not to be ignored, but something else with regard to America is still more remarkable.

'While the coroner was investigating one of the Whitechapel murders he told the jury a very queer story. You will remember that Dr. Phillips, the divisional surgeon, who made the post-mortem examination, not only spoke of the skilfulness with which the knife had been used, but stated that there was overwhelming evidence to show that the criminal had so mutilated the body that he could possess himself of one of the organs. The coroner, in commenting on this, said that he had been told by the sub-curator of the pathological museum connected with one of the great medical schools that some few months before an American had called upon him and asked him to procure a number of specimens. He stated his willingness to give £20 for each. Although the strange visitor was told that his wish was impossible of fulfilment, he still urged his request. It was known that the request was repeated at another institution of a similar character in London. The coroner at the time said: 'Is it not possible that a knowledge of this demand may have inspired some abandoned wretch to possess himself of the specimens? It seems beyond belief that such inhuman wickedness could enter into the mind of any man; but, unfortunately, our criminal annals prove that every crime is possible!'

'It is a remarkable thing,' Mr. Abberline pointed out, 'that after the Whitechapel horrors America should have been the place where a similar kind of murder began, as though the miscreant had not fully supplied the demand of the American agent.

'There are many other things extremely remarkable. The fact that Klosowski when he came to reside in this country occupied a lodging in George Yard, Whitechapel Road, where the first murder was committed, is very curious, and the height of the man and the peaked cap he is said to have worn quite tallies with the descriptions I got of him. All agree, too, that he was a foreign-looking man, but that, of course, helped us little in a district so full of foreigners as Whitechapel. One discrepancy only have I noted, and this is that the people who alleged that they saw Jack the Ripper at one time or another, state that he was a man about thirty-five or forty years of age. They, however, state that they only saw his back, and it is easy to misjudge age from a back view.'

Altogether Mr. Abberline considers that the matter is quite

beyond abstract speculation and coincidence, and believes the present situation affords an opportunity of unravelling a web of crime such as no man living can appreciate in its extent and hideousness.

Critics of the theory immediately alleged a dissimilarity in character between Chapman and the Ripper. A week after his original interview Abberline responded:

'As to the question of the dissimilarity of character in the crimes which one hears so much about,' continued the expert, 'I cannot see why one man should not have done both, provided he had the professional knowledge, and this is admitted in Chapman's case. A man who could watch his wives being slowly tortured to death by poison, as he did, was capable of anything; and the fact that he should have attempted, in such a cold-blooded manner, to murder his first wife with a knife in New Jersey, makes one more inclined to believe in the theory that he was mixed up in the two series of crimes. What, indeed, is more likely than that a man to some extent skilled in medicine and surgery should discontinue the use of the knife when his commission – and I still believe Chapman had a commission from America – came to an end, and then for the remainder of his ghastly deeds put into practice his knowledge of poisons? Indeed, if the theory be accepted that a man who takes life on a wholesale scale never ceases his accursed habit until he is either arrested or dies, there is much to be said for Chapman's consistency. You see, incentive changes; but the fiendishness is not eradicated. The victims, too, you will notice, continue to be women; but they are of different classes, and obviously call for different methods of despatch.'[12]

H. L. Adam, writing in 1930, tells us how Abberline followed up his theory:

Chief Inspector Abberline, who had charge of the investigations into the East End murders, thought that Chapman and Jack the Ripper were one and the same person. He closely questioned the Polish woman, Lucy Baderski, about Chapman's nightly habits at the time of the murders. She said that he was often out until three or four o'clock in the morning, but she could throw little light upon these absences. Both Inspector Abberline and Inspector

Godley spent years in investigating the Ripper murders. Abberline never wavered in his firm conviction that Chapman and Jack the Ripper were one and the same person. When Godley arrested Chapman Abberline said to his confrère, 'You've got Jack the Ripper at last!'[13]

The source of this information was almost certainly Godley himself for in his preface Adam expressed his gratitude to Godley for 'much information' received. In one particular, though, Godley's memory undoubtedly played him false. Abberline could not have made the remark 'You've got Jack the Ripper at last!' when Godley arrested Chapman in October 1902. At that time almost nothing was known about Chapman. Besides, Abberline himself implied in his *Pall Mall Gazette* interview that he did not suspect Chapman of the Ripper crimes until the Solicitor-General's opening address at the Central Criminal Court on 16 March 1903. I do not doubt that Abberline made such a comment at some time during the Chapman affair. But it is more likely to have been made on or soon after 19 March, when he congratulated Godley on having secured a conviction.

In 1932 the voice of ex-Superintendent Arthur Neil joined the chorus. Coming from a detective who had worked on the Chapman inquiry, the case he makes against Chapman, published in *Forty Years of Man-Hunting*, is valuable:

The Polish Jew, Kloskovski [Chapman] . . . got a job at a barber's shop in High Street, Whitechapel. He was right on the scene of these atrocities [the Ripper murders] during the whole period . . .

The first 'Ripper' crime occurred in August 1888. Chapman worked in Whitechapel at this time, and was there during the whole period of these wholesale killings. 'The Ripper,' by the account of four medical men, was testified as to having surgical knowledge. Severino Kloskovski, alias George Chapman, had this qualification. Also it was thought, by the expert manner of the mutilations examined on the various bodies of his victims, that the 'Ripper' was ambidextrous, that is left- and right-handed. Chapman was seen to use his hands in this way during the time he lived in the Borough. The only living description ever given by an eyewitness of the 'Ripper,' tallied exactly with Chapman, even to the height, deep-sunk black eyes, sallow complexion and thick, black moustache.

Towards the end of 1888, Severino Kloskovski left Britain for the United States. The 'Ripper' murders had by this time ceased, so far as London was concerned. But a series of equally terrible crimes, causing a precisely similar reign of terror, began in America. These crimes ceased when, in 1892, Kloskovski returned to this country.

We were never able to secure definite proof that Chapman was the 'Ripper'. But the strong theory remains just the same. No one who had not been trained as a surgeon and medical man, could have committed the 'Ripper' crimes. As we discovered, Chapman had been a surgeon in Poland, and would, therefore, be the only possible fiend capable of putting such trained knowledge into use against humanity, instead of for it. 'Jack the Ripper' was a cold-blooded, inhuman monster, who killed for the sake of killing.

The same could be said of Severino Kloskovski, alias George Chapman, the Borough poisoner.

Why he took to poisoning his women victims on his second visit to this country can only be ascribed to his diabolical cunning, or some insane idea or urge to satisfy his inordinate vanity.

In any case, it is the most fitting and sensible solution to the possible identity of the murderer in one of the world's greatest crime mysteries.

Neil conceded that police inquiries failed to procure proof that Chapman and the Ripper were one. Nevertheless, 'as every detective, and come to that, any active crime reporter, very quickly learns,' he added, 'there are things you cannot prove in a court of law but of which you may feel quite certain in your own mind.'[14]

A coterie of top detectives – Abberline, Godley and Neil – thus developed the strong conviction that Severin Klosowski, the man hanged at Wandsworth as George Chapman, was also Jack the Ripper. Were they right?

In certain respects there is no doubt that Chapman is the most promising suspect we have encountered. But before we consider his case in detail we had best clear out of the way some of the red herrings introduced into the discussion by his accusers.

The police claim that Chapman had a black bag was true. Harriet Greenaway, one of his neighbours in Hastings, saw it and told Southwark Police Court about it in 1903: 'Once Mrs Chapman [Mary Spink] showed me a black bag, secretly. Prisoner [Chapman] used to keep the bag.' Why Mary should have been so furtive about the bag is not clear. But since there is no reason to believe that the Ripper possessed such an article it does not matter. Similarly, Neil's claim that Chapman was ambidextrous is of doubtful relevance to our inquiry. For although two different weapons were used against Martha Tabram there is no persuasive evidence that the Ripper was an ambidexter. Perhaps the most patently bogus argument against Chapman, though, was one raised by H. L. Adam. He noted the Americanisms in the 'Dear Boss' letter and postcard and pointed out that Chapman was accustomed to use Americanisms and pass himself off as an American. Chapman certainly did sometimes pose as an American. Petitioning the Home Secretary for clemency after his trial in 1903, for example, he insisted that he was an American 'born in 1865 in the County of Michigan USA.' It is probable, too, that during his residence in Jersey City his speech acquired a smattering of Americanism. Unfortunately for Adam's argument, however, the 'Dear Boss' letter was penned in September 1888, more than two years *before* Chapman left for the States. In any case, as we have already learned, this letter was almost certainly a hoax.[15]

Even with the red herrings ruthlessly binned, an impressive array of circumstantial factors can still be alleged against Chapman.

A trained if relatively inexperienced surgeon, he possessed the medical expertise necessary to have perpetrated the Whitechapel murders.

Abberline said that Chapman lodged in George Yard. The White Hart, in the basement of which Chapman had a shop, was on the corner of George Yard and Whitechapel High Street. But Chapman did not move there until 1890. At the time of the murders he was ensconced at 126 Cable Street. This was within walking distance of all the murder sites. And Goulston Street, where the bloody remnant of Kate Eddowes' apron was discovered, could easily have been traversed by a murderer escaping to Cable Street from Mitre Square.

Chapman's personal circumstances mirrored those we have already deduced for the Ripper. He was in regular work. So, too, if the dates of the murders be any guide, was the Ripper. He was single. In other words, again probably like the Ripper, he was free of family entanglements. And Lucy Baderski, who met Chapman in 1889, tells us that he was in the habit of staying out late into the early hours of the morning. We have no certain knowledge of it but, ardent womanizer as he was, Chapman may well have been a regular patron of prostitutes.

There are remarkable affinities between the descriptions witnesses gave of the Whitechapel murderer and the known appearance of Chapman. As we have noted, the murderer seems to have been a white male in his twenties or thirties, of medium height, respectably dressed and possibly of foreign origin. Chapman fits this profile. At the time of the murders he was twenty-three. He was of medium height. And even in his working clothes, as a hairdresser, he would have been expected to dress respectably. Furthermore, three of the witnesses who may have seen the Ripper (Marshall, Schwartz and Lawende) describe a man who wore a round cap with a peak, like that of a sailor, and there is no doubt that Chapman's wardrobe once held just such a cap. In a photograph of Chapman and Bessie Taylor, taken about 1898–1900, he is clearly to be seen wearing it. If Chapman really was the Ripper he may even help to explain the inconsistency among the witnesses as to whether the murderer was a foreigner or not. Chapman was, of course, a foreigner, but one who might easily have passed for an Englishman. This was a point noted by the newspapers in 1903. 'Although born and bred near Warsaw,' commented one, 'Klosowski is not in appearance a typical Russian Pole. He is an undersized man, with small, sharp features, and in repose his face does not suggest a foreigner.'[16]

The resemblance between George Hutchinson's suspect and Chapman is particularly striking. Hutchinson described a foreigner of medium height, dark, very well dressed and sporting a dark moustache curled up at the ends. Any one of these details might accurately be applied to Chapman. Levisohn, it will be remembered, credited Chapman with a penchant for flashy dressing even in the early years of their acquaintanceship, testimony which suggests that the barber's assistant was not the impoverished immigrant that many of his compatriots were.

There are some difficulties in matching Chapman with the Ripper evidence. One is age. Hutchinson thought that the man he saw was about thirty-four or thirty-five. Chapman was then twenty-three. Certainly Hutchinson may have been mistaken. The estimation of age in strangers can be exceedingly difficult at the best of times, as those of my readers who care to experiment for themselves will readily discover, and it is not unreasonable to suppose that in a dimly-lit street a man with a heavy moustache could have passed for one older than his years. But no other witness made the Ripper as young as Chapman. PC Smith's estimate of age was twenty-eight, Schwartz's and Lawende's both thirty. The fact that almost all of our Chapman material comes from 1902–3 does not help either. It is true that Levisohn, Stanislaus Baderski (Lucy's brother) and Mrs Rauch (her sister) all testified that Chapman's general appearance changed little during the period of his residence in England, but the fourteen-year gap between the murders and the Chapman evidence inevitably introduces uncertainties into the case against him. Did Chapman own his peaked cap in 1888, for example, or was it a relic of his nautical expeditions out of Hastings during 1896–7?

Notwithstanding such caveats, it has to be conceded that, as a whole, Chapman matches up with the Ripper evidence on appearance very well.

Some students of the Whitechapel crimes have dismissed Chapman as a serious suspect because of an alleged dissimilarity in character between him and the Ripper. In fact, as Abberline pointed out, there were also many affinities of character between the two.

Chapman, like the Ripper, had a powerful sex drive, and he was regularly violent to women. A moral oaf, indifferent to the sufferings of others, the Pole physically beat at least two of his 'wives', went for one with a knife, threatened another with a revolver and ultimately condemned three to agonizing deaths by poison. Alone among the major Ripper suspects he was a known homicide. There must have been few men, even in late Victorian London, capable of multiple murder. The Ripper was one. Chapman was another.

In normal circumstances the Whitechapel killer's appearance and behaviour must have been disarming and reassuring. This, according to the Solicitor-General, Sir Edward (later Lord) Carson, who led for the prosecution at Chapman's trial, could scarcely be said of Chapman. 'I have never seen such a villain,' he recalled afterwards. 'He looked like some evil wild beast. I almost expected him to leap over the dock and attack me.'[17] Carson's reminiscence is much quoted but that does not make it accurate. Had Chapman typically presented such an appearance he would never have ensnared a succession of doting mistresses and the truth, as contemporary records amply demonstrate, is that he was possessed of a remarkable capacity for ingratiating himself with those around him.

His employers found him quiet, steady and industrious. The families of his victims were completely deceived. Having visited her son-in-law at the Monument, Bessie Taylor's mother, for example, averred that she had 'never seen a better husband'. Chapman's ability to allay suspicion is well illustrated in the case of Robert Marsh, father of Maud Marsh, the last victim.

On the day before Maud died, the worried father visited the Chapmans at the Crown.

'I think my daughter will pull through now, George,' he ventured hopefully.

Chapman prepared him for the worst: 'She will never get up no more.'

Marsh had heard rumours about Bessie Taylor, the previous wife, and understandably they troubled him. He probed Chapman on the matter. 'Have you seen anyone else like it?' he asked.

'Yes,' said Chapman.

'Was your other wife like it?'

Chapman realized that any attempt to conceal the fact would simply undermine his credibility. Without batting an eyelid he replied: 'Just about in the same way.'

All in all Marsh was impressed by his son-in-law. At the trial he testified that Chapman 'always answered my inquiries about my daughter perfectly frankly. He used to come down sometimes to see me with Maud, and, as far as I could see, she was very happy with him. I thought he treated her very well.'[18]

There were moments during the fatal illnesses of his wives when Chapman's mask slipped and witnesses like Martha Doubleday and Elizabeth Waymark glimpsed the callous indifference beneath. But their testimony was greatly overborne by those who could only see in him the solicitous husband. He ministered to his victims' needs, monitored their pulse and heart rates, prepared and administered their medicines and shed tears for their passing. Even Dr Stoker, who treated Bessie Taylor and Maud Marsh for the same symptoms, entertained no suspicion of foul play until after Grapel had alerted him to the possibility of poison.

Most remarkable of all Chapman retained the affection and trust of his victims. We have seen this in the case of Mary Spink and it is equally evident in that of Maud Marsh. At the trial Maud's mother was asked if Maud had uttered one word to suggest that she had ever doubted her husband. 'No,' she replied, 'she appeared perfectly happy and contented to the last.'[19]

'The tiger's heart was masked by the most insinuating and snaky refinement.' Such was de Quincey's description of John Williams, the supposed Ratcliff Highway murderer.[20] Recent research has tended to exonerate Williams of those crimes but the quality noticed by de Quincey might realistically be surmised of the Ripper and it was undoubtedly true of Chapman.

There was one other respect in which Chapman's personality may have replicated that of Jack the Ripper. If, as Mrs Long and George Hutchinson indicated, the Ripper was a foreigner, the chalk message – 'The Juwes are the men that will not be blamed for nothing' – was a gesture of overweening arrogance. And self-incriminating braggadocio was not uncharacteristic of Chapman. On one occasion Louisa Morris, Maud Marsh's sister, told him that it seemed strange that the doctor could not find out what was ailing Maud. 'I could give her a bit like that,' said Chapman snapping his fingers, 'and fifty doctors could not find out.'[21]

Why Abberline found Chapman such a compelling suspect should now be apparent. Here was a much more likely suspect than Macnaghten's depressed Blackheath barrister or Anderson's inoffensive scavenger of the streets. Here was a man who had the medical qualifications, the opportunity, the appearance, the cunning and the cruelty to have been Jack the Ripper.

At this point it would give me immense satisfaction to announce that we had unmasked the killer. Unfortunately I can't. Because although Chapman is undoubtedly the best suspect on offer the case against him still contains serious flaws.

The absence of any direct evidence linking Chapman with the killings is the major weakness. Lucy Baderski's statement that he was often out at night at the time of the murders will not bear scrutiny. Chapman met Lucy in a Polish club in St John's Square, Clerkenwell, and they were married on 29 October 1889. Now, according to the later testimony of Stanislaus Baderski, Lucy's brother, their courtship was a rapid affair: 'She met the accused at the Polish club, and they kept company together for four or five weeks, after which they got married.'[22] Stanislaus was vague on chronology and dates. In his Central Criminal Court testimony, for example, he erroneously dated the marriage August Bank Holiday 1889. Nevertheless, the import of his statement is clear. Lucy cannot have met Chapman before the summer of 1889 and thus knew nothing about his movements during the previous autumn. The only Ripper-type murders upon which she might conceivably have been questioned were those of Alice McKenzie and Frances Coles in July 1889 and February 1891.

There are other difficulties in identifying Chapman with the Ripper.

Would an immigrant, unfamiliar with the locality as well as the English language, have been capable of the crimes? We do not know the extent of the Ripper's command of English but some of our best witnesses – Long, Cadosch, Lawende and Hutchinson – attest to some ability to converse with English-speaking victims.

This is a difficult question to answer. Much depends upon how long Chapman had been resident in Britain. Arthur Neil, in the autobiography already referred to, tells us that he first came to this country in June 1887 but I have been unable to discover any corroboration of this statement. Papers in Russian and Polish, found in Chapman's possession when he was arrested in 1902, closely document his early life in Poland. Their abrupt termination, in February 1887, suggests to me that he emigrated soon after that date. At the height of the Ripper scare, then, he may have been resident the best part of eighteen months in the East End, long enough one would think to acquire some local knowledge and sufficient conversational English to pick up a Whitechapel whore. Wolff Levisohn's testimony on this point is inconclusive. He said that Chapman could only speak Polish and a little Yiddish when he met him in 1890. It should be remembered, however, that since Levisohn was himself a Russian Pole it would have been unnatural and unnecessary for Chapman to have attempted to communicate with him in English.

A much more serious objection to Chapman as a Whitechapel murder suspect is the dissimilarity in character between the Ripper-type slayer and the poisoner. For if Chapman was the Ripper we would have to accept that he abandoned the knife for fear of detection and adopted poison as a safer method of killing. Is this a credible scenario?

John Douglas of the FBI tells us: 'Some criminologists and behavioural scientists have written that perpetrators maintain their modus operandi, and that this is what links so-called signature crimes. This conclusion is incorrect. Subjects will change their modus operandi as they gain experience. This is learned behaviour.'[23] Point taken. It is also possible, as noted in an earlier chapter, to find examples of serial killers who lay dormant for extended periods or baffled police by changing their methods. But to exchange knife for hammer, gun or rope, weapons of violence all, is one thing. To forsake violence in favour of subterfuge, as is alleged of Chapman, quite another. I can think of only one possible parallel – California's still uncaught Zodiac killer.

In four horrific incidents in 1968–9 Zodiac shot or stabbed seven victims, five of them fatally. The attacks then ceased. But the murderer continued to taunt the police and press with letters until as late as 1978. He even boasted in his macabre correspondence of fresh killings. These later victims may have been figments of a perverted imagination. Yet it is also possible that they were real and that they had not been officially attributed to Zodiac because of differences of locale or technique. Indeed, in a letter of November 1969, Zodiac warned of just such an impending change in his modus operandi: 'I shall no longer announce to anyone when I commit my murders, they shall look like routine robberies, killings of anger, and a few fake accidents, etc. The police shall never catch me, because I have been too clever for them.' Robert Graysmith, who studied the case, took Zodiac at his word and presented evidence to link him with various unsolved murders of hitchhikers in California, Washington and Oregon between 1969 and 1981. The victims were stabbed, poisoned, strangled, drowned or smothered. 'The truly horrifying part to me,' he wrote, 'was that it seemed that someone was experimenting in different ways of killing people.'[24]

Whether Chapman was capable of such versatility in murder it is impossible now to say. 'You don't know what he is.' Maud Marsh's rejoinder to her sister might well serve as a caution to those eager to pontificate about what the Pole was or was not capable of doing. The fact is that he still remains very much an enigma. We do not even know why he poisoned three women. Apart from Mary Spink, with her £500 legacy, there were no substantial economic advantages in any of his 'marriages'. Bessie Taylor was the favourite daughter of comparatively affluent parents but Chapman killed her before she could inherit. And Maud Marsh was the daughter of a labourer. Since Chapman did not legally marry any of his victims, moreover, he had no need to resort to murder in order to free himself of one so that he might live with another. George Elliott, defending Chapman at the Central Criminal Court, made an effective point out of this lack of tangible motive, a point to which Carson could but protest Chapman's record of 'unbridled, heartless and cruel lust'.

A restless adventurer, never staying long in one place, Chapman slipped easily into fantasy worlds of his own creation. He posed as an American, displaying the stars and stripes prominently in his public houses, and boasted of his exploits at sea and in hunting big game. An American revolver, fully loaded, was found at the Crown after his arrest, but the most ferocious quarry he is known to have pursued with it were the rats he was accustomed to shoot in his cellar. Perhaps the lies served to mask a deep-rooted sense of inferiority. Whatever, despite his macho image and undoubted success with women, Chapman seems to have made no close male friends at all. Asked in the death cell whether he wanted to see any friends, he replied bitterly, 'I have none!'

Poison was an obvious weapon for Chapman given his knowledge of medicine and his desire to murder his 'wives'. And the fact that he was a poisoner in one set of circumstances does not, as Abberline intimated, preclude the possibility of his perpetrating different types of slayings in another. The Pole has a demonstrable record of physical violence against women and he is the only serious Ripper suspect who has. But perhaps it is stretching credibility too far to believe that the man who committed six horrific, often frenzied, knife murders in just three months in 1888 could have quietly gone into retirement and then re-emerged a decade later in the covert guise of domestic poisoner.

The case against Chapman would unquestionably look stronger if it could be shown that his movements correlated with other recorded sex murders or assaults. In this context the slayings of Alice McKenzie and Frances Coles and the alleged American attacks of 1890–92 are interesting.

The incident which inspired police references to American crimes was the murder of an aged prostitute in a room of the East River Hotel on the Manhattan waterfront of New York during the night of 23–24 April 1891.

The victim was Carrie Brown, known to locals as 'Old Shakespeare' because of her fondness for quoting the bard when she was tipsy. She checked into the hotel, a squalid lodging house on the southeast corner of Catherine Slip and Water Streets, between 10.30 and 11.00 at night with a man. Only Mary Miniter, the assistant housekeeper, saw her companion. She described him as 'apparently about thirty-two years old, five feet eight inches in height, of slim build, with a long, sharp nose and a heavy moustache of light colour. He was clad in a dark-brown cutaway coat and black trousers, and wore an old black derby hat, the crown of which was much dented. He was evidently a foreigner, and the woman's impression was that he was a German.'

The next morning the night clerk found Carrie lying dead on the bed in her room. She was naked from the armpits down and had been strangled and mutilated. The man had vanished.

Press notices of the autopsy suppressed the details of the injuries to the lower part of Carrie's trunk but noted that there were cuts and stab wounds 'all over it'. Dr Jenkins, who performed the autopsy, was reported as believing that the murderer had tried entirely to cut out his victim's abdomen but that his fury and her struggles had prevented him. At the later trial of Ameer Ben Ali, an Algerian Arab, for the crime, however, Jenkins said that the woman had been strangled first and mutilated after death. A black-handled table-knife, the blade ground or broken to a sharp point, was found on the floor of the room. It was stained with blood.

Inevitably newspaper headlines raised the spectre of Jack the Ripper. Those in the *New York Times* proclaimed:

CHOKED, THEN MUTILATED.
A MURDER LIKE ONE OF JACK THE RIPPER'S DEEDS.
WHITECHAPEL'S HORRORS REPEATED
IN AN EAST SIDE LODGING HOUSE.

The police refused to comment but the press made the most of the possibility that the Ripper had come to New York. 'There has not been a case in years that has called forth so much detective talent,' piped the *New York Times* again. 'Inspector Byrnes has said that it would be impossible for crimes such as Jack the Ripper committed in London to occur in New York and the murderer not be found. He has not forgotten his words on the subject. He also remembers that he has a photographed letter, sent by a person who signed himself Jack the Ripper, dated 'Hell', and received eighteen months ago.'

The man who brought Carrie Brown to the East River Hotel was never traced. However, in July 1891 the New York City police secured a conviction against Ameer Ben Ali, alias 'Frenchy', for the murder. Frenchy had occupied a room across the hall from Carrie's on the fatal night and it was their contention that when the first man left Frenchy crept to Carrie's room, robbed and killed her, and then slipped back to his own room. Their case was supported by the discovery of bloodstains in the hallway between the two rooms, on both sides of Frenchy's door and in his room. Frenchy protested his innocence to the last. 'They say that the man who was with the woman had large and lovely moustaches,' he wailed. 'Just look at my moustaches. They are neither long nor thick.' He was found guilty of murder in the second degree and sentenced to life imprisonment. Eleven years later, after fresh evidence suggested that the incriminating bloodstains may only have appeared *after* the coroner, police and reporters had been over the premises, Governor Benjamin Odell ordered his release.

The conviction of Frenchy was unquestionably unsafe. So who did kill Carrie Brown? We just don't know. In 1901 new evidence emerged to accuse a Danish farmhand working in Cranford, New Jersey, at the period of the murder. Absent on the fatal night, he returned home the next morning and left without notice a few days later. His employer allegedly discovered a key like those used at the East River Hotel and a bloodstained shirt in his room after he had gone. Had this information real substance one would have expected it to have been made public at the time. As it is the employer said nothing until approached by the press ten years later and that has to make his tale suspect.[25]

Mary Miniter did not get a good look at Old Shakespeare's companion on the fatal night. When the couple booked into the hotel he stayed in the background and appeared 'anxious to avoid observation'. Nevertheless, some of the details she remembered about him recall Chapman. The Pole is a possible suspect – but only just. For on 5 April 1891, when the English census was taken, he was still living in Tewkesbury Buildings, Whitechapel. We don't know when Chapman took passage for New York. If his decision to emigrate owed anything to the illness and death of his son in March it might have been in April. And that could place him in New York in time for the Carrie Brown killing. It is undoubtedly food for thought that the American press began to speculate that Jack the Ripper had appeared on the New York waterfront at about the time Chapman, who would become Abberline's chief suspect in the Ripper case, disembarked there. But clearly it will take nothing short of proof that Chapman was in the city when Carrie died to invest the American connection with real credibility.

The matter must rest there for the present.

George Chapman could have been Jack the Ripper. We have uncovered nothing to eliminate him from our inquiry. And he fits the evidence better than any other police suspect. But that does not make him a strong suspect. It is obvious that neither Abberline nor his colleagues were able to establish any tangible link between Chapman and the murders, and coincidences in opportunity, medical qualifications, appearance, social circumstances and character, however intriguing, inevitably fail to persuade by themselves. In his recent comments on the Ripper case Jonathan Goodman, doyen of true crime writers, hit the nail squarely on the head: 'Of those [suspects] named, I think the least unlikely is George Chapman.'[26]

I have little hesitation in declaring Druitt, Kosminski and Ostrog 'Not Guilty'. In the case of Chapman I prefer recourse to a verdict long recognized only in Scottish law – 'Not Proven'.

Last Thoughts

'WE ARE INUNDATED with suggestions and names of suspects!' Thus wrote Sir Charles Warren, Commissioner of the Metropolitan Police, to Sir James Fraser, his counterpart in the City, on 9 October 1888.[1]

It is a complaint that is as true today as it was a century ago. Year by year we are presented with a fresh crop of improbable identity theories. In the twelve months before this book went to press we have had William Westcott (surgeon and occultist), Thomas Cutbush, James K. Stephen and Montague Druitt (again, and this time in tandem!), Dr William Thomas (the Welsh Ripper) and James Maybrick. And next year? Who knows?

When I began my own search for Jack the Ripper I decided to concentrate upon the contemporary police suspects because I felt that it would be amongst these, if anywhere, that I would find him. Sadly, by the end of my study two things had become painfully apparent.

First, there was no single police view on the subject. Different officers espoused different theories. Indeed, just about every detective in the CID, even those who took no part in the Whitechapel investigation, seems at one time or another to have had a pet theory on the identity of Jack the Ripper.

Benjamin Leeson did not join the force until 1891. Nevertheless, we find him hinting in his memoirs that a 'certain doctor' known to him, who was never far away when the crimes were committed, could have 'thrown quite a lot of light' on the mystery. Detective Inspector Sewell of Brixton, retiring in 1898, put out a different theory: 'Although the exact identity of the man was never discovered, most of us believe that he was a Lascar sailor, who came to London at pretty frequent intervals. When the crimes ceased in London they commenced after a short interval abroad, and generally they were either in or near a port. In the police force today the belief is that the murderer is either dead or is confined in some criminal lunatic asylum.' Yet another suspect is referred to by John Littlechild, ex-head of the Special Branch, in a letter of 1913 to the journalist George R. Sims.[2]

The second conclusion suggested by a study of police records is that, with the exception of Lawende's dubious identification of Kosminski, none of their theories seem to have been based upon tangible evidence linking a suspect to the crimes. Rather, men were suspected because one detective or another thought them the type of person the police should be looking for. We hear a lot about insanity, medical knowledge, cruelty to women and the like, precious little about real *evidence*.

Chapman is the most likely of the known suspects to have been Jack the Ripper. But in all honesty I cannot find a convincing case against any of them. And there is every possibility that the man the Victorians called 'the master murderer of the age' was in reality a complete nobody whose name never found its way into the police file . . . some sad social cripple who lived out his days in obscurity, his true identity a secret now known only to the dead.

Fortunately, it is not quite the end of the search.

Our study of the historical facts has already enabled us to deduce a certain amount about the killer. We are pretty safe in thinking of him as a local man, white but possibly of continental origin, in his twenties or thirties. He dressed respectably and was of average or slightly less than average height. A single man in regular employment, he was right-handed and possessed some degree of anatomical knowledge and surgical skill.

History cannot take us further. But perhaps psychology can.

Anyone who has read or seen *The Silence of the Lambs* will know that criminal psychological profiling has become an invaluable instrument in the detection of serial murderers and rapists. Essentially it is the task of the profiler to help police prioritize suspects. In order to do this he carefully examines the scene of crime information and then, drawing upon his knowledge of similar offenders and behavioural science, attempts to provide an outline of the likely behavioural and personality traits of the unknown perpetrator.

Fiction claims too much for the technique. It cannot be expected to produce a word portrait of the criminal that is accurate in every detail because human behaviour is so very complex and unpredictable. And there are obvious problems inherent in applying it to historical cases. Few profilers are also historians. Yet any profile is only as good as the data upon which it is based. Which means that for past cases the historical evidence must first be competently researched and evaluated. Few historic cases, too, can be recovered in the wealth of detail ideally required by the profiler. A good profiler, for instance, will wish to see scene of crime photographs that depict the scene from every angle. Such photographs were taken in only one of the nine Whitechapel killings. However, I quibble. Psychological profiling can and does catch murderers and we ignore it at our peril.

The modern use of psychological profiling in criminal investigation was pioneered by the famous Behavioral Science Unit of the FBI academy in Quantico, Virginia. In 1988, a century after the Whitechapel murders, Supervisory Special Agent John E. Douglas of the FBI attempted a reconstruction of the killer's personality.[3]

Douglas opines that the Ripper was raised in a family with a domineering mother, probably fond of drink and the company of different men, and a weak and/or absent father. The boy thus grew up without consistent care or contact with stable adult role models. He became socially detached and developed 'a diminished emotional response toward people in general'. His anger was internalized. But, in his younger years, his pent-up destructive emotions were expressed by lighting fires and torturing animals. He developed a fantasy life which, as he grew older, included the domination, abuse and mutilation of women. As an adult the Ripper was an asocial loner. At work he was seen as quiet, shy and obedient, and his dress was neat and orderly. He would look for employment in positions in which he could work alone and experience vicariously his destructive fantasies, perhaps as a butcher or hospital or mortuary attendant. He was not adept at meeting people socially and his sexual relationships were mostly with prostitutes. He may have contracted venereal disease. If so it would have fuelled his hatred and disgust of women. He is unlikely to have been married. He carried a knife in order to protect himself against possible attack. 'This paranoid type of thinking would in part be justified by his poor self-image.' He lived or worked in the

Whitechapel area and his first homicide would have been close to his home or place of work.

The FBI distinguish two main types of serial murderer. The disorganized offender does not plan his crimes or stalk his victims. He attacks on impulse. The crime scene will betray confusion, the body left there unhidden, weapons and other clues thoughtlessly abandoned for investigating officers to find. By contrast the organized offender thinks his crime through in advance. Victims are selected and stalked with care. The crime scene is neat and orderly. It reflects control. And the murderer takes care to escape detection. He is unlikely to leave obvious clues at the scene and may transport and hide bodies elsewhere. The differences in method displayed by these two types of murderer are believed to reflect differences in personality. The disorganized offender will likely prove a loner, socially inept, single and employed, if at all, in positions demanding little skill or communication with the public. The organized offender, on the other hand, will be intelligent and articulate, the type of man who may have considerable educational achievements, who usually lives with a female partner and holds down steady skilled work. In the organized offender situational stress, like marital problems, may precipitate murder. In the disorganized offender no external trigger is needed. The impetus to kill, a prevailing sense of rage and hostility, lurks deep within his personality.[4]

To judge from John Douglas' profile of Jack the Ripper, he would place him in the disorganized category. But caution is necessary here. However useful the FBI typology is as a starting point for discussion it is a simplistic analysis. Many offenders will exhibit characteristics of both types. The Ripper is clearly one. In some ways (the probability that he was single, the local nature of his crimes and his disposition to leave bodies unhidden at the murder scene) he undoubtedly does fit into the disorganized group. But in others (his ability to engage victims in conversation, the disciplined character of his mature modus operandi and his care to remove weapons and clues from the scene) he sounds much more like an organized offender.

Perhaps the finest exponent of offender profiling in Britain is David Canter, Professor of Psychology at the University of Surrey, still best known for his uncannily accurate profile of John Duffy, the 'Railway Rapist', in 1986. Professor Canter believes that Jack the Ripper felt himself at odds with society, venting his anger and resentment on those he saw as easy victims. There was probably some history of psychological disturbance in his background of which those who had dealings with him would have been aware. Friends may have found him a loner, withdrawn and difficult to relate to. He may have been married but if so the degree of relationship between his wife and himself would not have been the norm. At some time in his life the Ripper probably held down a position requiring some skill. He was able to initiate contact with potential victims so his work may have involved limited social contact with people. Canter is convinced that the Ripper lived or had some sort of base within the Whitechapel area and that the first murder attributed to him was not the first crime he committed.[5]

As our experience with offender profiling grows the technique will undoubtedly be honed to a greater degree of refinement. We may, of course, also get lucky and uncover fresh documentary evidence on the Ripper case itself. But any new evidence is unlikely to change the general picture of the case presented in these pages. The development of offender profiling, though, should enable us to look at our facts in new ways, to suggest fresh avenues of research. For example, both John Douglas and David Canter advise us that the Ripper probably committed other offences in the same area before the first murder attributed to him. Is it not possible, then, that a search of local magistrates' court records for the five years preceding the murders may turn up a new suspect, regularly accused perhaps of indecent assault, rape or street robbery, a suspect who fits the facts and the profiles we have noticed? If so it will have uncovered a better suspect than any we have inherited from the police file.

In 1903 Inspector Abberline, that most celebrated of Ripper hunters, bemoaned the fact that Scotland Yard was 'really no wiser on the subject than it was fifteen years ago'. A century after the Metropolitan Police file was closed the case remains unsolved. But these are exciting times for those who would seek out Jack the Ripper. We still cannot put a name to him. Not yet. But a combination of sound historical scholarship and the latest profiling techniques is beginning to tell us more about him than Abberline would have dreamed possible.

Sources

A great many books, newspapers and journals have been consulted during the preparation of this book. Printed sources, primary and secondary, are relatively well-known. Where they have proved of value they are acknowledged in the notes. For a full listing, see Alexander Kelly, *Jack the Ripper: A Bibliography and Review of the Literature* (London, 1973; second edition, 1984) and Alexander Kelly, 'A Hundred Years of Ripperature,' in Colin Wilson & Robin Odell, *Jack the Ripper: Summing-up and Verdict* (London, 1987), pp. 280–314. A new edition of the bibliography is in preparation.

The following archival sources have been searched.

Public Record Office, Kew
(a) Metropolitan Police:
MEPO 1/48. Commissioner's letters, confidential & private, 1867–91.
MEPO 1/54. Out letters, 1890–1919.
MEPO 1/55. Letters to Home Office etc., 1883–1904.
MEPO 1/65. Letters from Receiver to Home Office etc., 1868–91.
MEPO 2/227. Police reinforcements for Whitechapel after Pinchin Street murder, 1889.
MEPO 3/140. Files on each of the Whitechapel Murders.
MEPO 3/141. Whitechapel Murders, miscellaneous correspondence and suspects.
MEPO 3/142. 'Jack the Ripper' letters.

MEPO 3/3153. Documents on Whitechapel Murders returned to Yard in November 1987.

MEPO 3/3155. Photographs of Whitechapel Murder victims.

(b) Home Office:

HO 8/194–6, 201–7. Quarterly returns of prisoners, Chatham (1872–3) and Portland (1874–6).

HO 27/140, 143, 167. Registers of persons charged at Assizes and Quarter Sessions, 1865, 1866 and 1874.

HO 45/9744/A56376. Police repudiate press interviews, 1894.

HO 140/25, 98. After-trial calendars of prisoners tried at Assizes and Quarter Sessions, 1874, 1887.

HO 144/220/A49301. Whitechapel Murders: suspects.

HO 144/220/A49301B. Whitechapel Murders: rewards.

HO 144/221/A49301C. Whitechapel Murders: steps taken to apprehend the murderer.

HO 144/221/A49301D. Whitechapel Murders: suspects.

HO 144/221/A49301E. Whitechapel Murders: use of dogs.

HO 144/221/A49301F. Miller's Court Murder, 1888.

HO 144/221/A49301G. Whitechapel Murders: police allowances.

HO 144/221/A49301H. Poplar Murder, 1888.

HO 144/221/A49301I. Castle Alley Murder, 1889.

HO 144/221/A49301K. Pinchin Street Murder, 1889.

HO 144/680/101992. George Chapman.

HO 145/5. Criminal Lunacy Warrant Book, 1884–7.

HO 151/4–5. Confidential Entry Books, 1887–95.

(c) Miscellaneous:

ASSI 2/39. Oxfordshire Assize, Lent 1863, crown minute book.

ASSI 5/183/12. Oxfordshire Assize, Lent 1863, indictments.

ASSI 31/37. Kent Assize, Summer 1866, agenda book.

ASSI 35/306, Part 2. Kent Assize, Summer 1866, indictments.

BT 27/66–8. Board of Trade passenger lists, outwards, January-July 1891.

MH 94/6, 11, and 85. Registers of patient admissions to lunatic asylums.

PCOM 2/4. Chatham Prison register, 1871–81.

PCOM 2/55. Millbank Prison register, 1873–5.

PCOM 2/75. Pentonville Prison register, 1873–5.

PCOM 2/364. Portland Prison, governor's journal, 1872–5.

PCOM 3/342, 605–29. Licenses for release of prisoners, 1873, 1882–3.

WO 97/1450, 2083, 3274, 5324. Soldiers: attestation & discharge papers.

Public Record Office, Chancery Lane
CRIM 1/84. Central Criminal Court, George Chapman case, 1903, depositions.
CRIM 4/1215. Central Criminal Court, George Chapman case, indictments.
National Census Returns, 1841–91.

Public Record Office of Northern Ireland, Belfast
D1507. Sir Edward Carson, correspondence & papers.

Office of Population Censuses & Surveys, St Catherine's House, London
Registers of births, marriages & deaths.

British Library
Additional MS. 57,485. Letters from George R. Sims to Sir Melville Macnaghten.

Bodleian Library, Oxford
MS. Eng. hist. c. 723. Letter: Matthews, 5 October 1888, to Ruggles-Brise, on offer of reward for Whitechapel murderer.

Corporation of London Records Office, Guildhall
Southwark Inquests 1865, No. 229. Charles White inquest, 1865.
Coroner's Inquest (L), 1888, No. 135. Catharine Eddowes inquest, 1888.
INQ/S/1902/274. Maud Marsh inquest, 1902.
Police Boxes 3.13–3.23. Letters, mainly from general public, to City Police about Whitechapel Murders.

Guildhall Library, Aldermanbury
MS. 10445/33. City of London Cemetery, Little Ilford, burial register, 1888.
MS. 6012A/17–19. Land Tax Books, Mile End Old Town, 1886, 1890–1.
MS. 6015A/4–5. Land Tax Books, Whitechapel, 1887–90.

Greater London Record Office, Northampton Road
MJ/SPC, NE 1888 Box 3 Case Paper 19. Mary Jane Kelly inquest, 1888.
PS/TH/A1/8–24 and PS/TH/A2/5–16. Thames Police Court registers, 1887–91.

H12/CH/B2/2. Colney Hatch Lunatic Asylum, male admissions register, 1888–1906.

H12/CH/B13/36, 39–42. Colney Hatch Lunatic Asylum, male casebooks, 1887, 1890–95.

H12/CH/B6/2. Colney Hatch Lunatic Asylum, discharge register, 1891–6.

StBG/Wh/123/19–20. Whitechapel Workhouse Infirmary, admission & discharge books, 1887–9.

StBG/ME/114/4–5. Mile End Old Town Workhouse, admission & discharge books, 1890–91.

StBG/ME/117/12–13. Mile End Old Town Workhouse Infirmary, admission & discharge books, 1890–91.

X/20/355. Mile End Old Town Workhouse, religious creed register, 1890–92, microfilm.

X/20/362. Mile End Old Town Workhouse Infirmary, religious creed register, 1887–92, microfilm.

StBG/ME/107/8. Mile End Old Town, orders for reception of lunatics into asylums, 1889–91.

StBG/ME/112/4. Mile End Old Town, orders for admission of imbeciles into asylums, 1886–1903.

HO.BG/541/71. Holborn Workhouse, City Road, admission & discharge book, 1900.

At time of writing the following records of Leavesden Asylum had not been allocated references:
Admission order book, Nos. 7351–7400.
Male case register, Vol. 12A, p. 29.
Male medical register, 1870–1917.
Male medical journal, 1918–21.
Admission & discharge book, 1919–20.
Aaron Kosminski file from 'case files 1919'.

Westminster City Library (Victoria Library), Buckingham Palace Road
D358, D362 and D366. Rate books, Rupert Street, St James Piccadilly, 1887–90.

Holborn Library (Local Studies), Theobalds Road
Rate books, Great Ormond Street, 1887–8.

Royal London Hospital Archives & Museum, Whitechapel
London Hospital, patient admission register, 1888.

MC/S/1/1. London Hospital Medical College, index register of students, 1741–1914.

MC/S/1/6. London Hospital Medical College, register of students, 1876–1889.

Whitechapel Murders: The E. K. Larkins Collection.

Maps and sketches by Dr Gordon Brown and Frederick Foster, Mitre Square Murder, 1888. Originals now framed in Secretary's Office, London Hospital Medical College, Turner Street, photographs in archives.

Harperbury Hospital, Radlett, Herts
Leavesden Asylum, admissions & deaths registers.

Springfield Hospital, Glenburnie Road, London
Surrey Lunatic Asylum, Male Patients Admission Book, 1880–88.
Surrey Lunatic Asylum, Criminal Lunatics Book, 1885–1950.

St Olave's & St Saviour's Grammar School Foundation, New Kent Road
St John's Charity School, admissions register 1842–7, and charity minutes up to 1857.

Gloucestershire Record Office, Gloucester
Q/Gc 6/5. Gloucester Gaol register, 1865–71.
Q/Sm 1/7. Gloucestershire Quarter Sessions, Epiphany Sessions, 1866, court minute book.
Q/SD2 1866. Gloucestershire Quarter Sessions, Epiphany Sessions, 1866, depositions.

Surrey Record Office, Kingston upon Thames
Acc 1523/3/1/5. Brookwood Lunatic Asylum, admission register, 1887.

Staffordshire Record Office, Stafford
Bushbury, Staffs., parish register, 1832.

The following abbreviations are employed throughout the notes:

CLRO	Corporation of London Records Office.
CPL	Coroner's Papers, Langham: Eddowes inquest, see under Corporation of London Records Office.
CPM	Coroner's Papers, Macdonald: Kelly inquest, see under Greater London Record Office.
DN	*Daily News*

DT   *Daily Telegraph*
ELA   *East London Advertiser*
ELO   *East London Observer*
GL   Guildhall Library
GLRO   Greater London Record Office
PMG   *Pall Mall Gazette*
PRO   Public Record Office
RLHAM   Royal London Hospital Archives & Museum
T   *The Times*
WCL   Westminster City Library (Victoria)

Notes

1 A Century of Final Solutions

1 *ELA* 6 October 1888; *Southern Guardian*, 5 January 1889.
2 Warren, 17 October 1888, to Matthews, HO 144/220/A49301B/12; Lusk, 7 October 1888, to Matthews, HO 144/220/A49301B/7.
3 Brian Marriner, *A Century of Sex Killers* (London, 1992), p. 19.
4 *DT* 1 October 1888; *Star* 10 November 1888.
5 *Star* 10 November 1888.
6 *Star* 11 September 1888.
7 Dan Farson, *Jack the Ripper* (London, revised edition, 1973), p. 45; *DT* 10 and 11 September 1888; *Hansard's Parliamentary Debates*, Third Series, Vol. CCCXXX, pp. 902–4; L. Forbes Winslow, *Recollections of Forty Years* (London, 1910), p. 252; Terence Robertson, 'Madman who Murdered Nine Women', *Reynolds' News*, 29 October 1950.

Even where newsmen purport to quote the words of persons actually interviewed by them their reports must be used with care. When Frances Coles was slain in 1891 a Press Association report quoted Sir Edward Bradford, then Commissioner of Metropolitan Police, as saying that she had been murdered by 'the same assassin who had previously struck terror in the East End' in 1888. Bradford could remember making no such statement and his chief clerk wrote to the Press Association and asked them to retract it (W. Staples, 16 February 1891, to Press Association, PRO, MEPO 1/54, ff. 51–2). In September 1894 the *Evening News* published a long 'chat' with Dr Anderson, head of CID, about anthropometry, and *Le Matin* a two-column interview with Chief Inspector Melville about foreign Anarchists. Both officers denied that the interviews had ever taken place. Anderson, in a note to the Home Office on 24 September, said that although he remembered a reporter visiting him at New Scotland Yard he had been 'positively rude to the man & declined altogether to be interviewed.' The documents will be found at PRO, HO 45/9744/A56376.

8 For interviews with elderly East Londoners, see especially Farson, *Jack the Ripper*, pp. 25, 26, 48–9, 53–4; Tom Cullen, *Autumn of Terror: Jack the Ripper, His Crimes and Times* (London, 1965), pp. 17–19, 52–3, 129.

9 The Sickert-Knight theory may be followed in: Elwyn Jones and John Lloyd, *The Ripper File* (London, 1975); Stephen Knight, *Jack the Ripper: The Final Solution* (London, 1976); *The Sunday Times*, 18 June 1978; *The Bloodhound*, March 1987; Donald Rumbelow, *The Complete Jack the Ripper* (London, revised edition, 1987), pp. 200–217; Martin Howells & Keith Skinner, *The Ripper Legacy* (London, 1987), pp. 37–52; Melvin Harris, *Jack the Ripper: The Bloody Truth* (London, 1987), pp. 136–69; Neal Shelden, 'Victims of Jack the Ripper', *True Detective*, January 1989, pp. 49–51; Melvyn Fairclough, *The Ripper and the Royals* (London, 1991).

10 The case for the diary is expounded at length in Shirley Harrison, *The Diary of Jack the Ripper* (London, 1993). It should be read in conjunction with: Nick Warren, 'Diary of an "extraordinarily nervous man"', *Ripperana*, No. 5, July 1993, pp. 24–7; Phillip Knightley, 'Is this man Jack the Ripper?', *The Independent on Sunday*, 29 August 1993; Maurice Chittenden & Christopher Lloyd, 'Fake!', *The Sunday Times*, 19 September 1993; Nick Warren, 'Ten reasons why I believe the Ripper diary to be bogus,' *Ripperana*, No. 7, January 1994, pp. 2–5. Kenneth Rendell, a specialist in the authentication of historical documents, concludes that the Ripper diary is a hoax in his forthcoming book, *Forging History: The Detection of Fake Letters and Documents*, to be published by University of Oklahoma Press in March 1994.

11 William Stewart, *Jack the Ripper: A New Theory* (London, 1939), p. 220.

12 Donald McCormick, *The Identity of Jack the Ripper* (London, 1959), pp. 149, 151.

13 See, especially: Cullen, *Autumn of Terror*; Rumbelow, *Complete Jack the Ripper*; Paul Begg, *Jack the Ripper: The Uncensored Facts* (London, 1988); Paul Begg, Martin Fido & Keith Skinner (ed.), *The Jack the Ripper A to Z* (London, 1991); Alexander Kelly, *Jack the Ripper: A Bibliography and Review of the Literature* (London, revised edition, 1984). For serious students a subscription to the aficionados' quarterly, *Ripperana*, edited by Nicholas P. Warren, is essential.

14 Neil Gaiman, Eugene Byrne and Kim Newman, 'Who was Jack the Ripper?', *The Truth*, No. 12, 20 October 1988, pp. 17–19.

2 *Mysterious Murder in George Yard*

1 Depositions of Elizabeth Mahoney, Alfred George Crow and John Saunders Reeves at inquest, 9 August 1888, *ELO* and *ELA* 11 August, *T* and *DN* 10 August; report of Inspector E. Ellisdon, 10 August 1888, MEPO 3/140, f. 34; report of Chief Inspector Donald S. Swanson, September 1888, HO 144/221/A49301C/8a. Walter Dew's reminiscent account of the Tabram murder must be used with care, *I Caught Crippen* (London, 1938), pp. 95–104.
2 Deposition of PC Thomas Barrett, 9 August 1888, *ELO* 11 August.
3 Deposition of Dr Timothy Robert Killeen, 9 August 1888, *ibid.*
4 Deposition of Dr Killeen, 9 August 1888, *ELO* 11 August and *DN* 10 August.
5 Report of Inspector Ellisdon, 10 August 1888, MEPO 3/140, f. 34; statement of Francis Hewitt and wife, *ELO* 18 August 1888; *Illustrated Police News* 18 August 1888.
6 *Star* 7 August 1888.
7 *ELO* and *ELA* 11 August 1888; For the St Jude's Vigilance Committee, see Secretary of Committee, Toynbee Hall, 9 September 1888, to *DN*, *DN* 11 September; *Star* 12 September 1888; *ELO* 15 September 1888; Cullen, *Autumn of Terror*, pp. 92–3.
8 The fullest notices of the inquest proceedings are in *ELO* and *ELA* 11 August 1888. Unless otherwise credited all details in the text relating to the inquest have been derived from these sources.
9 *T* 10 August 1888.
10 Biographical information on Martha Tabram has been drawn from the registers of births, marriages & deaths, St Catherine's House, from the censuses of 1851 (HO 107/1565) and 1871 (RG 10/606), PRO, and from the depositions of Henry Samuel Tabram, Henry Turner, Mary Bousfield and Ann Morris at the resumed inquest on 23 August 1888. For inquest reports, see *T* and *DN* 24 August, *ELO* and *ELA* 25 August, and report of Inspector Edmund Reid, 24 August 1888, MEPO 3/140, ff. 49–51. For James Bousfield, see Cullen, *Autumn of Terror*, p. 36 n. 1.
     The coroner's papers for the inquest on Charles Samuel White, held on 18 November 1865, will be found at CLRO, Southwark Inquests, 1865, No. 229. They contain the depositions of Mary Ann White (his daughter), Rebecca Grover (his landlady) and Henry O'Donnell (his doctor). White's wife also testified but her deposition is missing from the file. See also, *South London Chronicle* 25 November 1865.
11 Report of Inspector Reid, 16 August 1888, MEPO 3/140, f. 46; report of Chief Inspector Swanson, Sept. 1888, HO 144/221/A49301C/8a.

12 Report of Inspector Reid, 25 September 1888, MEPO 3/140, ff. 52–7. See also report of Inspector Reid, 16 August 1888, MEPO 3/140, ff. 46–7, and report of Chief Inspector Swanson, Sept. 1888, HO 144/221/A49301C/8a.

13 *Kelly's Kingston, Norbiton, Surbiton, and District Directory* for 1891 lists a John Benjamin as the landlord of the Canbury Arms, 49 Canbury Park Road, Kingston.

14 John Leary (regimental No. 6031), WO 97/3274, and John Leary (No. 172), WO 97/5324, PRO.

15 For Pearly Poll's story, see reports of Inspector Reid, 16 and 24 August 1888, MEPO 3/140, ff. 44–5, 50; report of Chief Inspector Swanson, Sept. 1888, HO 144/221/A49301C/8a; deposition of Mary Ann Connelly, 23 August 1888, *ELA* and *ELO* 25 August.

16 *ELO* 18 August 1888.

17 Reports of Inspector Reid, 16 August and 25 September 1888, MEPO 3/140, ff. 45, 47–8, 57–9; report of Chief Inspector Swanson, Sept. 1888, HO 144/221/A49301C/8a.

18 Dew, *I Caught Crippen*, pp. 102–3; report of Chief Constable Melville Macnaghten, 23 February 1894, MEPO 3/141, f. 182.

19 Summing up of George Collier, 23 August 1888, *ELA* 25 August.

20 Report of Chief Inspector Swanson, Sept. 1888, HO 144/221/A49301C/8a; deposition of Dr Killeen, 9 August 1888, *DN* 10 August.

21 McCormick, *Identity of Jack the Ripper* (1959), p. 17.

22 'Detail of reports in tabular form for reference,' MEPO 3/140, ff. 35–6.

23 Paul Harrison, *Jack the Ripper: The Mystery Solved* (London, 1991), p. 99.

24 *ELA* 18 August 1888. Unknown to each other Jon Ogan and I researched the Tabram murder at the same time. We both concluded that the evidence against the soldiery was unsatisfactory. See his perceptive article, 'Martha Tabram – the Forgotten Ripper Victim?', *Journal of Police History Society*, Vol. V (1990), pp. 79–83.

25 Whitechapel Workhouse Infirmary, Admission & Discharge Book, 1888–9, GLRO, StBG/Wh/123/20; death certificate, St Catherine's House; *Eastern Post* 7 April 1888; Russell Whitaker, 'A New Ripper Victim,' *Ripperana*, No. 7, January 1994, pp. 15–6.

26 *ELO* 31 March 1888; London Hospital, Patient Admissions Register, 1888, RLHAM.

27 *DN* 6 April 1888.

28 The file upon Emma Smith is now missing from MEPO 3/140. Most of the information in the present account has been drawn from press notices of the inquest on 7 April 1888: *Star* 7 April; *T, DT* and *DN* 9 April. See also: London Hospital, Patient Admissions Register, 1888,

RLHAM; Dew, *I Caught Crippen*, pp. 91–4; Rumbelow, *Complete Jack the Ripper* (1975), pp. 56–7.

29 For the movements of Polly Nichols on the night of 30–31 August, see *T* 1 September 1888; report of Inspector Joseph Helson, 7 September 1888, MEPO 3/140, f. 237; report of Inspector Frederick G. Abberline, 19 September 1888, MEPO 3/140, ff. 246–7; deposition of Ellen Holland, 3 September 1888, *ELO* 8 September.

3 *Without the Slightest Shadow of a Trace*

1 Cross and Paul told their stories at the Nichols inquest, Cross on 3 September and Paul on 17 September. The most useful notices of Cross' testimony are in *Star*, 3 September; *DT*, 4 September; *DN*, 4 September. There is a brief notice of Paul's testimony in *T*, 18 September, and even briefer ones in *DT*, 18 September, and *ELA*, 22 September. Their discovery of the body is also described in the report of Inspector Abberline, 19 September 1888, MEPO 3/140, ff. 242–3.

2 This account of police activities consequent upon the discovery of Nichols' body rests primarily upon inquest depositions. For those of PC John Neil and Dr Rees Ralph Llewellyn, 1 September 1888, see *T*, 3 September; *DT*, 3 September; *DN*, 3 September. For those of PC Jonas Mizen and Inspector John Spratling, 3 September, see *Star*, 3 September; *DN*, 4 September. And for that of PC Thain, 17 September, see *T*, 18 September; *DT*, 18 September.

Llewellyn's press statement of 31 August 1888 is printed in *DT*, 1 September, and *DN*, 1 September. Finally, the events are briefly covered in two police reports – that of Inspector Spratling, 31 August 1888, MEPO 3/140, f. 239, and that of Inspector Abberline, 19 September 1888, MEPO 3/140, ff. 243–4.

3 Report of Inspector Spratling, 31 August 1888, MEPO 3/140, ff. 239–240; report of Chief Inspector Swanson on Nichols murder, 19 October 1888, HO 144/221/A49301C/8a.

4 Deposition of Dr Llewellyn, 1 September 1888, see n. 2 above.

5 Much on Polly Nichols' history will be found in: report of Inspector Helson, 7 September 1888, MEPO 3/140, ff. 235–6; report of Inspector Abberline, 19 September 1888, MEPO 3/140, ff. 244–6; deposition of Edward Walker, 1 September 1888, *T*, *DT* and *DN*, all for 3 September; depositions of William Nichols and Ellen Holland, 3 September 1888, *ELO*, 8 September, for best coverage, but see also *DT*, 4 September, and *DN*, 4 September; statement of William Nichols, not dated, *DT*, 10 September 1888; registers of births, marriages and deaths, St Catherine's House.

I have also derived great benefit from the pioneering researches of Donald Rumbelow, *The Complete Jack the Ripper* (revised edition, 1987), pp. 41–2, and Neal Shelden, 'Victims of Jack the Ripper', *True Detective*, January 1989, p. 49.

6 Quoted in *DN*, 3 September. Since Polly did not leave Lambeth Workhouse until 12 May 1888 the date of 17 April given for this letter in *DT*, 3 September, must be incorrect and may be a misprint for 17 May.

7 Helson, in his report of 7 September, identifies the 'White House' as No. 55 Flower and Dean Street. Abberline, writing twelve days later, makes it No. 56.

8 *DT*, 3 September; *ELO*, 8 September. Both Edward Walker and William Nichols found it difficult to live with Polly's drinking. Nichols told the inquest: 'I did not leave my wife but she left me of her own accord. She had no occasion for so doing. If it had not been for her drinking habits we would have got on all right together.' See deposition of William Nichols, 3 September 1888, cited in n. 5 above.

9 *ELO*, 17 December 1887. For convenient sketches of Abberline's career, see 'On Duty in Plain Clothes (A Detective Officer's Reminiscences)', *Cassell's Saturday Journal*, Vol. X, No. 452, 28 May 1892, p. 852; Paul Begg, Martin Fido and Keith Skinner, *The Jack the Ripper A to Z*, pp. 5–8.

10 This account of the police investigation is drawn from the report of Inspector Spratling, 31 August 1888, MEPO 3/140, ff. 240–1, and from inquest testimony. For the depositions of Spratling and Helson, 3 September, see *Star*, 3 September, and *DN*, 4 September. For those of Spratling, PC Thain, Emma Green, Walter Purkis and Patrick Mulshaw, 17 September, see *T*, 18 September, and *DT*, 18 September.

11 *T* prints the watchman's name as Patrick Mulshaw, *DT* as Alfred Malshaw.

12 Deposition of Henry Tomkins, 3 September 1888, *Star*, 3 September; *DN*, 4 September; *DT*, 4 September. For Neil, *DN*, 3 September.

13 Report of Inspector Helson, 7 September 1888, MEPO 3/140, f. 237; report of Inspector Abberline, 19 September 1888, MEPO 3/140, f. 247; report of Chief Inspector Swanson, 19 October 1888, HO 144/221/A49301C/8a.

14 *DT*, 18 September 1888.

15 For Llewellyn's press statement, 31 August 1888, see n. 2 above.

16 For depositions of Inspectors Spratling and Helson, 3 September 1888, see n. 10 above.

17 Statement of Inspector Helson, 2 September 1888, *DN*, 3 September; report of Inspector Helson, 7 September 1888, MEPO 3/140, f. 236; report of Inspector Abberline, 19 September 1888, MEPO 3/140, f.

253; for Helson's inquest deposition, see n. 10 above.

18 Statement of Dr Llewellyn, 31 August 1888, *T*, 1 September.

19 Rumbelow, *Complete Jack the Ripper* (1987), p. 162; Arthur Douglas, *Will the Real Jack the Ripper* (Chorley, Lancs., 1979), p. 10.

20 Report of Inspector Spratling, 31 August 1888, MEPO 3/140, f. 240; report of Chief Inspector Swanson, 19 October 1888, HO 144/221/A49301C/8a; deposition of Dr Llewellyn, 1 September 1888, *DN*, 3 September, and *DT*, 3 September.

21 McCormick, *Identity of Jack the Ripper*, p. 30.

22 Colin Wilson & Robin Odell, *Jack the Ripper: Summing Up and Verdict* (London, 1987), p. 139.

23 *T*, 1 September 1888.

24 For full text, see Daniel Farson, *Jack the Ripper*, pp. 45–6.

4 Leather Apron

1 Summing up by George Collier, Tabram inquest, 23 August 1888, *DT* 24 August; *The Illustrated Police News*, 18 August 1888; *ELO*, 11 August 1888. Cries of murder, as Francis Hewitt and his wife observed, may have been commonplace in the East End but murder itself evidently was not. It is interesting that Superintendent Thomas Arnold, Head of H Division, noted that although Whitechapel had a considerable population of 'low and dangerous classes' that frequently indulged in rowdyism and street offences, 'with the exception of the recent murders crime of a serious nature is not unusually heavy in the district.' See, report of Supt. Arnold, 22 October 1888, MEPO 3/141, ff. 164–5. Cf. Cullen, *Autumn of Terror*, p. 32.

2 *DT*, 4 September 1888. After an investigation by Wilton Friend, the manager of the Foresters' Music Hall, the journalist who sent the report to the news agency confessed that he 'had absolutely no foundation for the story . . . that, in fact, it existed only in his own imagination.' See, *ELO*, 6 October 1888.

3 *DN*, 1 September 1888.

4 *Star*, 31 August and 1 September 1888.

5 *ELO*, 8 September 1888.

6 *DN*, 5 September 1888.

7 *T* 7 September 1888; *ELA* 8 September 1888; burial register, City of London Cemetry, Little Ilford, GL, MS. 10445/33.

8 L. & P. Walter & Son, 31 August 1888, to Matthews, and E. Leigh-Pemberton, 4 September 1888, to Messrs. Walter & Son, HO 144/220/A49301B.

9 For general accounts of Warren's career, see *T*, 24 January 1927;

Dictionary of National Biography, 1922–30, pp. 889–891; Watkin W. Williams, *The Life of General Sir Charles Warren* (Oxford, 1941).

Warren's commissionership of the Metropolitan Police is treated in Sir Charles Warren, 'The Police of the Metropolis,' *Murray's Magazine,* Vol. IV, No. 23, November 1888, pp. 577–594; Charles Clarkson & J. Hall Richardson, *Police!* (London, 1889), ch. vi, ix, xv; George Dilnot, *The Story of Scotland Yard* (London, 1926), pp. 95–105, 261–4; Sir John Moylan, *Scotland Yard and the Metropolitan Police* (London, 1934), pp. 48–52; Douglas G. Browne, *The Rise of Scotland Yard* (London, 1956), pp. 201–211; Paul Begg and Keith Skinner, *The Scotland Yard Files* (London, 1992), pp. 111–36. On public order, see Lisa Keller, 'Public Order in Victorian London,' Ph.D. thesis, Cambridge University, 1976.

10 Williams, *Life of Warren,* pp. 216, 218.

11 On the search, see Warren's press notice, 17 October 1888, *DT,* 18 October; minute of Robert Anderson, 23 October 1888, HO 144/221/A49301C/8a; *DN,* 19 October 1888.

12 For good examples of press criticism, see *DN,* 31 August 1888; *PMG* 8 October 1888.

13 The best account of the Warren–Monro feud is Bernard Porter, *The Origins of the Vigilant State* (London, 1987), pp. 82–7; there is a good assessment of Monro in Begg, Fido & Skinner, *Jack the Ripper A to Z,* pp. 190–1.

14 Sir Robert Anderson, 'The Lighter Side of My Official Life,' *Blackwood's Magazine,* Vol. CLXXXVII, No. 1132, February 1910, pp. 250–1; *T,* 16 November 1888.

15 Memorandum of Dr Anderson, now in private hands, quoted by Begg, *Jack the Ripper,* p. 51; Anderson, 'Lighter Side of My Official Life,' *Blackwood's Magazine,* Vol. CLXXXVII, No. 1133, March 1910, p. 356. The memorandum is not dated by Begg but Chief Inspector Swanson's entry in Begg, Fido & Skinner, *Jack the Ripper A to Z,* p. 283, implies a date of 1 September 1888. A. P. Moore-Anderson, *Sir Robert Anderson, KCB LLD, and Lady Agnes Anderson* (London & Edinburgh, 1947) is an indifferent biography.

16 Memorandum of Dr Anderson, quoted by Begg, *Jack the Ripper,* pp. 51–2.

17 Anderson, 'Lighter Side of My Official Life,' February 1910, p. 251; *Star,* 4 October 1888.

18 Quoted by John J. Tobias, *Crime and Industrial Society in the Nineteenth Century* (Pelican edition, Harmondsworth, 1972), p. 148.

19 Charles Booth, *Life and Labour of the People in London* (London, 1902), 3rd Series, Vol. II, p. 7. See also Lloyd P. Gartner, *The Jewish Immigrant in England, 1870–1914* (London, 1973), pp. 41–4; V. D.

Lipman, 'Jewish Settlement in the East End of London, 1840–1940,' pp. 31–4, in Aubrey Newman (ed.), *The Jewish East End 1840–1939* (London, 1981). For a colourful portrait of East London in the year of the Ripper murders, see William J. Fishman, *East End 1888* (London, 1988).

20 For the full ramifications of this fascinating case, see T. A. Critchley & P. D. James, *The Maul and the Pear Tree* (London, 1971).

21 Quoted by Clarkson & Richardson, *Police!*, p. 280.

22 C. E. Howard Vincent, *A Police Code, and Manual of the Criminal Law* (London, 1881), p. 253.

23 *ELA*, 18 August and 8 September 1888.

24 *DN*, 3 September 1888; *T*, 4 September 1888.

25 *DT*, 24 September 1888.

26 *DT*, 6 September 1888.

27 *Star*, 5 and 6 September 1888. According to Lincoln Springfield, *Some Piquant People* (London 1924), pp. 45–7, the author of the articles was an American journalist named Harry Dam.

28 Report of Inspector Helson, 7 September 1888, MEPO 3/140, f. 238; report of Inspector Abberline, 19 September 1888, MEPO 3/140, f. 248.

29 Sir Melville Macnaghten, *Days of My Years* (London, 1914), pp. 64–5; Dew, *I Caught Crippen*, p. 102.

30 Nick Ross & Sue Cook, *Crimewatch UK* (London, 1987), p. 159.

31 *DN*, 3 September 1888.

32 *ELA*, 8 September 1888.

5 Dark Annie

1 For details of Annie Chapman's background and character, see depositions of Amelia Palmer, Timothy Donovan and John Evans, 10 September 1888, in *DT* and *DN*, 11 September; deposition of Fountain Smith, 12 September 1888, in *DT* and *DN*, 13 September, and *ELA*, 15 September; deposition of Timothy Donovan, 13 September 1888, in *DT* and *DN*, 14 September; depositions of Eliza Cooper and Ted Stanley, 19 September 1888, in *DT* and *DN*, 20 September; report of Inspector Joseph Chandler, 8 September 1888, MEPO 3/140, ff. 10–11; report of Inspector Abberline, 14 September 1888, MEPO 3/140, f. 17; report of Inspector Abberline, 19 September 1888, MEPO 3/140, ff. 250–252; report of Chief Inspector Swanson, 19 October 1888, relating to Hanbury Street murder, HO 144/221/A49301C/8a; registers of births, marriages and deaths, St Catherine's House; Shelden, 'Victims of Jack the Ripper,' pp. 49–50.

T, 11 September 1888, prints Amelia Palmer's name as Amelia Farmer. In five other inquest reports checked by the author the name is given as Palmer and this name has been adopted in the present text.

2 Her name is not recorded in the Admissions & Discharge Book of the Whitechapel Workhouse Infirmary, 1888–9, GLRO, StBG/Wh/123/20.

3 Statement of Frederick Simpson, *Star*, 8 September 1888.

4 The times stated are those given by Donovan at the inquest, 10 September, see n. 1. They are consistent with the report of Inspector Chandler, written on the day of the murder, which states that Annie was approached for her lodging money at 1.45. John Evans, testifying on 10 September, said that Annie left the lodging house at about 1.45. Abberline's report of 19 September makes it later, at about 2.00.

5 Frustratingly, names are often reported differently in different newspapers. Thus Mrs Hardiman's first name is most commonly given as Harriet but also as Annie and Mary. Tyler is called Francis in some reports and John in others. All the contemporary references I have seen to the residents of the first floor back call them Waker but Begg, Fido & Skinner, *Jack the Ripper A to Z*, enter them under Walker. While the surname of the two unmarried sisters from the second floor back is variously given as Cooksley, Copsey and Huxley. The report in *T* even refers to them (erroneously) as *Mr and Mrs* Copsey.

6 This account of the discovery of Annie Chapman's body rests largely upon inquest testimony. See, deposition of John Davis, 10 September 1888, in *DT* and *DN*, 11 September; depositions of Amelia Richardson, Harriet Hardiman, James Kent, James Green and Henry John Holland, 12 September 1888, in *DT* and *DN*, 13 September; summing up of Coroner Wynne E. Baxter, 26 September 1888, in *T*, 27 September. See also, report of Inspector Abberline, 19 September 1888, MEPO 3/140, f. 249.

7 Report of Inspector Chandler, 8 September 1888, MEPO 3/140, f. 9.

8 Dew, *I Caught Crippen*, pp. 115–6.

9 Deposition of Dr George Bagster Phillips, 13 September 1888, in *DT*, 14 September.

10 Report of Inspector Chandler, 8 September 1888, MEPO 3/140, ff. 9–10; depositions of Inspector Chandler and Dr Phillips, 13 September 1888, in *DT*, *DN* and *T*, 14 September. The date of the postmark, 23 August, is taken from Swanson's summary report (see n.1). Dates of 3, 20 and 28 August are given in the press.

11 For Chandler's evidence, see n. 10.

12 Deposition of Dr Phillips, 13 September 1888, in *DT*, *DN* and *T*, 14 September; deposition of Dr Phillips, 19 September 1888, in *DT*, *DN* and *T*, 20 September; 'The Whitechapel Murders', *The Lancet*, 1888,

Vol. II, 29 September 1888, p. 637; report of Chief Inspector Swanson, 19 October 1888, HO 144/221/A49301C/8a.

13 Endorsement of Acting Superintendent West to report of Inspector Chandler, 8 September 1888, MEPO 3/140, f. 11.

14 For these police activities, see report of Inspector Chandler, 8 September 1888, MEPO 3/140, f. 11; report of Inspector Abberline, 19 September 1888, MEPO 3/140, ff. 252–3; report of Chief Inspector Swanson, 19 October 1888, HO 144/221/A49301C/8a. On the leather apron, see the inquest depositions of Amelia Richardson, 12 September 1888, and Inspector Chandler and Dr Phillips, 13 September 1888, cited in n. 6 and 10.

15 Report of Inspector Chandler, 14 September 1888, MEPO 3/140, f. 16; report of Inspector Chandler, 15 September 1888, MEPO 3/140, ff. 18–20; deposition of William Stevens, 19 September 1888, in *DT* and *T*, 20 September.

16 Deposition of John Richardson, 12 September 1888, in *DT* and *DN*, 13 September; report of Chief Inspector Swanson, 19 October 1888, HO 144/221/A49301C/8a.

17 Deposition of Mrs Elizabeth Long, 19 September 1888, in *DT*, *DN* and *T*, 20 September; report of Chief Inspector Swanson, 19 October 1888, HO 144/221/A49301C/8a.

There are frequent discrepancies between our sources. The only one which concerns the description of the suspect is about his hat. According to *DN* (quoted in the text) and *T*, Mrs Long described it as a brown deerstalker. The *DT* report, however, quotes her as saying that it was a 'brown, low-crowned, felt hat.'

Mrs Long's address seems to have been recorded differently by almost everyone who heard it. The main inquest reports print it as Church Row, Whitechapel (*DT*), 3 Church Row (*DN*) and 198 Church Row, Whitechapel (*T*). Baxter, summing up on 26 September, referred to it as Church Street, Whitechapel. And Swanson, reviewing the case on 19 October, gave it as 32 Church Street. There were Church Streets in Bethnal Green, Minories and Spitalfields. Mrs Long could have lived in any one of the three, or in Church Lane, by Whitechapel Church. All these four had house numbers up to or beyond 32 but none as high as 198.

18 The times given in the text follow Cadosch's inquest deposition of 19 September 1888. See, *DT*, *DN* and *T*, 20 September. Swanson, probably drawing upon a lost statement to the police, gave 5.25 and 5.28 as the times of Cadosch's experiences in the yard of No. 27.

19 Coroner Baxter's summing up, 26 September 1888, in *DT*, 27 September.

20 *DT*, 10 September 1888.

21 Baxter's summing up, 26 September 1888, *DT*, 27 September.
22 See, *Star*, 12 September 1888; *DT, DN* and *T*, 13 September 1888.
23 *T*, 13 September 1888; *DT* and *ELA*, 15 September 1888; for Fountain Smith's demeanour at inquest, *DN*, 13 September, and *ELA*, 15 September 1888.

6 *The Man in the Passage*

1 Leonard Matters, *Mystery of Jack the Ripper* (London, 1929), p. 61; Stewart, *Jack the Ripper*, pp. 56–7; Robin Odell, *Jack the Ripper in Fact and Fiction* (London, revised edition, 1966), p. 31; McCormick, *Identity of Jack the Ripper* (1959), p. 41; Peter Underwood, *Jack the Ripper: One Hundred Years of Mystery* (London, 1987), p. 8.
2 Stewart, *Jack the Ripper*, pp. 19, 58.
3 Deposition of Amelia Palmer, 10 September 1888, *DN* 11 September.
4 McCormick, *Identity of Jack the Ripper* (1959), p. 37.
5 *Star* 8 September 1888.
6 Victor Neuburg, *Gone for a Soldier* (London, 1989), pp. 25–6; Edward Spiers, *The Army and Society 1815–1914* (London, 1980), ch. 2.
7 Begg, *Jack the Ripper*, p. 53, citing *Yorkshire Post* 11 September 1888.
8 Deposition of Timothy Donovan, 10 September 1888, *DN* 11 September.
9 Terence Sharkey, *Jack the Ripper: 100 Years of Investigation* (London, 1987), p. 28.
10 Deposition of Timothy Donovan, 13 September 1888, *DN* and *DT* 14 September.
11 Allen's report is known only from Stewart, *Jack the Ripper*, p. 55. The 8 September 1888 issue of *PMG* consulted by the present writer did not carry the item but it is possible that it was given in another edition. For the farthings, *DT* 10 September 1888. For Reid and Smith, deposition of Inspector Reid, 18 July 1889, at Alice McKenzie inquest, *DT* 19 July 1889, and Sir Henry Smith, *From Constable to Commissioner* (London, 1910), p. 148.
12 Matters, *Mystery of Jack the Ripper*, p. 64; Stewart, *Jack the Ripper*, pp. 55, 215; McCormick, *Identity of Jack the Ripper* (1959), p. 35.
13 Harrison, *Jack the Ripper*, p. 39; Begg, Fido & Skinner, *Jack the Ripper A to Z*, p. 49.
14 Knight, *Jack the Ripper: The Final Solution*, pp. 168–9, 171–2.
15 Report of Inspector Chandler, 8 September 1888, MEPO 3/140, ff. 9–10; deposition of James Kent, 12 September 1888, *DT* and *DN* 13 September; depositions of Inspector Chandler and Dr Phillips, 13

September 1888, *DT*, *DN* and *T* 14 September; report of Inspector Abberline, 19 September 1888, MEPO 3/140, f. 252.

16 Knight, *Jack the Ripper: The Final Solution*, pp. 166–71; Fairclough, *Ripper and the Royals*, pp. 55, 58–9.

17 McCormick, *Identity of Jack the Ripper*, pp. 39, 49, 50.

18 *Star* 12 and 13 September 1888; *T*, *DT* and *DN* 13 September 1888.

19 *DT* 10 September 1888; *T* 11 September 1888.

20 Cullen, *Autumn of Terror*, p. 59.

21 *DN* 11 September 1888.

22 *DT* 10 September 1888.

23 Deposition of Amelia Richardson, 12 September 1888, *DT* 13 September.

24 *DT* 10 September 1888.

25 Report of Chief Inspector Swanson, 19 October 1888, HO 144/221/A49301C/8a.

7 The Panic and the Police

1 *Star*, 8 September 1888; *DT*, 10 September 1888.

2 *ELO*, 15 September 1888.

3 *DN*, 11 September 1888.

4 Dew, *I Caught Crippen*, pp. 117–122.

5 *Star*, 8 September 1888. The identity of 'Squibby' has not yet been established. Possibilities, culled from the records of the police courts, include George Squibb, a young carman charged at Worship Street with cutting and wounding a woman in Commercial Road and with violently assaulting two policemen in September 1886; William Squibb, charged at Thames Police Court in February 1888 with the theft of a watch; and Charles Squibb, who threatened to blind a policeman when arrested for attempted theft in August 1888.

6 *ELO*, 15 September 1888.

7 *The Jewish Chronicle*, 14 September 1888; *DN*, 10 September 1888; *Star*, 11 September 1888; *ELA*, 22 September 1888.

8 Montagu's note of authorization, 10 September 1888; Bruce, 10 September 1888, to Under Secretary of State; Leigh-Pemberton, 13 September 1888, to Warren; Montagu, 18 September 1888, to Warren; Warren, 19 September 1888, to Montagu. All these documents will be found at HO 144/220/A49301B/2 and MEPO 3/141, ff. 170–6.

9 *ELO*, 22 September 1888.

10 *ELO*, 15 September 1888.

11 *ELO*, 22 September 1888; *ELA*, 22 and 29 September 1888.

12 B. Harris, 16 September 1888, to Matthews, and Leigh-Pemberton,

17 September 1888, to Harris, HO 144/220/A49301B/3; Home Office minute on letter of Mile End Vigilance Committee, 24 September 1888, to Matthews, HO 144/221/A49301C/1.

13 Lusk's petition, 27 September 1888, to Queen Victoria, and Leigh-Pemberton, 6 October 1888, to Lusk, HO 144/220/A49301B/5; George Lusk and Joseph Aarons, 29 September 1888, to *DT*, *DT* 1 October 1888.

14 *Star*, 8 and 10 September 1888.

15 *DT*, 12 September 1888.

16 'A Night in Whitechapel,' *Star*, 11 September 1888.

17 *ELO*, 22 September 1888; *DT*, 17, 20 and 21 September 1888; *Star*, 19 and 20 September 1888.

18 *Star*, 8 September 1888; *T*, 10 September 1888; *DT*, 12 September 1888; *ELO* and *ELA*, 15 September 1888; Montagu Williams, *Round London: Down East and Up West* (London, 1892); Cullen, *Autumn of Terror*, p. 54; Underwood, *Jack the Ripper*, p. 171.

19 *T*, 18 September 1888.

20 Winslow publicized his views in *T*, 12 September 1888, and *The Lancet*, 22 September 1888, p. 603. There was little agreement within the medical profession on such matters. For other contemporary views, see *The Lancet*, 15 September 1888, pp. 533–4, and 22 September 1888, p. 603; George H. Savage, 'Homicidal Mania', *The Fortnightly Review*, New Series, Vol. XLIV, July–December 1888, pp. 448–463.

21 *DT*, 14 September 1888; *DN*, 20 September 1888.

22 Coroner Baxter's summing-up, 26 September 1888, *DT*, 27 September.

23 *T*, 27 September 1888.

24 James Risdon Bennett, 27 September 1888, to *T*, in *T*, 28 September; see also Central News interview with Bennett, 1 October 1888, *Evening News*, 1 October.

25 *DT*, 29 September 1888.

26 *The British Medical Journal*, 6 October 1888.

27 *ELA*, 15 September 1888; *DT*, 12 and 19 September 1888; *T*, 18 and 24 September 1888.

28 *DN*, 11 September 1888; *Star*, 8 and 10 September 1888; *DT*, 24 September 1888; Home Office memo., 19 September 1888, to Matthews, HO 144/221/A49301C/8.

29 *Star*, 8 September 1888; J. H. Ashforth, 12 September 1888, to Warren, HO 144/221/A49301E/4; deposition of Dr Phillips, 19 September 1888, *DT* 20 September.

30 'Brain Pictures – A Photo-Physiological Discovery,' *British Journal of Photography*, Vol. XXXV, No. 1450, 17 February 1888, p. 105; *Star* 13 September 1888; deposition of Dr Phillips, 19 September

1888, *DT*, 20 September; Matthews, 5 October 1888, to Warren, HO 144/221/A49301C/8; Dew, *I Caught Crippen*, p. 148; Kelly, *Jack the Ripper: A Bibliography and Review of the Literature* (1973), p. 20.
31 For background on reward question, see Sir Leon Radzinowicz, *A History of English Criminal Law* (London, 1948–86), espec. II, pp. 57–111; CET, 'Memoranda on the Question of the Offer of Rewards by Government in Criminal Cases,' 6 and 19 October 1888, HO 144/220/A49301B/19.
32 For comment at Nichols inquest, *DT*, 18 September 1888, and at Chapman inquest, *DT*, 14 and 20 September 1888.
33 *Star*, 14 September 1888; *DT*, 12, 19 and 24 September 1888.
34 Home Office minute, 11 September 1888, HO 144/220/A49301B/2.
35 *Star*, 10 and 12 September 1888; *DT* and *T*, 11 September 1888.

8 The King of Elthorne Road

1 *DN* 11 September 1888; Farson, *Jack the Ripper* (1973), p. 25.
2 *DT* 11 September 1888; Dew, *I Caught Crippen*, p. 110; Cullen, *Autumn of Terror*, p. 61.
3 Report of Chief Inspector Swanson, 19 October 1888, HO 144/221/A49301C/8a; deposition of John Pizer, 12 September 1888, *DN*, *DT* and *T* 13 September.
4 *T* and *DT* 12 September 1888.
5 *DN* 13 September 1888; *ELO* 15 September 1888; depositions of John Pizer and Sergeant Thick, 12 September 1888, *DN*, *DT* and *T* 13 September; *ELA* 15 September 1888.

   John Pizer, the son of Israel and August Pizer, died at the London Hospital in 1897 from gastro-enteritis. His death certificate makes him 47 years old at time of death and therefore 38 at the time of the Chapman murder. In the Thames Magistrates' Court registers his age is given as 36 in both 1887 and 1888. In September 1888 press reports ascribe ages of 33, 35 and 36 to him.

   On Thursday, 11 October 1888, Pizer successfully prosecuted Emily Patzwold at Thames Magistrates' Court for calling him 'Old Leather Apron' and assaulting him; see *DN* 5 October and *DT* 12 October. For Pizer's libel actions, *ELA* 13 October 1888 and Lincoln Springfield, *Some Piquant People*, pp. 45–7.
6 Report of Inspector Abberline, 19 September 1888, MEPO 3/140, ff. 248–9.
7 For statements of Pizer's relatives, *Star* 10 September 1888, *DT* 11 and 12 September 1888; for his court appearances, *T* 8 July 1887, and Thames Magistrates' Court Registers, GLRO, PS/TH/Al/9 and 12.

8 *DT* 12 September 1888; *Star* 11 September 1888. This incident was probably the basis for the *Star*'s claim, on 6 September, that Leather Apron had temporarily fallen into the hands of two J Division constables the previous Sunday. See ch. 4.

9 Numerous press reports relate to Piggott during the week but see, especially, *T* 11–12 and 14–15 September 1888; *DT* and *Star* 11 September 1888. Also, Whitechapel Workhouse Infirmary, Admission & Discharge Book, 1888–9, GLRO, StBG/Wh/123/20.

Piggott was no stranger to the infirmary. He had been admitted there from 19 Brick Lane on 8 June 1888 for alcoholism and discharged on 30 July. Infirmary records describe him as a ship's cook. Press reports aver that he was the son of an insurance agent in Gravesend and once prospered as a publican, giving £8000 to go into a house at Hoxton in 1880 or 1881. He died in 1901.

10 For Ludwig's activities, depositions of John Johnson, Alexander Finlay and PC 221H, Thames Magistrates' Court, 18 September 1888, *DT* and *T* 19 September; statement of Alexander Finlay, 18 September 1888, *DT* 19 September; Thames Magistrates' Court Register, 18 and 25 September 1888, GLRO, PS/TH/Al/11.

11 See, especially, *DT* 19 September 1888, which carries statements by C. A. Partridge and Mr Richter, and *DN* 20 September 1888, which prints a statement of the landlord of a hotel in Finsbury in which Ludwig sometimes stayed.

12 Ludwig is sometimes referred to in contemporary records as Wetzel. He eventually accounted for his whereabouts on the nights of the previous murders and, having spent two weeks on remand, was discharged on 2 October 1888. Just a fortnight later he was reported to have been seen acting strangely and flourishing a knife in the neighbourhood. See, *Star* 2 and 17 October. He often appears in the subsequent registers of Thames Magistrates' Court.

13 Cullen, *Autumn of Terror*, p. 199.

14 Warren, 19 September 1888, to Ruggles-Brise, HO 144/221/A49301C/8.

15 Philip Sugden, 'Puckridge: A Cautionary Tale,' *Ripperana*, No. 3, January 1993, pp. 55–62.

16 Admissions Register, Metropolitan Licensed Houses, 1886–1900, PRO, MH 94/6.

17 Register of births, marriages & deaths, St Catherine's House; 1841 census, PRO, HO 107/1093/2; Holborn Workhouse, City Road, Admission & Discharge Book, April-September 1900, GLRO, HO.BG. 541/71.

18 Report of Inspector Abberline, 14 September 1888, MEPO 3/140, f. 17; report of Chief Inspector Swanson, 19 October 1888, HO

144/221/A49301C/8a; student registers, London Hospital Medical College, 22 April 1879, RLHAM, MC/S/1/6; report of Inspector Abberline, 1 November 1888, MEPO 3/140, f. 206; admissions register, provincial licensed houses, 1880–1900, PRO, MH 94/11; Begg, *Jack the Ripper*, pp. 66–9, 188–9; Begg, Fido & Skinner, *Jack the Ripper A to Z*, pp. 244–5; Jon Ogan, 'The Third Man', *Ripperana*, forthcoming.

19 Smith, *From Constable to Commissioner*, pp. 147–8.

20 Index Register of Students 1741–1914, London Hospital Medical College, RLHAM, MC/S/1/1; rate books, Rupert St, St James Piccadilly, 1887–90, WCL, D358, D362, D366; 1881 and 1891 census returns, PRO.

21 The 1881 census records Henry Orford's household at 39 Rupert Street. From it we know that he had three sons. Alfred, like his father, was a carman. The other two – Harry and Charles – were still at school. They would have been twenty-eight, twenty-three and twenty-one respectively in 1888. Rate books and Post Office directories prove that by then Henry had moved to 40b Rupert Street. He was still there in 1891, living with his wife and two unmarried daughters, one a clerk, the other an actress.

22 Report of Inspector Abberline, 18 September 1888, MEPO 3/140, f. 25; for Warren, see above n. 14; *Star* 17 September 1888.

23 At the time of the Whitechapel murders it was possible to determine whether blood was mammalian but not specifically whether it was human.

24 On 4 February 1890 Isenschmid was discharged from Grove Hall to Banstead Asylum, where he was held, apparently, until late 1890. Within a month of his release from there he began to abuse his wife and children and on 12 October 1891 was brought to St Mary's Infirmary, St John's Road, in such a maniacal state that it took the combined efforts of four policemen to hold him. Three days later he was committed to Colney Hatch and he was held there until September 1892. Isenschmid was returned repeatedly to Colney Hatch for treatment and died there in March 1910. Cause of death was registered as 'recurrent mania over 1 year and 5 months lobar pneumonia and exhaustion 4 days.' According to the death certificate he was sixty-three when he died. Colney Hatch records make him forty-three in 1887 and hence sixty-six in 1910. Police reports refer to him incorrectly as 'Joseph' Isenschmid.

The police reports are at MEPO 3/140. See those by Inspector J. Styles of Y Division, 11 September 1888, ff. 12–13; Acting Superintendent West, 13 September 1888, f. 14; Sergeant Thick, 17 and 19 September 1888, ff. 21–3, 26–8; Inspector Abberline, 18 and 19 September 1888, ff. 24–5, 254–6; Inspector Helson, 19 September 1888, ff. 29–31.

For biographical data on Isenschmid, Registers of births, marriages & deaths, St Catherine's House; Lunacy Commission, Admissions Register, Metropolitan Licensed Houses, 1886–1900, PRO, MH 94/6; Colney Hatch Asylum, male patient casebooks, GLRO, H12/CH/B13/36, 40, 42; Colney Hatch Asylum, male admissions register, 1888–1906, GLRO, H12/CH/B2/2; statement of Mary Isenschmid, 18 September 1888, *Star* 18 September.
25 *DN* 27 September 1888.

9 *Double Event*

1 Statement of Morris Eagle, 30 September 1888, in *DN*, 1 October. For a contemporary description of a visit to the International Working Men's Educational Club, see John Henry Mackay, *The Anarchists* (Boston: B. R. Tucker, 1891), pp. 182–8.
2 Depositions of William West and Morris Eagle, 1 October 1888, in *DT*, *DN* and *T*, 2 October; statements of Joseph Lave and Morris Eagle, 30 September 1888, in *DN*, 1 October.
3 The gateway, according to Eagle, was nine feet two inches wide.
4 For the discovery of the body, see depositions of Morris Eagle and Louis Diemschutz, 1 October 1888, in *DT*, *DN* and *T*, 2 October; depositions of Edward Spooner and PC Henry Lamb, 2 October 1888, in *DT*, *DN* and *T*, 3 October; statements of Morris Eagle, Louis Diemschutz and Isaac Kozebrodski, 30 September 1888, in *DN* and *Star*, 1 October; statement of Mrs Diemschutz, 1 October 1888, in *DN*, 2 October.
5 Deposition of Dr Blackwell, 2 October 1888, in *DT*, *DN* and *T*, 3 October; depositions of Edward Johnston and Dr Phillips, 3 October 1888, in *DT*, *DN* and *T*, 4 October; depositions of Dr Blackwell and Dr Phillips, 5 October 1888, in *DT*, *DN* and *T*, 6 October; statement of Dr Blackwell, 30 September 1888, in *DN*, 1 October.
6 'Clavicle', given in *DT* and *DN*, and 'brow', given in *T*, are both errors. On 5 October Phillips said that the abrasion was on the right side of the neck, and Chief Inspector Swanson was probably correct when he reported a fortnight later that it was below the right angle of the jaw (Swanson's report, 19 October 1888, on Stride murder, HO 144/221/A49301C/8a).
7 *DN*, 1 October 1888.
8 This account of the discovery of the body in Mitre Square rests principally upon the following depositions in the coroner's papers – Coroners' Inquests (L), 1888, No. 135, Corporation of London Records Office, hereinafter referred to as CPL (Coroner's Papers, Langham): PC Edward Watkins, 4 October 1888, ff. 6–7; George

James Morris, 11 October 1888, ff. 31–32; PC James Harvey, 11 October 1888, ff. 33–34; Inspector Edward Collard, 4 October 1888, ff. 9–10, 11; Dr George William Sequeira, 11 October 1888, f. 24.

See also press statements of PC Watkins, date uncertain, *DN*, 2 October 1888; George James Morris and Inspector Collard, 30 September 1888, *DT*, 1 October; PC Watkins and George Morris, 30 September 1888, and Dr Sequeira, date uncertain, *Star*, 1 October.

9 Deposition of Dr Brown, 4 October 1888, CPL, ff. 12–14.

10 Francis E. Camps, 'More About Jack the Ripper,' *The London Hospital Gazette*, Vol. LXIX, No. 1, April 1966. The originals are now (1992) framed and hanging in the Secretary's Office of The London Hospital Medical College, Turner Street, London E1 2AD.

11 Sir Henry Smith, *From Constable to Commissioner*, pp. 149–150.

12 Smith, *Ibid.*, pp. 148, 151–2. The reality of these instructions has been questioned by some writers but they are substantiated by McWilliam's report of 27 October 1888 to the Home Office, HO 144/221/A49301C/8b, f. 1. Also *DT*, 1 October 1888, and *T*, 2 October 1888.

13 Deposition of Daniel Halse, 11 October 1888, CPL, f. 40; report of Inspector McWilliam, 27 October 1888, HO 144/221/A49301C/8b, ff. 1–2.

14 See the following depositions in CPL: PC Watkins, 4 October 1888, ff. 6–7; PC Harvey, 11 October 1888, ff. 33–4; PC Pearce, 11 October 1888, f. 35; George James Morris, 11 October 1888, ff. 31–2; George Clapp, 11 October 1888, ff. 34–5. Statements by Watkins, Morris and Pearce, all 30 September 1888, may be turned up in *Star*, 1 October.

15 Statement of George Morris, 30 September 1888, *DT*, 1 October.

16 Deposition of Inspector Collard, 4 October 1888, and of Daniel Halse, 11 October 1888, CPL, ff. 10 and 40 respectively.

17 Deposition of PC Long, 11 October 1888, CPL, ff. 37–39; report of PC Long, 6 November 1888, HO 144/221/A49301C/8c.

The writing in Goulston Street was probably the only tangible clue ever left by the Whitechapel murderer. The precise wording of the message cannot now be recovered. Begg, Fido & Skinner, *The Jack the Ripper A to Z*, pp. 96–7, speak of Metropolitan and City Police versions but this is misleading in that there was no unanimity in either force on the matter.

The form of the writing given in the present text was that transmitted by Warren himself to the Home Office (Warren, 10 October 1888, to Lushington, PRO, MEPO 1/48; Warren's report, 6 November, HO 144/221/A49301C/8c). The wording, but not the spelling 'Juwes', is confirmed by PC Long. On 11 October he told the inquest that the words were: 'The Juews are the men that will not be blamed for nothing.'. When Long delivered the apron to the inspector at Commercial Street the inspector returned to Goulston Street with him to see the writing for himself. 'I wrote [the words] down into my book,' testified Long, 'and the Inspector noticed that Jews was spelt Juews.' (Long's deposition, CPL, f. 38). This may be correct because both Long and Superintendent Arnold, in their reports of 6 November, record the message thus: 'The Juews are the men that will not be blamed for nothing' (HO 144/221/A49301C/8c) and Dr Adler, replying on 13 October to a query of Warren, refers to the spelling 'Juewes' (Chaim Bermant, *Point of Arrival*, London, 1975, p. 117).

Chief Inspector Swanson's summary report on the Mitre Square case gives the rendering 'The Juwes are the men who will not be blamed for nothing' (HO 144/221/A49301C/8c), which generally substantiates Warren, but Swanson, as far as we know, did not see the writing. Neither did Dr Anderson. He was not even in the country at the time of the double murder yet he assured a daily paper in April 1910 that the exact words were 'The Jewes are not the men to be blamed for nothing' (J. Hall Richardson, *From the City to Fleet Street*, London, 1927, p. 217), which is different again. Sir Melville Macnaghten's version is 'The Jews are the men who will not be blamed for nothing.' Unfortunately Macnaghten did not join the Metropolitan Police until 1889 and wrote most of his 1914 reminiscences from memory. (See, Macnaghten, *Days of My Years*, pp. ix, 60.) Dew, *I Caught Crippen*, p. 137, is the same as Macnaghten and almost certainly copied from him.

The ranks of the City Police are in similar disarray. We have three City renderings, only one – that given by Daniel Halse to the inquest on 11 October 1888 – coming from an eyewitness: 'I took a note of the writing before it was rubbed out. The exact words were "The Juwes are not the men that will be blamed for nothing."' (CPL, ff. 41–42). Press versions of his testimony add that there were three lines in 'a good schoolboy's round hand', the capital letters about three quarters of an inch high and the others in proportion. (Halse's deposition, 11 October, *DT*, 12 October). Since Halse was there and argued for the preservation of the writing it might be supposed that he took the trouble to record it accurately. But Inspector McWilliam, drawing up a report for the Home Office on 27 October, opted for a version closer to Warren's: 'The Jewes are the men that will not be blamed for nothing' (HO 144/221/A49301C/8b, f. 2). Finally, many years later, Smith remembered the message as 'The Jews are the men that won't be blamed for nothing' (*From Constable to Commissioner*, p. 153).

The reminiscent versions should be discounted. Nevertheless, in view of the conflicting contemporary testimony, the exact nature of the murderer's message must remain in doubt.

18 This paragraph rests on the deposition of Daniel Halse, 11 October 1888, CPL, ff. 40–2, and the report of Inspector McWilliam, 27 October 1888, HO 144/221/A49301C/8b, ff. 2–3. Where the two conflict Halse is preferable. McWilliam did not get to the Detective Office until 3.45 and Mitre Square later still. There is no evidence that he ever visited Goulston Street. Halse, on the other hand, was involved in the events at both places almost from the beginning. His account, moreover, was set down more than a fortnight before that of the inspector.

19 Report of Superintendent Arnold, 6 November 1888, and report of Sir Charles Warren, 6 November 1888, to the Under Secretary of State, HO 144/221/A49301C/8c.

20 Depositions of PC Long and Daniel Halse, both 11 October 1888, CPL, ff. 39 and 41–2 respectively.

21 Deposition of Dr Brown, 4 October 1888, CPL, ff. 22–3.

22 Smith, *From Constable to Commissioner*, pp. 147, 153.

Smith's memoir is repeatedly inaccurate. This is true even on matters, like the Mitre Square murder, with which he was directly concerned. Daniel Halse, the City Detective, went through Goulston Street twice on the night of the double murder, once at about 2.20 in search of suspects and subsequently to check out Long's discoveries. If the apron was there at 2.20 Halse did not notice it. And by the time he returned it had been taken away by PC Long. Smith, however, fuses Halse's two visits into one and describes him turning up in time to see the piece of apron, folded up and lying immediately beneath the chalk message. The site of these finds is incorrectly stated by Smith to have been at 'the door of one of the model workmen's dwellings erected by Peabody' (p. 153). It was, in fact, in the entry to 108–119 Wentworth Model Dwellings, a site first identified by Richard Whittington-Egan, *A Casebook on Jack the Ripper* (London, 1975), p. 123. I know of no evidence to substantiate Smith's belief (p. 161) that Warren wiped out the chalk message with his own hand and, given the fact that Superintendent Arnold sent an inspector to Goulston Street with a sponge expressly for that purpose, find the suggestion unlikely. It is perhaps needless to add that Smith's account of the Berner Street murder (pp. 150–1), an event that fell to the investigation of the Metropolitan force, is grossly misleading and should not be used.

The Scotland Yard library holds a copy of Smith's memoir annotated by George H. Edwards, Secretary to the Metropolitan Police from 1925 to 1927, thus: 'A good raconteur and a good fellow, but not strictly veracious . . . In dealing with matters within his own knowledge he is often far from accurate as my own knowledge of the facts assures me.' (Begg, Fido & Skinner, *Jack the Ripper A to Z*, pp. 92–3). Edwards' last stricture, quite frankly, might truthfully be said of most volumes of reminiscences. As far as Smith's veracity is concerned he was refreshingly honest in admitting his failure on the Ripper case, which can by no means be said of all the officers involved in the investigations.

23 Smith, *Ibid.*, pp. 153, 161–2; report of Inspector McWilliam, 27 October 1888, HO 144/221/A49301C/8b, ff. 3–4; Warren, 6 November 1888, to Under Secretary of State, HO 144/221/A49301C/8c.

10 Long Liz

1 Deposition of Inspector Reid, 5 October 1888, in *T* and *DT*, 6 October; report of Sergeant Stephen White, 4 October 1888, MEPO 3/140, f. 212; report of Chief Inspector Swanson on Berner Street murder, 19 October 1888, HO 144/221/A49301C/8a; report of Inspector Abberline, 1 November 1888, MEPO 3/140, f. 205.

   Dr Phillips later discovered a collection of further trifles in the pocket of the victim's underskirt. They comprised a key (as of a padlock), a small piece of lead pencil, a comb, a broken piece of comb, a metal spoon, six large and one small button, a hook (as if from a dress), a piece of muslin and one or two small pieces of paper. Deposition of Dr Phillips, 3 October 1888, in *DT* and *DN*, 4 October.

2 Deposition of Mary Malcolm, 2 October 1888, in *DT*, *T* and *DN*, 3 October; deposition of Elizabeth Stokes, 23 October 1888, in *DT*, *DN* and *T*, 24 October; Begg, Fido & Skinner, *Jack the Ripper A to Z*, pp. 277–8.

3 *DN*, 6 October 1888.

4 Deposition of Dr Phillips, 5 October 1888, *DT* 6 October.

5 Unless otherwise noted the account of Elizabeth Stride rests upon: depositions of Elizabeth Tanner, Catherine Lane, Charles Preston and Michael Kidney, 3 October 1888, in *DT*, *DN* and *T*, 4 October; depositions of Sven Olsson and Michael Kidney, 5 October 1888, in *DT*, *DN* and *T*, 6 October; depositions of Inspector Reid and Walter Stride, 23 October 1888, in *DT*, *DN* and *T*, 24 October; statement of Thomas Bates, *Star*, 1 October 1888, and *DN*, 2 October; statement of 'old artilleryman', i.e. Michael Kidney, 2 October 1888, *DN*, 3 October; registrations of births, marriages and deaths, St Catherine's House; Begg, *Jack the Ripper*, pp. 92–5; Shelden, 'Victims of Jack the Ripper', p. 50.

6 For these and other details of Elizabeth's life in Sweden, communicated by Klas Lithner, see Rumbelow, *Complete Jack the Ripper* (1987), 74–5.

7 Statement of 'old artilleryman' (Kidney), 2 October 1888, *DN*, 3

October; deposition of Sven Olsson, 5 October 1888, *DT*, 6 October; Begg, *Jack the Ripper*, p. 94, citing Sven Evander, former Rector of the Swedish Church; deposition of Catherine Lane, 3 October 1888, *DT*, 4 October.

8 *DN*, 1 October 1888.

9 Thames Magistrates' Court, Court Register, 6 April 1887, GLRO, PS/TH/A1/8.

10 Thomas J. Barnardo, 6 October 1888, to *Times*, 'The Children of the Common Lodging Houses,' *T*, 9 October.

11 Report of Chief Inspector Swanson, 19 October 1888, HO 144/221/A49301C/8a.

12 For the medical evidence, see chapter 9, note 5.

13 We have three accounts of PC Smith's sighting. The report of Chief Inspector Swanson, 19 October 1888, HO 144/221/A49301C/8a, was probably based upon the constable's original statement, now lost. Smith gave another account to the inquest on 5 October 1888, see *DT*, *DN* and *T*, 6 October. And finally, Scotland Yard circulated Smith's description of the suspect in *The Police Gazette*, New Series, Vol. V, No. 502, 19 October 1888.

14 Report of Chief Inspector Swanson, 19 October 1888, HO 144/221/A49301C/8a. Schwartz's description of the first man was also published in *The Police Gazette*, New Series, Vol. V, No. 502, 19 October 1888.

15 *Star*, 1 October 1888. I have broken this long report into paragraphs.

16 Deposition of William Marshall, 5 October 1888, *DT*, *DN* and *T*, 6 October. The time of 11.45 given for this sighting was apparently that at which Marshall first saw Elizabeth and her consort by No. 58 but this is not made explicitly clear in the sources. If correct, it must have been about 11.55 when he last saw them, walking towards Ellen Street.

In the different renderings of Marshall's deposition the man's coat is variously described. *DT* gives it as a 'black cutaway coat', *DN* as a 'black small coat'. In *T* it is first described as a small, black coat, and later as a cutaway coat. *Star*, 6 October 1888, makes Marshall speak of it as 'a black coat (not an overcoat).'

17 Deposition of James Brown, 5 October 1888, *DT*, *DN* and *T*, 6 October. *DT* prints Brown's occupation as that of dock labourer. The *DN* reporter heard it as 'box maker'.

18 'Was he thin or stout?' The answer to this question, put to Brown by the coroner, is conflictingly reported by the press. In *T* Brown is made to reply that the man he saw 'appeared to be stoutish built.' This seems to have been an error. Both *DT* and *DN* print Brown's answer as: 'He was of average build.' A report in the *Star*, 6 October 1888, renders it: 'Not so very stout.'

19 Statement of Mrs Mortimer, 30 September 1888, *DN*, 1 October. The news report will be found in the same issue and may be inspired by Mrs Mortimer's statement.

20 Deposition of Dr Phillips, 3 October 1888, *DT*, 4 October.

21 Depositions of Morris Eagle and Louis Diemschutz, 1 October 1888, *DT*, 2 October; statement of Mrs Diemschutz, 1 October 1888, in *DN*, 2 October; for Mrs Mortimer, see n. 19.

22 Deposition of Dr Phillips, 5 October 1888, *DT*, 6 October. An assistant of Roderick Macdonald, Coroner for Northeast Middlesex, had suggested that the victims might have been drugged by the murderer offering them a vial of rum or brandy drugged with an opiate such as a solution of morphia. See, Macdonald, 3 October 1888, to *DT*, in issue of 4 October.

23 Baxter's summing-up, 23 October 1888, *T*, 24 October.

24 Deposition of Dr Phillips, 5 October 1888, *DT*, 6 October.

25 *Star*, 1 October 1888.

26 For early release of Smith's account to press, see report of Chief Inspector Swanson, 19 October 1888, HO 144/221/A49301C/8a; *DN*, *DT* and *Star*, 1 October 1888.

27 Deposition of Louis Diemschutz, 1 October 1888, *DT*, 2 October. *DN*, same date, renders it thus: 'I noticed the time at a tobacco shop in Commercial Road.'

28 Deposition of Edward Spooner, 2 October 1888, *T*, 3 October; statements of Matthew Packer, *Evening News*, 4 October 1888; deposition of PC James Harvey, 11 October 1888, CPL, f. 34.

Other witnesses were almost as badly adrift in their times as Spooner. Isaac Kozebrodski told the press that Diemschutz first called him into the yard to see the body at about 12.40 and Abraham Heshburg that he was alerted to the tragedy by the sound of a policeman's whistle at about 12.45. Diemschutz was positive that he did not get home until one. See, statements of Kozebrodski and Heshburg, 30 September 1888, *DN* 1 October.

29 Deposition of PC Lamb, 2 October 1888, *DT* 3 October.

30 Deposition of PC Smith, 5 October 1888, *T* 6 October; depositions of William West, Morris Eagle and Louis Diemschutz, 1 October 1888, *DT* 2 October; statements of Barnett Kentorrich, Charles Letchford and Mrs Mortimer, 30 September 1888, *DN* 1 October.

31 Warren, 24 October 1888, to Under-Secretary of State; Lushington annotation to Swanson's report on Stride, 19 October 1888, f. 3; minute of Henry Matthews, 27 October 1888; all HO 144/221/A49301C/8a.

32 Under-Sec. of State, 29 October 1888, to Com. Met. Police, HO 144/221/A49301C/8a.

33 Report of Inspector Abberline, 1 November 1888, MEPO 3/140, ff. 204–6.

34 Abberline's comment on the use of Lipski's name as an anti-semitic taunt
is substantiated by a complaint in *Die Tsukunft* for 12 August 1887:
'When an ordinary person kills a person everything is quiet. It will not
occur to anyone to call another person by the name of the murderer.
But when Lipski is sentenced to death, the ordinary people taunted other
Jews 'Lipski!' Two weeks ago Saturday it happened in Brick Lane. Last
Saturday in Church Lane there was a great fight between Jews and
locals, and all because of Lipski.' Quoted by Martin L. Friedland, *The
Trials of Israel Lipski* (London, 1984), p. 118.

11 False Leads

1 Report of Sergeant Stephen White, 4 October 1888, MEPO 3/140,
ff. 212–3.
2 The investigations of Grand and Batchelor are described in *The Evening
News*, 4 October 1888.
3 *Evening News*, 4 October 1888.
4 Report of Inspector Henry Moore, 4 October 1888, and report
of Sergeant White, same date, MEPO 3/140, ff. 211 and 213–4
respectively.
5 Statement of Matthew Packer, 4 October 1888, MEPO 3/140, ff.
215–6.
6 DT, 6 October 1888; J. Hall Richardson, *From the City to Fleet Street*,
pp. 218–9.
7 *The Police Gazette*, 19 October 1888.
8 For release of Smith's account to press, see ch. 10, n. 26.
9 Statements of Louis Diemschutz, Isaac Kozebrodski and Mrs Mortimer,
30 September 1888, *DN*, 1 October.
10 Depositions of Dr Phillips and Dr Blackwell, 5 October 1888, *DT*, 6
October.
11 Statement of Louis Diemschutz, 30 September 1888, *DN*, 1 October;
deposition of Louis Diemschutz, 1 October 1888, *T*, 2 October.
12 Report of Chief Inspector Swanson, 19 October 1888, HO 144/221/
A49301C/8a.
13 *Star*, 2 October 1888. Rewards are discussed in chap. 14.
14 *Evening News*, 20 and 31 October 1888; *DT*, 15 and 16 November
1888; HO 144/221/A49301C/20; *Star* 24 November 1888.
15 Dew, *I Caught Crippen*, pp. 130–1; McCormick, *Identity of Jack the
Ripper* (1959), p. 72.
16 Report of Chief Inspector Swanson, 19 October 1888, HO 144/221/
A49301C/8a; statement of William West, *DN*, 3 October 1888.

12 'Don't Fear for Me!'

1 A list of the woman's clothes and belongings, submitted to the inquest by Inspector Edward Collard, is preserved amongst the coroner's papers at the Corporation of London Records Office, Coroner's Inquests (L), 1888, No. 135; see also, *DT* and *T* 1 October 1888.

2 *DT* 2 October 1888.

3 Whitechapel Workhouse Infirmary records give Kelly's age as forty-six in December 1886 and forty-nine in November 1887. See notes 5 and 6 below.

4 This account of Kate's family and early life has been reconstructed from the following sources: statement of John Kelly, 2 October 1888, *T* 3 October; statement of John Kelly, 3 October 1888, *Star* 3 October; statements of Eliza Gold and Emma Jones, 3 October 1888, *DN* 4 October; depositions of Eliza Gold, John Kelly and Frederick William Wilkinson, 4 October 1888, and of Annie Philips, 11 October 1888, CPL, ff. 1–5, 26–7; statement of Elizabeth Fisher, *Wolverhampton Chronicle*, 10 October 1888; parish register of Bushbury, Staffordshire, County Record Office, Stafford; registers of births, marriages, and deaths, St Catherine's House; 1841 (Wolverhampton) and 1851 (Wolverhampton and Birmingham) censuses, Birmingham Public Library, microfilms; 1851 census (West Street, Bermondsey), PRO, HO 107/1562; Shelden, 'Victims of Jack the Ripper', p. 51.

5 Surviving records are often very imprecise on the matter of age. In the 1841 census George Eddowes is set down as thirty and in that of 1851 as forty-two. Catharine, his wife, is recorded as twenty-five (1841), thirty-six (1851) and forty-two (death certificate, 1855).

6 Whitechapel Workhouse Infirmary, Admission & Discharge Book, 1887–8, GLRO, StBG/Wh/123/19.

7 Walter Besant, *East London* (London, 1901), p. 309.

8 This account of Kate's last days with John Kelly rests on: depositions of John Kelly and Frederick William Wilkinson, 4 October 1888, in CPL ff. 2–5 and *DT* 5 October; statement of John Kelly, 2 October 1888, *T* 3 October; statement of John Kelly, 3 October 1888, *Star* 3 October; statement of John Kelly, undated, *DT* 4 October 1888.

Kelly repeatedly said that Kate pawned his boots on the morning of Saturday, 29 September, but the pawnticket recovered from Kate's body was unquestionably dated 28 September. Mr Crawford, the City Solicitor, thereby deduced that the pawning took place on Friday evening, and at the inquest he combined with Coroner Langham to browbeat Kelly into admitting that he could not remember whether it occurred on Friday or Saturday, that he had been drinking at the time and was 'all muddled up.' However, a date of 28 September for the pawning doesn't make sense because if Kate had the money for the boots on Friday why was she compelled to spend that night in the casual ward? Frederick Wilkinson, the deputy at Cooney's, confirmed some of Kelly's chronology, including the fact that Kelly, though *not* Kate, slept at his house on Friday night. Perhaps Joseph Jones, the pawnbroker, simply made a clerical error.

 9 Depositions of PC Robinson, Sergeant Byfield and PC Hutt, 11 October 1888, CPL ff. 28–31 and *DT* 12 October.
10 Depositions of John Kelly and Frederick Wilkinson, 4 October 1888, CPL, ff. 2–3 and 5 respectively.
11 Statement of Eliza Gold, 3 October 1888, *DN* 4 October.
12 Descriptions of Kate's injuries are quoted from the official transcript of Dr Brown's inquest deposition, 4 October 1888, CPL, ff. 14–21.
13 For Foster's sketches, see ch. 9, n. 10; deposition of Dr Brown, CPL, f. 14.
14 Statement of Dr Brown, *Star* 1 October 1888; deposition of Dr Brown, 4 October 1888, CPL, ff. 19, 21, 22; deposition of Dr Brown, 11 October 1888, *DT* 12 October.
15 Deposition of Dr Brown, 4 October 1888, CPL, ff. 20, 21–2.
16 Deposition of Dr Brown, 4 October 1888, *DT* 5 October.
17 Deposition of Dr Brown, 4 October 1888, *DT* and *DN* 5 October; *Star* 1 October 1888.
18 Depositions of Doctors G. W. Sequeira and William Sedgwick Saunders, 11 October 1888, CPL, ff. 24, 25.
19 Statement of Dr Sequeira, *Star* 1 October 1888.
20 Report of Chief Inspector Swanson, 6 November 1888, HO 144/221/A49301C/8c. See also, statement of Dr Brown, *Evening News* 1 October 1888, and Baxter's summing up at Stride inquest, 23 October 1888, *T* 24 October.
21 Unless otherwise stated my account of this sighting rests upon the depositions of Joseph Lawende and Joseph Hyam Levy, 11 October 1888, CPL, ff. 35–6 and 37 respectively. Lawende's address was given by Inspector McWilliam as 79 Fenchurch Street (HO 144/221/A49301C/8b) and in the inquest record as 45 Norfolk Road, Dalston.
22 Deposition of Joseph Lawende, 11 October 1888, *DT* 12 October.
23 *The Police Gazette*, New Series, Vol. V, No. 502, 19 October 1888; report of Chief Inspector Swanson, 19 October 1888, HO 144/221/A49301C/8a.
24 Deposition of Joseph Lawende, 11 October 1888, CPL, f. 36; report of Inspector McWilliam, 27 October 1888, HO 144/221/A49301C/8b;

report of Chief Inspector Swanson, 6 November 1888, HO 144/221/A49301C/8c; Smith, *From Constable to Commissioner*, pp. 158–9.

25 *DT* 1 October 1888; *T* 2 October 1888; Smith, *From Constable to Commissioner*, p. 152; rumours of the 'appointment theory' seem to have inspired the confused and ill-informed piece of nonsense in the *Philadelphia Times* of 3 December 1888, clipping in MEPO 3/140, f. 7.

26 For the factual information on the murder noticed here, see depositions of Inspector Collard and Dr Brown, 4 October 1888, CPL, ff. 11, 13, 19–20, 22; depositions of Doctors Sequeira and Saunders, 11 October 1888, ff. 24, 25; list of Kate's clothes and property, submitted by Inspector Collard, 4 October 1888, to inquest and filed with CPL.

27 Francis E. Camps, *Camps on Crime* (Newton Abbot, 1973), p. 38; Camps, foreword to Farson, *Jack the Ripper*, p. 12; N. P. Warren, cited by Begg, Fido & Skinner, *Jack the Ripper A to Z*, p. 41.

28 Deposition of PC Harvey, 11 October 1888, CPL, ff. 33–4. There was a post office on Harvey's beat, in Aldgate between Houndsditch and Duke Street. If this was the only point at which he could verify the time his estimate for Church Passage might have been out by several minutes.

29 Rumbelow, *Complete Jack the Ripper*, p. 159.

30 Dew, *I Caught Crippen*, p. 129.

31 Dew, *I Caught Crippen*, p. 137; report of Chief Inspector Henry Moore, 18 October 1896, MEPO 3/142, f. 158; letter of Sir Robert Anderson, April 1910, to a daily paper, quoted by Richardson, *From the City to Fleet Street*, p. 217; deposition of Detective Constable Halse, 11 October 1888, CPL, f. 42.

32 Adler, 13 October 1888, to Warren, quoted in Chaim Bermant, *Point of Arrival*, p. 117; statement of Sir Charles Warren, *DN* 15 October 1888.

33 Reports of Chief Inspector Swanson and Sir Charles Warren, 6 November 1888, HO 144/221/A49301C/8c; minute of Sir Charles Warren, 13 October 1888, HO 144/221/A49301D/1; Smith, *From Constable to Commissioner*, pp. 161–2.

34 Warren, 10 October 1888, to Lushington, PRO, MEPO 1/48; Adrian Morris, 'Goulston Graffito – A New Angle?', *Ripperana*, No. 7, January 1994, pp. 16–18.

35 Knight, *Jack the Ripper: The Final Solution*, p. 179; Fairclough, *Ripper and the Royals*, p. 67; Begg, *Jack the Ripper*, pp. 127–8.

36 Statement of Dr Blackwell, 30 September 1888, *DN* 1 October; report of Inspector McWilliam, 27 October 1888, HO 144/221/A49301C/8b; Smith, *From Constable to Commissioner*, p. 151; for Phillips, see statement of Dr Brown, *Evening News* 1 October 1888, and Coroner Baxter's summing up, 23 October 1888, *T* 24 October.

37 Friedland, *Trials of Israel Lipski*, pp. 200–3.

38 *Star* 1 October 1888.

13 Letters from Hell

1 Stewart, *Jack the Ripper*, p. 102.
2 The 'Dear Boss' letter was written in red ink except for the postscript, set at right angles to the rest of the letter, which was in red crayon. The postcard no longer survives but to judge by facsimiles was probably written in red crayon.

   The letter, with its envelope and the Central News editor's cover note of 29 September 1888, disappeared from Metropolitan Police archives before 1928. In 1950 Philip Loftus evidently saw it in the possession of Gerald Donner, Sir Melville Macnaghten's grandson, but after Donner's death eighteen years later it disappeared again (Loftus, *The Guardian*, 7 October 1972). Then, in 1987, these documents were among a small bundle of Ripper records returned to the Curator of the Yard's Black Museum in a plain brown envelope and they can now be seen at the Public Record Office, MEPO 3/3153, ff. 1–4. The bundle had been posted in Croydon but all attempts to trace the sender failed (Neil Darbyshire, 'Jack the Ripper letter and pictures returned to Yard 100 years after killings', *DT*, 19 August 1988). Facsimiles of both letter and postcard are at MEPO 3/142, ff. 2–3.
3 The Metropolitan Police collection will be found at MEPO 3/142. For City Police examples, CLRO, Police Box 3.18, Nos. 224–6; Police Box 3.22, Nos. 369, 381–2; Police Box 3.23, Nos. 394–6.
4 My account of the 'From hell' parcel rests principally upon: report of Inspector McWilliam, 27 October 1888, HO 144/221/A49301C/8b; report of Chief Inspector Swanson, 6 November 1888, HO 144/221/A49301C/8c; statement of Joseph Aarons, 18 October 1888, *DT* 19 October; Smith, *From Constable to Commissioner*, pp. 154–5.
5 After being handed in at Leman Street the original letter was forwarded to Scotland Yard. On 20 October Swanson loaned it to Inspector McWilliam of the City Police, who had it photographed and returned it four days later. Like so many other important Ripper documents it has since disappeared from the Metropolitan Police file. The present text is taken from a contemporary photograph, collected by E. K. Larkins and preserved at the Royal London Hospital Archives & Museum.
6 Statement of Joseph Aarons, 18 October 1888, *DT* 19 October; *DN* 19 October 1888; statement of Dr Openshaw, 19 October 1888, *Star* 19 October.
7 Report of Chief Inspector Swanson, 6 November 1888.
8 Smith, *From Constable to Commissioner*, pp. 154–5.
9 *DT* 20 October 1888; report of Chief Inspector Swanson, 6 November 1888.

10 Statement of Emily Marsh, 19 October 1888, *DT* 20 October.

11 McCormick, *Identity of Jack the Ripper*, pp. 78–9.

12 Whittington-Egan, *Casebook on Jack the Ripper*, p. 109; Knight, *Jack the Ripper: The Final Solution*, p. 221.

13 *Star* 1 October 1888; *T* 2 October 1888; *DT* 4 October 1888.

14 *DN* and *DT* 1 October 1888.

15 *Star* 1 October 1888. An evening paper, it appeared on the streets after the Jack the Ripper postcard had been delivered.

16 Warren, 10 October 1888, to Lushington, PRO, MEPO 1/48; Anderson, 'Lighter Side of My Official Life', March 1910, p. 358; Begg, *Jack the Ripper*, p. 90.

17 The documents have become separated in the file. Chief Inspector Moore's report is at MEPO 3/142, ff. 157–9. The letter (undated) and its covering note (dated 14 October 1896) will be found in the same file at ff. 234–5 and 211 respectively.

18 Macnaghten, *Days of My Years*, pp. 58–9. According to Mr Stewart P. Evans of Bury St Edmonds, the identity of the police suspect is revealed in a private letter of Ex-Inspector John Littlechild to George Sims, written in 1913. Since this document has not yet been made available to the public I am unable to comment upon its contents.

19 Examples are right ('right track', 'right away') and write ('to write with'), caught, laughed, whores, squeal, enough, straight, and knife.

20 Begg, Fido & Skinner, *Jack the Ripper A to Z*, pp. 27–8.

21 *Star* 19 October 1888; *Evening News*, 20 October 1888.

22 In addition to Swanson and Smith, cited above n. 4, my account of the kidney rests on: deposition of Dr Gordon Brown, 4 October 1888, CPL, f. 20; *DT*, 20 October 1888; statement of Dr William Sedgwick Saunders, *Evening News*, 20 October 1888; Whittington-Egan, *Casebook on Jack the Ripper*, pp. 51–65; N. P. Warren, 'A Postal Kidney,' *The Criminologist*, Vol. 13, No. 1, Spring 1989, pp. 12–15; statement of Dr Brown, 20 October 1888, quoted by Stewart Evans, 'The Lusk Kidney', *Ripperana*, No. 6, October 1993, p. 12.

23 Thomas J. Mann, 'The Ripper and the Poet: A Comparison of Handwritings,' *WADE Journal* (Chicago), Vol. 2, No. 1, June 1975, pp. 1–31; cf., Derek Davis, '"Jack the Ripper" – The Handwriting Analysis', *The Criminologist*, Vol. 9, No. 33, Summer 1974, pp. 62–9.

24 Mann, 'The Ripper and the Poet', pp. 9–10; Joseph Wright, *The English Dialect Dictionary* (London, 1905), VI, p. 201; William Matthews, *Cockney Past and Present: A Short History of the Dialect of London* (London, 1938), pp. 181–2, 184; P. W. Joyce, *English as We Speak It in Ireland* (1910; reprinted, Dublin, 1979), pp. 93, 99; Jeremiah J. Hogan, *The English Language in Ireland* (Dublin, 1927), pp. 69, 75–6.

25 The most influential such claim originated in the handwritten crime

diaries of a medical man – Dr Thomas Dutton, MD, MRCP, LRCS, who died in Shepherds Bush in 1935. His diaries, compiled over sixty years and entitled *Chronicles of Crime*, disappeared after his death but author Donald McCormick claimed to have seen and taken notes from them as long ago as 1932 and, in his own book, *The Identity of Jack the Ripper*, published in 1959, printed what purport to be quotations and opinions from them. To judge from what McCormick tells us about Dutton the doctor made some quite extraordinary claims in connection with the murders.

He professed, for example, to have procured enlargements of 128 specimens of the alleged correspondence of Jack the Ripper by photographing them through a microscope attached to a camera and then to have deduced from his photographs that at least 34 were 'definitely in the same handwriting'.

Thomas Mann is frankly sceptical about this claim. Nowhere, he points out, does McCormick offer any proof of the similarity in handwriting of any two Ripper letters let alone the 34 alleged by Dutton. Since a plausible case for the Ripper's authorship can only be made on behalf of the Lusk letter it would be instructive to learn whether this was one of the doctor's thirty-four. We are not told. It is interesting to note, however, that McCormick seems to regard both the Lusk letter and that received by the Central News on 27 September as genuine when, as Mann confirms, these scripts are definitely *not* in the same hand.

Sadly, one's doubts about Dutton go beyond the validity of any handwriting comparisons he may have made because neither this, nor many of the other claims attributed to him, ring true. His assertions that the police asked him to photograph the chalk message in Goulston Street and that his photograph 'definitely established that the writing was the same as that in some of the letters' is demonstrably fictitious. The contemporary records of the Ripper investigation do not once mention Dutton. And, as the wording in Smith's memoir and, more importantly, Warren's report of 6 November 1888, makes absolutely clear, the Goulston Street writing was rubbed out *before* it could be photographed. Indeed, this was what the subsequent dispute between the Metropolitan and City forces was all about. Had Dutton's story been true there would have been no occasion for McWilliam and Smith to condemn Warren's action, there would have been no confusion as to how the message actually read, and Chief Inspector Swanson would never have reported to the Home Office, as he did on 6 November, that 'to those police officers who saw the chalk writing, the handwriting of the now notorious letters to a newspaper agency bears no resemblance at all.'

Among the letters Dutton decided were genuine were two said to have been posted in Liverpool. The first read:

> Beware, I shall be at work on the 1st and 2nd inst. in Minories at twelve midnight, and I give the authorities a good chance, but there is never a policeman near when I am at work.
>
> Yours,
Jack the Ripper.

By McCormick's account this was written on 29 September. Some time later it was supposedly followed by a second:

> Prince William Street, Liverpool.
>
> What fools the police are. I even give them the name of the street where I am living.
>
> Yours,
Jack the Ripper.

The problem with these documents is the implausible date ascribed to the first. It was almost certainly not written as early as 29 September 1888 because at that date the only use of the name Jack the Ripper had been in the letter of 25 September to the Central News and this would not be released to the press until 30 September. There is, in fact, an earlier text of these Liverpool letters extant. They are printed verbatim in J. Hall Richardson's *From the City to Fleet Street*, published in 1927. Interestingly, Richardson there prints the date of the first as '29th inst' – which means that it could have been written on 29 October or in any succeeding month during the Ripper scare. Dutton apparently claimed to have seen the originals but he could just as easily have cribbed the letters from Richardson. Wherever he got them from, one wonders why he falsified the date. Was it simply a transcription error? Or did the good doctor seek to invest the letters with a bogus authenticity by implying that they carried a forewarning of the double murder of 30 September?

Details like this destroy Dutton's credibility. If McCormick has drawn accurately upon the diaries, and without the original manuscripts we cannot be certain of it, then only one conclusion is possible – the doctor was a charlatan.

For Dutton's various statements on the letters, see McCormick, *Identity of Jack the Ripper*, revised edition, 1970, espec. pp. 99, 103–5, 111. The other references are: Mann, 'The Ripper and the Poet', p. 15 n. 9; reports of Sir Charles Warren and Chief Inspector

Swanson, 6 November 1888, HO 144/221/A49301C/8c; Smith, *From Constable to Commissioner*, pp. 153, 162; Richardson, *From the City to Fleet Street*, p. 219. There is no trace of the Liverpool letters in the Scotland Yard collection of Ripper communications at MEPO 3/142.

14 *In the Shadow of the Ripper*

1 *DN* 1 October 1888.
2 *Star* 1 October 1888.
3 *DN* 4 October 1888; *Star* 3 October 1888.
4 *ELO* 6 October 1888; Montagu, 15 October 1888, forwards petition of Whitechapel traders, HO 144/221/A49301C/10; traders' petition, October 1888, MEPO 3/141, ff. 136–7; report of Supt. T. Arnold, 22 October 1888, MEPO 3/141, f. 166; *DT* 19 October 1888.
5 *Star* 5 October 1888; *ELO* 6 October 1888.
6 For this collection of grisly anecdotes, *Star* 18 September 1888; *DT* 18 October 1888; *DN* 12 and 25 October 1888.
7 *ELO* and *ELA* 13 October 1888; *DT* and *DN* 9 October 1888; burial register, City of London Cemetery, GL, MS. 10445/33.
8 *DN* 12 October 1888.
9 Report of Inspector McWilliam, 27 October 1888, HO 144/221/A49301C/8b; *The Police Gazette*, 5 October 1888; *T* and *DT* 2 October 1888; *DT* and *DN* 5 October 1888.
10 Harris, 30 September 1888, to Matthews, and Home Office minutes thereon, HO 144/221/A49301C/3; Lusk, 7 October 1888, to Matthews, and Home Office draft to Lusk, 12 October, HO 144/220/A49301B/7.
11 This was the estimate mooted by the press (*DN* 2 October) and thereafter bandied about in Home Office correspondence. It is probably too small. How much a successful informer might have actually realized is impossible to say. A total of £1,475, however, had been offered by 2 October; Samuel Montagu (£100); *Illustrated Police News* (£100); foreman of the jury at Nichols inquest (£25); City Corporation (£500); *Financial News* (£300); Colonel Kirby (£100); Henry White, a Middlesex JP, in a letter to the *Times*, 2 October (£50); subscriptions to the Mile End Vigilance Committee reward fund, according to *DT* 1 October (£300).
12 For the Mile End Committee, *DT* 4 and 5 October 1888; for the Working Mens' Committee, *DN* 4, 8 and 9 October 1888, and Cullen, *Autumn of Terror*, pp. 135–6.
13 Dew, *I Caught Crippen*, pp. 124–5; *DN* 8 October 1888.
14 *DT* 1 and 2 October 1888; *Star* 1 October 1888; *ELA* 6 October 1888; *PMG* 10 October 1888.

15 Warren, 3 October 1888, to Chairman of Whitechapel Board of Works, *T*, *DT* and *DN* 4 October.

16 Wensley, *Detective Days* (London, 1931), p. 4. Interestingly, Warren ordered trials of several varieties of boots with 'india-rubber, waterproof or silent soles' but constables complained that they were tiring to wear and made their feet sore (Memo on noiseless boots sent to Mr Bulling of the Central News, 6 October 1888, PRO, MEPO 1/55, ff. 321–3).

17 *DT* and *DN* 10 and 17 October 1888; *T* 31 October 1888.

18 *Star* 1 October 1888; *DT* 2 October 1888.

19 Police notice, 30 September 1888, MEPO 3/141, f. 184.

20 Warren, 3 October 1888, to Chairman of Whitechapel Board of Works, *T* 4 October; report of Chief Inspector Swanson, 19 October 1888, on Stride murder, HO 144/221/A49301C/8a; *Star* 4 October 1888.

21 Ellis, 3 October 1888, to Matthews; Warren, 4 October 1888, to Ruggles-Brise; Matthews, 5 October 1888, to Warren; all in HO 144/221/A49301C/8.

22 The officers engaged in the search recorded their findings in small notebooks, none of which, sadly, have survived. My account rests on: official notice of Warren, 17 October 1888, *DT* 18 October; report of Chief Inspector Swanson, 19 October 1888, and minute of Dr Anderson, 23 October 1888, HO 144/221/A49301C/8a; *DN* 13 and 19 October 1888; *Star* 17 October 1888; *DT* 19 October 1888.

23 *T* 1 and 2 October 1888; HO 144/221/A49301E/1. Edwin Brough (*T* 8 October 1888) said that the dog used in the 1876 case was 'a mongrel with little or no trace of bloodhound about it.'

24 Macnaghten, *Days of My Years*, pp. 202–3; Dew, *I Caught Crippen*, pp. 145–6; H. M. Mackusick, in *DT* 19 October 1888; Edwin Brough, 5 October 1888, in *T* 8 October.

25 Warren, undated, to Lindley, PRO, MEPO 1/48; Warren, 5 October 1888, to Under Sec. of State, and minute of Henry Matthews, 7 October 1888, HO 144/221/A49301E/2.

26 *DN* 10 October 1888.

27 *T* 19 October 1888; statement of Mr Taunton, *T* 13 November 1888.

28 Taunton's statement, *T* 13 November 1888.

29 Warren, 23 October 1888, to Under Sec. of State, HO 144/221/A49301E/3.

30 *DT* 10 November 1888; for a Radical lampoon, see Howells & Skinner, *The Ripper Legacy*, p. 86; for the view that the dogs constituted a deterrent to the murderer see H. M. Mackusick in *DT* 19 October 1888 and Watkin W. Williams, Sir Charles Warren's grandson, in a

letter to Tom Cullen, *Autumn of Terror*, p. 160.

31 The whole question was reviewed in two Home Office memorandums of 6 and 19 October 1888, HO 144/220/A49301B/19.

32 Matthews, 5 October 1888, to Ruggles-Brise, Bodleian Library, MS. Eng. hist. c. 723, ff. 132–7; Warren, 6 October 1888, to Matthews, and Matthews, 7 October, to Warren, HO 144/220/A49301B/9; Lushington, 17 October 1888, to Warren, HO 151/4, ff. 251–4; Warren, 17 October 1888, to Matthews, HO 144/220/A49301B/12.

33 Warren, 6 October 1888, to Matthews, HO 144/220/A49301B/9; Warren, 9 October 1888, to Under Sec. State, and Lushington, 10 October, to Matthews, HO 144/220/A49301B/8; Warren, 17 October 1888, to Matthews, HO 144/220/A49301B/12; Warren, same date, to Murdoch, PRO, MEPO 1/48.

34 *PMG* 8 October 1888; Anderson, *Lighter Side of My Official Life*, p. 136; draft letter of Warren, 25 October 1888, to Lushington, MEPO 3/141, ff. 158–9.

35 Swanson's report, 19 October 1888, HO 144/221/A49301C/8a.

36 Dew, *I Caught Crippen*, p. 112; for Abberline, 'On Duty in Plain Clothes', *Cassell's Saturday Journal*, Vol. X, No. 452, 28 May 1892, p. 852, and *PMG* 24 March 1903.

37 Report of Inspector McWilliam, 27 October 1888, HO 144/221/A49301C/8b; Rumbelow, *Complete Jack the Ripper* (1987), p. 227.

38 Minute of Sir Charles Warren, 13 October 1888, HO 144/221/A49301D/1; Anderson's minute, 23 October 1888, and Warren, 24 October, to Under Sec. State, HO 144/221/A49301C/8a.

39 For Texas murders, *DN* 2 October 1888; *DT* 6 October 1888; *Star* 12 October 1888.

40 Statements of Albert Backert, 30 September and 1 October 1888, *DN* 1 and 2 October.

41 *DN* 10 and 17 October 1888; *DT* 10 October 1888; *ELA* 20 October 1888.

42 Statements of James Risdon Bennett and L. Forbes Winslow, 1 October 1888, *Evening News* 1 October; Edgar Sheppard, 1 October, to *T*, in *T* 2 October 1888; statements of Dr Blackwell, 30 September 1888, in *DN* 1 October, and Dr Brown, *Evening News* 1 October 1888.

43 *DT* 31 October 1888.

44 Dew, *I Caught Crippen*, pp. 86, 95–6, 150.

15 'I Want to go to the Lord Mayor's Show'

1 Thames Magistrates' Court register, GLRO, PS/TH/A1/11.

2 For Barnett's accounts of Mary's past and his life with her, see his statement to the police, 9 November 1888, copy filed with CPM; his inquest deposition, 12 November 1888, CPM; and his press statements in *DN* and *Star* 10 November and *DT* 12 November 1888.

All attempts to verify Barnett's statements have been unsuccessful or unconvincing. For gallant attempts see Begg, *Jack the Ripper*, pp. 211–2; Mark Madden, 'The Tragedy of Mary Kelly', *Ripperana*, No. 6, October 1993, pp. 26–8. Barnett himself has been the subject of more productive research. A tall, fair-complexioned fish porter, he was thirty at the time of the murders and died of bronchitis at 106 Red Lion Street in 1926. See, Bruce Paley, 'A New Theory on the Jack the Ripper Murders,' *True Crime Monthly*, April 1982, pp. 3–13; Mark Madden, 'Jack the Ripper?', *Ripperana*, No. 6, October 1993, pp. 2–6.

3 *Star* 12 November 1888.

4 Statement of 'another girl' who knew Kelly, 9 November 1888, *DN* 10 November 1888.

5 Statements of Elizabeth Phoenix, 11 November 1888, *Star* 12 November; Elizabeth Prater, 9 November 1888, *DN* and *Star* 10 November; Caroline Maxwell, 9 November 1888, *DN* 10 November.

6 Statement of Julia Venturney, 9 November 1888, to police, copy filed with CPM.

7 The identity of the prostitute cannot be established. Barnett (*DT* 12 November 1888) calls her 'Julia' which suggests that she might have been Julia Venturney. However, by 8 November Venturney was definitely living at 1 Miller's Court and neither in her statement to the police nor in her inquest testimony did she give any hint of a former residence with Mary Kelly.

8 Barnett's inquest testimony reads: 'I identify her [Mary's body] by the ear and the eyes.' Both ears, however, had been partially severed by the murderer and I suspect Barnett was misheard and really testified that he had identified the body by the hair and eyes.

9 Statement of Mrs Prater, 9 November 1888, *DN* 10 November.

10 My reconstruction of the finding of Mary's body rests principally upon the statements of Thomas Bowyer and John McCarthy, 9 November 1888, to police, copies filed with CPM; depositions of Thomas Bowyer and John McCarthy, 12 November 1888, CPM, ff. 1–3; press statements of John McCarthy, 9 November 1888, *T* and *DN* 10 November.

Bowyer speaks of the 'blinds' or 'curtain' at the broken window of

514	*The Complete History of Jack the Ripper*

No. 13. A report in *DT* 12 November 1888, and Inspector Dew in his reminiscences, both aver that the 'curtain' was merely an old coat hung across the inside of the window to exclude the draught. It may have been the man's black overcoat Maria Harvey left at No. 13 the previous evening.

11 Dew's memories of the Kelly murder will be found in *I Caught Crippen*, pp. 86, 143–55. *DT* 10 November 1888 calls Bowyer 'a pensioned soldier'. He certainly does not look like a 'youth' in the sketches of him in *The Penny Illustrated Paper* 17 November 1888 and on the front cover of *The Illustrated Police News* 24 November 1888.

12 Depositions of Dr Phillips and Inspector Abberline, 12 November 1888, CPM, ff. 9, 11.

13 Deposition of Dr Phillips, 12 November 1888, CPM, f. 9.

14 Anderson, 25 October 1888, to Bond, extract enclosed with Anderson, 13 November 1888, to Under Sec. State, HO 144/221/A49301C/21.

15 This was one of a series of unsolved murders, contemporaneous with the Ripper crimes, in which dismembered female remains were deposited in and around the River Thames. See, Elliott O'Donnell, *Great Thames Mysteries* (London, 1930), pp. 111–36.

16 Dr Thomas Bond, 'Notes of examination of body of woman found murdered & mutilated in Dorset Street,' MEPO 3/3153, ff. 12–14. Although stamped 16 November 1888 by the Metropolitan Police authorities the document itself is not dated. It is, however, almost certainly the special 'annexed report' on Mary's injuries referred to in Bond's general report to Anderson of 10 November (MEPO 3/140, ff. 220–3; HO 144/221/A49301C/21). The annexed document was detached from the general report at some early date and has, until now, been presumed lost. Hitherto our understanding of the appearances in Miller's Court has primarily rested upon erroneous press reports, especially *T* and *DN* 10 November 1888, and *Illustrated Police News* 17 November 1888. Neither these nor Bond's report substantiate the remarks allegedly made by Chief Inspector Henry Moore to the American journalist R. Harding Davis in August 1889: 'He cut the skeleton so clean of flesh that when I got here I could hardly tell whether it was a man or a woman. He hung the different parts of the body on nails and over the backs of chairs. It must have taken him an hour and a half in all.' (*PMG* 4 November 1889)

17 *Star* 10 November 1888.

18 *T* 10 November 1888. McCarthy's account of the disposition of the various parts of Mary's body was, understandably in the circumstances, inaccurate.

19 *DN* 10 November 1888.

20 *T* 10 November 1888.

21 Warren, 9 November 1888, to Lushington, and 'Telephone message from Police', 9 November 1888, HO 144/221/A49301F/1; E. S. Johnson, 9 November 1888, to Mr Wortley, HO 144/221/A49301C/8.

22 *T* 12 November 1888; deposition of Inspector Abberline, 12 November 1888, *T* and *DT* 13 November.

23 Compare, for example, the reports in *T* and *DT* 12 and 13 November 1888.

24 Bond, 'Notes of examination of body of woman found murdered & mutilated in Dorset Street', MEPO 3/3153, ff. 15–18.

25 Bond, 10 November 1888, to Anderson, HO 144/221/A49301C/21 and MEPO 3/140 ff. 220–3.

26 Matthews, 10 November 1888, to Lushington, HO 144/220/A49301B/15; Lushington, 10 November 1888, to Warren, enclosing draft bill, MEPO 3/3153, ff. 5–8; *T* 12 November 1888.

27 *Hansard's Parliamentary Debates*, Third Series, Vol. CCCXXX, pp. 902–4; Vol. CCCXXXI, pp. 15–6.

28 Quoted by Cullen, *Autumn of Terror*, p. 186.

29 *Star* and *T* 10 November 1888.

16 'Oh! Murder!'

1 *Western Mail*, 12 November 1888, quoted in Begg, *Jack the Ripper*, pp. 149–50.

2 Deposition of Thomas Bowyer, 12 November 1888, CPM, f. 2.

3 GLRO: MJ/SPC, NE 1888, Box 3, Case Paper 19, cited in present work as CPM.

4 Statement of Maria Harvey to police, 9 November 1888, copy filed with CPM; deposition of Maria Harvey, 12 November 1888, CPM, f. 10.

5 For Barnett, see chap. 15, n. 2.

6 Statement of Mary Ann Cox to police, 9 November 1888, copy filed with CPM; deposition of Mary Ann Cox, 12 November 1888, CPM, ff. 3–5.

7 Statement of Elizabeth Prater to police, 9 November 1888, copy filed with CPM; deposition of Mrs Prater, 12 November 1888, CPM, ff. 5–6.

8 Statement of Sarah Lewis to police, 9 November 1888, copy filed with CPM; deposition of Sarah Lewis, 12 November 1888, CPM, ff. 7–8.

9 The Britannia, kept by Walter and Matilda Ringer, at the corner of Dorset and Commercial Streets.

10 Statment of Caroline Maxwell to police, 9 November 1888, copy filed with CPM; statement of Caroline Maxwell, 9 November 1888, *DN* 10

November; and deposition of Caroline Maxwell, 12 November 1888, CPM, ff. 6–7.

11 *T* 12 November 1888.

12 Statement of George Hutchinson, 12 November 1888, MEPO 3/140, ff. 227–9.

13 Statement of George Hutchinson, 13 November 1888, *T* and *Star* 14 November.

14 Report of Inspector Abberline, 12 November 1888, MEPO 3/140, ff. 230–1.

15 *ELA* 24 November 1888.

17 The End of the Terror

1 *DT* 16 November 1888.

2 *DT* 13 and 14 November 1888.

3 Queen Victoria, 10 November 1888, to Salisbury; Victoria, 13 November 1888, to Matthews. G. E. Buckle (ed.), *Letters of Queen Victoria* (London, 1930), 3rd Series, Vol. I, pp. 447, 449.

4 Warren, 'The Police of the Metropolis,' *Murray's Magazine*, Vol. IV, No. 23, November 1888, pp. 577–94.

5 *Hansard's Parliamentary Debates*, 3rd Series, Vol. CCCXXXI, p. 148.

6 He was discharged on 23 November. *T* and *Star* 19 November 1888; *DT* 24 November 1888.

7 *Star* 16 November 1888.

8 *T* 12 November 1888.

9 Cullen, *Autumn of Terror*, pp. 93, 214.

10 Monro, 18 July 1889, to Ruggles-Brise, HO 144/220/A49301B/20. The documents relating to the extra allowance will be found at HO 144/221/A49301G/1–7 and MEPO 3/141, ff. 1–7.
  Anderson, replying to the Queen's queries of 13 November 1888, also gave details of police reinforcements in Whitechapel. He said that the 'special "detection" force', i.e. officers in plain clothes, numbered 3 inspectors, 9 sergeants and 6 constables after the Chapman murder of 8 September. In October this strength was increased by 51 men and another 28 were employed to carry out the house-to-house search. 'The force at present,' he wrote after the Kelly murder, 'consists of 2 inspectors and 56 constables.' Anderson also indicated that the strength of the uniformed sergeants and constables on night duty in H Division was 120 in November 1888. Of this number 43 had been provided by a special augmentation of the division and 77 had been 'supplied nightly from other divisions to fill the vacancies caused by men being supplied in plain clothes as above.' (Quoted by Howells & Skinner,

The Ripper Legacy, p. 193). Without more information these details cannot be reconciled with Monro's figures.

11 Deposition of John McCormack, 17 July 1889, *DT* 18 July.

12 Deposition of Elizabeth Ryder, 17 July 1889, *DT* 18 July; depositions of Margaret Franklin and Catherine Hughes, 18 July 1889, *DT* 19 July; statements of Elizabeth Ryder and Margaret Franklin, 22 July 1889, MEPO 3/140, ff. 275–6; report of Sergeant John McCarthy, 24 July 1889, MEPO 3/140, f. 278.

13 Depositions of PC Allen, PC Andrews, Sergeant Badham and Sarah Smith, 17 July 1889, *DT* 18 July; deposition of Inspector Reid, 18 July 1889, *DT* 19 July; reports of PC Andrews and Sergeant Badham, 17 July 1889, MEPO 3/140, ff. 272–4.

14 For the medical evidence, see: depositions of Dr Phillips, 18 July and 14 August 1889, *DT* 19 July and 15 August; medical report of Dr Phillips, 22 July 1889, MEPO 3/140, ff. 263–71; Bond, 18 July 1889, to Anderson, MEPO 3/140, ff. 259–62.

15 Monro, 17 July 1889, to Under Sec. State, and report of Superintendent Arnold, 17 July 1889, HO 144/221/A49301I/1; Anderson 'Lighter Side of My Official Life', *Blackwood's Magazine* (March 1910) p. 357 n. 1. For Bond, see n. 14 above. For plain clothes patrols and uniformed reinforcements, HO 151/4, ff. 480–1; MEPO 3/141, ff. 9, 12, 14; HO 144/220/A49301B/20; HO 144/221/A49301G/9.

16 Reports of Chief Inspector Swanson, 10 September 1889, and Monro, 11 September 1889, MEPO 3/140, ff. 128–33, 139; deposition of Dr Phillips, 24 September 1889, *Evening Standard*, 24 September.

17 There is a prodigious amount of evidence on the Coles murder. My account rests principally upon the inquest proceedings in *DT* 16, 18, 21, 24 and 28 February 1891, the police court proceedings against Sadler, reported in *DT* 17 and 25 February and 4 March 1891, and the police reports in MEPO 3/140, ff. 65–121. See also reminiscent accounts: Richardson, *From the City to Fleet Street*, pp. 277–9; Wensley, *Detective Days*, pp. 4–6; Dew, *I Caught Crippen*, pp. 160–1; Benjamin Leeson, *Lost London* (London, N. D.), pp. 54–60.

18 Wensley, *Detective Days*, p. 5

19 *T* 27 February, 7 and 28 March 1895; *PMG* 7 May 1895; Winslow, *Recollections of Forty Years*, pp. 280–3.

18 Murderer of Strangers

1 *Morning Advertiser*, 30 March 1903; *PMG* 2 April 1903; *Eastern Post*, 3 February 1893.

2 Report of Dr Phillips, 22 July 1889, MEPO 3/140, f. 270.

3 Report of Melville Macnaghten, 23 February 1894, MEPO 3/141, ff. 178–9; Macnaghten, *Days of My Years*, p. 55; *Cassell's Saturday Journal*, 28 May 1892; *PMG* 24 March 1903; Anderson, *Lighter Side of My Official Life*, pp. 135, 137; Dew, *I Caught Crippen*, pp. 91, 93–4, 97, 106, 156.

4 Sean P. Day, in Peter Underwood, *Jack the Ripper: One Hundred Years of Mystery*, pp. 158–61; Jon Ogan, 'Martha Tabram – the Forgotten Ripper Victim?', *Journal of Police History Society*, Vol. V (1990), pp. 79–83.

5 *ELO* 1 September 1888.

6 Quoted by Howells & Skinner, *The Ripper Legacy*, p. 25.

7 *Star* 1 October 1888.

8 Knight, *Jack the Ripper: The Final Solution*, pp. 144–9.

9 *ELA* 10 November 1888.

10 *Morning Advertiser*, 30 March 1903.

11 Dew, *I Caught Crippen*, pp. 126, 149–50.

12 *PMG* 4 November 1889.

13 Begg, Fido & Skinner, *Jack the Ripper A to Z*, p. 229.

14 *T* 4 October 1888.

15 See, William G. Eckert, 'The Ripper Project,' *American Journal of Forensic Medicine and Pathology*, Vol. 10, No. 2 (1989), pp. 168–70.

16 David Canter, *Criminal Shadows* (London, 1994), pp. 100–103.

17 Deposition of Frederick Wilkinson, 4 October 1888, *DT* 5 October.

18 *Cassell's Saturday Journal*, 28 May 1892.

19 Camps, *Camps on Crime*, p. 38; Farson, *Jack the Ripper*, p. 12.

20 Nick Warren, 18 November 1993, to author; Nick Warren, 'The Thames Torso Murders 1887–9', *The Criminologist*, Vol. 17, No. 2, Summer 1993, pp. 80–82.

21 Minute of Godfrey Lushington, 13 October 1888, HO 144/221/A49301D/1; report of Chief Inspector Swanson, 19 October 1888, on Stride murder, HO 144/221/A49301C/8a.

22 *PMG* 24 March 1903.

23 I am deliberately discounting the description attributed to Sergeant Stephen White in *The People's Journal*, 26 September 1919. This is clearly fiction developed out of memories of the Berner Street and Mitre Square murders and of Mrs Mortimer.

24 Bermant, *Point of Arrival*, pp. 118–20.

25 Colin Wilson & Donald Seaman, *The Serial Killers* (London, 1990), pp. 63–4.

19 Found in the Thames

1 Introduction by Colin Wilson to Alexander Kelly, *Jack the Ripper: A Bibliography and Review of the Literature*, p. 14.
2 Cullen, *Autumn of Terror*, pp. 238–9.
3 Howells & Skinner, *The Ripper Legacy*, pp. 91, 108–10.
4 Rumbelow, *Complete Jack the Ripper* (Penguin edition, 1988), Addendum, pp. 293–5.
5 The quotations are from *The Referee*, 13 July 1902 and 5 April 1903; see also, *Ibid.*, 16 February 1902 and 29 March 1903; Sims, *Mysteries of Modern London* (London, 1906), pp. 72–3; Sims, *My Life* (London, 1917), pp. 141–2.
6 Griffiths, *Mysteries of Police and Crime* (London, 1899), I, pp. 28–9.
7 Farson, *Jack the Ripper*, p. 16.
8 Farson, *Jack the Ripper*, pp. 16, 111, 117–8; *The New Statesman*, Vol. LVIII, No. 1495, 7 November 1959, p. 628; Cullen, *Autumn of Terror*, pp. 218–9; Odell, *Jack the Ripper in Fact and Fiction*, revised edition, 1966, p. 186.
9 Macnaghten, *Days of My Years*, pp. viii-ix.
10 See, especially, Rumbelow, *Complete Jack the Ripper*, pp. 129–31; Howells & Skinner, *Ripper Legacy*, pp. 62, 123–6; Begg, *Jack the Ripper*, pp. 167–72; Begg, Fido & Skinner, *Jack the Ripper A to Z*, pp. 175–81.
11 Philip Loftus, reviewing Farson's book, *The Guardian*, 7 October 1972.
12 'Memorandum on articles which appeared in the Sun re JACK THE RIPPER on 13 Feb. 1894 and subsequent dates' by 'my Father Sir M. M.', copied by Christabel Aberconway, pp. 5–6, 6A, 6B. Document in private ownership.
13 Report of Melville Macnaghten, 23 February 1894, MEPO 3/141, ff. 179–80.
14 Cullen, *Autumn of Terror*, pp. 223–30, 239–40; Farson, *Jack the Ripper*, pp. 112–6, 134, 140–1, 142–3; Irving Rosenwater, 'Jack the Ripper – Sort of a Cricket Person?', *The Cricketer*, Vol. 54, No. 1, January 1973, pp. 6–7, 22; Howells & Skinner, *Ripper Legacy*, pp. 119–21, 155–6; Begg, *Jack the Ripper*, pp. 173–6; Begg, Fido & Skinner, *Jack the Ripper A to Z*, pp. 71–5.
15 This paragraph rests principally upon *The Acton, Chiswick, and Turnham Green Gazette*, 5 January 1889, which prints summaries of the depositions of William Druitt, Henry Winslade and PC George Moulson, made on 2 January at the inquest into Druitt's death.
16 Macnaghten, *Days of My Years*, p. 62.

17 Macnaghten, *Ibid.*, p. 54.
18 'Secret of Scotland Yard: The End of "Jack the Ripper"', *Daily Mail*, 2 June 1913.
19 Macnaghten, *Days of My Years*, pp. 61–2.
20 Francis Camps, foreword to Farson, *Jack the Ripper*, pp. 11–12; see also p. 131.
21 No independent accusation of Druitt, official or unofficial, is known to exist. A careful study of the wording of Griffiths' account demonstrates clearly that it rested upon the draft version of Macnaghten's report. Sims saw neither version of the report. But he knew Griffiths' book and, more to the point, Macnaghten himself, referring to him in his autobiography as 'my friend of many long years' (*My Life*, 1917, p. 175). There are several personal letters from Sims to Macnaghten in the British Museum (Additional MS. 57, 485, ff. 166–70). We have no reason to believe that the very late but much published references to the killer's suicide by Sir John Moylan and Sir Basil Thomson were anything more than confused derivatives, directly or indirectly, of Macnaghten (Moylan, *Scotland Yard and the Metropolitan Police*, p. 191; Thomson, *The Story of Scotland Yard*, London, 1935, p. 178).
22 Quoted by Cullen, *Autumn of Terror*, p. 77.
23 Rumbelow, *Complete Jack the Ripper*, pp. 149–50, 154; Howells & Skinner, *Ripper Legacy*, p. 150.
24 Those who seek the full ramifications of the Australian connection will find them in Farson, *Jack the Ripper*, pp. 109, 117–21; Knight, *Jack the Ripper: The Final Solution*, pp. 129–33; Harris, *Jack the Ripper: The Bloody Truth*, pp. 76–80; Howells & Skinner, *Ripper Legacy*, pp. 128–38; Begg, Fido & Skinner, *Jack the Ripper A to Z*, pp. 77–9.
25 Mr Knowles was then in his eighties and must now be dead. Attempts to identify and trace him have not been successful. See, Farson, *Jack the Ripper*, pp. 118–9, 146; Howells & Skinner, *Ripper Legacy*, p. 130.
26 The *Globe* report is reprinted in Melvin Harris, *The Ripper File* (London, 1989), pp. 112–3. For the fullest discussion of Deeming's links with the Ripper case, see Wilson & Odell, *Jack the Ripper: Summing up and Verdict*, pp. 240–8. See also, Barry O. Jones, 'Frederick (Bailey) Deeming,' in *Australian Dictionary of Biography*, Vol. VIII, 1891–1939, pp. 268–9.
27 Camps, foreword to Farson, *Jack the Ripper*, p. 12.
28 The only crumb of comfort I can offer Druittists is the presence of Druitts on the Mile End Old Town Vestry and Board of Guardians in 1890. It is unlikely that they had any connection with Montague's family from Wimborne but detailed genealogical research might clarify the point.

29 *Bournemouth Guardian*, 4, 11 and 18 August, 1 and 8 September 1888; Rosenwater, 'Jack the Ripper – Sort of a Cricket Person?', pp. 7, 22. We cannot be certain of Montague's presence at Salisbury because the press report of the match does not specify which Druitt took part. It may have been William, Montague's brother, who also sometimes played for Bournemouth, or even Mr A. Druitt, who played for Canford with Montague ten days later.

30 *PMG* 31 March 1903.

20 Caged in an Asylum

1 Anderson's public utterances on the identity of Jack the Ripper will be found in: *Criminals and Crime* (London, 1907), pp. 3–4; 'The Lighter Side of My Official Life. VI. At Scotland Yard,' *Blackwood's Magazine*, Vol. CLXXXVII, No. MCXXXIII, March 1910, pp. 357–8; *The Lighter Side of My Official Life* (London, 1910), pp. 137–9; H. L. Adam, *The Police Encyclopaedia* (London, ND), Vol. I, pp. xi–xii.

2 Macnaghten, 'Memorandum on articles which appeared in the Sun re JACK THE RIPPER on 13 Feb 1894 and subsequent dates', p. 6B; report of Melville Macnaghten, 23 February 1894, MEPO 3/141, f. 180.

3 Charles Nevin, 'Whitechapel Murders: Sensational New Evidence' (p. 1) and 'Has this man revealed the real Jack the Ripper?' (p. 19), *DT* 19 October 1987; Begg, *Jack the Ripper*, pp. 189, 195–6.

4 Fido, *Crimes, Detection and Death of Jack the Ripper* (London, 1987), pp. 215–6, 228–9; revised edition (1989) pp. 225–6.

5 Mile End Old Town Workhouse, Admission & Discharge Books, 1890–1, GLRO, StBG/ME/114/4–5; Mile End Old Town Workhouse, Religious Creed Register, 1890–2, GLRO, Microfilm X/20/355; Orders for Reception of Lunatics into Asylums, 1889–91, GLRO, StBG/ME/107/8, No. 1558.

6 Mile End Old Town Board of Guardians, Orders for Reception of Lunatics into Asylums, 1889–91, GLRO, StBG/ME/107/8, No. 1558; Colney Hatch Lunatic Asylum, Male Admissions Register, 1888–1906, GLRO, H12/CH/B2/2; Colney Hatch Lunatic Asylum, Discharge Register, 1891–6, GLRO, H12/CH/B6/2; Colney Hatch Lunatic Asylum, Male Patient Casebook, 1890–91, GLRO, H12/CH/B13/39, No. 11, 190; Leavesden Asylum, Orders for Admission of Patients, No. 7367, GLRO.

7 Aaron's elder brother, Wolf, survived him. A master tailor, he died on 6 April 1930 at the age of eighty-six. His address at that time was 23 Baker Street, Stepney.

The records of Leavesden Hospital, recently transferred to the Greater London Record Office, have not yet been catalogued. I have searched the following: Orders for Admission of Patients, No. 7367; Admission & Discharge Book, 1919–20; Male Patients' Medical Register, 1870–1917; Male Patients' Medical Journal, 1918–21; Male Patients' Case Register, Vol. 12A, p. 29; file on Kosminski from 'case files 1919'. See also Mile End Old Town Board of Guardians, Orders for Admission of Imbeciles into Asylums, 1886–1903, GLRO, StBG/ME/112/4, No. 441; registers of deaths, St Catherine's House.

8 The contention sometimes made by modern writers that there *was* a sighting of Kate Eddowes with a man near Mitre Square by a City policeman, but that the documentation has not survived, is untenable. Both Chief Inspector Swanson of the Metropolitan Police and Inspector McWilliam of the City prepared confidential summary reports on this murder for the Home Office and it is inconceivable that had there been such a sighting they would not have mentioned it. The wording of McWilliam's report, moreover, explicitly precludes the possibility of a 'lost' sighting by a City constable: 'The police are at a great disadvantage in this case in consequence of the want of identity, no one having seen the deceased from the time she was discharged from Bishopsgate Station until her body was found at 1.45 a.m., except three gentlemen [Lawende, Levy and Harris] who were leaving the Imperial Club in Duke Street at 1.35 a.m. ... No other person can be found who saw either of them [Kate or her killer].' (Report of Inspector McWilliam, 27 October 1888, HO 144/221/A49301C/8b).

9 Macnaghten, *Days of My Years*, preface, p. ix.

10 Friedland, *Trials of Israel Lipski*, pp. 91–4, 144.

11 For documentation, see ch. 12, n. 24.

12 *DT* 18 February 1891; *PMG* 7 May 1895.

13 Some writers have claimed that when Kosminski was admitted to Mile End Old Town Workhouse in July 1890 he had been insane for two years. This is incorrect and is based upon an erroneous interpretation of an entry in the workhouse admission and discharge book.

14 Quoted by Richardson, *From the City to Fleet Street*, p. 217.

15 Anderson, *Lighter Side of My Official Life*, pp. 136–7.

16 Reports of Chief Inspector Swanson and Sir Charles Warren, 6 November 1888, HO 144/221/A49301C/8c; minute of Dr Anderson, 23 October 1888, HO 144/221/A49301C/8a.

17 *PMG* 24 and 31 March 1903. In order to escape the implications of this evidence supporters of the Kosminski theory have argued that Anderson and Swanson somehow managed to withhold their knowledge of the Polish Jew from Abberline. Not only does this view defy common

sense but it is unsupported by anything so vulgar as fact. The lack of explicit references to Kosminski in Abberline's interviews is not evidence that he did not know about him. He refuted the Druitt and Cream theories only in response to specific questions. He was not asked about Kosminski and did not volunteer information on any past suspect.

18 Smith, *From Constable to Commissioner*, pp. 159–62.

19 For Arnold, *Eastern Post and City Chronicle*, 3 February 1893; for Reid, *Morning Advertiser*, 30 March and 6 April 1903, and *PMG* 2 April 1903; for the reference in Littlechild, 23 September 1913, to Sims, I am indebted to Mr Stewart P. Evans of Bury St Edmunds, letter of Stewart Evans, 12 August 1993, to author.

20 *PMG* 7 May 1895 says that Swanson believed the Ripper murders to have been committed by 'a man who is now dead'. Given Swanson's belief that Kosminski died soon after being committed to Colney Hatch this could be a reference to Kosminski. It suggests that Swanson held to the theory twelve years before it was mentioned by Anderson.

21 See ch. 13.

22 *The Parliamentary Debates, Official Report*, 5th Series, Vol. XVI (1910), 2359.

23 *Ibid.*, 2322–2323.

24 Anderson, 6 February 1893, to Home Office, HO 144/221/A49301C/34; Anderson, *Lighter Side of My Official Life*, p. 135.

21 The Mad Russian

1 Draft report of Melville Macnaghten, February 1894, p. 6B; official report, 23 February 1894, MEPO 3/141, f. 180.

2 Oxfordshire Assize, Lent 1863, PRO, indictments, ASSI 5/183/12, No. 37, and crown minute book, ASSI 2/39; *Oxford Times* and *Jackson's Oxford Journal*, 7 March 1863.

3 *Cambridge Chronicle*, 6 and 13 February 1864; *Cambridge Independent Press*, 6 February 1864.

4 Registers of persons charged with indictable offences at Assizes and Quarter Sessions, PRO, HO 27/140; *Exeter and Plymouth Gazette* and *Western Times*, 6 January 1865.

5 The records are held at the Gloucestershire Record Office. See: depositions, Gloucestershire Quarter Sessions, Epiphany Sessions, 1866, Q/SD2 1866; court minute book, Q/Sm 1/7; register of prisoners, Gloucester Gaol, 1865–71, Q/Gc 6/5.

6 Kent Assize, Summer 1866, PRO, indictments, ASSI 35/306, Part 2, Nos. 11, 15–16, and agenda book, ASSI 31/37, pp. 55–6; *Maidstone*

Telegraph, 28 July and 4 August 1866.

7 Chatham Prison register, 1871–81, PRO, PCOM 2/4, p. 34; quarterly returns of prisoners, Chatham, December 1872 and June 1873, PRO, HO 8/194 and 196; licenses for release of convicts, No. 25779, 30 April 1873, PRO, PCOM 3/342.

8 Testimony of Supt. Oswald, 5 January 1874, County Hall, Aylesbury, *Bucks. Advertiser*, 10 January 1874. Oswald is called Oswell in some reports.

9 For Ostrog's trial and conviction, Aylesbury, 1874, see: register of persons charged with indictable offences, PRO, HO 27/167, f. 30; 'after-trial' calendar of prisoners, Bucks. Quarter Sessions, January 1874, PRO, HO 140/25; *Bucks. Herald* and *Bucks. Advertiser*, 10 January 1874.

10 Pentonville Prison register, 1873–5, PRO, PCOM 2/75, No. 2364; Millbank Prison register, 1873–5, PRO, PCOM 2/55, No. 225; quarterly returns of prisoners, Portland, September 1874-March 1876, PRO, HO 8/201–7; governor's journals, Portland Prison, 1872–6, PRO, PCOM 2/364–5.

11 *The Police Gazette*, 1 October 1883.

12 *T* 10 August 1887; GL, *Old Bailey Sessions Papers*, Vol. 106, 1886–7, pp. 509–10; after-trial calendar of prisoners, Central Criminal Court, September 1887, PRO, HO 140/98; register of pauper admissions to county asylums, 1887, PRO, MH 94/85; criminal lunacy warrant book, 1884–7, PRO, HO 145/5, f. 556; Surrey County Lunatic Asylum, male patients admission book 1880–88, and criminal lunatics book 1885–1950, Springfield Hospital, London.

13 The telegram is postmarked 2 October 1888 and endorsed: 'Answered by Com^r.' It will be found at CLRO, Police Box 3.17, No. 197.

14 Report of Inspector McWilliam, 27 October 1888, HO 144/221/A49301C/8b.

15 Dew, *I Caught Crippen*, p. 156.

16 Warren, 9 October 1888, to Fraser, PRO, MEPO 1/48; report of Chief Inspector Swanson, 6 November 1888, HO 144/221/A49301C/8c.

17 John Beddoe, 'On the Stature and Bulk of Man in the British Isles,' *Memoirs of the Anthropological Society of London*, Vol. 3, 1870, pp. 384–573; DT 9 October 1888.

18 See above, chaps. 5 and 12.

22 'You've got Jack the Ripper at last!'

1 Under Sec. State, Home Office, 29 October 1888, to Warren, HO 144/221/A49301C/8a; report of Inspector Abberline, 1 November 1888, MEPO 3/140, f. 204; Anderson draft, 5 November 1888, MEPO 3/140, f. 207; Warren, 6 November 1888, to Under Sec. State, HO 144/221/A49301C/8d.

2 *PMG* 24 and 31 March 1903.

3 Maud Marsh inquest, coroner's papers, CLRO, INQ/S/1902/274; Central Criminal Court files, including depositions taken at Southwark Police Court 1902–03, PRO, CRIM 1/84 and CRIM 4/1215; Home Office file, including Judge Grantham's trial notes, PRO, HO 144/680/ 101992; H. L. Adam (ed.), *Trial of George Chapman* (Edinburgh & London, 1930); registers of births, marriages & deaths, St Catherine's House. I have restricted precise documentation to points especially relevant to the Ripper case but unless credited otherwise my information on Chapman is derived from the above sources.

4 Deposition of Ethel Radin, 14 January 1903, Southwark Police Court, ff. 314–6, PRO, CRIM 1/84. The *Post Office London Directory* lists Radin at 70 West India Dock Road only in 1888.

5 My reconstruction of Chapman's early years rests principally upon the depositions of Wolff Levisohn, Stanislaus Baderski and Mrs Rauch, 7 January 1903, Southwark Police Court, ff. 273–6, 280, 286–95, PRO, CRIM 1/84; testimony of the same witnesses, 16 March 1903, Central Criminal Court, in Adam, *Trial of Chapman*, pp. 62–5; registers of births, marriages & deaths, St Catherine's House; *Post Office London Directory*; 1891 census, PRO, RG 12/280. To judge from a letter of Neal Shelden (*Ripperana*, No. 6, October 1993, pp. 17–8) he has been conducting parallel investigations to my own into Chapman's movements. I am relieved to learn that our conclusions largely coincide.

6 I have searched those at the PRO for the period March-July 1891 inclusive, BT 27/66–8.

7 Deposition of Annie Helsdown, 14 January 1903, Southwark Police Court, f. 322, PRO, CRIM 1/84; testimony of Annie Helsdown, 18 March 1903, Central Criminal Court, Judge Grantham's notes of evidence, ff. 64–5, PRO, HO 144/680/101992/6.

8 Deposition of Elizabeth Painter, 28 January 1903, Southwark Police Court, ff. 447–8, 449, 457, PRO, CRIM 1/84; testimony of Elizabeth Painter, 18 March 1903, Central Criminal Court, Grantham's notes of evidence, f. 76, HO 144/680/101992/6.

9 Deposition of Louisa Morris, 18 November 1902, CLRO, INQ/S/1902/

274, depositions, p. 25.

10 *Echo*, 20 September 1888; *DN* 9 October 1888; Begg, Fido & Skinner, *Jack the Ripper A to Z*, pp. 95, 259.

11 A. F. Neil, *Forty Years of Man-Hunting* (London, 1932), pp. 26–7.

12 See n. 2.

13 Adam, *Trial of Chapman*, p. 52,

14 Neil, *Forty Years of Man-Hunting*, pp. 17, 25–6. Neil's reference to the eyewitness who gave the 'only living description' of Jack the Ripper is inspired by vague memories of George Hutchinson.

15 Deposition of Harriet Greenaway, 14 January 1903, Southwark Police Court, ff. 326–7, PRO, CRIM 1/84; Adam, *Trial of Chapman*, p. 51; petition of Chapman, 25 March 1903, to Home Sec., PRO, HO 144/680/101992/10.

16 *The Daily Mail*, 20 March 1903.

17 H. Montgomery Hyde, *Carson* (London, 1953), p. 182.

18 Adam, *Trial of Chapman*, p. 83.

19 Adam, *Trial of Chapman*, p. 78.

20 Thomas de Quincey, 'On Murder, Considered as one of the Fine Arts,' p. 65, *De Quincey's Works*, Vol IV (Edinburgh, 1862).

21 Deposition of Louisa Morris, 18 November 1902, CLRO, INQ/S/1902/274, depositions, p. 24; deposition of Louisa Morris, 28 November 1902, Southwark Police Court, ff. 58–9, PRO, CRIM 1/84; Adam, *Trial of Chapman*, p. 85.

22 Adam, *Trial of Chapman*, p. 64.

23 See, William G. Eckert, 'The Ripper Project,' *American Journal of Forensic Medicine and Pathology*, Vol. 10, No. 2 (1989), p. 169.

24 Robert Graysmith, *Zodiac* (London, 1992), p. 255.

25 My account of the Carrie Brown murder rests upon: *New York Times*, 25 April–11 July 1891, 17–25 April 1902; *State of New York: Public Papers of Benjamin B. Odell, Jr, Governor, for 1902* (Albany, 1907), pp. 272–7; Edwin M. Borchard, *Convicting the Innocent* (New York, 1970), pp. 67–73.

26 Quoted in *Ripperana*, No. 1, July 1992, p. 14.

Last Thoughts

1 Warren, 9 October 1888, to Fraser, PRO, MEPO 1/48.

2 Leeson, *Lost London*, p. 60; *DT* 11 October 1898; Stewart Evans, 12 August 1993, to author.

3 William G. Eckert, 'The Ripper Project: Modern Science Solving Mysteries of History,' *American Journal of Forensic Medicine & Pathology*, Vol. 10, No. 2 (1989), pp. 168–70; cf. VHS video, *The*

Secret Identity of Jack the Ripper, Castle Communications PLC release, 1988 (Castle Hendring: CASH 5026).

4 R. M. Holmes & James DeBurger, *Serial Murder* (Thousand Oaks, California, 1987), pp. 82–111.

5 See, David Canter, *Criminal Shadows*, pp. 100–104, 111; Jon Ogan, 'A Light in the Shadows', *Ripperana*, No. 7, January 1994, pp. 18–20.

Index